Classics In
Child Development

Classics In
Child Development

BIBLIOGRAPHY OF
CHILD STUDY: 1898 - 1912

Louis N. Wilson

ARNO PRESS

A New York Times Company

New York — 1975

Reprint Edition 1975 by Arno Press Inc.

Reprinted from a copy in
   The Clark University Library

Classics in Child Development
ISBN for complete set: 0-405-06450-0
See last pages of this volume for titles.

Manufactured in the United States of America

———◆———

Library of Congress Cataloging in Publication Data

Wilson, Louis N   1857-1937.
   Bibliography of child study.

   (Classics in child development)
   Reprint of the 1899-1912 ed. published by Clark
University Press, Worcester, Mass. and the U. S. Govt.
Print. Off., Washington, in series: Publications of
the Clark University Library, v. 1, no. 2, 4, 7; v. 2,
no. 2, 5, 6; and in U. S. Bureau of Education bulletin,
1911, no. 11; 1912, no. 26.
   Includes index.
   1.   Child study--Bibliography. I. Title.
II. Series. III. Series: Clark University, Worcester,
Mass. Library. Publications ; v. 1, no. 2, etc.
IV. Series: United States. Office of Education.
Bulletin ; 1911, no. 11, etc.
Z5814.C5W7 1975   016.1554   74-21433
ISBN 0-405-06482-9

BIBLIOGRAPHY

OF

CHILD STUDY.

BY

LOUIS N. WILSON,

BIBLIOGRAPHY

OF

CHILD STUDY.

BY

LOUIS N. WILSON,

LIBRARIAN, CLARK UNIVERSITY.

The Clark University Press,
WORCESTER, MASSACHUSETTS,
APRIL, 1898.

O. B. WOOD, PRINTER,
WORCESTER, MASSACHUSETTS.

BIBLIOGRAPHY OF CHILD STUDY.[1]

As Librarian of Clark University, I have received hundreds of requests by letter for references on Child Study, and am constantly required to assist special investigators here. To meet this demand I have drawn up the following list of books, memoirs and brief articles up to date, selected from a far larger list kept here. The alphabetical arrangement by authors has been chosen because it brings together the contributions of each writer, but to make the bibliography of use for topical reference there is appended at the end an index of the more important subjects arranged under the leading captions.

Under section II the titles of the leading serial publications dealing with Child Study are given ; under section III the Reports, Serial Studies, and Transactions of Societies, and, finally, under section IV, a brief list of current text books on themes most nearly allied to the work in this field. For a larger bibliography, which is contemplated, I should be glad to receive other publications, titles, or suggestions.

This list represents works of all degrees of merit, for I have chosen to err on the side of inclusion rather than of exclusion, and have tried to meet the needs of teachers and parents as well as psychologists.

In the brief notes appended to the publications I have had the assistance of several members of the Psychological department who have kindly looked over the list. I am also indebted to the Bibliographies of Professor Earl Barnes (No. 22), Dr. W. H. Burnham (No. 86), Dr. A. F. Chamberlain (No. 95), Dr. O. Chrisman (No. 105), Dr. G. S. Hall and J. M. Mansfield (No. 210), Dr. E. M. Hartwell (No. 222), Professor Will S. Monroe (No. 321), the Index Catalogue of the Library of the Surgeon-General's Office (No. 590), the Transactions of the Illinois Society for Child Study (No. 559), to Mr. Frederic Burk, whose paper in the current issue of the *American Journal of Psychology* has 109 titles on the growth of children, and to a list of titles on the various phases of adolescence kindly supplied by Dr. G. S. Hall, who is preparing a book on this subject.

---

[1] This Bibliography can be had on application by mail for the sum of 50 cts.

I.

1. **Adler, Felix** The moral instruction of children. Int. Ed. Series. Vol. 21. D. Appleton and Co., N. Y., 1892. pp. 270.
   Valuable, instructive and inspiring.

2. **Adler, Mrs. Felix** Hints for the scientific observation and study of children. Reprint from The Teacher. 51 E. 9th St., N. Y., 1891. pp. 15.

3. —— —— Child study in the family. Child Study Monthly, July-August, 1896. Vol. 2, pp. 138-151.

4. **Alcott, Louisa M.** Comic tragedies. Roberts Bros., Boston, 1893. pp. 317.
   A collection of dramas written by girls for a study of dramatic activity.

5. **Aldrich, Auretta R.** Children: Their models and critics. Harper and Bros., N. Y., 1893. pp. 158.

6. **Aldrich, T. B.** The story of a bad boy. Houghton, Mifflin and Co., Boston, 33d ed. pp. 261.
   Supposed to be largely autobiographical.

7. **Allen, Mrs. J. G.** Child study and religious education. Child Study Monthly, Oct., 1896. Vol. 2, pp. 289-293.

8. —— —— Child study from the mother's standpoint. Rochester, N. Y., 1896. pp. 36.

9. **Allen, Mary Wood** Child study in the home. A series of articles in the North Western Monthly, Lincoln, Neb. First article Sept., 1897. Vol. 8, pp. 128-130.

10. **Allport, Frank** Tests for defective vision in school children. Ed. Rev., N. Y., Sept., 1897. Vol. 14, pp. 150-159.

11. **Atkins, T. Benjamin** Out of the cradle into the world, or self-education through play. The Sterling Co., Columbus, O., 1895. pp. 364.

11a. **Atkinson, F. W.** Child study in secondary schools. School Review, Sept., 1897. Vol. 5, pp. 461-466.

12. **Babcock, W. H.** Games of Washington children. Am. Anthropologist, July, 1888. Vol. 1, pp. 243-284.

13. **Baldwin, J. Mark** Bashfulness in children. Ed. Rev., N.Y., Dec., 1894. Vol. 8, pp. 434-441.

14. —— —— Mental development in the child and the race. Methods and processes. The Macmillan Co., N. Y., 1895. pp. 496.

15. —— —— Social and ethical interpretations in mental development. A study in social psychology. The Macmillan Co., N. Y., 1897. pp. 574.

16. **Balliet, Thomas M.** Manual training: its educational value. Am. Phys. Ed. Rev., Sept.-Dec., 1896. Vol. 1, pp. 60-75.

17. **Barnes, Earl** Feelings and ideas of sex in children. Ped. Sem., March, 1893. Vol. 2, pp. 199-203.

18. —— —— Theological life of a California child. Ped. Sem., Dec., 1893. Vol. 2, pp. 442-448.
   This is the first careful inductive study of children's ideas of God, heaven, etc. It is pregnant with suggestion to mothers and teachers.

19. —— —— A study on children's drawings. Ped. Sem., Dec., 1893. Vol. 2, pp. 455-463.
   Suggestive for a new dispensation in methods of teaching drawing.

20. —— —— Punishment as seen by children. Ped. Sem., Oct., 1895. Vol.3,pp. 235-245. See also Proceedings N. E. A.,1895. pp.914-924.
   An inductive study presenting facts of which parents and teachers should not be ignorant.

21. —— —— The art of little children. Ped. Sem., Oct., 1895. Vol. 3, pp. 302-307.

22. —— —— Studies in education. A series of ten numbers devoted to child study and the history of education. Stanford University, Cal., 1896-97. pp. 400. (See No. 557.)
   Especially important both as showing methods of study and for results contributed. The most important of Professor Barnes's studies are contained in this volume.

23. **Barnes, Mary Sheldon** The teaching of local history. Ed. Rev., N. Y. Dec. 1895. Vol. 10, pp. 481–488.

24. —— —— Studies in historical method. D. C. Heath and Co., Boston, 1896. pp. 144.
   Several chapters deal with the historic sense in children and primitive people.

25. **Bartholomäi, F.** Psychologische Statistik. Allg. Schulzeitung, 1871. Anfänge des Tastens, Sehens und Hörens des Kindes (nach Sigismund u. Fröbel). Jahrb. d. Vereins f. wissenschaftl. Pädag. IV.

26. **Bartholomäi u. Schwabe** Der Vorstellungskreis der Berliner Kinder beim Eintritt in die Schule. Berl.Städt. Jahrb.,1879.
   Almost the pioneer work of child study in the school.

27. **Barus, Annie Howes** The history of a child's passion. The Woman's Anthropological Soc., Washington, D. C., March 2, 1895. pp. 8.
   Study of a child's passion for collecting botties.

28. —— —— Methods and difficulties of c ild study. Forum, Sept., 1895. Vol. 20, pp. 113–119.

29. **Bashkirtseff, Marie** The journal of a young artist. Trans. by Mary J. Serrano. Cassell and Co., N. Y., 1889. pp. 434.
   An introspective study of early girlhood.

30. **Behnke, E. and Brown, L.** The child's voice: its treatment with regard to after development. A. N. Marquis and Co., Chicago, 1885. pp. 109.
   A poorly printed, but valuable contribution.

31. **Bell, Alex. Graham** Memoir upon the formation of a deaf variety of the human race. Mem. Nat'l Acad. Sc., 1883. Wash-

ington, 1884. Reprint, Washington, D. C., 1885. pp. 86, with a chart.
An important statistical study.

32. **Bentley, Ella Hart** Sex differences that have been brought out by child study. North Western Monthly;Lincoln,Neb.,Nov., 1897. Vol. 8, pp. 257–261.

33. **Bergmann, H.** Statistische Erhebungen. H. Böhlau, Weimar, 1891. pp. 23.

34. **Bergström, John A.** An experimental study of some of the conditions of mental activity. Am. Jour. of Psy., Jan., 1894. Vol. 6, pp. 247–274.
Especially on psychic fatigue.

35. **Beyer, Henry G.** The influence of exercise on growth. Am. Physical Ed. Rev., Sept., Dec., 1896. Vol. 1, pp. 76–87.
The most important contribution to the subject yet made.

36. **Bezold, Friedrich** Schuluntersuchungen über das kindliche Gehörorgan. J. F. Bergmann, Wiesbaden, 1885. pp. 94.
One of the most important scientific investigations of the hearing of school children.

37. **Binet, Alfred** Perceptions d'enfants. Revue Philosophique, Dec., 1890. Vol. 30, pp. 582–611.

38. —— —— Recherches sur les mouvements chez quelques jeunes enfants. Revue Philosophique, March, 1890. Vol. 29, pp. 297–309.

39. —— —— La perception des longueurs et des nombres chez quelques petits enfants. Revue Philosophique, July, 1890. Vol. 30, pp. 68–81.

40. —— —— La mesure des illusions visuelles chez les enfants. Revue Philosophique, July, 1895. Vol. 40, pp. 11–25.

41. —— —— La peur chez les enfants. L'Année Psychologique. Vol. 2, 1895. pp. 223–254.

42. **Binet, A. et Henri, V.** De la suggestibilité naturelle chez les enfants. Revue Philosophique, Oct., 1894. Vol. 38, pp. 337–348.

43. **Boas, Franz** Anthropological investigations in schools. Ped. Sem., June, 1891. Vol. 1, pp. 225-228. Also in Science, June 26, 1891. Vol. 17, pp. 351-352.

44. —— —— The growth of children. Science, May 6 and 20, 1892. Vol. 19, pp. 256-257; 281-282; Dec. 23, 1892. Vol. 20, pp. 351-352.

45. —— —— The correlation of anatomical or physiological measurements. Am. Anthropologist, July, 1894. Vol. 7, pp. 313-324.

46. —— —— Zur Anthropologie der Nordamerikanischer Indianer. Verhandlungen der Berliner Anthropologischen Gesellschaft, 1895. pp. 367-411.

47. —— —— On Dr. Wm. T. Porter's Investigations of the growth of the school children of St. Louis. Science, March 1, 1895. N. S. Vol. 1, pp. 225-230.

48. —— —— Growth of first-born children. Science, April 12, 1895. N. S. Vol. 1, pp. 402-404.

49. —— —— Indianische Sagen von der nordpacifischen Küste Amerikas. A. Asher and Co., Berlin, 1895. pp. 363.
Exhaustive. Excellent for comparative purposes.

50. —— —— The limitations of the comparative method of anthropology. Science, Dec. 18, 1896. N. S. Vol. 4, pp. 901-908.
Ought to be read by every teacher.

51. —— —— The growth of children. Science, April 9, 1897. N. S. Vol. 5, pp. 570-573.

52. —— —— Remarks on the theory of anthropometry. Papers on Anthropometry, pp. 16-22. (See No. 551.)

53. **Bohannon, E. W.** A study of peculiar and exceptional children. Ped. Sem., Oct., 1896. Vol. 4, pp. 3-60.
Of great and immediately practical importance for every teacher and parent.

54. **Bolton, H. C.** The counting-out rhymes of children, their antiquity, origin, and wide distribution. A study in folk-lore. N. Y., 1888. pp. 123.
A classic work.

55. **Bolton, T. L.** The growth of memory in school children. Am. Jour. of Psy., April, 1892. Vol. 4, pp. 362-380.

56. —— —— Rhythm. Am. Jour. of Psy., Jan., 1894. Vol. 6, pp. 145-238. Important and comprehensive.

57. **Boone, Richard G.** Child traits in the adult. Inland Educator, Sept., 1895. Vol. 1, pp. 65-68.

58. **Bowditch, H. P.** The growth of children. Eighth annual report of the State Board of Health of Mass., 1877. Vol. 8, pp. 275-323. Reprinted in Papers on Anthropometry, Am. Statis'l Ass'n., Boston, 1894. pp. 65-116. With 15 plates and tables.
The first report of the classic studies of growth by this investigator. Specially important.

59. —— —— The growth of children. A supplementary investigation with suggestions in regard to methods of research. Tenth annual report of the State Board of Health of Mass., Jan., 1879. Boston, 1879. Vol. 10, pp. 33-62. 11 tables.
Devoted chiefly to determining the effects of nutrition and race upon growth.

60. —— —— Relation between growth and disease. Trans. of the Am. Med. Ass'n, 1881. Collins, Printer, Phila. Reprint. pp. 9.

61. —— —— The physique of women in Massachusetts. 21st Annual Report State Board of Health of Mass., 1889. Boston, 1890. Vol. 21, pp. 287-304. Also reprinted.

62. —— —— The growth of children studied by Galton's method of precentile grades. 22d Annual Rep. State Board of Health of Mass., 1890. Boston, 1891. Vol. 22, pp. 479–522. Also reprinted.

63. **Bowles, Mary E.** Emotions of deaf children compared with emotions of hearing children. Ped. Sem., Oct., 1895. Vol. 3, pp. 330–334.

64. **Bramhall, Mae St. John** The wee ones of Japan. Harper and Brothers, N. Y., 1894. pp. 137.
Interesting and instructive for comparison.

65. **Brewer, W. H.** The instinctive interest of children in bear and wolf stories. Proc. Am. Ass'n Adv. Sci., Salem, Mass., 1894. Vol. 42, pp. 309–311.

66. **Brown, Elmer E.** Notes on children's drawings. Univ. of Cal. Studies, Vol. 2, No. 1. Published by the University, Berkeley, Cal., 1897. pp. 75.
Contains four detailed observations of individual children for several years.

67. **Brown, H. W.** Some records of the thoughts and reasonings of children. Ped. Sem., Dec., 1893. Vol. 2, pp. 358-396.

68. **Bruns, L.** Die Hysterie im Kindesalter. Sammlung zwangloser Abhandlungen aus dem Gebiet der Nerven-und Geisteskrankheiten. Bd. 1, Heft 5 und 6. Halle, 1897.

69. **Bryan, W. L.** On the development of voluntary motor ability. Am. Jour. of Psychology, Nov., 1892. Vol. 5, pp. 125-204.
An important scientific contribution to the science of development.

70. —— —— Child study, systematic and unsystematic. The Child Study Monthly, May, 1895. Vol. 1, pp. 13-21.

71. —— —— Suggestions on the study of children. Inland Educator. Terre Haute, Ind., Aug. and Sept., 1895. Vol 1, pp. 21-23; 94-95.

72. **Bryan, W. L. and Harter, Noble** Studies in the physiology and psychology of the telegraphic language. Psychol. Rev., N. Y., Jan., 1897. Vol. 5, pp. 27-53.

73. **Bryant, Mrs. Sophie** Experiments in testing the character of school children. Jour. Anthrop. Inst., Nov., 1885. Vol. 15, pp. 338-349.

74. **Buckman, S. S.** Babies and monkeys. 19th Century, Lond., Nov., 1894. Vol. 36, pp. 727-743. Also in Pop. Sci. Mo., Jan., 1895. Vol. 46, pp. 371-388.

75. **Burdette, Robt. J. and others** Before he is twenty. Five perplexing phases of the boy question considered by Robt. J Burdette, Frances Hodgson Burnett, Edward W. Bok, Mrs. Burton Harrison, and Mrs. Lyman Abbott. Fleming H. Revell Co., N. Y., 1894. pp. 104.

Burgerstein, Leo. See Axel Key (No 264).

76. **Burgerstein und Netolitzky** Handbuch der Schulhygiene.

Mit 154 Abbildungen. Weyl's Handbuch der Hygiene. Part 1, Vol. 7. Jena, 1895. pp. 429.

Shares with the treatise of Eulenberg and Bach (No. 144) the distinction of being the best handbook of school hygiene.

77. **Burk, Frederic L.** Teasing and bullying. Ped. Sem., April, 1897. Vol. 4, pp. 336-371.

78. **Burnett, Frances H.** The one I knew best of all. A memory of the mind of a child. Charles Scribner's Sons, N. Y., 1893. pp. 325. First appeared in Scribner's Magazine, Jan.-June, 1893. Vol. 13. (Autobiographical.)

79. **Burnham, Wm. H.** The study of adolescence. Ped. Sem., June, 1891. Vol 1, pp. 174-195.

The most important brief introduction to the study of the adolescent problem.

80. —— —— Observation of children at the Worcester Normal School. Ped. Sem., June, 1891. Vol. 1, pp. 219-224.

81. —— —— Outlines of school hygiene. Ped. Sem. June, 1892. Vol. 2, pp. 9-71.

82. —— —— A scheme of classification for child study. Ped. Sem., March, 1893. Vol. 2, pp. 191-198.

83. —— —— Individual differences in the imagination of children. Ped. Sem., March, 1893. Vol. 2, pp. 204-225.

84. —— —— Child study as the basis of pedagogy. Add. and Proc. of the N. E. A., Chicago, July 25-28, 1893. Pub. by the Ass'n, N. Y., 1895. pp. 718-720.

85. —— —— Motor ability in children: development and training. 64th Annual Meeting Am. Inst. of Instruction, Bethlehem, N. H., July 9-12, 1894. Am. Inst. of Instruction, Boston, 1894. pp. 127-140. Discussion of same. pp. 140-150.

86. —— —— Bibliographical notes to lectures in school hygiene. Worcester, Mass., 1897. pp. 11.

Privately printed in connection with a special course of lectures on a part of the field.

87. —— —— Suggestions from the psychology of adolescence. School Review, Chicago, Dec., 1897. Vol 5, pp. 652-665.

88. **Butler, N. M.** Is there a new education? Ed. Rev., N. Y., Jan. 1896. Vol. 11, pp. 58-71.

89. —— —— The meaning of infancy and education. Ed. Rev., N. Y., Jan., 1897. Vol. 13, pp. 58-75.

90. **Carter, R. Brudenell** Report on the vision of children attending elementary schools in London. Eyre and Spottiswoode, London, 1896. pp. 16.

91. **Cattell, James McK.** Tests of the senses and faculties. Ed. Rev., N. Y., March, 1893. Vol. 5, pp. 257-265.

92. **Cattell, J. McK. and Farrand L.** Physical and mental measurements of the students of Columbia University. Psychol. Rev., Nov., 1896. Vol. 3, pp. 618-648.

93. **Chaille, Stanford E.** Infants, their chronological progress. New Orleans, Med. and Surg. Jour., June, 1887, N. S. Vol. 14, pp. 893-912.

94. **Chamberlain, A. F.** Notes on Indian child language. Am. Anthropologist, July, 1890. Vol. 3, pp. 237-241 ; July, 1893. Vol. 6, 321-322.
     The only study on the subject yet published.

95. —— —— The child and childhood in folk-thought. (The child in primitive culture.) Macmillan and Co., N. Y., 1896. pp. 464.
     Contains an excellent bibliography of over 550 titles. The only work in English treating of the child's place in the history of the race. The result of wide anthropological reading.

96. **Champneys, F. H.** Notes on an infant. Mind, Jan., 1881. Vol. 6, p. 104-107.

97. **Chance, W.** Children under the poor law: their education, training and after care, together with a criticism of the report of the departmental committee on metropolitan poor law schools. London, 1897. pp. 443.

98. **Channing, Walter** The importance of physical training in childhood. Ed. Rev., N. Y., Oct., 1895. Vol. 10, pp. 262-272.

99. —— —— The significance of palatal deformities in idiots. Jour. of Mental Science, London, Jan., 1897. Vol. 43, pp. 72-84.

100. **Chapin, H. D.** Child study in the hospital. A record of 600 cases. Forum, March, 1894. Vol. 17, pp. 125-128.

101. **Chrisman Oscar** Secret language of children. Science, Dec. 1, 1893. Vol. 22, pp. 303. Child Study Monthly, Sept., 1896. Vol. 2, pp. 202-211. North Western Monthly, Lincoln, Neb., Oct., 1897. Vol. 8, pp. 187-193.

102. —— —— The hearing of children. Ped. Sem., Dec., 1893. Vol. 2, pp. 397-441.
     A very valuable résumé of the different investigations up to date of its publication.

103. —— —— Child study, a new department of education. Forum, Feb., 1894. Vol. 16, pp. 728-736.

104. —— —— One year with a little girl. Ed. Rev., N. Y., Jan., 1895. Vol. 9, pp. 10-26.

105. —— —— Paidologie. Entwurf zu einer Wissenschaft des Kindes. B. Vopelius, Jena, 1896. pp. 96.
     Contains a bibliography 517 titles.

106. —— —— How a story affected a child. Child Study Monthly, April, 1897. Vol. 2, pp. 650-661.
     A good lesson of adult indiscretion.

107. **Christopher, W. S.** Three crises in child life. Child Study Monthly, Dec., 1897. Vol. 3, pp. 324-335.

108. **Clapp, H. L.** Scientific method with children. Pop. Sci. Monthly, Nov., 1893. Vol. 44, pp. 57-68.

109. **Clarke, Edward H.** The building of a brain. Houghton, Mifflin and Co., Boston, 1874. 4th ed., pp. 153.

110. —— —— Sex in education: or, a fair chance for girls. Houghton, Mifflin and Co., Boston, 1886. 17th ed. pp. 181.
A classic work still important.

111. **Clarus, Albrecht** Ueber Aphasie bei Kindern. Teubner, Leipzig, 1874. pp. 32.

112. **Clouston, T. S.** The neuroses of development. (Morison Lectures for 1890.) Oliver and Boyd, Edinburgh, 1891. pp. 138.
A suggestive contribution to the psychology of adolescent development. Very important.

113. —— —— Developmental insanities and psychoses. The delirium and night terrors of children. The insanities of puberty and adolescence. Tuke's Dictionary of Psy. Med. Vol. 1, pp. 357-371.

114. **Cohn, H.** The hygiene of the eye in schools. An English translation. Ed. by W. P. Turnbull. Simpkin, Marshall and Co., London, 1886. pp. 236.
Contains 7 pp. of "literature" and many important practical suggestions.

115. —— —— Lehrbuch der Hygiene des Auges. Urban u. Schwarzenberg, Wien u. Leipzig, 1892. pp. 855.

116. **Comby, J.** Les maladies de croissance. (Extrait des Archives générales de médecine.) Asselin et Houzeau, Paris, 1890. pp. 42.

117. **Compayré, G.** L'Evolution intellectuelle et morale de l'enfant. Hachette et Cie, Paris, 1893. pp. 371.

118. —— —— The intellectual and moral development of the child. Trans. by Mary E. Wilson. Int. Ed. Series. Vol. 35. D. Appleton and Co., N. Y., 1896. pp. 298.

119. **Culin, S.** Street games of Brooklyn. Jour. Am. Folk-Lore, July-Sept., 1891. Vol. 4, pp. 221-237.
A model essay.

120. —— —— Exhibit of games in the Columbian Exhibition. Jour. Am. Folk-Lore, July-Sept., 1893. Vol. 6, pp. 205-227.

121. **Daffner, Franz** Das Wachstum des Menschen. Antropologische studie. W. Engelmann, Leipzig, 1897. pp. 129.

122. **Daniels, Arthur H.** The new life: a study of regeneration. Am. Jour. of Psychology, Oct., 1893. Vol. 6, pp. 61-106.
A co-ordination of the anthropology of adolescence with the theology of conversion.

123. **Darwin, Charles.** Biographical sketch of an infant. Mind, July, 1877. Vol. 2, pp. 285-294.
Useful for comparison with the later life of the same child.

124. **David, J. W.** Über die Schwankungen in der geistigen Entwickelung des Kindes. 3te Internationaler Congress für Psychologie in München, 1896. München, 1897. pp. 449-453.

125. **Dawson, George E.** A study in youthful degeneracy. Ped.
Sem., Dec., 1896. Vol. 4, pp. 221-258.

126. **Deland, Margaret** The story of a child. Houghton, Mifflin
and Co., Boston, 1892. pp. 226.

127. **Dewey, John** Psychology of infant language. Psychol. Review, N. Y., Jan., 1894. Vol. 1, pp. 63-66.

128. **Donaldson, H. H.** Education of the nervous system. Ed.
Rev., N. Y., Feb., 1895. Vol. 9, pp. 105-121.

129. —— —— The growth of the brain. A study of the nervous
system in relation to education. The contemporary Science
Series. Charles Scribner's Sons, N. Y., 1895. pp. 374.
The best and most scientific account of brain development with two final
chapters on education.

130. **Donkin, H. Bryan** The diseases of childhood (Medical).
Charles Griffin & Co., London, 1893. pp. 433.

131. **Dorsey, J. O.** Games of the Teton-Dakota children. Am.
Anthropologist, Oct., 1891. Vol. 4, pp. 329-344.
One of the few really good studies of Indian games.

132. **Down, J. Langdon** On some of the mental affections of
childhood and youth.J. and A.Churchill, London, 1887. pp. 307.
A presentation of the medical aspects of the education of mentally deficient children.

133. **Dresslar. F. B.** Fatigue. Ped. Sem., June, 1892. Vol. 2, pp.
102-106.

134. —— —— Studies in the psychology of touch. Am. Jour. of
Psychology, June, 1894. Vol. 6, pp. 313-368.

Earle, Alice Morse (See No. 524.)

135. **Eaton, Susie W.** Children's stories. Ped. Sem., Oct., 1895.
Vol. 3, pp. 334-338.

136. **Egger, M. E.** Observations et réflexions sur le développement
de l'intelligence et du langage chez les enfants. A.Picard,Paris,
1887. pp. 102.

137. **Ellis, A. Caswell** Sunday school work and Bible study in
the light of modern pedagogy. Ped. Sem., June, 1896. Vol. 3,
pp. 363-412.

138. —— —— Suggestions for a philosophy of education. Ped. Sem.,
Oct., 1897. Vol. 5, pp. 159-201.
Attempts a digest of the most important practical results of child study
up to its date, and especially before adolescence.

139. **Ellis, A. C. and Hall, G. S.** A study of dolls. Ped. Sem.,
Dec., 1896, Vol. 4, pp. 129-175.
An important inductive and reminiscent study on the development of the
play instinct.

140. **Emminghaus, H.** Die psychischen Störungen des Kindes-
alters. (Reprint from Handb. d. Kinderkrankheiten.) H.
Laupp, Tübingen, 1887. pp. 293.
A standard book on the subject.

141. **Enebuske, Cläes J.** An anthropometrical study of the effects
of gymnastic training on American women. Papers on Anthropometry, pp. 47-57.

142. —— —— Pedagogical gymnastics. Am. Physical Ed. Rev., June,
1897. Vol. 2, pp. 81-88.

143. —— —— Diagram of working capacity and resistance as mani-
fest in gymnasium exercises. Report Tenth Annual Meeting A.
A. A. P. E., 1895. pp. 11-18.

144. **Eulenberg u. Bach** Schulgesundheitslehre. Das Schulhaus
und das Unterrichtswesen vom hygienischen Standpunkte. J. J.
Heines, Berlin, 1891. pp. 636.
A revised edition of this standard handbook is now being published.

145. **Fackenthal, Katharine** The emotional life of children.
Ped. Sem., Oct., 1895. Vol. 3, pp. 319-330.

146. **Fahrner, Dr.** Das Kind und der Schultisch. F. Schulthess,
Zurich, 1865. pp. 64.
An important classic.

147. **Fewkes, J. W.** Dolls of the Tusayan Indians. Intern. Arch.
f. Ethnographie, 1894. Vol. 7, pp. 45-73. Also issued as a reprint, Leiden, 1894. 30 pp. 4°, with 5 colored plates.
Valuable for comparative purposes.

148. **Fitz, George W.** A study of types of respiratory movements.
Jour. of Experimental Med., N. Y., Nov., 1896. Vol. 1, pp. 677-
692. Reprint. pp. 16, with a plate.

149. —— —— A study of measurements in curvature of the spine.
Am. Physical Ed. Rev., Sept., 1897. Vol. 2, pp. 185-187.

150. —— —— Play as a factor in development. Am. Physical Ed.
Rev., Boston, Dec., 1897. Vol. 2, pp. 209-215.

151. **Fitz, H. G.** Free-hand drawing in education. Pop. Sci. Monthly, Oct., 1897. Vol. 51, pp. 755-765. Reprint. pp. 11.

152. **Fletcher, Alice C.** Glimpses of child life among the Omaha
Indians. Jour. Am. Folk-Lore, July-Sept., 1888. Vol. 1, pp.
115-123.

153. **Fletcher, Robert** Human proportion in art and anthropometry. Moses King, Cambridge, Mass., 1883, pp. 37. (With a bibliography. Important.)

154. **Fothergill, J. M.** The physiologist in the household. Part 1.
Adolescence. Bailliere, Tindall and Cox, London, 1880. pp. 24.

155. **Fougeray, Hamon du et Couëtoux, L.** Manuel pratique
des méthodes d'enseignement spéciales aux enfants anormaux

(sourds-muets, aveugles, idiots, bègues, etc.,) méthodes—statistique—institutions—législation, etc. Préface du Dr. Bourneville. F. Alcan, Paris, 1896. pp. 288.

156. **Frear, Caroline** Imitation : A study based on E. H. Russell's observations. Ped. Sem., April, 1897. Vol. 4, pp. 382-386.

157. **Friedrich, J.** Untersuchungen über die Einflüsse der Arbeitsdauer und der Arbeitspausen auf die geistige Leistungsfähigkeit der Schulkinder. Zeitschrift fur Psychologie und Physiologie der Sinnesorgane, Dec., 1896. Band 13, pp. 1-53.

158. **Froebel, Friedrich** Pedagogics of the kindergarten; or, his ideas concerning the play and playthings of the child. Trans. by Josephine Jarvis. Int. Education Series, Vol. 30. D. Appleton and Co., N. Y., 1895. pp. 337 and 13 plates.

159. **Gallaudet, E. M.** Values in the education of the deaf. Ed. Rev., N. Y., June, 1892. Vol. 4, pp. 16-26.

160. **Galton, Francis** (Editor) Life history album. Prepared by direction of the collective investigation committee of the Brit. Med. Ass'n. Macmillan and Co., London, 1884. pp. 172.
One of the best of many now before the public.

161. —— —— Remarks on replies by teachers to questions respecting mental fatigue. Jour. Anthrop. Institute, April, 1888. Vol. 18, pp. 157-167.

162. —— —— On the principles and methods of assigning marks for bodily efficiency. Nature, Oct. 31, 1889. Vol. 40, pp. 649-653.

163. —— —— Useful anthropometry. Proc. of the Am. Ass'n for Adv. of Phys. Ed. 6th Annual Meeting, April, 1891. Ithaca, N. Y., 1891. Vol. 6, pp. 51-57

164. **Garbini, Adriano** Educazione fisica del bambino. Verona, 1889. pp. 212.

165. —— —— Evoluzione della voce nella infanzia. G. Franchini, Verona, 1892. pp. 53.

166. —— —— Evoluzione del senso cromatico nei bambini. Verona, 1894.
The most exhaustive treatment of the subject yet published.

167. —— —— Evoluzione del senso olfattivo nella Infanzia. Archivio per l'Antrop. e la Etnol. Firenze, 1896. Vol. 26, pp. 239-286.

168. **Gayley, Julia G.** The classics for children. Ped. Sem., Oct., 1895. Vol. 3, pp. 342-346.

169. **Gelpke, Theodor** Die Augen der Elementarschüler und Elementarschülerinnen der Haupt- und Residenzstadt Karlsruhe. Eine statistische Untersuchung. H. Laupp, Tübingen, 1891. pp. 136.

170. **Genzmer, Alfred** Untersuchungen über die Sinneswahrnehmungen des neugeborenen Menschen. Halle, 1882. pp. 28.

171. **Gihon, Albert L.** Physical measurements. Wood's Reference Hand-book of the Medical Sciences. Wm. Wood and Co., New York, 1887. Vol. 5, pp. 667-673.

172. **Gilbert, J. Allen** Experiments on the musical sensitiveness of school children. Studies from the Yale Psy. Lab., Oct., 1893. Vol. 1, pp. 80-87.

173. —— —— Researches on the mental and physical development of school children. Studies from the Yale Psy. Lab., Nov., 1894. Vol. 2, pp. 40-100. Remarks on same by Dr. E. W. Scripture, pp. 101-104.
    A careful study of development in a large number of school children.

174. —— —— Researches upon school children and college students. Univ. of Iowa Studies in Psychology. Iowa City, Ia., 1897. Vol. 1, pp. 1-39.

175. **Godkin, E. L.** The illiteracy of American boys. Ed. Rev., N. Y., Jan., 1897. Vol. 13, pp. 1-9.

176. **Goethe, Johann W. von** Autobiography. From the German by John Oxenford. Cambridge edition, 2 vols. Estes and Lauriat, Boston, 1883.
    Full of suggestion and interest.

177. **Goltz, B.** Buch der Kindheit. (Selbstbiographie.) O. Janke, Berlin, 1847. 4th ed., pp. 532. (A classic.)

178. **Gomme, Alice B.** Children's singing games, with the tunes to which they are sung. The Macmillan Co., New York, 1894. pp. 70. (Old nursery standards.)

179. —— —— The international games of England, Scotland and Ireland, with tunes, singing rhymes, and method of playing according to the variants extant, and recorded in different parts of the kingdom. London, 1894. Vol. 1, pp. 453.
    Valuable for comparative purposes.

180. **Greenwood, J. M.** On children's vocabularies. Annual report of the Kansas City public schools. Kansas City, Mo., 1887. pp. 52-65.

181. —— —— Heights and weights of children. Am. Public Health Ass'n Rep., 1891. Republican Press Ass'n, Concord, N. H., 1892. Vol. 17, pp. 199-204.

182. **Griesbach, H.** Energetik und Hygiene des Nerven-Systems in der Schule. R. Oldenbourg. München und Leipzig, 1895. pp. 97.
    Reports important tests of fatigue by means of the æsthesiometer.

183. **Grimard, Ed.** L'enfant, son passé, son avenir. Hetzel et Cie., Paris. pp. 388
    A suggestive, though somewhat disconnected book.

184. **Groos, Karl** Die Spiele der Thiere. G. Fischer, Jena, 1896. pp. 359.
    A very valuable study preliminary to a promised work on the plays of children.

185. **Groszmann, M. P. E.** A working system of child study for schools. C. W. Bardeen, Syracuse, N. Y., 1897. pp. 70.

186. **de Guimps, Roger** Pestalozzi, his life and work. Trans. by J. Russell from the second French edition. Int. Education Ser., vol. 14. D. Appleton and Co., N. Y., 1890. pp. 438. (See particularly pp. 62-72.)

187. **Gulick, Luther** Manual for physical measurements. Int. Com. Y. M. C. A., N. Y., 1897. pp. 48.

188. **Guttzeit, Johannes** Grundzüge einer Gesundheitspflege der Kindesseele. W. Besser, Leipzig, 1895. pp. 80.

189. **Gutzmann, H.** Des Kindes Sprache und Sprachfehler. Gesundheitslehre der Sprache für Eltern, Erzieher und Aerzte. J. J. Weber, Leipzig, 1894. pp. 264.

190. —— —— Die praktische Anwendung der Sprachphysiologie beim ersten Leseunterricht. Mit einer Tafel. Samml. von Abh. aus dem Geb. der Päd. Psy. u. Phys. Band I, Heft 3. Reuther u. Reichard, Berlin, 1897. pp. 52.
    Practical suggestions by a distinguished specialist.

191. **Hall, G. Stanley** The moral and religious training of children. Princeton Review, Jan., 1882. Vol. 10, pp. 26-48.

192. —— —— The education of the will. Princeton Review, Nov., 1882. Vol. 10, pp. 306-325 Reprinted in Ped. Sem., June, 1892. Vol. 2, pp. 72-89.

193. —— —— Contents of children's minds on entering school. Princeton Review, May, 1883. Vol. 11, pp. 249-272. Reprinted by E. L. Kellogg and Co., N. Y.

194. —— —— The moral and religious training of children and adolescents. Ped. Sem., June, 1891. Vol. 1, pp. 196-210.

195. —— —— The study of children. (Privately printed.) N. Somerville, Mass., 1883. pp. 13.

196. —— —— Overpressure in schools. Nation, Oct. 22, 1885. Vol. 41, pp. 338-339.

197. —— —— The story of a sand pile. Scribner's Magazine, June, 1888. Vol. 3, pp. 690-696. Reprinted by E. L. Kellogg and Co., N. Y., 1897. pp. 20. Price 25 cents.

198. —— —— Children's lies. Am. Jour. of Psy., Jan., 1890. Vol. 3, pp. 59-70. Ped. Sem., June, 1891. Vol. 1, pp. 211-218.

199. —— —— Boy life in a Massachusetts country town thirty years ago. Proc. Am. Antiq. Soc., Worcester, Mass., Oct. 21, 1890. New Series, vol. 7, pp. 107-128.

200. —— —— Notes on the study of infants. Ped. Sem., June, 1891. Vol. 1, pp. 127-138.

201. —— —— Health of school children as affected by school build-

ings. Report of the Proc. of the Dept. of Supt. held in Brooklyn, N. Y., Feb., 1892. pp. 163-172.

202. —— —— Child study as a basis for psychology and psychological teaching. Rep. Commissioner of Ed., 1892-93. Washington, D. C., 1895. Vol. 1, pp. 357-358 ; 367-370.

203. —— —— Child study the basis of exact education. Forum, Dec., 1893. Vol. 16, pp. 429-441.

204. —— —— Child study in summer schools. Regents Bulletin, Univ. of the State of N. Y., No. 29. July, 1894. Regents Report, 108. Albany, 1895. Vol. 1, pp. 333-336.

205. —— —— Practical child study. Jour. of Ed., Dec. 13, 1894. Vol. 40, pp. 391-392.

206. —— —— Generalizations and directions for child study. North Western Jour. of Ed., July, 1896. Vol. 7, p. 8.

207. A study of fears. Am. Jour. Psy., Jan., 1897. Vol. 8, pp. 147-249.
His fullest topical study.

208. —— —— Topical Syllabi, **1894-1895.** I. Anger ; II. Dolls; III. Crying and Laughing; IV. Toys and Playthings ; V. Folk-Lore Among Children ; VI. Early forms of Vocal Expression ; VII. The Early Sense of Self ; VIII. Fears in Childhood and Youth ; IX. Some Common Traits and Habits ; X. Some Common Automatisms, Nerve Signs, etc.; XI. Feeling for Objects of Inanimate Nature ; XII. Feeling for Objects of Animate Nature ; XIII. Children's Appetites and Foods ; XIV. Affection and its Opposite States in Children ; XV. Moral ¡and Religious Experiences.

1895-96. I. Peculiar and Exceptional children, with E. W. Bohannon; II. Moral Defects and Perversions, with G. E. Dawson ; III. The Beginnings of Reading and Writing, with Dr. H. T. Lukens ; IV. Thoughts and Feelings about Old Age, Disease and Death, with C. A. Scott ; V. Moral Education, with N. P. Avery ; VI. Studies of School Reading Matter, with J. C. Shaw ; VII. Courses of Study in Elementary Grammar and High Schools, with T. R. Crosswell; VIII. Early Musical Manifestations, with Florence Marsh ; IX. Fancy, Imagination, Reverie, with E. H. Lindley ; X. Tickling, Fun, Wit, Humor, Laughing, with Dr. Arthur Allin ; XI. Suggestion and Imitation, with M. H. Small ; XII. Religious Experience, with E. E. Starbuck ; XIII. Kindergarten, with Miss Anna E. Bryan and Miss Lucy Wheelock ; XIV. Habits, Instincts, etc., in Animals, with Dr. R. R. Gurley ; XV. Number and Mathematics, with D. E. Phillips; XVI. The Only Child in the Family, with E. W. Bohannon.

1896-97. I. Degrees of Certainty and Conviction in Children, with Maurice H. Small ; II. Sabbath, and Worship in General, with J. P. Hylan ; III. Migrations, Tramps, Truancy, Running

Away, etc., *vs.* Love of Home, with L. W. Kline; IV. Adolescence, and its Phenomena in Body and Mind, with E. G. Lancaster; V. Examinations and Recitations, with John C. Shaw; VI. Stillness, Solitude, Restlessness, with H. S. Curtis; VII. The Psychology of Health and Disease, with Henry H. Goddard; VIII. Spontaneously Invented Toys and Amusements, with T. R. Crosswell; IX. Hymns and Sacred Music, with Rev. T. R. Peede; X. Puzzles and their Psychology, with Ernest H. Lindley; XI. The Sermon, with Rev. Alva R. Scott; XII. Special Traits as Indices of Character and as Mediating Likes and Dislikes, with E. W. Bohannon; XIII. Reverie and Allied Phenomena, with G. E. Partridge; XIV. The Psychology of Health and Disease, with H. H. Goddard.

1897-98. I. Immortality, with J. Richard Street; II. Psychology of Ownership vs. Loss, with Linus W. Kline; III. Memory, with F. W. Colegrove; IV. Humorous and Cranky Side in Education, with L. W. Kline; V. The Psychology of Shorthand Writing, with J. O. Quantz; VI. The Teaching Instinct, with D. E. Phillips; VII. Home and School Punishments and Penalties, with Chas. H. Sears; VIII. Straightness and Uprightness of Body, by G. Stanley Hall; IX. Conventionality, with Albert Schinz; X. Local Voluntary Association among Teachers, with Henry D. Sheldon; XI. Motor Education, with E. W. Bohannon; XII. Heat and Cold, by G. Stanley Hall; XIII. Training of Teachers, with W. G. Chambers; XIV. Educational Ideals, with Lewis Edwin York; XV. Water Psychoses, with Frederick E. Bolton; XVI. The Institutional Activities of Children, with Henry D. Sheldon; XVII. Obedience and Obstinacy, with Tilmon Jenkins; XVIII. The Sense of Honor Among Children, with Robert Clark.

Leaflets, of from one to four pages each, privately printed at Worcester, Mass., upon the results of which 35 studies have been printed in the Am. Jour. of Psychology and the Pedagogical Seminary.

—— —— See also Ellis, A. C. and Hall G. S. (No. 139.)

209. **Hall, G. S. and Allin, A.** The psychology of tickling, laughing, and the comic. Am. Jour. of Psy., Oct., 1897. Vol. 9, pp. 1-41.

210. **Hall, G. S. and Mansfield, John M.** Hints toward a select and descriptive bibliography of education. D. C. Heath and Co., Boston, 1886. pp. 309. (The study and observation of children. pp. 85-92.)

211. **Hall, Mrs. W. S.** First 500 days of a child's life. Child Study Monthly, Nov., Dec., 1896, Jan., Feb., March, 1897. Vol. 2, pp. 330, 394, 458, 522, 586 and 650.

212. **Halleck, Reuben P.** The education of the central nervous system. A study of foundations, especially of sensory and motor training. The Macmillian Co., N. Y., 1897. pp. 258.
Suggestive and helpful. Somewhat popular.

213. —— —— The bearings of the laws of cerebral development and modification on child study. Proc. N. E. A., 1897. pp. 833-843.

214. **Hancock, John A.** A preliminary study of motor ability. Ped. Sem., Oct., 1894. Vol. 3, pp. 9-29.
Very widely read and quoted; a fine piece of work.

215. —— —— The relation of strength to flexibility in the hands of men and children. Ped. Sem., Oct., 1895. Vol. 3, pp. 308-313.

216. —— —— Children's ability to reason. Ed. Rev., N. Y., Oct., 1896. Vol. 12, pp. 261-268.

217. —— —— Mental differences of school children. Proc. N. E. A., 1897. pp. 851-859.

218. **Harrison, Elizabeth** A study of child nature from the kindergarten standpoint. Kindergarten College, Chicago, 1891. pp. 207.

219. **Hartland, E. S.** The science of fairy tales. An inquiry into fairy mythology. London, 1891. pp. 372.
The best presentation of the subject extant.

220. **Hartmann, Berthold** Die Analyse des kindlichen Gedankenkreises als die naturgemässe Grundlage des ersten Schulunterrichts. Hermann Graser, Annaberg, 1890. pp. 116.
One of the earlier and most important studies of the contents of children's minds.

221. **Hartwell, Edward M.** On the physiology of exercise. Boston Med. and Surg. Jour., March 31 and April 7, 1887. Vol. 116, pp. 297-302 ; 321-324.

222. —— —— Preliminary report on anthropometry in the U. S., with a provisional list of works, articles, books and tables, relating to anthropometry in the U. S.; including 117 titles arranged in classes I-VI. Quar. Pub. of the Am. Statist'l Ass'n. New series, 24. Vol. 3, Dec., 1893, pp. 554-568. Class II. Titles 4-33 relate to the anthropometry of children. See also Papers on Anthropometry. pp. 1-15. (No. 551.)

223. —— —— Application of the laws of physical training to the prevention and cure of stuttering. Proc. of the Intern. Cong. of Ed., Chicago, 1893. Proc. N. E. A., 1893: pp. 739-749.

224. —— —— Report of the director of physical training, Boston Normal Schools. School Document, No. 8, Boston, 1894. pp. 151.
Contains special study of correlation of growth and death rates of Boston children; also a study of stuttering as a developmental school disease.

225. —— —— Report of the director of physical training. Reprinted from School Document, No. 4, Boston, 1895. pp. 82.
Contains a special study of the seating of school children in relation to their height, etc. The best monograph yet published on the subject of school seating.

226. —— —— Bowditch's law of growth and what it teaches. Reprinted from the Tenth Annual Proc. of the Am. Ass'n for the Adv. of Physical Ed., Concord, N. H., 1896. pp. 8. (No. ——. pp. 23-30.)

227. —— —— Physical training, its function and place in education. Am. Physical Ed. Rev., Boston, Sept., 1897. Vol. 2, pp. 133-151.

228. **Haskell, Ellen M.** Imitation in children. 'Ped. Sem., Oct., 1894. Vol. 3, pp. 30-47.

229. —— —— Child observations. First series : Imitation and allied activities. With an introduction by E. H. Russell. D. C. Heath and Co., Boston, 1896. pp. 267.
    An unclassified collection of observations made by the pupils of the Worcester Normal School.

230. **Hasse, Paul** Die Ueberbürdung unserer Jugend auf den höheren Lehranstalten mit arbeit im Zusammenhange mit der Entstehung von Geistesstörungen. F. Vieweg u. Sohn. Braunschweig, 1880. pp. 92.

231. **Hellwig, Bernhard** Die vier Temperamente bei Kindern. Ihre. Aeusserung und Behandlung in Erziehung und Schule. J. Esser, Paderhorn, 1888.

232. **Hemmen, N.** Das Stottern. Statistik, Folgen, Abhülfe. Ein Beitrag zur Heilpädagogik. St. Paulus-Gesellschaft. Luxemburg, 1890. pp. 56.

233 **Herrainz, D. Gregorio** Tratado de antropologia y pedagogia. Madrid, 1896. pp. 564.
    One of the first fruits of Child Study in Spain.

234. **Herrick, Mary A.** Children's drawings. Ped. Sem., Oct., 1895. Vol. 3, pp. 338.339.

235. **Heydner, Georg** Beiträge zur Kenntnis des kindlichen Seelenlebens. R. Richter, Leipzig, 1894. pp. 96.

236. **Hitchcock, E.** Physical measurements, fallacies, and errors. Proc. Am. Ass'n for Adv. of Physical Ed., 1887. Brooklyn, N. Y., 1887. Vol. 3, pp. 35-42.

237. —— —— The anthropometric manual of Amherst College. (These tables are issued each year in pamphlet form and are of great value. Amherst, Mass.)

238. **Hitchcock, E. and Seelye, H. H.** An anthropometric manual, giving the average and physical measurements and tests of male college students and methods of securing them. Amherst, Mass., 1889. pp. 37.

239. **Holden, Edward S.** On the vocabularies of children under two years of age. Trans. Am. Philol. Ass'n, 1877. pp. 58-68. Reprint. Case, Lockwood and Brainard Co., Hartford, Ct., 1878.

240. **Holmes, Bayard** A study of child growth, being a review of the work of Dr. Wm. T. Porter, of St. Louis. N. Y., Med. Jour., Oct. 6, 1894. Vol. 60, pp. 417-423.

241. **Holmes, Marion E.** The fatigue of a school hour. Ped. Sem., Oct., 1895. Vol. 3, pp. 213-234.

242. **Holt, L. Emmett** The care and feeding of children. A catechism for the use of mothers and children's nurses. D. Appleton and Co., N. Y., 1894. pp. 66.

243. **Hornbrook, Adelia R.** The pedagogical value of number forms. A study. Ed. Rev., N. Y., May, 1893. Vol. 5, pp. 467-480.

244. **Howard, F. E.** The child voice. Proc. N. E. A., 1897. pp. 784-790.

245. **Howells, W. D.** A boy's town. Harper and Bros., N. Y. pp. 247.
    Largely personal reminiscence.

246. **Hoyt, Wm. A.** The love of nature as the root of teaching and learning the sciences. Ped. Sem., Oct., 1894. Vol. 3, pp. 61-86.

247. **Hughes, James L.** Educational value of play. Ed. Rev., N. Y., Nov., 1894. Vol. 8, pp. 327-336.

248. **Humphreys, Milton W.** A contribution to infantile linguistics. Trans. Am. Philol. Ass'n, 1880. Case, Lockwood and Brainard Co., Hartford, Ct., 1880. Vol. 11, pp. 5-17.

249. **Hurd, Henry M.** Some mental disorders of childhood and youth. Boston Med. and Surg. Jour., Sept. 20, 1894. Vol. 131, pp. 281-285. Reprint. The Friedenwald Co., Baltimore, 1895. pp. 16.

250. **Hurll, Estelle M.** Child life in art. Joseph Knight Co., Boston, 1895. pp. 176.

251. **Jacobi, Mary P.** Applications of psychology to education. Ed. Rev., N. Y., June, 1891. Vol. 2, pp. 1-27.

252. **Jastrow, Joseph** The psychological study of children. Ed. Rev., N. Y., March, 1891. Vol. 1, pp. 253-264.

253. —— —— A statistical study of memory and association. Ed. Rev., N. Y., Dec., 1891. Vol. 2, pp. 442-452.

254. **Jeffreys, B. Joy** Color-blindness: its dangers and its detection. Houghton, Osgood and Co., Boston, 1879. pp. 312.

255. —— —— Report of the examination of 27,927 school children for color-blindness. School Document No. 13. Rockwell and Churchill, Boston, 1880. pp. 9.

256. **Johnson, G. E.** Education by plays and games. Ped. Sem., Oct., 1894. Vol. 3, pp. 97-133.
    A suggestive study of about 500 plays of children, grouped so as to teach each school branch.

257. —— —— Contributions to the psychology and pedagogy of feeble-minded children. Ped. Sem., Oct., 1895. Vol. 3, pp. 246-301.

258. **Johnson, John, Jr.** Rudimentary society among boys. Johns Hopkins Univ. Studies in Historical and Political Science, 2d Series, No. 11. Baltimore, 1884. pp. 56. Reprint of same. McDonogh, Md., 1893. pp. 66.
    Remains the best study on the subject.

3

259. —— —— The savagery of boyhood. Pop. Sci. Mo., Oct., 1887. Vol. 31, pp. 796-800.

260. **Johnson, Richard O.** Deaf mutes and their education. Inland Educator, Nov., 1895. Vol. 1, 215-221; Jan., 1896. Vol. 1, 338-341; Feb., 1896. Vol. 2, 11-16; March, 1896. Vol. 2, pp. 77-78; April, 1896. Vol. 2, 131-134.

261. **Just, Karl** Der Wechsel der Stimmung im Gemütsleben des Kindes. Jahrbuch des Vereins für wissenschaftl. Pädag. Bleyl and Kaemmerer. Dresden, 1894. Vol. 26, pp. 201-210.

262. **Kafemann, R.** Schuluntersuchungen des kindlichen Nasen- und Rachenraumes. Kafemann, Danzig, 1890. pp. 29.

263. **Kennedy, Helen P.** Effect of high school work upon girls during adolescence. Ped. Sem., June, 1896. Vol. 3, pp. 469-482. (Menstruation.)

264. **Key, Axel** Schulhygienische Untersuchungen. In deutscher Bearbeitung. Herausgegeben von Dr. Leo Burgerstein. L. Voss, Hamburg, 1889. pp. 346.

265. —— —— Die Pubertätsentwickelung. Verhandl. des X. Internat. Med. Cong., 1890. Berlin, 1891. Vol. 1, pp. 66-130.
    Gives a condensed statement of the results of the investigations by the Swedish Commission into the growth, diseases and hygienic conditions of 15,000 boys and 3,000 girls.

266. **Kiefer, Konrad** Die Natur des Kindes hinsichtlich seiner sittlichen und intellektuellen Anlage. F. Reinboth, Leipzig, 1897. pp. 73.

267. **Kirkpatrick, E. A.** An experimental study of memory. Psychol. Rev., Nov., 1894. Vol. 1, pp. 602-609.

268. **Koch, J. L. A.** Psychopathische Minderwertigkeiten. Otto Maier, Ravensburg, 1893. pp. 427.

269. **Kotelmann, Ludwig** Ueber Schulgesundheitspflege. Handb. d. Erz. u. Unterr. f. höhere Schulen. München, 1895. Zweiter Band. 2 Abt. pp. 225-395.

270. **Kratz, H. E.** Characteristics of the best teachers as recognized by children. Ped. Sem., June, 1896. Vol. 3, pp. 413-418.

271. **Krohn, W. O.** The most critical period of school life. Child Study Monthly, June, 1895. Vol. 1, pp. 33-44.

272. —— —— Practical child study; how to begin. Child Study Monthly, Dec., 1895. Vol. 1, pp. 161-176.

273. —— —— Nervous diseases of school children. Child Study Monthly, April, 1896. Vol. 1, pp. 354-368.

274. **Kroner, Traugott** Ueber die Sinnesempfindungen der Neugeborenen. Grass, Barth and Co., Breslau, 1882. pp. 14.

275. **Kussmaul, Adolf** Untersuchungen über das Seelenleben des

neugeborenen Menschen. 2 Aufl. A. Moser, Tübingen, 1884. pp. 32.
Still remains an important scientific contribution.

276. **Laing, Mary E.** Child study. A teacher's record of her pupils. Forum, May, 1894. Vol. 17, pp. 340-344.

277. **Lancaster, E. G.** The psychology and pedagogy of adolescence. Ped. Sem., July, 1897. Vol. 5, pp. 61-128.
Reviews the literature upon the subject, and gives the results of an investigation by the questionnaire method.

278. **von Lange, Emil** Die normale Körpergrösse des Menschen von der Geburt bis zum 25. Lebensjahre nebst Erläuterungen über Wesen und Zweck der Skala-Messtabelle zum Gebrauche in Familie, Schule und Erziehungs-Anstalten. J. F. Lehmann, München, 1896. pp. 38. (With two measuring charts, which should be in every family and school.)

279. **Lesshaft, P.** De l'éducation de l'enfant dans la famille et de sa signification. A. Schulz, Paris, 1894. pp. 268.
A very good presentation of the child-type theory.

280. **Leuba, James H.** A study in the psychology of religious phenomena. Am. Jour. Psy., April, 1896. Vol. 7, pp. 309-385.
Attempts an analysis of conviction of sin and conversion.

281. **Lewis, Henry K.** The child, its spiritual nature. The Macmillan Co., N. Y., 1896. pp. 222.

282. **Levy, Miriam B.** How the man got in the moon. Ped. Sem., Oct., 1895. Vol. 3, pp. 317-318.

283. **Lincoln, D. F.** Anthropometry individualized. Reprinted from Mind and Body, May, 1896. pp. 8. (Also printed in No. 547.)
Points out important lines for research.

284. —— —— The motor element in education. Am. Physical Ed. Rev., June, 1897. Vol. 2, pp. 65-72.

285. **Linde, Antonius von der** Kaspar Hauser. Eine neugeschichtliche Legende. Chr. Limbarth, Wiesbaden, 1887. 2 vols., pp. 408-416.

286. **Lindley, E. H.** A preliminary study of some of the motor phenomena of mental effort. Am. Jour. Psy., July, 1896. Vol. 7, pp. 491-517.
A study of automatic movements in co-ordinated and incipient chorea.

287. —— —— A study of puzzles with special reference to the psychology of mental adaptation. Am. Jour. Psy., July, 1897. Vol. 8, pp. 431-493.
A careful and suggestive study.

288. **Lindley, E. H. and Partridge, G. E.** Some mental automatisms. Ped. Sem., July, 1897. Vol. 5, pp. 41-60.

289. **Löbisch, J. E.** Entwickelungsgeschichte der Seele des Kindes. Haas, Wien, 1851. pp. 134.

290. **Loffler, Helene** Mutter und Kind. Rathgeber für die Wochen und Kinderstube. Hoffmann und Ohnstein, Leipzig, 1882. pp. 221.

291. **Lombroso, Paola** Saggi di psicologia del bambino. Torino e Roma, 1894. pp. 284.
   One of the best studies of childhood ever written.

292. —— —— L'instinct de la conservation chez l'enfant Revue Philosophique, Oct., 1896. Vol. 42, pp. 379-390.

293. **Lord, Frances and Emily** Mother's songs, games and stories. (Froebel's Mutter und Kose Lieder), W. Rice, London, 1890. Text, pp. 212. Music, pp. 75.

294. **Loti, Pierre** The romance of a child. Translated by Mary L. Watkins. Rand, McNally and Co., Chicago, 1891. pp. 179.
   A suggestive reminiscent study.

295. **Louch, Mary** Difference between children and grown up people from the child's standpoint. Ped. Sem., July, 1897. Vol. 5, pp. 129-135.

296. **Luckey, G. W. A.** Comparative observations on the indirect color range of children, adults, and adults trained in color. Am. Jour. of Psychology, Jan., 1895. Vol. 6, pp. 489-504.
   This study suggests a means of making a reasonably accurate examination of a child's color sense.

297. —— —— Children's interests. North Western Monthly. Lincoln, Neb. Vol. 7, pp. 67, 96, 133, 156, 221, 245, 306, and 335.

298. —— —— Child study in its effects upon the teacher. Child Study Monthly, Feb., 1896. Vol. 1, pp. 230-247.

299. —— —— Lines of child study for the teacher. Ed. Rev., N. Y., Nov., 1897. Vol. 14, pp. 340-347. Also in Proc. N. E. A., 1897. pp. 826-833.

300. **Lukens, Herman T.** Preliminary report on the learning of language. Ped. Sem., June, 1896. Vol. 3, pp. 424-460.

301. —— —— A study of children's drawings in the early years. Ped. Sem., Oct., 1896. Vol. 4, pp. 79-110.
   The best study yet made in this field.

302. —— —— Child study for superintendents. Ed. Rev., N. Y., Feb., 1897. Vol. 13, pp. 105-120.

303. **Mackenzie, Morell** The hygiene of the vocal organs. Macmillan and Co., London, 1886. pp. 223.

304. **Maitland, Louise M.** What children draw to please themselves. Inland Educator, Sept. 1895. Vol. 1, pp. 77-81.
   One of the most valuable and practical studies for pedagogy.

305. **Manton, W. P.** The development of the young child with reference to exercise. Am. Physical Ed. Rev., Sept. 1897. Vol. 2, pp. 174-184.

306. **Marenholtz-Bülow,** (Baroness.) The child and child nature. 5th ed. Sonnenschein and Co., London, 1890. pp. 186.

307. **Marro, Antonio** La pubertà studiata nell' uomo e nella donna in rapporto all' antropologia, alla psichiatria, alla pedagogia ed alla sociologia. Fratelli Bocca, Torino, 1898. pp. 507.
   The best discussion to date. Many charts and tables.

308. **Marsh, Harriet A.** Child study in the mothers' club. Robt. Smith Printing Co., Lansing, Mich., 1896. pp. 31.
   Helpful pamphlet for mothers' clubs. Price 15 cts. Address Miss H. A. Marsh, Hancock School, Detroit, Mich.

309. —— —— A new aspect of child study. Ped. Sem., July, 1897. Vol. 5, pp. 136-145.

310. **Meyer, Adolf** On the observation of mental abnormalities in school children. Child Study Mo., May, 1895. Vol. 1, pp. 1-12.

311. —— —— Suggestions to those beginning the systematic observation of children. Child Study Monthly, June, 1895. Vol. 1, pp. 45-49.

312. **Meyer, Bertha** The child physically and mentally. Advice of a mother according to the teaching and experience of hygienic science. Trans. by R. Salomon. M L. Holbrook and Co., N. Y., 1893. pp. 155.

313. **Mill, John Stuart** Autobiography. Henry Holt and Co., N. Y., 1887. pp. 313.
   A study of child and adolescent thoughts, feelings and actions.

314. **Minot, C. S.** Growth. Reference Hand-book of the Med. Sciences. Wm. Wood and Co., N. Y., 1886. Vol. 3, pp. 394-400.

315. **Monroe, Will S.** Feeble-minded children in the public school. An address read before the Ass'n of Med. Officers of Am. Institutions for Idiotic and Feeble-Minded Persons at Fort Wayne, Ind., May, 1894, and reprinted from the Proc. of the Ass'n. Westfield, Mass., 1897. pp. 11.
   An investigation of over 10,000 California children with reference to the percentage of mentally dull children in the public schools.

316. —— —— (Editor.) Comenius' school of infancy. An essay on the education of youth during the first six years. D. C. Heath and Co., Boston, 1896. pp. 99.
   One of the earliest methodical treatises on the first years of the child's life.

317. —— —— Historic sense of children. Jour of Ed., Boston, June 24, 1897. Vol. 45, pp. 406-407.
   Gives the basis of the child's belief in historical facts.

318. —— —— The social sense in childhood. Jour. of Ed., Boston, Nov. 18, 1897. Vol. 46, pp. 291-292.
   A study of the kinds of chums children like the best.

319. —— —— Child study and school discipline. Ed. Rev., N. Y., Dec., 1897. Vol. 14, pp. 451-456.
   Presents the question of testifying against evil doers.

320. —— —— Class responsibility. N. Y. Teachers' Quarterly, N. Y., Dec., 1897. Vol. 1, pp. 316-318.
Gives the views of over 3,000 school children on this question.

321. —— ——Bibliography of education. Int. Education Series. Vol. 42. D. Appleton and Co., N. Y., 1897. pp. 202.
One section devoted to child study, but gives only the books and pamphlets published in English.

322. **Moon, Schuyler B.** Measurements of the boys of the McDonough School for the years 1888-1891; arranged in order of height, summed and averaged. Also a percentile table for 115 boys 13-14 years of age. McDonough, Md., 1892. pp. 46.
Indicates the lines of physical growth of orphans.

323. —— —— The growth of boys. Reprinted from the Proc. Am. Ass'n for the Adv. of Physical Ed. Republican Press Ass'n, Concord, N. H., 1896. pp. 9, 5 plates. (No. 547. pp. 19-23.)

324. **Moore, Kathleen Carter** The mental development of a child. Psy. Rev. Monograph Supp. No. 3, Oct., 1896. The Macmillan Co., N. Y. pp. 150.
A careful study by a mother of her own child during the first three years of its life.

325. **Morrison, W. D.** Juvenile offenders. D. Appleton and Co., N. Y., 1897. pp. 317.
The most comprehensive recent treatment.

326. **Mosher, Eliza M.** Habitual postures of school children. Ed. Rev., N. Y., Nov., 1892. pp. 339-349.

327. **Motet, Auguste** Les faux témoignages des enfants devant la justice. Bailliere et fils, Paris, 1887. pp. 20.

328. **Moulton, A. R.** Body weight and mental improvement. Am. Jour. of Insanity, Oct., 1894. Vol. 51, pp. 209-220.

329. **Mulford, Henry J.** The throat of the child. Ed. Rev., N. Y., March, 1897. Vol. 13, pp. 261-272.

330. **Müller, George** Spinal curvature and awkward deportment; their causes and prevention in children. English edition. The Scientific Press, Ltd., 428 Strand, London, 1894. pp. 88.

331. **Mumford, Alfred A.** Survival movements of human infancy. Substance of an address given before the Manchester Branch of the British Association for Child Study, March 2, 1897. Brain, London, Autumn, 1897. (No. 79.) Vol. 20, pp. 290-307.

332. **Murray, J. Clark** The education of the will. Ed. Rev., N. Y., June, 1891. Vol. 2, pp. 57-68.

333. **Necker de Saussure, Mme.** Education progressive ou étude du cours de la vie, précédée d'une notice sur la vie et les écrits de l'auteur. 6e édition. Garnier Frères, Paris, n. d. 2 vols., pp. 347, 572.
The best of the older French studies of education and development. The appendix contains one of the earliest systematic records of infant life made by a mother.

334. **Newell, W. W.** Games and songs of American children. Harper and Bros., N. Y., 1884. pp. 242.

335. **Nicolay, Fernand** Les enfants mal élevés. Etude psychologique, anecdotique et pratique. Perrin et Cie., Paris, 1890. pp. 530.
Very discursive but suggestive.

336. **Oppenheim, Nathan** Why children lie. Pop. Sci. Mo., July, 1895. Vol. 47, pp. 382-387.

337. **Osborn, F. W.** Ethical contents of children's minds. Ed. Rev., N. Y., Sept., 1894. Vol. 8, pp. 143-146.

338. **O'Shea, M. V.** Physical training in the public schools. Atlantic Monthly, Feb., 1895. Vol. 75, pp. 246-254.

339. —— —— Method and scope of child study for teachers in service. Child Study Monthly, Nov., 1895. Vol. 1, pp. 129-134. Also Proc. N. E. A., 1895. pp. 924-928.

340. —— —— Educational values in the elementary school. Pop. Sci. Mo., March, 1896. Vol. 48, pp. 675-686.
A suggestive paper, based largely upon recent studies of fatigue.

341. —— —— Child study. Chautauquan, June, 1896. Vol. 23, pp. 302-307.

342. —— —— The training of childhood. Outlook, May 15, 1897. Vol. 56, pp. 164-167.

343. —— —— Interests in childhood. Child Study Monthly, Oct., 1896. Vol. 2, pp. 266-278. Also Proc. N. E. A., 1896. pp. 873-881.

344. —— —— When character is formed. Pop. Sci. Mo., Sept., 1897. Vol. 51, pp. 648-662.

345. —— —— Some aspects of drawing. Ed. Rev., N. Y., Oct., 1897. Vol. 14, pp. 263-284.

346. —— —— The purpose, scope, and method of child study. Jour. of Pedagogy, Syracuse, N. Y., Dec., 1897. Vol. 11, pp. 9-23.

347. **Ottolenghi, S.** La sensibilità e l'età. Arch. di psichiat. Torino, 1895. Vol. 16, pp. 540-551.

348. **Ouroussov, Mary** (Princess.) Education from the cradle. Translated by Mrs. E. Fielding. George Bell and Sons, London, 1890. pp. 168.

349. **Patrick, G. T. W.** The memory in education. Ed. Rev., N. Y., Dec., 1892. Vol. 4, pp. 463-474.

350. —— —— Is child study practicable for the teacher? Proceedings of the N. E. A., Denver, Colo., 1895. pp. 906-914.

351. **Paulsen, Ed.** Ueber die Singstimme der Kinder. Archiv für die ges. Physiologie, Aug., 1895. Vol. 61, pp. 407-426.
Based on the study of several thousand children.

352. **Peckham, Geo. W.** The growth of children. Sixth Annual

Rep. State Bd. of Health of Wis., 1881. Madison, Wis., 1882. Vol. 6, pp. 28-73. Reprint pp. 46.

With 9,500 children of school age it parallels Dr. Bowditch's study of Boston children. (See No. 58.)

353. —— —— Various observations on growth. 7th Annual Rep. Wis. State Board of Health, 1882. Madison, Wis., 1883. Vol. 7, pp. 185-188.

354. **Peckham, Grace** Infancy in the city. Pop. Sci. Mo., March, 1886. Vol. 28, pp. 683-689.

355. **Percy, J. F.** Causes of deafness in school children and its influences upon education. Child Study Monthly, Oct., 1895. Vol. I, pp. 97-109.

356. **Perez, Bernard** L'éducation morale dès le berceau. F. Alcan, Paris, 1888. pp. 320.

357. —— —— The first three years of childhood. Ed. and trans. by Alice M. Cristie. With an introduction by James Sully. C. W. Bardeen, Syracuse, N. Y., 1889. pp. 294.

Collection of notes, valuable chiefly as data.

358. —— —— Le caractère de l'enfant à l'homme. F. Alcan, Paris, 1892. pp. 308.

359. —— —— L'enfant de trois à sept. ans. 3e édition revue et augmentée d'un supplément. F. Alcan, Paris, 1894. pp. 330.

360. **Phillips, D. E.** Genesis of number-forms. Am. Jour. of Psy., July, 1897. Vol. 8, pp. 506-527.

361 —— —— Number and its application psychologically considered. Ped. Sem., Oct., 1897. Vol. 5, pp. 221-281.

A new view of both the psychology and pedagogy of the subject.

362. **Pierce, John M.** Interest of the child in physical training. Am. Physical Ed. Rev., March, 1897. Vol. 2, pp. 19-21.

363. **Ploss, H.** Das kleine Kind vom Tragbett bis zum ersten Schritt. Ueber das Legen, Tragen und Wiegen, Gehen, Stehen und Sitzen der kleinen Kinder bei verschiedenen Völkern der Erde. L. Fernau, Leipzig, 1881. pp. 121.

364. —— —— Das Kind in Brauch und Sitte der Völker. Anthropologische Studien. Leipzig, 1884. 2 vols., pp. 394, 478.

A classic. Exhaustive and suggestive.

365. **Pollock, F.** An infant's progress in language. Mind, July, 1878. Vol. 3, pp. 392-401.

366. **Porter, W. T.** The physical basis of precocity and dullness. Trans. of the Acad. of Sci., St. Louis, Mo. Issued March, 1893. Vol. 6, pp. 161-181. Also Am. Physical Ed. Rev., Sept., 1897. Vol. 2, pp. 155-173.

367. —— —— On the application to individual school children of the means derived from anthropological measurements by the gener-

alizing method. Paper read Sept. 16, 1893, before the Internat. Statist. Inst., at Chicago. Quarterly Publications of the Am. Statist. Ass'n. Boston, Dec., 1893. Vol. 3, pp. 576-587.

368. —— —— The growth of St. Louis children. Trans. of the Acad. of Sci., St. Louis, Mo. Issued April 14, 1894. Vol. 6, pp. 263-380, 46 plates. See also papers on anthropometry. (See No. 551, pp. 58-64.)

369. —— —— The use of anthropometrical measurements in schools. Ed. Rev., N. Y., Feb., 1896. Vol. 11, pp. 126-133 (See also No. 547, pp. 158-164.)

370. —— —— The relation between the growth of children and their deviation from the physical type of their sex and age. Trans. of the Acad. of Science of St. Louis. St. Louis, Mo., 1893. Vol. 6, pp. 233-250.

371. —— —— Ueber Untersuchungen der Schulkinder auf die Physischen Grundlagen ihrer geistigen Entwickelung. Read in Berliner Gesellschaft für Anthropologie, Ethnologie, und Urgeschichte, 15 July, 1893. Zeits. f. Ethnologie, Berlin, 1894. pp. 337-354.

372. **Potel, Maurice** De l'accroissement en poids des enfants nés avant terme. Soc. d'Editions Scientifiques. Paris, 1895. pp. 40.

373. **Poulsson, Emilie.** Finger plays for nursery and kindergarten. (18 plays with music.) D. Lothrop Co., Boston, 1893. pp. irregular.

374. **Powell, F. M.** Backward and mentally deficient children. Child Study Monthly, March, 1896. Vol. 1, pp. 290-305.

375. **Preyer, W.** The mind of the child. Part 1. The senses and the will. (Translated by H. W. Brown.) D. Appleton and Co., N. Y., 1888. pp. 346.

376. —— —— The mind of the child. Part 2. The development of the intellect. (Translated by H. W. Brown.) D. Appleton and Co., N. Y., 1889. pp. 317.

377. —— —— Die gesitige Entwickelung in der ersten Kindheit. Union, Stuttgart, 1893. pp. 201.

378. —— —— Mental development in the child. (Translated by H. W. Brown.) D. Appleton and Co., N. Y., 1893. pp. 170.

379. —— —— Die Seele des Kindes, Beobachtungen über die geistige Entwickelung des Menschen in den ersten Lebensjahren. Vierte Aufl. L. Fernau, Leipzig, 1895. pp. 462.

380. —— —— Die Psychologie des Kindes. Verhandlungen des 3te Internat. Congress für Psychologie in München, 1896. J. F. Lehmann, München, 1897. pp. 80-94.

381. **Prior, Mary D.** Notes on the first three years of a child. Ped. Sem., Oct., 1895. Vol. 3, pp. 339-341.

382. **Proudfoot, A. H.** A mother's ideals. A kindergarten mother's conception of family life. Pub. by the author, 1400 Auditorium, Chicago, 1897. pp. 270.

383. **Queyrat, F.** L'imagination et ses variétés chez l'enfant. F. Alcan, Paris, 1893. pp. 162.

384. **Raehlmann, E.** Physiologisch-psychologische Studien über die Entwickelung der Gesichtswahrnehmungen bei Kindern und bei operierten Blindgeborenen. Zeits. f. Psychologie und Physiologie der Sinnesorgane, Feb., 1891. Vol. 2, pp. 53-96.

385. **Rassier, M.** Valeur du témoignage des enfants en justice. Lyons, 1893. pp. 88.

386. **Rauber, A.** Homo sapiens ferus oder die Zustände der Verwilderten in ihrer Bedeutung für Wissenschaft, Politik und Schule. Biologische Untersuchung. Zweite Aufl. Leipzig, 1888. pp. 134.
   A valuable chapter.

387. **Renkauf, A.** Abnorme Kinder und ihre Pflege. H. Beyer u. Söhne, Langensalza, 1893. pp. 19.

388. **Riccardi, A.** Antropologia e pedagogia. Parte Prima. Introduzione ad una scienza della educazione (Osservazioni psicologiche; ricerche statistiche; misure antropologiche, ecc.). Modena, 1892. pp. 172.
   A valuable study of child-sociology.

389. **Ricci, Corrado.** L'arte dei bambini. N. Zanichelli, Bologna, 1887. pp. 84.
   Very suggestive. (For condensed translation see No. 21.)

390. **Richter, Gustav** Unterricht und geistige Ermüdung. Eine schulmännische Würdigung der Schrift Kraepelins "Ueber geistige Arbeit." Lehrproben und Lehrgänge, Halle A. S., Oct., 1895, Heft 45. pp. 1-37.

391. **Richter, Jean Paul** Levana; or, the doctrine of education. Trans. from the German. With a short biography of the author and his autobiography. George Bell and Sons, London, 1889. pp. 413.
   Child-life interpreted by an author who did not forget his childhood.

392. **Risley, S. D.** Defective vision in school children. Ed. Rev., N. Y., April, 1892. Vol. 3, pp. 348-354.

393. **Roberts, Charles** A manual of anthropometry, or a guide to the physical examination and measurement of the human body. With final report of the Anthropometric Committee of 1882-83. J. and A. Churchill, London, 1878. pp. 54.

394. **Robinson, L.** Darwinism in the nursery. 19th Century, Nov., 1891. Vol. 30, pp. 831-842.

395. —— —— Infantile atavism. Brit. Med. Jour., Dec. 5, 1891, II. pp. 1226-1227.

396. —— —— The primitive child. N. A. Review, Oct., 1894. Vol. 159, pp. 467-478.

397. **Rousseau, J. J.** Émile; a treatise on education. Translated by W. H. Payne. Int. Education Ser., vol. 20. D. Appleton and Co., N. Y., 1893. pp. 355. Selections from the same, by Jules Steeg. Trans. by Eleanor Worthington. D. C. Heath and Co., Boston, 1888. pp. 157.

398. **Royce, Josiah** Mental defect and disorder from the teacher's point of view. Ed. Rev., N. Y., Oct., Nov., Dec., 1893. Vol. 6, pp. 209-222; 322-331; 449-463.

399. —— —— The imitative functions and their place in human nature. Century Magazine, May, 1894. Vol. 48. (N. S. Vol. 26.) pp. 137-145.

400. **Russell, E. H.** Observation and experiment essential in pedagogical inquiry. The Academy, Syracuse, N. Y., Sept., 1889. Vol. 4, pp. 335-348.

401. —— —— The study of children at the State Normal School, Worcester, Mass. Ped. Sem., Dec., 1893. Vol. 2, pp. 343-357.

402. —— —— Exceptional children in school. Ed. Rev., N. Y., Dec., 1893. Vol. 6, pp. 431-442.

403. —— —— Blanks for the study of children. State Normal School, Worcester, Mass. (See also No. 229.)

404. **Ryerson, G. S.** Defective vision in the public schools. (Results of examination of 5,253 children in Toronto. Paper read March 22, 1890.) Trans. Canadian Inst., 1889-90. Toronto, 1891. Vol. 1, pp. 26-27.

405. **Sachs, B.** A treatise on the nervous diseases of children, for physicians and students. Baillière, Tindall and Cox, London, 1895. pp. 666.

406. **Schallenberger, Margaret E.** A study of children's rights as seen by themselves. Ped. Sem., Oct., 1894. Vol. 3, pp. 87-96.
 A careful scientific study.

407. **Schechter, S.** The child in Jewish literature. Jewish Quarterly, vol. 2, London, 1889.

408. **Scholz, Friedrich** Die Charakterfehler des Kindes. Eine Erziehungslehre für Haus und Schule. E. H. Mayer, Leipzig, 1891. pp. 233.

409. **Schubert, Conrad** Elternfragen, eine notwendige Ergänzung der Hartmannschen psychologischen Analyse. Aus dem Päd. Universitäts-Seminar zu Jena. Fünftes Heft. H. Beyer and Söhne, Langensalza, 1894. pp. 80-140.

410. **Schubert, P.** Die Steilschrift während der letzen fünf Jahre. Zeits. f. Schulgesundheitspflege, Apr., 1895. Vol. 8, pp. 193-215

411. **Schultze, Fritz** Die Sprache des Kindes. Eine Anregung zur

Erforschung der Gegenstandes. E. Günther, Leipzig, 1880. pp. 46.

412. **Schuschny, H.** Über die Nervosität der Schuljugend. Gustav Fischer, Jena, 1895. pp. 31.

413. **Schuyten, C.** Influence des variations de la température atmosphérique sur l'attention volontaire des élèves. Recherches expérimentales faites dans les écoles primaires d' Anvers, 1895-1896. Bull. de l'Acad. Roy. des Sciences, des. Lettres et des Beaux-Arts de Belgique, Bruxelles, 1896. 3e série, vol. 52, pp. 315-326, with two plates.

414. **Scott, Colin A.** Old age and death. Am. Jour. of Psy., Oct., 1896. Vol. 8, pp. 67-122.

415. —— —— The psychology of puberty and adolescence. Proc. N. E. A., 1897. pp. 843-851.

416. **Scovil, Elizabeth F.** The care of children. H. Altemus, Phila., 1895. pp. 348.

417. **Scripture, E. W.** Tests on school children. Ed. Rev., N. Y., Jan., 1893. Vol. 5, pp. 52-61.

418. —— —— Aims and status of child study. Ed. Rev., N. Y., Oct., 1894. Vol. 8, pp. 236-239.

419. **Scudder, H. M.** Childhood in literature and art, with some observations on literature for children. Houghton, Mifflin and Co., Boston, 1894. pp. 245.

420. **Search, P. W.** (Editor.) The Holyoke school children's Christmas annual, 1897. A budget of Christmas stories by real boys and girls. The first Christmas Annual of the girls and the boys of the Holyoke schools. Holyoke, Mass., 1897. pp. 96. Price 25c.

421. **Seaver, E. P.** Truants and incorrigibles. Ed. Rev., N. Y., May, 1894. Vol. 7, pp. 423-438.

422. **Seaver, Jay W.** Anthropometry and physical examination. Pub. by the author, New Haven, Conn., 1896. pp. 200. Bibliography, pp. 3.

423. **Seguin, Edward** Idiocy and its treatment by the physiological method. Wm. Wood & Co., N. Y., 1866. pp. 457.
This work is the basis of most of the instruction of feeble-minded children in America.

424. —— —— Prenatal and infantile culture. Pop. Sci. Mo., Nov., 1876. Vol. 10, pp. 38-43.

425. —— —— The psycho-physiological training of an idiotic hand. Archives of Medicine, N. Y., 1879. Vol. 2, pp. 149-156, with plate.

426. —— —— The psycho-physiological training of an idiotic eye. Archives of Medicine, Dec., 1880. Vol. 4, pp. 217-233, with 2 plates.

427. —— —— Rapport et mémoires sur l'éducation des enfants normaux et anormaux. F. Alcan, Paris, 1895. pp. 376.

428. **Seligmüller, Adolph** Wie bewahren wir uns und unsere Kinder vor Nervenleiden. Eduard Trewendt, Breslau, 1891. pp. 60.

429. **Semmig, Hermann** Das Kind, Tagebuch eines Vaters. 2te Aufl. Hartung und Sohn. Rudolstadt, 1876. pp. 240.

430. **Sergi, Giuseppe** Un primo passo alla pedagogia scientifica e la carta biografica. Enrico Trevisini, Milano. pp. 35.

431. **Shaw, Edward R.** Vertical script and proper desks as related to education. Proc. Am. Assoc., Adv. of Phys. Ed., 10th Ann. Meeting, April, 1895. Concord, N.H., 1896. pp. 110-123. (No. 547.)

432. —— —— Some observations upon teaching children to write. Child Study Monthly, Feb., 1896. Vol. 1, pp. 226-229.

433. —— —— A comparative study on children's interests. Child Study Monthly, July, August, 1896. Vol. 2, pp. 152-167.

433 a. —— —— The employment of the motor activities in teaching. Pop. Sci. Mo., 1896. Vol. 50, pp. 56-67.

434. **Shaw, John C.** A test of memory in school children. Ped. Sem., Oct., 1896. Vol. 4, pp. 61-78.

435. —— —— What children like to read. W. Va. School Journal, Charleston, W. Va., Oct., 1897. Vol. 17, pp. 5-6.

436. **Shinn, Milicent W.** The visible world of a little child. The Univ. of Cal. Mag., March, 1893. Vol. 1, pp. 13-18.

437. —— —— Notes on the development of a child. Univ. of Cal. Studies. Pub. by the Univ., Berkeley, Cal., 1893. pp. 178.
An excellent collection of classified notes on a single child.

438. —— —— The baby's mind : a study for college women. A paper presented to the Ass'n of Collegiate Alumnæ, Oct., 27, 1894. Series 2, No. 52, pp. 11.
Very valuable studies of a single child.

439. **Shuttleworth, G. E.** Mentally deficient children : their treatment and training. H. K. Lewis, London, 1895. pp. 140.
Deals with the mental and physical characteristics of mental deficiency.

440. **Siegert, Gustav** Problematische Kindesnaturen; eine Studie für Schule und Haus. Voigtländ, Leipzig, 1889. pp. 79.

441. —— —— Die Periodicität in der Entwickelung der Kindesnatur. Voigtländ, Leipzig, 1891. pp. 92.

442. —— —— Problem der Kinderselbstmorde. Voigtländ, Leipzig.

443. **Sigismund, Berthold** Kind und Welt. Vätern, Müttern und Kinderfreunden gewidmet. I. Die fünf ersten Perioden des Kindesalters. F. Vieweg u. Sohn, Braunschweig, 1856. pp. 221.
A delightfully written work.

444. —— —— Kind und Welt: für Eltern und Lehrer, sowie für

Freunde der Psychologie mit Einleitung und Anmerkungen neu herausgegeben von Chr. Ufer. *F*. Vieweg u. Sohn, Braunschweig, 1897. pp. 199.

445. **Sikorsky, M.** Du développement du langage chez les enfants. Archives de Neurologie, Nov., 1883. Vol. 6, pp. 319-336.

446. **Simpson, Walter G.** A chronicle of infant development and characteristics. Jour. of Mental Science, July, Oct., 1893. Vol. 39, pp. 378-389; 498-505.

447. **Slack, H. W.** Mirror writing and left-handedness. (Author incorrectly given in the Pedagogical Seminary as M. Strack.) Ped. Sem., March, 1893. Vol. 2, pp. 236-244.

448. **Small, Maurice H.** The suggestibility of children. Ped. Sem., Dec., 1896. Vol. 4, pp. 176-220.
A comprehensive and valuable study of imitation.

449. **Smith, Jessie R.** The story of Washington. A children's book by children. Illustrations by the children themselves. W. B. Harison, N. Y., 1896. pp. 30.

450. —— —— Four true stories of life and adventure. (Stories of Columbus, Capt. John Smith, Miles Standish, and Benjamin Franklin, written by children.) W. B. Harison, N. Y., 1897. pp. 106.

451. **Springer, Maurice** La croissance, son rôle en pathologie. Essai de pathologie générale. F. Alcan, Paris, 1890. pp. 196.

452. **Stableton, J. K.** Study of boys entering the adolescent period of life. Series of articles in the North Western Monthly, Lincoln, Neb., begun in the issue for Nov., 1897. Vol. 8, pp. 248-250.

453. **Starbuck, Edwin Diller** A study of conversion. Am. Jour. of Psy., Jan., 1897. Vol. 8, pp. 268-308.

454. —— —— Some aspects of religious growth. Am. Jour. of Psy., Oct., 1897. Vol. 9, pp. 70-124.

455. **Stenzl, Anton** Ansteckende Kinderkrankheiten. Belehrung über deren Erkenntniss nebst einem Anhang über Diätetik und Prophylaxis. Karl Graeser, Wien, 1883. pp. 39.

456. **Stevenson, R. L.** Child's play. Virginibus Puerisque and Other Papers. C. Kegan Paul & Co., London, 1881. pp. 237-260.

457. —— —— A child's garden of verses. Chas. Scribner's Sons, N. Y., 1893. pp. 101.

458. **Stockton-Hough, J.** Statistics relating to 700 births (white) occurring in the Philadelphia Hospital, between 1865 and 1872. Phila. Med. Times, 1885-86. Vol. 16, pp. 92-94.

459. **Stratton, George M.** Child study and psychology. Ed. Rev., N. Y., Sept., 1897. Vol. 14, pp. 132-139.

460. **Street, J. R.** A study in language teaching. Ped. Sem., April, 1897. Vol. 4, pp. 269-293.

Comparing different current methods of teaching modern languages,with criticism.

461. —— —— A study in moral education. Ped. Sem., July, 1897. Vol. 5, pp. 5-40.

462. **Strümpell, Ludwig** Die pädagogische Pathologie oder die Lehre von den Fehlern der Kinder. Versuch einer Grundlegung für gebildete Aeltern, Studirende der Pädagogik, Lehrer, sowie für Schulbehörden und Kinderärzte. Georg Böhme, Leipzig, 1890. pp. 225.

463. **Sudborough, Mrs. G. B.** What children imitate. North Western Monthly, Lincoln, Neb. Vol. 7, pp. 99, 136, 162, 226, 300 and 332.

464. **Sully, J.** Babies and science. Cornhill Mag., May, 1881. Vol. 43, pp. 539-554.

465. —— —— Baby linguistics. Eng. Illustrated Mag., Nov., 1884. Vol. 2, pp. 110-118.

466. —— —— The service of psychology to education. Ed. Rev., N. Y., Nov., 1892. Vol. 4, pp. 313-327.

467. —— —— Studies of childhood. D. Appleton and Co., N. Y., 1896. pp. 527.

The most important of the author's contributions to the subject.

468. —— —— Children's ways. Being selections from the author's Studies of Childhood with some additional matter. D. Appleton and Co., N. Y., 1897. pp. 193.

469. **Taine, M.** De l'acquisition du langage chez les enfants et dans l'espèce humaine. Revue Philosophique. Jan., 1876. (The acquisition of language by children. Translation of above. Mind, April, 1877. Vol. 2, pp. 252-259.)

470. **Talbot, Mrs. Emily** (Editor.) Papers on infant development. Pub. by the Education Dept. of the Am. Soc. Sci. Ass'n, Jan., 1882. pp. 52.

A collection of brief miscellaneous papers.

471. **Tarbell, G. G.** On the height, weight, and relative rate of growth of normal and feeble-minded children. Proc. 6th Annual Session, Ass'n of Med'l Officers, Am. Institutions for Idiotic and Feeble Minded Persons. J. B. Lippincott & Co., Phila., 1883. pp. 188-189, with diagram.

472. **Taylor, Henry L.** American childhood from a medical standpoint. Pop. Sci. Mo., October, 1892. Vol. 41, pp. 721-732.

473. **Taylor, John M.** The insane disorders of childhood. Archives of Pediatrics, Feb., 1894. Vol. 11, pp. 100-115. Reprint pp. 16.

474. **Thurber, Charles H.** Hints on child study. Also study of children's hopes. Rept. of State Supt. Pub. Instruction, Albany, N. Y., 1896. Vol. 2, pp. 977-1042. (See No. 556.)

475. —— —— The relation of child study to Sunday school work. North Western Monthly, Sept., 1897. Vol. 8, pp. 137-141.

476. **Tiedemann, D.** Beobachtungen über die Entwickelung der Seelenfähigkeiten bei Kindern. O. Bonde, Altenburg, 1897. pp. 56.
Contains a bibliography of 14 pp., by Chr. Ufer. Originally published in 1782. An English trans. of the French edition of 1863, published by C. W. Bardeen, Syracuse, N. Y., 1890. pp. 46. Price, 15 cts.

477. **Tolstoi, L.** Boyhood, adolescence and youth. Translated by Constantine Popoff. Elliott Stock, London, 1890. pp. 480. American translation by Isabel F. Hapgood. T. Y. Crowell and Co., N. Y., 1886. pp. 244.
A searching reminiscent study of boyhood.

478. **Tracy, Frederick** The language of childhood. Am. Jour. Psy., Oct., 1893. Vol. 6, pp. 107-138.

479. —— —— The psychology of childhood. D. C. Heath and Co., Boston, 1894. pp. 170.

480. **Trüper, J.** Psychopathische Minderwertigkeiten im Kindesalter. Ein Mahnwort für Eltern, Lehrer und Erzieher. C. Bertelsmann, Gütersloh, 1893. pp. 90.
Discusses the care and training of mentally dull children, and their legal responsibility.

481. **Tsanoff, Stoyan V.** Educational value of the children's playgrounds. A novel plan of character building. Pub. for the author, 1305 Arch St., Phila., Pa., 1897. pp. 203.

482. **Tucker, Mrs. E. F.** The development of the number sense. North Western Monthly, Lincoln, Neb. Vol. 7, pp. 70, 101, 158, 248, 302 and 333.

483. **Tucker, M. S.** Pedonomics. Child Study Monthly, April, 1896. Vol. 1, pp. 368-373.

484. **Ufer, Christian** Geistesstörungen in der Schule. Ein Vortrag, nebst 13 Krankenbildern. J. F. Bergmann, Wiesbaden, 1891. pp. 50.

485. —— —— Ueber Sinnestypen und verwandte Erscheinungen. (Heft 3 der Beiträge zur pädagog. Pathopsychologie.) Beyer u. Sohn, Langensalza, 1895. pp. 20.

486. —— —— Ueber Handschrift und Individualitat bei Schulkindern. Verhandlungen des 3te Intern. Congress für Psychologie zu München, 1896. J. F. Lehmann, München, 1897. pp. 442-443.

487. —— —— Kinderpsychologie. Ency. Handb. d. Pädagogik, von W. Rein. Langensalza, 1897. Band 4, pp. 113-123.
—— —— See also No. 476.

488. **Uffelmann, Julius** Manual of the domestic hygiene of the child. For the use of students, physicians, sanitary officials, teachers and mothers. Edited by Mary Putnam Jacobi, M. D., translated by Harriot R. Milinowski. G. P. Putnam's Sons, N. Y., 1891. pp. 221.

489. **Van Liew, C. C.** Some educational bearings of the principle of imitation. North Western Monthly, Lincoln, Neb., Dec., 1897. Vol. 8, pp. 320-327.

490. **Vaughn, Marion** The mother's record of the physical, mental and moral growth of her child for the first fifteen years. D. Lothrop Co., Boston, 1882.

491. **von Vierordt, Karl** Physiologie des Kindesalters. Reprint from Handb. d. Kinderkrankheiten. H. Laupp, Tübingen, 1881. pp. 496.
  A standard; cf. also his Physiologische Daten u. Tabellen.

492. **Wagner, Charles** Youth. Translated by Ernest Redwood. Dodd, Mead, and Co., N. Y., 1893. pp. 291.

493. **Ward, Effie M.** Geographic interests of children. Education, Boston, Dec., 1897. Vol. 18, pp. 235-240.
  An account of the places which 4,000 school children would like most to visit, and the reasons given for desiring to visit certain places.

494. **Warner, Charles D.** Being a boy. Houghton, Mifflin and Co., Boston, 1894. pp. 244.

495. **Warner, Francis** Recurrent headaches in children. Brain, Oct., 1880. Vol. 3, pp. 309-313. Reprint, W. Clowes and Sons, London, 1880. pp. 5.

496. —— —— Physical expression: its modes and principles. Int. Sci. Series, vol. 51. D. Appleton and Co., N. Y., 1886. pp. 372.

497. —— —— The anatomy of movement: a treatise on the action of nerve centers and modes of growth. Three lectures delivered at the Royal College of Surgeons. K. Paul, Trench and Co., London, 1887. pp. 135.

498. —— —— The children: how to study them. F. Hodgson, London, 1887. pp. 80.

499. —— —— Deviations from normal development among 50,000 children. Jour. of the Anthrop'l Institute. Session, June 13, 1893. London, 1894. Vol. 23, pp. 206-214.

500. —— —— A method of examining children in schools as to their development and brain condition. Brit. Med. Jour., Sept. 22, 1888. Vol. 2 for 1888, pp. 659-660.

501 —— —— Muscular movements in man and their evolution in the infant. Jour. Mental Science, April, 1889. Vol. 35, pp. 23-44.

502. —— —— A course of lectures on the growth and means of training the mental faculty. Delivered in the Univ. of Cambridge. Macmillan and Co., N. Y., 1890. pp. 222.

503. —— —— Report to the Brit. Med. Ass'n and Charity Organization Soc. of London, on the physical and mental condition of 50,000 children seen in 106 schools of London. Rep. of the Commissioner of Ed. for 1890-91. Washington, 1894. Vol. 2, pp. 1081-1138.

504. —— —— An inquiry as to the physical and mental condition of school children. Reprint from the Brit. Med. Jour., March 12–19, 1892. Brit. Med. Ass'n, London, 1892. pp. 14.

505. —— —— Report on the scientific study of the mental and physical conditions of childhood. With particular reference to children of defective constitution, and with recommendations as to education and training. (The report is based upon the examination of 50,000 children seen in 1888–91, and of another 50,000 seen in 1892–94.) Pub. by the Committee, Parkes Museum, Margaret St. W., London, 1895. pp. 117.

506. —— —— The study of children and their school training. The Macmillan Co., N. Y., 1897. pp. 264.
    Gives a very popular statement of the results of his previous studies.

507. **West, Gerald M.** Eye tests on children. Am. Jour. of Psy., Aug., 1892. Vol. 4, pp. 595-596.

508. —— —— Worcester school children. The growth of the body, head and face, Science, Jan. 6, 1893. Vol. 21, pp. 2-4.

509. —— —— Anthropometrische Untersuchungen über die Schulkinder in Worcester, Mass., Amerika. Archiv für Anthropologie. Braunschweig, July, 1893. Vol. 22, pp. 13-48.

510. —— —— The anthropometry of American school children. Memoirs of the International Congress of Anthropology, 1893. The Schulte Pub. Co., Chicago, 1894. pp. 50-58.

511. **Whitney, A. S.** Some practical results of child study. Child Study Monthly, May, 1896. Vol. 2, pp. 14-21.

512. **Wiener, Christian** Das Wachsthum des menschlichen Körpers. Vorträge gehalten im naturwissenschaftlichen Verein zu Karlsruhe. Karlsruhe, 1890. pp. 3-23.

513. **Wiggin, Kate D.** The relation of the kindergarten to the public school. C. A. Murdock and Co., San Francisco, 1881. pp. 25.

514. —— —— Children's rights. A book of nursery logic. Houghton, Mifflin and Co., Boston, 1893. pp. 235.

515. **Williams, Lillie A.** How to collect data for studies in genetic psychology. Ped. Sem., June, 1896. Vol. 3, pp. 419-423.

516. **Wilmarth, A. W.** A report on the examination of one hundred brains of feeble-minded children. Alienist and Neurologist, Oct., 1890. Vol. 11, pp. 520-533. Reprint, St. Louis, Mo., 1890. pp. 16.

517. **Wiltse, Sara E.** Stories for kindergartens and primary schools. Ginn and Co., Boston, 1885. pp. 75.

518. —— —— Hearing. (Sound blindness.) Under "Experimental." Am. Jour. of Psy., Aug., 1888. Vol. 1, pp. 702-705.

519. —— —— Mental imagery of boys. Under "Observations on General Terms," Am. Jour. of Psychology, Jan., 1890. Vol. 3, pp. 144-148.

520. —— —— The place of the story in early education, and other essays. Ginn and Co., Boston, 1892. pp. 132.

521. —— —— A brave baby. Ginn and Co., Boston, 1894. pp. 142.

522. —— —— A preliminary sketch of the history of child study in America. Ped. Sem., Oct., 1895. Vol. 3, pp. 189-212.

523. —— —— A preliminary sketch of the history of child study for the year ending Sept., 1896. Ped. Sem., Oct., 1896. Vol. 4, pp. 111-125.

524. [**Winslow, Anna Green**] Diary of Anna Green Winslow, a Boston school girl of 1771. Edited by Alice Morse Earle. Houghton, Mifflin and Co., Boston, 1894. pp. 121.

525. **Wolfe, H. K.** The color vocabulary of children. Univ. of Nebraska Studies, July, 1890. Vol. 1, pp. 205-234.

526. —— —— Study of children. Education, Boston, Dec., 1890. Vol. 11, pp. 201-207.

527. —— —— Common defects of school children. North Western Monthly, Lincoln, Neb. Vol. 7, pp. 22, 69, 137, 161 and 274.

528. —— —— Heredity. North Western Monthly, Lincoln, Neb., Oct., 1897. Vol. 8, pp. 200-205.

529. **Wolff, Hermann** Ueber das Seelische im Kinde. F. Tempsey, Prag., 1881. pp. 35.

530. **Worrell, J. P.** Deafness among school children. Transactions Ind. State Medical Soc. 33d Annual Seesion, Indianapolis, Ind., 1883. pp. 25-33.
Examined 491 children ; 72 imperfect in both ears, 53 in one ear.

531. **Wyckoff, Adelaide E.** Constitutional bad spellers. Ped. Sem., Dec., 1893. Vol. 2, pp. 448-450.

532. —— —— Infant study in the class-room. Ped. Sem., Dec., 1893. Vol. 2, pp. 454-455.

533. **Yale, Leroy M.** (Editor.) Nursery problems. Contemp. Pub. Co., N. Y. and Phila., 1893. pp. 274.

534. **Yoder, A. H.** The study of the boyhood of great men. Ped. Sem., Oct., 1894. Vol. 3, pp. 134-156. (Two hundred biographies).

535. **Young, A. G.** School hygiene and schoolhouses. 7th Ann. Rep. Maine State Bd. of Health, Augusta, Maine, 1892. pp. 83-399.
The most comprehensive report yet made by any State Board of Health. Very valuable.

II. JOURNALS.

536. **American Journal of Psychology** Edited by G. Stanley Hall, E. C. Sanford and E. B. Titchener. Commenced in Nov., 1887, now in its 9th volume. Quarterly, each vol. about 600 pages. J. H. Orpha, Worcester, Mass. Subscription price $5.00 a year.

537. **American Physical Education Review** Published quarterly by the committee on publication and information of the council of the A. A. A. P. E. Am. Association for the Advancement of Physical Education, Boston. Vols. 1-2, 1896-97. Price $1.50 per annum.

538. **The Child Study Monthly** Edited by W. O. Krohn and Alfred Bayliss. The Werner Co., Chicago. Monthly, except July and Aug. Now in its third vol. $1.00 a year.

539. **The Educational Review** Edited by Nicholas Murray Butler. Founded, 1891. Henry Holt and Co., N. Y. Monthly, except July and Aug. Price $3.00 a year.

540. **Jahrbuch des Vereins für Wissenschaftliche Pädagogik** hrsg. v. Th. Ziller, Langensalza, 1869-92. hrsg. v. Th. Vogt, Dresden, 1892. Bleyl and Kämmerer.

540a. **Journal of Pedagogy** Edited by Albert Leonard. Now in its 11th vol. Syracuse, N. Y. Quarterly. Price $1.50 a year.

540b. **Journal of Psycho-asthenics** Edited by A. C. Rogers, Faribault, Minn. Commenced Sept., 1896. Published quarterly. Price $1.50 a year. Devoted to the care and training of feeble-minded and epileptic children.

541. **Die Kinderfehler** Zeits. f. Pädagogische Pathologie und Therapie in Haus, Schule und sozialem Leben. Herausgegeben von J. L. A. Koch, Chr. Ufer, Dr. Zimmer, und J. Trüper. Beyer und Söhne, Langensalza. Vol. 1, 1896. Vol. 2, 1897. Six Nos. a year. (See Review of above by C. C. Van Liew in Ed. Rev., N. Y., Dec., 1897. Vol. 14, pp. 508 ff. Devoted to the interests of defective children. Although published in German, the contributors represent every country in the world.)

542. **The North Western Monthly,** Lincoln, Neb. Issued monthly. Now in its 8th volume. $1.50 a year. Has an excellent "Child Study Department," conducted by Prof. G. W. A. Luckey of the Univ. of Nebraska. The issue for July, 1896, is devoted entirely to the general subject of child study. The issue for July, 1897, to the physical child, health, food, exercise, etc.

543. **The Pedagogical Seminary** A quarterly international record of educational literature, institutions and progress. Edited by G. Stanley Hall. J. H. Orpha, Worcester, Mass. Commenced Jan., 1891. Now in its 5th volume. Vols. 1, 2, 3, 4, con-

tain only 3 numbers each, and cost $25.00 unbound. Subscription price to vol. 5 $4.00. Has reviewed most of the titles mentioned in this list.

544. **The Psychological Review** Edited by J. McKeen Cattell and J. Mark Baldwin. Commenced Jan., 1894. The Macmillan Co., N. Y. Published bi-monthly. Price $4.00 a year.

545. **Sammlung von Abhandlungen aus dem Gebiete der Pädagogischen Psychologie und Physiologie** Herausgegeben von H. Schiller und Th. Ziehen. Reuther und Reichard, Berlin, vol. 1,1897.

546. **Zeitschrift für Schulgesundheitspflege** Redigiert von Dr. L. |Kotelmann. L. Voss, Hamburg. Commenced in 1888. Monthly. Devoted to school hygiene in the broad sense. Contains many reports of school children. To be edited in the future by Fr. Erismann, of Zürich. Price $2.00 a year.

III. REPORTS, SERIAL STUDIES, AND TRANSACTIONS OF SOCIETIES.

547. **Am. Ass. for the Advancement of Physical Education** Report of the 10th Annual Meeting, N. Y., April, 1895. Repub. Press Ass'n, Concord, N. H., 1896. pp. 228. Contains many excellent papers from the physical side. The vol. may be procured from Dr. G. W. Fitz, Cambridge, Mass. Price 50 cts.

548. **Handbook of the Minnesota Child Study Association,** containing suggestions for the study of children. Printed by the Ass'n for the use of Members. Winona, Minn., 1897. pp. 60. With History and Constitution of the Association. S. H. Rowe, Sec'y, Winona, Minn. Price 50 cts.

549. **Michigan Manual of Child Study** Issued by the department of public instruction. Robt. Smith and Co., State Printers, Lansing, Mich., 1896. pp. 32. Sent gratis. Apply to Supt. J. Hammond, Lansing, Mich.

550. **National Congress of Mothers** The work and words of the first annual session held at Washington, D. C., Feb., 1897. D. Appleton and Co., N. Y., 2d ed., 1897. pp. 285. Contains a list of books (pp. 275-280), with prices, and gives information of interest to mothers' clubs. Price 35 cts.

551. **Papers on Anthropometry** Am. Statis'l Ass'n, Boston, 1894. pp. 116, and 15 tables. An important pamphlet. Contains articles by Drs. Boas, Bowditch, Enebuske, Hartwell, Hitchcock and Porter. Also a bibliography on anthropometry in the U. S., including 117 titles. May be obtained of Davis R. Dewey, Ph. D., Mass. Inst. of Tech., Boston. Price 50 cts.

552. **Proceedings** of the Association of Medical Officers of American Institutions for Idiotic and Feeble-Minded Persons. Commenced

in 1876.   Contains many valuable papers on care and training of feeble-minded children.   May be obtained from A. C. Rogers, M. D., Faribault, Minn.

553. **Proceedings of the National Educational Association** Child study department, 1894, pp. 995-1023; 1895, pp. 891-943; 1896, pp. 836-892; 1897, pp. 278-297; 585-603; 825-869. The proceedings have of late years reported many papers on child study as the National Association has accorded recognition to the child study section.   Irwin Shepard, Sec'y and Treas., Winona, Minn. Price $2.00 per vol.

554. **Report of the Committee on Color Vision** Proceedings of the Royal Society of London.   Harrison and Sons, St. Martin's Lane, July, 1892.   Vol. 51, pp. 281-396, with 2 colored plates.

555. **Report of the Commissioner of Education** Government Printing Office, Washington, D. C. Contains many valuable child study articles in the later volumes.   Report for the year 1892-93 (vol. 1, pp. 357-391), contains an article on child study, with a bibliography of 232 titles.

556. **Report of the State Superintendent of Public Instruction, New York** The 42nd and 43rd annual reports (1896 and 1897), contain about 100 pages each of reports and original articles on child study.   Reprints of these papers by State Supt. Charles R. Skinner of Albany, N. Y., form valuable reports of special investigations in child study.

557. **Studies in Education** Edited by Earl Barnes. Contains many very suggestive and valuable articles on child study, such as methods of studying children, by Earl Barnes.   A study of children's own stories, by Clara Vostrovsky.   Eight articles on discipline, by Earl Barnes.   The development of the historical sense in children, by Mary Sheldon Barnes.   Bibliographies of child study, by Earl Barnes and C. J. C. Bennett.   A study of children's superstitions, by Clara Vostrovsky. A study on children's interests, by Earl Barnes.   Children's ambitions, by Hattie Mason Willard.   Children's sense of money, by Anna Köhler, etc., etc.   Earl Barnes, Stanford University, 1896-97. pp. 400.   Price, in paper $1.50, in cloth $2.00.

558. **Studies from the Yale Psychological Laboratory** Edited by E. W. Scripture, Yale Univ., New Haven, Conn.   Vol. 1, 1892-93 ; issued Oct. 1, 1893, pp. 100; vol. 2, Nov. 1, 1894, pp. 124; vol. 3, 1895, pp. 110 ; vol. 4, 1896, pp. 141.

559. **Transactions of the Illinois Society for Child Study** Vol. 1, 1894-95, 4 nos.; vol. 2, 1896.

560. **Transactions of the Seventh International Congress of Hygiene and Demography** Eyre and Spottiswoode,

London, 1892. pp. 273. Contains, in addition to other valuable papers, one volume on infancy, childhood and school life.

561. **University of Iowa Studies in Psychology** Edited by G. T. W. Patrick and J. Allen Gilbert. Published annually. The Univ. of Iowa, Iowa City, Ia. Vol. 1 (issued June, 1897), pp. 92. Price 50 cts. Contains three original studies and gives a review of some recent literature on fatigue in school children, right and left handedness, etc.

562. **Verhandlungen des Internationalen Kongresses** für Ferienkolonien und verwandte Bestrebungen der Kinderhygieine in Zürich am 13 u. 14, August, 1888. L. Voss, Hamburg, 1889. pp. 115.

IV. WORKS OF STANDARD REFERENCE ON ALLIED TOPICS.

563. **Bain, Alexander** The emotions and the will. D. Appleton and Co., N. Y., 1876. pp. 604.

564. —— —— The senses and the intellect. D. Appleton and Co., N. Y., 1879. pp. 714.

565. —— —— Mind and body : the theories of their relation. D. Appleton and Co., N. Y., 1882. pp. 200.

566. **Baldwin, J. Mark** Handbook of Psychology. Henry Holt and Co., N. Y., 1892. 2 vols., pp. 343 ; 394.

567. —— —— Elements of psychology. Henry Holt and Co., N. Y., 1893. pp. 373.

568. **Ball, Sir Robert S.** A manual of scientific enquiry, prepared for the use of officers in her majesty's navy and travellers in general. 5th ed. Eyre and Spottiswoode, London, 1886. pp. 450. Directions to travellers how to collect data, by eminent experts.

569. **Bibliographie der deutschen Zeitschriften-Litteratur** Fr. Andra's Nachfolger, Leipzig, 1897. Vol. 1 for 1896, pp. 184. Price $1.75. A German Poole. Indexes 277 German periodicals.

570. **Binet, Alfred** L'Année psychologique. Publiée par M. Alfred Binet avec la collaboration de MM. H. Beaunis et Th. Ribot, Paris. Vols. 1-3, 1894-96. Published about June. Each volume contains an excellent bibliography of the psychological publications of the year.

571. **Brinton, Daniel G.** Races and peoples. Lectures on the science of ethnography. N. D. C. Hodges, N. Y., 1890. pp. 313.

572. **Carpenter, William B.** Principles of mental physiology, with their applications to the training and discipline of the mind and the study of its morbid conditions. D. Appleton and Co., N. Y., 1874. pp. 737.

573. **Claus and Sedgwick** Text book of Zoölogy. 2d ed., Macmillan and Co., London and N. Y., n. d. 2 vols., pp. 615 ; 352.

574. **Clouston, T. S.** Clinical lectures on mental diseases. J. and A. Churchill, London, 1887. pp. 643.

575. **Darwin, Charles** Origin of species. D. Appleton and Co., N. Y., 1878. pp. 458.

576. —— —— The descent of man, and selection in relation to sex. D. Appleton and Co., N. Y., 1878. pp. 688.

577. —— —— The expression of the emotions in man and animals. D. Appleton and Co., N. Y., 1896. pp. 374.

578. **Drummond, Henry** The ascent of man. James Pott and Co., N. Y. 3d ed. 1894. pp. 346.

578 a. **Edinger, Ludwig** Vorlesungen über den Bau der nervösen Centralorgane des Menschen und der Thiere. F. C. W. Vogel, Leipzig, 1896. pp. 386, with 258 figures.

579. **Ellis, Havelock** The criminal. Contemporary Science Series. Walter Scott, London. Chas. Scribner's Sons, N. Y., 1890. pp. 337.

580. —— —— Man and woman. A study of human secondary sexual characters. Contemporary Science Series. Walter Scott, London. Chas. Scribner's Sons, N. Y., 1897. pp. 398.

581. **Euler, Carl** Encyklopädisches Handbuch des gesamten Turnwesens und der verwandten Gebiete. Herausgegeben von Dr. Carl Euler. 3 vols. Wien and Leipzig, 1894-1896.

582. **Ferrier, David** The functions of the brain. D. Appleton and Co., N. Y., 1886. pp. 498.

583. **Flechsig, Paul** Gehirn und Seele. Veit and Co., Leipzig, 1896. pp. 112. (See also the phrenology of Gall and Flechsig's doctrine of association centres in the cerebrum, by Lewellys F. Barker, M. B., in Bull. of the Johns Hopkins Hospital, vol. 8, No. 70. Baltimore, Jan., 1897. pp. 7-14.)

584. **Galton, Francis** Inquiries into human faculty and its development. Macmillan and Co., London, 1883. pp. 387.

585. —— —— Natural inheritance. Macmillan and Co., London and N. Y., 1889. pp. 259.

586. **Geddes, P. and Thompson, J. A.** The evolution of sex. Contemporary Science Series. Walter Scott, London. Chas. Scribner's Sons, N. Y., 1894. pp. 322.

587. **Gerhardt, C.** Handbuch der Kinderkrankheiten. Herausgegeben von Dr. C. Gerhardt. Zweite umgearbeitete und vermehrte Auflage. H. Laupp, Tübingen. 6 vols., 1878-1893.

588. **Horsley, Victor** The structure and functions of the brain and spinal cord. Chas. Griffin and Co., London, 1892. pp. 223.

589. **Howell, W, H.** American Text Book of Physiology. By Drs. H. P. Bowditch, J. G. Curtis, H. H. Donaldson, W. H. Howell, F. S. Lee, W. P. Lombard, G. Lusk, W. T. Porter, E. T. Reichert and H. Sewall. Edited by Wm. H. Howell. W. B. Saunders, Phila., 1896. pp. 1052.

590. **Index Catalogue of the Library of the Surgeon-General's Office, U. S. Army** Government Printing Office, Washington, D. C. Vols. 1-16, 1880-95. New series, vols. 1-2, 1896-97. (A monumental work and a credit to the nation.)

591. **Index Medicus** A monthly classified record of the current medical literature of the world. Edited by Dr. John S. Billings and Dr. Robert Fletcher. Published by the editors, Washington, D. C., monthly. Vol. 1 issued in 1879. Vol. 19 issued in 1897.

592. **James, William** Principles of Psychology. Henry Holt and Co., N. Y., 1896. 2 vols., pp. 689; 704.

593. **Koelliker, A.** Handbuch der Gewebelehre des Menschen. W. Englemann, Leipzig, 2 vols., 1889 and 1896. pp. 409; 874.

594. **Kraepelin, Emil** Psychologische Arbeiten. Erster Band, mit 13 Figuren im Text. W. Englemann, Leipzig, 1896. pp. 678.

595. **Kussmaul, Adolf** Die Störungen der Sprache. Versuch einer Pathologie der Sprache. F. C. W. Vogel, Leipzig, 1877. pp. 299.

596. **Ladd, George T.** Elements of physiological psychology : a treatise of the activities and nature of the mind from the physical and experimental point of view. Charles Scribner's Sons, N. Y., 1887. pp. 696.

597. —— —— Psychology, descriptive and explanatory. Charles Scribner's Sons, N. Y., 1894. pp. 676.

398. **Lubbock, John** On the senses, instincts, and intelligence of animals, with special reference to insects. D. Appleton and Co., N. Y. pp. 292.

599. —— —— Ants, bees, and wasps. A record of observations on the habits of the social hymenoptera. D. Appleton and Co., N. Y., 1882. pp. 448. 5 plates.

600. **Luys, J.** The brain and its functions. D. Appleton and Co., N. Y., 1882. pp. 327.

600a. **Mercier, Charles** The nervous system and the mind. Macmillan and Co., London, 1888. pp. 374.

601. **Minot, Charles S.** Human Embryology. Wm. Wood and Co., N. Y., 1892. pp. 815.

602. **Moll, Albert** Hypnotism. 4th ed., revised and enlarged. Contemporary Science Series. Walter Scott, London. Chas. Scribner's Sons, N. Y., 1897. pp. 448.

603. **Morgan, C. Lloyd** Animal life and intelligence. Ginn and Co., Boston, 1891. pp. 512.

604. —— —— An introduction to comparative psychology. Charles Scribner's Sons, N. Y., 1894. pp. 382.

605. —— —— Psychology for teachers. With a preface by J. G. Fitch. E. Arnold, London, 1894. pp. 251.

606. —— —— Habit and instinct. Edward Arnold, London, 1896. pp. 351.

607. **Morris, Malcolm** The book of health. Edited by Malcolm Morris. Cassell and Co., N. Y., 1884. pp. 1079. Contains chapters, by various English writers, upon the throat, eye, ear, and the influence of food, stimulants, exercise, dress, climate, etc., on health.

608. **Notes and Queries on Anthropology** for the use of travellers and residents in uncivilized lands. Printed by Taylor and Francis, Fleet St., London. pp. 146.

609. **Paulsen, Friedrich** Introduction to philosophy. Trans. from the 3d German edition by Frank Thilly. Henry Holt and Co., N. Y., 1895. pp. 437.

610. **Reference Handbook of the Medical Sciences** Being a complete and convenient work of reference for information upon topics belonging to the entire range of scientific and practical medicine, and consisting of a series of concise essays, and brief paragraphs, arranged in the alphabetical order of the topics of which they treat. Prepared by writers who are experts in their respective departments. Edited by Albert H. Buck, M. D. 8 volumes. William Wood and Co., N. Y., 1885-87.

611. **Regis, E.** A practical manual of mental medicine, Press of Am. Jour. of Insanity, Utica, N. Y., 2nd ed., 1894. pp. 692.

612. **Rein, W.** Encyklopädisches Handbuch der Pädagogik. Herausgegeben von W. Rein. Beyer und Söhne, Langensalza, 1894. Now in course of publication. The 1st volume appeared in 1894, and the 4th volume (down to Myopie) in 1897. Contains numerous articles on child study.

613. **Ribot, Th.** Heredity : a psychological study of its phenomena, laws, causes and consequences. D. Appleton and Co., N. Y., 1889. pp. 393.

614. —— —— The psychology of attention. Open Court Pub. Co., Chicago, 1890. pp. 121. Price 25 cts.

615. —— —— Diseases of memory. Trans. by W. H. Smith. D. Appleton and Co., N. Y., 1893. pp. 209.

616. —— —— The diseases of the will. Trans. by M. M. Snell. Open Court Pub. Co., Chicago, 1894. pp. 134. Price 25 cts.

617. —— —— The diseases of personality. Open Court Pub. Co., Chicago, 1896. pp. 157. Price 25 cts.

618. —— —— The psychology of the emotions. Chas. Scribner's Sons, N. Y., 1897. pp. 455.

619. **Romanes, George J.** Animal intelligence. D. Appleton and Co., N. Y., 1883. pp. 520.

620. —— —— Mental evolution in animals. With a posthumous essay on instinct, by Charles Darwin. D. Appleton and Co., N. Y., 1884. pp. 411.

621. —— —— Mental evolution in man: origin of human faculty. D. Appleton and Co., N. Y., 1889. pp. 452.

622. **Ross, James** On aphasia. Being a contribution to the subject of the dissolution of speech from cerebral disease. J. and A. Churchill, London, 1887. pp. 128.

623. **Sanford, Edmund C.** A course in experimental psychology. D. C. Heath and Co., Boston, 1897. pp. 449.

624. **Schmidt, Emil** Anthropologische Methoden. Anleitung zum Beobachten und Sammeln für Laboratorium und Reise. Veit and Co., Lepzig, 1888. pp. 336.

625. **Spencer, Herbert** The principles of psychology. D. Appleton and Co., N. Y., 1883. 2 vols., pp. 642 ; 648.

626. **Sprockhoff, A.** Grundzüge der Anthropologie für höhere Lehranstalten, Lehrer-Seminare und Lehrer, sowie zur Selbstbelehrung für Jedermann. Der Körper des Menschen. Carl Meyer, Hannover, 1892. pp. 292.

627. **Stanley, Hiram M.** Studies in the evolutionary psychology of feeling. Macmillan and Co., N. Y., 1895. pp. 392.

628. **Stewart, G. N.** A manual of physiology. With practical exercises. Numerous illustrations, including 5 colored plates. Bailliere, Tindall and Cox, London, 1896; also Medical Pub. Co., Cleveland, O. pp. 796.

629. **Sully, James** Outlines of psychology, with special reference to the theory of education. D. Appleton and Co., N. Y., 1884. pp. 711.

630. **Titchener, E. B.** An outline of psychology. The Macmillan Co., N. Y., 1896. pp. 352.

631. —— —— A primer of psychology. The Macmillan Co., N. Y., 1898. pp. 314.

632. **Topinard, Paul** Elements d'anthropologie générale. Delahaye et Lecrosnier, Paris, 1885. pp. 1157.

633. **Tuke, D. Hack** Dictionary of Psychological Medicine, giving the definition, etymology, and synonyms of the terms used in medical psychology, with the symptoms, treatment, and pathology of insanity, and the law of lunacy in Great Britain and

Ireland.   Edited by D. Hack Tuke, M. D., London.   J. and A.
Churchill, 1892. 2 vols., pp. 1-642 ; 643-1477.   Contains many
articles on the pathological conditions of child life.

634. **Van Gehuchten, A.** Anatomie du système nerveux de l'homme. Deuxième Edition, avec 619 figures dans le texte. Dieu-
donné, Louvain, 1897. pp. 941.

635. **Vierordt, Hermann** Anatomische, Physiologische und Phy-
sikalische Daten und Tabellen zum Gebrauche für Mediciner.
Gustav Fischer, Jena, 1888. pp. 303.

636. **Weber, Alfred** History of philosophy. Translated from the
5th French edition by Frank Thilly. Charles Scribner's Sons,
N. Y., 1897. pp. 630.

637. **Weismann, August** Essays upon heredity and kindred biological problems. Clarendon Press, Oxford, 1889. pp. 455.

638. **Whitaker, J. Ryland** Anatomy of the brain and spinal
cord. 2d ed. E. and S. Livingstone, Edinburgh, 1892. pp. 173.

639. **Wundt, Wilhelm** Grundzüge der Physiologischen Psychologie. 4th ed. W. Engelmann, Leipzig, 1893. 2 vols., pp. 600;
684. (Professor E. B. Titchener, of Cornell University, is preparing an English translation of this standard text book in
physiological psychology.)

640. —— —— Outlines of Psychology. Trans. by C. H. Judd. W.
Englemann, Leipzig, 1897. pp. 342. Gustav E. Stechert, N. Y.
City. Price $2.00.

641. **Ziehen, Theodor** Introduction to physiological psychology.
Translated by C. C. Van Liew and Otto Beyer. Macmillan and
Co. N. Y., 1895. pp. 305.

SUBJECT INDEX.

Abnormal, 310, 427, 499.

Adolescence, 4, 6, 17, 18, 29, 30, 32, 53, 68, 75, 77, 79, 87, 109, 110, 112, 113, 116, 122, 132, 154, 173, 174, 192, 194, 198, 207, 249, 259, 261, 263, 265, 271, 277, 307, 386, 415, 452, 477, 492, 494, 557, 574.

Ambitions, 474, 534, 556, 557.

American Indians, 46, 49, 152.

Animals and Insects, 598, 599, 603, 619, 620.

Anthropological, 6, 29, 31, 43, 45, 46, 49, 50, 52, 78, 95, 122, 126, 176, 199, 233, 245, 294, 313, 363, 364, 388, 391, 568, 571, 608, 624, 626, 632.

Anthropometry, 35, 43, 44, 45, 46, 47, 48, 50, 51, 52, 58, 59, 60, 61, 62, 121, 141, 149, 153, 162, 163, 171, 173, 174, 181, 187, 222, 223, 236, 237, 238, 240, 278, 283, 322, 323, 352, 353, 366, 367, 368, 369, 370, 371, 372, 393, 422, 429, 507, 509, 510, 551, 558, 635.

Aphasia, 111, 622.

Art, 19, 21, 66, 234, 250, 389, 419, 557.

Association, 253.

Atavism, 74, 77, 207, 394, 395, 396.

Attention, 413, 614.

Autobiographical, 6, 29, 78, 126, 176, 199, 245, 294, 313, 477, 494, 524.

Bashfulness, 13.

Bibliographies, 22, 86, 95, 105, 210, 222, 321, 557, 559, 569, 570, 590, 591.

Blind, 155, 384.

Brain, 109, 128, 129, 213, 500, 582, 583, 588, 593, 600, 600a, 634, 638.

Bravery, 521.

Bullying, 77.

Character, 73, 344, 358.

Child evidence, 327, 385.

Child in literature, 407, 419.

Child literature, 420, 449, 450.

Chorea, 286.

Color and color sense, 166, 254, 255, 296, 525, 554, 558, 623.

Color Blindness, 254, 255.

Comenius, 316.

Conversion, 122, 280, 453, 454.

Crime, 325, 421, 579.

Crying, 107.

Darwinism, 394, 575, 576, 577.

Deaf and deafness, 63, 102, 155, 159, 260, 355, 530.

Death, 414.

Defective children, 53, 155, 387, 398, 402, 462, 473, 480, 484, 499, 503, 505, 552, 560, 633.

Degeneration, 125.

Delinquents, 325.

Dependent children, 97.

Development, 150.

Discipline. See Punishment.

Disease, 60, 68, 100, 111, 112, 113, 116, 125, 130, 132, 249, 455, 495, 587, 607, 610, 611, 622.

Dolls, 78, 139, 147.

Dramatic Instincts, 4.

Drawing, 19, 21, 66, 151, 234, 301, 304, 345, 389.

Ear, 36, 102, 607.

Emotions, 27, 41, 63, 145, 207, 209, 563, 577, 592, 618, 627.

Ethics, 15, 337.

Exceptional children, 53, 208, 402.

Exercise, 35, 141, 143, 221, 305.

Eye, Eyesight, 10, 25, 90, 114, 115, 169, 384, 392, 404, 426, 507, 554, 607, 612, 623.

Faculties. See Senses.

Fairy Tales, 219.

Fatigue, 34, 133, 143, 157, 161, 182, 230, 241, 286, 340, 390, 413, 561.

Fears, 41, 113, 207.

Feeble Minded, 257, 315, 516, 552.

Feeling, 627. See also Emotions.

Folk-lore. See Myths.

Food, 242, 607.

Firstborn, 48.

Froebel, 293.

Geographic Interests, 493.

Growth, 35, 43, 44, 45, 47, 48, 51, 58, 59, 60, 62, 109, 116, 121, 129, 153, 173, 181, 187, 211, 224, 226, 236, 237, 238, 240, 278, 305, 314,

322, 323, 328, 352, 353, 366, 368, 370, 371, 372, 451, 471, 490, 497, 502, 508, 510, 512, 551, 558, 561.
Gymnastics, 141, 142, 143.

Habit and Instinct, 603, 606, 619, 620.
Hand, 425, 447.
Hauser, Casper 285.
Headache, 495.
Health, 76, 201, 607.
Hearing, 25, 31, 36, 63, 102, 260, 355, 518, 530.
Heredity, 528, 585, 603, 606, 613, 619, 620, 621, 637.
Historic sense, 24, 317, 557.
History of Child Study, 522, 523.
Home, 3, 8, 9, 268, 279, 443.
Human embryology, 601.
Hygiene, 76, 81, 86, 114, 115, 144, 145, 188, 201, 264, 269, 303, 312, 488, 535, 560.
Hypnotism, 42, 448, 602.
Hysteria, 68.

Idiocy, 99, 155, 423, 426, 427.
Illiteracy, 175.
Illusions, 40.
Imagination, 83, 383, 519, 584.
Imbecility, 249.
Imitation, 156, 228, 229, 399, 463, 489.
Incorrigibles, 421.
Infants, 74, 89, 93, 95, 96, 123, 127, 130, 160, 170, 200, 211, 239, 242, 248, 324, 331, 333, 348, 354, 357, 365, 381, 394, 395, 416, 424, 436, 437, 438, 446, 458, 464, 465, 470, 521, 532, 533, 587.
Instincts, 27, 65.
See also Habit and Instinct.
Interests, 37, 65, 297, 343, 433, 557.

Kindergarten, 158, 218, 293, 373, 382, 513, 517.

Language, 72, 94, 95, 101, 127, 136, 180, 189, 190, 239, 248, 292, 300, 365, 411, 445, 460, 465, 469, 477, 478.
Laughing, 209.
Lefthandedness, 447.
Lies, 198, 336.

Manual Training, 16.
Mathematics. See Number.
Memory, 55, 253, 267, 349, 434, 615.
Mental automatisms, 288.
Mental defect, 230, 249, 257, 268, 315, 374, 423, 439, 471, 480, 516, 574.

Mental development, 14, 15, 117, 118, 124, 136, 173, 174, 193, 217, 220, 235, 251, 252, 253, 257, 266, 281, 286, 289, 324, 328, 333, 356, 359, 366, 374, 375, 380, 381, 409, 436, 438, 440, 441, 485, 502, 503, 504, 505, 564, 572, 578, 583, 584, 588, 600, 606, 620, 621, 634, 638.
Mental fatigue, 34.
Mirror writing, 447.
Money sense, 557.
Moral and religious training, 1, 117, 118, 122, 137, 191, 192, 194, 198, 208, 266, 356, 461. See also Religion.
Mother, 290, 293, 308, 312, 382, 549, 550, 557.
Mothers' clubs, 308, 549.
Motor ability, 69, 85, 208, 214, 215, 284, 433a, 501.
Motor ideas, 16, 38.
Motor training, 284.
Movements, 38.
Music, 172.
Myopia. See Eye.
Myths and mythology, 49, 54, 95, 219, 282.

Nature study, 246.
Nervous diseases, 273, 405, 412, 423.
Nervousness, 412, 428.
Nervous system, 128, 182, 212, 600a, 634.
Neurasthenia, 273, 405.
New born child, 274, 275.
Number and number forms, 39, 243, 360, 361, 482.

Offenders, 325.
Old Age, 414
Overpressure, 196, 230.

Palatal Deformities, 99.
Passions, 27.
Peculiar Children, 53, 108.
Perception, 26, 37, 39, 40, 193, 220, 246, 433.
Pestalozzi, 186.
Philosophy, 609, 636.
Philosophy of Education, 139.
Physical training, 98, 141, 142, 143, 162, 221, 223, 224, 225, 227, 338, 362, 547, 581.
Physiology, 589, 628, 634, 635.
Play, 78, 139, 150, 158, 184, 197, 373, 148.
Plays and Games, 4, 11, 12, 54, 119, 120, 131, 137, 150, 178, 179, 184, 199, 247, 256, 258, 293, 334, 373, 456, 481.

Playthings, 147, 152.
Poetry, 457.
Postures, 74, 326, 330.
Precocity, 366.
Prematurely born, 372.
Primitive child, 396.
Psychology, 202, 251, 252, 563, 564, 565, 566, 567, 570, 572, 592, 594, 596, 597, 604, 605, 613, 614, 615, 616, 617, 618, 621, 623, 625, 627, 629, 630, 631, 639, 640, 641.
Punishment, 20, 319, 320, 557.
Puzzles, 287.

Race Psychology, 14, 15, 95, 571.
Reading, 168, 435.
Reasonings, 67, 216.
Religion and religious ideas, 1, 7, 18, 280, 281, 453, 454, 475. See also moral and relig. training.
Reminiscent, 176, 199, 245, 294, 313, 456, 477, 494.
Respiration, 148.
Rhythm, 54, 56, 441.
Rights, 406, 514.

Schoolhouses, 535.
Secret languages, 101.
Senses and Faculties, 91, 92, 170, 274, 275, 564, 598, 599, 603, 606, 619, 620, 621.
Sex, 17, 31, 32, 110, 557, 576, 580, 586.
Sight. See Eye.
Singing. See Voice.
Smell, 167.
Social sense, 15, 258, 318, 320, 406, 599.
Songs, 293, 334.
Speech, 30, 189, 190, 223, 232, 239, 244, 248, 292, 303, 329, 365, 411, 445, 460, 465, 469, 478, 595, 622,
Spelling, 531.
Spinal curvature, 149, 326, 330.

Stammering. See Stuttering.
Story, 65, 106, 135, 219, 420, 449, 450, 520, 557.
Stuttering, Stammering, 223, 232.
Suggestibility, 42, 448.
Suicide, 442.
Summer Schools, 204.
Sunday School, 137, 475.
Superstitions, 49, 282, 557.
Syllabi, 195, 208.

Taste, 25.
Teacher, 270, 298, 299, 302, 339, 350, 433a, 605, 629.
Teasing, 77.
Technique of Child Study, 2, 3, 9, 28, 43, 50, 52, 70, 71, 80, 82, 83, 103, 105, 108, 160, 162, 163, 185, 202, 206, 208, 272, 283, 299, 308, 309, 310, 311, 339, 341, 346, 349, 393, 400, 401, 403, 416, 418, 422, 429, 474, 475, 506, 510, 515, 522, 523, 526, 556, 557.
Temperament, 231.
Thoughts, 67.
Throat 329, 607. See also Voice.
Tickling, 209.
Topical Syllabi, 208.
Touch, 134.
Tragedies, 4.
Truants, 421.

Vision. See Eye.
Voice, 30, 165, 208, 244, 261, 303, 351. See also Throat.
Volition, 69.

Will, 69, 192, 332, 563, 592, 616.
Women, 61.
Worcester State Normal School, 80, 401, 403.
Writing, 410, 431, 432, 447, 486.

Zoölogy, 573.

BIBLIOGRAPHY

OF

CHILD STUDY.

BY

LOUIS N. WILSON,

LIBRARIAN, CLARK UNIVERSITY.

The Clark University Press,

WORCESTER, MASSACHUSETTS,

SEPTEMBER, 1899.

BIBLIOGRAPHY OF CHILD STUDY

For the year 1898.

By LOUIS N. WILSON, Librarian, Clark University.

1. **Adsersen, H.** (On growth in height and mental derangements in childhood.) Nordiskt Med. Arkiv. 1898. Vol. 31, pp. 39.

2. **Aicard, Jean** L'âme d'un enfant. E. Flammarion, Paris, 1898. pp. 384.

3. **Alden, Annie Fields** My Collection of Dolls. Ladies' Home Journal, Nov., 1898. Vol. 15, p. 17; Dec., 1898; Jan., 1899. Vol. 16, pp. 13 and 19.

4. **Allport, Frank** The eyes and ears of school children. Reprint. The author, 92 State St., Chicago, Ill. pp. 30.

   Contains, also, articles on Refraction in Schools; Defective Eyesight in American Children; Tests for Defective Vision in School Children; Physical Defects in Pupils.

5. —— —— Report of eye examinations in the Minneapolis public schools. Jour. of Am. Med. Ass., 1898. Vol. 30, pp. 207-211.

6. **Altenburg, Oskar** Die Kunst des psychologischen Beobachtens. Praktische Fragen der pädagogischen Psychologie. Samml. v. Abh. a. d. Geb. d. Päd. Psy. u Physiol. Band 2, Heft 3, 1898. pp. 76.

   Contains interesting items concerning the effect of environment, family life, etc., on the child before entering school.

7. **Alvarez, B. Gonzales** Anatomia y fisiologia especiales del niño de su alimentacion y crecimiento y preliminares de clinica pediátrica. Carrion Hermanos, Madrid, 1895. pp. 344.

   A good *résumé* of the anatomy and physiology of childhood, with original contributions. The best book in Spanish on the subject.

8. **Aly, Max Voigt** Die Welt im Munde. Frankfurt, A. M., 1898. pp. 87.

   Practical rules for the care of the teeth and mouth.

9. **American, Sadie** Child training by the Froebel system. The Woman's Home Companion, N. Y. Sept., 1898. Vol. 25, No. 6, p. 12.

10. —— —— The movement for small play grounds Am. Jour. of Sociology, Sept. 1898. Vol. 4, pp. 159-170.

11. —— —— The movement for vacation schools. Am. Jour. of Sociology, Nov., 1898. Vol. 4, pp. 309-325.

12. **Atkinson, Fred. W.** A year's study of the entering pupils of the Springfield, Mass., high school. Proc. N. E. A., 1898. pp. 903-910.
    A suggestive application of child study to secondary education.

13. **Austin, Ellen M.** Child study in the high school. North Western Monthly, March, 1898. Vol. 8, pp. 487-490.

14. **Baginsky, Adolf and Janke, Otto** Handbuch der Schul-Hygiene zum Gebrauche für ärme Sanitätsbeamte, Lehrer, Schul-Vorstände und Techniker. F. Enke, Stuttgart, 1898. Vol. 1, pp. 748.

15. **Bailey, T. P.** Child Study and Ethology. North Western Monthly, Nov. 1897; Jan. 1898. Vol. 8, pp. 250-256; 370-375.

16. **Baker, Seth** Fatigue in school children. Ed. Review, Jan., 1898. Vol. 15, pp. 34-39.
    A brief statement of some of the premonitions of fatigue.

17. **Baldwin, J. Mark** The story of the mind. D. Appleton & Co., N. Y., 1898. pp. 236.
    The fourth chapter discusses the mind of the child.

18. **Balliet, Thomas M.** Value of motor education. Jour. of Education, Nov. 17, 1898. Vol. 48, p. 317.

19. —— —— School Baths. Jour. of Education Oct. 20, 1898. Vol. 48, pp. 251-252.

20. **Barnes, Earl** Childish ideals. North Western Monthly, Oct., 1898. Vol. 9, pp. 91-93.
    One of the very few comparisons between the English and the American child that are of any value.

21. —— —— The way young children think: a study of their pictures. Child Life (London), June, 1898. Vol. 1, pp. 120-122.
    Application of recent studies in children's drawings to the Kindergarten.

22. —— —— Effect of social ideas on choice of occupation. Jour. of Education, Sept. 8, 1898. Vol. 48, pp. 155-156.
    A brief study of the ambitions of English school children.

23. —— —— Corporal punishment in England. Education, Oct., 1898. Vol. 19, pp. 72-75.
    Corporal punishment discussed with special reference to juvenile delinquents.

24. —— —— Corporal punishment as a means of social control. Education, March, 1898. Vol. 18, pp. 387-395.
    A study of discipline in English schools.

25. **Barr, M. W.** The training of mentally deficient children. Pop. Sci. Mo., Aug., 1898. Vol. 53, pp. 531-535.

26. **Bastian, H. C.** Aphasia and other speech defects. Lewis, London, 1898. pp. 314.

27. **Baumann, Julius** Ueber Willens—und Characterbildung auf physiologisch—psychologischer Grundlage. Samml. von Abh, a. d. geb. d. Paed. Psy. u. Physiol. Vol. 1, Hft. 1. Reuther u. Reichard, Berlin, 1897. pp. 86.

28. **Bayr, Emanuel**   Über Beleuchtungsversuche in Lehrzimmern.
    Zeit für Schulgesundheitspflege, March, 1898. Vol. 11, pp.
    129-160.
    An exhaustive study of the lighting of school rooms.

29. **Beach, Fletcher**   Insanity in children. Jour. of Mental Sci.,
    July, 1898. Vol. 44, pp. 459-473.

30. **Beale, Dorothy** (and others)   Work and play in girls' schools.
    Longmans, Green & Co., London, 1898. pp. 433.
    A comprehensive presentation of the ways and means of educating ma-
    turing girls.

31. **Bellianine, C.**   Troubles de la parole dans l' hémiplégie infan-
    tile. Maloine, Paris, 1898. pp. 33.

32. **Bergen, F. D.**   Notes on the theological development of a
    child. Arena, 1899. Vol. 19, pp. 254-266.

33. **Bergey, D. H.**   School architecture. Heating, ventilation,
    lighting, and sanitary arrangements. Proc. N. E. A., 1898. pp.
    524-534.

34. **Berthelemy, H.**   La répression des violences commises envers
    les enfants. Rev. Pédagogique, April, 1898. Vol. 32, pp. 289-302.

35. **Binet, A., et Henri, V.**   La fatigue intellectuelle. Schleicher
    Freres, Paris, 1898. pp. 338 and 3 plates.
    An excellent presentation of the physiological and psychological effects
    of mental overwork ; presents the results of many investigations carried
    on in France, Germany, Italy, and America.

36. **Binet, A., and Vaschide, N.**   La psychologie à l'école pri-
    maire. Expériences de force musculaire et de fond chez les
    jeunes garçons. Épreuves de vitesse chez les jeunes garçons.
    Expériences sur la respiration et la circulation du sang chez les
    jeunes garçons. Mesures anatomiques chez 40 jeunes garcons.
    Échelle des indications données par les différents tests. Cor-
    rélation des épreuves physiques. La mesure de la force muscu-
    laire chez les jeunes gens. La force de pression de la main, la
    traction, la corde lisse, le saut. Expériences de vitesse chez les
    jeunes gens. Données anatomiques, capacité vitale et vitesse
    du coeur chez 40 jeunes gens. Échelle des indications données
    par les tests. Corrélation des tests de force physique. Année
    Psychol., 1897. Vol. 4, pp. 1-244.

37. **Bluhm, R.**   Die Schulsparkassen in Frankreich. Deuts-Zeits,
    f. Ausl. Unterr, Jan., 1898. Vol. 3, pp. 115-125.

38. **Blum, E.**   Le mouvement pédologique et pédagogique. Rev.
    Philos., Nov. 1898. Vol. 46, pp. 504-518.
    Review of literature of child study.

39. **Boas, Franz**   The growth of Toronto children.   Report
    Comm. of Ed., 1896-97. Washington, 1898. Vol. 2, pp. 1541-
    1599.
    Besides giving the growth of the Toronto children the paper discusses the
    influence of the order of birth on development.

40. **Bohannon, E. W.** The only child in a family. Ped. Sem., April, 1898. Vol. 5, pp. 475-496.

41. **Bolton, T. L., and Haskell, Ellen, M.** Knowledge from the standpoint of association. Ed. Review, May, 1898. Vol. 15, pp. 474-499.

42. **Bon, L. C.** Les châtiments corporels dans les écoles allemandes. Rev. Pédagogique, Jan., 1898. Vol. 32, pp. 59-65.

43. **Bradford, E. H.** (and others) The education of crippled children. American Physical Education Review, September, 1898. Vol. 3, pp. 188-207.
    A series of articles on the care and training of deformed and crippled children.

44. **Brauckmann, K.** Behinderte Nasenatmung. Rein's Ency. Handb. d Pädagogik. Vol. 5, pp. 6-12.

45. —— —— Ohrenkrankheiten. Rein's Ency. Handb. d Pädagogik. Vol. 5, pp. 121-124.

46. **Brinton, D. G.** The factors of heredity and environment in man. Am. Anthropologist, Sept., 1898. Vol. 11, pp. 271-277.
    Gives an excellent idea of the disagreement of eminent authorities as to the rôle of these factors. Emphasizes the *rôle* of character and temperament.

47. **Brodeur, Clarence A.** Child study in Westfield and vicinity. Jour. of Education, Jan. 6, Jan. 20, Feb. 3 and March 17, 1898. Vol. 47.

48. **Brower, Daniel R.** The judicious training of neurotic children an aid to the prevention of insanity. Proc. of the Am. Med.-Psy. Assn. 54th annual meeting, St. Louis, Mo., May 10-13, 1898. Vol. 5, pp. 143-146.

49. **Brown, Ernest N.** Child study. Educational Record, Province of Quebec, Montreal, March, 1898. Vol. 18, pp. 51-63.
    Discusses the subject from the teachers' point of view.

50. **Bruns, L.** Hysteria in children. Alienist and Neurologist, July, 1898. Vol. 19, pp. 373-430.

51. **Bryant, Sophie** The teachings of morality in the family and school. Macmillan Co., N. Y., 1897. pp. 146.
    Very general.

52. **Bucher, M. K.** Arbeit und Rhythmus. Allg. Phil. Hist. Classe Sächs. Ges. der Wiss. Bd. 17, No. 5, Leipzig, 1896. pp. 130.
    An important and fascinating monograph. Rhythm is born of the "intoxication of work."

53. **Buchner, E. F.** Reports of child study at state teachers' associations. North Western Monthly, Feb., 1898. Vol 8, pp. 429-431.

54. **Buck, Winifred** Boys' Clubs. N. A. Review, Oct., 1898. Vol. 167, pp. 509-512.

55. **Buisson, F.** L'école primaire en France et la part de responsibilité dans l'éducation morale du pays. Rev. Pédagogique, Feb., 1898. Vol. 32, pp. 121-134.

56. **Burk, Frederic** The graded system vs. individual pupils. North Western Monthly, March, 1898. Vol. 8, pp. 481-484.

57. —— —— Growth of children in height and weight. Am. Jour. of Psy., April, 1898. Vol. 9, pp. 253-326.
    An excellent summing up of work done in this field. Gives a bibliography of 109 titles.

58. —— —— Physical measurements. North Western Monthly, May, 1898. Vol. 8, pp. 586-588.

59. —— —— From Fundamental to accessory in the development of the nervous system and of movements. Ped. Sem., Oct., 1898. Vol. 6, pp. 5-64.

60. **Burke, Mrs. B. Ellen** Children's secrets. Trans. Ill. Soc. for Child Study, April, 1898. Vol. 3, pp. 56-61.

61. **Burkhard, P.** Die Fehler der Kinder. Nemnich, Karlsruhe, 1898. pp. 102.

62. **Burnham, Wm. H.** Bibliography of school hygiene. Proc. N. E. A. for 1898. pp. 505-523.
    A select list of 436 titles with a few descriptive and critical notes.

63. **Burton, Richard** Literature for children. N. A. Review, Sept., 1898. Vol. 167, pp. 278-286.

64. **Calkins, Mary Whiton** Short studies in memory and association. Psychol. Rev., Sept., 1898. Vol. 5, pp. 451-462.
    A study of the immediate and of the delayed recall of the concrete and of the verbal.

65. **Camerer, Wilhelm** Der Stoffwechsel des Kindes von der Geburt bis zur Beendigung des Wachstums meist nach eigenen Versuchen dargestellt. Zweite Ausgabe mit Ergänzungen. H. Laup'schen Buchhandlung, Tübingen, 1896. pp. 160.
    An important study of assimilative and excretive processes.

66. **Canton, William** W. V. Her book and various verses. Stone & Kimball, N. Y., 1898. pp. 146.
    Records of very 'cute doings and sayings of a child, with the author's poetic elaboration of some of them.

67. **Carlier, Jules** Les colonies scolaires et "l'œuvre du grand air" de Bruxelles. Rev. Pédagogique, Jan., 1898. Vol. 32, pp. 42-52.

68. **Carson, J. C.** The importance of a high grade of physical health in feeble-minded inmates of public institutions, with a view to their right development, and the best method of securing such health. Reprint from 31st Annual Report, N. Y. State Board of Charities, Jan. 24, 1898. pp. 10.

69. **Carter, Marion H.** Darwin's idea of mental development. Am. Jour. of Psy., July, 1898. Vol. 9, pp. 534-559.

70. —— —— Educational paper dolls. Jour. of Pedagogy, April, 1898. Vol. 11, pp. 133-144.
     An excellent exposition of the use to be made of paper dolls in the study of myths, history, and literature.

71. **Chamberlain, Alex. F.** The lesson of "the little child." North Western Monthly, Feb., 1898. Vol. 8, pp. 435-439.

72. **Chase, Susan F.** Choice of reading for the early adolescent years. Proc. N. E. A., 1898. pp. 1011-1015.

73. **Chrisman, Oscar** The secret language of children. North Western Monthly, Jan. and June, 1898. Vol. 8, pp. 375-379; 649-651.

74. —— —— Results of child study. Education, February, 1898. Vol. 18, pp. 322-332.
     Based on replies to a questionnaire sent to teachers.

75. —— —— Religious ideas of a child. Child Study Mo., March, 1898. Vol. 3, pp. 516-528.

76. —— —— Paidology, the science of the child. Ed. Rev., March, 1898. Vol. 15, pp. 269-285.
     A summary of the author's dissertation submitted to the University of Jena for the degree of Doctor of Philosophy.

77. —— —— The secret language of childhood. Century, May, 1898. Vol. 56, pp. 54-58.

78. —— —— Religious periods of child-growth. Ed. Rev., June, 1898. Vol. 15, pp. 40-48.

79. —— —— Child and parent. North Western Monthly, Nov., Dec., 1898. Vol. 9, pp. 135-138; 180-183.

80. **Clapp, Henry L.** School gardens. Pop. Sci. Mo., Feb., 1898. Vol. 52, pp. 445-456.

81. **Coe, George A.** The morbid conscience of adolescents. Trans. Ill. Soc. for Child Study, Oct., 1898. Vol. 3, pp. 97-108.

82. **Cohn, Hermann** Die Schulartz frage in Breslau. Zeit. für Schulgesundheitspflege, Nov. 1898. Vol. 11, pp. 579-596.

83. **Collins, Joseph** The genesis and dissolution of the faculty of speech : a clinical and psychological stndy of aphasia. Macmillan Co., N. Y., 1898. pp. 432.
     The most valuable treatment of speech disturbances to be found in the English language.

84. **Collins, Patti Lyle** What children ask of Santa Claus. Ladies' Home Journal, Dec., 1898. Vol. 16, p. 31.

85. **Colozza, G. A.** Del potere dell'inibizione ; nota di pedagogia. Paraira, Roma, 1898. pp. 128.
     A good study of inhibition.

86. **Compayré, Gabriel** Saturday teachers' class at the Westfield normal school. Education, Feb., 1898. Vol. 18, pp. 261-264.
     The translation of an article published in Manuel Général de l'Instruction Primaire (Paris), for Oct. 16, 1897.

87. **Core, E. B.** Getting good pictures of children. Ladies' Home Journal, Feb., 1898. Vol. 15, No. 3, p. 13.

88. **Curtis, Henry S.** Inhibition. Ped. Sem., Oct. 1898. Vol. 6, pp. 65-113.

89. **Curtis, H. S., and Partridge, G. E.** Child study in connection with the vacation schools. Report on the vacation schools and playgrounds, N. Y. City. Borough of Manhattan and the Bronx, 1898. pp. 51-97.

90. **Curtiss, Frank Homer,** Some investigations regarding loss in weight and gain in height during sleep. Am. Phys. Ed. Rev., December, 1898. Vol. 3, pp. 270-273.

91. **Darrah, Estelle M.** A study of children's ideals. Pop. Sci. Mo., May, 1898. Vol. 53, pp. 88-98.
An excellent statistical study of children's estimate of character.

92. **Dawson, Geo. E.** Child study. A series of articles in the International Evangel, Sept., 1897 to Sept., 1898.

93. **Defert, Louis** L'enfant et l'adolescent dans la société moderne. Préface de M. Th. Roussel. Montgrédien et Cie, Librairie Illustrée, Paris, 1898. pp. 221.
A popular work, devoted chiefly to infancy. Author maintains absolute neutrality, seeks only to present facts.

94. **Delabarre, E. B.** A method of recording eye movements. Am. Jour. of Psy., July, 1898. Vol. 9, pp. 572-574.

95. **Delpench, A.** La période prépubére. Presse Méd, Paris, 1898. Vol. 2, pp. 89-94.

96. **Delvaille, C.** L'hygiène scolaire au congrès international d'hygiène de Madrid. Rev. Pédagogique, Aug., 1898. Vol. 33, pp. 115-126.

97. **Demolins, Edmond** Anglo-Saxon superiority: to what it is due. R. F. Fenno & Co., N. Y., 1898. pp. 343.
In part I, asks whether the French, German and English school system forms men, and how to bring up our children.

98. **Deucker, R.** Das Kind und die geschlechdiche Entwickelung. Spohr, Leipzig, 1898. pp. 36.

99. **Dewey, John** Some remarks upon the psychology of number. Ped. Sem., Jan., 1898. Vol. 5, pp. 426-434.

100. **Dexter, Edwin G.** The child and the weather. Ped. Sem., April, 1898. Vol. 5, pp. 512-522.
See, also, North Western Monthly, Oct., 1898. Vol. 9, pp. 93-97.

101. **Dieckhoff, Chr.** Die Psychosen bei psychopathisch-minderwertigen. Allg. Zeits. f. Psychiat., 1898. Vol. 55, pp. 215-250.

102. **Dinsmore, J. W.** Running away. North Western Monthly, Dec., 1898. Vol. 9, pp. 183-186.

103. **Dodd, C.** A study in school children. National Rev., 1898. Vol. 32, pp. 66-74.

104. **Donath, Julius** Die Anfänge des menschlichen Geistes. Fest-Vortrag, gehalten in der Jahresversammlung der Gesellschaft der Budapester Hospitalsärzte, am 29. Dezember, 1897. Stuttgart, F. Enke, 1898. 47 s.

A very interesting discussion of the mind of the child in relation to the savage and the race.

105. **Du Bois, Patterson** The Sunday school as a force. North Western Monthly, Feb., 1898. Vol. 8, pp. 439-442.

106. **Elliott, Delia M.** Use of the voice in teaching. Am. Phys. Ed. Rev., Sept., 1898. Vol. 3, pp. 216-219.

107. **Ellis, A. Caswell** Play in education. North Western Monthly, Nov., 1898. Vol. 9, pp. 140-143.

108. **Ellis, Havelock** Auto-erotism : A psychological study. Alienist and Neurologist, April, 1898. Vol. 19, pp. 260-299.

A thorough general study of some sex-phenomena.

109. **Erdmann, Benno und Dodge, Raymond** Psychologischen Untersuchungen über das Lesen auf experimenteller Grundlage. Niemeyer, Halle A. S., 1898. pp. 360.

Considers rest and motion of the eye in reading. Gives descriptions of apparatus.

110. **Evellin, F.** Rapport sur l'enseignement de la morale dans les écoles primaires de l'academie de Paris. Rev. Pédagogique, Feb., 1898. Vol. 32, pp. 97-120.

111. **Fall, Delos** School diseases and medical inspection. Proc. N. E. A., 1898. pp. 534-544.

112. **Fauth, Franz** Das Gedächtnis, Samml. von Abh. a. d. geb. d. Paed. Psy. u. Physiol. Band 1, Heft 5. Reuter & Reichard, Berlin, 1898. pp. 88.

113. **Felker, Allie M.** Play as a means of idealizing and extending the child's experience. Proc. N. E. A., 1898. pp. 624-632.

114. **Féré, Ch.** La famille neuropathique. 2d ed. F. Alcan, Paris, 1898.

Valuable as a guide to the literature of the subject. Large list of authors cited.

115. **Ferrari, G. C.** Manifestazioni artistiche accessuate in una bambina. Archiv. di Psichiat., 1898. Vol. 19, pp. 238-256.

116. **Fitz, Geo. W.** The hygiene of instruction in primary schools. Proc. N. E. A., 1898. pp. 544-550. Also, in Am. Physical Ed. Rev., Dec., 1898. Vol. 3, pp. 242-248.

A strong plea for the correlation of mental and physical development.

117. **Fletcher, Horace** That lost waif or social quarantine, Chicago : Kindergarten Literature Co., 1898. pp. 270.

A study of neglected and abandoned children.

118. **Freud, S.** Die infantile Cerebrallähmung. Hölder, Vienna, 1897. pp. 327.

119. **Galbreath, Louis H.** The study of children by teachers. North Western Monthly, April, 1898. Vol. 8, pp. 541-544.

120. —— —— Child study for class work. Trans. Ill. Soc. for Child Study, April, 1898. Vol. 3, pp. 18-28.

121. —— —— Child study in the art of teaching. Journal of Pedagogy, July, 1898. Vol. 11, pp. 237-252.
Discusses some of the more direct pedagogic bearings of child study.

122. —— —— Practical course in child study for teachers. Trans. Ill. Soc. for Child Study, Oct., 1898. Vol. 3, pp. 153-170.

123. **Gallaudet, E. M.** The deaf and their possibilities. Proc. N. E. A., 1898. pp. 207-214.

124. **Gates, Fanny B.** Musical interests of children. Journal of Pedagogy, October, 1898. Vol. 11, pp. 265-284.
A statistical study of the song preferences of 2000 school children with the reasons for preferences; also, discusses briefly the music sense among primitive people.

125. **Gattel, F.** Ueber die sexuellen Ursachen der Neurastheni u. Angstneurose, Hirschwald, Berlin, 1898. pp. 68.

126. **Gélineau,** —— Hygiène de l'oreille et des sourds. Maloine, Paris, 1897. pp. 127.

127. **Gilles, L.** Du calcul de la mortalité des enfants placés en nourrice. Gy. Ronen, 1898. pp. 20.

Gonzales-Alvarez, B. See **Alvarez, B. Gonzales**

128. **Gordy, J. P.** What can child study contribute to the science of education ? Proc. N. E. A., 1898. pp. 348-354.

129. **Götze, C.** Das Kind als Künstler, Hamburg. Lehrervereinigung für die Pflege der künstlichen Bildung, 1898. pp. 36 and 8 plates.
Summarizes the results of inductive studies on children's drawings.

130. **Gould, George M.** Child fetiches. Ped. Sem., Jan., 1898. Voi. 5, pp. 421-425.

131. **Griffith, E. W.** Interest from the child study point of view. Child Study Monthly, Nov. 1898. Vol. 4, pp. 285-287.

132. **Groos, Karl** The play of animals (Trans. by Elizabeth L. Baldwin). D. Appleton & Co., N. Y., 1898. pp. 341.
Although dealing primarily with the play instinct in animals there is much in the book bearing on the plays of children.

133. —— —— Uber die Necklust. Die Kinderfehler, March, 1898. Vol. 3, pp. 33-39.
An account of the teasing and bullying instincts of children.

134. **Groszmann, M. P. E.** Language teaching from a child study point of view. Child Study Monthly, Nov., 1898. Vol. 4, pp. 266-278.

135. **Gulick, Luther** The religion of boys. The Asssociation Outlook, Springfield, Mass. Vol. 8, pp. 33-48.

136. —— —— Sex and religion. Series of articles published during 1897-98, in Association Outlook, Springfield, Mass.

137. —— —— Some psychical aspects of muscular exercise. Pop. Sci. Mo., Oct., 1898. Vol. 53, pp. 793-805.
An admirable statement of the psychological basis of play.

138. **Gutzmann, H.** Das Stottern. Rosenheim, Frankfort a. M., 1898. pp. 467.

139. **Haddon, Alfred C.** The study of man. G. P. Putnam's Sons, N. Y., 1898. pp. 410.
Contains chapters on measurements and their importance in anthropometry, toys and games, and the singing, counting and funeral games.

140. **v. Hagen, Karl** Die Geschlechts-Bestimmung des werdenden Menschen und was wir über die geschlechtliche Vorausbestimmung wussten und wissen. H. Steinitz, Berlin, 1898. pp. 60.

141. **Hall, G. Stanley** Some aspects of the early sense of self. Am. Jour. of Psy., April, 1898. Vol. 9, pp. 321-395.

142. —— —— New phases of child study. Child Study Monthly, May, 1898. Vol. 4, pp. 35-40.
A brief statement of some characteristics of adolesence.

143. —— —— Initiations into adolescence. Proc. Am. Antiq. Soc., Worcester, Mass., Oct. 21, 1898. Vol. 12, pp. 367-400.

144. —— —— The love and study of nature: a part of education. Agriculture of Mass., 1898. pp. 134-154.
Lectures delivered before the Mass. State Board of Agriculture at Amherst, Dec. 6, 1898. Treats of child's attitude toward nature.

145. —— —— Topical Syllabi, 1898-99. I. The organizations of American Student Life with Henry D. Sheldon; II. Mathematics in Common Schools, with E. B. Bryan; III. Mathematics in the Early Years, with E. B. Bryan ; IV. Unselfishness in children, with Willard S. Small; V. The Fooling Impulse in Man and Animals, with Norman Triplett; VI. Confession, with Erwin W. Runkle; VII. Pity ; VIII. Perception of Rhythm by Children, with Chas. H. Sears.

146. **Hall, Jeanette W.** The period of adolescence. Child Study Monthly, June, 1898. Vol. 4, pp. 68-82.
Contains a bibliography of 21 titles but most of the references are incomplete.

147. **Halleck, Reuben Post** Some contributions of child study to the science of education. Proc. N. E. A., 1898. pp. 254-262.

148. —— —— The education of the motor centers. Trans. Ill. Soc. for Child Study, April, 1898. Vol. 3, pp. 46-55.

149. **Hancock, John A.** Children's tendencies in the use of written language forms. North Western Monthly, June, 1898. Vol. 8, pp. 646-649.

150. **Haney, James P.** The hundredth child. Reprint from the Teachers' Quarterly, N. Y. City, 1898. pp. 13.

151. **Harris, William T.** (and others) The psychology of the initiative functions in childhood as related to the process of learning. Rep. Comm. of Ed. for 1896-97. Vol. 1, pp. 676 681.

152. —— —— Effect of exercise on the vital organs. Proc. N. E. A., 1898. pp. 930-933.

153. **Hartwell, Edward M.** School hygiene—what it is and why we need it. Proc. N. E. A., 1898. pp. 498-505.
Haskell, Ellen M. See Bolton and Haskell (No. 41).

154. **Henie, C.** Untersuchungen über die Zähne der Völksschuler zu Hamar in Norwegen. Zeit. für Schulgesundheitspflege, Feb. 1898. Vol. 11, pp. 65-71.
A careful investigation of the condition of the teeth of the school children in a Norwegian town of 5000 inhabitants.

155. **Henri, Victor and Catherine** Earliest recollections. Pop. Sci. Mo., May, 1898. Vol. 53, pp. 108-115.
Reminiscent study of childhood.

156. **Hogan, Louise A.** A study of a child. Harper & Bro., N. Y., 1898. pp. 220.
A rather diffuse history of a child during the first seven years of its life. Illustrated.

157. **Holmes, Manfred J.** Apperception and child study. Trans. Ill. Soc. for Child Study, Oct., 1898. Vol. 3, pp. 145-152.

158. **Hrdlicka, Ales** Report on anthropological work in the state institution for feeble-minded children, Syracuse, N. Y. Supplemental to 48th Annual Report, 1898. pp. 98.

159. —— —— Anthropological investigations on 1000 white and colored children of both sexes. 47th Annual Report, N. Y. Juvenile Asylum. State Printers, N. Y. and Albany, 1899. pp. 86.
An excellent piece of work. Commendable for its conservative tone.

160. —— —— The medico-legal aspect of the case of Maria Barbella. State Hospitals' Bulletin, Utica, N. Y., April, 1897. pp. 1-87, with 2 charts and 19 figures.

161. **Huey, Edmund B.** Preliminary experiments in the physiology and psychology of reading. Am. Jour. of Psy., July, 1898. Vol. 9, pp. 575-586.

162. **Hugh, D. D.** Formal education from the standpoint of physiological psychology. Ped Sem., April, 1898. Vol 5, pp. 599-605.

163. **Itard, ——** Rapports et mémoires sur le sauvage de l' Aveyron, l'idiotie et la surdi—mutité. Avec une appréciation de ces rapports par Delasiauve. Préface par Bourneville. Eloge d'Itard par Bousquet. Félix Alcan, Paris, 1894. pp. 144.
A reprint, with notes and introduction, of a classic.

164. **Ireland, William W.** The mental affections of children, idiocy, imbecility, and insanity. J. & A. Churchill, London, 1898. pp. 442.
An authoritative work on the care and training of mentally deficient children.

165. **Jacobi, Mary Putnam** Care of the adolescent girl. The Mother's Voice, Jan., 1898. Vol. 2, pp. 2-3; 13-15.

166. **Jegi, John I.** Children's ambitions. Trans. Ill. Soc. for Child Study, Oct., 1898. Vol. 3, pp. 131-144.
Treats of German children in Milwaukee. Conservative in general tone, and valuable.

167. **Johnson, George E.** Play in physical education. Proc. N. E. A., 1898. pp. 948-958.

168. **Juvenile Offenders.** A report based on an inquiry instituted by the committee of the Howard Association. Wertheimer, Lea & Co., London, 1898. pp. 39.
The opinions are almost universally opposed to imprisonment and in favor of whipping.

169. **Kemsies, Ferdinand** Arbeitshygiene der Schule auf Grund von Ermüdungsmessungen. Samml. v. Abh. a. d. Geb. d. Päd. Psy. u. Physiol. Band 2, Heft I, 1898. pp. 64.
A study of the effect of fatigue on the quality and quantity of mathematical work made by means of the ergograph.

170. **Keyes, Chas. H.** What can child study do for our schools ? North Western Monthly, June, 1898. Vol. 8, pp. 641-644.
Abstract of an address before meeting of the Conn. Teachers' Ass'n, Willimantic, Conn., May 6, 1898.

171. **Kiernan, James G.** The periods of stress in childhood. Trans. Ill. Soc. for Child Study, Oct., 1898. Vol. 3, pp. 91-96.

172. **Kirkpatrick, E. A.** The problem of children's reading. North Western Monthly, June, 1898. Vol. 8, pp. 651-654.

173. —— —— Children's reading I. North Western Monthly, Dec., 1898. Vol. 9, pp. 188-191.

174. —— —— Defects in the eyes of children. State Normal School, Fitchburg, Mass., 1898. pp. 7.
A little pamphlet sent out to parents of children whose eyes are found defective.

175. **Kittredge, F. E.** Adenoids and their complications in children. N. Y. Med. Jour., Nov. 12, 1898. Vol. 68, pp. 702-706.

176. **Kline, Linus W.** Truancy as related to the migrating instinct. Ped. Sem., Jan., 1898. Vol. 5, pp. 381-420.

177. —— —— The migratory impulse vs. love of home. Am. Jour. of Psy., Oct., 1898. Vol. 10, pp. 1-81.

178. **Knapp, Ludwig** Der Scheintod der Neugeborenen. Braumüller, Wien u. Leipzig, 1898. pp. 163.
Largely on the development of the various methods of reanimating apparently dead new born children. Bibliography of 13 pp.

2

179. **Kohlbrugge, I. H. F.** Der Atavismus. Scrineriüs, Utrecht, 1897. pp. 31.

180. **Krauss, W. C.** The stigmata of degeneration. Am. Jour. of Insanity, July, 1898. Vol. 55, pp. 55-88.

181. **Kraus-Boelte, Maria** The development of the inner life of the child. Proc. N. E. A., 1898. pp. 608-614.

182. **Krohn, William O.** Minor mental abnormalities in children as occasioned by certain erroneous school methods. Child Study Monthly, Oct., 1898. Vol. 4, pp. 201-214.

183. **Kuhn, Maurice** Les enfants degénérés dans les écoles publiques. Rev. Pédagogique, Jan., 1898. Vol. 32, pp. 53-58.
    Translation and discussion of a paper on feeble-minded children in the public schools, by Will S. Monroe.

184. **Laing, Mary E.** An inductive study of interest. Ed. Review, Nov., 1898. Vol. 16, pp. 381-390.

185. **Lancaster, E. G.** The vanishing character of adolescent experiences. North Western Monthly, June, 1898. Vol. 8, pp. 644-646.

186. **Lang, Ossian H.** Some cautions to be observed in child study. Proc. N. E. A., 1898. pp. 898-902.

187. **Law, Frederick H.** Age at which children leave school. Ed. Rev., Jan., 1898. Vol. 15, pp. 40-49.
    Discusses the extent of school training of children in N. Y. City.

188. **Lay, W. A.** Führer durch den Rechtschreibunterricht. Nemnich, Karlsruhe, 1897. pp. 230.
    Contains an account of important investigations in regard to spelling.

189. **Lay, Wilfred** Mental imagery. Experimentally and subjectively considered. The Psychol. Review Monograph Supp. Vol. 2, No. 3, May, 1898. pp. 59.

190. **Leclère, A.** Description d'un objet. L'Année Psychol., 1897. Vol. 4, pp. 379-389.

191. **Lemox, D., and Sturrock, A.** The elements of physical education. A teacher's manual. Wm. Blackwood & Sons, London, 1898. pp. 241.
    A practical and interesting book.

192. **Letchworth, Wm. Pryor** Dependent children and family homes. The Sanitarian, N. Y., Jan., 1898. Vol. 40, pp. 3-14.

193. **Lietz, Hermann** Emlohstobba. Berlin, 1897. pp. 192.

194. **Loeper, F.** Ueber Organisation von Hilfsschulen. Die Kinderfehler, Nov., 1898. Vol. 3, pp. 167-177.
    A discussion of the question of separate classes for the mentally dull.

195. **Lombroso, Paolo** (The logical consistency of the ideas of children) Voprosi Philos. Moscow, Jan., Feb.; Mch., Apr., 1898. Year 9, pp. 23-40; 99-110.

Luckey, G. W. A. (See Child Study Department, North Western Monthly, 1898. Lincoln, Neb.)

196. **Lui, Aurelio** L'isterismo infantile. Riv. Sper. di Freniat, 1898. Vol. 24, pp. 745-771.
Résumé of recent studies on hysteria in children.

197. **Lukens, Herman T.** The school fatigue question in Germany. Ed. Review, March, 1898. Vol. 15, pp. 246-254.
An excellent statement of recent investigations in Germany and especially of the labors of Kraepelin and Griesbach.

198. —— —— The method of suggestion in the cure of faults. North Western Monthly, May, 1898. pp. 592-595.

199. —— —— Notes abroad. Ped. Sem., Oct., 1898. Vol. 6, pp. 114-125.

200. **Mackenzie, John Noland** The physiological and pathological relations between the nose and the sexual apparatus of man. Bull. of the Johns Hopkins Hospital, Jan., 1898. Vol. 9, pp. 10-17.

201. **McKenzie, R. Tait** Influence of school life on curvature of the spine. Proc. N. E. A., 1898. pp. 939-948.

202. **McLeish, Mrs. Andrew** Observations in the development of a child in the first year. Trans. Ill. Soc. for Child Study, Oct., 1898. Vol. 3, pp. 109-124.
A rather careful bit of individual child study made by an observing mother.

203. **MacLennan, S. F.** Method in child study, with special reference to the psychological point of view. Trans. Ill. Soc. for Child Study, April, 1898. Vol. 3, pp. 29-45.

204. **McMurry, Lida Brown** Relation between parents and teachers. School and Home Education, Sept., 1898. Vol. 18, pp. 17-18.

205. **Mall, Franklin P.** Development of the human intestine and its position in the adult. Bull. of the Johns Hopkins Hospital, Sept., Oct., 1898. Vol. 9, pp. 197-208.
First attempt to trace the position and growth of the intestine from the embryo to the adult.

206. **Mansfield, Edith** Conflict of authority. Child Study Monthly, March, 1898. Vol. 3, pp. 529-539.
A good statistical study of school discipline from the child's standpoint.

207. **Marina, Giuseppe** Ricerche antropologiche ed etnografiche sui ragazzi. Bocca, Torino, 1896. pp. 86.
Anthropometric studies of Italian boys. Has a good bibliography.

2c8. —— —— Studi antropologici sugli adulti. Bocca, Torino, 1897. pp. 38.
Companion Vol. to preceding.

209. **Marshall, Henry R.** Instinct and reason. The Macmillan Co., N. Y., 1898. pp. 574.

210. **Mead, George H.** The child and his environment. Trans. Ill. Soc. for Child Study, April, 1898. Vol. 3, pp. 1-11.

211. **Merrill, Jennie B.** Children's gardens. North Western Monthly, Oct., 1898. Vol. 9, pp. 89-90. Also, Proc. N. E. A., 1898. pp. 598-602.

212. **Milliken, O. J.** Chicago vacation schools. Am. Jour. of Sociology, Nov., 1898. Vol. 4, pp. 289-308.

213. **Mills, Wesley** The nature and development of animal intelligence. The Macmillan Co., N. Y., 1898. pp. 307.
A valuable addition to the literature of the subject. Well indexed.

214. **Moll, A.** Das nervöse Weib. F. Fontane et Cie., Berlin. pp. 226.

215. **Möller, P.** Ueber Intelligenzprüfungen. Ein Beitrag zur Diagnostik des Schwachsinns. Berlin, 1897. pp. 32.

216. **Monroe, Will S.** Vocational interests of children. Education, Jan., 1898. Vol. 18, pp. 259-264.
A statistical study of the ambitions of 1,755 elementary school children.

217. —— —— Über die Behandlung der Verbrecher. Die Kinderfehler, Jan., 1898. Vol. 3, pp. 19-22.
Describes the training of adolescent delinquents in America.

218. —— —— Chorea among public school children. American Physical Education Review, March, 1898. Vol. 3, pp. 19-24.
Translated into German by Johann Trüper and published in Die Kinderfehler, Sept., 1898. Vol. 3, pp. 155-160.

219. —— —— Das Studium der Kindesseele in Amerika. Deutsche Zeit. für Ausländisches Unterrichtswesen, April, 1898. Vol. 3, pp. 193-203.
Historical and descriptive account of the child study movement in America.

220. —— —— Development of the social consciousness of children. North Western Monthly, Sept., 1898. Vol. 9, pp. 31-36. Also Proc. N. E. A., 1898. pp. 921-928.
Traces briefly the genesis of the social sense in animals, primitive man, and the child.

221. —— —— Child study outlines. Second series: 1. Children's spontaneous drawings. 2. The money sense of children. 3. Memory types of children. 4. Perception of children. 5. Fatigue in school children. 6. Growth of children. 7. Psychology of adolescence. 8. Imitation in childhood. 9. Suggestibility of children. Wright & Potter Printing Co., Boston, 1898.
A series of nine outlines suggesting specific studies, hints for the collation of the material collected, and bibliographic references to the literature of the subject.

—— —— See, also, No. 183.

222. **Morton, Aima B.** Child study and education. Public School Journal, Feb., 1898. Vol. 17, pp. 289-293.

223. **Mott, T. A.** Contagious diseases in school. Proc. N. E. A., 1898. pp. 381-386.

Muffang, H. See **Ammon O.**

224. **Munro, Mary F.** Three years in the life of a child. Ed. Review, Nov., 1898. Vol. 16, pp. 367-377.

225. **Mutke, Robert** Die Behandlung stammelnder und stotternder Schüler. Breslau, 1898. pp. 30.

Relates largely to the pedagogic and didactic treatment of stammerers who relapse. Author is director of the curative course of the Breslau Institution for stammering children.

226. **Neuman, B. P.** Take care of the boys. Fortnightly Rev., Sept., 1898. Vol. 70, pp. 410-421. Also Living Age, Nov. 19, 1898. Vol. 219, pp. 503-513.

227. **Noikov, D.** Das Aktivitätsprincip in der Pädagogik J. J. Rousseau's. Schmidt, Leipzig, 1898. pp. 160.

228. **Noss, Theo. B.** Child study record. The Author, Southwestern State Normal School, California, Pa.

A convenient individual record book prepared for the author's classes in pedagogy.

229. **Oltuszevski, W.** Die geistige und sprachliche Entwickelung des Kindes. H. Cornfeld, Berlin, 1897. pp. 43.

Gives monthly details of linguistic development of a Polish child, Valuable for comparison with Preyer, whose work the author has carefully collated with his own.

230. **Oppenheim, Nathan** The development of the child. Macmillan Co., N. Y., 1898. pp. 296.

Contents: Facts in the comparative development of the child; importance of heredity and environment; the primary school; religion; the child as a witness in suits of law; the child-criminal; the genius and the defective; the child and institutional life; the profession of maternity.

231. **Osborn, F. W.** Wordsworth's poems of children and childhood. Education, Oct., 1898. Vol. 18, pp. 93-99.

A brief study of the child in literature.

232. **O'Shea, M. V.** "Spare the rod and spoil the child." The Outlook, Jan. 8, 1898. Vol. 58, pp. 128-130.

Results of child study applied to corporal punishment.

233. —— —— The purpose, scope and method of child study. Jour. of Pedagogy, Jan., 1898. Vol. 11, pp. 9-23.

A forceful statement of the practical utility of child study.

234. —— —— Some adolescent reminiscences. Jour. of Pedagogy, Oct., 1898. Vol. 11, pp. 299-317.

A study based on replies to a questionnaire from forty college students on their recollections as to growth, intellectual and emotional phenomena, dress, etc., during early adolescence.

235. **Oswald, Felix L.** The secret of atavism. Pop. Sci. Mo., June, 1898. Vol. 53, pp. 192-196.

236. **Partridge, George E.** Reverie. Ped. Sem., April, 1898. Vol. 5, pp. 445-474.

—— —— See, also, No. 89.

237. **Pearson, Karl** On a scale of intelligence in children. Jour. of Ed., London, Sep., 1898. N. S. Vol. 20, pp. 509-510.

238. **Peck, E. A.** Defective vision. Child Study Monthly, June, 1898. Vol. 4, pp. 100-104.

239. **Pelopi,** —— De la precocité et des perversions de l'instinct sexuel chez les enfants. Bordeau, 1898.

240. **Petit, Edouard** Autour de l'école du soir : I. Chez les adolescents ; II. Chez les ouvriers ; III. Chez les soldats. Revue Pédagogique, April, 1898. Vol. 32, pp. 303-322.

241. —— —— Ames d'écoliers. Rev. Pédagogique, Nov., 1898. Vol. 33, pp. 377-387.

242. **Phelps, G. M.** Care of children's teeth. Child Study Monthly, Oct., 1898. Vol. 4, pp. 225-233.

243. **Pierce, A. H.** The illusion of the Kindergarten pattern. Psychological Review, May, 1898. Vol. 5, pp. 233-253.

244. **Pierce, John M.** Psychological aspects of physical education. Am. Phys. Ed. Review, March, 1898. Vol. 3, pp. 30-37.

245. **Phillips, Daniel E.** Some remarks on number and its application. Ped. Sem., April, 1898. Vol. 5, pp. 590-598.

246. **Plummer, Edward M.** The Olympic games in ancient times. Am. Phys. Ed. Review, March and June, 1898. Vol. 3, pp. 1-18 ; 93-106.

247. —— —— Toys and games for children among the ancient Hellenes. Am. Phys. Ed. Review, Sept., 1898. Vol. 3, pp. 157-169.

248. **Pollock, Susan P.** Ideal play in the Kindergarten. Proc. N. E. A., 1898. pp. 604-608.

249. **Porter, Isaac, Jr.** Photographing children at home. Ladies' Home Journal, Dec., 1898. Vol. 16, No. 1, p. 35.

250. **Powell, W. B.** Medical inspection of schools. Proc. N. E. A., 1898. pp. 454-462.

251. **Quantz, J. O.** Dendro-psychoses. Am. Jour. of Psy., July, 1898. Vol. 9, pp. 449-506.

252. **Quincy, Josiah** Playgrounds, baths, and gymnasia. Am. Phys. Ed. Review, Dec., 1898. Vol. 3, pp. 234-241.

253. **Ragozin, Zenaide A.** Tales of the heroic age ; Siegfried & Boewulf. G. P. Putnam's Sons, N. Y., 1898. pp. 332.
     Addressed to childhood under the conviction that myth is essential. Timely and valuable for every teacher of literature.

254. **Regnault, F. et Raoul** Comment on marche. Lavanzelle, Paris, 1898. pp. 188.

255. **Report** of the Chicago Vacation School Committee of Women's Clubs, Chicago, 1898. pp. 44.

256. **Report** of the Departmental Committee on Defective and Epileptic Children. Vol. 1. The Report, pp. 42 ; Vol. 2. Minutes of Evidence, Appendices, etc., pp. 283. Eyre & Spottiswood, London, 1898.
Recommends that teachers be trained to make special observations upon these children.

257. **Robinson, Harriet H.** Loom and spindle, or life among the early mill girls. T. Y. Crowell & Co., N. Y., 1898. pp. 216.
Valuable for its details and economic history.

258. **Rohleder, H.** Die Masturbation. Fischer's Med., Buchhandlg, Berlin, 1898. pp. 319.
A monograph for physicians and teachers. Elaborate and systematic.

259. **Rosenfeld, Leonhard** Arbeitsschulen für Verkrüppelte. Zeit. für Schulgesundheitspflege, Jan., 1898. Vol. 11, pp. 4-18.
An account of the European movement to give special training to crippled and deformed children.

260. **Roubinovitch, Dr.** L'alcool, l'enfance et l'école. Rev. Pédagogique, Jan., 1898. Vol. 32, pp. 35-41.

261. **Rowe, S. H.** Fear in the discipline of the child. The Outlook, Sept. 24, 1898. Vol. 60, pp. 232-234.

262. **Royce, Josiah** The new psychology and the consulting psychologist. Proc. N. E. A., 1898. pp. 554-570.

263. —— —— The psychology of invention. Psychological Review, March, 1898. Vol. 5, pp. 113-144.

264. **Rude, A.** Jugendlektüre und Schülerbibliotheken. Rein's Ency. Handb. d. Pädagogik. Vol. 3, pp. 934-945.

265. **Sachse, L.** Das Kind und die Zahl. Eine psychologisch-pädagogische Skizze. Zeits. f. Philosophie u. Pädagogik. Langensalza, 1898. Band 5, pp. 356-360.

266. **Salge, B.** Hysterie bei Kindern. Berlin, 1898.

267. **Sanborn, Alvan F.** About boys and boys' clubs. N. A. Review, Aug., 1898. Vol. 167, pp. 254-256.

268. **Sanders, W. H.** Attitude of Rensselaer pupils toward school. North Western Monthly, Jan., 1898. Vol. 8, pp. 382-385.

269. **Schiller, Hermann** Der Stundenplan. Ein Kapitel aus der pädagogischen psychologie und physiologie. Samml. von Abh. Geb. a. d. Päd. Psy. u. Physiol. Reuther & Reichard, 1897. pp. 65.

270. —— —— Studien und Versuche ueber die Erlernung der Orthographie. Samml. v. Abh. a. d. Geb. d. Päd. Psy. u. Physiol. Band 2, Heft 4, 1898. pp. 63.
An excellent experimental study on spelling made in the elementary classes of the Gymnasium at Giessen.

271. **Schinz, Albert** La moralité de l'enfant. Rev. Philos., March, 1898. Vol. 45, pp. 259-295. Also, translation, by Ch. Ufer, Die Sittlichkeit des Kindes. Beyer u. Söhne, Langensalza, 1898. pp. 42.

272. **Schwalbe, B.** Schulhygienische Fragen und Mittheilungen, H. Heyfelder, Berlin, 1898. pp. 37.
    Presents many measurements of height, weight, etc.

273. **Scott, Colin A.** Children's fears as material for expression and a basis of education in art. Trans. Ill. Soc. for Child Study, April, 1898. Vol. 3, pp. 12-17.

274. **Seeley, Levi** The daily programme in schools. Child Study Monthly, March, 1898. Vol. 3, pp. 544-549.
    Summarizes briefly Friedrich's study on fatigue and Schuyten's study on voluntary attention.

275. **Seerley, Homer H.** The dangers of the adolescent period. Educational Foundations. E. L. Kellogg & Co., N. Y., 1898.

276. **Sheffield, Herman B.** A contribution to the study of hysteria in childhood as it occurs in the United States of America. N. Y. Med. Jour., Sept. 17-24, 1898. Vol. 68, pp. 412-416 ; 433-436.

277. **Sheldon, Henry D.** The institutional activities of American children. Am. Jour. of Psy., July, 1898. Vol. 9, pp. 425-448.

278. **Shinn, Millicent W.** Comparative importance of the senses in infancy. North Western Monthly, April, 1898. Vol. 8, pp. 544-547.

279. **Small, M. H.** Methods of manifesting the instinct for certainty. Ped. Sem., Jan., 1898. Vol. 5, pp. 313-380.

280. —— —— An experiment borrowed from the schoolroom. North Western Monthly, Nov., 1898. Vol. 9, pp. 134-135.

281. **Smith, A. T.** Psychological tendencies. The study of imitation. Rep. U. S. Comm. of Ed., 1896-97. Vol. 1, pp. 671-676.

282. **Smith, Nora A.** The children of the future. Houghton, Mifflin & Co., Boston, 1898. pp. 165.
    Contains chapters on the study of children ; training for parenthood ; sand and the children ; kindergarten training.

283. —— —— The kindergarten made possible in every home, village, or small neighborhood. Ladies' Home Journal, Nov., 1898. Vol, 15, No. 12, p. 20; Dec., 1898, Vol. 16, No. 1, p. 34 ; Jan., 1899, No. 2, p. 16 ; Feb., 1899, No. 3, p. 22.

284. **Soldevilla, Carrera, M.** La infancia y la criminalidad. Lérida, 1897. pp. 240.

285. **Solotaroff, H.** The origin of the family. Am. Anthropologist, Aug., 1898. Vol. 11, pp. 229-242.

286. **Stableton, J. K.** The study of boys entering the adolescent period. III-IV. The relation of the sexes. V. An untruthful character. VI. The passionate boy. VII. Arrested development. North Western Monthly, Jan., March, April, May, Dec., 1898. Vol. 8, pp. 385-386 ; 484-487 ; 539-541 ; 589-592. Vol. 9, pp. 138-140 ; 179-180.

287. **Stanley, Hiram M.** On the early sense of self. Science, 1898. N. S. Vol. 8, pp. 22-23. (See No. 141.)

288. **Stern, Herman I.** The gods of our fathers. Harper & Brothers, N. Y., 1898. pp. 269.
A work on Saxon mythology that every student and teacher should read.

289. **Stryker, Mabel F.** Children's joys and sorrows. Child Study Monthly, Oct., 1898. Vol. 4, pp. 217-225.
A statistical study of the happiest and saddest days ever experienced by 1,800 school children.

290. **Stuart, Ruth McEnery** Sonny. A Christmas guest. The Century Co., N. Y., 1898. pp. 135.
Should be read by every teacher who has a tendency to magnify his office.

291. **Sudduth, W. X.** Nervous and backward children. Child Study Monthly, March, 1898. Vol. 3, pp. 540-543.
This series of articles continued in the issues for April, May, June and Sept., 1898.

292. **Sutherland, Alexander** The origin and growth of the moral instinct. Longmans, Green & Co., London, 1898. 2 Vols., pp. 461 ; 336.

293. **Swift, Edgar James** Heredity and environment. A study in adolescence. North Western Monthly, Sept., 1898. Vol. 9, pp. 36-41. Am. Phys. Ed. Rev., Sept., 1898. Vol. 3, pp. 170-178. Proc. N. E. A., 1898. pp. 910-916.
A study of juvenile delinquency.

294. **Szentesy, Béla** Die geistige Ueberanstrengung des Kindes. I. Theil : Von der Wiege bis zur Mittelschule. II. Theil : Die Psycho.-Physiologie des Musicirens. Pester Buchdruckerei Aktien-Gesellschaft, Budapest, 1898. pp. 123.
Part 1. A general characterization of childhood. Part 2. Describes the author's theory of playing the piano.

295. **Talbot, Eugene S.** Degeneracy. Its causes, signs and results. Contemp. Sci. Ser. Charles Scribner's Sons, N. Y., 1898. pp. 372.

296. —— —— A study of the stigmata of degeneracy among the American criminal youth. Jour. Am. Med. Ass'n, 1898. Vol. 30, pp. 849-856.

297. —— —— Defects of development in childhood. Trans. Ill. Soc. for Child Study, Oct. 1898. Vol. 3. pp. 75-90.

298. **Taylor, A. R.** The study of the child. D. Appleton & Co., N. Y., 1898. pp. 215.
A brief treatise on the psychology of the child with suggestions for teachers, students, and parents.

299. **Taylor, J. L.** The amount of work the growing brain should undertake. Bull. Am. Acad. Med., 1898. Vol. 3, pp. 469-482.

300. **Taylor, John Madison** The nervous mother. Reprint from University Med. Magazine (Phila.), July, 1895. pp. 8.

301. —— —— Puberty in girls and certain of its disturbances. A practical lesson. Reprint from Pediatrics, July 15, 1896. pp. 6.

302. —— —— Children of feeble resistance : their care and management. Reprint from Int. Med. Mag., Aug., 1896. pp. 26.

303. **Taylor, Joseph S.** Some practical aspects of interest. Ped. Sem., April, 1898. Vol. 5, pp. 497-511.

304. **Thompson, John G.** Child study in the training of teachers. North Western Monthly, Sept., 1898. Vol. 9, pp. 41-43. Also Proc. N. E. A., 1898. pp. 916-921.

305. **Titchener, E. B.** A primer of psychology. The Macmillan Co., N. Y., 1898. pp. 314.

306. —— —— Ebbinghaus's method for the study of fatigue in school hours. Journal of Education, June 30, 1898. Vol. 48, pp. 7-8.

307. **Trüper, Johann** Minor mental abnormalities in childhood. Child Study Monthly, May, June, Sept., and Dec., 1898. Vol. 4, pp. 2-15 ; 88-97 ; 130-138 ; 342-346.
This is a translation by C. C. Van Liew from the German of Trüper's excellent monograph on Psychopathische Minderwertigkeiten im Kindesalter.

308. —— —— Psychopathisches im Kindesleben. Rein's Ency. Handb. d. Pädagogik. Vol. 5, pp. 588-597.

309. **Truslow, Walter** Exercise during adolescence. Am. Phys. Ed. Review, June, 1898. Vol. 3, pp. 111-121.

310. **Tucker, Emmeline F.** Nebraska society for child study. North Western Monthly, Jan., 1898. Vol. 8, pp. 387-389.

311. —— —— The child and his school reader. North Western Monthly, June, 1898. Vol. 8, pp. 654-655.

312. **Tümpel, R.** Ueber die Versuche geistige Ermüdung durch mechanische Messungen zu untersuchen. Zeits. f. Philos. u. Pädagogik, 1898. Vol. 5, pp. 31-38 ; 108-114 ; 195-198.

313. **Ufer, Chr.** Zur Beobachtung der Kinder. Die Kinderfehler, Jan., 1898. Vol. 3, pp. 1-8.
Presents the claims of child study to parents.

314. —— —— Über Kinderpsychologie. Die Kinderfehler, May, 1898. Vol. 3, pp. 65-74.

Vaschide, N. See **Binet and Vaschide.** (No. 36.)

315. **Vitali, V.** Studi anthropologici in servizio della pedagogia. Vol. 1, I Romagnoli. Forli, 1896. pp. 116. Vol. 2, Le Romagnole. Turin, 1898. pp. 130.
Anthropometric and psychological studies of Italian boys and girls.

316. **Vivier, H.** Sur l'infantilisme. Jouve, Paris, 1898. pp. 58.

317. **Wagner, Ludwig** Unterricht und Ermüdung. Ermüdungsmessungen au Schülern des neuen Gymnasiums in Darmstadt. Samml. von Abh. a. d. Geb. d. Paed. Psy. u. Physiol. Vol. 1, Heft 4. Reuter u. Reichard, Berlin, 1898. pp. 134.
A study of fatigue in the gymnasium at Darmstadt by means of the compass æsthesiometer.

318. **Weir, James** The dawn of reason, or mental traits in the lower animals. Macmillan Co., N. Y., 1898. pp. 234.
Takes too high a view of animal mentality.

319. **Wessely, Rudolf** Der Geschmack der Quintaner und Quartaner. Zeits f. d. deuts. Unterricht, 1898. Vol. 12, pp. 449-460.

320. **Westermarck, Edward** The essence of revenge. Mind, July, 1898. N. S. Vol. 7, pp. 289-310.

321. **What** can child study contribute to the science of education ? North Western Monthly, April, 1898. Vol. 8, pp. 535-539.

322. **Wilke, G.** Die Hauptberührungs Unterscheidungspunkte der Erziehungsgedanken John Locke's und J. J. Rousseau's. Erlangen, 1898. pp. 65.

323. **Wille, W.** Die Psychosen des Pubertätsalters. F. Deuticke, Wien, 1898. pp. 218.

324. **Wilson, Louis N.** Bibliography of child study. Pedagogical Seminary, April, 1898. Vol. 5, pp. 541-589. The same reprinted in pamphlet form, Clark University Press, Worcester, 1898. pp. 49
A list of 535 books and pamphlets on child study ; 13 journals; 16 reports, serial studies, and translations of societies ; and 81 works of standard reference on allied topics. With a subject index.

325. **Winship, Albert E.** Fitting the curriculum to the different ages of childhood and youth. Journal of Education, Nov. 17, 1898. Vol. 48, pp. 320-321.
A discussion of Pres. G. Stanley Hall's address before the New England Association of School Superintendents.

326. **Wissler, Clark** The interests of children in the reading work of the elementary schools. Ped. Sem., April, 1898. Vol. 5, pp. 523-540.

327. —— —— Pupils' interest as influenced by the teacher. Child Study Monthly, Sept., 1898. Vol. 4, pp. 139-146.
A statistical study of the preferences of pupils and teachers for certain school subjects.

328. **Wolfe, H. K.** Moral training of children. North Western Monthly, Feb., 1898. Vol. 8, pp. 431-435.

329. **Woods, Alice** Child study. Jour. of Ed., London, July, 1898. N. S. Vol. 20, pp. 396-397.

330. **Yoder, A. H.** Pubescence. North Western Monthly, May, 1898. Vol. 8, pp. 597-600.

331. **Ziehen, Th.** Die Ideenassoziation des Kindes. Erste Abhandlung. Abh. a. d. Geb. d. Paed. Psy. u. Physiol. Band 1, Heft 6. Reuter & Reichard, Berlin, 1898. pp. 66.
A study of the association of ideas of boys from 8 to 14 years.

332. —— —— Nervensystem. Rein's Ency. Handb. d. Pädagogik. Vol. 5, pp. 89-92.

333. **Zueblin, Charles** Municipal playgrounds in Chicago. Am. Jour. of Sociology, Sept., 1898. Vol. 4, pp. 145-158.

SUBJECT INDEX.

Abandoned Children, 117, 158.
Abnormalities, 182, 307.
Accessory, 59.
Activity, 88, 227.
Adenoids, 175.
Adolescence, 12, 13, 72, 81, 93, 95, 135, 142, 143, 146, 165, 171, 185, 217, 221, 234, 240, 275, 286, 293, 301, 309, 323, 330.
Affirmation, 279.
Age of Leaving School, 187.
Alcohol, 260.
Ambition, 91, 166, 216.
Amnesia, 83.
Anatomy, 7.
Anger, 320.
Anglo Saxon, 97.
Animals, 132, 213, 318.
Anthropology, 97, 139, 158, 159, 160, 315.
Anthropometry, 1, 36, 39, 57, 58, 139, 158, 159, 160, 207, 208, 315.
Aphasia, 26, 83.
Apperception, 157.
Architecture, 33.
Art, 21, 87, 115, 129, 221, 231.
Association, 41, 64, 195, 331.
Atavism, 179, 235, 251, 295.
Atmosphere, 100.
Attention, 274.
Auto-erotism, 108.

Baths, 19, 252.
Bibliography, 38, 62, 221, 324.
Boys, 54, 135, 226.
Brain, 299.
Breathing (Nose), 44.
Bullying, 133.

Cerebral Paralysis, 118.
Ceremonies, 143.
Certainty, 279.
Character, 15, 27, 46, 91, 181.
Child as Teacher, 71.
Child Life, 66, 75, 156, 202, 224.
Child Study Societies, 310.
Chorea, 218.
Circulation, 36.
Clubs, 54, 267.
Collections, 3.

Confession, 145.
Conscience, 81.
Crime, 23, 34, 160, 168, 217, 230, 284, 295, 296.
Crippled. See Defectives.
Curriculum, 269, 325.

Darwin, 69.
Deaf and Deaf Mutes, 123, 126, 163.
Death (Apparent), 178.
Defects, 1, 61, 174, 297, 308.
Defectives, 25, 26, 31, 43, 48, 68, 101, 150, 163, 164, 182, 194, 198, 230, 238, 256, 259.
Deformed. See Defectives.
Degeneracy, 160, 180, 183, 295, 296.
Delinquents, 217, 293, 296.
Dendro-Psychoses, 251.
Dentition. See Teeth.
Dependent Children, 192.
Desires, 84.
Development, 69, 98, 104, 141, 181, 202, 220, 230, 292.
Digestion, 65.
Discipline, 23, 24, 42, 168, 198, 206, 217, 232, 261.
Disease, 45, 111, 218, 223.
Dolls, 3, 70.
Drawing, 21, 129, 221.
Dreaming, 236.

Ears and Hearing, 4, 45, 126.
Emotions, 273, 289.
England, 22, 23, 24.
Environment, 6, 46, 100, 210, 230, 293, 295.
Ethology, 15.
Evidence, 230.
Exercise, 152, 308.
Eye-movements, 94.
Eyes and Eyesight, 4, 5, 109, 174, 238.

Factory Life, 257.
Family, 6, 39, 40, 51, 192, 285.
Fatigue, 16, 35, 169, 197, 221, 274, 306, 312, 317.
Fear, 261, 273.
Feeble Minded, 25, 29, 68, 150, 164, 183, 215, 307, 308.

Fetiches, 130.
Food, 65.
Fooling, 145.
Formal Education, 162.
Froebelianism, 9.
Fundamental, 59.

Games, 139, 246, 247.
Gardens, 80, 211.
General, 7, 30, 47, 49, 53, 66, 74, 76, 92, 93, 103, 119, 121, 122, 128, 147, 156, 170, 186, 219, 222, 233, 290, 298, 313, 314, 321, 329.
Genius, 230.
Girls, 30, 165.
Gradation, 56.
Growth, 1, 39, 57, 59, 158, 221, 299.
Gymnasia, 252.
Gymnastics, 36.

Hearing. See Ears and Hearing.
Heating, 28, 33.
Height, 1, 57, 90.
Heredity, 46, 230, 293, 295.
High School. See Secondary Education.
Home, 177, 192, 249.
Honor, 279.
Hygiene, 14, 28, 33, 62, 96, 116, 126, 153, 272.
Hygiene (School), 96, 153.
Hypnotism, 198.
Hysteria, 50, 196, 266, 276.

Ideals, 20, 22, 91, 113.
Idiocy, 163, 164.
Illusion, 243.
Imbecility, 164.
Imitation, 151, 221, 281.
Imprisonment, 168.
Individual, 56.
Inhibition, 85, 88.
Initiation, 143.
Insanity, 29, 48, 164.
Instinct and Reason, 209, 318.
Instruction, 116, 317.
Intelligence, 215, 237.
Interest, 124, 131, 166, 184, 216, 303, 326, 327.
Invention, 263.

Juvenile Delinquents, 158.

Kindergarten, 9, 21, 243, 248, 282, 283.

Language, 26, 31, 73, 77, 83, 134, 138, 149, 225, 229.
Language Teaching, 134.

Lighting, 28, 33.
Literature, 63, 231, 264.
Locke, 322.
Lying, 279,

Masturbation, 258.
Maternity, 230.
Mathematics, 145.
Medical, 200, 205.
Medical Inspection, 82, 111, 250.
Memory, 64, 112, 156, 221, 270, 331.
Mental, 17, 29, 35, 101, 104, 114, 215, 237, 241, 291, 294, 308, 312, 323.
Mental Imagery, 189.
Mentally Deficient, 25, 194.
Method, 6, 94, 109, 119, 120, 121, 122, 186, 203, 221, 228, 233.
Migration, 176, 177.
Mind, 17, 21, 69, 141, 181, 213, 307.
Money Sense, 37, 221.
Morals and Morality, 51, 55, 110, 271, 292, 328.
Morbidity, 81.
Mortality, 127.
Mother, 300.
Motor Education, 18, 148.
Motor Ability, 59.
Mouth, 8.
Muscles, 36.
Muscular Exercise, 137.
Music 124, 294.
Myths and Mythology, 253, 288.

Nature and Nature Study, 144, 290.
Negroes, 159.
Nervousness, 214, 291, 300.
Neurology, 59, 114, 332.
Neuroses and Neurasthenia, 1, 48, 125, 295, 297, 300, 302, 308, 332.
Neuropathic, 114.
New-Born, 178.
Nose, 44, 200.
Number, 99, 245, 265.
Nursing, 127.

Oaths, 279.
Observation, 6
Occupations, 22, 216.
Only Child, 40.
Orphans, 158.
Outings and Out of Doors, 67.
Overexertion and Overwork, 35, 294.

Paidology, 76.
Parents, 79, 204, 282, 313.
Perception, 190, 221.

Perversions, 239.
Photography, 87, 249.
Physical Education, 137, 152, 167, 191, 244.
Physiology, 7, 65.
Play and Playgrounds, 3, 10, 30, 70, 89, 107, 113, 132, 137, 139, 167, 246, 248, 252, 333.
Poetry, 52, 66, 231.
Precocity, 239.
Psychology, 2, 17, 27, 36, 109, 132, 151, 161, 162, 203, 213, 262, 294, 298, 305, 318.
Psychopathy, 101, 308.
Punishment, 23, 24, 42, 168, 206, 232.

Questions, 84.

Race, 97.
Reading, 63, 72, 109, 161, 172, 173, 264, 311, 326.
Recollections, 155.
Record Book, 228.
Religion and Theology, 32, 75, 78, 105, 135, 136, 230.
Reminiscences, 234.
Respiration, 36.
Rest, 88.
Revenge, 320.
Reverie, 236.
Rhythm, 52, 124, 145.
Rousseau, 227, 322.
Running Away, 102.

Sanitation, 33.
Santa Claus, 84.
Savings Banks, 37.
School, 13, 51, 97, 183, 187, 194, 230, 260, 268, 280.
Schools (Evening), 240.
School Diseases, 111, 223.
School Libraries, 264.
School Physician, 82, 250.
School System, 97.
Secondary Education, 12, 13.
Secrets and Secret Language, 60, 73, 77.
Self, 141, 287.
Senses, 278, 319.
Sex, 98, 108, 125, 135, 136, 140, 165, 171, 200, 214, 239, 258, 285, 301, 315.

Sight. See Eyes and Eyesight.
Sleep, 90.
Social Sense, 22, 54, 220, 267, 277.
Sociology, 22, 54, 93, 117, 145, 220, 230, 257, 267, 277.
Speech and Speech Defects, 26, 31, 83, 138, 225, 229.
Spelling, 188, 270.
Spine, Curvature of, 201.
Stammering, 138, 225.
Strength, 36.
Stuttering, 138.
Suggestion, 198, 221.
Sunday School, 105.

Teacher, 71, 86, 119, 204, 290, 304, 327.
Teasing, 133.
Teeth, 8, 154, 242.
Temperament, 46.
Theology. See Religion and Theology.
Thrift, 37.
Toronto, 39.
Toys, 139, 247.
Tree Lore, 251.
Truancy, 176.

Unselfishness, 145.

Vacations, 22.
Vacation Schools, 11, 89, 212, 255.
Ventilation, 28, 33.
Violence, 34.
Vision. See Eyes and Eyesight.
Vital Capacity, 36.
Vocations, 166, 216.
Voice, 106.

Waifs, 117.
Walking, 254.
Wandering, 177.
Weather, 100.
Weight, 57, 90.
Whipping, 168.
Wild Boy, 163.
Will, 18, 27, 206.
Woman, 214.
Wordsworth, 231.
Work, 30, 52, 299.
Working Classes, 240.

BIBLIOGRAPHY

OF

CHILD STUDY.

BY

LOUIS N. WILSON,

LIBRARIAN, CLARK UNIVERSITY.

The Clark University Press.

WORCESTER, MASSACHUSETTS,

JANUARY, 1901.

BIBLIOGRAPHY OF CHILD STUDY

For the year 1899.

By LOUIS N. WILSON, Librarian, Clark University.

1. **Aars, K. P.** Der ästhetische Farbensinn bei Kindern. Zeits. f. päd. Psy., July, 1899. Vol. 1, pp. 173-179.

2. **Agahd, Konrad.** Die Erwerbsfähigkeit schulpflichtiger Kinder im Deutschen Reich. Zeits. f. Philos. u. Päd., 1899. Vol. 6, pp. 361-376.
   A detailed account, with tables, of the employment of the 214,954 children under 14 in the various industries of Germany.

3. **Albanel, Dr.** Étude sur les causes de progression de la criminalité des enfants. Jour. Soc. de Statist. de Paris, 1899. Vol. 40, pp. 94-99.

4. **Albanel et Legros** Les enfants menteurs. Semaine Méd., 1899. Vol. 14, clxii-clxiv.

5. **Alden, L. P.** Heredity versus environment. Char. Rev., N. Y., Apr., 1899. Vol. 9, pp. 85-87.

6. **Aldrich, C. A.** Head-nodding and head-rotation usually associated with nystagmus in very young children. Am. Jour. of Med. Sci., 1899. Vol. 117, pp. 158-168.

7. **Allin, Arthur** Social recapitulation. Ed. Rev., Nov., 1899. Vol. 18, pp. 344-352.

8. **Alterisio, Ilario** L'attenzione nei fanciulli delle scuole elementari. Note di psicologia scolastica. Paravia, Torino. 1899.

9. **Ament, Wilhelm** Die Entwicklung von Sprechen und Denken beim Kinde. E. Wunderlich, Leipzig, 1899, pp. 213.
   A characteristically German study of a girl's linguistic development, compared with that of several other children. Introduction on history of child study. Good author and subject indexes.

10. **de Amicis, Edmondo** Cuore, an Italian schoolboy's journal. A book for boys. Trans. from the 39th Italian ed., by Isabel F. Hapgood. T. Y. Crowell & Co., N. Y., 1895, pp. 326.
    One of the best books of its kind ever written. Character of the boys stands out in clear relief. Presents a most attractive and vivid picture of Italian school life.

11. **Anderson, W. G.** Studies in the effect of physical training. Am. Phys. Ed. Rev., Sept., 1899. Vol. 4, pp. 265-278.

12. **Andreae, C.** Zur Psychologie der Examina. Zeits. f. päd. Psy., May, 1899. Vol. 1, pp. 113-126.

13. **Armagnac, L.** De l'alimentation dans les internats et particulièrement à l'école normale. Rev. Pédagogique, Aug., 1899. Vol. 35, pp. 127-139.
   A good review of Dr. LeGendre's pamphlet on "school dyspepsia."

14. **Arnold, Mary L. H.** Bacteriological study of school utensils. Ped. Sem., Sept., 1899. Vol. 6, pp. 382-385.

15. **Association Review.** Edited by Frank W. Booth, Mt. Airy, Phila., Oct. and Dec., 1899. Vol. 1.
   An educational magazine published quarterly by the American Association to promote the teaching of speech to the deaf.

16. **Bailey Thomas P., Jr.** Character study in the kindergarten. Proc. N. E. A., 1899. pp. 541-547.

17. —— —— Ethological psychology. Psy. Rev., Nov., 1899. Vol. 6, pp. 649-651.

18. **Balliet, T. M.** Some new aspects of educational thought. Proc. A. A. A. S., 1898. Vol. 48, pp. 481-488.

19. **Barnes, Earl** Methods of studying children. Paidologist, April, 1899. Vol. 1, pp. 2-17.

20. —— —— Pour servir de préface. L'École Nouvelle [supplement], July 15, 1899. Vol. 2, pp. 377-378.

21. **Barr, Martin W.** Mental defectives and social welfare. Pop. Sci. Mo., April, 1899. Vol. 54, pp. 746-759.

22. —— —— The how, the why, and the wherefore of the training of feeble-minded children. Jour. of Psycho-Asthenics, Sept., 1899. Vol. 4, pp. 204-212.

23. **Barthel, Dr.** Die Zerstreutheit geistig normaler Schüler. Samml. päd Vortr., 1899. Band 12, Heft 5, pp. 18.

24. **Beaufils, Edouard** Études de méthode : conditions générales de l'observation des enfants. L'École Nouvelle [supplement], Oct. 21, 1899. Vol. 2. pp. 9-11.

25. **v. Bechterew, W.** Suggestion und ihre sociale Bedeutung. George, Leipzig, 1899.
   A very useful essay. See review in Centralblatt f. Nervenheilkunde, April, 1889. Vol. 22, pp. 250-252.

26. **Bell Sanford** Sex in secondary education. North Western Mo., May, 1899. Vol. 9, pp. 391-396.

27. **Belliol, Fernand** La curiosité à l'école. L'École Nouvelle. [Supplement]. July 15, 1899. Vol. 2, pp. 380-382.

28. **Benzoni, R.** Studi recenti di psicologia del bambino. Gio. Batta Carlini, Genova, 1898, pp. 37.
   Emphasizes the need of studying the evolution of morality. Warns against losing the scientific spirit.

29. **Bergen, Mrs. Fanny D.** Animal and plant lore. Collected from the oral tradition of English-speaking folk. Edited and Annotated by Fanny D. Bergen. With Introduction by J. Y.

Bergen. (Memoirs of the American Folk-Lore Society, Vol. 7).
Houghton, Mifflin & Co., Boston, 1899, pp. 180.
Contains a mass of data useful for comparative purposes.

30. **Berghold, K.** Schilderung der Spiele der Somâl-Jugend. ·Sitzungsber. der anthropol. Gesellsch. in Wien, 1899, pp. 39-41.
Treats of the games of the youth among the Somali of East Africa.

Bergström, John A. and Conradi, Edward Translation of Kotelmann's School Hygiene. (See No. 229.)

31. **Berkan, O.** Ueber den angeborenen und früh erworbenen Schwachsinn. Vieweg, Braunschweig, 1899, pp. 64.

32. **Bertola, G.** Il libro di testo nella scuola elementare al Congresso pedagogico di Torino : relazione, discussione e commenti. Mondovi, 1899.
A discussion of the *rôle* of the text-book in primary education—the result of the Turin Pedagogical Congress of 1898.

33. **Bethencourt-Ferreira, J.** La psychophysiologie des écoliers. Rev. de Psyc. Clin. et Thérap., 1899. Vol. 3, pp. 296-304.

34. **Von Bezold, Friedrich** Uber die Anfänge der Selbst-biographie und ihre Entwicklung im Mittelalter. Junge & Sohn, Erlangen. 1893, pp. 24.
A valuable contribution to the not very extensive literature of an important subject.

35. **Van Biervliet, J. J.** L'homme droit et l'homme gauche. Rev. Philosophique, Feb., Mar., Apr., 1899. Vol. 47, pp. 113-143 ; 276-296 ; 371-389.
Contains valuable data concerning the development of "right" and "left" at all periods of human life.

36. **Binet, A.** Note relative à l'influence du travail intellectuel sur la consommation du pain dans les écoles. Année Psychologique, 1898, Vol. 5, pp. 332-336.

37. **Blazek, B.** Ermüdungsmessungen mit dem Federæsthesiometer. Zeits. f. päd. Psy., Dec., 1899. Vol. 1, pp. 311-325.

38. **Blum, E.** La pédologie. Année Psychologique, 1898. Vol. 5, pp. 299-331.
Review of literature with reflections.

39. **Boardman, Charles A.** The fighting instinct. Association Outlook (Springfield, Mass.), Mar., 1899. Vol. 8, pp. 133-146.

40. **Boas, Franz** Some recent criticisms of physical anthropology. Am. Anthrop., Jan., 1899. n. s. Vol. 1, pp, 98-106.
Discussion of anthropometry good and bad by an expert.

41. **Boiadjieff, N.** La neurasthénie chez les enfants (Thèse, Fac. de Méd.). Bordeaux, 1899. pp. 87.

42. **Boisse, Louis** Société libre pour l'étude psychologique de l'enfant. Manuel Général de l'Instruction Primaire, Nov. 18, 1899, pp. 509-511.
An account of the French Child Study Association. (See also Buisson, No. 63.)

43. **Bolin, Jakob** On group contests. Am. Phys. Ed. Rev., March, 1899. Vol. 4, pp. 66-72.

44. **Bolton, F. E.** Scientific and practical child study : The province and the limitations of each. Wisconsin Jour. of Ed., May and June, 1899. Vol. 29, pp. 116-119; 138-141. Also in Child Study Mo., May, 1899. Vol. 5, pp. 7-24.

45. **Bondois, M.** L'étude de l'enfant et la pédagogie américaine. Manuel Général de l'Instruction Primaire, April 29, 1899. Vol. 35, pp. 178-180.

46. **Bonjean, G.** Enfants révoltés et parents coupables. Étude sur la désorganization de la famille et ses conséquences sociales. A. Colin et Cie, Paris, 1899. pp. 407.
   A valuable contribution to the literature of criminological pedagogy.

47. **Bonnier, P.** Un procédé simple d'Acoumétrie. Arch. Int. de Laryng. et d'Otol, 1899. Vol. 12, pp. 131-133.

48. **Bourneville, Dr.** Création de classes spéciales pour les enfants arriérés. Paris, 1898.
   Gives an account of special institutions for feeble-minded children in Switzerland, England, Belgium, etc., and argues for similar development in France.

49. **Bradford, E. H.** Variations in human gait. Med. Record, N. Y., July 8, 1899. Vol. 56, pp. 47-51.

50. **Bradley, John E.** Relation of play to character. Education, March, 1899. Vol. 19, pp. 406-412.

51. **Brown, Elmer E.** Art in education. Proc. N. E. A., 1899. pp. 112-121.

52. ———— Naughty children. Proc. N. E. A., 1899. pp. 564-570.

53. **Browne, C. R.** Report of the work done in the anthropometric laboratory of Trinity College, Dublin, from 1891 to 1898. Proc. Roy. Irish Acad., Dublin, 1899. 3d s. Vol. 5, pp. 269-293.

54. **Browne, T. J.** Boys' gangs. Association Outlook (Springfield, Mass.), Feb., 1899. Vol. 8, pp. 96-107.

55. **Bruce, Belle S.** Parents' meetings. Ed. Rev., Sept., 1899. Vol. 18, pp. 185-188.

56. **Bryan, William L.** Child study. Appleton's Universal Cyclopædia. Vol. 2, pp. 614-616.

58. **Bryan, W. L. and Harter, Noble** Studies on the telegraphic language : acquisition of a hierarchy of habits. Psy. Rev., July, 1899. Vol. 6, pp. 346-375.

59. **Bücher, Karl** Arbeit und Rhythmus. 2te. Auflage. Leipzig, 1899. pp. 412.
   A new edition of a valuable and suggestive work. Discusses the relations of labor and song among all peoples.

60. **Buchner, Edward F.** Attitudes towards child study. The Syracuse (N. Y.) Clinic, April and June, 1899. Vol. 2, pp. 40-42 ; 76-77.

61. **Buchner, Edward F.** New York society for child study. Rep. State Supt., N. Y., 1898. Vol. 2, pp. 882-887.
   Reprints of this paper have been issued by the Society and may be had by addressing Professor Buchner at New York University, N. Y. City.

62. **Buisson, F.** Education de la volonté. Rev. Pédagogique, Oct., 1899. Vol. 35, pp. 310-345.
   A comprehensive study of the will of the child from the standpoint of genetic psychology.

63. —— —— Société libre d'études pédagogiques sur la psychologie de l'enfant. Manuel Général de l'Instruction Primaire. Paris, Nov. 4 et 18, 1899. pp. 477-478; 509-511.
   The purposes of the society are to facilitate among its members the study of children, to publish results and to apply the same to the work of education.

64. **Bulkeley, J. E.** Social ethics in the schools. Forum, Jan., 1899. Vol. 26, pp. 615-620.

65. **Burk, Caroline Frear** Play: A study of kindergarten children. North Western Mo., Mar., Apr., 1899. Vol. 9, pp. 349-355.

66. **Burk, Frederick, and Caroline Frear** A study of the kindergarten problem. Whittaker & Ray Co., San Francisco, 1899. pp. 123.
   A noteworthy treatment of the problem of early education. Valuable chapters: Neurological conditions of the kindergarten child; physical culture; play; language; music; love of nature; connting and number; moral training.

67. **Burk, Frederic** The kindergarten child physically. Proc. N. E. A., 1899. pp. 570-574.

68. —— —— A curriculum of applied child study for the kindergarten and the primary school. Proc. N. E. A., 1899. pp. 1051-1057.

69. —— —— The influence of exercise upon growth. Proc. N. E. A., 1899, pp. 1067-1076. Am. Phys. Ed. Rev., Dec., 1899. Vol. 4, pp. 340-349.

70. **Burkhard, Ph.** Die Fehler der Kinder. O. Nemnich, Karlsruhe, 1898, pp. 102.

71. **Burne-Jones, E.** Letters of Burne-Jones to a child. The Strand Magazine, May, 1899. Vol. 17, pp. 375-380.

72. **Burnham, W. H.** The child in education. Nation, N. Y., Jan. 26, 1899. Vol. 68, pp. 72-73.

73. —— —— Mental hygiene. Appleton's Universal Cyclopædia, 1899. Vol. 8, pp. 601-604.

74. —— —— School diseases. Appleton's Universal Cyclopædia, 1899. Vol. 10, pp. 631-634.

75. —— —— School hygiene. Appleton's Universal Cyclopædia, 1899. Vol. 10, pp. 634-639.

76. **Butler, Nicholas Murray** Some criticisms of the kindergarten. Ed. Rev., Oct., 1899. Vol. 18, pp. 285-291.

77. **Butler, Nicholas Murray** Religious instruction in education. Ed. Rev., Dec., 1899. Vol. 18, pp. 425-436.

78. **Caldwell, W.** Social and ethical interpretations of mental development. Am. Jour. of Sociol., Sept., 1899. Vol. 5, pp. 182-192.

79. **Caley, Henry** (and others) A discussion on visual tests. Brit. Med. Jour., Sept. 23, 1899. Vol. 2, pp. 766-770.

80. **Camailhac, F.** Les enfants anormaux. Rev. Philanthropique, 1899. Vol. 5, pp. 182-189.

81. **Camerer, Wilhelm** Der Stoffwechsel des Kindes. Tübingen, 1896. pp. 160.
    Treats of first and second years of childhood. A painstaking and scientific work, with many tables.

82. **Carroll, Clarence F.** Place of the kindergarten in the common school system. Jour. of Ped., May, 1899. Vol. 12, pp. 126-136.

83. **Carter, M. H.** Romanes's Idea of Mental Development. Am. Jour. of Psy., Oct., 1899. Vol. 11, pp. 101-118.

84. **Carus, Paul** A few hints on the treatment of children. The Monist, Jan., 1899. Vol. 9, pp. 234-247.

85. —— —— Santa Claus. Open Court, Jan., 1899. Vol. 13; pp. 45-50.

86. —— —— Rationalism in the nursery. Open Court, Feb., 1899. Vol. 13, pp. 98-109.

87. —— —— The moral education of children. Open Court, March, 1899. Vol. 13, pp. 176-184.
    Treats of Imagination and love of truth; Wordly prudence; Square dealing; Sympathy with animals.

88. —— —— Parenthood. Open Court, April, 1899. Vol. 13, pp. 211-214.

89. —— —— Playful instruction, and genius. Open Court, Sept., 1899. Vol. 13, pp. 566-570.

90. —— —— The significance of naming things in the nursery. Open Court, Nov., 1899. Vol. 13, pp. 669-672.

91. —— —— Anticipate the School. Suggestions for the treatment of children. Open Court, Dec., 1899. Vol. 13, pp. 747-757.
    Treats of Counting; Natural science; Foreign languages; Mathematics.

92. **Cattell, J. McK.** New anthropometric methods. Proc. A. A. A. S., 1898. Vol. 48, pp. 357-358.

93. **Chabot, M. C.** Une enquête pédagogique dans les écoles primaires de Lyon. Rev. Pédagogique, April, 1899. Vol. 34, pp. 329-332.
    A study of the interests of children in elementary school subjects. See review in Ped. Sem., Sept., 1899. Vol. 5, pp. 412-413.

94. —— —— Les variations de l'attention à l'école primaire. Rev. Pédagogique, Oct., 1899. Vol. 35, pp. 346-351.

95. **Chamberlain, A. F.** Three shapers of childhood's genius—society, opportunity, travel. North Western Mo., June, 1899. Vol. 9, pp. 439-443.

Treats of the conditions favorable to the preservation of the genius of childhood.

96. —— —— The "child type." Ped. Sem., Dec., 1899. Vol. 6, pp. 471-484.

A brief attempt to state the place of the child in the physical and social evolution of man.

97. **Child-labor laws** and factory laws. Rep. U. S. Comm. of Ed., 1897-98. Vol. 2, pp. 1698-1700.

98. **Child Study.** Published monthly by the Kyo-iku-Ken-Kyu-Sho. Tokyo, Japan.

Published in Japanese. First-class in every respect. Price, 76 cents a year. See review in Ped. Sem., March, 1899, and July, 1900. Vol. 6, pp. 254-255. Vol. 7, pp. 290-294.

99. **Chrisman, Oscar** Pubescent period. Education, Feb., 1899. Vol. 19, pp. 342-347.

100. —— —— Child and teacher. Jour. of Ped., May, 1899. Vol. 12, pp. 112-125.

101. **Christian, J.** De la démence précoce des jeunes gens. Ann. Méd.-Psychol., 1899. Vol. 9, pp. 43-65; 200-216; 420-436. Vol. 10, pp. 5-23; 177-188.

102. **Clark, Kate Upson** Bringing up boys. T. Y. Crowell & Co., N. Y., 1899. pp. 227.

103. **Clouston, T. S.** What the brain has to do in youth besides getting educated. Paidologist, April, 1899. Vol. 1, pp. 17-23.

104. **Cohn, H.** Die Sehleistungen von 50,000 Breslauer Schulkindern. Schottlander, Breslau, 1899.

Valuable on account of comparisons with results obtained some years before in the same city.

105. **Cohn, J.** Was kann die Psychologie von den Pädagogen lernen? Zeits. f. päd. Psy., Jan. 1899. Vol. 1, pp. 20-27.

106. **Colegrove, F. W.** Individual memories. Am. Jour. of Psy., Jan., 1899. Vol. 10, pp. 228-257.

Conradi, Edward See Kotelmann (No. 229).

107. **Cook, Francis E** Relation of the kindergarten to primary education. Trans. Ill. Soc. for Child Study, April-July, 1899. Vol. 4, pp. 41-55.

108. **Cramer, A.** Ueber die ausserhalb der Schule liegenden Ursachen der Nervosität der Kinder (Samml. v. Abh. a. d. Geb. d. Pädag. Psychol. u. Physiol., II, 5 Heft). Reuther und Reichard, Berlin, 1899. pp. 28.

Author thinks the influence of the school in producing nervousness has been overestimated. Early home conditions (abnormal) count for much.

109. **Croswell, T. R.** Amusements of Worcester school children. Ped. Sem., Sept., 1899. Vol. 6, pp. 314-371.

110. **Culin, Stewart** Hawaiian games. Am. Anthropologist, April, 1899, N. S. Vol. I, pp. 201-247.
Very useful for comparative purposes. Notes many games of children.

111. **Dana, John Cotton** Children's reading. Rep. U. S. Comm. of Ed., 1897-98. Vol. I, pp. 680-684.

112. —— —— Public libraries and public schools. Proc. N. E. A., 1899. pp. 452-529.
A masterly report. Treats of the reading of children.

113. **Danger, O.** Helen Keller die Taubblinde. Die Kinderfehler, Jan., Mar. and May, 1899. Vol. 4, pp. 1-9, 49-57, 81-90.

114. **Daudé, G.** Douleurs osseuses de croissance. (Thèse, Fac. de Méd.). Montpellier, 1899, pp. 43.

115. **Davidson, S. G.** Relation of language teaching to mental development and of speech to language teaching. Assn. Rev., Dec., 1899. Vol. I, pp. 139-149.

116. **Delmas, N.** De la paralysie générale des adolescents. (Thèse, Fac. de Méd.). Bordeaux, 1899, pp. 152.

117. **Demolins, Edmond** L'éducation nouvelle. L'école des Roches. Librairie de Paris, Paris, 1899, pp. 320.
A most interesting study of a new educational movement and its realization in an institution of learning. See Ped. Sem., Vol. 7, pp. 479-491.

118. **Demoor, Jean** Les enfants anormaux et la criminologie. Rev. de l'Univ. de Bruxelles. April, 1899. Vol. 4, pp. 481-498.
Dr. Demoor is head of the special school in Brussels. Argues on behalf of special schools for epileptic, hysterical, and choreic children.

119. **Dendy, Mary** Individuality of the child. Ed. Rev. (London), April, 1899. Vol. I, pp. 225-230.

120. —— —— Importance of permanence in the care of the feebleminded. Ed. Rev. (London), Sept., 1899. Vol. I, pp. 574-580.

121. **Dewey, John** Principles of mental development as illustrated in early infancy. Trans. Ill. Soc. for Child-Study, Oct., 1899. Vol. 4, pp. 65-83.

122. —— —— The school and society. Supplemented by a statement of the University elementary school. The Univ. of Chicago Press. Chicago, 1899, pp. 125.

123. **Dexter, Edwin G.** The mental effects of the weather. Science, Aug. 11, 1899. N. S. Vol. 10, pp. 176-179. See also note by H. Helm Clayton. *Ibid.*, p. 378.

124. —— —— Conduct and the weather. (Psy. Rev. Monograph Suppl., No. 10.) The Macmillan Co., N. Y., 1899. pp. 105.

125. —— —— Influence of the weather upon crime. Pop. Sci. Mo., Sept., 1899. Vol. 55, pp. 653-659.

126. **Dinsmore, J. W.** Vices of childhood and youth. North Western Mo., Oct., 1899. Vol. 10, pp. 74-80.

127. **Dinsmore, J.W.** Some problems of the Sunday School. North Western Mo., Dec., 1899. Vol. 10, pp. 149-151. Also Proc. N. E. A., 1899. pp. 594-600.

128. **Douglas, A. R.** The improvable imbecile; his training and future. Jour. Mental Sci., Jan., 1899. Vol. 45, pp. 1-6.

129. **Dowdall, H. C.** Liverpool by-laws regulating juvenile street trading. Econ. Rev., Oct., 1899. Vol. 9, p. 50.

130. **Down, R. Langdon** A boy's imagination in play. Paidologist, April and June, 1899. Vol. 1, pp. 38-42 ; 94-100.

—— —— See also No. 201.

131. **Dresslar, F. B.** Genetic psychology. North Western Mo., March-April, 1899. Vol. 9, pp. 355-358.

132. —— —— Chinese pedagogics in practice. Education, Boston, Nov., 1899. Vol. 20, pp. 136-143.

133. **Drouot Edouard** Du rôle de l'instituteur des enfants anormaux. Rev. int. de Péd. comparative, April, 1899. Vol. 1, pp. 78-100.

134. **Drummond, W. B.** On the early training of blind children. Pediatrics, 1899. Vol. 7, pp. 533-538.

135. **Du Bois, Patterson** Beckonings from little hands. Eight studies in child life. John D. Wattles & Co., Phila., 1894. pp. 182.

136. —— —— The point of contact in teaching. A plea for the little children. John D. Wattles & Co., Phila., 1896. pp. 88.
Valuable for Sunday School teachers.

137. **Dutton, S. T.** Social phases of education. The Macmillan Co., N. Y., 1899. pp. 259.

138. **Dyche, William** Co-education: Some comparisons between boys and girls. Ed. Rev. (London), March, 1899. Vol. 1, pp. 173-178.

139. **Earle, Alice Morse** Child life in colonial days. The Macmillan Co., N. Y., 1899. pp. 418.
Contains interesting details of babyhood, children's dress, school life, discipline, manners, religious training, precocity, diaries, etc.

140. **Edmund, Gertrude** Child study in normal and training schools. Proc. N. E. A., 1899. pp. 1032-1038.

141. **Educational Review** A magazine of the science and art of education and review of current educational literature and events. Edited by William K. Hill, London.
Published monthly since Jan., 1899, at 5 shillings a year. Child study has not been neglected, and the editor gives excellent résumés of periodical literature.

142. **Ellis, Havelock** Evolution of modesty. Psy. Rev., March, 1899. Vol. 6, pp. 134-145.
An unprejudiced study with historical aperçu.

143. **Elsenhaus, Th.** Ueber individuelle und Gattungsanlagen. Zeits. f. päd. Psy., Sept. and Dec., 1899. Vol. 1, pp. 233-244; 334-342.

144. **Engelmann, Geo. J.** The health of the American girl as imperilled by the social conditions of the day. (Reprint from Trans. So. Surg. and Gyn. Assoc., 1890.) W. J. Dornan, Phila., 1891. pp. 29.

145. **Escorne, C.** De l'excitation cérébrale chez les enfants. (Thèse, Fac. de Méd.) Jouve, Paris, 1898. pp. 68.

146. **Féré, Ch.** L'instinct sexuel, évolution et dissolution. F. Alcan, Paris, 1899. pp. 346.
The best chapters are those devoted to sexual education and hygiene.

147. **Fernald, Walter E.** Quelques-unes des méthodes employées pour les soins et l'éducation des enfants les plus idiots. Rev. Int. de Péd. comparative, May, 1899. Vol. 1, pp. 148-154.

148. **Ferriani, L.** Nel mondo dell'infanzia. Cogliati, Milano, 1899.

149. **Field, A. G.** On the injury resulting to the eyes and vision of school children from want of proper regulation of light in the schoolroom; also proposed method of estimating the relative intensity of light for sanitary purposes. Proc. A. A. A. S., 1898. Vol. 48, pp. 479-480.

150. **Findlay, M. E.** An hour's study of girls' games in London. Paidologist, Nov., 1899. Vol. 1, pp. 158-160.

151. **Fitz, George W.** Hygiene of instruction in elementary schools. Jour. of Ped., Jan., 1899. Vol. 12, pp. 69-73.

152. —— —— Bed posture as an etiological factor in spinal curvature. Am. Phys. Ed. Rev., June, 1899. Vol. 4, pp. 136-138.

153. —— —— Conditions and needs of physical training. Proc. N. E. A., 1899, pp. 1065-1067. Am. Phys. Ed. Rev., Dec., 1899. Vol. 4, pp. 337-339.

154. **Flatau, G.** Ueber psychische Abnormitäten bei an Veitstanz leidenden Schulkindern. Zeits. f. päd. Psy., March, 1899. Vol. 1, pp. 85-88.

155. **de Fleury, Maurice** Le corps et l'âme de l'enfant. Armand Colin & Cie., Paris, 1899. pp. 341.
A characteristically verbose French book.

156. **Folks, Homer** The care of destitute, neglected and delinquent children. Char. Rev. Nov. and Dec., 1899. Vol. 9, pp. 392-407; 459-470.

157. **Forbush, William B.** A manual of boys' clubs. Warren, Mass., 1898. pp. 31.

158. **du Fougeray, Hamon** Pédagogie anormale; Etat actuel de l'enseignement spécial aux enfants anormaux en France. Rev. Int. de Péd. Comparative, March, 1899. Vol. 1, pp. 6-18.

159. **du Fougeray, Hamon** De l'enseignement du chant aux enfants sourd-muets. Rev. Int. Péd. Comparative, July, 1899. Vol. 1, pp. 260-283.

France, C. J. See Kline, L. W. and France, C. J.

160. **Francke, C.** Sprachenentwicklung der Kinder und der Menschheit. Rein's Encyclop. Handb. der Pädag., Langensalza, 1895-1899. Vol. 6, pp. 751-795. Also: Reprint, pp. 48. Very useful. Has good bibliography.

161. **Fraser, John.** Initiation among the Australian blacks. Am. Antiquarian, Chicago, July and Aug., 1899. Vol. 21, pp. 233-235.

162. **Fuchs, A.** Schwachsinnige Kinder, ihre sittliche und intellektuelle Rettung. C. Bertelsmann, Gütersloh, 1899. pp. 248.

163. **Garrod, Herbert B.** Co-education of boys and girls. Ed. Rev. (London), Jan., 1899. Vol. 1, pp. 37-47.

164. **Gellé, M. E.** L'audition et ses organes. F. Alcan, Paris, 1899. pp. 326.

165. **Germann, G. B.** On the invalidity of the æsthesiometric method as a measure of mental fatigue. Psy. Rev., Nov., 1899. Vol. 6, pp. 599-605.

166. **Giry. N.** Du rôle du médecin dans les écoles. Nancy, 1899. pp. 47.

167. **Graefe, A.** Das Sehen der Schielenden. Bergmann, Wiesbaden, 1899.

168. **Griffith, George** Course of reading for children. Ed. Rev., Jan., 1899. Vol. 17, pp. 65-69.
A well graded course of reading for children in grades 2 to 9 inclusive.

169. **Griffith, J. P. Crozer.** The care of the baby; a manual for mothers and nurses. W. B. Saunders, Phila., 1899. pp. 404.
Written by a clinical professor. A reliable book on the care of young children in sickness and in health.

170. **Grimm, Ludwig** Ueber die Bedeutung der Gebrüder Grimm in der Geschichte der Pädagogik. Zeits. f. d. deutschen Unterricht, 1899. Vol. 13, pp. 585-605; 641-671.
A sympathetic and critical estimate of the famous Grimm brothers.

171. **Groos, Karl** Die Spiele der Menschen. G. Fischer, Jena, 1899. pp. 538.
The theory of play is treated from the standpoints of psychology, biology, physiology, pedagogy, etc. A most valuable and suggestive book. Should be read by every student of the child.

172. **Groszmann, M. P. E.** Der Drang nach Gewissheit. Die Kinderfehler, July and Sept., 1899. Vol. 4, pp. 137-140; 157-164.

173. —— —— Criminality in children. Arena, Oct. and Nov., 1899. Vol. 22, pp. 509-525; 644-652.

174. **Gulick, Luther** Psychological, pedagogical, and religious aspects of group games. Ped. Sem., March, 1899. Vol. 6, pp. 135-151.

175. **Gutberlet, C.** Zur Psychologie des Kindes. Philos. Jahrb., 1899. Vol. 12, pp. 365-381.
Good review of recent literature in Child Study.

176. **Gutzmann, Hermann** Die Sprachlaute des Kindes und der Naturvölker. Zeits. f. päd. Psy., Jan., 1899. Vol. 1, pp. 28-40.
One of the few attempts to treat the subject upon a scientific basis.

177. —— —— Traitement diététique des troubles nerveux de la parole. Rev. Int. de Péd. Comparative, May, 1899. Vol. 1, pp. 132-140.

178. **Hague, J. Cecil** Athletics and fatigue. Jour. of Ed. (London), Feb. 1899. N. S. Vol. 21, pp. 104-106.

179. **Hall, G. Stanley** The methods, status and prospects of the child study of to-day. Trans. Ill. Soc. for Child Study, May, 1896. Vol. 2, pp. 178-191.

180. —— —— Heirs of the ages. Proc. of the N. J. Ass'n for the Study of Children and Youth, Newark, N. J., Mar. 11, 1899. The Brotherhood Press, Bloomfield, N. J., 1899. pp. 5-14.

181. —— —— Résumé of child study. North Western Mo., Mar., Apr., 1899. Vol. 9, pp. 347-349. Also as "Introductory Words" in the Paidologist, April, 1899. Vol. 1, pp. 5-8.

182. —— —— The education of the heart. (Abstract.) Kindergarten Mag., May, 1899. Vol. 11, pp. 592-595.

183. —— —— From fundamental to accessory in education. Kindergarten Mag., May, 1899. Vol. 11, pp. 599-600.

184. —— —— Needed modifications in the theory and practice of the kindergarten. Kindergarten Mag., May, 1899. Vol. 11, pp. 604-607.

185. —— —— The kindergarten. School and Home Ed., June, 1899. Vol. 18, pp. 507-509.

186. —— —— A study of anger. Am. Jour. of Psy., July, 1899. Vol. 10, pp. 516-591.

187. —— —— The line of educational advance. Outlook, Aug. 5, 1899. Vol. 62, pp. 768-770.

188. —— —— Note on early memories. Ped. Sem., Dec., 1899. Vol. 6, pp. 485-512.

189. **du Hamel, E.** De l'alcoolisme chez l'enfant. (Thèse, Fac. de Méd), Paris, 1899. pp. 118.

190. **Hanna D., and Spore, N. A.** Effect of college work on the health of women. Am. Phys. Ed. Rev., Sept., 1899. Vol. 4, pp. 279-280.

191. **Harrison, Elizabeth** The language of the body. Trans. Ill. Soc. for Child Study, Oct., 1899. Vol. 4, pp. 92-94.

192. **Hastings, William W.** A brief résumé of Quetelet's treatise
on man. Am. Phys. Ed. Rev., March, Sept. and Dec., 1899.
Vol. 4, pp. 56-55; 309-318; 366-376.
Gives in brief form the contents of one of the classical works on the study
of man, now rather antiquated.

193. —— —— Anthropometric studies in Nebraska. Proc. N. E. A.,
1899, pp. 1076-1084.

194. **Hawkins, Cecil** The physical measurements of public school
boys. Jour. of Ed. (London), Jan. and March, 1899. N. S. Vol.
21, pp. 33-35; 187-190.

195. **Hemprich, K.** Die Kinderpsychologie und ihre Bedeutung für
Unterricht und Erziehung. Dessau, 1899.

196. **Henri, V.** Influence du travail intellectuel sur les échanges
nutritifs. Année Psychologique, 1898. Vol. 3, pp. 179-189.

197. **Herbertson, Mrs.** The beginning of childhood; notes on the
first half of the third year. Paidologist, June, 1899. Vol. 1, pp.
83-93.

198. **Hirschlaff, Leo** Die angebliche Bedeutung des Hypnotismus
für die Pädagogik. Zeits. f. päd. Psy., May, 1899. Vol. 1, pp.
127-132.
Warns against the use of hypnotism, with its "mystic" associations, in
normal pedagogy.

199. **Hodge, C. F.** Foundations of nature study. I. Ped. Sem.,
Dec., 1899. Vol. 6, pp. 536-553.

200. **Holman, Henry** Imitativeness in school children. Paidologist,
April, 1899. Vol. 1, pp. 24-37.
Results of a statistical study.

201. **Holman Henry and J. Langdon-Down** Practical child
study; the baby—how to observe, understand, and train him.
London, 1899. pp. 35.
Some practical directions for the study of young children. Especially
valuable for mothers.

202. **Howard Francis E.** The child-voice in singing, treated from
a physiological and a practical standpoint, and especially
adapted to schools and boy choirs. Novello, Ewer & Co., N.
Y., 1898. pp. 138.
A convenient digest of voice physiology.

203. **Hrdlicka, Ales.** Abnormalities of the teeth and their positions.
Jour. of Psycho-Asthenics, June, 1899. Vol. 4, pp. 153-190.

204. **Hugh, D. D.** The animism of children. North Western Mo.,
June and Oct., 1899. Vol. 9, pp. 450-453. Vol. 10, pp. 71-74.

205. **Hull, S. E.** Education the restorer of vocal speech to the deaf.
Child Life, Oct., 1899. Vol. 1, pp. 211-214.

206. **Huther, A.** Die psychologische Grundlage des Unterrichts.
Berlin, 1889. pp. 83.

207. **Ilberg, G.** Das Jugendirresein (Hebephrenie und Katatonie). Samml. Klin. Vortr. (N. F., No. 224), 1898. Vol. 8, pp. 1287-1308.
Detailed discussion. A good *résumé* of the subject.

207A. **Jahrbuch** für Volks- und Jugendspiele. Achter Jahrgang, 1899. Herausgegeben von E. von Schenckendorff u. Dr. med. F. U. Schmidt. Voigtländer, Leipzig, 1899.
Contains many useful articles (medical, hygienic, critical, historical) concerning the various aspects of popular games and plays of children.

208. **James, William** Talks to teachers on psychology, and to students on some of life's ideals. Henry Holt & Co., N. Y., 1899. pp. 301.
Contains chapters on habit, interest, attention, memory.

209. **Jastrow, Joseph** Practical aspects of psychology. Ed. Rev., Feb., 1899. Vol. 17, pp. 135-153.
Discusses the utility of child study.

210. **Jegi, J. J.** Children's ambitions. Trans. Ill. Soc. for Child Study. Chicago, 1899. Vol. 3, pp. 131-144.

211. **Johnson, E. R.** Value of nature study in sense training. Jour. of Psycho-Asthenics, Sept., 1899. Vol. 4, pp. 213-217.

212. **Johnson, George E.** An educational experiment. Ped. Sem., Dec., 1899. Vol. 6, pp. 513-522.
Describes the work of the Andover, Mass., Play School. A school for boys ranging from 10 to 14 years.

213. —— —— General principles of school management and instruction. Report of the Supt. of Schools for the year 1899. Andover, Mass. pp. 8-35.
A model superintendent's report.

214. **Johnson, Walter B.** Defective vision of school children. Ed. Rev., June, 1899. Vol. 18, pp. 15-22.

215. **Johnson, W. S.** Researches in practice and habit. Studies from Yale Psy. Lab., 1898. Vol. 6, pp. 51-103.

216. **Joteyko, J.** Revue générale sur la fatigue musculaire. Année Psychologique, 1898. Vol. 5, pp. 1-54.

217. **Judd, Charles H.** Psychology and the individual teacher. Jour. of Ped., May, 1899. Vol. 12, pp. 136-148.

218. **Kafemann, R.** Die Erkrankungen der Sprechstimme, ihre Ursachen u. Behandlung, nebst einer kurzen Hygiene für Lehrer, Geistliche, Advokaten u. Offiziere. A. W. Kafemann, Danzig, 1899. pp. 48.
A primer of the more important points that bear upon the hygiene of the speaking voice.

219. **Kaler, A.** Contribution à l'étude de l'hystérie chez les enfants (Thèse, Fac. de Méd.). Nancy, 1899. pp. 88.

220. **Kelsey, Carl** Proposed child legislation in Illinois. Char. Rev., Jan., 1899. Vol. 8, pp. 511-513.

221. **Kemsies, Ferdinand** Fragen und Aufgaben der Pädagogischen Psychologie. Zeits. f. Päd. Psy., Jan., 1899. Vol. 1, pp. 1-20.

222. —— —— Die häusliche Arbeitszeit meiner Schüler. Zeits. Päd. Psy., March, May and July, 1899. Vol. 1, pp. 89-95; 132-134; 192-196.

223. **Kirkpatrick, E. A.** Promising line of child study for parents. Trans. Ill. Soc. for child study, Jan., 1899. Vol. 3, pp. 179-182.
Suggestions for the study of children's vocabularies.

224. —— —— Children's reading, II, III, North Western Mo., Jan. 2, March, April, 1899. Vol. 9, pp. 229-233; 338-342.

225. —— —— Development of voluntary movement. Psy. Rev., May, 1899. Vol. 6, pp. 275-281.
Gives results of children learning to walk.

226. **Kline, L. W. and France, C. J.** The psychology of ownership. Ped. Sem., Dec., 1899. Vol. 6, pp. 421-470.

227. **Kooistra, J.** Sittliche Erziehung. E. Wunderlich, Leipzig, 1899. pp. 100.
Treats of rewards, punishments, honor, education of girls, etc. Ought to be translated into English.

228. **Körösi, Joseph** An estimate of the degrees of legitimate natality as derived from a table of natality compiled by the author from his observations made at Budapest. Phil. Trans. Rev. Soc., London (B), 1895. Vol. 186, Part 2, pp. 781-875.
Treats in great detail the age conditions of fecundity for married couples.

229. **Kotelmann, Ludwig** School hygiene. Translated by John A. Bergström and Edward Conradi. Bardeen, Syracuse, N. Y., 1900. pp. 391.
Important material added since the German edition was published in 1895. A valuable book.

230. **Kratz, H. E.** How may fatigue in the schoolroom be reduced to the minimum? Proc. N. E. A., 1899. pp. 1090-1096. Am. Phys. Ed. Rev., Dec., 1899. Vol. 4, pp. 358-364.

231. **Krohn, William O.** Physical growth periods and appropriate physical exercises. Forum, June, 1899. Vol. 27, pp. 445-451.

232. **Kuhn, Maurice** Études méthode. L'École Nouvelle [supplement], July 15, 1899. Vol. 2, pp. 378-380.
Methods of studying children.

233. —— —— La Science de l'éducation L'École Nouvelle [supplement], July 15, 1899. Vol. 2, pp. 750-753.
An excellent statement of the aims and purposes of child study.

234. **Kupferschmid, Adalbert** Ueber das Muskelgefühl bei Schwachsinnigen. Die Kinderfehler, July and Sept., 1899. Vol. 4, pp. 113-123; 145-157.

235. **Laisant, M.** Mathematics for children. Pop. Sci. Mo., Oct., 1899. Vol. 55, pp. 800-811.

236. **Laloy, L.** Die Stellung des Menschen in der Tierwelt mit besonderer Berücksichtigung der neueren Entdeckungen im Gebiete der Gehirnphysiologie. Ztschr. f. Morphol. u. Anthropol., 1899. Vol. 1, pp. 313-324.
   Differences between human reason and animal instinct are of degree not of kind. Man is not somatically separate from the rest of the animal world. A very good paper.

237. **Lancaster, E. G.** The adolescent at home and in school. Proc. N. E. A., 1899. pp. 1039-1043.

238. **Lange, K.** Ueber Apperception. Eine psychologische-pädagogische Monographie. 6 Aufl. R. Voigtländer, Leipzig, 1899.
   A new edition of a familiar classic.

239. **Larguier des Bancels, J.** Essai de comparaison sur les différentes méthodes proposées pour la mesure de la fatigue intellectuelle. Année Psychologique, 1898. Vol. 5, pp. 190-201.

240. **Lawrence, Isabel** Children's interests in literature. Proc. N. E. A., 1899. pp. 1044-1051.

241. **Le Dantec, F.** Le mécanisme de l'imitation. Rev. Philosophique, Oct., 1899. Vol. 48, pp. 337-382.

242. L'éducation physique. Rev. Encyclop., 1899. Vol. 9, pp. 681-764 (Numéro spécial).

243. **Ledyard, Mary F.** Relation of imitation to originality and consequent freedom. Proc. of N. E. A., 1899. pp. 547-551.

244. **Le Gendre, Paul** La dyspépsie chez les collégiens. Rev. pratique d'obstétrique et de pédiatrie, Oct., 1898. Vol. 11, pp. 300-328.
   An interesting and valuable study of the alimentation of school children (male and female) between the ages of seven and eighteen. The author reaches the conclusion that digestive troubles are more common with children and adolescents than is ordinarily believed, and also more common at school.

245. **Letourneau, C.** L'évolution mentale chez les animaux. Rev. de l'école d'anthrop. de Paris, 1899. Vol. 9, pp. 137-152.

246. **Leuba, J. H.** On the validity of the Griesbach method of determining fatigue. Psy. Rev., Nov., 1899. Vol. 6, pp. 573-598.

247. **Ley, A. et Sano. F.** De la pédologie. Jour. de Neurol., 1899. Vol. 4, pp. 161-164.

248. **Lichtenberger, H.** Richard Wagner. Der Dichter und Denker. C. Reissner, Dresden, 1899. pp. 571.
   Gives an account of Wagner's childhood and youth, his first opera, experience in Paris, etc.

249. **Lindner, Gustav** Aus dem Naturgarten der Kindersprache. Ein Beitrag zur kindlichen Sprach- und Geistesentwickelung in den ersten vier Lebensjahren. L. Fernan, Leipzig, 1898. pp. 122.
   Treats of the stages of development of the language of his own children during the first year. A very interesting little book.

250. **Little, E. Graham** The causation of night terrors. Pediatrics, 1899. Vol. 8, pp. 357-362. Brit. Med. Jour., Aug. 19, 1899. Vol. 2, pp. 464-465.

251. **Lobsien, M.** Aufgaben, Quellen und Methoden der Kinderforschung. Deutsche Schule, Berlin, 1899. Vol. 3, pp. 97-

252. **Locke, Josephine E.** Æsthetic occupations. Trans. Ill. Soc. for Child Study, Jan., 1899. Vol. 3, pp. 183-195.

253. **Lombroso, Paola** La evoluzione delle idee nei bambini. Riv. di Sci. Biologiche, Torino, Italy, Aug.-Sept., 1899. Vol. 1, pp. 641-664.

254. **Luckey, G. W. A.** The development of moral character. Proc. N. E. A., 1899. pp. 127-136.

255. **Lukens, Herman T.** The Joseph story. Illustrated by children. Teacher's Mag., N. Y. City, April, 1899. Vol. 1, pp. 331 334.

256. —— —— Mental fatigue. Am. Phys. Ed. Rev., March and June, 1899. Vol. 4, pp. 19-29 and 121-135.
An admirable summary with fatigue results; also good bibliography.

257. —— —— Drawing in the early years. Proc. N. E. A., 1899. pp. 945-951.

258. **Lynch, Hannah** Autobiography of a child. Wm. Blackwood and Sons, Edinburgh and London, 1899. pp. 299.
Written in an interesting style. Of some value on several child study topics.

259. **Lyttelton, E.** Instruction of the young in sexual knowledge. Int. Jour. of Ethics, July, 1899. Vol. 9, pp. 452-466.

260. **MacDonald, Arthur** Ueber Körpermessungen an Kinder. Deuts. Zeits. f. Ausländischen Unterricht, July, 1899. Vol. 4, pp. 253-266.
A study of the growth of school children in Washington, D. C.

261. —— —— Observations et expériences psycho-physiologiques sur les enfants. Rev. Scientifique, July 15, 1899. Vol. 12, pp. 70-73.

262. —— —— Experimental study of children, including anthropometrical and psycho-physical measurements of Washington school children. Rep. U. S. Comm. of Ed., 1897-98. Vol. 1, pp. 985-1204.

263. —— —— Child study in the United States. Rep. U. S. Comm. of Ed., 1897-98. Vol. 2, pp. 1281-1390.

264. —— —— Colored children: A psychological study. Jour. Am. Med. Ass'n, 1899. Vol 32, p. 14.

265. **McGee, W. J.** The beginning of mathematics. Am. Anthrop., Oct., 1899. N. S., Vol. 1, pp. 646-674.

266. **Maitland, Louise** Notes on Eskimo drawings. North Western Mo., June, 1899. Vol. 9, pp. 443-450.
Compares Eskimo (adult and child) drawings with those of other children.

267. **Makowsky, A.** Mannbarkeitsgebräuche bei den Kaffern. Globus, Braunschweig, 1899. Vol. 75, p. 230.

268. **Makuen, G. Hudson** Falsetto voice in the male. Report of five cases. Reprint from Jour. of Am. Med. Ass'n, March 4, 1899. Chicago, 1899. pp. 7.

268A. **de Manacéine, Marie** Sleep: Its physiology, pathology, hygiene, and psychology. Chas. Scribner's Sons, N. Y. (Cont. Sci. Ser.), 1897. pp. 341.
A subject of great importance and one too often neglected by parents.

269. **Manheimer, Marcel** Le troubles mentaux de l'enfance. Précis de psychiatrie infantile avec les applications pédagogiques et médico-légales. Preface de M. le Professeur Toffroy. Société d'Editions Scientifiques, Paris, 1899. pp. 188.
A good book. Rich in data and bibliography.

270. **Mapes, C. C.** More about the ethics of adolescence. N. Y. Med. Jour., June 4, 1898. Vol. 67, pp. 794-795.
Refers to articles on *Age of Consent* which appeared in the same journal, Feb. 25 and Aug. 10, 1896, and May 14, 1898.

271. **Marion, Henri** Les mouvements de l'enfant au premier âge; premiers progrès de la volonté. Rev. Scientifique, June 21, 1890. Vol. 45, pp. 769-777.

272. **Mark, H. T.** An outline of the history of educational theories in England. Swan Sonnenschein & Co., London, 1899. pp. 139.
Short chapters on physical, practical, and moral education in England.

273. **Marro, Antoine** Le rôle sociale de la puberté. Rev. Philosophique, June, 1899. Vol. 47, pp. 606-631.

274. —— —— Influence of the puberal development upon the moral character of children of both sexes. Amer. Jour. of Sociol., Sept., 1899. Vol. 5, pp. 193-219.

275. **Martin, E. S.** Children. Harp. Mag., Dec., 1899. Vol. 100, pp. 7-17.

276. **Matthews, W.** The study of ethics among the lower races. Jour. Amer. Folk-Lore, 1899. Vol. 12, pp. 1-9.
Treats of lying, stealing, etc.

277. **Melza, C.** Antropologia pedagogica. Arona; Tipografia economica, 1899. pp. 246.
Gives an account of "Pedagogical anthropology" (child study) in Italy. Also discusses the education of the sexes. A valuable and suggestive book by a teacher and educational reformer.

278. **Messer, August** Die Wirksamkeit der Apperception in den persönlichen Beziehungen des Schullebens. Berlin, 1899. pp. 69.

279. **Meurice, J.** Les fugues chez les enfants. (Thèse, Fac. de Méd.). Jouve, Paris, 1899. pp. 60.

280. **Meyer, Max** Die Tonpsychologie, ihre bisherige Entwicklung und ihre Bedeutung für die musikalische Pädagogik. Zeits. f. Päd. Psy., March, July and Sept., 1899. Vol. 1, pp. 74-85; 180-189; 245-254.

281. **Mitter, Peary C.** The spoilt child. A tale of Hindu domestic life. Translated by G. D. Oswell. Thacker, Sprink & Co., Calcutta, 1893. pp. 234.

An interesting picture of a Hindu child made bad by faulty education, but finally reformed.

282. **Möbius, P. J.** Ueber J. J. Rousseau's Jugend. Beitr. z. Kinderforschung. Heft 2. Langensalza, 1899. pp. 29.

An interesting study of Rousseau's early life by one of the most distinguished European alienists.

283. **Monroe, Will S.** Individual child study. Jour. of Ped., Jan., 1899. Vol. 12, pp. 46-68.

284. —— —— The money sense of children. Ped. Sem., March, 1899. Vol. 6, pp. 152-158.

285. —— —— Les enfants dégénérés dans les écoles publiques. Rev. Int. de Péd. comparative, March, 1899. Vol. 1, pp. 2-6.

286. —— —— Education des enfants idiots en Californie. Rev. Int. de Péd. comparative, April, 1899. Vol. 1, pp. 63-70.

287. —— —— Play interests of children. Trans. Ill. Soc. for Child Study, April-July, 1899. Vol. 4, pp. 1-9. Also published in Proc. N. E. A., 1899. pp. 358-364; and in the Am. Phys. Ed. Rev., Dec., 1899. Vol. 4, pp. 358-365.

A statistical study of the favorite games and counting-out rhymes of 2,050 Massachusetts school children.

288. —— —— La chorée dans les écoles publiques d'enfants. Rev. Int. de Péd. comparative, June, 1899. Vol. 1, pp. 195-208.

289. —— —— Fatigue among school children. Proc. N. E. A., 1899. pp. 90-93.

290. —— —— Status of child study in Europe. Ped. Sem., Sept., 1899. Vol. 6, pp. 372-381.

291. —— —— Das Studium defekter Kinder in Amerika. Die Kinderfehler, Nov., 1899. Vol. 4, pp. 183-188.

Summarizes briefly the American studies on the eyesight, hearing and mental ability of school children.

292. —— —— Child study outlines. Third series. Study of defective children. Wright and Potter Printing Co., Boston, 1899.

A series of eight outlines covering the following subjects: 1. Mental deficient children; 2. Hearing of school children; 3. Eyesight of school children; 4. Truants and juvenile delinquents; 5. Nervousness of school children; 6. Functional neuroses among school children; 7. Spinal curvature and locomotor ataxia; 8. Defective speech, stammering and stuttering.

293. —— —— Die Entwickelung des sozialen Bewusstseins der Kinder: Studie zur Psychologie und Pädagogik der Kinder. Berlin, 1899. pp. 88.

Chapters: 1. Origin of the social sense (in animals, primitive man, and the child). 2. Reactions to the social environment (companions, occupations, and societies). 3. Social utility of play (toys and games). 4. Social content of school instruction (singing, history, and geography). 5. Social aspects of proprietary notions (money sense and thrift, rights and altruism). 6. Discipline as a social factor (esprit de corps, class responsibility and punishments). 7. Social suggestibility of emotional states (fears and superstitions).

294. **Montaigne, Michel de** The education of children. Selected, translated and annotated by L. E. Rector. Int. Ed. Ser. D. Appleton & Co., N. Y., 1899. pp. 191.

295. **Montgomery, C.** The religious element in the formation of character. Proc. N. E. A., 1899. pp. 121-127.

296. **Montheil, E.** L'équitation, ses effets physiologiques, psychiques et pédagogiques. (Thèse, Fac. de Méd.). Bordeaux, 1899. pp. 97.

297. **Moon, S. B.** Growth at puberty. Am. Phys. Ed. Rev., Sept., 1899. Vol. 4, pp. 294-298.

298. **Morey-Errant, Derexa** The unity of the periods of growth in man. Trans. Ill. Soc. for Child Study, Oct., 1899. Vol. 4, pp. 84-91.

299. **Morgan, C. Lloyd** Our double acrostic. Paidologist, April and June, 1899. Vol. I, pp. 43-52; 78-93.
   An able discussion of the aims of child study and the means by which those aims may be attained.

300. —— —— Psychology for teachers. Ed. Rev. (London), June, 1899. Vol. I, pp. 360-366.

301. **Morrison, W. D.** Physische Einflüsse auf das jugendliche Verbrecherthum. Naturw. Wochenschr. Berlin, 1899. Vol. 14, pp. 13-20.

302. —— —— Einfluss der Eltern auf die jugendlichen Uebelthäter. Naturw. Wochenschr. Berlin, 1899. Vol. 14, pp. 69-74.

303. **Moses, Julius** Pathologie der kindlichen Schüchternheit. Die Kinderfehler, Nov., 1899. Vol. 4, pp. 177-182.

304. **Mosher, Eliza M.** Hygenic desks for school children (illustrated). Ed. Rev., June, 1899. Vol. 18, pp. 9-14.

305. **Muffang, H.** Écoliers et étudiants de Liverpool. Anthropologie, Paris, 1899. Vol. 10, pp. 21-41.
   Gives results of numerous anthropometric investigations.

306. **Muthesius, K.** Kindheit und Volkstum. Beitr. z. Lehrerbildung u. Lehrerforthildung, Heft 13. Thienemann, Gotha, 1899. pp. 54.
   Discusses the literature and phenomena of folk-life as bearing upon child-life.

307. **Nacla, Vicomtesse** L'enfant. Toutes ses éducations. Flammarion, Paris, 1899. pp. 203.
   Has a chapter on physical and another on moral defects.

308. **Natorp, P.** Herbart, Pestalozzi und die heutigen Aufgaben der Erziehungslehre. F. Frommann, Stuttgart, 1899. pp. 151.
   See paper on above by W. Rein in Zeits. f. Philos. u. Päd., 1889. Vol. 6, pp. 296-315.

309. —— —— Socialpädagogik. F. Fromman, Stuttgart, 1899. pp. 352.

310. **Netsch, A.** Spielbuch für Mädchen im Alter von 6-16 Jahren. Mit einem Vorworte von Schulrat Professor Dr. Euler. Carl Meyer, Hannover and Berlin, 1899. pp. 291.
Describes 240 games for girls, with brief bibliography.

311. **Nüsse, H.** Die Schreibstütze. Zeits. f. Päd. Psy., July, 1899. Vol. 1, pp. 189-192.

312. **Olhert, Arnold** Das Studium der Sprachen und die geistige Bildung. Berlin, 1899. pp. 50.

313. **Olivier, P.** Le bégarément dans la littérature médicale. La Parole, 1899. Vol. 9, pp. 721-745.

314. **O'Shea, M. V.** Some practical phases of mental fatigue. Pop. Sci. Mo., Aug., 1899. Vol. 55, pp. 511-524.

315. —— —— Conservation of mental energy. Jour. of Ped., Dec., 1899. Vol. 12, pp. 195-230.

316. **Oliphant, James** The relations of the sexes. Int. Jour. of Ethics, April, 1899. Vol. 9, pp. 273-296.
A plea for coeducation and personal purity.

317. **Oppenheim, H.** Nervenleiden und Erziehung. Vortrag, gehalten im psychologischen Verein zu Berlin am 20. Juli, 1899. S. Karger, Berlin, 1899.
Epitomizes the chief things about nervous affections. Ought to be read by teachers and parents.

318. **Ottolenghi, S.** Il tatuaggio nei minorenni corrigendi. Arch. di psichiatr., Torino, 1899. Vol. 20, pp. 157-163. Also: Riv. di med. leg., Milano, 1899. Vol. 2, pp. 347-350.

319. **Paidologist:** organ of the British child study association. Edited by Miss Mary Louch, Chiltenham, England, April, June, and Nov., 1899.
A well edited child study journal published three times a year.

320. **Papillault, G.** Quelques lois touchant la croissance et la beauté du visage humain. Rev. Scientifique, July 29, 1899. 4 s., Vol. 12, pp. 129-138. Also: Bull Soc. d'Anthr. de Paris, 1899. pp. 220-241.
A very interesting and valuable study. Treats of the influence of the social and "extra-organic" factors in the development of the form and beauty of the human face.

321. —— —— Ontogénèse et phylogénèse du crâne humain. Rev. de l'École d'anthropol. de Paris, 1899. Vol. 9, pp. 105-133.
Discusses the origin and development of the skull with man and with the animals beneath him.

322. **Pappenheim, Karl** Bemerkungen über Kinderzeichnungen. Zeits. päd. Psy., March, 1899. Vol. 1, pp. 57-73.

323. **Parsons, F. C.** Childhood's three ages. Journal of Education, 1899. Vol. 21, pp. 686-688.

324. **Partridge, George E.** Report of the tests of the vision and hearing of the school children of Worcester. Report of the Worcester (Mass.) schools, 1899. pp. 68-79.

325. **Patrick, G. T. W.** Should children under ten learn to read and write? Pop. Sci. Mo., Jan., 1899. Vol. 54, pp. 382-392.
A good presentation of the case against premature instruction.

326. —— —— Analysis of perceptions of taste. Univ. of Iowa Studies in Psychology. Vol. 2, pp. 85-127.

327. —— —— Some peculiarities of the secondary personality. Univ. of Iowa Studies in Psychology. Vol. 2, pp. 128-152.

328. **Pauper Children** An open letter on the care and control of London pauper children, addressed to the Rt. Hon. Viscount Peel. P. S. King & Son, London, 1897. pp. 30.

329. **Payot, Jules** L'éducation du caractère. Rev. Philosophique, Dec., 1889. Vol. 48, pp. 594-614.

330. **Perrone-Capano, R.** Infanticidio ed esposizione d'infante negli animali inferiori e nei popoli selvaggi. Riv. mens. di psichiatr. forense, Napoli, 1899. Vol. 2, pp. 1-15.
A very useful statement of the facts concerning infanticide and the exposure of offspring among the lower animals and among savage peoples.

331. **Perry, Charles S.** Training period of deaf as compared with hearing youth. Ass'n Rev., Dec., 1899. Vol. 1, pp. 150-157.

332. **Petit, Edouard** La fête de l'adolescence. Rev. Pédagogique, Sept., 1899. Vol. 35, pp. 193-210.
An interesting account of the "adolescence festival" at Paris, July 30, 1899—founded with the idea of "creating a holiday for adolescents."

333. **Pfitzner, F.** Social-anthropologische Studien. I. Der Einfluss des Lebensalters auf die anthropologischen Charaktere. Ztschr. f. Morphol. u. Anthropol., Stuttgart, 1899. Vol. 1, pp. 325-377.
The first portion of an elaborate study of the relations between the periods of life and the anthropological characters of man.

334. **Phillips, D. E.** Some aspects of the child study movement. North Western Mo., Jan., 1899. Vol. 9, pp. 233-237.

335. —— —— The teaching instinct. Ped. Sem., March, 1899. Vol. 6, pp. 188-245.

336. **Pidancet, J.** Le travail intellectuel dans ses relations avec la thermogénèse. Nancy, 1899. pp. 87.

337. **Plettenberg, P.** Die neuesten Abhandlungen und Untersuchungen über die Ermüdung der Schuljugend. Ztschr. f. Hypnot., 1899. Vol. 8, pp. 228-249.

338. **Proceedings** of the seventh annual meeting of the American Psychological Association, New York, Dec., 1898. Psy. Rev., Mar., 1899. Vol. 6, pp. 146-179.

339. **Proceedings** of the New Jersey association for the study of children and youth. The Brotherhood Press, Bloomfield, N. J., 1899. pp. 68.
Contains eleven articles and reports. A valuable pamphlet and a good *vade mecum* for those interested in organizing such institutions.

340. **Quick, R. H.** Life and remains. Edited by F. Storr. The Macmillan Co., N. Y., 1899. pp. 544.

Contains chapters on public schools, boys and masters, child nature, language, memory, religious beliefs, etc.

341. **Rayner, H.** The early recognition and treatment of mental defects in children. Medical Mag., 1899. Vol. 8, pp. 451-461; 591-600.

Rector, L. E. See Montaigne. (No. 294.)

342. **Reis, J.** Ueber einfache psychologische Versuche an Gesunden und Geisteskranken. Psy. Arbeiten, 1899. Vol. 2, pp. 587-694.

343. **Report** of the educational commission of the city of Chicago. Chicago, 1899. pp. 248.

Contains chapters on public kindergartens, vacation schools and school playgrounds, parental schools, pupil government, etc.

344. **Report** of the state superintendent of public instruction in New York. (44th.) For the school year ending July 31, 1897. State Printers, N. Y. and Albany, 1898. 2 vols., pp. 1304. With appendix, pp. 228.

Pp. 873-913 devoted to child study. Contains the following papers: Report on child study, by Anna K. Eggleston—New York Society for Child Study; and scientific child study, by Edward F. Buchner. The relation of the home and the school in child study, by Mrs. M. H. McElroy. Child study for the practical teacher, by L. H. Galbreath. Child study in the high school, by John G. Allen. The dullard, by James P. Haney. Child study by a woman's club, by Mrs. Ella Hastings.

345. **Revue** Internationale de Pédagogie Comparative. Auguste Mailloux, Rédacteur en chef. Nantes, France.

Begun in March, 1899. Price, 10 francs a year. Published in the interests of defective children. See review of first issue in Ped. Sem., Sept, 1899. Vol. 5, p. 411.

346. **Ribot, Th.** The general ideas of infants and deaf-mutes. Open Court, March, 1899. Vol. 13, pp. 164-175.

347. —— —— The evolution of speech. Open Court, May, 1899. Vol. 13, pp. 267-278.

348. —— —— Abstraction prior to speech. Open Court, Jan., 1899. Vol. 13, pp. 14-20.

349. —— —— The higher forms of abstraction—their nature. Open Court, July, 1899. Vol. 13, pp. 433-443.

350. —— —— Intermediate forms of abstraction. Open Court, June, 1899. Vol. 13, pp. 349-359.

351. —— —— The evolution of general ideas. (Auth. transl. by F. A. Welby), Chicago and London, 1899. pp. 231.

352. **Richmond, Ennis** Through boyhood to manhood. Longmans, Green & Co., London and N. Y., 1899. pp. 194.
A plea for unselfishness, self-control, and purity.

353. **Rider, Edward C.** Kindergarten work in schools for the deaf. Ass'n Rev., Oct., 1899. Vol. 1, pp. 35-41.

354. **Rohleder, Hermann** Die Masturbation. Eine Monographie f. Ärzte u. Pädagogen. Fischer's medicin. Buchh., Berlin, 1899. pp. 319.

355. **Roussey, C.** Notes sur l'apprentissage de la parole chez un enfant. La Parole, 1899. Vol. 9, pp. 791-799; 870-880.

356. **Roux, Joanny** Psychologie de l'instinct sexuel. J. B. Baillière & fils, Paris, 1899. pp. 96.

357. **Rowe, Stuart H.** The physical nature of the child and how to study it. The Macmillan Co., New York, 1899. pp. 207.
Chapters: Sight; hearing; motor ability; enunciation; nervousness; fatigue; disease; posture; movements; growth and adolescence.

358. **Ruyssen, Th.** L'École et le crime. Manuel Général de l'Instruction Primaire, June 3, 1899. pp. 237-239.
Study of juvenile delinquents.

359. **Rzesnitzek, Emil** Zur Frage der psychischen Entwickelung der Kindersprache. G. P. Aderholz, Breslau, 1899. pp. 35.

360. **Sante de Sanctis, —.** I sogni: studi psicologici e clinici. Bocca, Turin, 1899. pp. 388.
Perhaps the best book on dreams we have. Chapter IV treats of children's dreams. Dreams of animals and of adults are also discussed.

361. **Schaefer, F.** Schule und Arbeit. I. Wie erzieht die Schule zur Arbeitsfreudigkeit? II. Gegen den Handfertigkeitsunterricht in den Schulen. Mayer, Leipzig, 1898. pp. 90.

362. **Schiller, H.** Die Schularztfrage. Ein Wort zur Verständigung. Reuther und Reichard, Berlin, 1899. pp. 56.
Hopes more from the hygienic education of the teacher than from the institution of the school physician.

363. **Schröter, Dr.** Wird bei jungen Unverheirateten zur Zeit der Menstruation stärkere sexuelle Erregtheit beobachtet? Allg. Ztschr. f. Psychiatr., 1899. Vol. 56, pp. 321-334.

364. **Schwendt, A.** Examen clinique et acoustique de 60 sourds-muets. La Parole, 1899. Vol. 9, pp. 641-672.

365. —— —— Les restes auditifs des sourds-muets peuvent-ils être utilisés pour leur apprendre à mieux parler? La Parole, 1899. Vol. 9, pp. 845-869.

366. **Schwendt, A., und Wagner, —** Untersuchungen von Taubstummen. B. Schwabe, Basel, 1899. pp. 187.

367. **Sciascia, P.** La psicogenesi dell' instinto e della morale secondo C. Darwin. Palermo, 1899. pp. 190.

368. **Scott, Jas. Foster** The sexual instinct: Its use and dangers as affecting heredity and morals. E. B. Treat & Co., 1899.

369. **Sears, Charles H.** Home and school punishments. Ped. Sem., March, 1899. Vol. 6, pp. 159-187.

370. **Seashore, C. E.** Motor ability, reaction, time, rhythm, and time sense. Univ. of Iowa Studies in Psychology. Vol. 2, pp. 64-84.

371. **Shinn, Milicent W.** Notes on the development of a child. Parts 3-4. Univ. of Cal. Studies, pub. by the Univ., Berkeley, Cal., 1899. pp. 179-424.

372. **Shuttleworth, George E.** Exceptional children. Paidologist, Nov., 1899. Vol. 1, pp. 138-144.

373. **Sicchirollo, Angelo** Psicologia infantile popolare. A. Vallardi, Milano, 1899.

374. **Siviter, Anna P.** Fears of childhood discovered by a mother. Kindergarten Mag., Oct., 1899. Vol. 12, pp. 82-87.

375. **Skinner, Charles R.** See Report of the State Supt. of Pub. Instruction, N. Y. No. 344.

376. **Spahr, Charles B.** Child labor in England and the United States. Chautauquan, Oct., 1899. Vol. 30, pp. 41-43.

377. **Spencer, Frank C.** Education of the Pueblo child. A study in arrested development. Columbia Univ. Contrib. to Philos. Psy. and Ed., Vol. 7, No. 1. The Macmillan Co., N.Y., 1899. pp. 97.
 A valuable contribution to the study of the problems involved in individual and racial development.

378. **Spicer, —** Elementary schools (children working for wages). Eyre & Spottiswoode, London, 1899. Parts I and II, pp. 51-110.
 Parliamentary report on children attending school and working for wages in England and Wales.

379. **Spitzner, Alfred** Psychogene Störungen der Schulkinder. Ein Kapitel der pädagogischen Pathologie. E. Ungleich, Leipzig, 1899. pp. 45.
 Contains suggestions on overcoming psychic and nervous abnormalities in children.

380. **Stableton, J. K.** The study of boys entering the adolescent period of life. IX. The boy developed by business training. North Western Mo., March-April, 1899. Vol. 9, pp. 342-344.

381. **Stanley, Hiram M.** Professor Gross and theories of play. Psy. Rev., Jan., 1899. Vol. 6, pp. 86-92.

382. —— —— Education and individuality. Ed. Rev., June, 1899. Vol. 18, pp. 80-84.

383. **Starbuck, E. D.** Child study and its possibilities as a science. North Western Mo., March-April, 1899. Vol. 9, pp. 358-362.

384. —— —— The psychology of religion. (Contemporary Science Series.) Scribner's Sons, N. Y., 1899. pp. 420.
 Attempts to bring conversion and other stages of religious development into line with the biological facts of life.

385. **State** care of dependent children. Ann. Amer. Acad. Pop. Soc. Sci., Sept., 1899. Vol. 14, pp. 120-123.

386. **Steffens, C.** Die Indianerpuppensammlung von Frau A. L. Dickerman. Globus, Braunschweig, 1899. Vol. 75, pp. 354-356.

387. **Stevens, Kate** Lessons from the standpoint of the child. Child Life, July and Oct., 1899. Vol. 1, pp. 160-162; 231-236.
A statistical study of the interests of children in the subjects taught in elementary schools.

388. **Stickney, Lucia** Homes of our down-town children. Proc. N. E. A., 1899. pp. 388-395.

389. **Stimpfl, Joseph** Die Pflege der Kinderpsychologie in Nordamerika. Blätter für die Schulpraxis in Volksschulen und Lehrerbildungs-anstalten, 1899. Vol. 10, pp. 24.
A comprehensive study of the child study movement in America.

390. —— —— Stand der Kinderpsychologie in Europa und Amerika. Zeits. f. Päd. Psy., Dec., 1899. Vol. 1, pp. 344-361.
A comprehensive study of the present status of child study.

391. —— —— Translation of Tracy's psychology of childhood. (See No. 412.)

392. **Stockham, Alice B.** Games in education. School and Home Ed., Bloomington, Ill., Dec., 1899. Vol. 19, pp. 187-189.

Storr, F. (Editor.) See **Quick, R. H.** (No. 340.)

393. **Strauss, P.** Enfants maltraités et jeunes délinquants. Rev. Philanthr., 1899. Vol. 5, pp. 298-304.

394. **Street, J. Richard** A genetic study of immortality. Ped. Sem., Sept., 1899. Vol. 6, pp. 267-313.

395. **von Strümpell, L.** Die Pädagogische Pathologie oder die Lehrer von den Fehlern der Kinder. 3. Aufl. Hrsg. von Alf. Spitzner. E. Ungleich, Leipzig, 1899.

396. **Sully, James** Dollatry. Contemp. Rev., Jan., 1899. Vol. 75, pp. 58-72.

397. **Swift, Edgar J.** Some causes of reflex neuroses in children. Am. Phys. Ed. Rev., March, 1899. Vol. 4, pp. 34-41.

398. **Taylor, Charlotte** The series method: A comparison. Pop. Sci. Mo., Feb., 1899. Vol. 54, pp. 537-541.

399. **Thiemich, M.** Ueber die Diagnose der Imbecillität im frühen Kindesalter. Deutsche Medic. Wochenschr., 1900. Nr. 2, p. 34.
Discusses the symptoms of imbecility noticeable as abnormalities in the second and third years of life.

400. **Thomas, Félix** L'enseignement visuel. Rev. Pédagogique, Dec., 1899. Vol. 35, pp. 481-497.

401. **Thomas, P. F.** Morale et éducation. Alcan, Paris, 1899. pp. 171.

402. —— —— L'éducation des sentiments. Alcan, Paris, 1899. pp. 287.

403. **Thorndike, Edward** Mental fatigue. Science, May 19, 1899. N. S., Vol. 9, pp. 712-713.

404. **Thulié, H.** Education des dégénérés supérieurs. Réflexe de l'obéissance. Rev. Mensuelle de L'Ecole d'Anthrop. de Paris, Jan., 1899. Vol. 9, pp. 1-16.
Emphasizes the hygiene of movement.

405. **Thurber, Charles H.** Plans for the development of child study in the State through the State department. Trans. Ill. Soc. for Child Study, Jan., 1899. Vol. 3, pp. 195-198.

406. —— —— Child study in the Sunday school. Bib. World, July, 1899. Vol. 14, pp. 42-46.

407. —— —— Little critics. Trans. Ill. Soc. for Child Study, Oct., 1899. Vol. 4, pp. 95-99.

408. **Tissier, P.** De l'influence de l'accouchement anormal sur le développement des troubles cérébraux de l'enfant. (Thèse, Fac. de Méd.) Steinheil, Paris, 1899. pp. 100.

409. **Toischer, W.** Die Sprache der Kinder. (Samml. gemein-nütz., Vortr. 248.) F. Haerpfer in Komm., Prag., 1899.

410. **Toulouse and Vaschide** Mesure de l'odorat chez les enfants. C. R. Soc. de Biol., 1899, 11th Ser. Vol. 1, pp. 381-387; 487-489.

411. **Tracy, Frederick** Left-handedness. Paidologist, June, 1899. Vol. 1, pp. 100-106.

412. —— —— Psychologie der Kindheit. Mit Erlaubnis des Verfassers nach der vierten neubearbeiteten Auflage des Originals aus dem Englischen übertragen von Dr. J. Stimpfl. Mit 28 Abbildungen im Text. E. Wunderlich, Leipzig, 1899. pp. 158.
A good translation minus the bibliography given in the English edition.

413. **Troublesome Child** in School (The) Proceedings of the Kansas Society for Child Study. Child Study Mo., Feb., 1899. Vol. 4, pp. 451-488.
A section of the Kansas State Teachers' Association devoted to the discussion of this subject. Rather chatty.

414. **Trüper, J.** Bemerkungen zu den Verhandlungen der IX. Konferenz für das Erziehungswesen der Schwachsinnigen. Die Kinderfehler, Jan. and March, 1899. Vol. 4, pp. 21-28; 57-68.

415. **Valentine, Maude** Two studies of school children. Trans. Ill. Soc. for Child Study. April-July, 1899. Vol. 4, pp. 56-61.

416. **Van Liew, C. C.** Mental and moral development of the kindergarten child. Proc. N. E. A., 1899. pp. 551-559.

417. —— —— Racial traits in the group activity of children. North Western Mo., Sept., 1899. Vol. 10, pp. 34-38. Also Proc. N. E. A., 1899. pp. 1057-1064.

418. **de Varigny, Henry** Croissance. Dictionnaire de physiologie, 1899. Vol. 4, pp. 488-545.
Discusses the question of growth from all points of view. A good *résumé* of the subject.

419. **Viali, F.** L'enseignement moral à l'école primaire. Challamel, Paris, 1898.

420. **von Voss, G.** Ueber die Schwankungen der geistigen Arbeits-leistung. Psy. Arbeiten, 1898, Vol. 2, pp. 399-449.

421. **Vostrovsky, Clara** A study of children's reading tastes. Ped. Sem., Dec., 1899. Vol. 6, pp. 523-535.

422. **Ward, A. O.** The vision of school children. Brit. Med. Jour., 1899, I, p. 443.

423. **Warner, Charles Dudley** The making of criminals. Arena, Jan., 1899. Vol. 21, pp. 15-28.

424. **Warner, Francis** Mental abilities and disabilities of children. Lancet, 1899. I, pp. 1137-1138.

425. —— —— The nervous system of the child. Its growth and health in education. The Macmillan Co., N. Y., 1909. pp. 233.

426. **Warren, H. C., and others** The Psychological Index for 1898. The Macmillan Co., N. Y., 1899. pp. 173.

427. **Warwick, Countess of** (Editor.) Progress in women's education in the British empire. Being the report of the education section, Victorian Era Exhibition, 1897. Longmans, Green & Co., London and N. Y., 1898. pp. 370.

   Under education of children are papers on the pauper child; teaching of defective children, and the children's guild of play.

428. **Washburn, M. F.** Recent discussions of imitation. Philos. Rev., Jan., 1899. Vol. 8, pp. 101-104.

429. **Wegener, H.** Die Spiegelschrift. Zeits. f. Päd. Psy., Sept., 1899. Vol. 1, pp. 254-269.

430. **Weir, James, Jr.** The dawn of reason, or mental traits in the lower animals. The Macmillan Co., N. Y., 1899. pp. 234.
   Welby, F. A. See No. 351.

431. **Welsh, Charles** The early history of children's books in New England. New Eng. Mag., April, 1899. N. S., Vol. 20, pp. 147-160.

432. **Weygandt, W.** Römer's Versuche über Nahrungsaufnahme und geistige Leistungsfähigkeit. Psy. Arbeiten, 1899. Vol. 2, pp. 695-706.

433. **Williams, Lillie A.** How to collect data for studies in genetic psychology. Ped. Sem., June, 1896. Vol. 3, pp. 419-423.
   Miss Williams has probably collected more child study data by the sylla-bus method than any other teacher.

434. **Wilson, Louis N.** Bibliography of child study for the year 1898. Ped. Sem., Sept., 1899. Vol. 6, pp. 386-410.

435. **Wiltse, Sara E.** Children's autobiographies. Paidologist, Nov., 1899. Vol. 1, pp. 155-157.

436. **Winterburn, Florence Hull** From the child's standpoint. Views of child life and nature. A book for parents and teachers. The Baker & Taylor Co., N. Y., 1899. pp. 278.
   Brief papers from popular journals. Interesting, but of little scientific value.

437. **Wolf, O.** Die Hörprüfung mittelst der Sprache. Zeits. f. Ohrenheilk., 1899. Vol. 34, pp. 289-311.

438. **Woodworth, R. S.** The best movement for handwriting. Science, Nov. 10, 1899. N. S. Vol. 10, pp. 679-681.

439. **Wright, Carroll D.** Outlines of practical sociology. Longmans, Green & Co., N. Y., 1899. pp. 431.

Parts III, IV, V, deal with population, family, and labor.

440. **Zeitschrift** für Pädagogische Psychologie. Herausgegaben von Ferdinand Kemsies. Herman Walther, Berlin.

Begun in Jan., 1899. Price 8 marks a year. See review of the first number in Ped. Sem., March, 1899. Vol. 5, p. 255.

441. **Zucke, A.** Ueber Schuld und Strafe der Jugendlichen Verbrecher. Stuttgart, 1899. pp. 127.

Argues against punishment by fines and for a reduction of the age for punishment.

SUBJECT INDEX.

Abnormal, 80, 118, 133.
Abstraction, 348, 349, 350.
Accouchement, 408.
Adolescence, 99, 101, 103, 116, 237, 270, 297, 332, 352, 380. See also Puberty.
Æsthetics, 1, 252.
Africa, 30.
Alcoholism, 189.
Alimentation, 13.
Ambition, 210, 293.
Amusements, 109.
Anger, 186.
Animal and plant lore, 29.
Animals, 430.
Animism, 204.
Anthropology, 96.
Anthropometry, 40, 53, 92, 192, 193, 194, 260, 262, 305.
Apperception, 238, 278.
Art, 51.
Athletics, 178.
Attention, 8, 94.
Australia, 161.
Autobiography, 34, 258, 435.

Baby. See Infants and infancy.
Backward children, 372.
Bacteria, 14.
Bashfulness, 303.
Bibliography, 160, 175, 262, 263, 426, 434.
Birth rate, 228.
Blind, 113, 134.
Body, 155.
Boys, 102, 380.
Boys' clubs, 157.
Boys' gangs, 54.
Brain, 103, 145.

California, 286.
Certainty, 172.
Character, 329.
Childhood, 126, 139, 148.
Child labor, 2, 97, 376, 378.
Child laws, 97, 220.
Child and race, 96, 160.
Child study (in Europe), 190.
Child study (General), 17, 18, 20, 23, 28, 42, 44, 45, 47, 56, 60, 61, 63, 70, 71, 72, 84, 100, 102, 117, 121, 122, 126, 131, 135, 136, 140, 175, 179, 180, 181, 187, 195, 213, 232, 233, 251, 261, 263, 275, 283, 290, 292, 293, 294, 299, 334, 339, 340, 344, 357, 361, 373, 383, 389, 390, 398, 405, 406, 407, 412, 413, 415, 433, 436.
Child type, 96.
Children's reading, 224.
Chorea, 154, 288, 292.
Co-education, 138, 163, 316.
Color sense, 1.
Colored children, 264.
Companions, 293.
Conduct, 124.
Conversion, 384.
Counting out rhymes, 287.
Craniology, 321.
Crime, 3, 118, 125, 173, 292, 301, 302, 358, 393, 423.
Curiosity, 27.

Darwin, 367.
Deaf and deaf mute, 15, 113, 159, 205, 331, 346, 353, 364, 365, 366.
Defectives, 21, 291, 346, 427. See also Feeble minded.
Defects (moral and physical), 307

Delinquent, 156.
Dementia praecox, 101, 207.
Dentition, 203.
Dependent classes, 328, 385.
Desks, 304, 311.
Development, 183, 356, 371, 377.
Discipline, 293.
Disease, 357.
Dolls, 386, 396.
Drawing, 51, 66, 255, 257, 266, 322.
Dreams, 360.
Dyspepsia, 244.

Ear, 164.
Emotions, 182, 402.
Environment, 5, 95.
Eskimo, 266.
Ethics, 276.
Evolution of ideas, 253.
Examinations, 12.
Excitation, 145.
Exercise, 69, 357.
Eyesight. See Vision.

Face, 320.
Fairy tales, 170.
Family, 46, 439.
Fatigue, 37, 178, 216, 222, 230, 239,
    246, 256, 289, 314, 337, 357, 403.
Faulty education, 281.
Fear, 250, 293, 374.
Feeble minded, 22, 31, 48, 120, 133,
    147, 158, 162, 234, 285, 286, 291,
    292, 372, 414. See also Abnor-
    mal, and defectives.
Festivals, 332.
Fighting, 39.
Flightiness, 279.
Folk Lore, 306.
Food, 13, 36, 196, 315, 432.
France, 42, 63.
Fright, 250.

Games. See Play.
Genius, 89, 95.
Geography, 293.
Girls, 144, 227, 310.
Groos, 381.
Group games, 417.
Growth, 69, 81, 114, 192, 193, 231,
    260, 297, 298, 357, 418.

Habit, 215.
Hawaii, 110.
Head nodding, 6.
Health, 144, 169, 190, 315.
Hearing, 164, 291, 292, 324, 357, 437.
Hebephrenia, 101, 207.
Heredity, 5.
History, 293.
Home education, 185.

Home study, 222.
Horse riding, 296.
Hygiene, 151, 169, 191, 315, 362.
Hypnotism, 198.
Hysteria, 219, 292.

Ideas, 351.
Idiots, 286.
Ill treatment, 393.
Imagination, 130.
Imbecile, 128, 399.
Imitation, 200, 241, 243, 428.
Indians, 386.
Individual, 143, 283.
Individuality, 119, 382.
Infants and infancy, 86, 90, 121,
    169, 197, 201, 271, 346, 371.
Infanticide, 330.
Initiation, 161.
Instinct, 236, 367.
Instruction, 151, 206.
Intellectual work, 36.
Interests, 93, 240, 387.
Italy, 277.

Japan, 98.
Journals, 98, 141, 207A, 319, 345,
    440.

Kindergarten, 16, 65, 66, 67, 68,
    76, 82, 107, 184, 185, 343, 353,
    416.

Labor, 439.
Language, 9, 58, 66, 115, 176, 223,
    249, 340, 355, 359, 364, 365, 409.
Languages, 91.
Laws, 129.
Left-handedness, 411.
Libraries, 112.
Light, 149.
Literature, 112, 168, 240, 431.
Liverpool, 305.
Lying, 4.

Manual Training, 361.
Masturbation, 354.
Mathematics, 91, 235, 265.
Medical Inspection, 166, 362.
Memory, 106, 188, 340.
Menstruation, 363.
Mental, 336, 432.
Mental Ability, 420, 424.
Mental defects, 269, 341.
Mental disturbances, 379.
Mental evolution and develop-
    ment, 9, 78, 83, 245, 249.
Mental hygiene, 73, 165.
Mental traits, 430.
Method, 19, 24.
Mind, 155.

Modesty, 142.
Money sense, 284, 293.
Moral training, 66, 87.
Morals and religion, 77, 254 ,272,
    274, 295, 340, 367, 384, 394, 401,
    419.
Motor ability, 357, 370.
Movement, 225, 271, 272, 357, 404.
Muscles, 225.
Music, 66, 159, 280, 293.
Myths, etc., 85.

Natural science, 91.
Nature study, 66, 199, 211.
Neglected children, 388.
Nervous system, 425.
Nervousness, 108, 177, 292, 317.
Neurasthenia, 41.
Neurology, 66.
Neuroses, 397.
Night terrors, 250.
Normal schools, 140.
Number, 66.
Nurses, 169.

Originality, 243.
Ownership, 226.

Parents and parenthood, 55, 88,
    228, 302.
Pathology, 395.
Pauper children, 328.
Pedagogy, 105, 132.
Pedology, 38, 247.
Perception, 326.
Periods, 323, 333.
Personality, 327.
Pestalozzi, 308.
Physical defects, 307.
Physical training, 11, 67, 153, 242,
    272.
Play, 50, 65, 66, 110, 130, 150, 171,
    174, 207A, 287, 293, 310, 343,
    381, 392, 427.
Play school, 212.
Posture, 152, 357.
Primitive man, 96, 176.
Property sense, 226.
Psychology, 28, 105, 208, 209, 217,
    221, 300, 338, 342, 412.
Psychophysiology, 33.
Puberty, 99, 267, 273, 274.
Punishment, 227, 293, 369, 441.
Purity, 352.

Race, 417.
Reading, 111, 112, 168, 240, 325, 421.
Reason, 236.
Recess, 289.

Reflexes, 397.
Religion. See Morals.
Rhythm, 59, 370.
Right and left, 35.
Rights, 293.
Rousseau, 282.

Santa Claus, 85.
School and school life, 10, 48.
School diseases, 74.
School hygiene, 75, 166, •229, 362.
Senses, 211, 410.
Sex, 26, 99, 138, 142, 146, 163, 259,
    277, 316, 356, 368.
Sight. See Vision.
Singing. See Music.
Sleep, 268A.
Social, 137.
Social ethics, 64.
Social sense, 7, 43, 293.
Sociology, 309, 439.
Sound, 280.
Speech, 116, 160, 205, 223, 291, 292,
    312, 347, 348, 357, 437.
Spinal curvature, 152, 292, 304.
Squinting, 167.
St. Vitus dance. See Chorea.
Stammering and stuttering, 291,
    292, 313.
Suggestion, 25.
Sunday School, 127, 136, 406.
Superstitions, 293.
Syllabus methods, 433.
Taste, 326.
Tattooing, 318.
Teaching instinct, 335.
Teeth, 203.
Text books, 32.
Time sense, 370.
Toys, 293.
Truants, 292.

Vacation schools, 212, 343.
Vice, 126.
Vision, 79, 104, 149, 167, 214, 291,
    292, 324, 357, 422.
Visual education, 400.
Vocabulary, 9, 223.
Voice, 202, 218, 268.

Wagner, 248.
Walking, 49.
Weather, 123, 124, 125.
Will, 52, 62.
Woman, 96, 190.
Worcester, 109, 324.
Writing, 311, 325, 429, 438.

Youth, 126, 207, 282.

BIBLIOGRAPHY

OF

CHILD STUDY.

BY

LOUIS N. WILSON,

LIBRARIAN, CLARK UNIVERSITY.

The Clark University Press.

WORCESTER, MASSACHUSETTS,

January, 1902.

BIBLIOGRAPHY OF CHILD STUDY.

For the Year 1900.

By LOUIS N. WILSON, Librarian, Clark University.

1. **Alexander, S.** Interest, Child Life, July, 1900. Vol. 2, pp. 138-145.
2. **Alrutz, Sydney** Studien auf dem Gebiete der Temperatursinne. Skandinavisches Archiv für Physiologie. Upsala, 1900. Vol. 10, pp. 340-352.
3. **Ament, W.** Die Entwickelung von Sprachen und Denken beim Kinde. Wunderlich, Leipzig, 1899, pp. 213.
   A valuable recent inductive study on the language of children.
4. **Babinski, ——** Quelques jeunes choréiques. Journ. Méd. Int. 1900. Vol. 4, pp. 512-513.
5. **Bailey, Thomas P.** Some difficulties of child study. Proc. N. E. A., 1900, pp. 582-584.
6. **Balliet, Thomas M.** Results from study of bodily growth. School Journal, Jan. 13, 1900. Vol. 60, p. 47.
7. **—— ——** Pedagogy of instincts. School Journal, Jan. 13, 1900. Vol. 60, p. 47.
8. **Bancroft, Margaret** The claims of the feeble minded. Proc. N. E. A., 1900, pp. 674-677.
9. **Barella, D.** Cantilene infantili della Sardegna centrale. Arch. p. l. Stud. d. Trad. Pop. Palermo, 1900. Vol. 19, pp. 307-321; 433-442.
   Children's songs collected in and about Nuoro.
10. **Barnes, Earl** Children's ideals. Ped. Sem., April, 1900. Vol. 7, pp. 3-12.
11. **—— ——** Freedom in education. Child Life, April, 1900. Vol. 2, pp. 79-82.
   A brief study of the ambitions of English children.
12. **—— ——** Young children's stories. Paidologist, April, 1900. Vol. 2, pp. 17-21.
13. **Barr, M. W.** Epilepsy modified by treatment and environment, with some notes of 200 cases. Alien. and Neurol., 1900. Vol. 21, pp. 85-95.
14. **Bartlett, J. H.** School breakdown. Med. News, 1900. Vol. 77, pp. 208-210.

15. **Batten, F. E.** Two cases of arrested development of the nervous system in children. Brain, 1900. Vol. 23, pp. 269-276.

16. **Baur, A.** Die Schulartzfrage in Stuttgart. Zeit. für Schulgesundheitspflege, 1900. Vol 13, pp. 78-88.

17. **Bawden, E. Heath** A study of lapses. Psy. Rev. Monograph Supplement. April, 1900. Vol. 3, No. 4, pp. 122.

18. **Bayr, Emanuel** Die Einführung der Hygiene, Volksgesundheitslehre, als obligatorischen Lehrgegenstand in den Gewerbeschulen. Zeit. für Schulgesundheitspflege, 1900. Vol. 13, pp. 11-13.

19. —— —— Schulstrafen. Zeit. für Schulgesundheitspflege, 1900. Vol. 13, pp. 429-457.

20. **Bell, Sanford** A study of the teacher's influence. Ped. Sem., Dec., 1900. Vol. 7, pp. 492-525.

21. **Bellei, G.** La stanchezza mentale nei bambini delle pubbliche scuole. Riv. Sper. di Freniatria, 1900. Vol. 26, pp. 692-698.
    Reports results of fatigue experiments on 460 children in the public schools of Bologna, Italy.

22. **Benedetti, V.** La pedagogia della volontà. Milano, 1899. pp. 312.

23. **Bernheim, P.** Les associations d'images verbales et l'aphasie chez les enfants. Gaz. d. Hôp., 1900. Vol. 73, pp. 41-47; 73-79.

24. **Beyer, Henry G.** The relation between physique and mental work. Am. Physical Ed. Rev., June, 1900. Vol. 5, pp. 149-161.
    Gives results of examination of 76 boys at Boston Navy Yard.

25. **Bezy et Bibent** L' hystérie infantile et juvénile, Vigot, Paris, 1900. pp. 215.

26. **Bielschovsky, A.** Untersuchungen über das Sehen der Schielenden. Arch. f. Ophthamologie, 1900. Vol. 50, pp. 406-509.

27. **Binet, Alfred** La mesure en psychologie individuelle. Rev. Philos. Aug., 1898. Vol. 46, pp. 113-123.

28. —— —— Nouvelles recherches sur la consommation du pain, dans ses rapports avec le travail intellectuel. Année Psychologique, 1899 (1900). Vol. 6, pp. 1-73.
    Treats of effects of school life on consumption of bread.

29. —— —— La suggestibilité. Paris: Schleicher Frères, 1900, pp. 395, with 32 cuts and 2 plates.
    An exhaustive experimental study of the suggestibility of school children.

30. **Blake, Isabella M.** Fatigue. Jour. of Pedagogy, March, 1900. Vol. 12, pp. 319-325.

31. **Blount, William A.** Sphere of the playground. Jour. of Pedagogy, June, 1900. Vol. 13, pp. 56-61.

32. **Bodenstein, K.** Das Ehrgefühl der Kinder. Wie weit darf und muss der Erzieher es anregen? Beyer, Langensalza, 1899. pp. 47.

33. **Boesch, Hans** Kinderleben in der deutschen Vergangenheit. Mit 149 Abbildungen und Beilagen nach den Originalen aus dem 15,—18. Jahrhundert. Verlegt bei Eugen Diederichs in Leipzig, 1900, pp. 131.

A most interesting sketch of German child life (in all aspects) of the past, illustrated by 149 cuts, etc., after originals belonging to the fifteenth-eighteenth centuries.

34. **Booth, Frank W.** Statistics of speech teaching in schools for the deaf in the United States. Proc. N. E. A., 1900, pp. 668-670.

35. **Bosina, Hendrik** Psychogenic disturbances. Paidologist, April, 1900. Vol. 2, pp. 10-16.

36. **Bourneville et Boyer** De l' hystérie mâle de l' enfance. Progrès Méd., 1900. 3rd. ser., Vol. 11, pp. 244-248.

37. **Brockway, Harriet** Common diseases of childern. Child Study Mo., March, 1900. Vol. 5, pp. 405-416.

38. **Brown, H.** Physical training in English schools. Am. Phys. Ed. Rev., Sept., 1900. Vol. 5, pp. 246-252.

39. **Bryan, Elmer B.** Nascent stages and their pedagogical significance. Ped. Sem., Oct., 1900. Vol. 7, pp. 357-396.

An interesting contribution to the literature of growth, physical and mental.

40. **Buckman, S. S.** Human babies—what they teach. Nature, July 5, 1900. Vol. 62, pp. 226-228.

Deals with atavistic and kindred traits of babyhood.

41. **Bullock, Royal W.** Some observations on children's reading. Proc. N. E. A., 1897, pp. 1015-1021.

42. **Bülow-Wendhausen,** (Baroness.) Frœbel's system of education and the spread of the kindergarten. Rep. Comm. Ed., 1899-1900. Vol. 1, pp. 883-894.

43. **Burk, Caroline Frear** Secretiveness of children. Child Study Mo., Feb., 1900. Vol. 5, pp. 355-369.

44. —— —— Promotions of bright and slow children. Ed. Rev., March, 1900. Vol. 19, pp. 296-302.

45. —— —— The collecting instinct. Ped. Sem., July, 1900. Vol. 7, pp. 179-207.

The best study on the subject.

46. **Burnham, Wm. H.** Health inspection in the schools. Ped. Sem., April, 1900. Vol. 7, pp. 70-94; Paidologist, July, 1900. Vol. 2, pp. 76-82.

An up-to-date discussion.

47. **Burton, Ernest D.** The adaptation of bible literature to the development of the child. Child-Study Mo., Nov. 1900. Vol. 6, pp. 164-172.

48. **Butler, Nicholas M.** The Quincy Movement. Ed. Rev., June, 1900. Vol. 20, pp. 80-84.

49. **Calkins, Mary W.** An attempted experiment in psychological æsthetics (Wellesley Coll. Psychol. Stud.). Psychol. Rev., 1900. Vol. 7, pp. 580-591.

50. **Camerer, W.** Gewichts- und Längenwachsthum der Kinder, insbesondere solcher im ersten Lebensjahre. Wiener klinische Rundschan, Jan. 14, 1900. Vol. 14, pp. 28-30.

51. **Campbell, C. Victor** Desks that fit. Child Study Mo., Oct., 1900. Vol. 6, pp. 141-145.

52. **Carmen, E. Kate** Cause of chronic bad spelling. Jour. of Pedagogy, Oct., 1900. Vol. 13, pp. 86-91.

53. **Chamberlain, A. F.** Die Entwickelungshemmung des Kindes bei den Naturvölkern und bei den Völkern von Halbkultur. Ztschr. f. päd. Psych., 1900. Vol. 2, pp. 303-309.-
An anthropological study of the "arrest at puberty."

54. —— —— Recent German discussions on folk-lore in the school. Ped. Sem., Oct., 1900. Vol. 7, pp. 347-356.

55. —— —— Recent Italian educational literature. Ed. Rev., Oct., 1900. Vol. 20, pp. 278-288.
Reviews the recent child-study literature of Italy.

56. —— —— The child. A study in the evolution of man. Scribner's, N. Y., 1900. Vol. 12, pp. 498.
A study of the child in the light of evolution. Bibliography contains 696 titles.

57. **Chalmers, Lillian H.** Studies in imagination. Ped. Sem., April, 1900. Vol. 7, pp. 111-123.

58. **Chancellor, W. E.** The organization of local societies. Proc. N. J. Assoc. for the study of Children and Youth, Jan., 1900, pp. 62-65.

59. **Channing, Walter** Special classes for mentally defective children. Jour. of Psycho-Asthenics, Dec., 1900. Vol. 5, pp. 40-46.

60. **Chapin, H. D.** Epidemic paralysis in children. Pediatrics, 1900. Vol. 17, pp. 807-812.

61. **Child Study** in France. School Journal, Feb. 24, 1900. Vol. 60, p. 209.

62. **Children's** claim upon childhood. Rep. Comm. of Ed., 1899-1900. Vol. 1, pp. 810-825.

63. **Children's** valuation of money. N. Y. School Jour., April 21, 1900. Vol. 60, p. 427.

64. **Chrisman, Oscar** (Editor) Paidology: the science of the child. Emporia, Kansas, 1900. Vol. 1.
A series of brief articles by the students in the State Normal School at Emporia, Kansas.

65. —— —— The purpose and place of paidology. Child Study Mo., Oct., 1900. Vol. 6, pp. 149-150.

66. **Christopher, W. S.** Child study in Chicago public schools. Child Study Mo., Oct., 1900. Vol. 6, pp. 127-140.
   Preliminary résumé. See next title.

67. —— —— Report on child study investigation. Reprinted from Annual Rep. Board of Ed. of Chicago, 1898-1899, pp. 48.
   Detailed account, with many tables and charts of anthropometric investigations on Chicago school children.

69. **Clark, A. C.** On epileptic speech. Jour. of Ment. Sci., 1900. Vol. 46, pp. 242-254.

70. **Clouston, T. S.** What the brain has to do in youth besides "getting educated." Child Study Mo., March, 1900. Vol. 5, pp. 417-424.

71. **Colegrove, F. W.** Memory: an inductive study. Henry Holt and Co., N. Y., 1900, pp. 369.
   The latest and best study of the psychology of memory. Contains a chapter on individual memories and one on pedagogical applications.

72. **Colozza, G. A.** Psychologie und Pädagogik des Kinderspiels. Aus dem Italienischen übersetzt von Chr. Ufer. O. Bonde. Altenburg, 1900, pp. 272.
   The translator has included in this useful handbook on the psychology and pedagogy of play a valuable introduction and many useful foot-notes.

73. **Compayre, Gabriel** Entwicklung der Kindesseele. Int. Päd. Bibliothek. Herausg. von Chr. Ufer. Band I. O. Bonde, Altenburg, 1900, pp. 460.
   The German translation of a standard French work, the first part of which has been translated into English.

74. **Corporal Punishment** in the elementary schools of Prussia. Rep. Comm. of Ed., 1899-1900. Vol. 1, pp. 878-883.

75. **Cotgreave, A.** A contents-subject index to general and periodical literature. Elliot Stock, London, 1900, pp. 744.
   Gives references to boys, girls, children, etc.

76. **Croswell, T. R.** L'École des Roches; a school of the twentieth century. Ped. Sem., Dec., 1900. Vol. 7, pp. 479-491.
   First extended American appreciation of this new institution.

77. **Crouter, A. L. E.** Teaching deaf mutes. N. Y. School Jour., July 28, 1900. Vol. 61, pp. 88-89.

78. **Cry** of children N. Y. School Jour., Jan. 27, 1900. Vol. 60, p. 99.

79. **Danger, O.** Die Erblichkeit der Taubheit. Die Kinderfehler, 1900. Vol. 5, pp. 44-47 ; 67-71.
   Based upon an American study by Fay. Argues for the inheritance of deafness.

80. **Danziger, F.** Die Missbildungen des Gaumes und ihr Zusammenhang mit Nase, Auge und Ohr. Bergmann, Wiesbaden, 1900.
   This discussion of palatal malformations in relation to nose, eye and ear, contains, among other things, measurements of 286 pupils of the Ratibor Institution for Deaf Mutes.

81. **Danziger, F.** Schädel und Auge. Eine Studie über die Bezie-
hungen zwischen den Anomalien des Schädelbaues und des
Auges. Bergmann, Wiesbaden, 1900, pp. 56.
A general discussion of the relations between cranial and eye anomalies.
Treats of growth of skull in years of childhood, myopia, etc.

82. **Darwin, Charles** A biographical sketch of an infant. Pop.
Sci. Mo., June, 1900. Vol. 57, pp. 197-205.
Reprint of a paper published in Mind. 1877. Vol. 2, pp. 285-294.

83. **Dawson, George E.** Children's interest in the bible. Ped.
Sem., July, 1900. Vol. 7, pp. 151-178.
A suggestive contribution to the psychology and pedagogy of religion.

84. **Deahl, J. N.** Imitation in education. Columbia Univ. Contrib.
to Philos. The Macmillan Co., New York, 1900, pp. 103.

85. **Dearborn, G. V. N.** The nature of the smile and laugh. Science, June 1, 1900, N. S. Vol. 11, pp. 851-855.

86. **Defective** children of the school age in Switzerland. Report
Comm. of Ed., 1899-1900. Vol. 1, pp. 855-858.

87. **Defective Vision** of board school children. (From the London
Times) Science, N. Y., Aug. 17, 1900, N. S. Vol. 12, pp. 274-275.

88. **Delitsch, Johs.** Über Schülerfreundschaften in einer Volks-
schulklasse. Kinderfehler, 1900. Vol. 5, pp. 150-163.
A statistical study of the school-friendships of boys.

89. **Delobel, J.** Hygiène de l' écolier. Ann. de Méd. et Chir. in-
fantiles, 1900. Vol. 4, pp. 265-276.

90. **Demoor, J.** Die physiologischen Grundlagen einer angemess-
enen körperlichen Erziehung abnormer Kinder. Kinderfehler,
1900. Vol. 5, pp. 174-177; 201-205.

91. —— —— Le traitement des idiots du premier degré. J. Méd.,
Bruxelles, 1900. Vol. 5, 161-164.

92. **Dennis, Margaret E.** A story of one child. Child Study Mo.,
Apr., 1900. Vol. 5, pp. 465.466.

93. **Dexter, Edwin G.** School deportment and the weather. Ed.
Rev., Feb., 1900. Vol. 19, pp. 160-168.

94. **Dodd, Catherine I.** A study of the early instruction of twin
boys. National Review (London), June, 1899. Vol. 33, pp. 622-
636.
Describes an experiment in individual education.

95. —— —— School children's ideals. National Review (London),
Feb., 1900. Vol. 34, pp. 875-889.

96. **Duprat, G. L.** Les troubles de la parole chez l' enfant. Manuel
Gén. de l' Instruction Primaire. May 5, 1900, No. 18, pp. 277-
279.

97. **Eby, Frederick** The reconstruction of the kindergarten. Ped.
Sem., July, 1900. Vol. 7, pp. 229-286.
Valuable for the new orientation of the kindergarten.

98. **Elmiger, Dr.** Ueber 49 Fälle von Pubertätsirresein. Allg. Ztsch. f. Psychiat., 1900. Vol. 57, pp. 490-494.

99. **Elsenhaws, T.** Ueber individuelle und Gattungsanlagen. Ztsch. f. päd. Psychol. u. Path., Feb., 1900. Vol. 2, pp. 41-49.

100. **Emmons, Bertha E.** Humane instincts of children. Jour. of Pedagogy, Oct., 1900. Vol. 13, pp. 110-116.

101. **Engelmann, Geo. J.** The American girl of to-day. (Reprint from the Am. Jour. of Obstetrics. Vol. 42, No. 6, 1900. Also Trans. Am. Gynec. Soc., 1900.) pp. 45.
    A careful and authoritative study.

102. **Everett, Ruth** Against kindergarten. Child Study Mo., Sept., 1900. Vol. 6, pp. 106-110.
    Based on Dr. W. Oppenheim's views.

103. **Feilchenfeld, W.** Medizinkasten für Schulen. Zeit. für Schulgesundheitspflege, 1900. Vol. 13, pp. 88-92.

104. **Forbush, William B.** How to help boys. "The men of tomorrow," Charlestown, Boston, 1900, pp. 52.
    Short articles by various writers. Contains also a directory of the principal kinds of boys' clubs in the U. S.

105. —————— The social pedagogy of boyhood. Ped. Sem., Oct., 1900. Vol. 7, pp. 307-346.

106. **Foster, H. W.** Child study personally applied. N. E. Jour. of Ed., July 12, 1900. Vol. 52, pp. 53-54.

107. **Frenzel, Fr.** Das Lebens- und Personalbuch im Dienste der Pädagogik und Schulhygiene. Zeit.für Schulgesundheitspflege, 1900. Vol. 13, pp. 607-615.

108. **Freudenberg, F.** Ueber Spiegelschrift. Psychische Studien, 1900. Vol. 27, pp. 346-351.

109. **Geheeb-Föhr, Paul** Ein Beitrag zur Behandlung der konstitutionellen Schwäche im Kindesalter. Zeit.für Schulgesundheitspflege, 1900. Vol. 13, pp. 215-225.

110. **Gelpke, T.** Ueber den Einfluss der Steilschrift auf die Augen und die Schreibhaltung der Karlsruher Volksschuljugend. Ztsch. f. Schulgesundheitspfl,, 1809. Vol. 12, pp. 247-319.

111. **Gerhardi,** —— Psychologie in Bezug auf Pädogogik und Schulgesundheitspflege. Zeit für Schulgesundheitspflege, 1900. Vol. 13, pp. 543-551.

112. **Gilbert, Charles B.** Youth study in the high school. Child Study Mo., Jan., 1900. Vol. 5, pp. 317-319.

113. **Gilman, Charlotte P.** Concerning children. Small, Maynard & Co., Boston, 1900. pp. 298.
    A practical talk by a mother.

114. **Ginsburg,** —— De épilepsie chez l' enfant dans ses rapports avec l' évolution dentaire (Thèse). Montpellier, 1900.

115. **Gonnelli-Cioni, C.** Phrénasthénie infantile. Journ. d' Hyg., 1900. Vol. 25, pp. 3-6.

116. **Goubert, Elie** Les maladies des enfants a Paris. Rapport de la mortalité avec la morbidité caractéristique de la maladie chez l' enfant. Baillière et Fils, Paris, 1891, pp. 164.
    A valuable statistical and sociological study.

117. **Gray, J. and Tocher, J. F.** The physical characteristics of adults and school children in East Aberdeenshire. Jour. Anthrop. Inst., London, 1900. N. S. Vol. 3, pp. 104-124.
    Results of investigation of shape of the nose, hair and eyes of 14,561 children, and 3,262 adults. Measurements of stature, etc.

118. **Greenwood, James M.** Report on high school statistics. Proc. N. E. A., 1900, pp. 340-351.
    Gives statistics of children leaving high schools and causes for same.

119. **Gregory, B. C.** The rationale of spelling. Proc. N. J. Ass. for the Study of Children and Youth, Jan., 1900, pp. 43-61.

120. **Grohmann, A.** Der Schwachsinnige und seine Stellung in der Gesellschaft. Für Eltern und Lehrer. Ed. Rascher, Zürich, 1900.
    A sociological study of the feeble-minded.

121. **Groszmann, M. P. E.** Perversion through environment. Child Study Mo., Sept., 1900. Vol. 6, pp. 116-117.

122. —— —— The ethics of child study. Monist, October, 1900. Vol. 11, pp. 65-86.

123. **Grothe, A.** Ueber Schuleinrichtungen für schwachbegabte Kinder. Zeit. für Schulgesundheitspflege, 1900. Vol. 13, pp. 557-559.

124. **Grünewald, H.** Ueber die Kinderfehler der Grausamkeit. Kinderfehler, 1900. Vol. 5, pp. 38-41.
    Cites cases of cruelty to animals on the part of a boy of eight, physically and intellectually sound.

125. —— —— Ueber die Kinderfehler des Eigensinns. Kinderfehler, 1900. Vol. 5, pp. 205-209.
    Credits the home with the development of hyperobstinacy in children.

126. **Guillet, Cephas** Recapitulation and education. Ped Sem., Oct., 1900. Vol. 7, pp. 397-445.
    A valuable discussion of the pedagogical import of the recapitulation of race-life in the individual.

127. **Gumbertz, K.** Beitrag zu den im Kindesalter auftretenden Seelenstörungen. Arch. für Psychiat., 1900. Vol. 33, pp. 326-331.

128. **Gutberlet, C.** Zur Psychologie des Kindes. Philos. Jahrb., 1899-1900. Vol. 12, pp. 365-381. Vol. 13, pp. 22-36.
    Devoted especially to a discussion of Baldwin's investigations and theory of development.

129. **Gutzmann, H.** Neueres über Taubstummheit und Taubstummbildung. Berl. Klinik, 1900. Vol. 142, pp. 20.

130. **Hakonson-Hansen, M. K.** Schulgebäude nach dem Pavillonsystem in Drontheim. Zeit. für Schulgesundheitspflege, 1900. Vol. 13, pp. 205-215.

131. **Hall, A.** Hysteria in boys aud youth. Quart. Med. Journ., 1900, pp, 393-405.

132. **Hall, G. Stanley** Some defects of the kindergarten in America. The Forum, Jan., 1900. Vol. 28, pp. 579-591.

133. —— —— The ministry of pictures. Perry Mag., Feb., Mar., Apr., May, 1900. Vol. 2, pp. 243-245; 291-292; 339-340; 387-388.

134. —— —— College philosophy. Forum, June, 1900. Vol. 29, pp. 409-422.

135. —— —— Child study and its relation to education. Forum, Aug., 1900. Vol. 29, pp. 688-702.

136. —— —— The educational value of the social side of student life. I. In America. Outlook, Aug. 4, 1900. Vol. 65, pp. 798-801.

137. —— —— The use of a doctrinal catechism in Sunday-School instruction. Biblical World, Sept., 1900. Vol. 16, pp. 175-176.

138. —— —— Student customs. Proc. Am. Antiq. Soc., Oct. 24, 1900. N. S. Vol. 14, pp. 83-124.

139. —— —— The religious content of the child mind. Chap. 7, in "Principles of Religious Education." Longmans, Green & Co., N. Y., 1900, pp. 161-189.

140. **Hall, G. S. and Saunders, F. H.** Pity. Am. Jour of Psy., July, 1900. Vol. 11, pp. 534-591.

141. **Hall, Mrs. W. S.** The beginnings of sensuality. Child Study Mo., Feb., 1900. Vol. 5, pp. 374-377.

142. **Halle, ——** Ueber Störungen der Atmung bei Stottern. Monatsschr. f. d. ges. Sprachhk., 1900. Vol. 10, pp. 225-236.

143. **Hanus, Paul H.** The school and the home. International Monthly, Dec., 1900. Vol. 2, pp. 647-671.

144. **Harris, William T.** The study of arrested development in the child as produced by injudicious school methods. Education, April, 1900. Vol. 20, pp. 453-467.

145. **Hastings, William W.** Anthropometric studies in Nebraska. Am. Phys. Ed. Rev., March, 1900. Vol. 5, pp. 53-66.
   Epitomizes researches on school children in Lincoln and Omaha. Detail to be published later.

146. **Headland, Isaac T.** Chinese mother goose rhymes. F. H. Revell Co., N. Y., 1900, pp. 157.
   Author thinks there are more nursery rhymes in China than in England or America.

147. **Heffron, John L.** Diet of school children. Jour. of Pedagogy, March, 1900. Vol. 12, pp. 285-294.

148. **Heller, T.** Ueber Ermüdungsmessungen bei schwachsinnigen Kindern. Zeits. f. d. Behandl. Schwachs. u. Epil., 1898. Vol. 14, pp. 136-150.

149. **Herfeldt, A.** Zur Casuistik des Irreseins bei Zwillingen. Allg. Ztschr. f. Psychiat., 1900. Vol. 57, pp. 24-39.

150. **Heubner, O.** Die Entwickelung des kindlichen Gehirns in den letzten Fœtal- und ersten Lebensmonaten. Zeits. f. Päd. Psy. u. Path., April, 1900. Vol. 2, pp. 73-83.

151. **Hill, C. H.** Dementia præcox. Amer. Jour. Insan., 1900. Vol. 57, pp. 319-324.

152. **Hodge, C. F.** Foundations of nature study. II-III. Ped. Sem., April and July, 1900. Vol. 7, pp. 95-110 ; 208-228.
Shortly to appear in book form under the title of Nature Study and Life.

153. **Hofer, Mari Ruef** The educational use of music for children. Kindergarten Rev., Sept., 1900. Vol. 11, pp. 15-20 ; Proc. N. E. A., 1900, pp. 397-402.

154. **Holden, W. A. and Bosse, K. K.** The order of development of color perception and of color preference in the child. Arch. of Ophthalmology, 1900. Vol. 29, pp. 261-278.

155. **Horrix, H.** Worin hat die Abneigung einzelner Eltern gegen die Hilfsschule ihren Grund, und wie ist sie zu beseitigen? Kinderfehler, 1900. Vol. 5, pp. 168-173.

156. **Howard, Frances E.** Gaining knowledge through the senses. N. Y. School Journal, March 10, 1900. Vol. 60, p. 271.

157. **Hubbell, George Allen** The child and the bible. Syllabus of a course of 25 lessons in education. For bible teachers, Sunday school teachers and parents. The Author, N. Y., Sept. 1900, pp. 76.

158. **Irving, Arthur P.** Home reading of school children. Ped. Sem., April, 1900. Vol. 7, pp. 138-140.

159. **Jenks, Albert E.** The childhood of Ji-shib, the Ojibwa, and sixty-four pen sketches. Am. Thresherman, Madison, Wis., 1900, pp. 130.
From this little volume we may really learn something of the Indian child.

160. **Jerome, Jerome K.** The German school boy. Literature (London), Oct. 27, 1900. Vol. 7, pp. 311-313.

161. **Johnson, George E.** Some facts of child-development and their relation to school work and school grading. Report of the Andover (Mass.), School Committee for the year 1900, pp. 10-24.
Deals with the relation of the physical and the mental.

162. **Johnson, N. C.** Habits of work and methods of study of high school pupils in some cities in Indiana. School Review (Chicago), May, 1899. Vol. 7, pp. 257-277.

163. **Johnston, Fanny L.** Physical education for little children. Kindergarten Rev., March, 1900. Vol. 10, pp. 410-414.

164. **Johnstone, E. R.** The training of normal and feeble minds. Proc. N. J. Association for the Study of Children and Youth, Jan., 1900, pp. 17-27 ; also Proc. N. E. A., 1900, pp. 677-680.

165. **Judd, Chas. H.** Movement and mental development. N. E. Jour. of Ed., Jan. 11, 1900. Vol. 51, pp. 19-20.

166. —— —— Studies in genetic psychology. Jour. of Pedagogy, Oct., 1900. Vol. 13, pp. 75-85.

167. **Kaler, A.** Hystérie chez les enfants (Thése), Crépin-Leblond-Nancy, 1900.

168. **Kemp, H.** Overwork in the schools. Am. Phys. Ed. Rev. March, 1900. Vol. 5, pp. 114-116.

169. **Kerr, James** School hygiene in its mental, moral and physical aspects. Jour. Roy. Statistical Soc., London, Sept., 1897. Vol. 60, pp. 613-680.

170. **Kemsies, F.** Gedächtnisuntersuchungen an Schülern. I und II. Zeits. f. Päd. Psy. u. Path., Feb.-April, 1900. Vol. 2, pp. 21, 30 ; 84-94.

171. **Kirkpatrick, E. A.** Individual tests of school children. Psy. Rev., May, 1900. Vol. 7, pp. 274-280.

172. **Knies, M.** On a frequent but hitherto unrecognized form of congenital violet-blindness and on color anomalies in general. Arch. of Ophthalmology, 1900. Vol. 29, pp. 491-502.

173. **Közle, J. F. G.** Die pädagogische Pathologie in der Erziehungskunde des 19. Jahrhunderts. C. Bertelsmann, Gütersloh, 1893. pp. 492.

174. **Kratz, H. E.** A study in musical interpretation. Proc. N. E. A., 1900. pp. 590-591.

175. **Kuhn, Maurice** Portraits d' enfants. L'Ecole Nouvelle, July 28, 1900. Vol. 3, pp. 172-174.

176. **Landmann, S.** Ein schlechtes Gedächtnis. Die Kinderfehler, 1900. Vol. 5, pp. 10-25; 49-66.

177. **Langsdorf, E.** Beiträge zum gegenwärtigen Stand der Steilschrift. Zeit. für Schulgesundheitspflege, 1900. Vol. 13, pp. 365-374.

178. **Lawrence, H. Cripps** Habit in childhood. Paidologist, April, 1900. Vol. 2, pp. 22-25.

179. **Lay, W. A.** Didaktisch-psychologisches Experiment, Rechtschreiben und Rechtschreibunterricht. Zeits. Päd. Psy. u. Path., April, 1900. Vol. 2, pp. 95-112.

180. **Lehmensiek, Fritz** Ueber das Prinzip des Arbeitsunterrichts und über die Sittlichkeit des Kindes. Kinderfehler, 1900. pp. 163-167.

181. **Leuba, James H.** The personifying passion in youth with remarks upon the sex and gender problem. Monist, July, 1900. Vol. 10, pp. 536-549.

182. **Liepmann, H.** Sprachstörung und Sprachentwickelung. Neurol. Centralbl., 1900. Vol. 19, pp. 695-703.

183. **Lindberg, K.** Zur Häufigkeit des Stotterns bei Schulkindern. Monatsschr. f. d. ges. Sprachlk., 1900. Vol. 10, pp. 281-286.

184. **Livi, Ridolfo** Antropometria. Ulrico Hoepli, Milano, 1900. pp. 237.
   A useful little manual of the chief facts and technique of anthropometry.

185. **Lobsien, M.** Ueber die psychologisch-pädagogischen Methoden zur Erforschung der geistigen Ermüdung. Zeits. f. päd. Psy. u. Path., 1900. Vol. 2, pp. 273-286.

186. **Loisel, G.** Précocité et périodicité sexuelles chez l' homme. C. R. Acád. d. Sci., 1900. Vol. 131, pp. 725-727.

187. **Lueddeckens, F.** Rechts- und Linkshändigkeit. Engelmann, 1900. pp. 82.

188. **Lyttelton, E.** Training of the young in laws of sex. Longmans, Green & Co., London and N. Y., 1900. pp. 117.
   Expansion of an article in Int. Jour. of Ethics, July, 1899.

189. **Maass, B.** Die Psychologie in ihrer Anwendung auf die Schulpraxis. (8. Aufl.) F. Hirt, Breslau, 1899. pp. 84.

190. **MacCunn, John** The making of character. Some educational aspects of ethics. The Macmillan Co., N. Y., 1900. pp. 226.

191. **MacDonald, Arthur** Neurere amerikanische Arbeiten auf dem Gebiet der Kinderforschung. Zeits. f. Päd. Psy. u. Path., April, 1900. Vol. 2. Heft 2, pp. 112-121.

192. **MacNamara, N. C.** The human brain in relation to education. Westminster Rev., 1900. Vol. 154, pp. 634-640.

193. **McGhee, Zach** A study in the play life of some South Carolina children. Ped. Sem., Dec., 1900. Vol. 7, pp. 459-478.
   Valuable by reason of the mass of data considered.

194. **McKenzie, R. T.** The place of physical training in a school system. Montreal, Med. Jour., 1900. Vol. 29, pp. 30-36.

195. **McLeish, Martha V.** Child study in the home. Child Study Mo., Nov., 1900. Vol. 6, pp. 188-196.

196. **McMillan, Margaret** Early childhood. With 5 illustrations. Swan, Sonnenschein & Co., London, 1900. pp. 211.

197. **Marro, Antonio** Pubertal hygiene in relation to pedagogy and sociology. Am. Jour. of Sociology, Sept., 1900. Vol. 6, pp. 224-237.
   Treats of food, sleep, emotions, games, occupations, etc., etc.

198. **Mathews, Byron C.** A sociological study of high school students out of school. Proc. N. J. Association for the study of Children and Youth, Jan., 1900. pp. 28-42.

199. **Mead, William E.** Is spelling a lost art? Ed. Rev., Jan., 1900. Vol. 19, pp. 49-58.

200. **Messer, August** Kritische Untersuchungen über Denken, Sprechen und Sprachunterricht. Sammlung Abh. a. d. Geb. d. Päd., Psy., u. Physiol., 1900. Heft. 6, pp. 51.

201. **Meyer, Max** How a musical education should be acquired in the public school. Ped. Sem., April, 1900. Vol. 7, pp. 124-131.

202. **Monroe, Will S.** Comenius and the beginnings of educational reform. Charles Scribner's Sons, N. Y., 1900. pp. 184.
    Chapter seven (pp. 109-122) gives Comenius's views on the earliest education of the child.

203. —— —— Das Studium der Kinderpsychologie in amerikanischen Normalschulen. Zeits. f. Päd. Psy. u. Path., Feb., 1900. Vol. 2, pp. 30-41.

204. —— —— Rights of children; a study in juvenile altruism. Ped. Sem., April, 1900. Vol. 7, pp. 132-137.

205. —— —— Moral Training of young children. N. Y. School Jour., April 28, 1900. Vol. 60, p. 452.

206. **Morgan, C. Lloyd** An unspoken address. Paidologist, July, 1900. Vol. 2, pp. 72-76.

207. —— —— Animal behavior. E. Arnold, London and New York, 1900. pp. 344.

208. **Mouton, J. M. C.** Ist es möglich die Mortalität infolge von Masern durch gesetzliche Bestimmungen herabzudrücken? Zeit. f. Schulgesundheitspflege, 1900. Vol. 13, pp. 374-379.

209. **Netschajeff, Alexander** Experimentelle Untersuchungen über die Gedächtnissentwickelung bei Schulkindern. Zeits. f. Psychologie, 1900. Vol. 24, pp. 321-351.
    A valuable study on school children. See review by Will S. Monroe in Psy. Rev., July, 1901. Vol. 8, pp. 436-437.

210. —— —— Zur Frage über die normale geistige Arbeit. Zeit. f. Schulgesundheitspflege, 1900. Vol. 13, pp. 137-153.

211. **Niel, Harriet** The kindergarten gifts. Proc. N. E. A., 1900. pp. 383-390.

212. **Nissen, Hartvig** Swimming a necessity in education. Am. Phys. Ed. Rev., March, 1900. Vol. 5, pp. 74-80.

213. **Nitobe, I.** Bushido, the soul of Japan. Leeds & Biddle Co., Phila., 1900. pp. 127.

214. **Norton, Abbey N.** Self activity in the student. Kindergarten Rev., Jan., 1900. Vol. 10, pp. 289-291.

215. **Noyes, William** Summer play grounds in Chicago. Am. Phys. Ed. Rev., March, 1900. pp. 186-187.

216. **O'Shea, M. V.** Aspects of mental economy. Bulletin of the
    University of Wisconsin, Madison, 1900. pp. 198.
    An essay in some phases of dynamics of mind, with particular observa-
    tion on the students in the University of Wisconsin. A most valuable
    contribution to the literature of dietaries from the standpoint of the psy-
    chologist and with special reference to the relative value of foods in the
    production of nervous energy.

217. **Observation** of some moral aspects of children. Paidologist,
    July, 1900. Vol. 2, pp. 64-72.

218. **Ohlert, A.** Das Studium der Sprachen und die geistige Bil-
    dung. Abh. a. d. Geb. d. päd. Psychol. Vol. 2, Heft. 7. Reu-
    ther & Reichard, Berlin, 1899. pp. 50.

219. **Olerich, H.** The cleverest child in the world. Strand Mag.,
    Sept., 1900. Vol. 20, pp. 130-136.

220. **Oliver, Thomas** An address on the physiology and pathology
    of inheritance, or what do we inherit from our parents? Lan-
    cet, Nov., 10, 1900. Vol. 2, 1900. pp. 1335-1341.
    A lecture delivered in the Newcastle-upon-Tyne Royal Infirmary, Oct.
    31, 1900.

221. **Olsen, J.** Children's ideas. Paidologist, November, 1900.
    Vol. 2, pp. 128-131.

222. **Oltuszewski, W.** Psychologie und Philosophie der Sprache.
    Monatss. f. d. ges. Sprachhk., 1900. Vol. 10, pp. 97-121; 140-184.

223. **Oppenheim, Nathan** The medical diseases of childhood,
    with 101 original illustrations and 19 charts. The Macmil-
    lan Co., N. Y., 1900. pp. 653.

224. **Overton, F.** The physician as a factor in education. Med.
    Record, 1900. Vol. 57, pp. 320-321.

225. **Paedologisch Jaarboek, Schuyten, M. C.** (Editor.) Ant-
    werp, 1900. pp. 210.
    This is the year-book of the pedagogical laboratory of the city of Ant-
    werp. It contains two noteworthy studies by Dr. Schuyten—one on the
    conditions affecting voluntary attention of school children (pp. 1-109), and
    the other on the adaptation of manual training to eyesight of girls. (See
    SCHUYTEN.)

226. **Pappenheim,K.** Die Kinderzeichnung im Anschauungsunter-
    richt. Ztschr. f. päd. Psychol., 1900. Vol. 2, pp. 161-190.

227. **Pater, Walter H.** The child in the house. Macmillan's
    Mag., Aug., 1878. Vol. 38, pp. 313-321.

228. **Perier, E.** Children's sleep. Paidologist, July, 1900. Vol. 2,
    pp. 82-83.

229. **Piper, ——** Wie können wir die sprachlosen schwachsinni-
    gen Kinder zum Sprechen bringen? Ztschr. f. d. Behandl.
    Schwachs. u. Epil., 1898. Vol. 14, pp. 100-108.

230. **Plettenberg, P.** Neuere Abhandlungen und Untersuchungen
    über das Gedächtnis. Zeits. f. Hypnotismus, 1900. Vol. 10,
    pp. 91-113.

231. **Poulsson, Emilie** The child's senses. Kindergarten Rev., Feb., 1900. Vol. 10, pp. 352-354.

232. **Powel, F. P.** Evolution and environment. School Journal, Sept. 22, 1900. Vol. 61, pp. 286-287.

233. —— —— Evolution and morals. School Journal, Oct. 6, 1900. Vol. 61, pp. 309-310.

234. —— —— Evolution and education. School Jour., Oct. 20, 1900. Vol. 61, pp. 369-370.

235. **Preiss, O.** Die heimlichen Jugendsünden als Ursache der Schwächlichkeit unseres Geschlechts. Kinderfehler, 1900. Vol. 5, pp. 102-109.
Argues for parental honesty and counsel in the matter of sexual development in children.

236. **Principles of** religious education. A course of lectures delivered under the auspices of the sunday school commission of the diocese of New York, with an introduction by the Rt. Rev. Henry C. Potter, D. D., Bishop of N. Y. Longmans, Green & Co., N. Y., 1900. pp. 292.

237. **Punishment of** children. Child Study Mo., Apr., 1900. Vol. 5, pp. 456-460.

238. **Ratzel, Friedrich** Mythen und Einfälle über den Ursprung der Völker. Globus, July 14-21, 1900. Vol. 78, pp. 21-25; 45-48.

239. **Rauber, A.** Der Ueberschuss an Knabengeburten und seine biologische Bedeutung. Georgi, Leipzig, 1900. pp. 220.
An attempt to account for the excess of male over female births with résumés of the literature of the subject.

240. **Reik, H. O.** Report on the examination of the ears of 440 school children. Johns Hopkins Hospital Bulletin, 1900. Vol. 11, pp. 318-321.
Treats of ear-measurements, anomalies, etc., of 215 boys and 225 girls, of whom 378 were between 7 and 17 years of age.

241. **Ribot, Th.** Essai sur l'imagination créatrice. Félix Alcan, Paris, 1900. pp. 304.
The second part (pp. 77-148) discusses the development of imagination in animals, the child, and primitive man.

242. —— —— The nature of the creative imagination. International Monthly, June-July, 1900. Vol. 1, pp. 648-675; Vol. 2, pp. 1-25.

243. **Riemann, G.** Taubstumm u. blind zugleich. Zeits. f. päd. Psy., 1900. Vol. 2, pp. 257-273.

244. **Riemann, P.** Beeinflussung des Seelenlebens durch Taubheit. Kinderfehler, 1900. Vol. 5, pp. 241-269.
A plea for early recognition and pedagogical treatment of the deaf child.

245. —— —— Hörübung in Taubstummenanstalten. Kinderfehler, 1900. Vol. 5, pp. 41-43.
Notes the value of acoustic exercises for the partially deaf.

246. **Rivers, W. H. R.** The senses of primitive man.   Science,
     May 11, 1900.   N. S., Vol. 11, pp. 740-742.
     Abstract of lectures delivered before the Royal Institution, London, Jan.
     and Feb., 1900.

247. **Robinson, Ida E.** Children's ideas of play.   Proc. N. J. Ass.
     for the Study of Children and Youth, Jan., 1900.   pp. 3-16.

248. **Rosin u. Fenyvessy** Ueber das Lipochron der Nervenzellen.
     Arch. f. path. Anat. u. Physiol., 1900.   Vol. 162, pp. 534-540.

249. **Rostowzeff, Gr.** Ueber die Notwendigkeit der Individuali-
     sierung der Schulbänke; eine neue individuelle Schulbank:
     Zeits. f. Schulgesundheitspflege, 1900.   Vol. 13, pp. 295-313.

250. **Roussey, C.** Notes sur l' apprentissage de la parole chez un
     enfant.   La Parole, 1900.   Vol. 10, pp. 23-41; 86-99.

251. **Sabin, Henry** Nurture of moral impulses.   Education, Jan.,
     1900.   Vol. 20, pp. 259-263.

252. **Saint-Paul, G.** Le visuélisme et l'étude des langues.   Rev.
     Scient., 1900.   4th. Ser.   Vol. 14, pp. 239-240.

     Saunders, F. H.   See **Hall and Saunders.**

253. **Saylor, J. F.** Child study—its importance to the home.   Child
     Study Mo., Jan., 1900.   Vol. 5, pp. 306-309.

254. **Schenk, Alwin** Zur Fürsorge für die Geistesschwachen in Hol-
     land, Belgium, Frankreich und Luxemburg.   Kinderfehler,
     1900.   Vol. 5, pp. 270-276.

255. **Schenkendorf, E. v.** Public playgrounds and vacation schools.
     Rep. Comm. of Ed., 1899-1900.   Vol. 1, pp. 895-904.

256. **Schiller, H.** Die Schulartzfrage.   Samml. v. Abh. a. d. Geb.
     d. päd. Psychol. u. Physiol., 1899.   Vol. 3, Part 1, pp. 56.

257. ———— Der Aufsatz in der Muttersprache.   Samml. v. abh.
     a. Geb. d. päd. Psy. u. Physiol., 1900.   Vol. 3, Part 1, pp. 68.

258. **Schneider, Georg** Die Zahl im Grundlegenden Rechenun-
     terricht.   Samml. v. Abh. a. d. Geb. d. päd. Psy. u. Physiol.,
     1900.   Vol. 3, Part 7, pp. 86.

259 **Schmid-Monnard** Ueber den Werth von Körpermassen zur
     Beurtheilung des Körperzustandes von Kindern.   Corresp. d.
     dents. Ges. f. Anthr.   München, 1900.   Vol. 31, pp. 130-133.
     Result of an investigation of 1,021 boys and 1,071 girls, from birth to 14
     years, in Halle.

260. ———— Die Ursachen der Minderbegabung von Schulkindern:
     Zeits. f. Schulgesundheitspflege, 1900.   Vol. 13, pp. 552-556.

261. **Schmidt, F.** Ueber den Reiz des Unterrichtens.   Samml. v.
     abh. a. d. Geb. d. päd. Psy. u. Physiol., 1900.   Vol. 3, Part
     3, pp. 36.

262. **Schmidtmann, Dr.** Medical inspection of the schools in Ger-
     many.   Rep. Comm. of Ed., 1899-1900.   Vol. 1, pp. 825-828.

263. **Schoen, W.** Die durch Krämpfe im Kindesauge bewirkten Veränderungen. Beitr. z. path. Anat., 1900. Vol. 28, pp. 318-322.

264. **Schoenrich, Carl Otto** Aus Jungamerikas Lehrjahren. Pädagogische Monatshefte. The Herold Co., Milwaukee, Wis., April, 1900. Vol. 1, pp. 20-25.

265. **Schreiber, H.** Für das Wohl der Dummen in unsern öffentlichen Schulen. Kinderfehler, 1900. Vol. 5, pp. 185-201.
    A plea for proper treatment of the dull children in the school; argues for the real teacher.

266. **Schreiber, Mae E.** How to direct children in their reading. Proc. N. E. A., 1900. pp. 636-642.

267. **Schreuder, A. J.** Gerrit W., ein psychopathisch minderwertiger Knabe der öffentlichen Schule. Kinderfehler, 1900. Vol. 5, pp. 119-133
    Detailed account of a ten-year-old psychopath in a Dutch public school.

268. **Schubert, Paul** Soll der Schulartz durch den Lehrer ersetzt werden? Zeits. f. Schulgesundheitspflege, 1900. Vol. 13. pp. 589-606.

269. **Schuschny, ——** Geistige Ermüdung kleiner Schulkinder. Arch. f. Verdaunngskr., 1900. Vol. 28, Hefte 5, 6.

270. **Schütte, E.** Die pathologische Anatomie der Idiotie. Centralb. f. allg. Path. u. path. Anat., 1900. Vol. 11, pp. 353-392.

271. **Schuyten, M. C.** Over de toename der spierkracht bij kinderen gedurende het schooljaar. Paedologisch Jaarboek, Antwerpen, 1900. Vol. 1, pp. 1-109.
    A valuable study with brief French résumé,well-provided with statistics of voluntary attention during the school year.

272. **—— ——** In hoeverre is het gezicht der meisjes aangepast bij het verrichten van handwerk in de gewone onderrichts klassen der Antwerpsche gemeentescholen? Paedologisch Jaarboek, Antwerpen, 1900. Vol. 1, pp. 110-125.
    Discusses the effect of manual work on the eyes of girls in Antwerp primary schools.

273. **Schwendt, A.** Des exercises acoustiques pour l' éducation des sourds-muets Ann. d. Mal. d. l' Oreille, 1900. Vol. 26, pp. 490-499.

274. **—— ——** Les restes auditifs des sourds-muets peuvent ils être utilisés pour leur apprendre à mieux parler? La Parole, 1900. Vol. 10, pp. 1-17.

275. **Shaw, Edw. R.** Some observations upon teaching children to write. Child Study Mo., Feb., 1896. Vol. 1, pp. 226-229.

276. **Shinn, Milicent W.** The biography of a baby. Houghton, Mifflin & Co., Boston, 1900. pp. 247.
    An excellent popular treatment. Perhaps the best single book for the mother.

277. **Shuttleworth, G. E.** Anatomie pathologique de l'idiotie. Arch. de Neurol., 1900. Vol. 10, pp. 301-320.

278. —— —— Mentally deficient children. H. K. Lewis, London, 1900. pp. 180.
A revised edition of the best brief treatment of the care and training of mentally deficient children.

279. **Simon, T.** Recherches anthropométriques sur 223 garçons anormaux âgés de 8 à 23 ans. Année Psychol., 1899, Paris, 1900. Vol. 6, 191-247.
Chiefly concerned with relation of physical and mental.

280. **Slack, Hiram W.** Origin and development of the emotional nature. Child Study Mo., Sept., 1900. Vol. 6, pp. 96-105.

281. **Sluys, A.** Abnormally alcoholic children. Rep. Comm. of Ed., 1899-1900. Vol. 1, pp. 604-606.

282. —— —— Methods of the anti-alcoholic school propaganda. Rep. Comm. of Ed., 1899-1900. Vol. 1, pp. 606-612.

283. **Small, Maurice H.** On some psychical relations of society and solitude. Ped. Sem., April, 1900. Vol. 7, pp. 13-69.

284. **Smedley, Fred W.** The work of the child study department in the Chicago public schools. Child Study Mo., May, 1900. Vol. 6, pp. 2-4.

285. —— —— Report of the department of child study and pedagogic investigation containing the report of the committee and report of director Fred W. Smedley. Child Study Report No. 2, Board of Ed. Chicago, 1899-1900. pp. 72. (See also CHRISTOPHER.)
Gives results of further anthropometric studies of Chicago children.

286. **Smith, Fred** [Pseudonym.] The boyhood of a naturalist. Blackie & Son., London, 1900. pp. 227.
A valuable account of the development of the scientific instinct in youth.

287. **Snyckers, ——** Le bégayement et les autres défauts de la parole. Leur traitement pédagogique. Librairie Falk fils, Bruxelles, 1900. pp. 45.

288. **Spaulding, Frank E.** The individual child and his education. A practical plan for the systematic study of children in the schoolroom. F. E. Spaulding, Supt. of Schools, Passaic, N. J., 1900. pp. 18.

289. **Spitzner, A.** Psychogene Störungen der Schulkinder. Ein Capitel der pädagogischen Pathologie. E. Ungleich, Leipzig, 1899. pp. 45.

290. **Stanley, Hiram M.** The psychology of pity. Science, 1900. N. S., Vol. 12, pp. 487-488.

291. **Steinhardt, Ignez** Zur Prophylaxe der Schulepidemien: Zeits. f. Schulgesundheitspflege, 1900. Vol. 13, pp. 1-11.

292. **Stevens, Kate** Lessons from the standpoint of the child. Child Life, Jan., April, July, 1900. Vol. 2, pp. 47-50; 113-115; 171-174.

293. **Stone, James S.** School furniture in relation to lateral curvature. Am. Phys. Ed. Rev., June, 1900. Vol. 5, pp. 142-149.

294. **Street, J. R.** The religion of childhood. Zion's Herald, Boston, Jan. 24, 1900. Vol. 78, pp. 108-109; 118-119.

295. **Stumpf, C.** Zur Methodik der Kinderpsychologie. Zeits. f. Päd. Psy. Path., Feb., 1900. Vol. 2, pp. 1-21.

296. **Sturge, Mary D.** The claims of childhood. Jour. of the Sanitary Institute, London, April, 1899. Vol. 20, pp. 88-96.

297. **Tardieu, E.** L' ennui aux différents âges de la vie. Rev. Bleue, Paris. 1900. 4e ser. Vol. 14, pp. 202-209.

298. **Thiemich, M.** Ueber die Diagonose der Imbecillität im frühen Kindesalter. Deutsche med. Wochensch., 1900. Vol. 26, pp. 34-36.

299. **Thorndike, Edward** Mental fatigue. Psy. Rev., Sept. and Nov., 1900. Vol. 7, pp. 466-482; 547-579.

300. —— —— The parent as a factor in mental development. Child Study Mo., Jan., 1900. Vol. 5, pp. 299-305.

301. **Townsend, E.** Education of the deaf and dumb in its relation to child study. Paidologist, April, 1900. Vol. 2, pp. 3-9.

302. **Töws, J.** Heilpädagogische Anstalten. Zeits. f. Philos. u. Pad. Langensalza, 1900. Vol. 7, pp. 24-40.

   Account, with statistics, of German educational institutions for blind, deaf and dumb, idiotic, feeble-minded children, and of correctional institutions for juvenile criminals.

303. **Trettien, A. W.** Creeping and walking. Am. Jour. of Psy., Oct., 1900. Vol. 12, pp. 1-57.

304. **Triplett, N.** The psychology of conjuring deceptions. Am. Jour. of Psy., July, 1900. Vol. 11, pp. 439-510.

305. **Truant Schools.** Rep. Comm. of Ed., 1899-1900. Vol. 1, pp. 85-219.

306. **Trüper, J.** Zum Gesetz über die Zwangserziehung Minderjähriger in Preussen. Kinderfehler, 1900. Vol. 5, pp. 137-150. (See also pp. 109-119.)

   Discusses the new Prussian law for the compulsory education of minors and the problems connected with it.

307. —— —— Fürsorge für unsere sittlich gefährdete Jungend. Kinderfehler, 1900. Vol. 5, pp. 209-211.

308. **Ufer, Chr.** Psychologie und Pädagogik der Kinderspiels. Kinderfehler, 1900. Vol. 5, pp. 286-288.

309. **Upham, A. A.** Transportation of rural school children at public expense. Ed. Rev., Oct., 1900. Vol. 20, pp. 241-251.

310. **Vaschide, N.** Experimental researches upon the creative imagination in the child. Paidologist, Nov., 1900. Vol. 2, pp. 111-113.

311. **Voisin, J.** The psychoses of puberty. N. Y. Med. Jour., 1900.
Vol. 72, pp. 634-636.

312. **Ward, Phyllis** The parental instinct. (Dolls.) Kindergarten Rev., Nov., 1900. Vol. 11, pp. 132-135.

313. **Watson, Foster** Mrs. Meynel and her historic account of childhood. Paidologist, Nov., 1900. Vol. 2, pp. 124-128.

314. **Wells, David W.** Sight and hearing of school children. N. E. Jour. of Ed., Feb. 15, 1900. Vol. 51, p. 99.

315. **Wiedeburg, ——** Ueber die Notwendigkeit der Erbauung von populär-medizinischen Unterrichtsanstalten. Kinderfehler, 1900. Vol. 5, pp. 71-77.

316. **Wiese, Dr.** Ueber Kinderfron und Kinderschutz. Kinderfehler, 1900. Vol. 5, pp. 32-36.
General discussion of child labor and its results in the various countries of Europe.

317. **Wilson, Louis N.** Bibliography of child study for the year 1899. Ped. Sem., Dec., 1900. Vol. 7, pp. 526-556.
A dictionary list of the books and articles on child study published during the year 1899.

318. **Wilson, T.** Criminology. Proc. Am. Ass. Adv. of Sci., 1900.
Vol. 49, pp. 294-300.
Rejects Lombroso's theory.

319. **Winship, A. E.** Jukes-Edwards; a study in education and heredity. R. L. Meyers & Co., Harrisburg, Pa., 1900. pp. 88.
An important study in heredity and degeneracy.

320. **Winterburn, R. V.** Some studies of children in teaching history. Education, Sept., 1899. Vol. 20, pp. 37-44.

321. **Wiskel, Anna Hamlin** The child and his book. Education, May, 1900. Vol. 20, pp. 544-548.

322. **Wreschner, A.** Eine experimentelle Studie ü. d. Association in einem Falle von Idiotie. Allg. Zeits. f. Psychiatrie, 1900.
Vol. 57, pp. 241-339.

323. **Wundt, Wilhelm** Völkerpsychologie: ein Untersuchung der Entwickelungsgesetze von Sprache, Mythus und Sitte. Englemann, Leipzig, 1900. Vol. 1, parts 1 and 2, pp. 627 and 642.
The first and second volumes of this comprehensive work deal with the origin and growth of language among primitive people and children.

324. **Wurdemann, H. V. and Allport, F.** The sight and hearing of school children. Jour. Am. Med. Ass'n, 1900. Vol. 34, pp. 1111-1116.

325. **Wylie, A. R. T.** A study of the senses of the feeble-minded. Jour. of Psycho-Asthenics, June, 1900. Vol. 4, pp. 137-150.

326. **—— ——** Motor ability and control of the feeble-minded. Jour. of Psycho-Asthenics, Dec., 1900. Vol. 5, pp. 52-58.

327. **Yan Phou Lee** When I was a boy in China. Lothrop Pub. Co., Boston (1887), pp. 111.

328. **Yule, G. U.** On the association of attributes in statistics, with examples from the material of the childhood society, etc. Proc. Roy. Soc., 1900. Vol. 66, pp. 22-23.

329. **Ziegler, K.** Zum Egoismus einziger Kinder. Kinderfehler, 1900. Vol. 5, pp. 89-101.
Treats in general fashion, of the egoism of "only children."

330. **Ziehen, Th.** Die Ideenassoziation des Kindes. Samml. v. Abh. a. d. Geb. d. Päd. Psy. u. Physiol., 1900. Heft. 4, pp. 59.
A valuable study of the association of ideas in the child.

331. —— —— Das Verhältnis der Herbartschen Psychologie zur Physiologisch-experimentellen Psychologie. Samml. von Abh. a. d. Geb. d. Päd. Psy. u. Physiol., 1900. Heft. 5, pp. 79.

SUBJECT INDEX.

Adolescence, 20, 98.
Æsthetics, 49.
Alcoholism, 281, 282.
Altruism, 204.
Ambitions, 10, 11, 95.
America, 264.
Anatomy, 270.
Animals, 207.
Anthropology, 53.
Anthropometry, 50, 66, 67, 80, 81, 117, 145, 184, 240, 279, 285.
Aphasia, 23.
Architecture, 130.
Arithmetic, 258.
Arrested Development, 8, 15, 53, 144, 265, 278.
Art, 56.
Association, 322, 330.
Asymetry, 187.
Association, 23.
Atavism, 40, 56.
Attention, 225, 271.
Auxiliary School, 155.

Baby, 40, 276.
Backward Children, 44.
Bible, 47, 83, 157.
Bibliography, 55, 75, 230, 317.
Biography, 107, 276.
Births, 239.
Blind, 243.
Boys, 104, 105, 131, 160, 239.
Brain, 70, 150, 192.
Breathing, 142.
Buildings, 130.

Catechism, 137.
Character, 190.
Chicago, 66, 67, 285.
Child and Savage, 56.

Childhood, 56, 62.
Child Labor, 316.
Child-Life, 33.
Child Study, 5, 58, 61, 64, 66, 67, 73, 82, 92, 106, 113, 122, 135, 195, 203, 206, 253, 284, 285, 288, 295, 301, 313, 317, 328.
Children's Songs, 9.
China, 327.
Chinese Nursery Rhymes, 146.
Chorea, 4.
Christmas, 138.
Clubs, 104, 105.
Collecting Instinct, 45.
Color Blindness, 172.
Color Sense, 154.
Comenius, 202.
Companions, 88.
Compulsory Education, 306.
Conduct, 93.
Conjuring, 304.
Creeping, 303.
Criminal, 56, 318.
Cruelty, 124.
Curriculum, 194.

Darwin, 82.
Deaf, 34, 77, 79, 129, 243, 244, 245, 273, 274, 301.
Deception, 304.
Defective Children, 59, 86, 90.
Degeneracy, 319.
Dementia praecox, 151.
Dentition, 114.
Desks, 51, 249.
Development, 92.
Diet, 147.
Diseases, 37, 116, 208, 223.
Dolls, 312.
Drawing, 56, 175, 226.

Dullness, 260, 265, 267.
Dumb, 129, 301.

Ears, 80, 240.
Egotism, 329.
Emotions, 280.
England, 38.
Environment, 121, 232.
Epidemics, 291.
Epilepsy, 13, 69, 114, 148.
Ethics, 122, 190.
Evolution, 39, 40, 126, 232, 233, 234.
Eye, 80, 81, 263.
Eyesight, 26, 87, 110, 272, 314, 324.

Fatigue, 21, 30, 148, 168, 185, 269, 297, 299.
Feeble Minded, 8, 120, 123, 148, 164, 229, 254, 278, 279, 302, 325, 326.
Fœtal Conditions, 150.
Folk Lore, 54, 238.
Food, 28, 147, 197, 216.
France, 61, 254.
Froebel, 42.
Furniture, 51, 249.

Games, 197.
Genetic Psychology, 166.
Germany, 160.
Gifts, 211.
Girls, 101.
Grading, 161.
Growth, 6, 39, 50, 56, 66, 67, 70, 90, 105, 112, 131, 134, 161, 165, 188, 259.

Habit, 178.
Health, 46, 315.
Hearing, 240, 273, 274, 314, 324.
Herbart, 331.
Heredity, 99, 220, 319.
High School, 112, 118, 162, 198.
Historical, 33, 48, 76, 313.
History, 320.
Holland, 254.
Home, 158, 195, 227, 253, 300.
Honor, 32.
Human Instincts, 100.
Hygiene, 16, 18, 89, 103, 109, 111, 169, 197, 208, 223, 224, 256, 262, 268, 296, 302, 315.
Hysteria, 25, 36, 131, 167, 284.

Ideals, 10, 11, 95.
Ideas, 221.
Idiots and Idiocy, 91, 270, 277, 279, 322.

Imagination, 57, 241, 242, 310.
Imbecility, 298.
Imitation, 84.
Indian children, 159.
Individual, 27, 92, 171, 249, 276, 286, 288.
Industrial, 18.
Infancy, 196, 202.
Infant, 82.
Instincts, 7, 100, 286.
Institutions, 76, 302, 315.
Instruction, 261.
Interest, 1, 83, 261.
Italy, 55.

Japan, 213.

Kindergarten, 42, 97, 102, 132, 211.

Language, 3, 34, 56, 96, 182, 200, 250, 252, 257, 323.
Language Study, 218.
Lapses, 17.
Laughing, 85.
Left-handedness, 187.
Life-album, 107.
Literature, 47.

Manual Training, 180, 225.
Manual Work, 272.
Medical, 103, 223.
Medical Inspection, 16, 46, 224, 256, 262, 268.
Memory, 71, 170, 176, 209, 230.
Mental, 269, 299.
Mental Development, 165.
Mental Work, 210.
Mental Affections, 115.
Mental Disturbances, 127, 149, 151, 289.
Mental and Physical, 28.
Methods, 185, 295.
Mirror-writing, 108.
Money Sense, 63.
Morals, 233, 251, 307.
Moral Training, 205.
Morality, 180, 217.
Morbidity, 116.
Mortality, 116, 208.
Mother tongue, 257.
Motor Ability, 326.
Motor Training, 6.
Movement, 165.
Music, 153, 174, 201.
Myths, 54, 238.

Nascencies, 39.
Nature Study, 152, 286.
Nebraska, 145.

Nerve-cells, 248.
Nervous Energy, 216.
Nervous System, 15.
Neurasthenia, 115.
Neurology, 70, 150.
Normal Schools, 203.
Nose, 80.
Number, 258.
Nursery Rhymes, 146.

Object-lessons, 226.
Obstinacy, 125.
Overwork, 14, 168.

Paidology, 64, 65.
Palate, 80.
Paralysis, 60.
Parental Instinct, 312.
Parents, 155, 300.
Parker (Frances W.), 48.
Passions, 181.
Pathology, 173, 267, 289.
Penmanship, 177, 275.
Pedagogical Laboratory, 225.
Periodicity, 56, 186.
Personal, 106, 107.
Personification, 181.
Perversion, 121.
Philosophy, 134.
Physical, 24.
Physical and Mental, 24.
Physical training, 38, 163, 194.
Physical weakness, 109.
Physiology, 101.
Pictures, 133.
Pity, 140, 290.
Play, 56, 72, 193, 197, 247, 308, 312.
Playground, 31, 215, 255.
Precocity, 186, 219.
Primitive Man, 246.
Promotion, 44.
Property, 204.
Prussia, 74.
Psychology, 27, 35, 44, 49, 73, 111,
    127, 128, 185, 189, 207, 244, 260,
    283, 290, 308, 331.
Psychoses, 311.
Puberty, 53, 101, 197, 311.
Pubescence, 98, 235.
Punishments, 19, 74, 237.

Quincy Movement, 48.

Reading, 41, 158, 266, 321.
Recapitulation, 126.
Religion, 47, 83, 137, 139, 157, 236,
    294.
Right handedness, 187.
Rights of children, 204.

Rural Schools, 309.

School Friendships, 88.
School and Home, 143.
School Furniture, 293.
School Life, 160.
School Methods, 144.
Secretiveness, 43.
Self activity, 214.
Senses, 156, 231, 246, 325.
Sensuality, 141.
Sex, 56, 88, 101, 104, 181, 186, 188,
    235, 239.
Sexual abuses, 225.
Skull, 81.
Sleep, 197, 228.
Smiling, 85.
Social Sense, 105, 136.
Society, 283.
Sociological, 198.
Solitude, 283.
Speech, 3, 34, 69, 96, 182, 200, 218,
    222, 229, 250, 287.
Spelling, 52, 119, 179, 199.
Spine, 293.
Squinting, 26.
Statistical, 118, 328.
Stature, 50.
Stories, 12.
Student Customs, 138.
Study and Studies, 162, 292.
Stuttering and Stammering, 142,
    183, 287.
Suggestion, 29.
Sunday School, 137, 157.
Swimming, 212.
Switzerland, 86.

Teeth, 114.
Temperature Sense, 2.
Tests, 171.
Thought, 3, 200.
Transportation, 309.
Truants, 305.
Twins, 94, 149.

Vacation Schools, 255.
Vertical writing, 110, 177.
Vision, 87, 252.
Voluntary attention, 225.

Walking, 303.
Weather, 93.
Weight, 50.
Will, 22.
Woman, 56.
Work, 162, 180.
Writing, 275.

BIBLIOGRAPHY

OF

CHILD STUDY.

BY

LOUIS N. WILSON,

LIBRARIAN, CLARK UNIVERSITY.

The Clark University Press.
WORCESTER, MASSACHUSETTS,
JANUARY, 1903.

BIBLIOGRAPHY OF CHILD STUDY.

For the Year 1901.

By LOUIS N. WILSON, Librarian, Clark University.

1. **Alengry, F.** L'école dans la prison. Rev. Péd, April, 1901. Vol. 38, pp. 313-334.

2. **Allen, Ezra** The Pedagogy of myth in the grades. Ped. Sem., June, 1901. Vol. 8, pp. 258-277.
   Shows how both sentiment and practice in many lands and places have tended in the direction of myth.

3. **Ament, William** Die Entwicklung der Pflanzenkenntnis beim Kinde und bei Völkern. Samml. von Abhandl. a. d. Gebiete der Päd. Psy. und Physiol., 1901. Vol. 4. Heft 4, pp. 60.
   See review in Journal of American Folk-Lore, 1901. Vol. 14, pp. 319, 320.

4. **Amigh, Orphelia L.** Alcoholism as a cause of degeneracy. Nat. Conf. Char. and Corr., Boston, 1901, pp. 282-283.

5. **Ammon, O.** Der Ursprung der sozialen Triebe. Zeits. f. Sozialwiss., Berlin, 1901. Vol. 4, Heft 1-2.
   Contends against the views of Schultze and Sutherland. Discusses sexual and family instincts.

6. **Anton, G.** Ueber geistige Ermüdung der Kinder im gesunden und kranken Zustande. Marhold, Halle, a. S., 1900, pp. 26.

7. **Ausset** A propos d' un cas de maturité précoce chez une fillette de quatre ans et neuf mois. Echo Méd. Nord, 1901. Vol. 5, pp. 293-295.

8. **Baer, A.** Der Selbstmord im kindlichen Lebensalter. Eine socialhygienische Studie. Leipzig, Thieme, 1901, pp. 84.
   Based upon 25 cases of suicide up to the fifteenth year. Interesting and valuable.

9. **Baginsky, Adolph** Ueber Suggestion bei Kindern. Zeit. für Päd. Psy., April, 1901. Vol. 3, pp. 97-103.

10. **Bagley, William C.** On the correlation of mental and motor ability in school children. Am. Jour. of Psy., Jan., 1901. Vol. 12, pp. 193-205.

11. **Balis, Sylvia Chapin** The deaf and their relations with the hearing. Association Rev., April, 1901. Vol. 3, pp. 141-145.

12. **Balliet, Thomas M.** A few lessons to be learned from European schools. Ped. Sem., March, 1901. Vol. 8, pp. 59-64.
    Advocates extension of the high school course, so as to make it fit for the professional school.

13. **Barnes, Earl** A forgotten student of child study. Paidologist, Nov., 1901. Vol. 3, pp. 120-123.

14. **Bashkirtseff, Marie** The last confession of Marie Bashkirtseff and her correspondence with Guy de Maupassant. With a foreword by Jeannette L. Gilder. F. A. Stokes Co., N. Y., 1901, pp. 157.
Less interesting than the previously published volume.

15. **Bawden, H. Heath** A bibliography of the literature on the organ and sense of smell. Jour. of Comp. Neurology, Granville, O., April, 1901. Vol. 11, pp. 1-11.
Contains 885 titles of books and articles, many of which relate to child study.

16. **Bayr, Emanuel** Alkohol und Kinder. Zeit. f. Schulgesundheitspflege, 1901. Vol. 14, pp. 365-388.

17. **Behringer, G.** Die Gefängnissschule. Ein Ueberblick über die geschichtliche Entwickelung, den heutigen Stand und die Bedeutung des Schul- und Bildungswesens in den Strafanstalten. C. L. Hirschfeld, Leipzig, 1901, pp. 132.

18. **Bellei, G.** Intorno alla capacità intellectuale di ragazzi e ragazze che frequentano la 5a classe elementare. Riv. Sperim. di Freniat. Reggio, 1901. Vol 27, pp. 446-455.
See review in Pedagogical Seminary, 1901. Vol. 8, pp. 246.

19. —— —— Mental fatigue in school children. Lancet, Lond., 1901. Vol. 97, pp. 1330-1331.

20 **Benda, T.** Nervenhygiene und Schule. O. Coblentz, Berlin, 1900, pp. 55.

21. **Bennett, Beulah** Value of child study to the primary Sunday school teacher. Kindergarten Mag., Jan., 1901. Vol. 13, pp. 259-263.

22. **Berillon, ——** Les applications de l'hypnotisme à l'éducation des enfants vicieux et dégénérés. Revue Int. de Péd. Comp., Nov., 1901. Vol. 3, pp. 257-265.

23. **Beyer, Henry G.** The relation between physique and mental work. (Reprinted from Jour. of Bost. Soc. of Med. Sci. Vol. 5, pp. 437-446.) Boston, 1901.
Thorough and suggestive.

24. **Bibliography** of literature upon medical pedagogy and curriculums published in 1899 to March 1900. Bull. Am. Acad. of Med. (Easton, Pa.), Feb., 1901. Vol. 5, pp. 236-238.

25. **van Biervliet, J. J.** Etudes de psychologie. L'homme droit et l'homme gauche. Gand, A. Siffer, 1901, pp. 143.
Valuable study of asymmetry, based upon the examination of 200 individuals. Parts have appeared previously in the Revue Philosophique.

26. **Binet, Alfred** Recherches préliminaires de céphalométrie. L'Année Psychologiqne, 1900. Paris, 1901. Vol. 7, pp. 369-429.

27. **Bion, Walter** Die Ferienkolonien und verwandte Bestrebungen auf dem Gebiete der Kinder—Gesundheitspflege. Zürich, 1901, pp. 296.
Gives illustrations of buildings, grounds and localities.

28. **Blümml, E. K. und Rott, A. J.** Die Verwendung der Pflanzen durch die Kinder in Deutschböhmen und Niederösterreich. Ztschr. d. Ver. f. Volkskunde, Berlin, 1901. Vol. 11, pp. 49-64.
See Chamberlain, A. F.

29. **Boas, F.** The mind of primitive man. Journal of American Folk-Lore, Jan.-Mch., 1901. Vol. 14, pp. 1-11. Also Science, N. Y., 1901, N. S. Vol. 13, pp. 281-289.
Ought to be read by all psychologists and students of the child.

30. **Bonnefoy, G.** Les questions d'éducation et d'assistance des sourds-muets. Revue Int. de Péd. Comp., Fév., 1901. Vol. 3, pp. 52-59.

31. **Bonzon, J.** Maisons d'éducation correctionnelle. Revue Int. de Péd. Comp., June and July, 1901. Vol. 3, pp. 165-175; 205-215.

32. **Boubier, A. M.** Les jeux de l'enfant pendant la classe. Arch. de Psychol. Suisse Rom., 1901. Vol. 1, pp. 44-68.

33. **Bourdon, B.** Le type grammatical dans les associations verbales. C. R. IVe Congrès Internat. de Psy., Paris, 1901, pp. 169-174.

34. **Boyd Hypatia** The deaf and their social relations with the hearing. Association Rev., June, 1901. Vol. 3, pp. 227-238.

35. **Boyer, J.** Notes psychologiques sur les idiots. Revue Int. de Péd. Comp., Nov., 1901. Vol. 3, pp. 266-270.

36. **Brandt, Francis Burke** The state in its relation to the defective child. Proceedings N. E. A., 1901, pp. 876-880.

37. **Brauckmann, Karl** Die psychische Entwicklung und pädagogische Behandlung schwerhöriger Kinder. Samml. von Abh. a. d. Gebiete der Päd., Psy., Physiol., 1901. Vol. 4, pp. 96.

38. **Briggs, Le Baron R.** School, college and character. Houghton, Mifflin & Co., Boston, 1901, pp. 148.

39. **British** Child-Study Ass'n Conference. Fourth annual meeting. Paidologist (Lond.), July, 1901. Vol. 3, pp. 104-108.

Browne, Edgar A. See Hope, Edw. W.

40 **Burzio, ——** Contributo allo studio delle stigmate psichiche degenerative degli epilettici. Arch. di Psichiat., 1901. Vol. 22, pp. 58-62.

41. **Butler, Amos W.** Saving the children. Nat. Conf. Char. and Corr. Boston, 1901, pp. 204-219.

42. **—— ——** Education and crime. Proceedings N. E. A., 1901, pp. 560-564.

43. **Calkins, Mary Whiton** An introduction to psychology. New York, Macmillan Co., 1901, pp. 509.
Chapter 26 (pp. 382-396) is devoted to the psychology of the child's consciousness.

44. **Carrara, M.** Les petits vagabonds de Cagliari. Rev. de l'Hypnot., 1901. Vol. 16, pp. 135-139.

45. **Carrière, P.** De la précocité physique et intellectuelle chez l'homme. Paris, 1901.

46. **Chaillons, François** Facteurs de la viciation morale du traitement méthodique des viciations par l'éducation et de l'application de la méthode dans les colonies d'enfants. C. R. IVE Congrès Int. de Psy., Paris, 1901, pp. 512-517.

47. **Chamberlain, Alex. F.** Some recent anthropometric studies. Ped. Sem., June, 1901. Vol. 8, pp. 239-257.
Notes in anthropometric literature in various countries. Bibliography of 21 titles.

48. —— —— Notes on Italian educational literature. Ped. Sem., Sept., 1901. Vol. 8, pp. 412-423.
Interesting for students of childhood from the point of anthropology, psychology and pedagogy.

49. —— —— Use of Plants by children. Jour. Amer. Folk-Lore, Apr.-June, 1901. Vol. 14, pp. 132-138.
Condensed translation and rearrangement of No. 28.

50. **Child Study** A systematic plan of. Paidologist (Lond.), Nov., 1901. Vol. 3, pp. 124-139.
Reptd. from the Report of the Dept. of Ed., Passaic, N. J.

51. **Children's** attitude towards rewards. Paidologist (Lond.), April, 1901. Vol. 3, pp. 22-28.

52. **Christian, J.** Dementia præcox. Am. Jour. of Insanity, Oct., 1901. Vol. 58, pp. 215-241.

53. **Claus, A.** Psychoglogische Betrachtungen zur Methodik des Zeichenunterrichts. Zeit. für Päd. Psy., Dec., 1901. Vol. 3, pp. 456-473.

54. **Clavière, —— ** Le travail intellectuel dans ses rapports avec la force musculaire. Bull. Soc. Etude Psy. de l'Enfant, 1901. Vol. 1, pp. 8-12.

55. **Coe, George A.** The philosophy of play. Kindergarten Mag., Feb.-Mch., 1901. Vol. 13, pp. 285-290; 356-363.

56. **Compayrè, G.** J. J. Rousseau et l'éducation de la nature. Delaplane, Paris, 1901.

57. **Couchoud, Paul Louis** La jeunesse de Spinoza. Rev. de Philos., Paris, April, 1901. Vol. 1, pp. 318-330.

58. **Coupin, H.** Le chant des oiseaux. Rev. Scientifique, Paris, 1901. Vol. 15, pp. 490-495, 555-561, 584-589.

59. **Csapodi, Istvàn** Ueber Steilschrift und Schrägschrift. Zeit. f. Schulgesundheitspflege, 1901. Vol. 14, pp. 238-243.

60. **Curtis, Henry S.** The play instinct. Kindergarten Mag., April, 1901. Vol. 13, pp. 424-432.

61. **Danger, O.** The "mixed method" and the "pure oral method" in Germany. Association Rev., June, 1901. Vol. 3, pp. 411-417.

62. **Demoor, Jean** Die anormalen Kinder und erziehliche Behandlung in Haus und Schule. O. Bonde, Altenberg, 1901, pp. 292.
A valuable work on special training for abnormal children bibliography.

63. **Demoor, et Daniel** Les enfants anormaux à Bruxelles. L' Année Psychologique, 1900, Paris, 1901. Vol. 7, pp. 296-313.

64. **Dodge, Raymond** The psychology of reading. Psy. Rev., Jan., 1901. Vol. 8, pp. 56-60.

65. **Dolbear, Katherine E.** A few suggestions for the education of women. Ped. Sem., Dec., 1901. Vol. 8, pp.'548-555.

66. **Donald, Dora** Linnie Haguewood. Association Rev., April, 1901. Vol. 3, pp. 97-105.

67. **Douchez, ——** Croissance des élèves d' une école professionnelle pendant l'année scolaire. Bull. Soc. Etude Psy., de l'Enfant, Paris, 1901. Vol. 1, pp. 34-51.
See review in Pedagogical Seminary, 1901. Vol. 8, pp. 247-248.

68. **Dresslar, F. B.** A morning's observation of a baby. Ped. Sem., Dec., 1901. Vol. 8, pp. 469-481.
A parent's careful observation of his child's (a boy 13½ months old) movements during one forenoon.

69. **Drummond, W. B.** The child: his nature and nurture. The Macmillan Co., N. Y. (Temple Primers) 1901, pp. 146.
A useful little manual.

70. **DuBois, Patterson** Adultism the rock of offense. Kindergarten Rev., Jan., 1901. Vol. 11, pp. 261-264.

71. **Dubranle, A.** Les arriérés dans les écoles des sourds-muets. Revue Int. de Péd. Comp., May, 1901. Vol. 3, pp. 129-136.

72. **Duché, E.** De la précocité intellectuelle; étude sur le génie. Paris, 1901.

73. **Ellis, Havelock** The development of the sexual instinct. Alienist and Neurologist, July-Oct., 1901. Vol. 22, pp. 500-521, 615-623.

74. **—— ——** A study of British genius. Pop. Sci. Mo., N. Y., 1901. Vol. 58, pp. 372-380; 540-547; 595-603. Vol. 59, pp. 59-67, 209-216, 266-272, 373-379, 441-446.
A study of the character, parentage, racial and social characteristics of British genius.

75. **Ellison, P. E.** Child saving under state supervision. Nat. Conf. Char. and Corr., Boston, 1901, pp. 230-233.

76. **Engelmann, Geo. J.** The age of first menstruation on the North American continent. Reprint from Trans. Am. Gynecol. Soc., 1901. W. J. Dorman,. Philadelphia, 1901., pp. 36.
About the only comprehensive and reliable study of its kind.

77. **Engelmann, Geo. J.** Rapport du développement mental au développement fonctionnel chez la jeune fille américaine. Analyse de 12,000 cas de Ier menstruation. Ann. de Gynécol. et d'Obstét., 1901. Vol. 55, pp. 30-44.

78. **Erdmann, Benno** Die Psychologie des Kindes und die Schule. F. Cohen, Bonn, 1901, pp. 51.
A lecture on child study in America. Too brief to have merit.

79. **Fairbanks, William G.** Girls' reformatories and their inherent characteristics. Nat. Conf. Char. and Corr., Boston, 1901, pp. 254-261.

80. **Féré, Ch.** Les variations de l'excitabilité dans la fatigue. L'Année Psychologique, 1900. Paris, 1901. Vol. 7, pp. 69-81.

81. **Ferrai, C.** Sul compenso sensoriale nei sordomuti. Riv. Sperim. di Freniat., Reggio, 1901. Vol. 27, pp. 341-368.

82. **Ferriani, L.** Delinquenza precoce e senile. Omarini, Como, 1901. pp. 460.
A very good book on crime in youth and old age.

83. **Finzi,** —— I sintomi organici della demenza precoce. Riv. di Patol. Nerv. e Ment., 1900. Vol. 5, pp. 63-97.

84. **Fisher, G.** Der Blinde. Kinderfehler, 1901. Vol. 6, pp. 14-19; 49-60.

85. **Forbush, William B.** The boy problem. A study in social pedagogy. (2nd edition.) Pilgrim Press, Boston, 1901, pp. 194.

86. —— —— (Editor.) How to help boys. A quarterly magazine. Boston, Mass.

87. **Fornari, P.** De l'état psychique des arriérés. Revue Int. de Péd. Comp., Oct., 1901. Vol. 3, pp. 225-241.

88. **Fornelli, N.** Getäuschte Erwartungen, Kinderfehler, 1901. Vol. 6, pp. 208-214; 241-258.

89. **Friedrich, Johann** Die Ideale der Kinder. Zeit. f. Päd. Psy., Feb., 1901. Vol. 3, pp. 38-64.

90. **Frood, Charlotte A.** Too late for the train. A study in child's drama. Paidologist (Lond.), April, 1901. Vol. 3, pp. 28-30.

91. **Gale, Harlow** The vocabularies of three children of one family to two and a half years of age. Psy. Studies, Univ. of Minn., July, 1900. No. 1, pp. 70-117.

92. **Galton, F.** The possible improvement of the human breed under the existing conditions of law and sentiment. Nature, London, Oct. 31., 1901. Vol. 64, pp. 659-665.
A suggestive discussion of human stirpiculture.

93. **Garnier, P.** La criminalité juvénile. Étiologie du meurtre. Arch. d'Anthropol. Crim., 1901. Vol. 16, pp. 576-586.

94. **Giuffrida-Ruggeri, V.** Sulla distribuzione delle intelligenze superiori in Italia. Riv. Ital. di Sociol., 1901. Vol. 5, pp. 331-338.

95. **Godin, P.** Du rôle de l'anthropométrie en éducation physique. Bull. et Mém. Soc. d'Anthr. de Paris, 1901, Ve S., 2. pp. 110-134.
See review in Pedagogical Seminary, 1902. Vol. 9, pp. 43-44.

96. **Gommes, Manheimer** L'instruction des enfants mentalement anormaux à l'étranger. Rev. Péd., Nov., 1901. Vol. 39, pp. 406-426.

97. **Gould, F. J.** Children's ethical classes. Int. Jour. of Ethics, Jan., 1901. Vol. 11, pp. 214-226.

98. **Greene, E.** The preponderance of male stammerers over female. N. Y. Med. Jour., N. Y., 1901. Vol. 73, pp. 635-638.

99. **Greenwood, James M.** Present duties. School Journal, Sept. 21, 1901. Vol. 63, pp. 275-277.
Refers to growth.

100. **Grohmann, O.** Ernstes und Heiteres aus meinen Erinnerungen im Verkehre mit Schwachsinnigen. Melusine, Zürich, 1901. pp. 133.

101. **Groos, Karl** The play of man. (Trans. by Elizabeth L. Baldwin with a preface by J. Mark Baldwin.) D. Appleton & Co., N. Y., 1901, pp. 412.
An admirable work in English dress.

102. —— —— Experimentelle Beiträge zur Psychologie des Erkennens. Zeit. f. Psy. und Physiol. der Sinnesorgane, Leipzig, 1901. Vol. 26, pp. 145-167.

103 **Groszmann, M. P. E.** The treatment of defectives. N. Y. Med. Ins., Feb. 1, 1902. Vol. 75, pp. 187-193.

104. **Gruber, Hugo** Pädagogische Irrtümer in Schule und Haus. Baedeker, Essen, 1900, pp. 72.
A contribution of some significance to pedagogical pathology.

105. **Gutenberg, Berthold** Zum Kapitel der Zähne und Zahnpflege bei den Schulkindern. Zeit. f. Schulgesundheitspflege, 1901. Vol. 14, pp. 452-466.

106. **Hall, G. Stanley** Confessions of a psychologist. Part 1, Ped. Sem., March, 1901. Vol. 8, pp. 92-143.
Frank statements of problems in university pedagogy.

107. —— —— The ideal school as based on child study. Forum, Sept., 1901. Vol. 32, pp. 24-39. Proc. N. E. A., 1901, pp. 475-488. Paidologist, Lond., Nov., 1901. Vol. 3, pp. 161-166.

108. —— —— Present tendencies in higher education. Regents' Bull. Univ. State of N. Y., No. 55, Sept., 1901, pp. 372-385.

109. —— —— Theory and play. Kindergarten Mag., Sept., 1901, Vol. 14, pp. 5-9.

110. —— —— Rhythm of work and play. Kindergarten Rev., Sept., 1901. Vol. 12, pp. 43-48.

111. **Hall, G. Stanley.** Some fundamental principles of Sunday school and Bible teaching. Ped. Sem., Dec., 1901. Vol. 8, pp. 439-468.
      Seeks to bring the laws now known concerning adolescence to bear in this field.

112. —— —— How far is the present high school and early college training adapted to the nature and needs of adolescents? School Review, Dec., 1901. Vol. 9, pp. 649-665.

113. **Hamlin, F. M.** Schools for the insane. Am. Jour. of Insanity, July, 1901. Vol. 58, pp. 141-150.

114. **Hancock, John A.** The observation of school children. Ped. Sem., Sept., 1901. Vol. 8, pp. 291-340.
      Methods of observation practical and convenient in schools. Bibliography of 50 titles.

115. **Harris, W. T.** School statistics and morals. Rep. Com. Ed., 1898-99 (Washington, 1900), pp. 1329-1333.

116. **Hartmann, Arthur** Die Schwerhörigen in der Schule. Zeit. f. Schulgesundheitspflege, 1901. Vol. 14, pp. 654-661.

117. **Hase, Karl von** Die psychologische Begründung der religiösen Weltanschauung. Zeit. f. Päd. Psy. u Path., Feb., 1901. Vol. 3, pp. 1-26.

118. **Headland, Isaac T.** The Chinese boy and girl. F. H. Revell Co., N. Y., 1901, pp. 176.
      A holiday book. Many photographs of Chinese children.

119. **Hemprich, K.** Die Kinderpsychologie in ihrer Bedeutung für Unterricht und Erziehung. Oesterwitz & Voigtländer, 1900, pp. 42.

120. **Henderson, Charles R.** Neglected children in neglected communities. Nat. Conf. Char. and Corr., Boston, 1901, pp. 219-224.

121. **Henderson, C. Hanford** Juvenile traders. Kindergarten Rev., June, 1901. Vol. 11, pp. 587-591.

122. **Herford, Caroline** The development of the will between the ages of five and thirteen. Paidologist (Lond.), July, 1901. Vol. 3, pp. 75-84.

123. **Hirschlaff, Leo** Ueber die Furcht der Kinder. Zeit. für Päd. Psy., August, 1901. Vol. 3, pp. 296-315.

124. **Hofer, Mari Ruef** Singing games and their sources. Kindergarten Mag., Sept., 1901. Vol. 14, pp. 46-51.

125. —— —— Study of children's games as played in Chicago's crowded districts. Kindergarten Mag., Oct., 1901. Vol. 14, pp. 105-110.

126. **Hoffa, A.** Die medizinisch-pädagogische. Behandlung gelähmter Kinder. Kinderfehler, 1901. Vol. 6, pp. 193-208.

127. **Hoffman, Hugo** The condition of the education of deaf-mutes in Germany at the end of the nineteenth century. Association Rev., Feb., 1901. Vol. 3, pp. 1-11.

128. **Hope, Edw. W. and Browne, Edgar A.** A manual of school hygiene. Univ. Press, Cambridge, 1901, pp. 207.
Hygiene of childhood as affected by school life.

129. **Huey, Edmund B.** On the psychology and physiology of reading. II. Am. Jour. of Psy., April, 1901. Vol. 12, pp. 292-312.

130. **Johnson, Geo. E.** The condition of the teeth of children in public schools. Ped. Sem., March, 1901. Vol. 8, pp. 45-58.
Advocates dental inspection of school children.

131. **Joire, P.** De l'emploi de la suggestion dans l'éducation artistique et en particulier pour l'étude de la musique. Rev. de l'Hypnot., Paris, 1901. Vol. 16, pp. 110-120.

132. **Jonckheere, T.** Ueber den Einfluss der Musik auf die Bewegungen bei schwachsinnigen Kindern. Kinderfehler, 1901. Vol. 6, pp. 113-120.

133. **Joteyko, J.** Distribution de la fatigue dans les organes centraux et périphériques. C. R. ive Congrès Inter. de Psy., Paris, 1901, pp. 77-78.

134. —— —— La fatigue comme moyen de défense de l'organisme. C. R. ive Congrès Int. de Psy., Paris, 1901, pp. 230-231.

135. **Kellner,** —— Ueber Kopfmaasse der Idioten. Allg. Zeits. f. Psychiatrie, Berlin, 1901. Vol. 58, pp. 61-78.
Discusses results of head-measurements of 220 idiots in the Hamburg Asylum at Alsterdorf.

136. **Kemsies, Ferdinand** Gedächtnisuntersuchungen an Schülern. III-IV. Zeits. f. Päd. Psy. u. Path., Berlin, 1901. Vol. 3, pp. 171-183; 281-291.

137. —— —— Arbeitstypen bei Schülern. Zeit. f. Päd. Psy., October, 1901. Vol. 3, pp. 348-362.

138. **Kerr, M. R. and F. M.** Our baby's journal, No. 1. Hope-Edgewood Press, New Haven, Conn., 1901. pp. 175.
Notes to the age of 5 yrs. Practical and of interest to parents.

139. **Kimmins, C. W.** The child as the director of the parent's education. Child Life, June, 1901. Vol. 3, pp. 128-134.

140. **Kirkpatrick, E. A.** A genetic study of space perception. Psy. Review, Nov., 1901. Vol. 8, pp. 565-577.

141. **Knortz, K.** Kindeskunde und häusliche Erziehung. Tittel, Altenburg, 1900, pp. 62.

142. **Koren, A.** Die Körperlänge norwegischer Soldaten. Corrbl. d. deutschen Ges. f. Anthr., München, 1901. Vol. 33, p. 46.
Indicates growth in height after 22nd and even after 28th year.

143. **Kraft-Ebing, R. von** Flagellatio puerum als Ausdruck des larvirten Sadismus eines paedophilen Conträrsexualen. Allg. Zeits. f. Psychiatrie, Berlin, 1901.   Vol. 58, pp. 545-557.

144. —— —— Psychopathia sexualis, with especial reference to antipathic sexual instinct. A Medico-Forensic study. (Only authorized English translation of tenth German edition.) W. T. Keener & Co., Chicago, 1900, pp. 585. 2d Ger. ed. Eucke, Stuttgart, 1901, pp. 419.

145. **Krohn, W. O.** Physical training as a corrective of brain disorderliness. Proceedings N. E. A., 1901, pp. 759-760.

146. —— —— Minor mental abnormalities in children as occasioned by certain erroneous school methods. Paidologist (London), April, 1901. Vol. 3, pp. 2-12. Also, Rep. Com. of Ed., Wash.

147. **Lange, O.** Zur Anatomie des Auges des Neugeborenen. I, II. Klin. Monatsbl. f. Augenhk, 1901. Vol. 39, pp. 1-5; 202-212.

148. **Lapicque, Louis** Sur le temps de réaction suivant les races ou les conditions sociales. C. R. Acad. d. Sci., June 17, 1901. Vol. 132, pp. 1509-1511.

149. **Laquer, L.** Die Hülfsschulen für schwachbefähigte Kinder, ihre ärztliche und sociale Bedeutung. Bergmann, Wiesbaden, 1901, pp. 64.

150. **Lasch, R.** Besitzen die Naturvölker ein persönliches Ehrgefühl? Zeits. f. Sozialwiss., Berlin, 1900. Vol. 3, Heft. 12, pp. 837 ff.
"Primitive honor," rather than "personal honor" in our sense exists among the lower races.

151. **Lavergne, ——** Education des enfants anormaux. Revue Int. de Péd. Comp., Jan., 1901. Vol. 3, pp. 13-18.

152. **Lee, James** Usefulness of the school physician. School Journal, May 18, 1901. Vol. 62, pp. 546-547.

153. **Lee, Joseph** Playground education. Ed. Rev., N. Y., Dec., 1901. Vol. 22, pp. 449-471.

Lee, Vernon See Paget, V.

154. **Lemaître, A.** Audition colorée observée chez des écoliers. Alcan, Paris, 1901, pp. 169.

155. **Lemon, James S.** Uses of the knowledge of skin psychology. C. R., ive Congrès Int. de Psy., Paris, 1901, pp. 418-419.

156. **Lenz, R.** Ueber Ursprung und Entwicklung der Sprache. Die Neueren Sprachen, Marburg, 1901. Vol. 8, pp. 449-472, 513-534, 577-589. Vol. 9, pp. 1-12.
Contains among other things, notes on the language of children.

157. **Libby, M. F.** Shakespeare and adolescence. Ped. Sem., June, 1901. Vol. 8, pp. 163-205.
A good article on Shakespeare's treatment of youth and adolescence.

158. **Lichtwark, Alfred**, editor Versuche und Ergebnisse der Lehrervereinigung für die Pflege der künstlerischen Bildung, Hamburg. Alfred Janssen, 1901, pp. 171.
Papers on the art interests of school children.

159. **Liebmann, A.** Die Sprachstörungen geistig zurückgebliebener Kinder (Samml. v. Abh. a. d. Geb. d. päd. Psychol.). Reuther & Reichard, Berlin, 1901. Vol. 4, No. 3, pp. 78.

160. —— —— Agrammatismus infantilis. Arch. f. Psychiat. u. Nervenhk., Berlin, 1901. Vol. 34, pp. 240-252.

161. **Lingreen, Ethel Roe** Rhythm in the kindergarten. Proceedings N. E. A., 1901, pp. 532-538. Also in Kindergarten Review, Sept., 1901. Vol. 12, pp. 7-13.

162. **Lobedank,** —— Ueber das Gedächtniss und das Auswendiglernen. Zeit. f. Schulgesundheitspflege, 1901. Vol. 14, pp. 443-452.

163. **Lobsien, M.** Experimentelle Untersuchungen über die Gedächtnissentwickelung bei Schulkindern. Zeits. f. Psychol., Leipzig, 1901. Vol. 27, pp. 34-76.

164. **Lombroso, C.** The determining of genius. Monist, Chicago, Oct., 1901. Vol. 12, pp. 49-64.

Lord, I. E. See Wyer, J. I., Jr.

Loti, Pierre See Smith, Caroline F.

165. **Louch, Mary** The relativity of truth. Paidologist (London), Nov., 1901. Vol. 3, pp. 141-155.
A study of children's lies by the questionnaire method.

166. **Luschan, F. von** Ueber kindliche Vorstellungen bei den sogen. Naturvölkern. Zeits. f. päd Psychologie, 1901. Vol. 3, pp. 89-96.
Should be read in connection with Boas's paper.

167. **McCormack, T. J.** Brushwork and inventional drawing. Open Court, Chicago, 1901. Vol. 15, pp. 30-42.

168. **MacDonald, Arthur** Study of man. Am. Jour. of Sociology, Chicago, 1901. Vol. 6, pp. 839-846.

169. **MacMillan, D. P.** Some results of hearing tests of Chicago school children. Proceedings N. E. A., 1901, pp. 876-880.

170. **Machado, B.** Notas d'um pae as creanças, Coimbra, Imprensa da Universidade, 1901, pp. 511.
A good child study book. See review in Pedagogical Seminary, 1902. Vol. 6, pp. 46, 47.

171. **Malapert. P.** Éducation des énfants anormaux. Revue Int. de Péd. Comp., June, 1901. Vol. 3, pp. 161-164.

172. **Manaceíne, Marie de** Sur l'hérédité psychique, C. R. ive Congrès Int. de Psy., Paris, 1901, pp. 545-548.

173. **Mansfield, E. D.** The relation between crime and education. Rep. Com. Ed., 1898-99, Washington, 1900, pp. 1290-1299.

174. **Maréchal, P.** Supériorité des animaux sur l'homme. Fischbacher, Paris, 1901, pp. 228.

175. **Marro, A.** Psychoses of puberty. Alien & Neurol., Oct., 1901. Vol. 21, pp. 658-660.
Abstract of paper read at the 13th Int. Med. Congress in 1900.

176. —— —— La puberté chez l'homme et chez la femme. Schleicher Frères, Paris, 1901, pp. 356.
Renders more accessible the valuable Italian original.

177. **Marsh, Harriet A.** Report of child study. 57th Annual Rep. Bd. of Ed., Detroit, Mich., 1900, pp. 142.
Practical utility in child study by a mothers' club.

178. **Di Mattei,** —— La sensibilità nei fanciulli in rapporto al sesso ed all'età. Arch. di Psichiat., 1901. Vol. 22, pp. 207-229.

179. **Meleney, Clarence E.** Education for defective children. School Journal, May 11, 1901. Vol. 62, pp. 523-525.

180. **Mingins, Mary W.** Sense training in Detroit kindergarten. Kindergarten Rev., Nov., 1901. Vol. 12, pp. 136-142.

181. **Moll, Albert** Ueber eine wenig beachtete Gefahr der Prügelstrafe bei Kindern. Zeit. f. Päd. Psy., June, 1901. Vol. 3, pp. 215-219.

182. **Monroe, Will S.** Notes on child study in Europe. Ped. Sem., Dec., 1901. Vol. 8, pp. 510-514.
Interesting observations during a year abroad.

183. —— —— Imagery in dreams. C. R. ive Congrès Inter. de Psy., Paris, 1901, pp. 175-177.

184. **Moore, Kathleen C.** Comparative observations of the development of movements. Ped. Sem., June, 1901. Vol. 8, pp. 231-238.
Compares movements of a boy and a girl during a period of six weeks from birth.

185. **Morgan, Charlotte L.** Outlook of kindergarten work for the deaf in leading cities. Kindergarten Mag., Dec., 1901. Vol. 14, pp. 198-203.

186. **Morgan, C. Lloyd** Child study. Paidologist (London), July, 1901. Vol. 3, pp. 62-75.

187. **Münch, Wilhelm** Zum Seelenleben des Schulkinder. Zeit. f. Päd. Psy., Dec., 1901. Vol. 3, pp. 448-455.

188. **Munroe, James P.** Sparing the rod. Ed. Rev., New York, Dec., 1901. Vol. 22, pp. 514-521.

189. **Murray, E. R. et al.** On kindergarten games. Child Life (Supplement), July, 1901, pp. 169-184.

190. **Netchaeff, A.** Zur Frage über Gedächtnissentwicklung bei Schulkindern. C. R. ive Congrès Int. de Psy., Paris, 1901, pp. 421-426.

191. **Nibecker, Franklin H.** The moral capacity of juvenile delinquents. Nat. Conf. Char. and Corr., Boston, 1901. pp. 262-268.

192. **O'Grady, C. Geraldine** Necessary elements in work and play and some practical consequences. Proceedings N. E. A., 1901, pp. 527-532. Also Kindergarten Magazine, October, 1901. Vol. 14, pp. 98-104.

193. **Ormond, A. T.** The social individual. Psy. Rev., Jan., 1901. Vol. 8, pp. 27-41.

194. **O'Shea, M. V.** Playing and learning. Kindergarten Rev., March, 1901. Vol. 11, pp. 389-394.

195. —— —— The psychology of number—a genetic view. Psy. Rev., July, 1901. Vol. 8, pp. 371-383.

196. **Otterson, Ira** The reform school officer. Nat. Conf. Char. and Corr., Boston, 1901, pp. 277-282.

197. **Paedologisch Jaarboek** (Stad Antwerpen.) Onder redactie van Prof. Dr. M. C. Schuyten. Tweede Jaargang, 1901. Antwerpen, De Nederlandsche Boekhandel, pp. 216.
Pages 149-240 contain annoted bibliography. See Schuyten, M. C.

198. **Paget, V.** (Vernon Lee) et Thomson, G. A. Le rôle d'élément moteur dans la perception esthétique visuelle. C. R. ive Cong. Int. de Psy., Paris, 1901, pp. 470-473.

199. **Parker, Francis W.** What child study has brought to the children. Kindergarten Rev., June, 1901. Vol. 11, pp. 597-598.

200. **Patrick, G. T. W.** The psychology of profanity. Psy. Rev., March, 1901. Vol. 8, pp. 113-127.

201. **Pearson, K.** On the inheritance of the mental characters in man. Proc. Roy. Soc., London, 1901. Vol. 69, pp. 153-156.

202. **Philippe, J.** Premiers mouvements d'enfant. C. R. ive Congrès Int. de Psy., Paris, 1901, pp. 239-241.

203. **Pickett, Wm.** A study of the insanities of adolescence. Jour. of Nervous and Mental Disease, Aug., 1901. Vol. 28, pp. 440-454.

204. **Pillon, F.** La mémoire affective. Son importance théorétique et pratique. Rev. Philosophique, Feb., 1901. Vol. 51, pp. 113-138.

205. **Potwin, Elizabeth B.** Study of early memories. Psy. Rev., New York, Nov., 1901. Vol. 8, pp. 596-601.

206. **Poulsson, Laura E.** Thoughts for toy-buyers. Kindergarten Rev., Dec., 1901. Vol. 12, pp. 190-196.

207. **Powe, Charlotte M.** Work and play in primary and grammar grades. Proceedings N. E. A., 1901, pp. 507-512. Also Kindergarten Magazine, October, 1901. Vol. 14, pp. 82-88.

208. **Prentice, May H.** The facetious attitude toward children. Kindergarten Rev., May, 1901. Vol. 11, pp. 521-524.

209. **Preston, Annie L.** Our sand-table work. Kindergarten Review, Jan.-Feb., 1901. Vol. 11, pp. 277-281, 341-345.

210. **Prinzig, Fr.** Die Kindersteblichkeit auf dem Lande und in der Stadt. Kinderfehler, 1901. Vol. 6, pp. 61-63.

211. **Putnam, Alice H.** Work and play in the kindergarten. Proceedings N. E. A., 1901, pp. 502-507. Also Kindergarten Magazine, Sept., 1901. Vol. 14, pp. 1-5.

212. **Quantz, J. O.** Problems in the psychology of reading. Psy. Rev. Monograph Supp., No. 5. Macmillan Co., New York., Dec., 1897, pp. 51.

213. **Quilter, H. H.** Can children be taught morality? Jour. of Education, 1901. Vol. 23, pp. 488-491.

214. **Randall, C. D.** Child saving work under state supervision. Nat. Conf. Char. and Corr., Boston, 1901, pp. 224-229.

215. **Rausch, F.** Die Suggestion im Dienste der Schule. Zeits. f. Philos. u. Päd., 1901. Vol. 8, (4-5).

216. **Régis, ——** Aliéné ou criminel? J. de Méd. de Bordeaux, 1901. Vol. 31, pp. 105-106.

217. **Reich, Edouard** De l'influence du système économique et social sur la criminalité. C. R. ive Congrès Int. de Psy., Paris, 1901, pp. 757-760.

218. **Reynaud, G.** The laws of orientation among animals. Rep. of Smith. Inst., 1898, Washington, 1899, pp. 481-498.

219. **Ribot, Th.** The nature of the creative imagination. Int. Monthly, June-July, 1900. Vol. 1. pp. 648-675; Vol. 2, pp. 1-25.

220. **Richet, Charles** Note sur un cas remarquable de précocité musicale. C. R. ive Congrès Int. de Psy., Paris, 1901, pp. 93-99.

221. **Richmond, Ennis** Boyhood. A plea for continuity in education. Longmans, Green & Co., N. Y., 1899, pp. 154.

222. —— —— The mind of a child. Longmans, Green & Co., N. Y., 1901, pp. 176.
A plea for avoiding cram, recognizing nature, health, etc. Very general. No index.

223. **Riggs, F. R.** Peculiarities of Indian education. Southern Workman, Hampton, Va., 1901. Vol. 30, pp. 66-71.
Notes power of custom and habit.

224. **Rivers, W. H. R.** The color vision of the Eskimo. Proc. Cambridge Philos. Soc., 1901. Vol. 11, pp. 143-149.
See review in Psychological Review, 1901. Vol. 8, pp. 396, 402.

225. —— —— Vision. Reports of the Camb. Anthrop. Ex. to Torres Straits. Vol. 2, Part 1, pp. 1-132. With appendix by C. G. Seligmann, pp. 133-140. Univ. Press, Camb. (Eng.), 1901.
Most valuable work on the subject of senses of primitive peoples.

226. **Robertson, Stewart A.** The money sense in children. Paidologist (London), April, 1901. Vol. 3, pp. 12-17.

227. **Robinovitch, L. G.** Idiot and imbecile children. Various causes of idiocy and imbecility. The relation of alcoholism in the parent to idiocy and imbecility of the offspring. Jour. of Mental Pathology, 1901. Vol. 1, pp. 14-24, 86-95.

228. —— —— L'idiotie et l'imbécillité chez les enfants. Jour. de Neurologie, 1901. Vol. 6, pp. 221-230.

Rott, A. J. See Blümml, E. K.

Sanford, E. C. See Triplett, Norman.

229. **Sano, Fr.** Van dolende kinderen. Paedol. Jaarb., 1901, pp. 137-147.

230. **Schliz, A.** Eine Schulkinderuntersuchung zum Zweck der Rassenbestimmung nach Farbencomplexion und primären Körpermerkmalen. Arch. f. Anthr., Braunschweig, 1901. Vol. 27, pp. 191-209.
See review in Pedagogical Seminary, 1902. Vol. 9, p. 43.

231. **Schultz, Fritz** La psychologie des peuples sauvages. C. R. IVe Congrès Int. de Psy., Paris, 1901, pp. 762-763.
Brief abstract of author's book Psychologie der Naturvölker, Leipzig, 1900,

232. **Schuyten, M. C.** Over de verandeilijkheid der spierkracht bij kinderen gedurende het kalender en het schooljaar. Paedol. Jaarb., 1901, pp. 1-112.
Elaborate study of muscular strength in children during the various seasons of the year.

233. —— —— Het oorspronkelijk teekenen also bijdrage tot kinder-analyse. Paedol. Jaarb., 1901, pp. 113-128.
Study of children's drawings as a basis for child analysis.

234. —— —— Steilschrift of schuinschrift. Paedol. Jaarb., 1901, pp. 129-136.
Favors vertical writing.

235. —— —— La force musculaire des élèves à travers l'année. C. R. IVe Congrès Int. de Psy., Paris, 1901, pp. 432-434.
See No. 232

236. **Scripture, E. W.** The color sense tester. C. R. IVe Congrès Int. de Psy., Paris, 1901, pp. 387-402.

237. —— —— A safe test for color vision. Studies from Yale Psychol. Lab., 1900, New Haven, 1901. Vol. 8, pp. 1-20.

238. **Sears, Charles H.** Studies in rhythm. Ped. Sem., March, 1901. Vol. 8, pp. 3-44.
A laborious and painstaking test of the rhythmic sense of school children from 6 to 18.

239. **Seashore, C. E.** Suggestions for tests on school children. Ed. Rev., N. Y., June, 1901. Vol. 22, pp. 69-82.

240. **Sérieux, P.** La démence précoce. Gaz. Hebd. de Méd. et de Chir., 1901. Vol. 48, pp. 229-233.

241. **Shaw, Edward R.** School hygiene. Macmillan Co., New York, 1901, pp. 260.
Sets forth the conditions which should surround children at school.

242. **Sheldon, Henry D.** The history and pedagogy of American student societies. D. Appleton & Co., N. Y., 1901, pp. 366.
Treats of American and foreign student life. Bibliography of 318 titles.

243. **Sikorsky,** —— Les principes d'une pédagogie conforme à l'évolution naturelle du cerveau humain. Rev. de Psychol. Clin. et Thér., Paris, 1901. Vol. 5, pp. 9-21.

244. **Simon,** —— De développement de la tête chez les enfants anormaux. Bull. Soc. Étude Psychol. de l'Enfant, 1901. Vol. 2, pp. 109-115.
See Ped. Sem., 1901. Vol. 8, p. 247.

245. —— —— L'interprétation des sensations tactile chez des enfants arriérés. L'Année Psychologique, Paris, 1901. Vol. 7, pp. 537-558.

246. **Smith, Caroline F.** The story of a child. Trans. from the French of Pierre Loti. Birchard, Boston, 1901, pp. 304.
Mainly autobiographical. Cannot fail to develop a deeper sympathy with childhood.

247. **Sollier, P.** Psychologie de l'idiot et de l'imbécile. (2nd edition.) Alcan, Paris, 1901, pp. 236.

248. **Spaulding, F. E.** The individual child; his education. School Journal, Feb. 2, 9, 16, March 16, 1901. Vol. 62, pp. 110-112, 146-147; 170-171; 281-284.

249. **Spitzka, E. A.** The redundancy of the preinsula in the brains of distinguished educated men. Med. Record, New York, 1901. Vol. 59, pp. 940-943.

250. **Squire, C. R.** A genetic study of rhythm. Am. Jour. of Psy., July, 1901. Vol. 12, pp. 492-589.

251. **Stahl, Fritz, et al.** Die Kunst im Leben des Kindes. Zeit. f. Päd. Psy., April, 1901. Vol. 3, pp. 126-140.

252. **Starr, Laura B.** A unique collection of dolls. Delineator, Dec., 1901. Vol. 58, pp. 927-931.

253. **Steel, R.** Imitation, or the mimetic force in nature and human nature. Simpkin, Marshall, London, 1901, pp. 197.

254. **Stelling, Heinrich** The care of backward children in the public schools and institutions for deaf-mutes. Association Review, Feb., 1901. Vol. 3, pp. 73-75.

255. **Stumpf, Carl** Eigenartige sprachliche Entwickelung eines Kindes. Zeit. f. Päd. Psy., Dec., 1901. Vol. 3, pp. 419-447.

256. **Study** of a Deaf Child. Some incidents of little Mary's first years at school. Am. Annals of the Deaf, March, 1901. Vol. 46, pp. 186-217.
Shows importance of caring for individuality.

257. **Sully, James** George Sands's childhood. Longman's Mag., Dec., 1889. Vol. 15, pp. 149-164.

258. —— —— A girl's religion. Longman's Mag., May, 1890. Vol. 16, pp. 89-99.

259. —— —— Child study and education. International Monthly, March, 1901. Vol. 3, pp. 314-343.

260. —— —— The laughter of savages. International Monthly, Sept., 1901. Vol. 4, pp. 379-402.
Résumés most of the literature on the subject.

261. —— —— The psychology of tickling. C. R. ive Congrès Int. de Psy., Paris, 1901, pp. 329-342.

262. **Swift, Edgar J.** Some criminal tendencies of boyhood. A study in adolescence. Ped. Sem., March, 1901. Vol. 8, pp. 65-91.
A valuable contribution to the embryology of crime.

263. **Talbot, E. S.** Juvenile female delinquents. Alienist and Neurologist, St. Louis, 1901. Vol. 22, pp. 689-694.

264. **Thomas, W. I.** The gaming instinct. Am. Jour. of Sociology, Chicago, 1901. Vol. 6, pp. 750-763.
Résumés the psychology of the subject.

Thomson, G. A. See Paget, V.

265. **Thorndike, Edw. Lee** The mental life of the monkeys. Psy. Rev., Monograph Supp., No. 15, 1901, pp. 57.

266. —— —— The intelligence of monkeys. Pop. Sci. Mo., N. Y., 1901. Vol. 59, pp. 273-279.
Abstract of No. 265.

267. —— —— The study of children. Teachers College Record, New York., May, 1901. Vol. 2, No. 3, pp. 110.

268. —— —— Notes on child study. Macmillan Co., N. Y., 1901, pp. 157. Columbia Univ. contributions to Philos., Psy. and Ed., June, 1901. Vol. 8, Nos. 3-4.

269. —— —— The evolution of the human intellect. Pop. Sci. Mo., Nov., 1901. Vol. 60, pp. 58-65.

270. **Thorndike, E. L., and Woodworth, R. S.** The influence of improvement in one mental function upon the efficiency of other functions. Psy. Rev., N. Y., 1901. Vol. 8, pp. 247-261, 384-395, 553-564.

271. **Tisserand, Pierre** Sur les théories Herbartienne et physiologiques du plaisir. C. R. ive Congrès Int. de Psy., Paris, 1901, pp. 272-273.

272. **Tissié, P.** La science du geste.   Rev. Scientifique, Paris, 1901. Vol. 16, pp. 289-300.

273. **Toulouse & Marchand** Démence précoce par paralysie générale.   Rev. de Psychiatrie, Paris, 1901.   Vol. 4, pp. 1-11.

274. **Trask, Mary G.** What is a good child?   Kindergarten Rev., Sept., 1901.   Vol. 12, pp. 1-6.

275. —— —— How shall we develop goodness?   Kindergarten Rev., Nov., 1901.   Vol. 12, pp. 126-132.

276. **Triplett, Norman and Sanford, E. C.** Studies of rhythm and meter.   Am. Jour. of Psy., April, 1901.   Vol. 12, pp. 361-387.

277. **Trömmer, E.** Das Jugendirresein (Dementia praecox).   Marhold, Halle a. S., 1901, pp. 28.

278. **Ufer, Chr.** Ueber Kinderspiel und Kinderspielsachen.   Kinderfehler, 1901.   Vol. 6, pp. 1-13.

279. **Urwick, H. M.** "If you found a shilling."   A study in children's property sense.   Paidologist (London), April, 1901.   Vol. 3, pp. 18-22.

280. **Van Epps, C.** The Babinski reflex.   Jour. Nerv. and Ment. Disease, April, 1901.   Vol. 28, pp. 214-223.
     See especially the normal plantar reflex in children. p. 217.

281. **Van Liew Charles C.** The curriculum of secondary education in the light of fundamental traits of adolescence.   Mysell-Rollins Co., San Francisco, 1901, pp. 15.

282. **Van Voorhes, Lillian C.** Children of yesterday and to-day.   Ledger Monthly, New York, June, 1901.   Vol. 57.   No. 8, pp. 1-2; 20-21.
     Popular; with a few pictures of children.

283. **Vaschide, N.** Recherches expérimentales sur l'imagination créatrice chez l'enfant.   C. R. ive Congrès Int. de Psy., Paris, 1901.   pp. 251-253.

284. **Voisin, J.** Puberty psychoses.   Alienist and Neurologist, St. Louis, 1900.   Vol. 21, pp. 653-657.

285. **Wachsmuth, H.** Cerebrale Kinderlähmung und Idiotie.   Arch. f. Psychiat. u. Nervenhk., Berlin, 1901.   Vol. 34, pp. 787-840.

286. **Wade W.** The deaf-blind.   Association Review, Feb., 1901. Vol. 3, pp. 41-42.

287. **Wagner, F. von** Von den Spielen der Tiere.   Biol. Centralblatt, Leipzig, 1901.   Vol. 21, pp. 329-336.

288. **Wardle, Phyllis** A little mathematician.   Kindergarten Rev., Feb., 1901.   Vol. 11, pp. 329-333.

289. —— —— Tools and a boy.   Kindergarten Rev., Jan., 1901. Vol. 11, pp. 267-270.

290. **Warner, F.** A discussion on feeble-minded children: diagnosis and treatment. Brit. Med. Jour., 1901. Vol. 2, pp. 1251-1254.

291. **Wateff, S.** Anthropologische Beobachtungen an den Schülern und Soldaten in Bulgarien. Corrbl. d. deutschen Ges. f. Anthr., München, 1901. Vol. 33, pp. 29-30.
See review in Ped. Sem., 1901. Vol. 8, pp. 244-245.

292. **Watson, James** Report of the school for defective youths. Association Review, June, 1901. Vol. 3, pp. 261.

293. **Wentworth, Edwin P.** Origin and development of the juvenile reformatories. Nat. Conf. Char. and Corr., Boston, 1901, pp. 245-254.

294. **Weygandt, W.** Die Behandlung idiotischer und imbeciller Kinder in ärztlicher und pädagogischer Beziehung. Kabitzsch, Würzburg, 1901, pp. 103.

295. **Wheeler, Marianna** The baby, his care and training. Harper & Bros., New York, 1901, pp. 189.

296. **White, Stella K.** The home instruction of a little deaf child. Association Review, Dec., 1901. Vol. 3, pp. 418-427.

297. **Wiedeburg, Dr.** Die Chorea im Kindesalter Kinderfehler, 1901. Vol. 6, pp. 145-157.

298. **Wikel, Anna Hamlin** The child's special gift. Kindergarten Rev., Feb., 1901. Vol. 11, pp. 334-337.

299. **Wilson, Louis N.** Bibliography of child study for the year 1900. Ped. Sem., Dec., 1901. Vol. 8, pp. 515-537.
331 titles of books and magazine articles.

300. **Wipf, H.** Steilschrift als Schulschrift. Zeit. f. Schulgesundheitspflege, 1901. Vol. 14, pp. 388-396.

301. **Wissler, Clark** The correlation of mental and physical tests. Psy. Rev. Monograph Supp., No. 16, 1901. pp. 62.

302. **Woodruff, C. E.** An anthropological study of the small brain of civilized man and its evolution. Am. Jour. of Insanity, 1901. Vol. 58, pp. 1-78.

Woodworth, R. S. See Thorndike, E. L.

303. **Wyckoff, Adelaide E.** Children's ideals. Ped. Sem., Dec., 1901. Vol. 8, pp. 482-494.
What children hope to be and do as adults.

304. **Wyer, J. I., Jr., and Lord, I. E.** Bibliography of education for 1900. Ed. Rev., New York, 1901. Vol. 21, pp. 382-421.

305. **Yocum, Albert D.** An inquiry into the teaching of addition and subtraction. Avil Printing Co., Philadelphia, 1901, pp. 92.
An effort to determine the contents of children's minds on entering school. Rich in methodic suggestions.

306. **Ziegler, K.** Unser Erziehungsberuf an Schwachsinnigen. Kinderfehler, 1901. Vol. 6, pp. 97-101.

307. **Zimmer, Hans** Was soll das Kind lesen? Zeit. f. Päd. Psy., June, 1901. Vol. 3, pp. 204-214.

SUBJECT INDEX.

Abnormal, 62, 63, 96, 146, 151, 171, 244.
Activity, 68.
Adolescence, 157, 203, 281.
Adultism, 70.
Æsthetics, 198.
Age, 178.
Alcohol, 16.
Ambidexterity, 25.
Animal Psychology, 58, 174, 218, 265, 266, 287.
Anthropometry, 26, 47, 67, 95, 135, 142, 244, 291.
Arithmetic, 305.
Art, 131, 158, 251.
Association, 33.
Asymmetry, 25.
Autobiography, 246.
Auxiliary School, 149.

Baby, 295.
Backward Children, 71, 87, 159, 245, 254.
Bibliography, 15, 24, 299, 304.
Biography, 57, 138.
Birds, 58.
Blind, 84, 286.
Boys, 85, 86, 221, 262, 302.
Brain, 243, 249.
Breeding, 92.

Character, 38.
Child Saving, 41, 75, 214.
Child Study, 13, 21, 50, 69, 78, 114, 119, 141, 170, 177, 182, 186, 199, 259, 267, 268.
China, 118.
Chorea, 297.
City, 210.
Colonies, 27, 46.
Color Hearing, 154.
Color Sense, 236.
Color Vision, 224, 237.
Confessions, 14, 106.
Consciousness, 43.
Country, 210.
Crime, 1, 17, 42, 82, 93, 173, 191, 216, 217, 263.
Criminal, 262.

Curriculum, 61, 281.

Deaf, 11, 34, 116, 185, 256, 286, 296.
Deaf Mutes, 30, 71, 81, 127, 254.
Defectives, 36, 103, 179, 292.
Degeneration, 4, 22, 40.
Dementia praecox, 52, 83, 240, 273, 277.
Development, 184.
Dolls, 252.
Drama, 90.
Drawing, 53, 167, 233.
Dreams, 183.

Economics, 217.
Energy, 68.
Epilepsy, 40.
Ethics, 97.
Europe, 182.
European Schools, 12.
Evolution, 243, 269.
Eye, 147.

Fatigue, 6, 19, 80, 133, 134.
Fear, 123.
Feeble Minded, 100, 290, 306.
Flagellation, 143.
Flowers, 28.

Games, 32, 124, 125, 189.
Gaming, 264.
General, 108, 112, 168, 197.
Genius, 72, 74, 94, 164, 249.
Germany, 61, 127.
Gesture, 272.
Girls, 65, 79.
Grammar, 33.
Growth, 67, 99.
Gymnastics, 95.

Hard Hearing, 37.
Hearing, 11, 37, 116, 169.
Heredity, 172, 201.
Historical, 13, 17, 282.
Home, 104, 141, 296.
Honor, 150.
Hygiene, 20, 27, 128, 152, 241.
Hypnotism, 22.

Ideal School, 107.
Ideals, 89, 303.
Idiots and Idiocy, 35, 135, 227, 228, 247, 285, 294.
Imagination, 219, 283.
Imbecility, 227, 228, 247, 294.
Imitation, 253.
Indian children, 223.
Individual, 193, 248.
Infant, 68.
Insane, 113, 203.
Instincts, 5, 60, 73, 101.
Intellect, 18, 23, 72, 94, 266, 269.
Italy, 48.

Journal, 138.

Kindergarten, 161, 180, 185, 189, 209, 211.

Language, 91, 156, 159, 255.
Laughter, 260.
Left-handedness, 25.
Lunacy, 216.

Manual Training, 289.
Mathematics, 288, 305.
Medical Inspection, 152.
Memory, 162, 163, 190, 204, 205.
Menstruation, 76.
Mental, 6, 10, 43, 45, 96, 159, 166, 172, 187, 201, 222, 265, 270, 301.
Mental Development, 87.
Mental Work, 23.
Methods, 61, 146.
Money Sense, 226, 279.
Monkey, 265, 266.
Morality, 213.
Morals, 115, 191.
Mortality, 210.
Movements, 184, 202.
Muscular strength, 54, 232, 235.
Music, 131, 132, 220.
Myths, 2.

Nature, 56.
Nature Study, 3, 28, 49, 59.
Neglected children, 120.
Nerve hygiene, 20.
New born, 147.
Number, 195.

Observation, 114.
Outings, 27, 46.

Paralysis, 126, 285.
Parents, 139.
Phonetics, 156.
Physical, 23, 26, 45, 54, 67, 135, 184, 244, 301.

Physical and Mental, 145, 301.
Physical training, 95, 145.
Physical characteristics, 142, 230, 291.
Physiology, 271.
Physique, 23.
Play, 32, 55, 60, 101, 109, 125, 192, 194, 207, 211, 278, 287.
Playground, 153.
Portugal, 170.
Precocity, 7, 45, 72, 82, 220.
Primary school, 21.
Primitive Man, 29, 150, 166, 231, 260, 302.
Prisons, 1, 17.
Profanity, 200.
Property sense, 279.
Psychology, 53, 64, 102, 106, 117, 119, 129, 148, 195.
Puberty, 175, 176, 284.
Punishments, 17, 31, 181, 188.

Reaction time, 148.
Reading, 64, 129, 212, 307.
Reform, 46, 63, 79, 196, 293.
Reform schools, 31.
Religion, 117, 257, 258.
Rewards, 51.
Rhythm, 110, 161, 238, 250, 276.
Right-handedness, 25.
Rousseau, 56.
Rural schools.

Sadism, 143.
School Physician, 152.
Schools, 12.
Seasons, 232, 235.
Senses, 15, 180.
Sex, 18, 65, 73, 76, 77, 79, 85, 98, 118, 143, 144, 178, 257, 258, 263.
Sexual abuses, 143, 144.
Shakespeare, 157.
Skin, 155.
Smell, 15.
Societies, 39, 242.
Sociological, 5, 34, 35, 193, 217.
Song, 58.
Spinoza, 57.
State, 36, 75, 214.
Statistical, 115.
Stature, 142.
Stirpiculture, 92.
Students, 242.
Stuttering and Stammering, 98.
Suggestion, 9, 131, 215.
Suicide, 8.
Sunday School, 21, 111, 280.

Teeth, 105, 130.

Tests, 114, 239.
Tickling, 261.
Touch, 245.
Toys, 206, 278.
Trade, 121.
Truth, 165.

Vagabondage, 44, 229.
Vertical writing, 59, 234, 300.
Vision, 225.

Vocabulary, 91.

Weak minded, 132, 149.
Will, 122.
Woman, 65.
Work, 54, 137, 192, 207, 211
Writing, 59, 234, 300.

Youth, 57.

PUBLICATIONS

OF THE

CLARK UNIVERSITY LIBRARY

WORCESTER, MASS.

| VOL. I | January, 1904 | No. 2 |

Bibliography of Child Study for the Year 1902.

Clark University Press

WORCESTER, MASS.

BIBLIOGRAPHY OF CHILD STUDY.

For the Year 1902.

By LOUIS N. WILSON, Librarian, Clark University.

1. **Abt, G.** L'écriture en miroir. L'Année Psychologique. **Paris,** 1902. Vol. 8, pp. 221-255.
    A study of 13 mirror writers found among 80 left-handed persons.

2. —— —— Note sur la lecture et l'écriture chez trois enfants anormaux. Bull. Soc. Étude Psychol. de l'Enfant, 1902, pp. 169-175.

3. **Adams, Cecilia** Hindrances to the development of language. Proc. N. E. A. for 1902, pp. 412-417. Also Kindergarten Magazine, Sept., 1902. Vol 15, pp. 20-24.
    Differentiates speech and language development and discusses speech defects.

4. **Alexander, G.** Zur Frage des postembryonalen Wachstumes des menschlichen Ohrlabyrinthes. Anat. Hefte, 1902. Vol. 19, pp. 569-578.
    —— —— See also Kreidle and Alexander.

5. **Aley, Robert J.** Arithmetic. Rev. of Ed., Jan., 1902. Vol. 7, pp. 235-236.

6. **D'Alfonso, N. R.** Le Anomalie del Linguaggio e la loro Educabilità, Roma, Soc. Ed. Dante Alighieri, 1902, pp. 47.

7. **Allin, Arthur** Some experimental observations on practice and habit. Jour. of Ped., March, 1902. Vol. 14, pp. 237-254.

8. **Allison, James** Practical thoughts on reformatory work. Nat. Conf. Char. and Corr., Boston, 1902, pp. 250-264.
    Deals with the nutrition, occupation, and punishment of delinquents.

9. **Ament, Wilhelm** Begriff und Begriffe der Kindersprache. Sammlung von Abhandlungen aus dem Gebiete der pädagogischen Psychologie und Physiologie. Berlin, 1902. Vol. 5, pp. 85.

10. **André, A. E.** L'œuvre des voyages scolaires. Rev. Péd., July, 1902. Vol. 41, pp. 23-42.
    An account of the school-journey movement in France.

11. **Apert, E.** Les enfants retardataires. Baillière, Paris, 1902, pp. 96.

12. **Arnett, L. D.** Origin and development of home and love of home. Ped. Sem., Sept., 1902. Vol. 9, pp. 324-365.

13. **Arnold, Sarah L.** Mission of the kindergarten. Rev. of Ed., March, 1902. Vol. 9, pp. 297-298.

14. **Axmann, ——** Zür Behandlung kranker Schulkinder durch Beihülfe der Lehrerschaft. Zeits. für Schulgesundheitspflege, No. 3-4, 1902. Vol. 15, pp. 148-156.

15. **Bacon, John** Thoughts on imitation. The Paidologist, July and Nov., 1902. Vol. 4, pp. 100-104; 160-163.

16. **Bair, J. H.** The practice curve; a study in the formation of habits. New York, 1902, pp. 70.
    This is supplement No. 19 of the Psychological Review monographs.

17. **Baker, C. D.** Biology as a means of inducing the pupil to think. Proc. N. E. A., 1902, pp. 468-470.

18. **Baldwin, J. M.** (Editor) Dictionary of philosophy and psychology in 3 vols. Vol. 1, 1901; Vol. 2, 1902, New York and London, Macmillans, pp. 644; 892.

19. **—— ——** Social and ethical interpretations in mental development. Macmillan Co., N. Y., 1902, pp. 606.

20. **Barnes, Anna Köhler** Children's ideas of lady and gentleman. Barnes' Studies in Education, June, 1902. Vol. 2, pp. 141-150.
    Study of class distinctions among English and American children.

21. **Barnes, Earl** Chautauqua lectures on the moral development of the child. Kindergarten Magazine, Oct., 1902. Vol. 15, pp. 73-84.

22. **—— ——** Children's attitude toward future occupation. Barnes' Studies in Education, Sept., 1902. Vol. 2, pp. 243-258.
    A statistical study of 2,360 English children—what they would like to do when they grow to be men and women.

23. **—— ——** Children's attitude towards theology. Barnes' Studies in Education, Oct., 1902. Vol. 2, pp. 283-307.
    Comparative English and American statistical studies on children's ideas of God, heaven, hell, and Old and New Testament preferences.

24. **—— ——** Children's ideas of war. Barnes' Studies in Education, Nov., 1902. Vol. 2, pp. 323-337.
    Compositions by English children on the causes of the South African war furnish the basis of this study. Its purpose is to throw light on the management of adult opinion.

25. **—— ——** Children's stories and poetry. Barnes' Studies in Education, March to Nov., 1902. Vol. 2, pp. 31-33; 71-73; 112-114; 155-156; 196-197; 234-236; 274-276; 317-318; 356-358.
    Stories and verses written by young children with comments on the same.

26. **—— ——** The development of children's political ideas. Barnes' Studies in Education, March, 1902. Vol. 2, pp. 5-24.
    Why English children wish to be like Queen Victoria.

27. **—— ——** Growth of social judgment. Barnes' Studies in Education, Aug., 1902. Vol. 2, pp. 203-217.
    Punishments advocated by English and American children. The study is based on the story of Jennie's paints.

28. **Barnes, Earl** How words get content. Barnes' Studies in Education, April, 1902. Vol. 2, pp. 43-61.
Study of the definition of common words by London and Boston school children.

29. —— —— Political ideas of American children. Barnes' Studies in Education, March, 1902. Vol. 2, pp. 25-30.
Why 1,800 New Jersey children would like to be like the late President McKinley.

30. —— —— The present and future of child study in America. Barnes' Studies in Education, Dec., 1902. Vol. 2, pp. 363-372.
The author seeks in the results of child study a basis in theory and practice in definite knowledge.

31. —— —— The prettiest thing. Barnes' Studies in Education, July, 1902. Vol. 2, pp. 180-194.
A study based upon the prettiest things seen by 700 London children.

32. —— —— Studies on children's drawings. Barnes' Studies in Education, March to June, Aug. to Dec., 1902. Vol. 2, pp. 34-35; 74-77; 109-111; 151-154; 231-233; 271-273; 314-317; 352-355; 388-391.
Collections of spontaneous drawings by children and comments on the same.

33. —— —— Truth versus lies. Kindergarten Magazine, Nov., 1902. Vol. 15, pp. 147-151.

34. —— —— Type study on ideals. Barnes' Studies in Education, March to Nov., 1902. Vol. 2, pp. 36-40; 78-80; 115-120; 157-160; 198-200; 237-240; 277-280; 319-320; 359-360.

35. **Barr, M. W.** Mental defectives; their classification and training. Phila. Med. Jour., 1902. Vol. 9, pp. 195-199.

36. —— —— The recognition and training of mental defectives. Phila. Med. Jour., 1902. Vol. 9, pp. 407-410.

37. **Baudrillart and Roussel** La mémoire de l'orthographe. Bull. Soc. Étude Psy. de l'Enfant, 1902, pp. 140-151.

38. **Beard, R. O.** The physiology of childhood as applied to education. Proc. N. E. A., 1902, pp. 720-727.
Motor training is made the basis of normal development.

39. **Bell, Sanford** A preliminary study of the emotion of love between the sexes. Am. Jour. of Psy., July, 1902. Vol. 13, pp. 325-354.

40. **Benda, Th.** Die Schwachbegabten auf den höheren Schulen. Zeits. f. Schulgesundheitspflege, 1902. Vol. 15, pp. 160-164.

41. **Bentley, I. Madison** The psychology of mental arrangement. Am. Jour. of Psy., April, 1902. Vol. 13, pp. 269-293.

42. **Berkhan,** —— Über den angeborenen oder früh sich zeigenden Wasserkopf (Hydrocephalus internus) und seine Beziehungen zur geistigen Entwickelung. Die Kinderfehler, 1902. Vol. 7, pp. 49-58.
Discusses the large heads of congenitally mentally deficient children.

43. **Bertrand, M.** L'infantilisme dysthyroïdien. (Thèse méd.) Paris, 1902, pp. 60.

44. **Besnard, A.** Dessins d'enfants. Bull. Soc. Étude Psychol. de l'Enfant, 1902, pp. 162-169.

45. **Binet, Alfred** La croissance du crâne et de la face chez les normaux entre 4 ans et 18 ans. L'Année Psychologique, Paris, 1902. Vol. 8, pp. 345-362.

46. —— —— Les proportions du crâne chez les aveugles. L'Année Psychologique, Paris, 1902. Vol. 8, pp. 369-384.

47. —— —— Les proportions du crâne chez les sourds-muets. L'Année Psychologique, Paris, 1902. Vol. 8, pp. 385-389.

48. **Bishop, William Warner and Manny, Frank A.** Do children know the alphabet. Rev. of Ed., April, 1902. Vol. 10, pp. 355-356.

49. **Boitel, J.** La criminalité juvenile. Manuel général de l'instruction primaire, 21 Mai, 1902. Vol. 38, pp. 324-325.

50. **Bolk, L.** De Oorzaken en Beteckenis der Rechtshandigheid. Haarlem, 1901.

51. **Bolton, Frederick E.** New lines of attack in child study. Proc. N. E. A., 1902, pp. 703-710.

52. **Bonser, F. G.** Chums: A study in youthful friendships. Ped. Sem., June, 1902. Vol. 9, pp. 221-236.
   An application of the questionnaire method to analyze the propensity of children to form strong individual attachments.

53. **Booth, F. W.** Lessons to be learned by the general teacher from teaching language to the deaf. Proc. N. E. A., 1902, pp. 831-836.

54. **Bourdon, B.** Recherches sur l'habitude. L'Année Psychologique, Paris, 1902. Vol. 8, pp. 327-340.

55. **Boyer, H.** Recherches sur les causes et les époques de la surdité accidentelle enfantine. Bull. de Laryngol., Otol., etc., 1902, pp. 23-25.

56. **Bradley, John E.** The educational value of play. Rev. of Ed., Jan., 1902. Vol. 7, pp. 226-231.

57. **Breton, M. E.** Le syndrome infantilisme: sa nature dysthyroïdienne. Thèse méd., Lille, 1901, pp. 130.

58. **Brinton, D. G.** (Farrand, L. ed.) The basis of social relations. Putnams, N. Y. and London, 1902, pp. 204.

59. **Brockman, F. S.** A study of the moral and religious life of 251 preparatory school students in the United States. Ped. Sem., Sept., 1902. Vol. 9, pp. 255-273.
   Shows that 17 is the age of most frequent conversions.

60. **Brown, George P.** Criticism on Stanley Hall's "School of the Future." Kindergarten Magazine, Feb., 1902. Vol. 14, pp. 331-333.

61. **Browne-Chrichton, Sir James** Address at the child study conference. Paidologist, Nov., 1902. Vol. 4, pp. 132-137.

62. **Buchner, Edward Franklin** Fixed visualization: Three new forms. Am. Jour. of Psy., July, 1902. Vol. 13, pp. 355-363.

63. —— —— Some characteristics of the genetic method. Psy. Rev., 1902. Vol. 9, pp. 490-507.

64. **Burgess, M. H.** Evolution of "children's house," Rev. of Ed., March, 1902. Vol. 9, pp. 299-301.

65. **Burk, Frederic** From fundamental to accessory in the development of the nervous system of movements. Rep. Commissioner of Ed., 1900-1901. Vol. 1, pp. 325-344.
    The republication of a valuable neurological study.

66. —— —— The genetic versus the logical order in drawing. Ped. Sem., Sept., 1902. Vol. 9, pp. 296-323.
    An excellent discussion of the psychologic basis and the pedagogic value of spontaneous drawing in the mental development of the child.

67. **Čáda, Franteŝek** (Editor) Českà Mysl. Prague, 1902.
    An excellent Bohemian journal published in the Czeck language with a department of child study, edited by Dr. Cadà.

68. —— —— Hodnota Pedopsychologie. Prague, 1902, pp. 49.
    A critical and comprehensive survey of the child study movement.

69. **Call, A. D.** Education versus crime. A study of the state reformatory at Elmira, N. Y., Education. Vol. 22, pp. 587-603.

70. **Cambell, C. Victor** Kindergarten training and motor development; a study of a thousand children. Kindergarten Magazine, Nov., 1902. Vol. 15, pp. 135-142.

71. **Carman, E. Kate** Notes on school activity. Ped. Sem., March, 1902. Vol. 9, pp. 106-117.
    Shows how the restless nature of the child chafes against the restrained life of the school.

72. **Carr, Harvey A.** Survival values of play. Investigations of the Dept. of Psychology and Education of the University of Colorado. Boulder, 1902, pp. 47.
    A valuable study with an excellent bibliography appended.

73. **Cash, K. G.** Children's pets: A side study. Barnes' Studies in Education, May, 1902. Vol. 2, pp. 100-108.
    A statistical study of the humane instincts of English children.

74. —— —— Children's sense of truth. Barnes' Studies in Education, Oct., 1902. Vol. 2, pp. 308-313.

75. **Chadwick-Pratt, Mrs. M. L.** Illustrations for children's stories. Paidologist, Nov., 1902. Vol. 4, pp. 166-170.

76. **Chamberlain, Alexander F.** The contact of "higher" and "lower" races. Ped. Sem., Dec., 1902. Vol. 9, pp. 507-520.

77. —— —— Some recent child-study literature. Ped. Sem., March, 1902. Vol. 9, pp. 43-49.

78. —— —— Work and rest; genius and stupidity. Pop. Sci. Mo., 1902. Vol. 60, pp. 413-423.

79. **Chapin, T. F.** Dietaries. Nat. Conf. Char. and Corr., Boston, 1902, pp. 453-462.
Nutrition suitable for juvenile delinquents.

80. —— ——. Play as a reformative agency. Nat. Conf. Char. and Corr., Boston, 1902, pp. 437-440.
Discusses play as an agency in the physical development of delinquents.

81. —— —— Punishments. Nat. Conf. Char. and Corr., Boston, 1902, pp. 426-427.
Use of punishment in reform schools.

82. **Chapple, B. P.** What Minnesota is doing for her blind children. Proc. N. E. A., 1902, pp. 840-844.

83. **Chase, Philo F.** Why children break down in school. Rev. of Ed., March, 1902. Vol. 9, pp. 296-297.

84. **Cheatle, A. H.** The report of an examination of the ears of 1,000 school children between the ages of three and sixteen years in Hanwell Dist. School. Jour. of Laryngol, Rhinol & Otol, 1902. Vol. 17, pp. 282-292.

85. **Cohn, Herm.** Ueber den Druck der Breslauer Schulbücher vom augenärztlichen Standpunkte. Zeits. für Schulgesundheitspflege No. 6, 1902. Vol. 15, pp. 331-333.

86. —— —— Die Augen der in Breslau Medicin Studirenden. Arch. f. Augenhk., 1902. Vol. 46, pp. 29-48.

87. **Colson, O.** Jeux d'enfants dans la Belgique. Archivio per le Tradizioni Popolari, Palermo, 1902. Vol. 21, pp. 104-110.
A collection of Belgian finger-rhymes.

88. **Colucci, ——** Sui criteri e metodi per l'educabilità dei deficienti e dei dementi. Vol. 2. I Dementi. Riv. Sperim. di Freniat., Reggio, 1902. Vol. 28, pp. 410-451.

89. **Colvin, Stephen S.** Invention versus form in English composition. An inductive study. Ped. Sem., Dec., 1902. Vol. 9, pp. 393-421.
Discusses the relations between content and form in teaching of English.

90. —— —— Rhythm, time and number. Am. Jour. of Psy., Jan., 1902. Vol. 13, pp. 80-97.

91. **Combe, A.** La nervosité de l'enfant. Paris, 1902, pp. 200.

92. **Compayré, Gabriel** Development of the child in later infancy. (Int. Ed. Series), Appleton, New York, 1902, pp. 300.
This is a translation of Part II of Compayré's intellectual and moral development of the child. It treats of the instincts, judgment and reasoning, language, voluntary activities, character and morbid tendencies.

93. **Cook, O. F.** Kinetic evolution in man. Science, June 13, 1902, N. S. Vol. 15, pp. 927-933.

94. **Crothers, Samuel M.** The humor of childhood. Kindergarten Rev., May, 1901. Vol. 12, pp. 515-517.

95. **Curtis, H. S.** Inhibition. Rep. Commissioner Ed., 1900-1901. Vol. 1, pp. 345-356.
Republished from the Pedagogical Seminary, Oct., 1898. Vol. 6, pp. 65-113.

96. **Davis, E. G** A Saturday school. The Paidologist, April, 1902. Vol. 4, pp. 38-40.

97. **DeCock, A.** Taalvervorming in den kindermond. Volkskunde, 1901-2. Vol. 14, pp. 89-100.

98. **Denoel et Epinoux** L'éducation sociale dans les écoles primaires de filles. Manuel général de l'instruction primaire, 5 Juillet, 1902. Vol. 38, pp. 417-419.

99. **Denoy, E.** Descendons-nous du singe? Schleicher, Paris, 1902.

100. **Deroy, F. C.** Psychoses post-typhiques chez les enfants. Thèse mèd., Lille, 1902, pp. 46.

101. **Dewey, John** Interpretation of the savage mind. Psy. Rev., May, 1902. Vol. 9, pp. 217-230.

102. **Dexter, Edwin G.** A study of calms. Pop. Sci. Mo., April, 1902. Vol. 60, pp. 521-528.

103. —— —— The survival of the fittest in motor training. Ed. Rev., Jan., 1902. Vol. 23, pp. 81-91.

104. **Dismorr, Blanche** Ought children to be paid for domestic services? Barnes' Studies in Education, April, 1902. Vol. 2, pp. 62-70.

105. **Doll, L.** Aerztliche Untersuchungen aus der Hilfsschule für schwachsinnige Kinder zu Karlsruhe. Macklot, Karlsruhe, 1902, pp. 62.

106. **Drouot, ——** État intellectuel du sourd muet. Rev. Phillanthr., 1902. Vol. 8, pp. 436-471.

107. **Dunton, Wm. Rush** Some points in the diagnosis of dementia præcox. Proc. Am. Medico-Psy. Ass'n, 1902, pp. 147-155.

108. **Eichholz, A.** The treatment of feeble-minded children. Brit. Med. Jour., 1902. Vol. 2, pp. 683-687.

109. **Eigenmann, Carl H.** Physical basis of heredity. Pop. Sci. Mo., May, 1902. Vol. 61, pp. 32-44.

110. **Ellis, G. Harold** Fetichism in children. Ped. Sem., June, 1902. Vol. 9, pp. 205-220.
Suggestive and interesting parallelism between the growth of the individual child and the race.

111. —— —— The pedagogy of Jesus. Ped. Sem., Dec., 1902. Vol. 9, pp. 441-459.

112. **Ellis, Havelock** The criminal. W. Scott, London, 1901, pp. 419.

113. —— —— Studies in the psychology of sex. 2 vols. Watford, Lond., and F. A. Davis Co., Phila., 1900-1902, pp. 204 and 314.
The author places the cause of sincerity against that of reticence in matters of sex. One vol. deals with sexual inversion.

Epinoux. See **Denoel et Epinoux.**

114. **Everett, R.** Educating the deaf-blind. Am. Review of Reviews, 1902. Vol. 35, pp. 435-442.

115. **Ewing, A. E.** Visual tests for children. Am. Jour. of Ophthal., 1902. Vol. 19, pp. 33-37.

116. **Fairweather, Elizabeth K.** The psychological and ethical value of music. Proc. N. E. A., 1902, pp. 621-625.

117. **Ferriani, L.** I drammi dei fanciulli. Como, Ormarini, 1902, pp. 312.
    Treats of child-labor, child-suicides and school-martyrdom.

118. **Féré, Charles** L'influence du rhythme sur le travail. L'Année Psychologique, Paris, 1902. Vol. 9, pp. 49-106.

119. **Fernald, Walter E.** The Massachusetts farm colony for the feeble-minded. Nat. Conf. Char. and Corr., Boston, 1902, pp. 487-490.

120. **Ferrari, Giulio C.** Oral method and its fitness for the deaf Ass'n Rev., Oct., 1902. Vol. 4, pp. 344-356.
    The superiority of articulate language to the mimic system in the education of deaf children.

121. —— —— Psychic development and pedagogical treatment of children who are hard of hearing. Ass'n Rev., June, 1902. Vol. 4, pp. 232-239.
    Pedagogic suggestions for the treatment of the semi-deaf child.

122. **Finck, Henry T.** Evolution of girlhood. Harper's Magazine, Jan., 1902. Vol. 104, pp. 235-238.

123. **Fischer, Heinrich** Geographische Spaziergänge. Zeits. für Päd. Psy., Dec., 1902. Vol. 4, pp. 442-452.
    Discusses home geography and school excursions.

124. **Folks, Homer** The care of destitute, neglected, and delinquent children. Macmillan Co., N. Y., 1902, pp. 251.
    An excellent treatment of the institutional aspects of juvenile pauperism and delinquency.

125. **France, J. Clemence** The gambling impulse. Am. Jour. of Psy., July, 1902. Vol. 13, pp. 364-407.

126. **French, F. C.** The mental imagery of students. Psy. Rev., Jan., 1902. Vol. 9, pp. 40-56.

Frenkel. See **Lafon and Frenkel.**

127. **Von Gabnay, F.** Ungarische Puppen., Globus, Braunschweig, 1902. Vol. 80, pp. 205-208.
    Describes Hungarian dolls. Báitsa in the country of Sáros is the Hungarian Nürnberg.

128. **Gale, H. and M. C.** Children's vocabularies. Pop. Sci. Mo., May, 1902. Vol. 61, pp. 45-51.

129. —— —— The vocabularies of three children in one family at two and three years of age. Ped. Sem., Dec., 1902. Vol. 9, pp. 422-435.
    Full of suggestion to teachers of modern languages on the natural method

130. **Galton, Francis** The possible improvement of the human breed under existing conditions of law and sentiment. Pop. Sci. Mo., 1902. Vol. 60, pp. 218-233; Man, 1901, 161-164.

131. **Garber, John P.** Co-education. Education, Dec., 1902. Vol. 23, pp. 235-241.

132. **Garnier, P.** La criminalité juvenile. Rev. Scient., 1902. Vol. 17, pp. 449-455.

133. **Gérard-Varet, L.** Le jeu chez l'homme et chez les animaux. Rev. Scient., 1902. Vol. 17, pp. 485-491.

134. **Giessler, C. M.** Die Gerüche vom psychogenetischen Standpunkte aus. Vtljsch. f. wiss. Philos. u. Sociol., 1902. Vol. 26, pp. 49-76.

135. **Goddard, Henry H.** Negative ideals. Barnes' Studies in Education, Dec., 1902. Vol. 2, pp. 392-398.
A statistical study of the people whom children would not wish to be like.

136. **Gordon, A.** A note on some psychoses of early puberty with report of a case in a boy, 12 years old. Phila. Med. Jour., 1902. Vol. 10, pp. 332-335.

137. **Gregor, K.** Untersuchungen über der Athmungsgrösse des Kindes. Arch. f. Anat. u Physiol., Physiol. Abth., 1902, Suppl. Bd., pp. 59-118, Arch. f. Kinderhlk., 1902. Vol. 35, pp. 272-304.

138. **Griggs, Edward Howard** Influence of parent and teacher in moral education. Kindergarten Mag., May, 1902. Vol. 14, pp. 553-556.

139. **Groszmann, M. P. E.** The treatment of defectives. N. Y. Med. Jour., 1902. Vol. 75, pp. 187-193.

140. **Guimaraens, F. da C.** Le besoin de prier et ses conditions psychologiques. Rev. Philos., 1902. Vol. 54, pp. 391-412.

141. **Gulick, L.** Interest in relation to muscular exercise. Am. Phys., Ed. Rev., 1902. Vol. 7, pp. 57-65.

142. **Gutzmann, Albert** Care of the speech of children in the family and in the school. Ass'n Review, April, 1902. Vol. 4, pp. 107-112.

143. **Gutzmann, H.** Ueber die Sprache der Schwerhörigen und Ertaubten. Deutsche med. Wochensch, 1902. Vol. 28, pp. 18-19.

144. ——— —— Ueber die Stummheit der Kinder. Fortsch. d. Med., 1902. Vol. 20, pp. 601-606.

145. **Hall, Frank H.** Transition in mental training from the spoken to the written symbol. Jour. of Ped., March, 1902. Vol. 14, pp. 214-223.

146. **Hall, G. Stanley** Adolescents and high school English, Latin, and algebra. Ped. Sem., March, 1902. Vol. 9, pp. 92-105.
A discussion of the logical and genetic order in the approach to secondary school studies.

147. **Hall, G. Stanley** Ausgewählte Beiträge zur Kinderpsychologie und Pädagogik. Aus dem Englischen uebersetzt von Joseph Stimpfl, Altenburg, 1902, pp. 454.
    A translation of 13 valuable papers on the psychology of childhood.

148. —— —— The ideal school as based on child study. Paidologist, April, 1902. Vol. 4, pp. 32-38.

149. —— —— Some social aspects of education. Ped. Sem., March, 1902. Vol. 9, pp. 81-91.

150. **Hall, G. Stanley and Wallin, J. E. W.** How children and youth think and feel about clouds. Ped. Sem., Dec., 1902. Vol. 9, pp. 460-506.
    Sheds light upon the position of sentiment in nature teaching.

151. **Hamilton, Samuel** The teacher's work. Rev. of Ed., May, 1902. Vol. 11, pp. 378-380.

152. **Harrison, Elizabeth** How the mastery of language is aided by the kindergarten. Kindergarten Rev., Sept., 1902. Vol. 13, pp. 42-44.

153. **Hattie W. H.** The role of education in the development of self-control. Proc. Am. Medico-Psy. Ass'n, 1902, pp. 252-260.

154. **Hefferan, Mrs. Helen M.** The organization of the associations of parents of deaf children as an aid to schools. Proc. N. E. A., 1902, pp. 848-850.

155. **Henri, Victor** Education de la mémoire. L'Année Psychologique, Paris, 1902. Vol. 8, pp. 1-48.
    An experimental study of the memory span.

156. **Hermann, A.** Ueber Kopfschmerzen bei Schulkindern und ihre Beeinflussung durch suggestive Behandlung. (Inaug. Diss.) Breslau, 1902, pp. 28.

157. **Hill, Patty S.** Punishment. Kindergarten Rev., Sept., 1902. Vol. 13, pp. 11-17.

158. **Hill, Walter B.** Psychology and ethics of fun. Kindergarten Mag., April and May, 1902. Vol. 14, pp. 451-458; 521-528. Also Proc. N. E. A., 1902, pp. 286-297.

159. **Hines, Jessie Scott** The middle ground in gift work. Kindergarten Mag., Nov., 1902. Vol. 15, pp. 152-161.

160. **Hirschlaff, L.** Ueber die Furcht der Kinder, II and III. Zeit. für Päd. Psy., 1902. Vol. 4, pp. 39-56; 141-156.

161. **Hitz, John** (Editor) International reports of schools for the deaf made to the Volta Bureau. Washington, 1902, pp. 56.
    This report furnishes conclusive proof of the growth of oral schools for the deaf in the different countries of the world.

162. **Hoche, A.** Ueber Dementia præcox. Deutsche Klinik, 1902. Vol. 6, pp. 207-224.

163. **Hoeve, J. van der** Beiträge zur Lehre vom Schielen. Arch. f. Augenhk, 1902. Vol. 46, pp. 172-183; 185-231.

164. **Hoffman, H.** Construction and activity of the brain with special regard to speaking and speech. Ass'n Review, Oct., 1902. Vol. 4, pp. 313-322.
Discusses the relation of mental efficiency to speech.

165. **Holman, H.** The philosophy of play. Paidologist, July, 1902. Vol. 4, pp. 92-97.

166. —— —— Principles and practices in education. Paidologist, Nov., 1902. Vol. 4, pp. 170-173.

167. **Howerth, I. W.** Education and social progress. Ed. Rev., April, 1902. Vol. 23, pp. 355-370.

168. —— —— Education and the individual. Jour. of Ped., June, 1902. Vol. 14, pp. 321-324.

169. **Hughes, James L.** Art as an educational factor. School Journal, July 19, 1902. Vol. 45, pp. 68-71.

170. **Hylan, J. P., and Kraepelin, Emil** Ueber die Wirkung kurzer Arbeitszeiten. Psychologische Arbeiten, 1902. Vol. 4, pp. 454-494.

171. **Jessen, Peter** Die Erziehung zur bildenden Kunst. Zeits. für Päd. Psy., Feb., 1902. Vol. 4, pp. 1-10.

172. **Johnson, W. S.** Experiments on motor education. Studies from the Yale Psy. Lab., 1902. Vol. 10, pp. 81-93.

173. **Jordan, W. R.** Heredity. Paidologist, April, 1902. Vol. 4, pp. 8-19.

174. **Judd, C. H.** Action as a condition of mental growth. Am. Phys. Ed. Rev., 1901. Vol. 6, pp. 199-203.

175. —— —— An experimental study in writing movements. Wundt's Philos. Studien, 1902. Vol. 19, pp. 243-259.

176. —— —— Practice and its effects on the perception of illusions. Psy. Rev., Jan., 1902. Vol. 9, pp. 27-39.

177. **Keasbey, L. M.** The descent of man. Pop. Sci. Mo., Feb., 1902. Vol. 60, pp. 365-376.

178. **Kielhorn, H.** Die Fürsorge für geistig minderwerthige. Jugendfürsorge, 1901. Heft. 7, pp. 18.

179. **Kimmins, C. W.** Child study in relation to the house. Paidologist, Nov., 1902. Vol. 4, pp. 141-143.

180. **Kirkpatrick, E. A.** Physiology of the nervous system in childhood as applied to education. Education, Dec., 1902. Vol. 23, pp. 193-203.

181. **Körte, Oswald** Gedanken und Erfahrungen über musikalische Erziehung. Zeits. für Päd. Psy., Feb., 1902. Vol. 4, pp. 11-39.

182. **Kovalcheff, N.** Les paralysies chez l'enfant. Toulouse, 1902, pp. 103.

183. **Kozlovski,** —— La psychogénèse de l'étendue. Rev. Philos., 1902. Vol. 54, pp. 570-594.

184. **Kraepelin, Emile** Die Arbeitscurve. Wundt's Philos. Studien, 1902. Vol. 19, pp. 458-507.
   A summary of the valuable researches made by Professor Kraepelin and his students on the problem of fatigue.
   —— —— See **Hylan and Kraepelin.**

185. **Krauss, W. C.** Heredity—with a study of the statistics of the New York State Hospital. Am. Jour. of Insanity, 1902. Vol. 58, pp. 607-624.

186. **Kreidle, A., and Alexander G.** Entwurf zu einer Statistik der körperlichen und geistigen Entwicklung Taubstummer in Oesterreich während der ersten Lebensjahre. Wien. klin. Wochensch., 1902. Vol. 15, pp. 418-420.

187. **Krenn, Regine** Das schwachbegabte Kind und dessen Unterricht im Elternhause und in der Schule. Zeits. für Schulgesundheitspflege, 1902. Vol. 15, pp. 93-100.

188. **Kropotkin, P.** Mutual aid: A factor of evolution. London, 1902, pp. 368.

189. **Lafon, G. and Frenkel** Etude graphique des oscillations rhythmiques de la tête chez les sujets sains. C. R. Soc. de Biol., 1902. Vol. 54, pp. 660-661.

190. **Landau, Richard** Zur geschichtlichen Entwickelung Schulhygiene. Zeits. für Schulgesundheitspflege, No. 10, 1902. Vol. 15, pp. 576-578.

191. **Laprade, A.** Contributions à l'étude de l'écriture en miroir. Paris, 1902, pp. 58.

192. **Largnier des Bancels, J.** Les méthodes de mémorisation. L'Année Psychologique, 1901. Vol. 8, pp. 184-204

193. —— —— Sur la Mémorisation. Bull. Soc. Étude Psy. de l'Enfant, 1902, pp. 137-139.

194. **Lefevre, G.** Notes d'écoliers: leurs relations avec l'âge, le sexe, et la couleur des cheveux. Revue Pédagogique, Sept., 1902. Vol. 41, pp. 201-220.
   A statistical study of the relation of the color of hair to mental efficiency of 22,000 French children.

195. **Lehne, G.** Wie kann der Lehrer die Lügenhaftigkeit der Jugend bekämpfen, Kinderfehler, 1902. Vol. 7, pp. 58-74.

196. **Leiteisen, G.** Rôle du surmenage physique dans l'éclosion des psychoses de puberté. Thèse med., Paris, 1902, pp. 54.

197. **Lemaître, A.** Le langage interieur chez les enfants. Viret-Genton, Lausanne, 1902.

198. **Liebmann, A.** Die Sprache schwerhöriger Kinder. Bresgen's Samml. Zwangl. Abhandl., 1901. Vol. 5.

199. **Liebmann, A.** Die sprachliche Entwicklung und Behand lung geistig zurückgebliebener Kinder. Zeits. für Päd. Psy., April, 1902. Vol. 4, pp. 97-120.
Discusses the speech defects of mentally deficient children.

200. **Lobsien, Marx** Schwankungen der psychischen Kapazität. (Sammlung von Abh. a. d. Gebiete d. Päd. Psy. u. Physiol.) Berlin, 1902. Vol. 5, pp. 110.

201. **Loesch Angeline** The child study department of the Chicago public schools. School Journal, Aug. 30, 1902. Vol. 45, pp. 164-165. Also in Proc. N. E. A., 1902, pp. 710-716.

202. **Loeschhorn, Karl** Einige Worte über die gemeinsame Erziehung der beiden Geschlechter. Zeits. für Päd. Psy., June, 1902. Vol. 4, pp. 223-228.

203. —— —— Ueber Kompensationen bei der Beurteilung der Schüler. Zeits. für Päd. Psy., April, 1902. Vol. 4, pp. 135-140.

204. **Lombroso, C.** Puberty and genius. Alienist and Neurologist, April and July, 1902. Vol. 23, pp. 176-182; 257-265.

205. —— —— Why criminals of genius have no type. International Quart., Dec., 1902. Vol. 6, pp. 229-240.

206. **Louch, Mary** Some common objections to child study. Paidologist, Nov., 1902. Vol. 4, pp. 137-141.

207. **MacDonell, W. R.** On criminal anthropology and the identification of criminals. Biometrika, 1902. Vol. 1, pp. 177-227.

208. **MacDougall, Robert** Relation of auditory rhythm to nervous discharge. Psy. Rev., Sept., 1902. Vol. 9, pp. 460-480.

209. —— —— Rhythm, time and number. Am. Jour. of Psy., Jan., 1902. Vol. 13, pp. 88-97.

210. **MacEacharn, Madeline** Domestic authority. Child Life (London), July, 1902. Vol. 4, pp. 137-139.

211. —— —— Education of the sense of humor. Child Life (London), Oct., 1902. Vol. 4, pp. 222-224.

212. **McKendrick, John G.** Experimental phonetics. Ass'n Review, Oct., 1902. Vol. 4, pp. 327-343.
An excellent brief statement of researches in the field of experimental phonetics.

213. **Maknen, G. Hudson** Speech as a factor in the diagnosis and prognosis of backwardness in children. Jour. of Psycho-Asthenics, March, June, 1902. Vol. 6, pp. 80-83.
It is the belief of the author that the best method of arriving at a proximately correct prognosis in cases of backward children is the speech-test.

214. **Malapert, ——** Une enquête sur la colère. Bull. Soc. Étude Psychol. de l'Enfant, 1902, pp. 241-244.

Manny. See **Bishop and Manny.**

215. **Marage,** —— Phonation et audition d'après les travaux récents publiés en France. L'Année Psychologique, Paris, 1902. Vol. 8, pp. 257-298.
   A valuable résumé of recent experimental studies in phonetics.

216. **Marsden, R. E.** Records from a parent's note book. Paidologist, July and Nov., 1902. Vol. 4, pp. 97-100; 155-159.

217. **Marsh, Mabel A.** Children and animals. Barnes' Studies in Education, May, 1902. Vol. 2, pp. 83-99.

218. **Masselon, R.** Psychologie des déments précoces. Thèse mèd., Paris, 1902, pp. 265.

219. **Maupate,** —— Du langage chez les idiots. Ann. Medico-Psychol., 1901. Vol. 15, pp. 37-49; 230-239; 401-413.

220. **Meeus, F.** De la démence précoce. Jour. de Neurol., 1902. Vol. 7, pp. 449-467.

221. **Milligen, M.** Schools for invalid children. Child Life (London), July, 1902. Vol. 4, pp. 140-144.
   An account of the London settlement movement to provide children who are incapacitated from attending the ordinary schools a means of obtaining an elementary education.

222. **Monroe, Will S.** Elective system and its limits. Rep. of the Board of Regents of the Univ. of the State of N. Y., 1902, pp. 209-212.
   Maintains that the course of study must take into account the interests of the child.

223. **Morgan, C. L.** The beginnings of mind. Internat. Qt., Dec., 1902. Vol 6, pp. 330-352.

224. **Moses, J.** Schulhygienische Betrachtungen über Gliederung und Organisation der deutschen Volksschule. Zeits. für Schulgesundheitspflege, No. 8, 1902. Vol. 15, pp. 427-434.

225. **Mouribal. A.** Contribution à l'étude de l'enfantilisme. Thèse méd., Toulouse, 1902, pp. 89.

226. **Müller, J.** Das sexuelle Leben der Naturvölker. Das sexuelle Leben der alten Kulturvölker. Th. Grieben, Leipzig, 1902.

227. **Murray, G.** The report of an examination of the ears of 400 school children. J. of Laryngol., Rhinol. and Otol., 1902. Vol. 17, pp. 293-294.

228. **Myers, C. S.** A study of Papuan Hearing. Arch. of Otol., 1902. Vol. 31, pp. 283-288.

229. —— —— The visual acuity of the natives of Sarawak. Jour. of Physiology, 1902. Vol. 28, pp. 316-318.

230. **Nandy,** —— L'éducation des enfants arriérés. Manuel général de l'instruction primaire, 2 Août, 1902. Vol. 38, pp. 481-483.

231. **Netschajeff, C.** Über Memorieren. Samml. von Abhand. a.d. Gebiete der Päd. Psy. u. Physiol., Berlin, 1902. Vol. 5, pp. 39.
   An excellent statistical study of the memory of Russian school children.

232. **Newell, W. W.** Fairy lore and primitive religion. Internat. Monthly, Mar., 1902. Vol. 5, pp. 316-337.

233. **Nibecker, F. H.** Punishments. Nat. Conf. Char. and Corr., Boston, 1902, pp. 427-431.

234. **Noss, Theodore B.** What our schools owe to child study. Proc. N. E. A., 1902, pp. 716-719.
The author maintains that the aim of education, course of study, and methods of teaching must be based upon child study.

235. **O'Shea, M. V.** Educational and social aspects of pictorial art. School Journal, Nov. 29, 1902. Vol. 65, pp. 531-533.

236. —— —— Work and play in adjustment to the school environment. Notes on Groos' The Play of Man. Am. Jour. of Sociology, Nov., 1902. Vol. 8, pp. 382-389.

237. **Oldys, H. W.** Parallel growth of bird and human music. Harper's Mag., Aug., 1902. Vol. 105, pp. 474-478.

238. **Oppenheim, Nathan** Mental growth and control. New York, 1902, pp. 296.
Contents: Character, the mind, attention, association, instinct, memory, habit, hypnotism and suggestion, imagination, emotions, reasoning, the will.

239. **Partridge, Geo. E.** Studies of individual children. Ped. Sem., Dec., 1902. Vol. 9, pp. 436-440.

240. **Partridge, Lena** Children's drawings of men and women. Barnes' Studies in Education, July, 1902. Vol. 2, pp. 163-179.

241. **Payton, C. L.** Feelings as factor in school training. N. Y., School Jour., May 24 and 31, 1902. Vol 64, pp. 594-595; 615.

242. **Peabody, Endicott** The relation of the home to the preparatory school. Rev. of Ed., Feb., 1902. Vol. 8, pp. 260-263.

243. **Pearson, K.** On the correlation of intellectual ability with the size and shape of the head. Proc. Roy. Soc., 1902. Vol. 69, pp. 333-342.

244. **Platt, W.** Children and disobedience. Paidologist, Nov., 1902. Vol. 4, pp. 164-166.

245. —— —— Children's tunes. Paidologist, April, 1902. Vol. 4, pp. 2-7.

246. **Poetter, A.** Die Schulärzte in Leipzig und ihre bisherige Thätigkeit mit besonderer Berücksichtigung der Untersuchung der in die Schule neu eingetretenen Kinder. Zeits. für Schulgesundheitspflege, No. 5, 1902. Vol. 15, pp. 214-259.

247. **Prentice, May H.** Myth and history in the elementary schools; the use and limits of each. Kindergarten Mag., Sept., 1902. Vol. 15, pp. 6-13. Also Proc. N. E. A., 1902, pp. 447-453.

248. **Putnam, Alice H.** How Froebel planned to foster the child's powers in language. Kindergarten Mag., Sept., 1902. Vol 15, pp. 14-19. Also Proc. N. E. A., 1902, pp. 417-421.

249. **Putnam, Alice H.** Work and play. Rev. of Ed., April, 1902. Vol. 10, pp. 356.

250. **Queyrat, F.** La logique chez l'enfant et sa culture. Paris, 1902, pp. 158.

251. **Randall, C. D.** The progress of State care of dependent children in the United States. Nat. Conf. Char. and Corr., Boston, 1902, pp. 243-249.

252. **Rheinhard, W.** Der Mensch als Thierrasse und seine Triebe. Beiträge zu Darwin und Nietzsche, Leipzig, 1902, pp. 235.

253. **Rhoades, Lillian Ione** Bibliography of child study. Board of Education, Phila., 1902, pp. 128.
    A list of 1,090 book and periodical references on child study in the pedagogical library of the Board of Education of Philadelphia.

254. **Rivers, W. H. R.** The color vision of the natives of Upper Egypt. Jour. of Anthropological Inst., N. S., 1901, July to Dec. Vol 4, pp. 229-247.

255. **Robin, F. R.** Surdi-cécité et moyens pour communiquer avec les sourds-aveugles. (Thèse méd.), Bordeaux, 1902, pp. 76.

256. **Robinson, George B.** The distinction between destitute and delinquent children. Nat. Conf. Char. and Corr., Boston, 1902, pp. 440-443.

257. **Rodiet, A.** Les enfants alcooliques. Rev. Philanthr., Oct., 1902, pp. 654-673; Nov., pp. 48-61.

258. **Rogers, A. C.** What Minnesota is doing for her feeble-minded and epileptics. Proc. N. E. A., 1902, pp. 845-846.

259. **Rose, H. A.** Unlucky children. Folk-Lore, London, 1902. Vol. 13, pp. 63-68.
    Customs and superstitions in India concerning the order of birth.

260. **Rowe, Stuart H.** School game for girls. Education, Nov., 1902. Vol. 23, pp. 155-160.

261. **Russell F.** Know, then, thyself. Science, N. S., 1902. Vol. 15, pp. 561-571. Jour. of Am. Folk-Lore, 1902. Vol. 15, pp. 1-13.
    Treats of educational value of anthropology.

262. **Saenger, A.** Neurasthenie und Hysterie bei Kindern. Berlin, 1902, pp. 32.

263. **Sanford, Edmund C.** Illustrations of the application of psychological principles to ethical problems. Ped. Sem., March, 1902. Vol. 9, pp. 18-27.
    The author contends that psychology has generalizations that throw light on spiritual experiences.

264. —— —— Mental growth and decay. Am. Jour. of Psy., July, 1902. Vol. 13, pp. 426-449.
    A comprehensive and scientific statement of the laws of growth with special reference to adolescence and senescence.

265. **Saunders, Una M.** Student life in India. Child Life (London), July, 1902. Vol. 4, pp. 147.
    Gives an account of the education of girls in India.

266. **Scherer, H.** Der Werkunterricht in seiner soziologischen und physiologisch-pädagogischen Begründung. (Samml. von Abhand. a. d. Gebiete d. Päd. Psy. Physiol.) Berlin, 1902. Vol. 6, pp. 50.

267. **Schiller, Hermann** Der Aufsatz in der Muttersprache. (Samml. von Abhand. a. d. Gebiete d. Päd. Psy. u. Physiol.) Berlin, 1902. Vol. 5, pp. 61.

268. **Schlesinger, ——** Ueber die Beziehungen zwischen Schädelgrösse und Sprachentwicklung. (Diss. med.) Breslau, 1902, pp. 29.

269. **Schulthess, Wilhelm** Schule und Rückgratsverkrümmung. Zeits. für Schulgesundheitspflege, No. 1, 1902. Vol. 15, pp. 11-26; 91-93.

270. **Schurtz, H.** Altersklassen und Männerbünde. Reimer, Berlin, 1902.

271. **Schuyten, M. C.** Over Geheugenvariatie bij Schoolkinderen. Paedol. Jaarb., 1902-3. Vols. 3-4, pp. 240-256.

272. **Sears, Charles H.** The psychology of rhythm. Am. Jour. of Psy., Jan., 1902. Vol. 13, pp. 28-61.
     An exhaustive study of the rhythmical sense in children and the utility of rhythm in instruction.

273. **Seashore, C. E.** A method of measuring mental work. (Univ. of Iowa Studies in Psy.), Iowa City, 1902. Vol. 3, pp. 1-17.

274. **Seglas, J.** Démence précoce et catatonie. Nouv. Icon. Salpêtriére, 1902. Vol. 15, pp. 330-346.

275. **Seligmann, C. G.** Sexual inversion among primitive races. Alienist and Neurologist, 1902. Vol. 23, pp. 11-15.

276 **Serieux and Masselon** Troubles psychiques chez les déments précoces. An. Medico-Psychol., 1902. Vol. 16, pp. 449-463.

277. **Sherrington** Child study and physiology. Paidologist, July, 1902. Vol. 4, pp. 75-84.

278. **Slaughter, J. W.** The moon in childhood and folk lore. Am. Jour. of Psy., April, 1902. Vol. 13, pp. 294-318.

279. **Smith, Anna Tolman** The recent reaction in France against Rousseau's negation of society in education. Proc. N. E. A., 1902, pp. 383-386.

280. **Snider, D. J.** Social institutions: In their origin, growth, and interconnection, psychologically treated. Sigma Pub. Co., St. Louis, Mo., 1901, pp. 615.

281. **Steiger, Adolf** Einige Bemerkungen über Methode und Resultate der Augenuntersuchungen in den Volksschulen der Stadt Zürich. Zeits. für Schulgesundheitspflege, No. 3 and 4. Vol. 15, pp. 123-141.

282. **Stern, L. W.** Ueber Psychologie der individuellen Differenzen. (Schriften der Gesellschaft für psychologische Forschung, Heft., 12.) J. A. Barth, Leipzig, 1900, pp. 146.
Contains bibliography on mental tests, memory types, temperament, etc.

283. **Street, J. R.** Adolescence. Jour. of Ped., 1902. Vol. 15, pp. 93-104.

284. **Stroszner, Edmund** Einiges über den Tabak namentlich mit Bezug auf das Rauchen der Schuljugend. Zeits. für Schulgesundheitspflege, No. 8, 1902. Vol. 15, pp. 419-427.
A discussion of the use of tobacco on the mental and physical development of children.

285. **Sully, James** An essay on laughter; its forms, its causes, its development and its value. Longmans, Green & Co., N. Y., 1902, pp. 441.

286. ―― ―― Les théories du risible. Rev. Philos., Aug., 1902. Vol. 54, pp. 113-139.

287. **Szeyko, J.** Influence de l'éducation sur le developpement de la neurasthénie. Thèse méd., Lyon, 1902, pp. 83.

288. **Talbot, Eugene S.** Juvenile female delinquents. Alienist and Neurologist, 1902. Vol. 23, pp. 16-27; 163-175.

289. **Tate, J. N.** What is Minnesota doing for her deaf children? Proc. N. E. A., 1902, pp. 836-840.

290. **Tews, J.** Institutions for the defective in Germany. Rep. Commissioner of Ed., 1900-1901. Vol. 1, pp. 40-48.

291. **Thiemich, M.** Ueber die Functionsfähigkeit der motorischen Rindenfelder beim Säuglinge. Ztsch. f. klin. Med., 1902. Vol. 45, 226-236.

292. **Tibbey, T. G.** The amateur and child study. Paidologist, Nov., 1902. Vol. 4, pp. 144-146.

293. **Titchener, E. B.** Were the earliest organic movements conscious or unconscious? Pop. Sci. Mo., Mar., 1902. Vol. 60, pp. 458-469.

294. **Tredgold, A. F.** Remarks on the subsequent history of children born whilst the mother was insane. Lancet, 1902. Vol. 1, pp. 1380-1385.

265. **Triplett, Norman** A contribution to individual psychology. Am. Jour. of Psy., Jan., 1902. Vol. 13, pp. 149-160.

296. **Trueper, J.** Ueber das Zusammenwirken von Medizin und Pädagogik bei Fürsorge für unsere abnormen Kinder. Kinderfehler, 1902. Vol. 7, pp. 97-122.

297. **Tschermak, A.** Ueber die absolute Localisation bei Schielenden. Arch. f. Ophthal. (v. Graefe's), 1902. Vol. 55, pp. 1-45.

298. **Upthoff, W.** Ein weiterer Beitrag zur angeborenen totalen Farbenblindheit. Ztsch. f. Psychol., 1902. Vol. 27, pp. 344-360.

299. **Urbantschitsch, V.** Exercices acoustiques méthodiques dans la surdi-mudité. Parole, 1902. Vol. 12, pp. 29-56.

300. **Van den Broeck, P., and A. D'Hooge** Kinderspelen uit het Land van Dendermond. Utrecht, Bracckmans, 1902, pp. 102.
A good collection of Flemish songs and games of children.

301. **Vanderwalker, Nina G.** Child life as recorded in history, and its place in kindergarten training. Rev. of Ed., May, 1902. Vol. 11, pp. 375-378.

302. **Vergely, P.** Hallucinations diurnes chez les enfants. Rev. Mens. d. Mal de l'Enfance, 1902. Vol. 20.

303. **Wade, W.** The deaf-blind. Indianapolis, 1902, pp. 80.

304. **Walker, M. R.** Caution in child study. Paidologist, April and July, 1902. Vol. 4, pp. 19-24; 84-92.

Wallin See **Hall and Wallin.**

305. **Wegener** Ein Beitrag zur Frage nach den Ursachen der Minderbegabung von Schulkindern. Zeits. für Schulgesundheitspflege, No. 11, 1902. Vol. 15, pp. 620-622.

306. **Wegschieder-Ziegler, Hildegard** Erfahrungen im Gymnasialunterricht für Mädchen als Beitrag zur Frage der gemeinschaftlichen Erziehung beider Geschlechter. Zeits. Päd. Psy., June, 1902. Vol. 4, pp. 212-222.

307. **Wetterwald, X.** Sprachstörungen. Kinderfehler, 1902. Vol. 7, pp. 145-176.

308. **Williams, Lillie A.** Children's interest in words. Ped. Sem., Sept., 1902. Vol. 9, pp. 274-295.
The immense importance of hearing in the affective side of language clearly shown.

309. **Williams, Mabel Clare** Normal illusions in geometrical forms. (Univ. of Iowa Studies in Psy.), Iowa city, 1902. Vol. 3, pp. 38-139.

310. **Wilson, Louis N.** Bibliography of child study for the year 1901. Ped. Sem., Dec., 1902. Vol. 9, pp. 521-542.
Bibliographic references to 307 books and periodical articles on child study.

311. **Wissler, Clark** A review of progress in school tests. Jour. of Ped., March, 1902. Vol. 14, pp. 203-213.

312. **Withers, O.** Children's early drawings. Paidologist, April, 1902. Vol. 4, pp. 25-32.

313. **Woods, Frederick Adams** Mental and moral heredity in royalty. Pop. Sci. Mo., Aug. to Dec., 1902. Vol. 61, pp. 369-378; 449-460; 506-513; Vol. 62, pp. 76-84; 167-182.

314. **Woolston, H. B.** Religious emotions. Am. Jour. of Psy., Jan., 1902. Vol. 13, pp. 62-79.

315. **Wray, C.** Civilization and eyesight. Brit. Med. Jour., 1902, pp. 1434-1435.

316. **Wuensch, R.** Aus der Kinderstube. Hessische Blätter für Volkskunde, Leipzig, 1902. Vol. 1, pp. 134-137.
Treats of such relics of exorcism and demonology as the mother's driving away pain by blowing on hurt, etc.

317. **Wylie, Arthur R. T.** On the psychology and pedagogy of the blind. Ped. Sem., June, 1902. Vol. 9, pp. 127-160.
An excellent recent statement of the mental and physical characteristics of blind children.

318. **York, E. E.** The cultivation of individuality. Nat. Conf. Char. and Corr., Boston, 1902, pp. 261-264.

319. **Young, Sarah** Children's travel interests. Barnes' Studies in Education, Nov., 1902. Vol. 2, pp. 338-351.
An account of enjoyable journeys made by 1,280 English children.

320. —— —— Delegated authority. Barnes' Studies in Education. Aug., 1902. Vol. 2, pp. 218-226.
With comments by Professor Earl Barnes (pp. 227-230) on the delegation of authority by parents and teachers.

321. —— —— School girls' ideas of women's occupations. Barnes' Studies in Education, Sept., 1902. Vol. 2, pp. 259-270.
A study of the motives which influence children with respect to prospective occupations.

322. —— —— A study in children's social environment. Barnes' Studies in Education, June, 1902. Vol. 2, pp. 123-140.
A study of the ambitions of English children.

323. —— —— The teaching of geography. Barnes' Studies in Education, Dec., 1902. Vol. 2, pp. 373-387.

324. **Ziehen, Th.** Die Geisteskrankheiten des Kindesalters. Samml. von Abhand. a. de Gebiete d. Päd. Psy., u. Physiol., Berlin, 1902. Vol. 5, pp. 79.
A valuable study of the mental diseases of childhood and of school factors inducing mental disease.

325. —— —— Ueber die allgemeinen Beziehungen zwischen Gehirn und Seelenleben. Leipzig, 1902, pp. 66.

326. **Zirkle, Homer** Medical inspection of schools. (Investigations of the Dept. of Psychology and Education of the Univ. of Colorado.) Boulder, 1902, pp. 66.
Besides discussing medical inspection and school diseases this monograph has brief but valuable paragraphs on mental and physical defects, eyesight and deafness.

---

327. British child study association: Proceedings of the Hampton Wick Conference. London, 1902, pp. 57.
A souvenir volume containing papers on child study by Dr. Langdon-Down, Sir James Crichton-Browne, Miss Mary Louch, Dr. C. W. Kimmins, Henry Holman, Dr. Geo. E. Shuttleworth, and E. E. Matherson.

328. Child labor in Germany outside of factories. Rep. Commissioner of Ed., 1900-1901. Vol. 1, pp. 54-80.

329. Child study records. N. Y. School Jour., Feb., 15, 1902. Vol. 64, p. 190.

330. Children's ideals. Paidologist, April, 1902. Vol. 4, pp. 40-41.

331. Co-education of the sexes in the United States. Rep. Commissioner of Ed., 1900-1901, Washington, 1902. Vol. 2, pp. 1217-1315.

  A valuable and exhaustive discussion with an excellent bibliography appended.

332. Compulsory attendance and child-labor laws. Rep. Commissioner Ed., 1900-1901, Washington, 1902. Vol. 2, pp. 2409-2415.

  Contains a résumé of statutory provisions relating to compulsory school attendance and child labor.

333. Educational results of child study. N. Y. School Jour., June 14, 1902. Vol. 64, p. 680.

334. First comprehensive attempts at child study. Rep. Commissioner of Ed., 1900-1901. Vol. 1, pp. 709-729.

  An account of the Berlin study of the contents of children's minds upon entering school.

335. First two years at school. N. Y. School Jour., Jan. 25, 1902. Vol. 64, p. 90.

336. Health of school children. N. Y. School Jour., March, 1902. Vol. 64, p. 235.

337. L'enfance abandonné ou coupable. Rev. Péd., 15 Janvier, 1902. Vol. 40, pp. 36-45.

338. Message of the child. N. Y. School Jour., May 17, 1902. Vol. 64, pp. 559-560.

339. New law concerning reformatory education of children in Prussia. Rep. Commissioner of Ed., 1900-1901. Vol. 1, pp. 48-54.

340. Physical exercise in afternoon recess. N. Y. School Jour., Feb. 8, 1902. Vol. 64, p. 175.

341. Sleep of children. Rev. of Ed., Jan., 1902. Vol. 7, pp. 231-232.

342. Training to think. N. Y. School Jour., May 3, 1902. Vol. 64, p. 492.

343. Will-training and school management. N. Y. School Jour., Jan. 25, 1902. Vol. 64, p. 89.

344. Worth of an individual child. N. Y. School Jour., May 10, 1902. Vol. 64, p. 545.

SUBJECT INDEX.

Abnormal, 2.
Acoustics, 299.
Action, 174.
Adolescence, 136, 147, 196, 204, 264, 283.
Æsthetics, 31.
Age, 270.
Alcoholic, 257.
Algebra, 146.
Alphabet, 48.
Ambitions, 22, 322.
Anger, 214.
Animals, 73, 133, 217.
Anthropology, 45, 58, 76, 207, 261.
Arithmetic, 5.
Art, 169, 171, 235.

Backward Children, 11, 213, 230, 326.
Bibliography, 72, 253, 282, 310.
Biology, 17.
Blind, 46, 82, 114, 255, 303, 317.
Brain, 164, 325.

Chicago, 201.
Child Labor, 117, 328, 332.
—— Life, 301.
Child Study in America, 30.
—— General, 51, 61, 63, 68, 77, 147, 148, 179, 201, 206, 216, 234, 239, 277, 292, 304, 327, 329, 333, 334, 338.
Chums, 52.
Civilization, 315.
Class Distinctions, 20.
Co-education, 131, 202, 203, 306, 331.
Color Blindness, 298.
—— Vision, 254.
Composition, 89.
Concepts, 28.
Conversion, 59.
Craniometry, 45, 46, 47, 268.
Crime, 69, 124.
Criminal, 112, 132, 205, 207.
Criminology, 337.

Deaf and Deafness, 47, 53, 55, 114, 120, 121, 143, 154, 161, 198, 255, 289, 303, 326.
Deaf-mutes, 186, 299.
Defectives, 35, 106, 139, 290, 296.
—— Mental, 36.

Delinquents, 8, 49, 80, 124, 256, 288, 339.
Dementia Præcox, 107, 162, 218, 220, 274, 276.
Dependents, 251, 256.
Development, 92, 252.
Dictionaries, 18.
Discipline, 210, 244, 320.
Disease, 14, 326.
Dolls, 127.
Drawing, 32, 44, 66, 240, 312.
Dumb, 144.

Education, 166, 167, 168, 261.
—— vs. Crime, 69.
Egypt, 254.
Electives, 222.
English, 146.
Epileptic, 258.
Ethics, 263.
Evolution, 93, 99, 130, 188.
Eyesight, 85, 86, 281, 315, 326.

Fairy lore, 232.
Fatigue, 118, 170, 184.
Fear, 160.
Feeble Minded, 40, 108, 119, 178, 187, 258, 305.
Feeling, 241.
Fetichism, 110.
Finger Rhymes, 87.
Folk lore, 278, 316.
Food, 79.
France 279.
Friendships, 52.
Fun, 158.
Fundamental to Accessory, 65.

Gambling, 126.
Genius, 78, 204.
Geography, 123, 319, 323.
Germany, 290, 339.
Girls, 98, 122, 265.
Growth, 45, 196, 264, 326.

Habit and Habits, 7, 16, 54.
Hair, 194.
Hallucinations, 302.
Head, 189, 243.
Headache, 156.
Health, 336.
Hearing, 84, 227, 228.

Heredity, 109, 173, 177, 185, 294, 313.
Higher and lower races, 76.
History, 247.
Home, 12, 242.
Human instincts, 73, 217.
Humor, 94, 158, 211.
Hydrocephaly, 42.
Hygiene, 190, 224.
Hysteria, 262.

Ideals, 22, 26, 34, 135, 330.
Idiots, 219.
Illusions, 176, 309.
Illustrations, 75.
Imagery, 150.
Imitation, 15.
India, 265.
Individual, 168, 344.
—— Psychology, 295.
Individuality, 318.
Infant, 182, 291,
Infantilism, 43, 225.
Inhibition, 95.
Insane mother, 294.
Instincts, 252.
Intellectual ability, 243.
Interest, 141, 308.
Invalids, 221.

Jesus, 111.
Journals, 67.

Kindergarten, 13, 70, 152, 159, 301.

Language, 3, 6, 128, 129, 143, 145, 152, 197, 198, 248, 267, 268.
Latin, 146.
Laughter, 285, 286.
Lefthandedness, 1.
Lies, 33, 195.
Localization, 297.
Logic, 250.
Love, 39.
Luck, 259.

Manual training, 266.
Massachusetts, 119.
Medical inspection, 246, 326.
Memory, 37, 155, 192, 193, 231.
Mental development, 19, 174, 238.
—— Disease, 324.
—— Arrangement, 41.
—— Work, 273.
Mentally deficient, 42, 88, 199.
Mind, 223.
Minnesota, 82, 289.
Mirror Writing, 1, 191.

Moral and religious, 59.
—— Development, 38.
—— Training, 21, 138.
Motor areas, 291.
—— Training, 38, 70, 103, 172.
Movements, 293.
Muscular exercise, 141.
Music, 116, 181, 237, 245.
Myth, 247.

Nervousness, 91.
Nervous system, 65, 180.
Neurasthenia, 262, 287.
New York, 185.
Number, 90, 209.

Obedience, 244.
Occupation, 22, 321.
Orthography, 37.

Paralysis, 182.
Parent, 138, 216, 242.
Pauperism, 124.
Pedagogy, 30.
Phonetics, 212, 215.
Physiology, 180, 277.
Play, 56, 72, 80, 133, 165, 236, 249, 260, 300.
Poetry, 25.
Political ideas, 26, 29.
Practice, 7, 166.
Prayer, 140.
Precocity, 326.
Primitive Peoples, 76, 228, 229, 232, 254, 275.
Psychology, 200, 263, 272, 282.
Psychoses, 100, 136.
Punishment, 27, 81, 157, 233.

Recess, 340.
Reform schools, 81.
Religion, 23, 232, 314.
Rest, 78.
Rhythm, 90, 118, 189, 208, 209, 262.
Righthandedness, 50.
Rousseau, 279.

Savage, 101.
School, 96, 97, 148, 236, 335.
—— Activity, 71.
—— Break down, 83.
—— for the deaf, 161.
—— of the future, 60.
—— Journey, 10.
Self control, 153.
Senescence, 264.
Sex, 39, 113, 226, 270, 275.
Sleep, 341.

Social, 58, 149, 167.
—— institutions, 280.
Songs, 300.
Space, 183.
Speech, 3, 9, 142, 164, 213, 219.
—— defects, 199, 307.
Spinal curvature, 269.
Squinting, 163, 297.
Stories, 26, 75.
Stupidity, 78.
Suggestion, 156, 239.
Suicide, 117.

Teacher, 138, 151.
Tests, 311.
Thinking, 17, 342.

Time, 90, 209.
Tobacco, 284.
Travel, 319.
Truth, 33, 74.

Variation, 271.
Vision, 115, 229.
Visualization, 62.
Vocabularies, 128, 129.

War, 24.
Weather, 102.
Will, 343.
Words, 28, 308.
Work, 78, 170, 184, 236, 249.
Writing, 175.

PUBLICATIONS

OF THE

CLARK UNIVERSITY LIBRARY

WORCESTER, MASS.

VOL. I   July, 1904   No. 4

Bibliography of Child Study for the Year 1903.

Clark University Press
WORCESTER, MASS.

BIBLIOGRAPHY OF CHILD STUDY.

For the Year 1903.

By Louis N. Wilson, Librarian, Clark University.

1. **Addams, Jane** Child labor and pauperism. Nat. Conf. Char. and Corr., 1903. pp. 114-121.
   Discussion of pauperism as caused by premature labor.

2. **Adler, Nettie** Children as wage-earners. Fortnightly, May, 1903. Vol. 79, pp. 918-927.

3. **Alcock, N. H.** On the rapidity of the nervous impulse in tall and short individuals. Proc. Roy. Soc., 1903. Vol. 72, pp. 419-424.

4. **Am Ende, Paul** Das Brausebad in der Volksschule. A. Arnold, Dresden, 1900. pp. 32.

5. **Andrews, B. R.** Habit. Am. Jour. of Psy., April, 1903. Vol. 14, pp. 121-149.
   Touches briefly on forming habits in childhood, in last few pages.

6. **Arnold, Sarah L.** Plans for busy work. Silver, Burdett & Co., N. Y., 1901, pp. 139.

7. **Arnould, Louis** Une âme en prison. H. Oudin, Paris, 1903, pp. 89.

8. **Aschaffenburg, Gustav** Ueber die Bedeutung der Stimmungs-schwankungen bei Epileptikern. Kinderfehler, Dec., 1903. Vol. 9, pp. 62-72.
   A discussion of the signs of epilepsy and their significance.

9. **Bach,** —— Die Logik des Kindes. Compte rendu du quatrième congrès scientifique international'des catholiques tenu à Fribourg (Suisse) du 16 au 20 août 1897. Troisième section, 1898, pp. 35-38.

10. **Baer,** —— Ueber jugendliche Mörder und Totschläger. Arch. f. Kriminalanthropol., 1903. Vol 11, pp. 103-170.

11. **Bagner, G.** La lecture sur les levres. Revue Int. de Péd. Comp., July 31, 1903. Vol. 5, pp. 305-309.
    Treats of instruction of deaf mutes by lip reading.

13. **Bailey, L. H.** The nature-study movement. Proc. N. E. A., 1903, pp. 109-116.
    What the nature-study movement is and its value.

Previous installments of the BIBLIOGRAPHY OF CHILD STUDY have appeared in the *Pedagogical Seminary*, as follows: April, 1898, Vol. 5, pp. 541-589; Sept., 1899, Vol. 6, pp. 386-410; Dec., 1900, Vol. 7, pp. 526-556; Dec., 1901, Vol. 8, pp. 515-537; Dec., 1802 Vol. 9, pp. 521-542; Dec., 1903, Vol. 10, pp. 514-536.

13. **Baldrian, Karl** Uber Schülerbefähigung. Kinderfehler, June, 1903. Vol. 8, pp. 145-157.

14. **Balliet, Thomas M.** Are there too many studies in the curriculum? Jour. of Ed., May 7, 1903. Vol. 57, pp. 291-292.

15. —— —— Educational rationale of manual training. School Jour., Feb. 7, 1903, pp. 143-145.
    Gives effects upon mind and body of manual training.

16. —— —— The instincts and education. Am. Phys. Ed. Rev., 1903. Vol. 8, pp. 1-7.

17. **Baracelli, S. E.** Deficienti e tardivi. La scuola per i tardivi. Tip. Fezzi, Cremona, 1903, pp. 77.

18. **Barbier, Karl** Ein Beitrag zu dem Kapitel psychopathische Minderwertigkeiten. Kinderfehler, Aug., 1903. Vol. 8, pp. 203-210.
    An individual case recorded to show the effect of trouble on the mental development of a child.

19. **Barnes, Earl** The child's favorite study in the elementary curriculum. Proc. N. E. A., 1903, pp. 420-425.

20. —— —— Ideals of New York Kindergarten children. Kindergarten Mag., Oct., 1903. Vol. 16, pp. 86-100.

21. —— —— The mentally defective child. School Jour., March 7, 1903, pp. 264-265.
    Advocates individual educating of defective children.

22. —— —— A study based on the children of a state. Proc. N. E. A., 1903, pp, 754-761.
    Concludes that child study has reached the comparative stage, needing support of city, state and national departments of education.

23. —— —— Two child study papers: (a) Study on the children of a state; (b) The child's favorite study in the elementary curriculum. Kindergarten Mag., Sept., 1903. Vol. 16, pp. 26-31.
    (a) Discusses comparative studies on ideals of children and national qualities of character.
    (b) Tests showing that newer subjects do not appeal to children as much as old ones.

24. —— —— Why children lie. Current Literature, Feb., 1903. Vol. 34, pp. 213-214.
    Gives six causes for children's lies and the cure for them.

25. **Barry, William F.** Hygiene of the school room. Snow, Providence, 1903, pp. 167.

26. **Barth, P.** Die Geschichte der Erziehung in soziologischer Beleuchtung. Vtljsch. f. wiss. Philos. u. Soz., 1903. Vol. 27, pp. 209-229.
    Treats of education among barbarous, semi-civilized and civilized peoples.

27. **Baudrillard, J.** L' education par le travail manuel. Rev. Pèdagogique, Feb., 1903. Vol. 42, pp. 120-133. April, 1903. Vol. 42, pp. 347-368.

28. **Baur, A.** Gesundheit in der Schule. Stuttgart, 1901. pp. 381.

29. —— —— Das kranke Schulkind. F. Enke, Stuttgart, 1903, pp. 367.

30. —— —— Organization des Schulhygienischen Unterrichts an den Schullehrerseminaren. Pädagogische Blätter, 1902, pp. 84-87.

31. **van Becclaere, F. L.** Les études sur la psychologie de l'enfant en Amérique. Revue Thomiste, 1903, pp. 702-716.
    Reviews the work of Dr. G. Stanley Hall in child study.

32. **Bell, A. M.** Faults of speech. Volta Bur. Wash., 1898, pp. 71.

33. **Bell, Sanford** Significance of activity in child life. Independent, April 16, 1903. Vol. 55, p. 911-914.

34. **Bellei, Guiseppe** An hour's work done by school children. Ed. Rev., April, 1903. Vol. 26, pp. 364-386.
    Results of mental work in an hour's lesson at the beginning and end of daily teaching, and at the beginning and end of scholastic year.

35. **Berkhan, O.** Ueber Störungen der Sprache und der Schriftsprache. A. Hirschwald, Berlin, 1889, pp. 89.

36. **Bernstein, A.** Ueber die Dementia praecox. Allg. Ztsch. f. Psychiat., 1903. Vol. 6, pp. 554-571.

37. **Betts, Lillian W.** Child labor in factories. Outlook, March 14, 1903. Vol. 73, pp. 637-41.

38. —— —— Child labor in shops and homes. Outlook, April 18, 1903. Vol. 73, pp. 921-927.

39. —— —— Children out of school hours. Outlook, Sept. 26, 1903. Vol. 75, pp. 209-216.

40. **Beyer, Otto Wilhelm** Deutsche Schulwelt des 19, Jahrhunderts in Wort und Bild. A. Pichler, Leipzig, 1903, pp. 392.

41. **Bienfait,** —— Enfants arriérés. Ann. Soc. Méd.-Chir. de Liège, 1902, pp. 171.

42. **Binet, A.** Les Simplistes. Enfants d'école et adultes. L'Année Psychol., 1902. Vol. 9, pp. 129-168.

43. —— —— Les distraits. L'Année Psychol., 1902. Vol. 9, pp. 169-198.

44. —— —— L'écriture pendant les états d'excitation artificielle. L'Année Psychol., 1902. Vol. 9, pp. 57-78.

45. —— —— Etude expérimentale de l'intelligence. Schleicher, Paris, 1903, pp. 309.

46. —— —— Les interprétateurs. L'Année Psychol., 1902. Vol. 9, pp. 199-234.

47. **Blackwell, L. S.** Later impressions of the non-heredity of acquired characters. Med. News, 1903. Vol. 83, pp. 500-501.

48. **Blake, C. J.** The importance of hearing tests in public schools. Proc. N. E. A., 1903, pp. 1013-1019.

49. **Bloch, Maurice** Le courage chez l'enfant. Alcide Picard & Kaan, Paris, 1901, pp. 29.

50. **Blusy, Eugène** Le mouvement pédologique et pédagogique. Rev. Philos., 1903. Vol. 55, pp. 649-666.

51. **Boas, Franz** Heredity in head form. Amer. Anthropol., N. S., 1903. Vol. 5, pp. 530-538.

52. **Bolton, Frederick E.** Unsoundness of the culture epochs theory of education. Jour. of Ped., Dec., 1903. Vol. 16, pp. 136-151.

    The individual is not a sum of racial experiences but rather a resultant of them, hence experiences have largely lost their identity.

53. **Bolton, H. C.** Early instance of tangible lip-reading. Science, N. S., 1903. Vol. 17, pp. 631-632.

54. **Bolton, Thaddeus L.** The fatigue problem. Jour. of Ped., Dec., 1903. Vol. 16, pp. 97-123.

    Deals with conditions, kinds and causes of fatigue and complexity of the problem, also difficulties in way of winning trustworthy results.

55. —— —— The relation of motor power to intelligence. Am. Jour. of Psy., 1903. Vol. 14, pp. 615-631 (351-367).

56. **Boone, Richard G.** The lock-step in the public school. Proc. N. E. A., 1903, pp. 408-412.

    The grouping of pupils for work. How this grouping ought to be determined. The method of dealing with these groups.

57. **Booth, F. W.** Report of committee on statistics of defective sight and hearing of public school children. Proc. N. E. A., 1903, pp. 1036-1037. Also Association Review, Dec., 1903. Vol. 5, pp. 436-443.

58. **Bosse, R.** Aus der Jugendzeit. Die Grenzboten. 62 Jahrg., 1903. 3 Viertelj., pp. 155-166; 285-294; 408-416; 525-537; 718-724. 4 Viertelj., pp. 237-244; 367-375; 693-704; 760-773.

59. **Bourneville, ——** Recherches sur l'épilepsie, l'hystérie et l'idiotie. Alcan, Paris, 1902, pp. 234.

60. **Boyden, Arthur C.** Home gardens in Bridgewater. Jour. of Ed., Nov. 19, 1903. Vol. 58, pp. 335-336.

62. **Bradford, Mary D.** The function of the story. Kindergarten Mag., Feb., 1903. Vol. 15, pp. 337-344.

    Deals with selection of stories, the needs of children as manifested by interest and how the story can be used as a school exercise.

63. **Breckenridge, Mary S.** James—an unusual pupil. Ass'n Rev., June, 1903. Vol. 5, pp. 228-230.

    Study of a defective child.

64. **Bremond, E.** L'inspection médicale quotidienne des écoles manual général de l'instruction primaire. March 14, 1903. pp. 124-125.

65. **Bretherton, Ralph H.** The child mind. J. Lane, London, 1903, pp. 229.
Describes typical experiences from the supposed standpoint of the child.

66. **Bright, Orville T.** School gardens, city school yards, and the surroundings of rural schools. Proc. N. E. A., 1903, pp. 77-85.

67. **Broca, A. and Sulzer D.** Comparison des diverser lettres au point de la vitesse de lecture. Formation d'un alphabet rationnel. C. R. Acad. d. Sci., 1903. Vol. 137, pp. 812-814.

68. **Brooks, Stratton D.** Causes of withdrawal from school. Ed. Rev., Nov., 1903. Vol. 26, pp. 362-393.
Classification and discussion of causes of withdrawal from school, and suggestions for the prevention of needless withdrawal.

69. **Brouard, Eugène** Essai d'histoire critique de l'instruciton primaire en France de 1789 jus qu' à nos jours. Hachette & Co., Paris, 1901, pp. 360.

Browne, C. E. See **Hall and Browne.**

71. **Bryant, Geo. H.** The boy and his handicraft at home. Proc. N. E. A., 1903, pp. 651-652.

72. **Buck, Winnifred.** Boys' self governing clubs. Macmillan Co., N. Y., 1903, pp. 218.

73. **Bucke, W. Fowler** Oliver, the tame crow. Ped. Sem., March, 1903. Vol. 10, pp. 13-26.
Reaction of the crow on the children of Westfield, Mass., showing the feelings of the children.

74. —— —— Cyno-psychoses. Ped. Sem., Dec., 1903. Vol. 10, pp. 459-513.
Statistical study of children's reactions and feelings toward pet dogs. Bibliography of 113 titles.

75. **Buisson, Ferdinand** Education of the will. Rep. of Commissioner of Ed. for 1902. Vol. 1, pp. 721-740.

76. **Bunge, G. von** Die zunehmende Unfähigheit der Frauen ihre Kinder zu stillen. E. Reinhardt, München, 1903, pp. 32.

77. **Byrd, Susie M.** Influences of the kindergarten. School Journal, Feb. 14, 1903, p. 186.
Treats influences upon the ethical and the æsthetic nature of the child.

78. **Čada, Frantešek** Paedopsychologické dotazniky ze skol severoamerickych. Beseda Usitelská, Rijna 15 and 29, 1903. Vol. 35, pp. 583-586; 614-617.
Account of the child study movement in the United States.

79. **Carr, H. A.** Recent essays emphasizing the social in education. Invest. Dept. of Psy. and Ed., Univ. of Colo., 1903. Vol. 1 (3), pp. 13-19.

80. **Cattaneo & Marimo.** Ricerche sur alcune sensibilità e sul senso stereognostico nella età infantile. Pediatria, 1903. Vol. 10, p. 593.

81. **Chamberlain, A. F.** Legal folk-lore of children. Jour. of Am. Folk-Lore, Boston, 1903. Vol. 16, p. 280. Résumés part of article by De Cock. See No. 103.

82. —— —— Primitive taste-words. Am. Jour. of Psy., 1903. Vol. 14, pp. 410-417 (146-153).

83. **Chambers, Will Grant** The evolution of ideals. Ped. Sem., March, 1903. Vol. 10, pp. 101-143.
    Established what is essentially a new standpoint for judging of certain educational values. Draws practical lessons for the education of girls. Annotated list of 23 other studies.

84. **Chancellor, W. E.** Higher education of boys. Education, Nov., 1903. Vol. 24, p. 167-177.

85. **Cheney, Frances E.** Mentally defective children in a public school. Jour. of Ed., Sept. 24, 1903. Vol. 58, pp. 208-209.
    Describes experiences of the author in teaching such a class in connection with the schools of Springfield, Mass.

86. **Chesebrough, Amos S.** Culture of child piety. Cong. S. S. Pub. Co., Boston, 1886, pp. 235.

87. **Clapp, Henry Lincoln** School gardens. Proc. N. E. A., 1903, pp. 85-88.

88. **Clevenger, S. V.** The evolution of man and his mind. Evolution Pub. Co., Chicago, 1903, pp. 615.

89. **Clouston, L. S.** Child Study. Paidologist, July, 1903. Vol. 5, pp. 66-77.
    In child study psychology, physiology, pathology, evolution, hygiene, medicine, educational sciences, must all be called in to elucidate its problems.

90. **Coburn, Frederick W.** Mr. Gibson's primary industrial school. Jour. of Ed., Sept. 3, 1903. Vol. 58, pp. 160-161.

91. **Conradi, Edward** Children's interests in words, slang, stories, etc. Ped. Sem., Sept., 1903. Vol. 10, pp. 359-404.
    Varying interests of children at each stage of development. Pedagogical value of choosing books.

92. **Consoni, F.** Mesure de l'attention des faibles d'esprit. Arch. de Psy., 1903. Vol. 2, pp. 209-252.

93. **Cooper, E. H.** Children's prayers and prayer manuals. Fortnightly, Oct., 1903. Vol. 80, pp. 663-671.

94. —— —— Punishment of children. Fortnightly, June, 1903. Vol. 79, pp. 1060-67. Also Eclectic Mag., Sept., 1903. Vol. 141, pp. 343-348; also Living Age, July 11, 1903. Vol. 238, pp. 110-115.

95. **Cornman, O. P.** (Witmer, L. *ed.*) Experimental studies in psychology and pedagogy. I. Spelling in the elementary school: an experimental and statistical investigation. Ginn & Co., Boston, 1902, pp. 98.

96. **Crockett, E. A., M. D.** Some diseases of the nose and throat of interest to teachers. Proc. N. E. A., 1903, pp. 1028-1031.

97. **Culin, S.** American Indian games (1902). Am. Anthropol., N. S., 1903. Vol. 5, pp. 58-64.

98. **Cunningham, D. J.** Right-handedness and left-brainedness. Jour. of Anthropol. Inst., 1902. Vol. 32, pp. 273-295.

99. **Dangueger, ——** L'enseignement de la musique vocale. Manual général de l'instruction primaire. Nov. 14, 1903, pp. 541-543.
Notes should be taught after the sounds have been learned.

100. **Davids, Eleanor** Note book of an adopted mother. E. P. Dutton, N. Y., 1903, pp. 259.

101. **Dawson, George E.** A boy's religion and other papers. Int. Comm., Y. M. C. A., N. Y., 1801, pp. 16.

102. **—— ——** An experiment in teaching history. Jour. of Ped., June, 1903. Vol. 15, pp. 313-338.
Method of teaching history planned to appeal to adolescent aptitudes and interest.

103. **De Cock, A.** Rechtshandelingen bij de Kinderen. Volkskunde, Gent, 1902-1903. Vol. 15, pp. 193-199.
First part of an article treating of the laws of children's finds.

104. **Demoor, J.** Les enfants anormaux et la criminologie. Rev. Int. de Péd. Comp., Nov. 30, 1903. Vol. 6, pp. 81-89.
Criminal tendencies in abnormal children.

105. **Demoor, J. and Jonckheere, T.** L'influence de la vei urbaine sur la dégénérescence des enfants jusqu'à la quatrième génération. Inst. de Sociol., Bruxelles, 1903.

106. **De Nardi, P.** Dell' animalità (sensitività corporea e temperamento fisico)di Vittorio Alfieri. Tip. Sociale, Forli, 1903, pp.46.

107. **—— ——** Dell' intelligenza di Vittorio Alfieri. Studio psico-fisiologico-etnico. Tip. Sociale, Forli, 1903, pp. 54.

108. **Deries, Leon** De la correction des épreuves écrites dans les examens. Rev. Péd., Nov., 1903. Vol. 43, pp. 491-507.
How to correct examination papers.

109. **Dexter, E. G.** High-grade men: in college and out. Pop. Sci. Mo., 1903. Vol. 62, pp. 429-435.

110. **Dewey, John** The child and the curriculum. Univ. Press, Chicago, 1902, pp. 40.

111. —— —— More freedom. School Journal, Jan. 24, 1903, pp. 93-94.
Advocates more freedom for teachers in choice of methods and materials.

112. **Diefendorf, A. R.** Early symptoms of dementia praecox.
Med. Record, 1903. Vol. 64, pp. 453-457.

113. **Diem, O.** Die einfach demente Form der Dementia praecox.
Arch. f. Psychiat., 1903. Vol. 37, pp. 111-187.

114. **Döring, A.** Ueber sittliche Erziehung und Moralunterricht.
Zeits. für päd. Psy., Path. und Hygiene, April, 1903. Vol. 5,
pp. 1-20.
Discussion of the value, mistakes made, and objects to be sought in ethical and religious instruction in school.

115. **Dresslar, F. B.** Are chromæsthesias variable ? A study of
an individual case. Am. Jour. of Psy., 1903. Vol. 14, pp. 632-
646 (368-382).

116. **Drouard, Ch.** La puériculture à l'école primaire. Manuel
général de l'instruction primaire, Feb. 14, 1903, pp. 73-74.
A plea for young mothers to learn the essential principles of childish hygiene.

117. **Drummond, W. B.** Child study. Paidologist, Feb., 1903.
Vol. 5, pp. 22-32.
Child Study is the study of children by the methods of modern science.

118. **Du Bois, Patterson** Natural way in moral training. Revell
Co., N. Y., 1903, pp. 328.

119. **Dugas, L.** L' imagination. O. Doin, Paris, 1903, pp. 350.

120. **Durand, K.** Child labor in Pennsylvania. Outlook, May 9,
1903. Vol. 74, pp. 124-127.

121. **Durkheim, E.** Pédagogie et sociologie. Revue de Méta-
physique et de Morale, Paris, 1903. Vol. 11, pp. 37-54.
Argues that sociology must give " guiding ideas " to pedagogy.

122. **Eastman, Charles A.** Indian boyhood. McClure, N. Y.,
1903, pp. 289.

123. **Eastman, Charlotte W.** Evolution of Dodd's sister. Rand-
McNally, Chicago, 1897, pp. 230.

124. **Elkins, W. B.** Early education in Hawaii. Ped. Sem., 1903,
Vol. 10, pp. 86-93.

125. **Ellis, A. Caswell** The percentage of boys who leave high
school and the reasons therefor. Proc. N. E. A., 1903, pp. 792-
798.

126. **Ellis, A. C. and Shipe, M. M.** A study of the accuracy of
the present methods of testing fatigue. Am. Jour. of Psy.,
1903. Vol. 14, pp. 496-509 (232-245).

127. **Ellis, H.** Studies in the psychology of sex. Davis & Co.,
Phila., 1903, pp. 275.
New edition.

128. —— —— Variation in man and woman. Pop. Sci. Mo., 1903. Vol. 62, pp. 237-253.
Maintains that man varies more than woman.

129. **Elmer, A.** IV me conférence suisse pour l'éducation des anormoux. Lucerne, 1903. Arch. de Psy., 1903. Vol. 3, pp. 111-114.

130. **Everett, Charles Carroll** Ethics for young people. Ginn & Co., Boston, 1893, pp. 185.

131. **Farquhar, A. B.** Child labor as an economic question. Nat. Conf. Char. and Corr., 1903, pp. 196-199.
Intelligent versus unintelligent labor.

132. **Faunce, W. H. P.** Moral education in the public school. Ed. Rev., April, 1903. Vol. 6, pp. 325-340.
Suggestions as to how we can prevent the ecclesiastical neutrality of the school from producing moral indifferentism in the pupil.

133. **Feindel, E.** Le gigantisme chez l'homme. Révue générale des Sciences, Paris, 1903. Vol. 14, pp. 209-216.
Discusses infantile and acromegalic types.

134. **Ferrari, G. C.** L'assistenza dei fanciulli deficienti in Italia, il suo passato e il suo avvenire. Riv. Sperim. di Freniat., 1903. Vol. 29, pp. 316-323.

135. **Ferriani, L.** Fanciulli nervosi. Nuova Antol., 1903. Vol. 107, pp. 637-641.

136. —— —— I drammi dei fanciulli. Studi di psicologia sociale e criminale. V. Omarini, Como, 1902, pp. 312.

137. **Flanigan, M.** When children deem spanking just. Jour. of Ed., April 23, 1903. Vol. 57, p. 260.
Test given 1,000 children in Vermillion, Illinois.

138. **Flatau, Georg** Die Psychologie der Zwangsvorstellungen. Zeits. für päd. Psy., Path. u. Hygiene. April, 1903. Vol. 5, pp. 21-35.

139. **Forbush, William B.** Boy problem. 4th ed. Pilgrim Press, Boston, 1902, pp. 207.

140. **Forster, A.** Kurzer Bericht über das Muskelsystem einer Papua-Neugeborenen. Anat.Anz., Jena, 1903. Vol. 24, pp. 183-186.
Compares muscular system of 8 months old Papuan with that of European child of like age.

141. **Fouché, Maurice** Si la morale évolue. Manuel général de l'instruction primaire, Dec. 5, 1903, pp. 577-578.
Does not believe in children being taught the evolution of morality.

142. **Freeman, Flora Lucy** Religious and social work amongst girls. Skeffington & Son, London, 1901, pp. 143.

143. **Friedeberger, Moritz** Psychologie der Sprache. Steiger & Co., Bern, 1896, pp. 71.

144. **Friedel, V. H.** L'Éducation physique dans les écoles d'Écosse. Rev. Péd., Dec., 1903. Vol. 43, pp. 579-587.
Physical education in the schools of Scotland.

145. **Fuchs, Arno** Beobachtungen an schwachsinnigen Kindern. Zeits. für päd. Psy., Path. und Hygiene, Aug., 1903. Vol. 5, pp. 179-193.
Types and characteristics of weak-minded children. Conversations with weak-minded children quoted.

146. **Galbraith, A. M.** Four epochs of woman's life. 2d ed. Saunders, Philadelphia, 1903, pp. 244.

147. **Galton, F.** Pedigrees. Nature, 1903. Vol. 67, pp. 586-587.

148. **Gasquet, ——** La pédagogie œuvre d'intelligence et de bonté Manuel général de l'instruction primaire, Jan. 3, 1903, pp. 2-3.
Upon necessity for teacher to be experienced, cautious and a man of heart.

149. **Géant, Clothilde** L'école et l'éducation des travailleurs d'après l'enquête Mosely. Manuel général de l'instruction primaire. May 2, 1903, pp. 208-209.
Extracts from reports of Mosely commission and praises for U. S. system.

150. **Gersch, ——** Zu dem Aufsatz: Kinderpsychologie und Pädagogik. Der Türmer. 6 Jahrg., 1903-04. Vol. 1, pp. 213-214.

151. **Gilder, Richard Watson** The kindergarten: an uplifting social influence in the home and the district. Proc. N. E. A., 1903, pp. 388-394.

152. **Giroud, G.** Observations sur le développement de l'enfant. Schleicher, Paris, 1902, pp. 53.

153. **Giuffrida-Ruggeri, V.** Considerazioni antropologiche sull' infantilismo e conclusioni relative all' origine delle varietà umane. Monitore Zoologico, Firenze, 1903. Vol. 21. Repr. pp. 1-21.
Argues against the "infantilism" of woman.

154. **von Gizycki, P.** Die Urteilen Schulkinder über Funddiebstahl? Kinderfehler, 1903. Vol. 8, pp. 14-27.
Deals with the lack of moral standards in children, and the attitude to be assumed towards it.

155. **Gladstone, R. J.** Preliminary communication on some cephalometric data bearing upon the relation of the size and shape of the head to mental ability. Jour. of Anat. and Physiol., 1903. Vol. 37, pp. 333-346.

156. **Goerth, A.** Das sittliche Gefühl beim männlichen und beim weiblichen Geschlecht. Die Deutsche Schule, Leipzig, 1903. Vol. 7, pp. 166-174.
Argues against placing women above men in office.

157. **Goldstein, K.** Beiträge zur Entwickelungsgeschichte des menschlichen Gehirnes. Arch. f. Anat. u. Physiol., 1903, pp. 29-60.

158. **Gould, G. M.** Biographic clinics; the origin of the ill-health of De Quincey, Carlyle, Darwin, Huxley and Browning. Blakiston, Philadelphia, 1903. 2 v. pp. 223 and 392.

159. —— —— The rôle of eyestrain in civilization. Brit. Med. Jour., 1903. Vol.2, pp. 663-666; 757-760.

160. **Gréard** —— Michelet et L'Éducation nationale. Rev. Péd., Jan., 1903. Vol. 42, pp. 1-23.

161. **Greenwood, Allen** Some eye defects of feeble-minded and backward children Proc. N. E. A., 1903, pp. 1023-1028.

162. **Groser, William H.** A hundred years work for the children. S. S. Union, London, 1903, pp. 196.

163. **Grosmolard, M.** Criminalité juvenile. Arch. d'Anthropol, Crim., 1903. Vol. 18, pp. 129-158; 193-209; 257-273.

164. **Grout, Carrie L.** Rights of children. Arena, March, 1903. Vol. 29, pp. 288-291.

165. **Gruber, M.** Führt die Hygiene zur Entartung der Rasse? E. H. Moritz, Stuttgart, 1903, pp. 35.

166. **Gruenenbaum, Ferdinand** Erklärung des Stotterns dessen Heilung und Verhütung. B. Konegen, Leipzig, 1897, pp. 63.

167. **Günther, Ed** Praktische Anleitung zur vollständigen Heilung des Stotterns fur Eltern und Lehrer sowie zum Selbstgebrauch. L. Heuser, Berlin, 1893, pp. 106.

168. **Guillermet, F.** Cas de mensonge infantile. Arch. de Psy., 1903. Vol. 2, p. 377.

169. **Gutzmann, Hermann** Die Sprachentwicklung des Kindes und ihre Hemmungen. Kinderfehler, 1902. Vol. 7, pp. 193-216.

170. —— —— Zur vergleichenden Psychologie der Sprachstörungen. Zeits. für päd. Psy., Path. und Hygiene, Aug., 1903. Vol. 5, pp. 162-178.
   Discussion of speech defects of children, their causes and cures.

171. **Hall, F. H.** Influence of the study of the unusual child upon the teaching of the usual. Proc. N. E. A., 1903, pp. 987-991.
   See also Johnson, G. E., on same subject.

Hall, Florence See **Howe, Maude and Hall, Florence.**

172. **Hall, G. Stanley** Note on moon fancies. Am. Jour. of Psy., Jan., 1903. Vol. 14, pp. 88-91.
   Supplements Dr. Slaughter's article. See Bibliog. for 1902, No. 278.

173. —— —— Child study at Clark University. An impending new step. Am. Jour. of Psy., Jan., 1903. Vol. 14, pp. 96-106.
   List of 102 questionnaires with list of books and articles based thereon.

174. **Hall, G. Stanley** Note on cloud fancies. Ped. Sem., March, 1903. Vol. 10, pp. 96-100.
Children's feeling about clouds.

175. —— —— Psychic arrest in adolescence. Proc. N. E. A., 1903, pp. 811-816.

176. **Hall, G. Stanley and Browne, C. E.** Children's ideas of fire, heat, frost and cold. Ped. Sem., March, 1903. Vol. 10, pp. 27-85.
Shows that children have some notion of range of temperature far beyond that of their immediate experience.

177. **Hall, G. Stanley and Smith, Theodate L.** Reactions to light and darkness. Am. Jour. of Psy., Jan. 1903. Vol. 14, pp. 21-83.

178. —— —— Showing off and bashfulness as phases of self-consciousness. Ped. Sem., June, 1903. Vol. 10, pp. 159-199.
Reports of mothers. Summary of results.

179. —— —— Marriage and fecundity of college men and women. Ped. Sem., Sept. 1903. Vol. 10, pp. 275-314.
Does a college education deter women from marrying?

180. —— —— Curiosity and interest. Ped. Sem., Sept., 1903. Vol. 10, pp. 315-358.
Data indicating prevailing directions of interest in children.

181. **Hammerschlag, V.** Beitrag zur Lehre von den Sprachstörungen im Kindesalter. Zeits. f. Ohrenhk., 1903. Vol. 45, pp. 254-262.

182. **Hammond, Edward Payson** Conversion of children. F. H. Revell Co., Chicago, u. d., pp. 274.

183. **Haney, James Parton** Manual training versus manual arts. Proc. N. E. A., 1903, pp. 658-664.

184. **Hapgood, H.** The autobiography of a thief. Fox Duffield, New York, 1903, pp. 349.

185. **Hart, Hastings H.** Common sense and co-operation in child saving. Nat. Conf. Char. and Corr., 1903, pp. 180-187.
Gives essentials of report by Hon. Thomas L. Mulvy at meeting of N. C. C. C. in 1899, and closes with the important steps for co-ordination.

186. **Haseltine, B.** The eye in childhood. Jour. of Ophthal., Otol. and Laryngol., 1903. Vol. 15, pp. 157-161.

187. **Hastings, Wm. W.** A manual for physical measurements for use in normal schools, public and preparatory schools, etc., with anthropometric tables for each height of each age and sex from 5 to 20 years, and vitality coefficients. The Author, Springfield, Mass., 1902, pp. 112.
An excellent book in this field.

188. **Hastings, Wm. W.** Physical examinations and exercise in public schools. Am. Phys. Ed. Rev., 1903. Vol. 13, pp. 259-268.

189. —— —— Health and growth of school children. Proc. N. E. A., 1903. Vol. 42, pp. 769-778.
How health and growth are estimated, retarded, increased.

190. **Heinmann, G.** Ein Beitrag zur Idioten-Statistik. Allg. Zeits. f. Psychiat., 1903. Vol. 6, pp. 443-454.

191. **Henninger, C. H.** Report of three cases of hystero-epilepsy. Jour. of Psycho-Asthenics, Dec., 1902, March, 1903. Vol. 7, pp. 34-38.

192. **Henry, Alice** Special moral training of girls. Int. Jour. of Ethics, 1903. Vol. 14, pp. 1-15.

193. **Herder** —— (Keller, L'Herausg.) Comenius und die Erziehung des Menschengeschlechts. 2d ed. Weidmann, Berlin, 1903, pp. 15.

194. **Heyse, P.** Jugenderinnerungen. Deutsche Rundschau. Vol. 101, 1899, pp. 92-123; 287-302; 453-477. Vol. 102, 1900, pp. 98-110; 188-207; 359-387. Sonderdruck u. d. T.: Jugenderinnerungen und Bekenntnisse, 1900. 2 Aufl.

195. **Hirschfeld, Magnus** Das urnische Kind. Kinderfehler, Sept., 1903. Vol. 8, pp. 241-258.
Discussion of the sexual pathology of children.

196. **Hirschlaff, L.** Bibliographie der psycho-physiologischen Literatur des Jahres, 1901. Zeits. f. Psy., 1903. Vol. 31, pp. 305-492.

197. **Hodge, C. F.** Nature study true to life. Proc. N. E. A., 1903, pp. 412-417.

198. **Hoffman, Frederick L.** The social and medical aspects of child labor. Nat. Conf. Char. and Corr., 1903, pp. 138-155.
Discussion of,—number of child employers, economics, rational, condition and physical basis of child labor, standard physical requirements, plea for strong and healthy children, data wanting mortality in industry, physical basis for school life, and moral value of child labor.

199. **Hoffman, L. W.** The pedagogical value of mediate interest. Jour. of Ped., Sept., 1903. Vol. 16, pp. 49-55.
Utility of permanent mediate interest.

200. **Houghton, Frederick** Co-operation of museums and schools, School Jour., Jan. 10, 1903, pp. 49-50.
Helps teachers in five lines. Co-operation strongly urged.

201. **Howe, Maude and Hall, Florence** Laura Bridgman. Dr. Howe's famous pupil and what he taught her. Little, Brown & Co., Boston, 1903, pp. 394.
Full and connected account of the education of this famous blind, deaf-mute.

202. **Hughes, C. H.** The evolution of the brain.   Alien. & Neurol., 1903. Vol. 24, pp. 153-167.

203. **Hughes, R. E.** The making of citizens. A study in comparative education.   Scott, London, 1902, pp. 405.
   Chap. XIII, treats of the ed. of girls in various countries; chap. XIV, the ed. of defective children.

204. **Hunt, James** Stammering and stuttering. Longmans, London, 1865, pp. 258.

205. **Hunter, R.** Child labor; a social waste. Independent, Feb. 12, 1904. Vol. 55, pp. 375-379.

206. **Hutchinson, Woods** Play as an education. Contemp. Rev., Sept., 1903. Vol. 84, pp. 375-394, also Liv. Age, Oct. 3, 1903. Vol. 239, pp. 28-44.
   Importance of play in the mental and physical development of the child. Suggestions for the introduction of play into the present system of education.

207. **Ide, Fannie Ogden** Character and charm in children. Outlook, Oct. 24, 1903. Vol. 75, pp. 447-453.

208. **Itschner, Hermann** Bildungsnöte der Volksschullehrer. T. Hofmann, Leipzig, 1901, pp. 78.

209. **Jahrmärker, Max** Zur Frage der Dementia praecox. C. Marhold, Halle, 1903, pp. 119.
   Gives number of interesting cases.

210. **James, A.** Deafness and blindness occurring acutely in chilren. Scot. Med. Surg. Jour., 1903. Vol. 13, pp. 47-50.

211. **James, Miss** Mentally defective child. Paidologist, July, 1903. Vol. 5, pp. 83-88.
   Description of the schools where the child is under special medical as well as educational supervision.

212. **Janke, Otto** Grundriss der Schulhygiene. L. Voss, Hamburg, 1901, pp. 309.

213. **Jarach, L.** Encore un mot sur la "puériculture" à l' école. Man. Gen., May 30, 1903.
   Necessity for girls to learn the needs, etc., of children.

214. **Jastrow, J.** Helen Keller; a psychological autobiography. Pop. Sci. Mo., 1903. Vol. 63, pp. 71-83.

215. **Jauregg, W.** Ueber Myxödem und sporadischen Kretinismus. Wien. med. Wochensch., 1903. Vol. 63, pp. 66-70; 134-138.

216. **Johnson, George E.** Influence of the study of the unusual child upon the teaching of the usual. Proc. N. E. A., 1903, pp. 992-996.
   See also Hall, F. H. on same subject.

217. **Johnstone, E. R.** Discipline. Jour. of Psycho-Asthenics, Dec., 1902—March, 1903. Vol. 7, pp. 38-46.
Method of treatment of feeble-minded at institutions, and discussion of same by experts.

218. **Jonckheere, T.** Notes sur la psychologie des enfants arriérés. Arch. de Psy., 1903. Vol. 2, pp. 253-268.

—— —— See **Demoor and Jonckheere.**

219. **Jones, L. H.** The place of physical training in education. Am. Phys. Ed. Rev., 1903. Vol. 8, pp. 164-167.

220. **Jordan, David Starr.** Voice of the scholar. P. Elder & Co., San Francisco, 1903, pp. 278.

221. **Judd, Charles H.** Genetic psychology for teachers. D. Appleton & Co., New York, 1903, pp. 329.
Contents: Teacher-study, its scope and aim; interpretation of experience; ideals; individuality, adaptation and expression; teachers' writing habit; racial development in writing; reading; number.

222. **Just, K.** Das religiöse Gefühl im Kindesalter. 28 Jahresbericht über die Bürgerschulen zu Altenburg auf das Schuljahr, 1894-1895. 1895, pp. 3-17.

223. **Keller, Helen** Story of my life. Doubleday, Page & Co., New York, 1903, pp. 441.
Story of the mental development of a child who at the age of eighteen months lost sight, hearing, and speech, but who subsequently learned to articulate and to read lips.

224. **Kelley, F.** Law of child labor. Ann. Am. Acad. Pol. Sci., May, 1903. Vol. 21, pp. 438-445.

225. **Kelly, Robert L.** Psychophysical tests of normal and abnormal children. (Stud. fr. Psychol. Lab., Univ. of Chicago, IV.) Psy. Rev., 1903, Vol. 10, pp. 345-372.
A statistical study.

226. **Kelso, J. J.** Reforming delinquent children. Nat. Conf. Char. and Corr., 1903, pp. 230-237.
What respect, trust, and useful employment will do for delinquent children.

227. **Kenyon, Walter** The drift of manual training. School Jour., March 21, 1903, pp. 324-327.
Brief history of manual training in the public schools. Gives value of manual training.

228 **Kiernan J. G.** Mixoscopic adolescent survivals in art, literature and pseudo-ethics. Alien. & Neurol., 1903. Vol. 24, pp. 167-188; 338-353; 457-465.

229. **King, C. H.** The reasoning powers of children. Paidologist, Nov., 1903. Vol. 5, pp. 157-162.
Investigations made to discover how far the actual evidence of the powers of thought in certain children accord with the usually accepted outline of intellectual progress.

230. **King, Irving** Psychology of child development. Univ. of Chicago Press, Chicago, 1903, pp. 265.

Contents: Child psychology, its validity and aims; problems relating to the child's earliest experience; earliest consciousness; emotional expressions in infancy; co-ordination of impulses; inhibition; imitation; moral ideas; interest, adolescence.

231. **Kirkpatrick, Edwin A.** Fundamentals of child study. Macmillan Co., New York, 1903, pp. 384.

Contents: Nature, scope and problems of child study; physical growth and development; native motor activities and general order of development; classification and development of instincts; imitation; play; heredity; individuality; abnormalities; child study applied in schools.

232. —— —— Plans and ambitions of adolescents in relations to school work—a statistical study from the Fitchburg normal school. Jour. of Ped., March, 1903. Vol. 15, pp. 189-220.

Do upper grades and high schools serve the peculiar needs of adolescents?

233. **Kline, Linus W.** A study in juvenile ethics. Ped. Sem., June, 1903. Vol. 10, pp. 239-266.

A study and comparison of the aims, ideals, emotions and judgments of right and justice of city and country children by the questionnaire method.

234. **Knopf, S. A.** Duties of school teacher in combat of tuberculosis. School Jour., Oct. 31, 1903, pp. 427-431.

Gives description of the disease and the duties of teachers in preventing it.

235. **Koch, J. L. A.** Die erbliche Belastung bei den Psychopathien. Kinderfehler, 1903. Vol. 8, pp. 1-15.

The inheritance of mental disease.

236. **König, A.** Die Entwicklung des musikalischen Sinnes bei Kindern. Kinderfehler, 1903. Vol. 8, pp. 49-62; pp. 97-111.

Deals with the musical appreciation of children of different ages and conditions.

237. **Koons, Wm. George** The child's religious life; a study of the child's religious nature and the best methods for its training and development. With an introduction by T. B. Neely. Eaton & Mains, New York, 1903, pp. 270.

238. **Krohn, William D.** Physical education and brain building. Proc. N. E. A., 1903, pp. 818-823.

239. **Lacombe, Paul** Faut-il enseignerl' histoire à rébours? Manuel général de l'instruction primaire, April 25, 1903, pp. 195-196.

Study of history should not begin with ancient history.

240. **Laignel-Lavastine** Audition colorée familiale. Rev. Neurol., 1901. Vol. 9, pp. 1152-1162.

241. **Langdon-Down, R.** Neurotic children. Paidologist, Feb., 1903. Vol. 5, pp. 2-11.

The nervous states of children depend upon, and are attended by, some changes in the nervous system.

242. **Langston, Rev. G. D.** The child and the farms. Nat. Conf.
Char. and Corr., 1903, pp. 204-205.
How to keep these children from the mills.

243. **Langwill, H. G.** Stammering and its treatment by the general practitioner. Practitioner, N. S., 1903. Vol. 17, pp. 24-43.

244. **Lawrence, Isabel** How shall children be led to love good books? Jour. of Ed., June 18, 1903. Vol. 57, p. 387.

245. **Lay, W. A.** Experimentelle Didaktik; ihre Grundlegung mit besonderer Rücksicht auf Muskelsinn, Wille und Tat. O. Nemnich, Wiesbaden, 1903, pp. 595.
Comparative treatment of motor education with recognition of the contributions of child study, etc. A valuable, solid work.

246. **Le Bon, G.** The crowd; a study of the popular mind. F. Unwin, London, 1903, pp. 239.

247. **Lee, A., Lewenz, M. A., and Pearson, K.** On the correlation of the mental and physical characters in man. Man, 1903, pp. 7-12.

248. **Lee, Joseph** Boston's play-ground system. N. E. Mag., N. S., Jan., 1903. Vol. 27, pp. 521-36.

249. —— —— Kindergarten principles in social work. Proc. N. E. A., 1903, pp. 378-382.

250. **Lefebure,** —— L'éducation physique en Suède. Lamertin, Bruxelles, 1903, pp. 198.

251. **Legarde, Ellen** Should the scope of the public school system be broadened so as to take in all children capable of education. Jour. of Ed., Oct. 8, 1903. Vol. 58, pp. 240, 245, 246.
Treats of schools opened for defective children, especially in Providence, R. I.

252. Législation against child labor. Chaut., Aug., 1903. Vol. 37, pp. 439-440.

253. **Leri, A.** Le réflexe des orteils chez les enfants. Rev. Neurol., 1903. Vol. 11, pp. 689-693.

254. **Leubuscher, G.** Schulhygienische Schullehrerseminaren. Pädagogische Blätter, 1902. No. 4, pp. 178-180.

255. **Levi-Bianchini, M.** Sull' età di comparsa e sull' influenza dell'ereditarietà nella patogenesi della demenza primitiva o precoce. Riv. Sperim. di Freniat., 1903. Vol. 29, pp. 558-575.

Lewenz See **Lee, Lewenz and Pearson.**

256. **Lewis, G. A.** Practical treatment of stammering and stuttering and a treatise on the cultivation of the voice. G. A. Lewis, Detroit, Mich., 1902, pp. 415.

257. —— —— Cure of stammering and stuttering. Am. Phys. Ed. Rev., 1903. Vol. 8, pp. 249-259.

258. **Ley** —— Les soi-disant mauvaises habitudes des enfants. Ann. Soc. Med. Angers, July, 1903.

259. **Liard, Louis** Psychologie de l'enfant. Manuel général de l'instruction primaire, Nov. 28, 1903, pp. 565-566.

260. **Liebmann, A.** Untersuchung und Behandlung geistig zurück gebliebener Kinder. Berlin, 1898, pp. 36.

261. —— —— Vorlesungen uber Sprachstörungen. O. Coblentz, Berlin, 1898.

262. —— —— Stotternde Kinder. Samml. von Abhand. a. d. Gebiete Päd. Psy. u. Physiol. Berlin, 1903. Vol. 6, Heft 2, pp. 96.
    Cites a number of cases of stuttering showing a family tendency through nervous disease. Distinguishes between stammering and stuttering.

263. **Lindsey, Ben. B.** The reformation of juvenile delinquents, through the juvenile court. Nat. Conf. Char. and Corr., 1903, pp. 206-230.
    Reports what has been done in the court over which Judge Lindsey presides, refers to principles of the methods.

264. **Livingstone, J. W.** Automatic action in elementary education. Jour. of Ed., Sept. 17, 1903. Vol. 58, pp. 192, 193, 197, 198.
    Utility of automatic acts in education.

265. **Lloyd, R. J.** Education of physically and mentally defective children. Westminster Rev., June, 1903. Vol. 159, pp. 662-674.

266. **Lobsien, Marx** Schwankungen der psychischen Kapazität; einige experimentelle Untersuchungen an Schulkindern. Schiller-Ziehen, 1902. Vol. 5, pp. 110.

267. —— —— Einige Untersuchungen über das Gedächtnis bei schwachbefähigten. Kinderfehler, June-Aug., 1903. Vol. 8, pp. 157-169; 193-204.
    A comparative study of the memory of normal and of weak minded children.

268. **Lombroso, C.** L'homme de génie. Schleicher, Paris, 1903, pp. 615.

269. **Lombroso P.** I capricci dei bambini. Nouva Antol., 1903. Vol. 107, pp. 257-262.

270. —— —— Il senso della gioia nei bambini. Nuova Antol., 1903. Vol. 108, pp. 601-606.

Lord See **Wyer and Lord**

271. **Loria, G.** Les femmes mathématiciennes. Rev. Scient., Paris, 1905. 4e s., Vol. 20, pp, 385-392.
    Historical sketch. Author believes that mathematics lie outside the sphere of woman.

272. **Louch, Mary** Adolescence. Paidologist, July, 1903. Vol. 5, pp. 101-110.

The author describes some of the characteristics of adolescence as known by the ordinary observer, and states educational problems connected with it as presented to educators.

273. **Love, J. K.** Developing the residual hearing power and speech of the deaf. Jour. of Laryngol., Rhinol. & Otol., 1903. Vol. 18, pp. 393-398.

274. **Lyttle, E. W.** Place of physical education in the curriculum —should it be fundamental or incidental? Proc. N. E. A., 1903, pp. 823-829.

275. **McClure, W. Frank** Cleveland Boy's Club. Munsey, Dec., 1903. Vol. 30, pp. 393-96.

McDougall See **Myers and McDougall.**

276. **McKenny, Charles** Social nature and needs of the child. Kindergarten Mag., March, 1903. Vol. 15, pp. 446-449.

Deals with three things needed to accomplish socialization of the child. The work of education is to socialize the child.

277. **Magnus, Laurie** Ed. National education. J. Murray, London, 1901, pp. 303.

278. **Malapert, P.** Enquête sur le sentiment de la colère chez les enfants. L'Année Psy., 1902 (1903). Vol. 9, pp. 1-40.

279. **Mancinni, E.** L'aritmetica degli animali. Nuova Antol., 1903. Vol. 187, pp. 658-670.

Marimo See **Cattaneo and Marimo.**

280. **Markscheffel, Karl** Internationaler Schülerbriefwechsel. Marburg, 1903, pp. 44.

281. **Marro, H.** La puberté chez l'homme et chez la femme, étudiée dans ses rapports avec l'anthropologie, la psychiatrie, la pédagogie, et la sociologie. Schleicher, Paris, 1903, pp. 530.

Good French version of the valuable Italian original.

282. **Marsden, Rufus** The study of the early color sense. Psy. Rev., Jan., 1903. Vol. 10, pp. 37-46.

Deals with three problems in genetic psychology, with three methods of performing experiments, and charts showing results of the experiments.

283. **Martin, Alexandre** L'éducation du caractère, Paris, 1896, pp. 377.

284. —— —— L'educazione del carattere. G. Laterza, Bari, 1903, pp. 600.

285. **Martinazzoli, A.** L'anthropologia e la scienza dell 'educazione. Rendic. Istit. Lombard., 2e. s., 1903. Vol. 36, pp. 569-581.

286. **Mass, O.** Einige Bemerkungen über das Stottern. Deutsche Zeits. f. Nervenhk., 1903. Vol. 24, pp. 390-403.

287. **Matiegka, H.** Ueber das Hirngewicht, die Schädelkapazität und die Kopfform, sowie deren Beziehungen zur psychischen Tätigkeit des Menschen. I. Ueber das Hirngewicht des Menschen. Prag. Verl. d. k. böhm. Gesellsch. d. Wissensch., 1902.

288. **Maurer, L.** Beobachtungen über das Anschauungsvermögen der Kinder. I. Zeits, für päd. Psy. Path. und Hygiene, April, 1903. Vol. 5, pp. 62-85.
     Tabulated results of experiments on the perception of children.

289. **Mautoux, P.** Anatole France on childhood. Academy, Feb. 7, 1903. Vol. 64, pp. 133-134; also Eclectic Mag., May, 1993. Vol. 140, pp. 631-33; also Living Age, March 28, 1903. Vol. 236, pp. 820-822.

290. **Maxwell, Samuel S.** Ambidexterity and mental development. Jour. of Ped., Sept., 1903. Vol. 16, pp. 64-67.
     Calls attention to the importance of scientific data on the question.

291. **Mayer A.** Ueber Einzel-und Gesamtleistung des Schulkindes. Arch. f. d. ges. Psy., 1903. Vol. 1, pp. 276-416.

292. **Meleney, Clarence E.** Vacation schools. Jour. of Ed., Jan. 15, 1903; Vol. 51, pp. 35-36; Jan. 22, 1903; Vol. 57, pp. 51-52.
     Vacation schools in New York City.

293. **Menpes, Dorothy** The world's children. A. and C. Black, London, 1903, pp. 246.

294. **Merkel, W.** Employment of partial hearing of pupils in institutions for the deaf. Ass'n Rev., April, 1903. Vol. 5, pp. 101-111.
     Systematic exercises for training the hearing.

295. **Messmer, O.** Zur Psychologie des Lesens bei Kindern und Erwachsenen. Arch. f. d. ges. Psy., 1903. Vol. 2, pp. 190-298.

296. **Metchnikoff, E.** Études sur la nature humaine. Masson, Paris, 1903, pp. 400.

297. **Meumann, E. F. W.** Die Sprache des Kindes. Zürcher and Furrer, Zürich, 1903, pp. 82.

298. **Meyer, R. M.** Die Wette. Arch. f. Kulturgesch., 1903. Vol. 1, pp. 1-17.

299. **Miles, S. S.** The eyes of school children. Jour. of Opthal., Otol., and Laryngol., 1903. Vol. 15, pp. 386-387.

300. **Miller, M. M.** Library work with children at Madison, N. J. Library Jour., April, 1903. Vol. 28, pp. 169-170.

301. **Mitchell, Clara J.** Principles underlying the use of the industrial arts in the kindergarten and the grades. Kindergarten Mag., Feb., 1903. Vol. 15, pp. 367-373.

302. **Modena, G.** L'acromegalia. Riv. Sper. di Freniat., Reggio-Emilia, 1903. Vol. 29, pp. 629-640.
First part of critical résumé of literature.

303. **Moebius** Ueber den physiologischen Schwachsinn des Weibes. 5th ed. Marhold, Halle, 1903, pp. 123.

304. **Moeli, C.** Die Imbecillität. Deutsche klin. Lief., 1903. Vol. 96, pp. 317-340.

305. **Mönkemöller,** —— Geistesstörung und Verbrechen im Kindesalter. Samml. von Abhand. a. d. Gebiete der Päd. Psy. u. Physiol., Berlin, 1903. Vol. 6, Heft 6, pp. 104.
Statistics of the great increase since 1873 of criminality of children. Mental conditions of child criminal; environment and heredity. Statistics of crimes of mentally deficient children.

306. **Monroe, Will S.** Tone perception and music interest of young children. Ped. Sem., March, 1903. Vol. 10, pp. 144-146.
Treats sex-differences and musical abilities.

307. **Montgomery, John B.** Common sense and co-operation. Nat. Conf. Char. and Corr., 1903, pp. 200-203.
Need of work in active period of child's life.

308. **Morgan, T. H.** Recent theories in regard to the determination of sex. Pop. Sci. Mo., 1903. Vol. 64, pp. 97-116.

309. **Morlat, A.** Infantilisme et insuffisance surrénale. J. Rousset, Paris, 1903, pp. 74.

310. **Morrison, Alice** Training a special sense. Jour. of Psycho-Asthenics, Dec., 1902, March, 1903. Vol. 7, pp. 46-50.
Report of cultivation of hearing of three apparently deaf children by training of other senses followed by discussion of training senses of the feeble-minded.

311. **Mosny, E.** Les devoirs de l'état envers l'enfant au point de vue de l'hygiène. Manuel général de l'instruction primaire, Jan. 3, 1903, pp. 51-52.
Demands a rigorous and periodical surveillance over public and private schools as a protection against contagious diseases.

312. **Mossier, H.** Nos Écoles primaires jugées par un Étranger. Rev. Péd., June, 1903. Vol. 42, pp. 560-573.

313. **Muir, J.** An analysis of twenty-six cases of Mongolism. Arch. of Pediatrics, 1903. Vol. 20, pp. 161-169.

314. **Murphy, Edgar Gardner** Child labor as a national problem; with especial reference to the southern states. Nat. Conf. Char. and Corr., 1903, pp. 121-134.

315. **Murray, E. R.** Symmetrical paper folding a waste of time. Child Life, Jan., 1903. Vol. 5, pp. 14-18.
Author argues that it should occupy a much less important place in school work.

316. **Myers, C. S., & McDougall, W.** Reports of the Cambridge Anthropological Expedition to the Torres Straits. Vol. 2. Physiology and psychology. Pt. 2. Hearing, smell, taste, cutaneous sensations, etc. Univ. Press, Cambridge, 1903, pp. 141-223.

317. **Nawratzki, E.** Rachenmandel und Gehörorgan der Idioten. Zeits. f. Ohrenhk., 1903. Vol. 45, pp. 105-127.

318. **Newell, William Wells** Games and songs of American children. Harper & Bros., New York, 1903, pp. 282.
A new edition of a classic.

319. **Newsholme, Arthur** Health of scholars. Jour. of the Sanitary Institute, July, 1900. Vol. 21, pp. 269-288.

320. **Niceforo, A.** Note préliminaire d' anthropologie sur 3147 enfants des écoles le Lausanne, étudiés en rapport à leur condition sociale. Scuola Posit., S. II, 1903. Vol. 1, pp. 417.

321. **Nichols, F. E.** Children of the coal shadow. McClure, Feb., 1903. Vol. 20, pp. 435-444.

322. **Nodes, Frances M.** Methods of dealing with dull and backward children in Germany. Child Life, April, 1903. Vol. 5, pp. 96-99.

323. **Nunes, J. J.** Jogos infantis. Portugalia, Porto, 1903. Vol. 1, pp. 853-858.
Describes in-door and out-door plays and games of Portuguese children of Algarve.

324. **Nussbaum, H. C.** Leitfaden der Hygiene. R. Oldenbourg, München, 1902, pp. 601.

325. **Oppenheim, ——** Ueber die ersten Zeichen der Nervosität des Kindesalters. Kinderfehler, Dec., 1903. Vol. 9, pp. 49-63.
The effect of heredity as seen in nervous children, the early appearance of nervous signs and their interpretation.

326. **Orth, Johannes** Gefühl und Bewusstseinslage: eine kritisch-experimentelle Studie. Samml. von Abhand. a. d. Gebiete der Päd. Psy. und Physiol., Berlin, 1903. Vol. 6, Heft. 4, pp. 131.
Contents: Historical terminology; Significance of word sensation, in usage of every-day life; Critique of modern teaching of sensation; Consciousness; Personal researches with tables.

327. **Pfalz, F.** Ein Knabenleben vor sechzig Jahren. Päd. Betrachtung eigener Erlebnisse. Pt. 1, 1901; Pt. 2, 1902.

328. **Pfister, H.** Ueber das Gewicht des Gehirns und einzelner Hirntheile beim Säugling und älteren Kinde. Neurol. Centralb., 1903. Vol. 22, pp. 562-572.

330. **Piggot, H. E.** Die Grundzüge der sittlichen Entwicklung und Erziehung des Kindes. Beiträge zur Kinderforschung. Jena, 1903, Pt. 7.

331. **Platzhoff-Lejeune, E.** Werk und Persönlichkeit. J. C. C. Bruns, Minden, 1903, pp. 246.

332. **Pace, Edward A.** The influence of religious education upon the motives of conduct. Ed. Rev., 1903. Vol. 26, pp. 332-338.
From Catholic point of view.

333. **Pappenheim, K.** Das Tierzeichnen der Kinder. Kindergarten, 1900. Vol. 41, pp. 180-182; 247-252.

334. **Parlin, Frank E.** Shorter primary sessions. Jour. of Ed., April 9, 1903. Vol. 57, p. 231.
Shows harm of keeping small children in school so much of the day.

335. —— —— Mentally defective children. Jour. of Ed., April 30, 1903. Vol. 57, p. 279.
Distinction between slightly abnormal and mentally defective children; the latter not to be allowed in the public schools.

336. **Pater, Walter** The child in the house. J. B. Mosher, Portland, 1902, pp. 45.

337. **Patrick, G. T. W.** The psychology of foot ball. Am. Jour. of Psy., 1903. Vol. 14, pp. 368-381 (104-117).

338. **Patten, S. N.** Heredity and social progress. Macmillan, New York, 1903, pp. 214.

339. **Pearson, K.** Inheritance of psychical and physical characters in man. Nature, 1903. Vol. 68, pp. 607-608.

340. —— —— Mathematical contributions to the theory of evolution. On homotyposis in homologous but differentiated organs. Proc. Roy. Soc., 1903. Vol. 71, pp. 288-313.

341. —— —— Mathematical contributions to the theory of evolution. XI. On the influence of natural selection on the variability and correlation of organs. Philos. Trans. Roy. Soc., 1903. Vol. 200 (Ser. A), pp. 1-66.

Pearson See **Lee, Lewenz and Pearson.**

342. **Pelisson, Maurice** La prophylaxie de la tuberculose dans les établissements universitaires. Rev. Péd., Sept., 1903. Vol. 43, pp. 232-240.
How tuberculosis is studied in universities.

343. **Permewan, W.** The waste of intelligence in the young. Paidologist, Feb., 1903. Vol. 5, pp. 20-21.
The author argues that there was going on in the elementary schools a waste of intelligence which could only be described as wanton.

344. **Poncet, A. et Leriche, R.** Nains d'aujour d'hui et nains d'antrefois. Rev. Scient., Paris, 1903. 4e s., Vol. 20, pp. 587-589.
Treats of ancient and modern dwarfs and their nature.

345. **Raelhmann, E.** Ueber die Entwicklung der Kunst im Leben des Kindes. Deutsche Revue, 1903. Vol. 3, pp. 201-212; 335-346.

346. **Rayot,** —— Psychologie de l'éducation. Manuel général de l'instruction primaire. Oct. 31, 1903, pp. 518-519.
Practice should always precede theory in education.

347. **Reddie, Cecil** Froebelian methods in the class-room. Child Life, Oct., 1903. Vol. 5, pp. 186-189.

348. —— —— Co-operation of successive teachers of the pupil. Child Life, Oct., 1903. Vol. 5, pp. 190-195.

349, **Rich, E. J.** Child labor in Europe. Ann. Am. Acad. Pol. Sci., May, 1903. Vol. 21, pp. 499-502.

350. **Rietz, E.** Das Wachstum Berliner Kinder während der Schuljahre. Arch. f. Anthrop., N. F. 1903. Vol. 1, pp. 30-42.

351. **Riis, Jacob A.** Children of the tenements. Macmillan, New York, 1903, pp. 387.

352. **Risley,** —— Examens oculaires des écoles publiques. Ann. d'Ocul., 1903. Vol. 127, pp. 234.

353. **Roth, W. E.** Games, sports and amusements. North Queensland Ethnology Bull., 1902. (4.)

354. **Sabin Edwin L.** A boy's loves. Century, July, 1903. Vol. 44, pp. 409-413.

355. **Sachs, B.** On amaurotic family idiocy; a disease chiefly of the gray matter of the central nervous system. Jour. of Nerv. and Ment. Dis., 1903. Vol. 6, pp. 1-13.

356. **Salsbury, Ambrosine** Troublesome children. Child Life, Jan., 1903. Vol. 5, pp. 33-35.
    Deals with methods of treating defective moral and physical development.

357. **Salter, Wm. M.** Society and its children with special reference to the problem of child labor. Kindergarten Mag., May, 1903. Vol. 15, pp. 537-550.
    Discusses educational needs of young children with special need for law to govern child's attendance at school instead of working, especially in the state of Illinois.

358. **Scammell, Amy C.** Boys. Jour. of Ed., Feb. 19, 1903. Vol. 57, pp. 117.
    Some ways of managing boys.

359. **Schaefer, F.** Einzelentwicklung und Gesamtentwicklung. Die Deutsche Schule, 1903. Vol. 7, pp. 156-165; 226-237.
    Treats of individual and mass-development from point of view of philosophy, biology, pedagogy.

360. **Schäfer, K. L.** Wie lernt das Kind Denken und Sprechen? Deutsche Revue, 21 Jahrg., 1896. Vol. 1, pp. 118-120.

361. **Schlöss, H.** Pflege und Behandlung von zu Geistesstörungen disponierten Kindern. Wien. med. Wochensch., 1903. Vol. 53, pp. 2344-2366.

362. **Schneider, O.** Die Schöpferische Kraft des Kindes in der Gestaltung seiner Bewustseinszustände bis zum Beginn des Schulunterrichts. (Ein Beitrag zur Kinderpsychologie, auf Grund der Beobachtung zweier Kinder.) Zeit. f. Philos. u. Philosophische Kritik, 1903. Vol. 121, pp. 153-175; Vol. 122, pp. 1-14.

363. **Schoenichen, Walther** Die Abstammungslehre in Unterrichte der Schule. Teubner, Leipzig, 1903, pp. 46.

364. **Scholz, L.** Abnorme Kindesnaturen. Kinderfehler, April, 1903. Vol. 8, pp. 61-76; pp. 110-124.

A discussion of physically, mentally, and morally abnormal children and what can be done for them.

365. **Schroeder, F.** Kindersprache und Sprachgeschichte. Die Grenzboten, 60 Jahrg., 1901. 2d Viertelj., pp. 412-421; 455-464.

366. **Schulze, Edward** Der erste Lese- und Schreib-Unterricht in der Hilfsschule. Kinderfehler, Oct., 1903. Vol. 9, pp. 1-22.

Statement of experiment in teaching elementary reading and writing in school for backward children.

367. **Schumacher, T.** Was ich als Kind erlebt. Stuttgart, 1901.

368. **Schunk, P.** Der Wortschatz eines dreivierteljährigen Kindes. Zeits. d. allg. deuts. Sprachvereins, 1900. Vol. 15, pp. 167.

369. **Schuster, G.** Aus den Kinderjahren unseres Heldenkaisers, 1898.

370. **Schwabach,** —— (Knapp, A. trans.) On the pathological anatomy of deaf mutism. Arch. of Otol., 1903. Vol. 32, pp. 378-385.

371. **Seggel, K.** Ueber das Verhältnis von Schädel-und Gehirnentwicklung zum Langenwachstum des Körpers. Arch. f. Anthrop. (der ganzen Reihe, Vol. 29), 1903, N. F. Vol. 1, pp. 1-25.

372. **Serbsky, W.** La démence précoce. Ann. Méd.-Psychol., 1903. Vol. 18, pp. 379-388.

373. **Seydel,** —— Rééducation visuelle d'enfants devenus aveugles. Ann. d'Ocul., 1903. Vol. 128, pp. 232.

374. **Shattuck, G. B.** The grading of defective public school children. Boston Med. and Surg. Jour., 1903. Vol. 148, pp. 349-350.

375. **Shaw, Edward R.** Introduction to outline. Jour. of Ped., March, 1903. Vol. 15, pp. 221-231.

Gives in analytical form, results of attempt to arrange requirements of an enriched course of study for elementary schools.

Shipe See **Ellis and Shipe**

376. **Shuttleworth, G. E.** Some slighter forms of mental defect in children and their treatment. Brit. Med. Jour., 1903. Vol. 2, pp. 828-830, also Lancet, 1903. Vol. 2, pp. 538-539.

377. **Sikorsky, J. A.** Die Seele des Kindes. J. A. Barth, Leipzig, 1902, pp. 80.

378. **Skeat, Walter** Fables and folk-tales from an Eastern forest. Univ. Press, Cambridge, 1901, pp. 92.

379. **Skinner, Charles R.** Surroundings of rural schools. Proc. N. E. A., 1903, pp. 89-96.

380. **Smith, Hoke**   Child labor and illiteracy.   Nat. Conf. Char. and Corr., 1903, pp. 188-191.

381. **Smith, M. K.**   The psychological and pedagogical aspect of language.   Ped. Sem., Dec., 1903.   Vol. 10, pp. 438-458.
Tells why high school and college students have so poor a command of their mother tongue.

382. **Smith, Theodate L.**   The questionnaire method in genetic psychology.   Ped. Sem., Sept., 1903.   Vol. 10, pp. 405-409.
Discusses the educational influence on those questioned also as a method of scientific study.

——— ——— See **Hall and Smith**

383. **Somasco, Ch.**   L'Instruction et l'éducation du jeune ouvrier. Rev. Péd., June, 1903.   Vol. 42, pp. 533-541, July, 1903.   Vol. 43, pp. 28-45.

384. **Sorley, W. R.**   Betting and gambling.   Int. Jour. of Ethics, 1903.   Vol. 13, pp. 421-430.

385. **Spalikowski, Ed.**   La tristesse chez l'enfant.   Rev. Scient., 1902. 4 e. ser.   Vol. 17, pp. 525-526.

386. **Spaulding, F. E.**   The teacher's practical application of the results of child study.   Proc. N. E. A., 1903, pp. 761-769, also Jour. of Ped., Sept., 1903.   Vol. 16, pp. 34-42.

387. **Speranza, Gino Carlo**   Criminality in children.   Green Bag, Nov., 1903.   Vol. 15, p. 516-520.

388. **Spitzka, E. A.**   The brain weight of Japanese.   Science, Sept. 18, 1903.   Vol. 18, pp. 371-394.
Brain weight of Japanese compared with those of Europeans, age 2 months to 14 years.

389. **Spratling, W. P.**   Results of brain surgery in epilepsy and congenital mental defect.   Am. Jour. of Insanity, 1903.   Vol. 60, pp. 27-52.

390. **Stableton, J. K.**   How to increase the attendance of boys at the high school.   Proc. N. E. A., 1903, pp. 801-807.

391. **Stadelmann, Heinrich**   Schulen für nervenkranke Kinder. Samml. von Abhand. a. d. Gebiete Päd. Psy. u. Physiol., Berlin, 1903.   Vol. 6, Heft 5, pp. 31.
The condition of nervous children in their abnormal, psychical expression. The importance of their individual and methodical treatment by physician and teacher.

392. **Standish, Miles, M. D.**   Facts and fallacies in the examination of school children's eyes.   Proc. N. E. A., 1903, pp. 1020-1023.

393. **Steel, F. A.**   Cult of the child.   Electic Mag., Aug., 1903. Vol. 141, pp. 261-63; also Living Age, June 20, 1903.   Vol. 237, pp. 761-63.

394. **Steiger, ——** Vision dans les écoles primaires de Zurich. Ann. d'Ocul., 1903. Vol. 127, pp. 75.

395. **Stetson, William Wallace** Some things the common school should do for the child. Jour. of Ed., Aug. 27, 1903. Vol. 58, pp. 144, 145, 150.

396. —— —— School surroundings. Proc. N. E. A., 1903, pp. 96-97.

397. **Stevens, Edward L.** Backward and defective children. School Jour., Dec. 26, 1903, pp. 687-688.
Suggestions for care and education of backward and defective children in graded schools.

398. **Stevenson, M. C.** Zuñi Games. Am. Anthropol., 1903. N. S. Vol. 5, pp. 468-497.

399. **Stilling, J.** Die Kurzsichtigkeit: ihre Entstehung und Bedeutung. Samml. von Abhand. a. d. Gebiete Päd. Psy. u. Physiol., Berlin, 1903. Vol. 6, pp. 75.
Statistics of the per cent. of shortsightedness in different schools and in the gymnasium. Statistics of the effect of illumination. Time when most cases originate. Physical conditions of the eye.

400. **Stookes, Alexander** Some educational problems. Paidologist, Feb., 1903. Vol. 5, pp. 32-36.
Education should be a preparation of the young for a successful life.

401. **Stoops, J. D.** Three stages of individual development. Int. Jour. of Ethics, 1903. Vol. 14, pp. 81-90.

402. **Strauss, Paul** Assistance et éducation des enfants anormaux. Rev. Int. de Péd. Comp., July 31, 1903, pp. 289-91; Nov. 30, 1903, pp. 29-32.

Sulzer See **Broca and Sulzer**

403. **Swift, Edgar J.** Standards of efficiency in school and in life. Ped. Sem., March, 1903. Vol. 10, pp. 3-22.
Illustrates phases of development in many distinguished men in their early years.

404. —— —— Studies in the psychology and physiology of learning. Am. Jour. of Psy., April, 1903. Vol. 14, pp. 201-251.
Reports experiments on tossing and catching balls, learning short hand, acquisition and control of the reflex wink. Bibliog. of 26 titles.

405. **Syrett, Netta** On the right choice of books for children. Academy, Dec. 5, 1903. Vol. 65, p. 641.

406. **Tannery, Jules** L'enseignement de la géométrie élémentaire. Rev. Péd., July, 1903. Vol. 43, pp. 1-27.

407. **Tappan, Eva March** Fads or not fads. Jour. of Ped., Dec., 1903. Vol. 16, pp. 152-166.
Deals with enrichment of school course, induction and interest.

408. **Tarde, G.** The laws of imitation; tr. by E. C. Parsons. Holt, New York, 1903, pp. 405.

409. **Tarrant, M. Eleanor** Louisville summer playgrounds. Chaut., Aug., 1903. Vol. 37, pp. 473-476.

410. **Taylor, Ellen E.** Kindergartens for the deaf. Assn. Rev., Feb., 1903. Vol. 5, pp. 1-11.
    The aims, the kindergarten as an assimilator, speech in the kindergarten, some things that have been done, the personnel of the class, joys of the work, play as an educational factor.

411. **Taylor, Joseph S.** Art of class management. E. L. Kellogg, New York, 1903, pp. 116.

413. **Thieme, P.** Ueber Sinnestypen und ihre Berücksichtigung im Unterrichte nach L'imagination et ses variétés chez l'enfant par Queyrat. Praxis der Erziehungsschule, 1895. Vol. 9, pp. 184-189; 220-225.

414. **Thieme, Robert** Der Humor in der Schule. A. Pichler, Wien, n. d., pp. 196.
    Interesting collection of specimens of children's humor.

415. **Thompson, H. B.** Mental traits of sex. Univ. Press, Chicago, 1903, pp. 188.
    Important. Too few cases considered.

416. —— —— Psychological norms in men and women. (Univ. of Chicago contrib. to Philos., IV, No. 1.) Univ. Press, Chicago, 1903, pp. 188.

417. **Thomson, J.** On lip reflex of new born children. Rev. of Neurol. and Psychiat., 1903. Vol. 1, pp. 145-149.

418. **Thomson, J. Arthur** Adolescence. Paidologist, Nov., 1903. Vol. 5, pp. 128-135.
    The author makes comparisons between young animals and young people.

419. **Thorndike, Edward Lee** Educational psychology. Lemcke and Buechner, New York, 1903, pp. 177.
    The work is written from the genetic viewpoint and contains several helpful chapters on children.

420. —— —— Notes on child study. Columbia Univ. Contrib. to Philos., 1903. Vol. 8, Nos. 3-4, pp. 181.

421. —— —— Heredity, correlation and sex differences in school abilities. Columbia Univ. Contrib. to Philos., 1903. Vol. 11, No. 2, pp. 60.

422. **Thorne, ——** Éducation des sourds à Londres. La Parole, 1903. Vol. 12, pp. 647.

423. **Thornton, William** On teaching the surd, or deaf, and consequently dumb to speak. Assn. Rev., Dec., 1903. Vol. 5, pp. 406-414.
    Discussion on the method of teaching the deaf to speak.

424. **Thorpe, E. J. Ellery** What teachers need to know about speech impediments. Proc. N. E. A., 1903, pp. 1031-1036.

425. **Timmermans, A.** L'onomatopée et fla ormation du langage. Rev. Scient., 4es., 1903. Vol. 19, pp. 395-400.

426. **Tompkins, Juliet Wilbor** A boy's love. Atlantic, July, 1903. Vol. 92, pp. 68-73.

427. **Trask, Bertha M.** What one baby learned in a summer. Kindergarten Mag., Feb., 1903. Vol. 15, pp. 377-380.
Study of a two year old baby boy of German parentage left to his own resources during the day, thus showing line of interest.

428. **Triplett, N.** A study of the faults of children. Ped. Sem., March, 1903. Vol. 10, pp. 200-238.
As seen by the children and as seen by teachers and parents.

429. **Tupper, F.** The comparative study of riddles. Mod. Lang. Notes, 1903. Vol. 18, pp. 1-8.

430. **Verney, Edmund** Children's country holiday in France. Eclectic Mag., April, 1903. Vol. 140, pp. 513-518; also Living Age, Feb. 21, 1903. Vol. 236, pp. 493-498.

431. **Vial, Francisque** La liberté d'enseignement. Rev. Péd., May, 1903. Vol. 42, pp. 429-447.
Liberty of instruction in schools.

432. **Villard, O. G.** A year of the children's court. Nation, Oct., 1903. Vol. 77, pp. 262-263.

433. **Vincent, George E.** The group morality of children. Kindergarten Mag., May, 1903. Vol. 15, pp. 559-565.
Deals with one source of the suggestions which pour in upon the growing child, *e. g.*, the influence of child's group life in the nursery, playground, gang or class.

434. **Vinson, J.** L'enseignement des langues. La grammaire. Rev. de l'École d'Anthropol., 1903. Vol. 13, pp. 213-229.

435. **Walker, Anna E.** Children's lies. Jour. of Ed., June 11, 1903. Vol. 57, pp. 372-373.

436. **Ward, Mrs. Humphrey** London schools for invalid and crippled children. Kindergarten Mag., Jan., 1903. Vol. 15, pp. 288-297.
Describes schools in London for physical defectives.

437. **Ward, L. F.** Pure sociology; a treatise on the origin and spontaneous development of society. Macmillan, New York, 1903, pp. 606.

438. **Warren, H. C., etc.** Psychological index for 1902. Macmillan, New York, 1903, pp. 178.

439. **Warren, Orson** Seen and heard in our large cities. Jour. of Ed., April 23, 1903. Vol. 57, pp. 262-263.
Teaching spelling so as to help both the ear- and eye-minded pupils.

440. **Washburn, M. F.** The genetic function of movement and organic sensations for social consciousness. Am. Jour. of Psy., 1903. Vol. 14, pp. 337-342 (73-78).

441. **Wateff, S.** Anthropologische Beobachtungen der Farbe der Augen, der Haare und der Haut bei den Schulkindern von den Türken, Pomaken, Tataren, Armeniern, Griechen und Juden in

Bulgarien. Co. Bl. d. deutschen Gesellsch. f. Anthrop. [etc.], München, 1903. Vol. 34, pp. 58-60.
Based on examination of some 54,000 children between the ages of 6 and 15.

442. **Watson, G. A.** The pathology and morbid histology of juvenile general paralysis. Arch. Neur., 1903. Vol. 2, pp. 621-726.

443. **Weininger, O.** Geschlecht und Charakter. Brawmüller, Leipzig, 1903, pp. 597.

444. **Wen, G. O.** Free paper cutting. Child Life, Oct., 1903. Vol. 5, pp. 198-201.
Deals with its use and value in the kindergarten.

445. **Wendt, F. M.** Psychologische Kindergartenpädagogik. K. Graesar & Co., Wien, 1903, pp. 142.

446. **Wernicke, O.** Angeborene Wortblindheit. Centralbl. f. Prak. Augenhk., 1903. Vol. 27, pp. 264-267.

447. **Wersely, K.** Auge und Immunität. Berl. Klin., 1903 (H. 182), pp. 23.

448. **Weule, K.** Aus dem afrikanischen Kinderleben. Westermanns Illustrierte deutsche Monatshefte., 43 Jahrg., 1899. Vol. 85, pp. 647-666.

449. **Weygandt** —— Beiträge zur Lehre von Kretinismus. Allg. Zeits. f. Psychiat., 1903. Vol. 6, pp. 933-939.

450. **Wiebe, Edward** Paradise of childhood. M. Bradley, Springfield, 1901, pp. 274.

451. **Weidersheim, R.** Der Bau des Menschen als Zeugnis für seine Vergangenheit. 3d ed. Laupp'sche Buchhandlung, 1902, pp. 243.

452. **Wilks, S.** Ambidexterity. Nature, 1903. Vol. 67, pp. 462.

453. **Williams, Alida S.** Visual inaccuracies in school children. Ed. Rev., Sept., 1903. Vol. 26, pp. 180-189.
Showing complications in the act of reading, and the difficulties which must be conquered by child before he can read, and the results of inaccuracies.

454. **Williams, Llewellyn W.** Education, disciplinary, civic and moral. Simpkin, London, 1903, pp. 192.

455. **Williams, Mornay** The street boy—who he is, and what to do with him. Nat. Conf. Char. and Corr., 1903, pp. 238-244.

456. **Williamson, Mrs. E. E.** The children's age. Nat. Conf. Char. and Corr., 1903, pp. 192-196.
Discussion of forces that are bringing about the development of children

457. —— —— Synopsis of report on legislation on child labor. Ann. Am. Acad. Pol. Sci., May, 1903. Vol. 21, pp. 446-451.

458. **Wilmer, Rev. C. B.** Humanity and economics, with special reference to child labor. Nat. Conf. Char. and Corr., 1903, pp. 166-180.

459. **Wilson, Louis N.** Bibliography of the published writings of President G. Stanley Hall. Am. Jour. of Psy., July, Oct., 1903, pp. 681-694; also Publications of the Clark Univ. Library, Vol. 2, pp. 3-16.
Lists all Dr. Hall's papers on child study down to Oct., 1903.

460. —— —— Bibliography of child study for the year 1902. Ped. Sem., Dec., 1903. Vol. 10, pp. 514-536; also Publications of Clark Univ. Library, Jan., 1904. Vol. 1, pp. 17-40.
A list of 344 books and articles on child study published during the year 1902.

461. **Winston, Annie Steger** Memoirs of a child. Longmans, New York, 1903, pp. 169.
Has a very rare quality of suggestiveness. Of value to teachers.

462. **Wissler, Clark** Growth of boys. Am. Anthropol., 1903, N. S. Vol. 5, pp. 81-88.

463. **Wölfflin, E.** Reduplikation in der Kindesprache. Zeits. f. deuts. Wortforschung., 1901. Vol. 1, pp. 263 f.

464. **Wood, Edith Elmer** Notes on oriental babies. Am. Anthropol., Oct.-Dec., 1903. Vol. 5, pp. 659-666.
A study ou the size and growth of children under six years of age.

465. **Wood, Thomas D.** School hygiene and its bearing on school life. Proc. N. E. A., 1903. pp. 778-784; also Jour. of Ed., July 9, 1903. Vol. 58, p. 71.

466. **Woods, Alice (Ed.)** Co-education. A series of essays by various authors. With an introduction by M. E. Sadler. Longmans, Green & Co., London, 1903, pp. 148.
Sympathetic papers from an English point of view.

467. **Woods, F. A.** Mental and moral heredity in royalty. VI-IX. Pop. Sci. Mo., 1903. Vol. 62, pp. 261-268; 316-322; 423-428; 497-503.

468. **Worth, C.** Squint. Blakiston's Son, Philadelphia, 1903, pp. 229.

469. —— —— Squint; its causes, pathology and treatment. Hale, Sons and Danielson, London, 1903, pp. 129.

470. **Wyer, J. J. Jr., and Lord, I. E.** Bibliography of education, 1902. Ed. Rev., 1903. Vol. 26, pp. 49-91.

471. **Wyllie, John** Disorders of speech. Oliver, Edinburg, 1894, pp. 495.

472. **Yoder, A. H.** Sex differentiation in relation to secondary education. Proc. N. E. A., 1903. Vol. 42, pp. 785-792.

473. **Young, Ella Flagg** Isolation in the school. Univ. Press, Chicago, 1901, pp. 111.

474. —— —— Ethics in the school. Univ. Press, Chicago, 1902, pp. 44.

475. **Zollinger, Friedrich**   Bestrebungen auf dem Gebiete der Schulgesundheitspflege und des Kinderschutzes. O. Füssli, Zurich, 1901, pp. 305.

---

476. Addresses and proceedings of the 42d annual meeting of the National Education Association held at Boston, Mass., July 6-10, 1903. Pub. by the Association, 1903, pp. 1080.

477. Boys, how they express themselves. Spectator, March 28, 1903. Vol. 90, pp. 486-487.

478. Boys' and girls' agricultural experiment club. School Journal, Oct. 10, 1903, pp. 358-360.
    An account of work done by pupils in experimenting with varieties of corn in varieties of soil. Gives value of this sort of work.

479. Child study in Chicago. Report of Commissioner of Education for 1902. Washington, 1903. Vol. 1, pp. 1095-1168.
    Brief summary of the investigations in child study carried on in the public schools of Chicago.

480. Garden work with school boys. School Journal, Feb. 21, 1903, pp. 209-210.
    Gives interesting account of results of School of Horticulture, Hartford, Connecticut.

481. The Individual Child and his Education. A quarterly journal, edited by Supt. F. E. Spaulding. Contributions by the teachers of Passaic, N. J. F. A. Owen Pub. Co., Dansville, N. Y. First issue Sept., 1903.

482. Illinois society for child study. Transactions. Chicago, 1899. Vol. 4, Nos. 1 and 2.

483. Recherches cliniques et thérapeutiques sur l'épilepsie, l'hystérie et l'idiotie, par M. Bourneville. F. Alcan, Paris, 1902. Vol. 22, pp. 236.
    Contains an interesting memoir on schools for abnormal children in all parts of the world.

484. Religious Educational Association. Proceedings of the first convention, Chicago, 1903. The Association, Chicago, 1903, pp. 422.

485. The school luncheon. School Journal, Dec. 5, 1903, p. 605.
    States importance of amount and character of food to be given to children.

486. Testing of the vision of school children. Lancet, 1903. Vol. 1, pp. 977-978.

SUBJECT INDEX.

Ability, 421.
Abnormal, 104, 129, 225, 364, 402.
Abnormalities, 231.
Acquired Characters, 47.
Acromegaly, 302.
Activity, 33.
Adolescence, 175, 228, 230, 272, 418.
Adolescents, 232.
Africa, 448.
Alfieri, 106, 107.
Ambidexterity, 290, 452.
Anatomical, 370.
Anger, 278.
Animal Psychology, 73, 74, 279.
Anthropology, 285, 320.
Anthropometry, 187, 287, 316, 320, 350, 371, 441, 462, 464.
Arithmetic, 279.
Arrest, 175.
Art, 345.
Artisan, 383.
Atavism, 451.
Athletics, 337.
Attendance, 390.
Attention, 43, 92.
Autobiography, 122, 184, 194, 214, 223, 327, 367.
Automatic Acts, 264.

Backward Children, 41, 161, 218, 260, 322, 397.
Bad Habits, 258.
Bashfulness, 178.
Bath, 4.
Betting, 384.
Bibliography, 31, 50, 78, 173, 196, 228, 420, 438, 459, 460, 470.
Biographical, 123, 158, 369, 461.
Biological, 363.
Blindness, 210, 214, 223, 373.
Boyhood, 122.
Boy Problem, 139.
Boys, 354, 358, 426.
Boys' Club, 275.
Brain, 157, 202, 238, 371.
Brain Surgery, 389.
Brain Weight, 287, 328, 388.
Bridgman, Laura, 201.

Capacity, 13.
Caprices, 269.
Cephalic Index, 51.
Cephalometry, 155.
Character, 203, 207, 283, 284, 443.

Childhood, 123, 289.
Child Labor, 1, 2, 37, 38, 120, 131, 198, 205, 224, 252, 314, 321, 349, 357, 380, 457, 458.
Child Mind, 65.
Child Saving, 185.
Child Study, 22, 89, 117, 150, 173, 230, 231, 245, 386, 393, 420.
Children's Court, 432.
Chromesthesia, 115.
City, 105.
Civilization, 159.
Class Management, 411.
Cloud Fancies, 174.
Clubs, 72, 275.
Coeducation, 466.
Cold, 176.
College, 109, 179.
Color Hearing, 240.
Color Sense, 282.
Comenius, 193.
Conduct, 332.
Consciousness, 326.
Conversion, 182.
Co-operation, 348.
Correction, 108.
Correspondence, 280.
Courage, 49.
Creative Power, 362,
Cretinism, 215, 449.
Crime, 10, 104, 136, 163, 184, 226, 263, 305, 387.
Crippled, 436.
Crow, 73.
Crowd, 246.
Culture Epochs, 52.
Curiosity, 180.
Curriculum, 14, 19, 110, 251, 274, 375, 395.

Darkness, 177.
Deaf, 11, 273, 294, 310, 410, 422.
Deaf Mute, 201, 223, 370, 423.
Deafness, 210.
Defectives, 17, 18, 57, 134, 171, 215, 313, 356, 366, 374, 397, 436.
Degeneration, 105, 165.
Delinquents, 226.
Dementia praecox, 36, 112, 113, 209, 255, 372.
Development, 152, 230, 401.
Discipline, 217, 411, 454.
Disease, 96.
Doctrine of Descent, 363.

3

Dog, 74.
Drawing, 333.
Dull, 322.
Dwarfs, 344.

Economics, 131.
Educational Problems, 400.
Educational Science, 285.
Efficiency, 403.
Emotion, 18, 230, 233, 270, 278.
Epilepsy, 8, 59, 389.
Errors, 108.
Ethics, 130, 233, 474.
Ethnological, 293, 448.
Evolution, 157.
Examination, 108.
Excursions, 430.
Experimental, 45, 95, 126, 225.
Eye, 186, 299, 352, 392, 394, 399, 412, 447, 453.
Eye Defects, 161.
Eye Strain, 159.

Fables, 378.
Fads, 407.
Farm, 242.
Fatigue, 34, 54, 126.
Faults, 428.
Fecundity, 179.
Feeble Minded, 92, 146, 161, 217, 267, 303.
Feeling, 326.
Fire, 176.
Football, 337.
France, 312, 430.
France, Anatole, 289.
Freedom, 11ʄ, 431.
Froebel, 347.
Frost, 176.

Gambling, 384.
Games, 81, 97, 103, 318, 323, 353, 398.
Genetic, 221, 419, 440.
Genius, 106, 107, 268.
Geometry, 406.
Giantism, 133.
Gibson, 90.
Girls, 142, 192.
Grading, 374.
Grammar, 434.
Group, 433.
Growth, 189, 231, 350, 371, 462.

Habit, 5.
Hall, G. S., 31, 459.
Handicraft, 71.
Hawaii, 124.
Head Form, 155, 287.

Health, 28, 189, 319.
Hearing, 57, 240, 273, 294, 310, 316, 317.
Hearing Tests, 48.
Heat, 176.
Heredity, 47, 51, 231, 235, 255, 262, 338, 339, 421, 467.
High School, 125, 390.
Higher Education, 84.
Historical, 40, 50, 69, 78, 124, 160, 173.
History, 102, 239.
History of Education, 26.
Home, 71, 151, 336.
Homotyposis, 340.
Humor, 414.
Hygiene, 25, 28, 158, 165, 166, 311, 324.
Hysteria, 59.
Hystero-epilepsy, 191.

Ideals, 20, 83, 232, 233.
Idiocy, 59, 190, 355.
Idiots, 317.
Illiteracy, 380.
Imagination, 119, 413.
Imbecility, 304.
Imitation, 230, 231, 408.
Immunity, 447.
Imperative Ideas, 138.
Indians, 97, 122, 398.

Individual, 291, 359, 401.
Industrial, 90.
Industrial Arts, 301.
Infantilism, 154, 309.
Infants, 76, 152.
Inhibition, 230.
Instincts, 16, 231.
Intelligence, 45, 55, 343.
Interest, 19, 23, 91, 180, 199, 230, 306, 427.
Interpretators, 46.
Isolation, 473.

Japanese, 388.
Judgment, 233.
Justice, 137.
Juvenile Court, 263.

Keller, Helen, 214.
Kindergarten, 77, 151, 249, 301, 410, 445.

Language, 91, 143, 169, 297, 360, 365, 368, 381, 425, 434, 463.
Learning, 404, 427.
Left-brainedness, 98.
Legal Folk-lore, 81, 103.

Letters, 67.
Library, 300.
Life, 296.
Light, 177.
Lip Reading, 11, 53.
Lip Reflex, 417.
Logic, 9.
Loves, 354, 426.
Lying, 24, 168, 435.

Manual Arts, 183.
Manual Training, 15, 27, 183, 227.
Marriage, 179.
Mathematics, 271.
Measurements, 187.
Medical, 198.
Medical Inspection, 64.
Melancholy, 385.
Memory, 267.
Mental, 247, 467.
Mental Ability, 155.
Mental Defects, 361, 376.
Mental Evolution, 88.
Mental Pathology, 305.
Mental Traits, 415.
Mentally Defective, 21, 85, 211, 235, 251, 265, 335.
Michelet, 160.
Mongolism, 313.
Moon Fancies, 172.
Morality, 433, 467.
Morals, 114, 118, 132, 141, 156, 192, 330, 454.
Moseley, 149.
Mothers, 100, 116.
Motor Activities, 231.
Motor Education, 245.
Motor Power, 55.
Movement, 440.
Murder, 10
Muscles, 140.
Museums, 200.
Music, 99, 306.
Musical Sense, 236.
Myxœdema, 215.

National Education, 160, 277.
Natural Selection, 341.
Nature Study, 12, 197.
Nervousness, 135, 241, 325, 391.
Neurology, 3, 202.
Neuroses, 329.
Newborn, 417.
Normal, 225.
Norms, 416.
Nose, 96.

Observation, 288.
Onomatopoeia, 425.

Optimism, 296.
Oriental, 464.

Paper Cutting, 444.
Paper Folding, 315.
Papuan, 140.
Paralysis, 442.
Pathology, 195, 370.
Pedigrees, 147.
Perception, 306.
Personality, 331.
Pets, 73, 74.
Physical, 187, 247, 436.
Physical Education, 144, 238, 250, 274.
Physical Examinations, 188.
Physical Exercise, 188.
Physical Training, 219.
Physically Defective, 265.
Piety, 86.
Play, 206, 231, 323.
Playgrounds, 248, 409.
Portugal, 323.
Practice, 346.
Prayer Manuals, 93.
Prayers, 93.
Primary Education, 69, 116.
Primary School, 90, 312.
Primitive People, 316, 353.
Psychic Capacity, 266, 287.
Psychological, 127, 143, 170, 175, 218, 221, 259, 295, 346, 377, 416, 419.
Psycho-physical, 107.
Puberty, 281.
Puericulture, 116, 213.
Punishment, 94, 137.
Pupils, 348.

Questionnaire Method, 382.

Race, 165.
Reading, 67, 244, 295, 366, 405.
Reasoning, 229.
Recapitulation, 52.
Recess, 39.
Reduplication, 463.
Re-education, 373.
Reflex, 253, 417.
Reform, 226.
Religion, 101, 142, 162, 182, 222, 237, 332.
Riddles, 429.
Right-handedness, 98.
Rights, 164.
Routine, 56.
Royalty, 467.
Rural Schools, 379.

Sadness, 385.
School Days, 334.
School Gardens, 60, 66, 87.
School Hygiene, 30, 212, 254, 465, 475.
School Influeuce, 403.
School Surroundings, 396.
School World, 40.
School Yards, 66.
Scotland, 144.
Self-consciousness, 178.
Self-government, 72.
Sense of Joy, 270.
Senses, 80, 82, 316, 413.
Sex, 101, 127, 128, 139, 142, 156, 179, 192, 195, 213, 271, 303, 308, 358, 415, 416, 421, 443, 466, 472.
Sex Perversion, 195.
Short-sightedness, 399.
Showing Off, 178.
Sickness, 29, 158.
Sight, 57, 186, 299, 352, 392, 394, 399, 412, 447, 453.
Skin Sensations, 316.
Skull, 371.
Skull Capacity, 287.
Slang, 91.
Smell, 316.
Social, 79, 142, 198, 249, 276, 320, 357.
Social Consciousness, 440.
Social Progress, 338.
Sociology, 26, 121, 136, 351, 437.
Songs, 318.
Spanking, 137.
Speech Defects, 32, 35, 169, 170, 181, 261, 424, 471.
Spelling, 95, 439.
Squint, 468, 469.
Stammering, 204, 243, 256, 257, 262.
Statistics, 190, 225, 232.
Stature, 3, 371.
Stereognostic Sense, 80.
Story, 62, 91.
Street Boy, 455.
Studies, 14, 19.
Study, 23.

Stuttering, 166, 167, 204, 256, 257, 262, 286.
Success, 109.
Suckling, 76.
Sunday School, 162.
Survivals, 228.
Sweden, 250.
Switzerland, 129.

Taste, 82, 316.
Teachers, 111, 208, 234, 348, 386.
Teaching, 102, 114, 132, 148, 201, 219, 239, 406, 431, 434.
Temperament, 106.
Tenements, 351.
Tests, 126.
Texts, 48.
Theory, 346.
Thought, 360.
Throat, 96.
Toe Reflex, 253.
Torres Straits, 316.
Troublesome Children, 356.
Tuberculosis, 234, 342.

Unusual Child, 216.
Unusual Pupil, 63.
Urban Life, 105

Vacation Schools, 292.
Variation, 128, 266, 341.
Vocabulary, 368.
Voice, 99.

Wager, 298.
Waste, 343
Weak Minded, 145.
Will, 75.
Withdrawal from School, 68, 125.
Woman, 153.
Word Blindness, 446.
Words, 91.
Works, 6, 34, 307, 331.
Writing, 35, 44, 280, 366.

Youth, 58, 130, 194.

Zuñi, 398.

PUBLICATIONS

OF THE

CLARK UNIVERSITY LIBRARY

WORCESTER, MASS.

| VOL. I. | July, 1905 | No. 7 |

Bibliography of Child Study for the Year 1904

Clark University Press
WORCESTER, MASS.

BIBLIOGRAPHY OF CHILD STUDY.

For the Year 1904.

By LOUIS N. WILSON, Librarian Clark University.

1. **Adams, Myron E.** Municipal regulations of street trades. Nat. Conf. of Char. and Corr., 1904, pp. 294-300.
   Plea for municipal supervision of newsboys, boot-blacks, and juvenile peddlers.

2. **Adersen, H.** Eine ästhesiometrische Untersuchung. Zeits. für Schulgesundheitspflege. No. 8, 1904. Vol. 17, pp. 540-543.
   Study of fatigue made with the Sieveking æsthesiometer.

3. **Ajam, Maurice** La parole en public. Soc. Parisienne, Paris, 1904, pp. 204.

4. **Altschul, Theodor** Morbiditätsstatistik in Schulen. Arch. f. Rassen und Gesellschaftsbiologie, 1904. pt. 5.

5. —— —— Wert der Experimente bei Schüleruntersuchungen. Päd. psy. Stud., 1904. Vol. 5, pp. 25-28; 37-40.

6. **Ament, Wilhelm** Fortschritte der Kinderseelenkunde, 1895-1903. W. Engelmann, Leipzig, 1904, pp. 68. Also Samml. von Abh. zur psy. Päd., 1904. Vol. 1, pp. 113-180.
   A very compact article giving a fairly comprehensive overview and classification of the most important contributions to child study from 1895 to 1903. Reviewed in Ped. Sem., June, 1904, Vol. 11, pp. 233-234.

7. —— —— Das psychologische Experiment an Kindern. Ber. ü. d. I. Kong. f. exper. Psy. Giessen, April, 1904. pp. 98-100. J. A. Barth, Leipzig, 1904.

8. **Aranzadi,** —— Antropometria de las colonias escolares de Bilbao, Gac. méd. del Norte, Vol. 10, pp. 40-46.

9. **Axmant, Dr.** Zur Auswahl der Ferienkolonisten. Zeits. für Schulgesundheitspflege. No. 7, 1904. Vol. 17, pp. 482-484.

10. **Badley, J. H.** Co-education in the secondary school. Child Life, July, 1904. Vol. 6, pp. 130-136.

11. **Bailward, Margaret E.** Mothers and their responsibilities. Longmans, London, 1904, pp. 145.

12. **Bair, Joseph H.** Factors in the learning process. Investigations in Psy. and Ed. Univ. of Colo., March, 1904. Vol. 2, pp. 43-51.

13. **Baldrian, Karl** Ein Fall, der lehrt, wie notwendig genaue ärztliche Untersuchung der Kinder in Schulen und Anstalten ist. Zeits. für Schulgesundheitspflege, 1904. Vol. 17, pp. 91-94.

14. **Baldrian, Karl**   Zur Gesundheitspflege der Taubstummen-kinder. Monatschr. für d. ges. Sprachhlk., 1904. Vol. 14, pp. 151-157.

15. **Bandler, H.** *ed.*   Mutter und Kind; illustrierte Halbmonats-schrift für Kinderpflege, Erziehung und Frauenhygiene. M. Perles, Wien, 1904.

16. **Barbe, Waitman**   Going to college; with the opinions of fifty leading college presidents and educators. Earhart and Rich-ardson, Cincinnati, 1899, pp. 104.

17. **Barnes, Earl**   America as a field for child study. Paidologist, June, 1904. Vol. 6, pp. 74-84.

18. —— —— The place of drawing in elementary education. Child Life, Oct., 1904. Vol. 6, pp. 177-180.

19. —— —— Student honor; a study in cheating. Int. Jour. of Ethics, July, 1904. Vol. 14, pp. 481-488.
   This study shows that even among university students the sense of the larger social self is only partially developed.

20. **Barr, Martin W.**   What can teachers of normal children learn from the teachers of defectives? Jour. of Psycho-Asthenics, Dec., 1903 to March, 1904. Vol. 8, pp. 55-59.

21. **Bartels, M.**   Pupillenverhältnisse bei Neugeborenen, Zeits. f. Augenhlk., 1904. Vol. 12, pp. 638-644.

22. **Bassenco, A.**   Ein Fall von hysterischen Aphasie im Kindes-alter. (Diss.) Berlin, 1904, pp. 25.

23. **Bateson, William**   Heredity and Evolution. Pop. Sci. Mo., Oct., 1904. Vol. 65, pp. 522-531.
   Treats of the law of natural and aided selection in plants and animals.

24. **Batten, F. E.**   The pathology of infantile paralysis (acute an-terior poliomyelitis). Brain, 1904. Vol. 27, pp. 376-387.

25. **Bell, Sanford**   An introductory study of the psychology of foods. Ped. Sem., March, 1904. Vol. 11, pp. 51-90.
   Shows new relations between ontogeny and phylogeny.

26. **Bellei, G.**   Ulteriore contributo allo studio della fatica mentale nei fanciulli. Riv. Sperim. di Freniat., 1904. Vol. 30, pp. 17-34.

27. **Benda, Karl**   Zur Frage der Disinfektion entliehener Bücher. Zeits. für Schulgesundheitspflege. Nos. 2 and 3, 1904. Vol. 17, pp. 94-97.
   Use of formalin as a disinfectant for books in order to prevent the spread-ing of contagious diseases.

28. **Benson, William E.**   Prevention of crime among colored children. Nat. Conf. Char. and Corr., 1904, pp. 257-268.
   Manual training as a preventive of delinquency among the negroes.

29. **Berg, W.**   Erziehung zum Sprechen. Teubner, Leipzig, 1904, pp. 55.

30. **Berkhan, O.**   Schule für epileptische Kinder. Zeits. für d. Behandlg. Schwachs. u. Epil., 1904. Vol. 20, pp. 117-122.

31. **Bernhart, Dr.** Medizin und Pädagogik in der Idotenanstalt. Kinderfehler, Feb., 1904. Vol. 9, pp. 111-115.

32. **Berze, J.** Paranoia oder Dementia Praecox? Psychiat. Wochensch., 1904. Vol. 6, pp. 39-43.

33. **Biervliet, J. J. van** L'éducation de la mémoire à l'école. Rev. Philos., 1904. Vol. 57, pp. 569-586.

34. —— —— Esquisse d'une éducation de la mémoire. Siffer, Gand, 1904. pp. 126.

35. **Bierwass, Richard** Arbeit im Knabenhort für Schwachbegabte. Zeits. für päd. Psy., Aug. to Dec., 1904. Vol. 6, pp. 210-221.

36. **Billotey, D.** La littérature enfantine. Revue Péd., Aug., 1904. Vol. 45, pp. 121-132.

37. **Binet, Alfred** La graphologie et ses révélations sur le sexe, l'âge et l'intelligence. L'Année Psy., 1903 (1904). Vol. 10, pp. 179-210.

38. —— —— Sommaire des travaux, en cours à la société de psychologie de l'enfant. L'Année Psy., 1903 (1904). Vol. 10, pp. 116-130. Also Leipziger Lehrerzeitung, Nov. 7 and 16, 1904. Vol. 12, pp. 91-94; 109-111.

39. **Bischoff, E.** Experimentelle Untersuchungen über die Beeinflussung associativer Vorgänge durch die Menstruation. (Diss.) Tübingen, 1904, pp. 15.

40. **Blitstein, Max** Alkohol und Schule. Zeits. für Schulgesundheitspflege. No. 8, 1904. Vol. 17, pp. 535-540.

41. **Blum, Eugène** Note sur le développement des recherches pédologiques en France. L'Année Psy., 1903 (1904). Vol. 10, pp. 311-316.
    Contains bibliography.

42. **Bonser, Frederick G.** Practical child study for teachers. Normal Seminar, March, 1904. Vol. 1, pp. 51-59.

43. **Book, William F.** Why pupils drop out of the high school. Ped. Sem., June, 1904. Vol. 11, pp. 204-232.
    Studied by the questionnaire method and gives the children's point of view.

44. **Boole, Mrs. M. E.** The preparation of the child for science. Clarendon Press, Oxford, 1904, pp. 157.

45. **Booth, Frank W.** Report of committee on statistics of defective sight and hearing of public school children. Proc. N. E. A., 1904, pp. 946-952.

46. —— —— Speech-teaching in American schools for the deaf. Ass'n Rev., April, 1904. Vol. 6, pp. 122-126.

47. **Borst, M.** Recherches expérimentales sur l' éducabilité et la fidélité du témoignage. Arch. de Psy., 1904. Vol. 3, pp. 233-314.

48. **Bosma, H.** Nervöse Kinder; medizinische pädagogische und allgemeine Bemerkungen. J. Ricker, Giessen, 1904, pp. 100.

49. **Bosmans, W.** La démence précoce. Presse Méd. Belge, 1904. Vol. 56, p. 291.

50. **Branson, E. C.** Traits in children indicative of future criminality. Proc. 37th meeting Georgia Ed. Ass., 1903, pp. 74-84. Foote and Davies Printers, Atlanta, Ga.

51. **Brousseau, Kate** L'éducation des nègres aux États-Unis. F. Alcan, Paris, 1904, pp. 396.
   A comprehensive work, but written for a French audience. Excellent bibliography on pp. 333-391.

Brown, C. E. See **Hall, G. S. and Brown, C. E.**

53. **Bryce, James** Relations of the advanced and backward races of mankind. Clarendon Press, Oxford, 1902, pp. 46.

54. **Buckbee, Anna** Fourth school year; a course of study with detailed selection of lesson material arranged by months and correlated. A. Flanagan Co., Chicago, 1904, pp. 241.
   An effort to correlate school studies upon a basis of children's interests and capacities.

55. —— —— Methods of teaching child study in normal schools. Proc. N. E. A., 1904, pp. 787-790.
   A distinct contribution to the literature of methods of instruction in elementary schools.

56. **Burnham, William H.** Contribution to the hygiene of teaching. Ped. Sem., Dec., 1904. Vol. 11, pp. 488-497.
   An important preliminary discussion of the hygienic conditions of normal schools.

57. —— —— The hygiene of the kindergarten child. Proc. N. E. A., 1904, pp. 416-422.

58. **Butler, Amos W.** Work for the children. Nat. Conf. Char. and Corr., 1904. pp. 246-250.
   Discussion of the habits of juvenile delinquents.

59. **Cahen, Brach** Zur Frage der Munduntersuchung der Schulkinder. Zeits. für Schulgesundheitspflege. No. 5, 1904. Vol. 17, pp. 91-92.

60. **Campbell, Charles F.** Spontaneous recreation and industrial training for the blind. Nat. Conf. Char. and Corr., 1904, pp. 419-421.

61. **Campbell, Mary R.** The Chicago hospital school for nervous and delicate children. Its educational and scientific methods. Proc. N. E. A., 1904, pp. 952-962.
   This article includes the methods of training in music, speech, and gymnastics.

62. —— —— Some laboratory investigations of sub-normal children. Proc. N. E. A., 1904, pp. 744-754.

63. **Chamberlain, Alexander F.** Child study and related topics in recent Italian scientific literature. Ped. Sem., Dec., 1904. Vol. 11, pp. 508-515.

64. **Chamberlain, Alexander F.** Child study and related topics in recent Russian scientific literature. Ped. Sem., Dec., 1904. Vol. 11, pp. 516-520.

65. ———— **and Isabel C.** Studies of a child. Ped. Sem., Sept. and Dec., 1904. Vol. 11, pp. 264-292; 452-483.
   Study of the linguistic and mental development of a child.

Chamberlain, Isabel C. See No. 65.

67. **Chambers, Will Grant** Questionnaire methods of child study. Proc. N. E. A., 1904, pp. 762-770.

68. **Chance, Lulu M.** Little folks of many lands. Ginn & Co., Boston, 1904, pp. 112.

69. **Chance, Lydia Gardiner** Public school classes for mentally deficient children. Nat. Conf. Char., and Corr., 1904, pp. 390-401.
   Excellent survey of the work being done for backward children in the public schools of Europe and the United States.

70. **Chancellor, William Estabrook** Our schools, their administration and supervision. D. C. Heath, Boston, 1904, pp. 434.

71. **Chapin, T. F.** Manual training work with white children. Nat. Conf. Char. and Corr., 1904, pp. 250-256.
   Utility of manual training in reform schools for boys.

72. **Cheney, Frances E.** Five years' experience in teaching mentally defective children in a public school. Jour. of Psycho-Asthenics, Dec., 1903, to March, 1904. Vol. 8, pp. 39-41.

73. **Chervin, Arthur** Bégaiement et autres maladies fonctionnelles de la parole. Paris, 1901, pp. 551.

74. **Chrisman, Oscar** Relation of the home to the wayward child. Proc. N. E. A., 1904, pp. 800-801.

75. ———— Sight and hearing in relation to education. Proc. N. E. A. 1904, pp. 939-946.

76. **Chubb, Percival** Avenues of language expression in the elementary school. Proc. N. E. A., 1904, pp. 452-459.
   A plea for a better comprehension of the child's nature on the æsthetic and literary side.

77. **Claparède, E.** L'illusion de poids chez les anormaux. Arch. de Psy., 1902. Vol. 2, pp. 22-32.

78. **Clark, L. P.** A comparative study of idiopathic epilepsy in animals and man. N. Y. Med. Jour., 1904. Vol. 80, pp. 1105-1111.

79. **Clarke, John** Short studies in education in Scotland. Longmans, London, 1904, pp. 269.

80. **Clough, G. Benson** Short history of education. Holland & Co., London, 1904, pp. 128.

81. **Coe, George Albert.** Education in religion and morals. F. H. Revell, Chicago, 1904, pp. 434.
   Contains bibliography.

82. **Cohn, H.** Ueber sexuelle Belehrung der Schulkinder. Allg. Med. Centralztg., 1904. Vol. 73, pp. 931-935.

83. —— —— Was haben die Augenärzte für die Schulhygiene geleistet und was müssen sie noch leisten ? O. Coblentz, Berlin, 1904. pp. 35. Also in Allg. Med. Centralztg., 1904. Vol. 73, pp. 433-436; 453-456; 473-477.

84. **Compton, Fanny A.** What four months has done for Walter. Jour. of Psycho-Asthenics, Dec., 1903, to March, 1904. Vol. 8, pp. 41-44.
   Shows what can be accomplished in teaching a defective child.

85. **Conradi, Edward.** Psychology and pathology of speech development in the child. Ped. Sem. Sept., 1904. Vol. 11, pp. 328-380.
   Order of development, recapitulation theory, stammering and stuttering; bibliography, pp. 376-380.

86. **Cook, O. F.** The biological evolution of language. Monist, 1904. Vol. 14, pp. 481-491.

87. **Corbin, John.** Precautions used by the New York City department of health. School Jour., Dec. 10, 1904. Vol. 69, pp. 622-627.
   Prevention of contagious diseases in schools of the city.

88. **Cotton, Fassett A.** Compulsory education in Indiana. Nat. Conf. Char. and Cor., 1904, pp. 274-279.
   Relation of compulsory school attendance to juvenile crime.

89. **Cramer, —.** Ueber Nervosität der Studirenden. Allg. Zeit. für Psychiat., 1903. Vol. 60, pp. 753-754.

90. **Crampton, C. Ward** Pubescence: a preliminary report. Am. Anthropologist, Oct. to Dec., 1904. Vol. 6. pp. 705-709.
   Study of the ages at which more than 1,200 New York city high school boys arrived at puberty.

91. **Curtis, Henry S.** The sub-conscious effect of the school-room. School Jour., April 2, 1904. Vol. 68, pp. 373-376.

92. **Dana, John Cotton** What books should children read ? School Jour., Nov. 5, 1904. Vol. 69, pp. 435-436.
   Books in the Newark public library for children.

93. **Danger, O.** Education of the deaf for life in human society. Ass'n Rev., April, 1904. Vol. 6, pp. 101-108.

94. **Darrow, Clarence S.** Farmington. A. C. McClurg & Co., Chicago, 1904, pp. 277.
   Memories of a boyhood in a Pennsylvania village.

95. **Daskam, Josephine** Memoirs of a baby. Harper & Bros., N. Y., 1904, pp. 272.

96. **Davidson, H. A.** The gift of genius. Jour. of Ped., June, 1904. Vol. 16, pp. 281-297.
   Method of training a child with such a gift.

97. **Davidson, Thomas** The education of the wage-earners. Ginn & Co., Boston, 1904, pp. 247.

98. **Decroly, Dr. and Rowma, G.** Troubles du langage et enfants arriérés. Policlinique, 1904. Vol. 13, p. 18.

De Croly, Dr. See **Demoor, J. and De Croly, Dr.**

100. **De Forest, J. L.** Education of backward children. Education, March, 1904. Vol. 24, pp. 401-406.

101. **Demoor, J. and De Croly, Dr.** Revue de pédagogie des anormaux. L'Année Psy., 1903 (1904). Vol. 10, pp. 317-327.

102. **Denver, Col.** Juvenile Court of the city and county. The problem of the children and how the State of Colorado cares for them. Denver, 1904, pp. 222.

103. **Deny, G.** La démence précoce. Mèd. mod., 1904. Vol. 15, p. 257.

104. **Devrient Hans** Das Kind auf der antiken Bühne. Gymnasial-programm, Weimar, 1904, pp. 20.

105. **Dewey, John** Educational psychology; syllabus of a course of twelve lecture studies. Univ. Press, Chicago, 1896, pp. 24

106. —— —— Die Schule und das öffentliche Leben. Zeits. für päd. Psy., April to June, 1904. Vol. 6, pp. 34-49; 81-117.
Translated from the English by Else Gurlitt.

107. **Dexter, T. F. and Garlick, A. H.** Object lessons in geography for standards 1, 2 and 3. Longmans, London, 1899, pp. 334.

108. **Dopp, Katharine E.** The natural activities of children as determining the industries in early education. Proc. N. E. A., 1904, pp. 437-443.

109. **Dörrich, H.** Ein Fall von motorischer Aphasie. Kinderfehler. Aug., 1904. Vol. 9, pp. 271-274.

110. **Dorsey, George A.** An Arikara story-telling contest. Am. Anthropologist, April to June, 1904. Vol. 6, pp. 240-243.
An account of the telling of personal stories of adventure among the Arikara Indians.

111. **Duche, Emile** La précocité intellectuelle: étude sur le génie. L. Boyer, Paris, 1901, pp. 92.

112. **Dugas, L.** Psychologie des examens. Rev. Philos., 1904. Vol. 58, pp. 379-399.

113. —— —— Sur la reconnaissance des souvenirs. Jour. de Psy. Norm. et Pathol., 1904. Vol. 1, pp. 513-523.

114. **Dunn, R.** Games of the city street boys. Outing, June, 1904. Vol. 44, p. 271.

115. **Ebert, E. and Meumann, E.** Ueber einige Grundfragen der Psychologie der Uebungsphänomene im Bereiche des Gedächtnisses. Samml. von Abh. zur psy. Päd., 1904. Vol. 1, pt. 5, pp. 437-668.

116. **Egger, E.** Beobachtungen und Betrachtungen über die Entwicklung der Intelligenz und der Sprache bei den Kindern. E. Wunderlich, Leipzig, 1903, pp. 73.

117. **Eggert, Bruno** Der psychologische Zusammenhang in der Didaktik des neusprachlichen Reformunterrichts. Samml. von Abhand. a. d. Gebiete der päd. Psy. u. Physiol. Berlin, 1904, Vol. 7, pt. 4, pp. 74.
    The author takes up the development of the art of presentation of modern languages, and discusses it from a psychological point of view.

118. **Ekstein, E.** Die Sexualfrage in der Erziehung des Kindes. Modern. Verlagsbur., Leipzig, 1904, pp. 38.

119. **Ellis, H.** A study of British genius. Hurst & Blackett, London, 1904, pp. 300.

120. **Elson, William H.** Relation of teacher and child. School Jour., March 19, 1904. Vol. 68, pp. 327-328.

121. **Engelhorn.** Welche Bedeutung für die Schulhygiene hat die Psychologie und Psychopathologie der Entwicklungsjahre? Kinderfehler, Aug., 1904. Vol. 9, pp. 253-261.

122. **Escherich, T.** Die Grundlage und Ziele der modernen Kinderheilkunde. Wien. klin. Woch., 1904. Vol. 17, pp. 1025-1027.

123. **Escarne, —.** De l'excitation cérébrale chez les enfants. H. Jouve, Paris, 1898, pp. 68.

124. **Fairbank, William G.** Religious and moral training [of juvenile delinquents]. Nat. Conf. Char. and Corr., 1904, pp. 327-331.

125. **Faulkner, C. E.** Institution care of dependent children. Nat. Conf. Char. and Corr., 1904, pp. 335-342.

126. **Feilchenfeld, W.** Vortäuschung von Myopie bei Schulkindern. Deutsche Med. Woch., 1904. Vol. 30, pp. 1541-1542.

127. **Fernald, Walter E.** Care of the feeble-minded. Nat. Conf. Char. and Corr., 1904, pp. 380-390.
    Brief survey of the growth of the 25 public institutions for the care of the feeble-minded in the United States.

128. —— —— Mentally defective children in the public schools. Jour. of Psycho-Asthenics, Dec., 1903, to March, 1904. Vol. 8, pp. 25-35.

129. **Ferreri, G.** Measurement and development of the hearing power of the deaf. Ass'n Rev., April, 1904. Vol. 6, pp. 127-129.

130. **Fetscherin, Eduard** Schule und Zahnpflege. Zeits. für Schulgesundheitspflege, No. 7, 1904. Vol. 17, pp. 490-494.

131. **Findlay, J. J.** Mental life at the age of eleven. Paidologist, Nov., 1904. Vol. 6, pp. 169-174.

132. **Fitch, Charles E.** The public school; history of common school education in New York from 1633 to 1904. J. B. Lyon Co., Albany, N. Y., 1904, pp. 124.

133. **Flachs, Albert** Zur Frage der sexuellen Aufklärung. Zeits. für Schulgesundheitspflege, No. 7, 1904. Vol. 17, pp. 471-482.
Opposes the instruction of youth in sex-knowledge.

134. **Fletcher, Margaret** School of the heart. Longmans, N. Y., 1904, pp. 109.

135. **Forster, —.** Das Muskelsystem eines männlichen Papua-Neugeborenen. Abh. d. K. Leop.-Car. Akad. d. Naturf., Vol. 82, pp. 1-140.
Detailed account of the muscular system of a new-born Papuan child.

136. **Forster F.** Kind und Alkohol. B. G. Teubner, Leipzig, 1904, pp. 35.

137. **Fox, Hugh F.** Boards of children's guardians. Nat. Conf. Char. and Corr., 1904, pp. 311-317.
Need of state guardianship of abandoned and neglected children.

138. **Frenzel, Franz** Notwendigkeit und Wirksamkeit des Arztes in der Hilfsschule. Zeits. für Schulgesundheitspflege, 1904. Vol. 17, Nos. 2 and 3, pp. 97-120.
Need of the medical supervision of schools.

139. **Frenzel, K.** Internationaler Kongress für Schulhygiene zu Nürnberg von 4-9, April, 1904. Kinderfehler, 1904. Vol. 9, pp. 221-230.

140. **Friedjung, J. K.** Eine typische Form der Hysterie des Kindesalters und ihre Beziehung zu der Anatomie der Linea alba. Zeits. für Heilk., 1904. Vol. 25, pp. 209-259.

141. **Fuchs, Arno** Dispositionsschwankungen bei normalen and schwachsinnigen Kindern. Beitr. zur Päd. Pathologie, 1904. Pt. 5, pp. 62.

142. **Von Gabnay, F.** Ungarische Kinderspiele. Globus, Braunschweig, Vol. 85, 1904, pp. 42-45; 60-63.
Brief descriptions of playthings, dolls, games, etc.

Garlick, A. H. See **Dexter, T. F. and Garlick, A. H.**

144. **Garnier and Santenoise** Sur un cas de rachitisme congénital avec nanisme, chez un enfant arriéré. Arch. de Neurol., 1903. Vol. 16, pp. 31-37.

145. **Gelpke, T.** Ueber die Beziehungen des Sehorgans zum jugendlichen Schwachsinn. C. Marhold, Halle a S., 1904. pp. 24. Also in Samml. zw. Abh. a. d. Geb. d. Augenhlk., 1904. Vol. 6, pt. 1, pp. 24.

146. **Gillette, Arthur J.** State care of indigent, crippled, and deformed children. Nat. Conf. Char. and Corr., 1904, pp. 285-294.
Need of instruction in trades for such children.

147. **Gobelbecker, L. F.** Das Kind in Haus, Schule und Welt. Nemnich, Wiesbaden, 1904, pp. 144.

148. **Godart, M.** La littérature enfantine. Rev. Ped., Nov., 1904. Vol. 45, pp. 464-474.

149. **Godin, Paul** Recherches anthropométriques sur la croissance des diverses parties du corps. L'Année Psychol. 1903 (1904). Vol. 10, p. 297-299.

150. **Gould, F. J.** Children's book of moral lessons. Series 1-3. Watts & Co., London, 1899-1904. 3 v.

151. **Gould, George M.** Righteyedness and lefteyedness. Science, N. S., April 8, 1904. Vol. 19, pp. 591-594.
      This article gives causes and results of acquired and inherited right-eyedness and lefteyedness.

152. **Gray, Mary Richard** What Chicago is doing for the abnormal child. School Jour., Dec., 3, 1904. Vol. 69, pp. 585-586.

153. **Greef, R.** Augenärztliche und hygienische Schuluntersuchungen. Klin. Jahrb., 1904. Vol. 12, pp. 1-92.

154. **Green, S. M.** What teachers may learn from the model school for the deaf and blind, and their exhibits. Proc. N. E. A., 1905, pp. 937-939.

155. **Griesbach, H.** Der Stand der Schulhygiene in Deutschland. Vogel, Leipzig, 1904, pp. 59.

156. **Grimmbart** Mittel, den Kindern unbekannte Begriffe zu erläutern, an Beispielen aus der Schulpraxis dargestellt nach Overbergs Anweisung. Westdeutsch. Lehrerztg., 1904. Vol. 12, pp. 197-198; 219-220; 232-234.

157. **Groos, Karl** Das Seelenleben des Kindes. Reuther & Reichard, Berlin, 1904, pp. 229.
      Shows great familiarity with American work. No general conclusions of importance attempted.

158. **Groszmann, Maximilian P. E.** To what extent may atypical children be successful in our public schools? Proc. N. E. A., 1904, pp. 754-759.

159. **Gruber, M.** Normen für Tageslichteinfall in Schulen. Zeits. für Schulgesundheitspflege, No. 5, 1904. Vol. 17, pp. 319-325.
      Some hints for producing better light in the schoolroom.

160. **Gugler, Philipp** Individuität und Individualisation des Einzelnen. Friedrich, Leipzig, 1900, pp. 435.

161. **Guillet, Cephas** A glimpse at a nature school. Ped. Sem., March, 1904. Vol. 11, pp. 91-98.
      Account of a Canadian school for boys in which about one-half of the school time is spent in getting knowledge first hand from the pupil's environment.

162. **Gulick, Luther Halsey** Physical education by muscular exercise. P. Blakiston, Phila., 1904, pp. 67.

163. **Gündel, A** Zur Organisation der Hilfsschule. Zeits. für d. Behandlg. Schwachs. u. Epil., 1904. Vol. 20, pp. 1-7; 26-40.

164. **Gunn, John** The infant school: its principles and methods. Thos. Nelson & Sons, Edinburgh, 1904, pp. 412.
      An excellent book written from the viewpoint of genetic psychology. A valuable chapter on child study.

165. **Gutberlet, C.** Der Mensch; sein Ursprung und seine Ent-wickelung. F. Schoningh, Paderborn, 1903, pp. 645.

166. **Haeberlin, Dr.** Ferienjugendhort in Zürich-Oberstrass. Sond.-Abdruck a. d. Arch. f. Soz. Med. u. Hygiene, 1904.

167. **Hagen, J. Chr.** Zur anstaltlichen Behandlung unserer sitt-lich gefährdeten Jugend. Kinderfehler, Feb., 1904. Vol. 9, pp. 132-137.
Intellect and morals of youth conditioned by good health.

168. **Hall, G. Stanley** Adolescence; its psychology and its rela-tion to physiology, anthropology, sociology, sex, crime, relig-ion and education, . . . New York, D. Appleton & Co., 1904. 2 vols., pp. 589; 784.
Contents: Growth in height and weight; growth of parts and organs dur-ing adolescence; growth of motor power and function; diseases of mind and body; juvenile faults, immoralities, and crimes; sexual development—its dangers and hygiene in boys; periodicity; adolescent in literature, biog-raphy, and history; changes in the senses and voice; evolution and the feelings and instincts characteristic of normal adolescence; adolescent love; adolescent feelings toward nature and a new education in science; savage public initiations, classical ideals and customs, and church con-firmation; the adolescent psychology of conversion; social instincts and institutions; intellectual development and education; adolescent girls and their education; ethnic psychology and pedagogy, or adolescent races and their treatment.

169. —— —— In how far may child psychology take the place of adult psychology or rational psychology in training of teach-ers ? Jour, of Ed., July 14, 1904. Vol. 60, p. 74.

170. —— —— The natural activities of children as determining the industries in early education. Proc. N. E. A., 1904, pp. 443-447.

171. —— —— Unsolved problems of child study and the method of their attack. Proc. N. E. A., 1904, pp. 782-787.

172. —— —— **and Brown, C. E.** The cat and the child. Ped. Sem., March, 1904. Vol. 11, pp. 3-29.
This article discusses the cat in geology; anatomy of the cat; naming, activities, anthropomorphism, moods and singing of cats, and the relation of the cat to child life.

173. **Hall, Percival** Defective sight and hearing of school chil-dren. School Jour., July 23, 1904. Vol. 69, p. 91.

174. **Hall, R. D.** Boys: Indian and white. Southern Workman, Hampton, Va. Vol. 25, 1904, pp. 269-272.
Compares as to character, temperament, etc.

175. **Hall, W. H.** On the education of the visual centres. Lancet, 1904. Vol. 2, pp. 205-206.

176. **Hamburger, C.** Ueber die einfachste Methode der Sehprü-fung bei Lernanfängern. Zeits. für Schulgesundheitspflege, No. 7, 1904. Vol. 17, pp. 485-490.

177. **Hammarberg, Carl** Studien über Klinik und Pathologie der Idiotie. E. Berling, Upsala, 1895, pp. 126.

178. **Hammerschlag, V.** Ueber Hörstörungen im Kindesalter and ihre Bedeutung für die psychische and intellektuelle Entwickelung des Kindes. Wien. Med. Presse, 1904. Vol. 45, pp. 657-662; 708-717.

179. **Hancock, H. Irving** Physical training for children by Japanese methods. Putnam, N. Y., 1904, pp. 153.

180. **Harrison, Elizabeth** The study of children by means of their hand work. Proc. N. E. A., 1904, pp. 792-794.

181. **Harvey, Anna E.** Value of pets in the kindergarten. Proc. N. E. A., 1904, pp. 432-437.

182. **Harvey, Lorenzo D.** The natural activities of children as determining the industries in early education. Proc. N. E. A., 1904, pp. 447-452.

183. **Haslett, Samuel B.** Pedagogical Bible School. Revell, N. Y., 1903, pp. 383.

184. **Heller, Theodor** Die Gefährdung der Kinder durch krankhaft veranlagte und sittlich defekte Aufsichtspersonen. Zeits. für Schulgesundheitspflege, No. 11, 1904. Vol. 17, pp. 759-770, also in Wien. klin. Woch., 1904. Vol. 17, pp. 669-672.

185. —— —— Grundriss der Heilpädagogik. W. Engelmann, Leipzig, 1904, pp. 366.
      Discusses idiocy, moral degeneracy, epilepsy, chorea, speech defects, etc.

186. —— —— Studien zur Blindenpsychologie. Engelmann, Leipzig, 1904, pp. 136.

187. **Hemprich, K.** Zur modernen Kinderforschung. Part 1. Jahrbuch des Vereins für wissens. Päd., 1904. Vol. 26, p. 161-208.

188. **Henderson, Charles R.** Theory and practice of juvenile Courts. Nat. Conf. Char. and Corr., 1904, pp. 358-369.

189. **Hensser, J.** Geschlechtertrennung oder Geschlechtervereinigung im Schulunterrichte. Zeits. für Schulgesundheitspflege, 1904. Vol. 17, Nos. 2 and 3, pp. 120-126.
      Discussion of co-education.

190. **Hermann, ——** Erziehung und Krankheit. Kinderfehler, Aug., 1904. Vol. 9, pp. 265-268.

191. **Hervey, Walter L.** How the American boy is educated. Chautauquan, Nov., 1904. Vol. 40, pp. 263-270.

192. **Hieronymus, D.** Der Stundenplan in hygienischer Beleuchtung. Zeits. für Schulgesundheitspflege, No. 1, 1904. Vol. 17, pp. 14-28.
      Plan of good arrangement of study in the school.

193. —— —— Vergabung und erbliche Belastung in ihrer Bedeutung für Jugend und Volkserziehung. Kinderfehler, Aug. 1904. Vol. 9, pp. 241-253.
      Study of heredity with an explanation of Weismann's theory.

194. **Hildebrandt, Paul** Das Spielzeug im Leben des Kindes. G. Söhlke, Berlin, 1904, pp. 421.

195. **Hilfiker, Schmid J.** Gemeinsamer Unterricht beider Geschlechter. Zeits. für Schulgesundheitspflege. Nos. 2 and 3, 1904. Vol. 17, pp. 126-127.
Discussion of co-education.

Hindshaw, Winifred See **Salmon, David and Hindshaw, W.**

197. **His, W.** Die Entwickelung des menschlichen Gehirns während der ersten Monate. Hirzel, Leipzig, 1904, pp. 176.

198. **Hocksinger, K.** Krämpfe bei Kindern. Dtsch. Klinik, 1904. Vol. 7, pp. 478-532.

199. —— —— Versuch einer pathogenetischen Einteilung der funktionellen Kinderkrämpfe. Wien. Med. Woch., 1904. Vol. 54, pp. 2409-2415.

200. **Hoffmann, Hugo** Division of [deaf] pupils according to capacity. Ass'n Rev., Feb., 1904. Vol. 6, pp. 35-40.

201. **Holcombe, Chester** The moral training of the young in China. Int. Jour. of Ethics, July, 1904. Vol. 14, pp. 445-468.
This article treats on primary and secondary education in China.

202. **Hollkomm, F.** Der erziehende Unterricht in der einklassigen Schule. H. Beyer and Söhne, Langensalza, 1904, pp. 257.

203. **Horsten, ——** Soll die Schule Staatsanstalt werden? Päd. Abhand., N. F., Vol. 10, pt. 8, pp. 153-163.

204. **Hosslin, R. von** Die Schwangerschaftslähmungen der Mütter. Arch. f. Psychiat. u. Nervenkr., 1904. Vol. 38, pp. 730-861.

205. **Hubbell, George Allen** Up through childhood. G. P. Putnam's Sons, New York, 1904, pp. 303.
Discussion of moral and religious training of youth in the school, the college, the Sunday school, and the Y. M. C. A.

206. **Idelberger, H. A.** Die Entwickelung der kindlichen Sprache. H. Walther, Berlin, 1904, pp. 87.

207. **Infeld, M.** Beiträge zur Kenntnis der Kinderpsychosen. Jahrb. für Psychiat. u. Neurol., 1902. Vol. 22, pp. 326-345.

208. **Jacobs, Bertha** Work of one state. Nat. Conf. Char. and Corr., 1904, pp. 317-320.
Family care of juvenile offenders, neglected children, and dependent children in Massachusetts.

209. **Jacoby, P.** Études sur la sélection chez l'homme. 2e éd. F. Alcan, Paris, 1904, pp. 920.

210. **Johnson, Clifton** Old-time schools and school books. Macmillan Co., New York, 1904, pp. 381.
A popular study of the school books that have been used by American children.

211. **Jones, Cora Stuart** What nature study should give. School Jour., March 12, 1904. Vol. 68, pp. 303-304.

212. **Jussuf, I.** Klinische Beiträge zur Kenntnis der cerebralen Diplegien des Kindesalters und der Mikrocephalie. Jahrb. für Kinderhlk., 1904. Vol. 60, pp. 843-883.

213. **Karr, Grant** Aim of education in school and home. Jour. of Ped., Sept., 1904. Vol. 17, pp. 26-42.
    Discussion of ways in which to make the home and school life of greater educative value.

214. **Keene, George F.** Genesis of the defective. Nat. Conf. Char. and Corr., 1904, pp. 407-408.

215. **Keller, Helen** The story of my life. Doubleday, N. Y., 1904, pp. 441.

216. **Kelley, Florence** Child labor laws. Nat. Conf. Char. and Corr., 1904, pp. 268-273.

217. **Kelly, Myra** Little citizens; the humors of school life. McClure, Phillips & Co., New York, 1904, pp. 352.

Kenwood, Henry See **Parkes, Louis C. and Kenwood, Henry.**

219. **Kenyon, Walter J.** The telling of a story. School Jour., June 11, 1904. Vol. 68, p. 691.

220. **Kiefer, O.** Hygienische und psychologische Bedenken der körperlichen Züchtigung bei Kindern. Kinderfehler, March, 1904. Vol. 9, pp. 157-160.
    Opposes corporal punishment of children.

221. **Kielhorn, K.** Die Gesundheitspflege in der Hilfsschule. Zeits. für die Behandlg. Schwachs. u. Epil., 1904. Vol. 20, pp. 149-162.

222. **King, Irving** Recent books on child psychology and education. Psy. Bulletin, April 15, 1904. Vol. 1, pp. 147-160.
    Review of recent books by Groos, Kirkpatrick, O'Shea, Laisant, Van Biervliet, and Thorndike.

223. **Kinkead, T. L.** State supervision of dependent children. Nat. Conf. Char. and Corr., 1904, pp. 342-349.

224. **Kline, Linus W.** The contributions of zoölogical psychology to child study. Proc. N. E. A., 1904, pp. 776-782.

225. **Koch, J. L. A.** Abnorme Charaktere. Bergmann, Weisbaden, 1900, pp. 40.

226. **Koenig, W.** Die Ætiologie der einfachen Idiotie verglichen mit derjenigen der zerebralen Kinderlähmungen. Allg. Zeits. für Psychiat., 1904. Vol. 61, pp. 133-168.

227. **Kolster, R.** Ueber Längenvariationen des Oesophagus und deren Abhängigkeit vom Alter. Zeitschr. f. Morph. Vol. 7, pp. 1-21.

228. **Kuhlmann, F.** Experimental studies in mental deficiency: three cases of imbecility and six cases of feeble-mindedness. Am. Jour. of Psy., July, 1904. Vol. 15, pp. 391-446. Bibliography, pp. 442-446.

229. **Langdon-Down, Reginald** Signs of development. Paidologist, Nov., 1904. Vol. 6, pp. 174-179.

230. **Langer, Leo.** Herder und die Kindesseele. Kinderfehler, Feb., 1904. Vol. 9, pp. 115-126.

231. **Lanner, A.** Wie lernt das Kind zählen? Zeits. für Philos. u. Päd., 1904. Vol. 11, pp. 23-38.

232. **Lay, W. A.** Ueber das Wesen und die Bedeutung der experimentellen Didaktik. Ber. ü. d. I. Kong. f. exper. Psy., Giessen, April, 1904, pp. 101-106. J. A. Barth, Leipzig, 1904.

233. **Legarde, Ellen** Should the scope of the public school system be broadened to take in all children capable of education? Jour. of Psycho-Asthenics., Dec., 1903, to March, 1904. Vol. 8, pp. 35-38.

234. **Le Gendre, ——** Les névroses dans le milieu scolaire; réactions réciproques entre élèves et maîtres au point de vue des influences morales. Bull. Méd., 1904. Vol. 18. p. 39.

235. **Lehmann-Nitsche, R.** Die dunklen Hautflecke der Neugeborenen bei Indianern und Mulatten. Globus, 1904. Vol. 85, pp. 297-301.
Discusses with bibliography the "Mongolian spot" in new-born American Indians, etc.

236. **Leland, C. Godfrey** The alternate sex; or, the female intellect in man and the masculine in woman. Funk & Wagnalls, New York, 1904, pp. 134.

237. **Lemaitre, Auguste** Observations sur le langage intérieur des enfants. Arch. de Psy., 1904. Vol. 4, pp. 1-43.

238. **Lewandowski, Alfred** Ueber die Hautkrankheiten der Schule. Zeits. für Schulgesundheitspflege, No. 5, 1904. Vol. 17, pp. 295-304.

239. **Ley, Auguste** L'arriération à l'étude de la pathologie infantile. J. Lebègue & Cie., Bruxelles, 1904, pp. 263.

240. **Libby, M. F.** Co-education and the raw material of the school. Investigations in Psy. and Ed. Univ. of Col., March, 1904. Vol. 2, pp. 39-42.

241. **Lindemann, Fedor** Das kunstreich gestaltete Schulhaus. Voigtlander, Leipzig, 1904, pp. 113.

242. **Lobsein, Marx** Ueber den relativen Wert verschiedener Gedächtnistypen. H. Beyer, Langensalza, 1902, pp. 22.

243. **—— ——** Ueber Farbenkenntnis bei Schulkindern. Zeits. für Psy. und Physiol. der Sinnesorgane, Jan. to Feb., 1904. Vol. 34, pp. 29-47.
A study of ability of school children to name and recognize colors.

244. **Lowinsky, Victor** Neuere amerikanische Arbeiten auf dem Gebiete der Kinderpsychologie. Zeits. für päd. Psy., April and Aug., 1904. Vol. 6, pp. 1-33; 222-254.
Discussion of the labors of G. Stanley Hall, Earl Barnes and others.

245. **Lund, Troels** Gesundheit und Krankheit in der Anschauung alter Zeiten. Teubner, Leipzig, 1901, pp. 233.

246. **McCowen, Mary** Dramatization as a factor in education [of the deaf]. Ass'n Rev., April, 1904. Vol. 6, pp. 109-115.

247. **MacDougall, Robert** Sex differences in the sense of time. Science, April 29, 1904. N. S., Vol. 19, pp. 707-708.

248. **Macmillan, D. P.** The diagnosis of the capabilities of school children. Proc. N. E. A., 1904, pp. 738-744.
Scheme for diagnosis of mental and physical capabilities of children, with reference to arrangement of school curricula.

249. **McMillan, Margaret** Fatigue. Child Life, July, 1904. Vol. 6, pp. 146-157.

250. **Macnamara, T. J.** Physical condition of the working-class children. 19th Century, April, 1904, Vol. 56, p. 307.

251. **MacIneany, T. H.** The truant and his treatment. School Jour., May 28, 1904. Vol. 68, pp. 610-612.

252. **Mall, F. P.** On the development of the blood-vessels of the brain in the human embryo. Amer. Jour. of Anat., 1904. Vol. 4, pp. 1-18.

253. **Mark, Thistleton** New movement in education. Charles & Dible, London, 1904, pp. 107.

254. **Masselon, R.** Forme fruste de démence précoce. Arch. de Neurol., 1904. Vol. 17, pp. 433-455.

255. **Matiegka, H.** Ueber die Bedeutung des Hirngewichts beim Menschen. Anat. Hefte, Abt. 1, 1904. Vol. 23, pp. 655-699.

256. **Mayer, August** Ueber Einzel-und Gesamtleistung des Schulkindes; ein Beitrag zur experimentellen Pädagogik. Samml. v. Abh. zur psy. Päd., 1904. Vol. 1, pt. 4, pp. 301-436.

257. **Mayor, G.** Hörstummheit. Kinderfehler, June, 1904. Vol. 9, pp. 230-236.
Defective speech of children and how to overcome it.

258. **Mehnert, M.** Ueber Sprachstörungen mit besonderer Berücksichtigung des Stammelns und Stotterns bei Schulkindern. A. Urban, Dresden, 1904, pp. 40.

259. **Messmer, Oskar** Zur Psychologie des Lesens bei Kindern und Erwachsenen. Samml. von Abh. zur psy. Päd., 1904. Vol. 1, pt. 1, pp. 1-109.

260. **Meumann, E.** Haus-und Schularbeit, Experimente an Kindern der Volksschule. Klinkhardt, Leipzig, 1904, pp. 64; also Die Deutsche Schule, May, 1904. Vol. 8, pp. 278-303.

261. **Meumann, E.** Ueber Oekonomie and Technik des Lernens. J. Klinkhardt, Leipzig, 1903, pp. 102; also die Deutsche Schule, 1903. Vol. 7, pts. 3-7, pp. 133-155; 205-225; 284-299 ; 354-368; 425-450.

—— —— See **Ebert, E. and Meumann, E.**

263. **Meyer, H. T. M.** Die Schulstätten der Zukunft. L. Voss, Leipzig, 1903, pp. 78.

264. **Michaelis, Karin** The child Andrea; trans. from the Danish by J. L. Laurrik. Duckworth, London, 1904, pp. 142.

265. **Miller, Mary Jean** What is kindergarten discipline? Proc. N. E. A., 1904, pp. 427-431.

266. **Minchen, J. G. Cotton** Our public schools, their influence on English history. Sonnenschein, London, 1901, pp. 462.

267. **Mobius, P. J.** Geschlecht und Kinderliebe. Beitr. z. Lehre v. den Geschlechts-Unterschieden, Halle, 1904. Pts. 7 and 8, pp. 72.

268. **Monroe, Will S.** Adolescence: Its psychology and pedagogy. Jour. of Ped., Sept., 1904. Vol. 17, pp. 8-23.
A review of G. Stanley Hall's great work.

269. —— —— Counting-out rhymes of children. Am. Anthropologist, Jan. to March, 1904. Vol. 6, pp. 46-50.
An inductive study of the counting-out rhymes of school children and the use of the same in plays and games.

270. —— —— Memory test of students. School Jour., Feb. 27, 1904. Vol. 68, pp. 242-243.
An inductive study of memory for faces.

271. —— —— De ontwikkeling van het Sociale Bewustzijn der Kinderen. G. P. Tierie, Amsterdam, 1904, pp. 120.
Translation from the German of the author's book on the development of the social consciousness of children.

272. —— —— Perception of children. Ped. Sem., Dec., 1904. Vol. 11, pp. 498-507.
An inductive study of the qualities of objects most readily perceived by children and a discussion of sex differences; also a bibliography.

273. —— —— Typical child-study methods at the St. Louis exhibit. Proc. N. E. A., 1904, pp. 759-762.

274. **Mooney, J.** The Indian navel-cord. Jour. Amer. Folk-Lore, Vol. 17, 1904, p. 197.
Notes on folk-lore as to disposition of navel-cord.

275. **Morrison, Alice** Entertainments as a practical factor in the training of the feeble-minded. Jour. of Psycho-Asthenics, June, 1904. Vol. 8, pp. 75-78.

276. **Morse, Fannie French** Methods most helpful to girls. Nat. Conf. Char. and Corr., 1904, pp. 306-311.
Institutional training of juvenile delinquents among girls.

277.　**Morten, Honnor**　Consider the children.　R. B. Johnson, London, 1904, pp. 80.

278.　**Moses, J.**　Die Schulbank in den Hilfsklassen für Schwachbefähigte.　Zeits. für Schulgesundheitspflege, No. 12, 1904.　Vol. 17, pp. 853-859.

279.　**Mosso, Angelo**　Les exercises physiques et le développement intellectuel.　F. Alcan, Paris, 1904, pp. 294.
　　Describes physical ed. in the universities, its relations to democracy and to women.

280.　—— —— Fatigue: Translated by Margaret Drummond and W. B. Drummond.　G. P. Putnam's Sons, New York, 1904, pp. 334.
　　This valuable Italian work lays emphasis on the part played by toxins in the production of fatigue.　It also contains useful chapters on attention, examinations, and overpressure.

281.　**Mouton, M. C.**　Eine staatliche Untersuchung der bei Schulkindern in Holland vorkommenden adenoiden Vegetationen.　Zeits. für Schulgesundheitspflege, Nos. 2 and 3, 1904.　Vol. 17, pp. 89-91.
　　The study of adenoid growths.

282.　**Muirhead, John H.**　Wordsworth's ideal of early education.　Int. Jour. of Ethics, April, 1904.　Vol. 14, pp. 339-352.
　　Extracts from Wordsworth's writings concerning his own child life, and a plea that children be permitted to educate themselves under the right conditions.

283.　**Muller, Hugo**　Höhere Schulwesen Deutschlands am Anfang des 20 Jahrhunderts.　Stuttgart, 1904, pp. 135.

284.　**Nausester, Walter**　Das Kind und die Form der Sprache.　Samml. von Abhand. a. d. Gebiete der päd. Psy. u. Physiol., Berlin, 1904.　Vol. 7, pt. 7, pp. 51.
　　Takes up the various accounts of the first words spoken by a child Tells its vocabulary is made up from his surroundings.

285.　**Netschajeff, A.**　Ueber Auffassung.　Samml. von Abhand a. d. Gebiete der päd. Psy. u. Physiol., Berlin, r904.　Vol. 7, pt. 6, pp. 26.
　　A sketch from the sphere of experimental pedagogical psychology.　Experiments are given which tested the ability of children to describe and remember things seen and heard.

286.　**Nibecker, F. H.**　Forward movement in the boarding schools for delinquents.　Nat. Conf. Char. and Corr., 1904, pp. 300-306.
　　Argument for the institutional care of juvenile delinquents.

287.　**Nicoll, S. A.**　How to bring up our boys.　Crowell & Co., N. Y., 1904, pp. 64.

288.　**Neitzold, Franz**　Prüfung der zur Volksschule angemeldeten Kinder, besonders im Gesange.　Kinderfehler, Oct., 1904.　Vol. 10, pp. 9-19.
　　Results obtained by testing the early reading and singing ability of children.

289.　**Nightingale, Eleanor M.**　Close thinking and accurate speech.　School Jour., April 2, 1904.　Vol. 68, pp. 378-379.

290. **Norman, C.** Dementia Praecox. Brit. Med. Jour., 1904. Vol. 2, pp. 972-975.

291. **Oppenheim, Hermann** Ueber die ersten Zeichen der Nervosität des Kindesalters. Kinderfehler, 1904. Vol. 9, pp. 49-62.

292. **Oppler, Therese** Zur Frage der sexuellen Aufklärung. Zeits. für Schulgesundheitspflege, No. 9, 1904. Vol. 17, pp. 629-633.
    In favor of instructing the youth in sex knowledge.

293. **O'Shea, M. V.** The relation of physical training to mental activity. Amer. Phys. Ed. Rev., 1904. Vol. 9, pp. 28-35.

294. **Page, Frank S.** Teaching arithmetic by playing store. School Jour., May 7, 1904. Vol. 68, pp. 521-522.

295. **Palmer, Luella A.** Method of child study in the kindergarten. Proc. N. E. A., 1904, pp. 794-797.

296. **Parkes, Louis C. and Kenwood, Henry.** Hygiene and public health. P. Blakiston, Philadelphia, 1902, pp. 763.

297. **Parsons, Bell Ragnar** Physical training by means of play. School Jour., Nov. 26, 1904. Vol 69, pp. 520-522.

298. **Partridge, Sophia S.** Children's drawings. Paidologist, Nov., 1904. Vol. 6, pp. 130-166.

299. **Patzak, Jul. Vinzenz** Schule und Schülerkraft; statistische Versuche über Arbeitsleistung an höheren Lehranstalten. A. Pichlers Witwe & Sohn, Wien, 1904, pp. 82.

300. **Paulsen, Friedrich** Höhere Schulen Deutschlands, and ihr Lehrerstand in ihrem Verhältnis zum Staat and zur geistigen Kultur. F. Vieweg, Brns., 1904. pp. 31.

301. **Payne, Bertha** The individual child. Proc. N. E. A., 1904, pp. 422-426.
    A plea for a small working community.

302. **Pfalz, Franz** Ein Knabenleben vor Jahren; pädagogische Betrachtung eigner Erlebnisse. C. Belser, Stuttgart, 1904. 2v.

303. **Pfersdorff, K.** Die Remissionen der Dementia Praecox. Zeits. für klin. Med., 1904. Vol. 55, pp. 488-507.

304. **Pfister,** —— Die Kapazität des Schädels (der Kopfhöhle) beim Säugling und älteren Kinde. Monatsschr. für Psychiat. n. Neurol., 1903. Vol. 13, pp. 577-589.

305. **Philpott, Hugh B.** London at school; the story of the school board, 1870-1904. T. F. Unwin, London, 1904, pp. 314.

Phulpin, —— See **Roubinovitch and Phulpin.**

307. **Pick, A.** Ueber einige bedeutsame Psycho-Neurosen des Kindesalters. Samml. Zwang. Abhand. a. d. Gebiete d. Nerven- u. Geisteskrankheiten, 1904. Vol. 5, Heft. 1, pp. 28.

308. **Pieron, H.** La psychologie des jeux. Rev. de Psychiat., 1904. Vol. 8, pp. 292-296.

309. **Platt, William** Child music; a study of tunes made up by quite young children. Simpkin, Marshall & Co., London, 1904, pp. 37.

310. **Podiapolsky, ——** Les impressions ou suggestions paternelles ou maternelles se transmettent elles aux enfants? Rev. de l'hypt., Vol. 18, pp. 212-220.

311. **Poincaré, Lucien** Du rôle des sciences expérimentales dans l'éducation. Rev. Péd., Jan., 1904. Vol. 45, pp. 1-19.

312. **Probst, M.** Gehirn und Seele des Kindes. Samml. von Abhand. a. d. Gebiete der päd. Psy. u. Physiol. Berlin, 1904. Vol. 7, pts. 2 and 3, pp. 148.
    Gives a comparison of the weights of boys' and girls' brains during infancy and childhood. Describes the appearance of the brain, peripheral nerves, brain of embryo, cerebrum, cerebellum, cortical areas, fibers, gray matter, and discusses the excitability of the peripheral nerves of the child, and the function of the cerebellum in the child.

313. **Pröbsting, August** Die künstliche Beleuchtung der Schulsäle. Zeits. für Schulgesundheitspflege, No. 4, 1904. Vol. 17, pp. 244-246.

314. **Puterman, J.** Ueber die Beeinflussung des Zirkulationssystems durch die Schulexamina. Wien. klin. Woch., 1904. Vol. 54, pp. 265-270.

315. **Ranschburg, P.** Der gegenwärtige Stand der Heilpädagogik in Ungarn. Kinderfehler, 1904. Vol. 9, pp. 262-265.

316. **Régis, E.** Note à propos de la démence précoce. Rev. de Psychiat., 1904.Vol. 8, pp. 150-156.

318. **Richmond, Mary E.** The early training of the imagination. Child Life, Oct., 1904. Vol. 6, pp. 193-198.

319. **Ridgeway, J. T.** Psychology of mobs as an educational factor. Jour. of Ed., August 25, 1904. Vol. 60, pp. 136-138.

320. **Rivers, W. H. R.** Investigations of the comparative visual acuity of savages and of civilized people. Brit. Med. Jour., 1904. Vol. 2, p. 1297.

Roberts See **Southard and Roberts.**

322. **Rogers, Helen W.** Probation system of the juvenile court of Indianapolis. Nat. Conf. Char. and Corr., 1904, pp. 369-379.

323. **Roller, K.** Neue Untersuchungen über Schulbücherdruck. Zeits. für Schulgesundheitspflege, No. 1, 1904. Vol. 17, pp. 7-14.
    How to prevent short-sightedness by having the proper print.

324. **Rorie, G. A.** Notes on adolescent insanity in Dorset. Jour. of Mental Sci., 1904. Vol. 50, pp. 266-272.

325. **Roubinovitch and Phulpin** Sur la démence précoce. Bull. Méd., 1904. Vol. 18, p. 93.

Rouma, G. See **Decroly, and Rouma, G.**

327. **Rowe, Stuart H.** Child study from a scientific point of view. Jour. of Ped., June, 1904. Vol. 16, pp. 328-335.

328. —— —— The light of schoolrooms. Longmans, Green & Co., N. Y., 1904, pp. 94.
    Appendix tells how to test the eyes of children in ways practicable in every schoolroom.

329. **Russell, E. Harlow** In how far may child psychology take the place of adult psychology or rational psychology in the training of teachers. Proc. N. E. A., 1904, pp. 571-575.

330. **Salisbury, Albert** The disparagement of memory. Jour. of Ed., Jan., 1904. Vol. 59, pp. 35-36.
    A discussion of the place of memory in the schools and its needs at the present time in school and out.

331. **Sallwürk, E. von** Ueber die Ausfüllung des Gemüts durch den erziehenden Unterricht. Samml. von Abhand. a. d. Gebiete der päd. Psy. u. Physiol., Berlin, 1904. Vol. 7, pt. 5, pp. 47.
    A criticism of the pedagogical doctrines of Herbart and Ziller.

332. **Salmon, David and Hindshaw, Winifred** Infant schools: Their history and theory. Longmans, N. Y., 1904, pp. 324.
    Part 2 treats of the beginnings of mental life, thinking and speaking, imagination, etc.

333. **Samosch, Dr.** Einige bemerkenswerte Ergebnisse von Schulkindermessungen und- Wägungen. Zeits. für Schulgesundheitspflege, No. 6, 1904. Vol. 17, pp. 389-403.
    Study of precocious and dull children.

334. **Sanborn, Bigelow T.** Care of the feeble-minded. Nat. Conf. Char. and Corr., 1904, pp. 401-407.

Santenoise See **Garnier and Santenoise.**

336. **Sayer, E.** The deterioration of vision during school life. Brit. Med. Jour., 1904. Vol. 1, pp. 1418-1420.

337. **Schanz, F.** Ueber das Sehenlernen blindgeborener und später mit Erfolg operierter Menschen. Zeits. f. Augenhlk., 1904. Vol. 12, pp. 753-762.

338. **Schaeffer, Nathan C.** Thinking and learning to think. Lippincott Co., Philadelphia, 1903, pp. 351.

339. **Schenk, A.** Gewinnung dauernder Unterrichtsergebnisse in Hilfsschulen und Erziehungsanstalten für schwachbegabte Kinder. Zeits. für d. Behandlg. Schwachs. u. Epil., 1904. Vol. 20, pp. 111-112.

340. **Scheppegrell, William** Voice, song and speech. Pop. Sci. Mo., Jan., 1904. Vol. 64, pp. 262-273.
    Author explains formation of various sounds made in speaking. He takes up the subject of defective speech and tells how this may be remedied.

341. **Schiffer, F.** Bericht über 1150 Fälle von Nervenkrankheiten im Kindesalter. Jahrb. für Kinderhlk., 1904. Vol. 60, pp. 388-406.

342. **Schmidt, F.** Experimentelle Untersuchungen über die Hausaufgaben des Schulkindes; ein Beitrag zur experimentellen Pädagogik. Arch. für d. ges. Psy., 1904. Vol. 3, pp. 33-152.

343. **Schmidt, Ferdinand A.** Unser Körper. Voigtlander, Leipzig, 1903, pp. 643.

344. **Schulze, E.** Humor in der Schule. Päd. Abhand., N. F. Vol. 10, pt. 2, pp. 17-28.

345. **Schuyten, M. C.** Comment doit-on mesurer la fatigue des écoliers? Arch. de Psy., 1904. Vol. 4, pp. 113-128.

346. —— —— (**Ed.**) Paedologisch Jaarboek; 5th year, 1904. Schleicher, Paris, 1904, pp. 263.

347. **Scudder, Doremus** Our children for Christ. F. H. Revell, New York, 1899, pp. 32.

348. **Seashore, C. E.** Experimental study of mental fatigue. Psy. Bulletin, March 15, 1904. Vol. 1, pp. 97-101.
    The article points out some errors and some lines of progress in the experimental study of fatigue.

349. **Serbsky, W.** Contribution à l'étude de la démence précoce. Ann. Méd. Psychol., 8e Sér., 1904. Vol. 19, pp. 188-203.

350. **Shearer, William J.** Children and Christmas. School Jour., Dec. 14, 1904. Vol. 69, pp. 670-671.

351. **Sheldon, Walter Lorenzo** Duties in the home and the family. W. M. Welch, Chicago, 1904, pp. 411.

352. —— —— Lessons in the study of habits, for use in school and home. W. M. Welch, Chicago, 1903, pp. 270.

353. —— —— The Old Testament Bible stories as a basis for the ethical instruction of the young. W. M. Welch, Chicago, 1902, pp. 326.

354. **Simkhovitch, Mrs. Vladimir.** Enlarged function of the public school. Nat. Conf. Char. and Corr., 1904, pp. 471-486.
    Playgrounds, baths for children, vacation schools and other outside functions of the New York City public schools.

355. **Smith, Frank Webster** The high school and the adolescent-physical relations. Jour. of Ped., Dec., 1904. Vol. 17, pp. 114-131.

356. **Smith, James L.** Experience in teaching idiomatic English [to the deaf]. Ass'n Rev., Feb., 1904. Vol. 6, pp. 18-34.

357. **Smith, Mrs. R. A.** The baby; its treatment and care. Drane, London, 1904, pp. 102.

358. **Smith, Theodate L.** Psychology of day dreams. Am. Jour. of Psy., Oct., 1904. Vol. 15, pp. 445-488.
    An inductive study of the day dreams, reveries, and fancies of children and adolescents, based upon returns from questionnaires.

359. **Smith, Theodate L.** Types of adolescent affection. Ped. Sem., June, 1904. Vol. 11, pp. 178-203.
Study of sex differences in adolescent love.

360. **Smith, W.** Why is the human ear immobile ? Pop. Sci. Mo., 1904. Vol. 55, pp. 228-237.

361. **Sommer, R.** Zur Kritik der Dementia Praecox. Beitr. z. Psychiat. Klinik, 1903. Vol. 1, pp. 182-187.

362. **Southard and Roberts** A case of chronic internal hydrocephalus in a youth. Jour. of Nerv. and Ment. Dis., 1904. Vol. 31, pp. 73-80.

363. **Spender, H. F.** The education of the Indians of Canada. Jour. African Soc., London, 1903, pp. 425-432.
Advocates the "scattered home" system in place of the "barracks schools."

364. **Speyer, R.** Die Liebe bei den Kindern. Kinderfehler, 1904. Vol. 9, pp. 21-25.

365. **Stadelmann, Heinrich** Wie kann die unterrichtliche Behandlung abnormer Kinder die Prophylaxe der Nerven-und Geisteskrankheiten unterstützen ? Zeits. für Schulgesundheitspflege, No. 7, 1904. Vol. 17, pp. 463-470.

366. **Stempel, Therese D.** Physical exercise for girls. Melrose, London., 1904, pp. 87.

367. **Stern, W.** Die Sprachentwicklung eines Kindes, insbesondere in grammatischer und logischer Hinsicht. Ber. ü. d. I. Kong. f. exper. Psy. Giessen, April, 1904, pp. 106-114. J. A. Barth, Leipzig, 1904.

368. **Stratz, C. H.** Der Körper des Kindes für Eltern, Erzieher, Aerzte u. Künstler. F. Enke, Stuttgart, 1904, pp. 250.
Describes the child to the age of full maturity, with 187 illustrations largely from the nude. Chapters on growth and proportions.

369. —— —— Die Körperformen in Kunst und Leben der Japaner. 2 Aufl., Stuttgart, Enke, 1904, pp. 196.

370. **Streeter, William B.** Admission of children to orphanages. Nat. Conf. Char. and Corr., 1904, pp. 331-335.

371. **Streib, W.** Die Augen der Schüler und Schülerinnen der Tübinger Schulen. F. Pietzcker, Tübingen, 1904, pp. 21.

372. **Stubbs, George W.** Mission of the juvenile court. Nat. Conf. Char. and Corr., 1904, pp. 350-357.
Account of the operations of the juvenile court at Indianapolis.

373. **Swift, E. J.** The acquisition of skill in type-writing; a contribution to the psychology of learning. Psychol. Bull., 1904. Vol. 1, pp. 295-305.

374. **Swoboda, H.** Die Perioden des menschlichen Organismus in ihrer psychologischen und biologischen Bedeutung. Deuticke, Wien, 1904, pp. 135.

375. **Talbot, W. T.**   Some abnormalities of boys.   Education, Jan., 1904.   Vol. 23, pp. 299-304.

376. **Tanner, Amy Eliza**   The child; his thinking, feeling, and doing.   Rand, Chicago, 1904, pp. 430.
Summarizes in simple and readable form the present condition of child study.

377. **Tawney, Guy Allan**   Period of conversion.   Psy. Rev., May, 1904.   Vol. 11, pp. 210-226.
Discussion of the value of the questionnaire method in the scientific study of religious experience.

378. **Taylor, William T.**   The color element in early education. Jour. of Ped., June, 1904.   Vol. 16, pp. 315-327.
Discussion of educative value of color with results of tests.

379. **Terman, Lewis M.**   Preliminary study of the psychology and pedagogy of leadership.   Ped. Sem., Dec., 1904.   Vol. 11, pp. 413-451.
Leadership among animals, primitive races and children, the latter based upon results obtained by a questionnaire.

380. **Tesdorph, ——**   Hysterische Geistesstörung im Kindesalter. Allg. Zeits. für Psychiat., 1903.   Vol. 60, p. 744.

381. **Thiry, J. H.**   School savings bank in the United States. School Jour., Aug. 20, 1904.   Vol. 69, p. 120.

382. **Tibbey, T. G.**   Child study and the new educational authorities.   Paidologist, April, 1904.   Vol. 6, pp. 28-33.

383. **Tokata, K.**   Ueber den Einfluss des Gemütszustandes und der Jahreszeit auf den Eintritt der ersten Menstruation.   Wien. Med. Woch., 1904.   Vol. 54, pp. 14-18.

Tomlinson, Agnes   See No. 385.

385. **Tomlinson, Ella and Tomlinson, Agnes.**   A summerful of children.   Dent, London, 1904, pp. 88.

386. **Tonzig, C.**   Ueber das Schülerfrühstück, mit besonderer Berücksichtigung der in der Stadt Padua bestehenden Einrichtungen.   Zeits. für Schulgesundheitspflege, No. 9, 1904.   Vol. 17, pp. 605-629.

387. **Treitel, Leopold**   Ueber die körperliche Entwicklung während der Schulzeit.   Zeits. für päd. Psy., June, 1904.   Vol. 6, pp. 135-140.
Mental capacity conditioned by bodily health.

388. **Trettien, A. W.**   Psychology of the language interest of children.   Ped. Sem., June, 1904.   Vol. 11, pp. 113-177.
General theories of language development; factors upon which the development of language depends and the periods of language development: (1) the primary language period; (2) the period of childhood; (3) period of adolescence; bibliography, pp. 174-177.

389. **Trüper, Johann**   Psychopathische Minderwertigkeiten als Ursache von Gesetzesverletzungen Jugendlicher.   Hermann Beyer und Söhne, Langensalza, 1904, pp. 57.   Repr. from Kinderfehler, 1904.   Vol. 9.
A valuable study of feeble-mindedness and other abnormalities as factors of juvenile crime.

390. **Tuer, Andrew W.** Stories from old-fashioned children's books. Simpkin, London, 1899-1900, pp. 439.

391. **Ufer, C.** Ueber das Spiel des Kindes. Elberfeld, 1904, pp. 11.

392. **Urbantschitsch, Victor** Value of methodical exercises in hearing. Ass'n Rev., Feb., 1904. Vol. 6, pp. 48-52.

393. **Urwick, E. J. ed.** Studies of boy life in our cities, written by various authors for the Toynbee trust. Dent, London, 1904, pp. 320.

394. **Van Liew, Charles C.** What is the net gain to education of recent investigations in physiological psychology? Proc. N. E. A., 1904, pp. 576-583.

395. **Veraguth, O.** Kultur und Nervensystem. Schulthess & Co., Zürich, 1904, pp. 42.

396. **Viali, F.** L'enseignement moral à l'école primaire. Challamel, Paris, 1898, pp. 272.

397. **Wachsmuth, H.** Beiträge zur cerebralen Kinderlähmung. Arch. für Psychiat. u. Nervenkr., 1904. Vol. 38, pp. 713-739.

398. **Waddle, Charles W.** Animal tendencies and the juvenile court. Proc. N. E. A., 1904, pp. 797-799.

399. **Warner, F.** Training of the feeble-minded. Lancet, 1904. Vol. 1, pp. 864-865.

400. **Webb, Sidney** London education. Longmans, London, 1904, pp. 219.

401. **Wendt, —** Psychologische Kindergarten-pädagogik. B. G. Teubner, Leipzig, 1904, pp. 142.
Describes senses, nerves, morals, habits, feelings, etc., of young children and gives methods for the training of each.

402. **Wendt, F. M.** Zur Psychologie der Eltern- und Kindesliebe. Kinderfehler, 1904. Vol. 10, pp. 1-9.

403. **Weygandt, W.** Epileptische Schulkinder. Psychiat. Wochensch., 1904. Vol. 6, pp. 253-256; 263-265; 271-273.

404. —— —— Ueber alte Dementia Praecox. Allg. Zeits. für Psychiat., 1904. Vol. 61, p. 884.

405. —— —— Ueber atypische juvenile Paralyse. Sitzber. d. Phys. Med. Ges. Würzburg, 1904, pp. 32-44.

406. **Wichmann, Ralf** Zur Statistik der Nervosität bei Lehrern. Zeits. für Schulgesundheitspflege, May, August and October, 1904. Vol. 17, pp. 304-318; 543-554; 713-718.
A preliminary study of the nervousness of teachers.

408. **Widowitz, J.** Ueber die geistige Ermüdung der Schulkinder. Wien. klin. Woch., 1904. Vol. 17, pp. 277-280; 306-308.

409. **Wildermuth, —** Schule und Nervenkrankheiten. Wien. klin. Woch., 1904. Vol. 17, pp. 727-730.

410. **Wilk, E.** Das Werden der Zahlen and des Rechnens im Menschen and in der Menschheit auf Grund von Psychologie u. Geschichte. Part 1. Jahrbuch des Vereins für wissens. Päd., 1903. Vol. 35, pp. 194-254.

411. **Williams, Alida S.** Elementary course of study in city schools. Jour. of Ped., June, 1904. Vol. 16, pp. 298-314.

412. **Williams, L. Wynn** Education disciplinary, cure and moral. Simpkin, London, 1904, pp. 192.
Essentially a plea against corporal punishment.

413. **Williams, Mabel Clare** Laboratory tests as a means of child study. Proc. N. E. A., 1904, pp. 770-776.

414. **Wilson, Louis N.** Bibliography of Child Study for the year 1903. Ped. Sem., Sept., 1904. Vol. 11, pp. 292-327.
A select bibliography of 486 books and articles relating to the study of children.

415. **Winch, W. H.** Immediate memory in school children. Brit. Jour. of Psy., 1904. Vol. 1, pp. 127-134.

416. **Winchester, Myra H.** Comparison of methods and results in child study. Proc. N. E. A., 1904, pp. 791-792.

417. **Wizel, A.** Ein Fall von phänomenalem Rechentalent bei einem Imbecillen. Arch. für Psychiat. and Nervenkr, 1904. Vol. 38, pp. 122-155.

418. **Wood, Alice** Co-education up to the age of twelve. Child Life, Oct., 1904. Vol. 6, pp. 181-184.

419. **Wroe, Margaret, A.** Sex in education. Child Life, April, 1904. Vol. 6, pp. 74-78.

420. **Wylie, A. R. T.** Contribution to the study of the feeble-minded in height and weight. Faribault, Minn., pp. 7.
Rapid growth followed by delay or rest seems typical for the feeble-minded.

421. **Yorke, M. A.** Mrs. Humphry Ward's vacation school. Child Life, Oct., 1904. Vol. 6, pp. 201-202.

422. **Young, Sarah.** Children's saving and spending. Paidologist, April, 1904. Vol. 6, pp. 6-17.
Study of the money sense and economic notions of children.

423. —— —— An investigation circle. Paidologist, April, 1904. Vol. 6, pp. 33-35.
The method of procedure in conducting a child-study class.

424. **Ziehen, Theodore** Die Geisteskrankheiten des Kindesalters mit besonderer Berücksichtigung des schulpflichtigen Alters. Samml. von Abhand, d. Gebiete der päd. Psy. u. Physiol., Berlin, 1904. Vol. 7, pt. 1, pp. 94.
The author describes the forms of insanity peculiar to adolescence. He takes up mania, melancholia, stupidity, hallucinations and delusions, night terrors, epilepsy, delirium, hysteria, and children's diseases associated with mental derangement.

425. Kind und Kunst. Monatsschrift für die pflege der Kunst im leben des Kindes Alex. Koch, Darmstadt.

Attractive, practical and helpful to elementary teachers. Devoted to the fostering of art in the child's life. The perspective is broad, including myth, poetry, and music on the one hand; practical school work in art and manual training on the other. Issued monthly. Begun in Oct., 1904.

426. Nocturnal emissions. Am. Jour. of Psy., Jan., 1904. Vol. 15, pp. 104-107.

Valuable individual study in the sexual hygiene of an adolescent.

427. Report of the Chicago Vacation School Committee of Women's clubs, Chicago, Ill., 1904, pp. 48.

428. The Seguin physiological school for the training of children of arrested mental development. Rept. Comm'r of Educ., 1902, pp. 2188-2190.

429. The Wide World. Ginn & Co., Boston, 1902, pp. 122.

Sketches of child life in foreign lands.

SUBJECT INDEX.

Abnormal, 101, 225.
Abnormal Children, 152.
Abnormalities, 375, 389.
Acting, 104.
Activities, 108, 170, 182.
Adenoid Growth, 281.
Adolescence, 168, 268, 355, 359, 424.
Adolescent Races, 168.
Æsophagus, 227.
Æsthesiometer, 2.
Age, 37.
Alcohol, 40, 136.
America, 17, 191.
Anthropology, 165, 168, 209.
Anthropometry, 8, 368.
Aphasia, 22, 109.
Arithmetic, 294.
Arithmetical Prodigy, 417.
Art, 241, 425.
Association, 39.
Attention, 280.
Atypical Children, 158.
Autobiographical, 94, 215, 282, 302.
Auxiliary Schools, 138, 163, 221.

Baby, 357.
Backward Children, 62, 69, 72, 98,
    100, 128, 158, 233, 239, 333.
Baths, 354.
Bible, 353.
Bible School, 183.
Bibliography, 6, 38, 41, 51, 63, 64, 81,
    85, 222, 228, 235, 244, 272, 388, 414.
Biological, 374.
Blind, 60, 154, 186, 215, 337.
Blood-vessels, 252.
Boarding-schools, 286.
Body, 149.
Books, 27, 92.

Boy-life in Cities, 393.
Boys, 287, 375.
Brain, 123, 197, 252, 312.
Brain-weight, 255.
Breakfast, 386.
British Genius, 119.

Cat, 172.
Cerebral, 397.
Cerebral Development, 197, 312.
Cerebral Diplegia, 212.
Cerebral Paralysis, 226.
Character, 174, 225.
Cheating, 19.
Chicago, 152.
Child, 36, 120, 147, 148, 301, 350, 376.
Child Labor, 1, 216.
Child-life, 282.
Child-life in Foreign Lands, 429.
Child Psychology, 222, 329.
Child Study, 6, 17, 38, 41, 42, 55, 63,
    64, 67, 164, 169, 171, 180, 187, 224,
    244, 273, 295, 327, 382, 413, 414,
    416, 423.
Childhood, 15, 277.
Children's Books, 390.
China, 201.
Christmas, 350.
Circulatory System, 314.
Co-education, 10, 189, 195, 240, 418.
College Education, 16.
Color-sense, 243, 378.
Colorado, 102.
Comparative Psychology, 78.
Compulsory Education, 88.
Conversion, 168, 377.
Corporal Punishment, 220, 412.
Counting, 231.
Counting-out Rhymes, 269.

Course of Study, 411.
Cramps, 198, 199.
Craniometry, 304.
Crime, 28, 58, 88, 102, 124, 168, 188, 322, 372, 389.
Criminal, 50.
Cripples, 146.
Culture, 395.
Curriculum, 54, 192, 248.

Day Dreams, 358.
Deaf, 46, 93, 129, 154, 200, 246, 356.
Deaf Mutes, 14.
Defectives, 20, 45, 60, 62, 69, 72, 84, 85, 93, 127, 128, 146, 152, 154, 173, 200, 214, 228, 337, 339, 365, 403, 405, 428.
Deformed Children, 146.
Delinquents, 74, 398.
Delusions, 424.
Dementia Praecox, 32, 49, 103, 254, 290, 303, 316, 324, 325, 349, 361, 404.
Dependent Children, 125, 208, 223.
Desks, 278.
Development, 121, 229.
Discipline, 265.
Diseases, 27, 87, 168, 184, 190, 238, 245.
Disinfection, 27.
Disposition, 141.
Domestic Animals, 172.
Drama, 104, 246.
Drawing, 18, 298.
Dwarfism, 144.

Ear, 360.
Education, 51, 79, 80, 97, 168, 191, 363, 400.
Elementary Schools, 18, 76.
Emotions, 168, 359.
England, 266, 324.
English, 356.
Entertainments, 275.
Environment, 91.
Epilepsy, 78, 403, 424.

Epileptics, 30.
Ethics, 353.
Ethnological, 68.
Europe, 69.
Evidence, 47.
Examinations, 112, 280, 288, 314.
Excitation, 123.
Experimental, 39.
Experimental Didactics, 232.
Experimentation, 5, 7.
Eye, 175, 371.
Eyesight, 45, 75, 83, 145, 151, 153, 173, 176, 323, 328, 336, 371.

Family, 208, 351.
Fatigue, 2, 26, 249, 280, 345, 348.
Feeble-minded, 20, 31, 35, 84, 127, 145, 228, 275, 278, 334, 365, 389, 399, 420, 424.
Folk Lore, 274.
Food, 25, 386.
France, 41.

Games, 114, 142.
General, 256.
Genius, 96, 111, 119.
Geography, 107.
Germany, 155, 300.
Girls, 168, 276, 366.
Graphology, 37.
Growth, 149, 168, 387, 420.
Guardianship, 137.

Habits, 352.
Hallucinations, 424.
Handwork, 180.
Health, 167, 245, 387.
Hearing, 45, 75, 129, 173, 178, 257, 392.
Heart, 134.
Herbart, 331.
Herder, 230.
Heredity, 23, 193.
High School, 43, 355.
"Higher" and "Lower" Races, 53.
Higher Education, 300.

Historical, 79, 80, 132, 210, 305.
Holiday-"settlements," 9.
Holidays, 427.
Holland, 281.
Home, 74, 147, 213, 351, 352.
Home Lessons, 260.
Home Study, 342.
Hospital School, 61.
Humor, 217, 344.
Hungary, 315.
Hydrocephalus, 362.
Hygiene, 13, 14, 27, 31, 56, 57, 59, 83, 87, 122, 130, 153, 167, 184, 185, 221, 281, 296.
Hysteria, 22, 140, 380.

Ideas, 156.
Idiocy, 177, 226.
Idiots, 31.
Illusion, 77.
Imagery, 358.
Imagination, 318.
Imbecility, 228, 417.
Indian, 174, 235, 274, 363.
Indiana, 88.
Indianapolis, 322.
Individual, 256, 264, 301.
Individuality, 160.
Industries, 108, 170, 182.
Infancy, 95, 357.
Infant Schools, 164, 332.
Infants, 21.
Initiations, 168.
Insanity, 424.
Instincts, 168.
Intelligence, 37.
Interest, 54.
Internal Speech, 237.
Italy, 63.

Japan, 179, 369.
Journals, 346.
Juvenile Courts, 102, 188, 322, 372, 398.
Juvenile Crime, 28.

Juvenile Delinquents, 58, 124, 208, 276, 286.
Juvenile Occupations, 1.

Kindergarten, 57, 181, 265, 295.

Language, 65, 76, 85, 86, 98, 116, 206, 284, 388.
Language-teaching, 29, 356.
Law, 216.
Leadership, 379.
Learning, 261.
Learning Process, 12.
Lessons, 260.
Lighting, 159, 313, 328.
Literature, 36, 148.
London, 305, 400.
Love, 168, 359, 364.
Love of Children, 267.

Mania, 424.
Manual Training, 60, 71.
Maternal Impressions, 310.
Measurements, 333.
Medical Inspection, 138.
Medical Supervision, 13.
Melancholia, 424.
Memory, 33, 34, 113, 115, 270, 285, 330, 415.
Memory Types, 242.
Menstruation, 39, 383.
Mental Ability, 248, 299.
Mental Activity, 293.
Mental Development, 157, 230, 279, 338, 428.
Mental Evolution, 65, 95, 116, 131, 236, 312, 376.
Mental Fatigue, 348, 408.
Methods, 67, 273, 295, 416, 423.
Methods of Teaching, 55.
Microcephaly, 212.
Mobs, 319.
Modern Language, 117.
Money-sense, 422.
"Mongolian Spot," 235.
Moods, 383.

Moral Instruction, 124, 396.
Moral Training, 201.
Morals, 81, 150, 167, 205, 234.
Morbidity, 4.
Motherhood, 204.
Mothers, 11, 15.
Motor, 109.
Motor Ability, 168, 373.
Mouth, 59.
Municipal, 1, 87.
Muscle, 135.
Music, 288, 309, 340.
Myopia, 126.

Nature Study, 161, 211.
Navel Cord, 274.
Neglected Children, 137.
Negroes, 28, 51. .
Nervous Defectives, 341.
Nervous System, 395.
Nervousness, 48, 61, 89, 234, 291, 365, 406, 409.
Neuroses, 307.
New York (state), 132.
Newborn, 21.
Normal Schools, 55, 56.
Number Concept, 410.

One-class Schools, 202.
Orphans, 370.
Overberg System, 156.
Overpressure, 280.

Padua, 386.
Paralysis, 24, 405.
Paranoia, 32.
Parental Love, 402.
Parents, 11, 402.
Pathology, 168, 239, 307.
Perception, 272, 285.
Periodicity, 168, 374.
Pets, 172, 181.
Physical Anthropology, 369.
Physical Development, 149, 368, 387.
Physical Exercise, 366.

Physical Training, 162, 179, 279, 293, 297, 343.
Physiological Psychology, 394.
Physiology, 168.
Physique, 250.
Pictures of Children, 385.
Play, 60, 269, 294, 297, 308, 391.
Playgrounds, 354.
Playthings, 142, 194.
Precocity, 111, 333.
Pregnancy, 204.
Printed Books, 323.
Probation System, 322.
Problems, 171.
Psychological, 7, 105, 112, 117, 121, 186, 319, 358, 379.
Psychology, 168, 311, 394, 402.
Psychoses, 207.
Puberty, 90.
Pubescence, 90.
Public Health, 296.
Public Schools, 132, 233, 266, 354.
Pupil (eye), 21.

Questionnaire Method, 67.

Race, 28, 51, 53, 71, 174.
Rachitis, 144.
Reading, 92, 259, 288, 390.
Recognition, 113.
Reform, 253.
Religion, 81, 168, 183.
Religious Instruction, 124.
Religious Psychology, 377.
Religious Training, 205, 347, 353.
Reverie, 358.
Right and Left, 151.
Russia, 64.

Savages, 320.
School Books, 210.
School Buildings, 241.
School for Defectives, 427.
School Furniture, 278.
School Hygiene, 121, 155, 192, 315.
School Hygiene Congress, 139.

School Savings Banks, 381.
School System, 70.
Schoolrooms, 91.
Schools, 190, 213, 263, 409.
Science, 44, 311, 327.
Scotland, 79.
Seasons, 383.
Secondary Schools, 10, 283.
Selection, 23.
Selection in Man, 209.
Seminal Emissions, 426.
Senses, 75, 168, 401.
Sex, 10, 37, 90, 118, 133, 168, 189, 236,
    240, 247, 267, 276, 287, 366, 375,
    418, 419.
Sex-knowledge, 82.
Sexual Hygiene, 133, 168, 292, 426.
Sexual Pathology, 168.
Skin-diseases, 238.
Social Consciousness, 271.
Social Psychology, 319.
Social Training, 106.
Sociology, 168.
Speech, 3, 29, 46, 65, 73, 85, 206, 257,
    284, 289, 340, 367, 388.
Speech-defects, 98, 258.
Stage, 104.
Stammering, 73, 258.
State, 208, 223, 281.
State School, 203.
Statistics, 4, 299.
Stories, 110, 219.
Story-telling, 110, 219.
Street Boys, 114.
Student Honor, 19.
Stupidity, 424.
Stuttering, 85, 258.
Sub-conscious, 91.

Sunday School, 183, 205.

Teachers, 20, 42, 120, 154, 169, 234,
    329, 406.
Teaching, 117.
Technique, 261.
Teeth, 59, 130.
Temperament, 174.
Testimony, 47.
Tests, 176, 413.
Therapeutics, 122.
Thought, 289.
Time Sense, 247.
Toys, 142, 194.
Truants, 251.

United States, 69.

Vacation-Colonies, 166.
Vacation Schools, 354, 421, 427.
Vacation Trips, 9.
Variation, 141.
Vision, 320.
Visual Centres, 175.
Voice, 168, 340.

Wage-earners, 97.
Wayward Children, 74.
Weight, 333.
Whites, 71.
Women, 168.
Wordsworth, 282.
Work, 35, 58.
Working Class, 250.

Ziller, 331.
Zoölogy, 224.

PUBLICATIONS

OF THE

CLARK UNIVERSITY LIBRARY

WORCESTER, MASS.

EDITED BY LOUIS N. WILSON, LITT. D., LIBRARIAN

| VOL. 2. | October, 1906. | No. 2. |

Bibliography of Child Study for the Year 1905

Clark University Press

WORCESTER, MASS.

BIBLIOGRAPHY OF CHILD STUDY

For the Year 1905

By LOUIS N. WILSON, Librarian, Clark University

1. **Adams, Myron E.** Children in American street trades. Ann. Am. Acad. Pol. and Soc. Sci., 1905. Vol. 25, pp. 437-458.

2. **Addams, Jane** Child labor. Journal of Education, March 16, 1905. Vol. 61, p. 289.

3. —— —— Child labor legislation, a requisite for industrial efficiency. Ann. Am. Acad. Pol. and Soc. Sci., 1905. Vol. 25, pp. 542-550.

4. **Adkins, Frank J.** Intellectual opportunities of manual instruction. Jour. of Ed. (Lond.), 1905. N. S.,Vol. 27, pp. 128-129.

5. **Adler, Felix** Child labor in the United States and its great attendant evils. Ann. Am. Acad. Pol. and Soc. Sci., 1905. Vol. 25, pp. 417-429.

6. **Anderson, Neal L.** Child labor legislation in the South. Ann. Am. Acad. Pol. and Soc. Sci., 1905. Vol 25, pp. 491-507.

7. **Andrews, Benjamin Richard** Auditory tests. Am. Jour. of Psy., July, 1905. Vol. 16, pp. 302-326.
   Extensive material on tests of general hearing, tests of musical capacity, and diagnostic tests.

8. **Arnett, L. D.** Counting and adding. Am. Jour. of Psy., July 1905. Vol. 16, pp. 327-336.
   Treats fundamentals of arithmetic, best methods of teaching them.

9. **Arnold, E. H.** The importance of the school yard for the physical well-being of school children. Proc. N. E. A., 1905, pp. 756-760.

10. **Baernreither, J. M.** Jugendfürsorge und Strafrecht in den Vereinigten Staaten von Amerika. Duncker und Humbolt, Leipzig, 1905. pp. 304.

11. **Ballowitz, E.** Ueber hyperdaktyle Familien und die Vererbung der Vielfingerigkeit des Menschen. Archiv f. Rassen-u. Gesellsch.–Biol. 1904. Vol, 1. pp. 347-365.

12. **Barrie, James Matthew** Tommy and Grizel. C. Scribner's Sons, N. Y., 1900, pp. 509.

13. **Baumann, Friedrich** Sprachpsychologie und Sprachunterricht. M. Niemeyer, Halle, 1905, pp. 142.

14. **Baumann, Julius** Wille und Charakter; eine Erziehungslehre auf moderner Grundlage. 2d ed. Reuther & Reichard, Berlin, 1905, pp. 98.

15. **Bergström, John Andrew** American school hygiene literature for the year 1904. Int. Archiv f. Schulhygiene. 1905. Vol. I (Literature section), pp. 25-34.

16. **Binet, Alfred** A propos de la mesure de l'intelligence. L'Année Psychol., 1905. Vol. II, pp. 69-82.
Determination and classification by teacher of the most intelligent.

17. —— —— Recherches sur la fatigue intellectuelle scolaire et la mesure qui peut en être faite au moyen de l'esthésiomètre. L'Année Psychol., 1905. Vol. II, pp. 1-37.
Gives nature of tests made after different studies, position of subject and results gained. Relation between tactile sensibility and intellectual fatigue. Proof that intellectual fatigue can be measured.

18. **Binet, Alfred** and **Simon, Th.** Application des méthodes nouvelles au diagnostic du niveau intellectuel chez des enfants normaux et anormaux d'hospice et d'école primaire. L'Année Psychol., 1905. Vol. II, pp. 245-336.
Grades of intelligence. Various classes of children and choice of those to be examined. Results of investigations. Tables of questions and answers.

19. —— —— Enquête sur le mode d'existence des sujets sortis d'une école d'arriérées. L'Année Psychol., 1905. Vol. II, pp. 137-145.
Advantage of backward children attending special schools; number following professions; and number returning home.

20. —— —— Méthodes nouvelles pour le diagnostic du niveau intellectuel des anormaux. L'Année Psychol., 1905. Vol. II, pp. 191-244.
Stages of inferiority. Distinctions necessary. Methods employed. Knowledge of objects and powers of comparison. Normal versus abnormal children. Physical conditions.

21. —— —— Sur la nécessité d'établir un diagnostic scientifique des états inférieurs de l'intelligence. L'Année Psychol., 1905. Vol. II, pp. 163-190.
Education of abnormal children. Advantage of special schools. Methods of determining whether children are abnormal. Series of questions given to show the extent of their ideas.

22. **Birney, Mrs. Alice McLellan** Childhood. F. A. Stokes Co., N. Y., 1905. pp. 254.

23. **Black, Clementina** Mental underwork of children. School Jour., Sept. 9, 1905. Vol. 72, p. 249.

24. **Boas, Franz** and **Wissler, Clark** Statistics of growth. Gov't Print., Wash., 1905. pp. 108. Preprinted from Rep. U. S. Comm. Ed. 1904, Vol. I, pp. 25-132.
A valuable monograph treating the anthropometric data obtained in the Schools of Worcester, Mass., 1891-1892.

25. **Boggs, Lucinda Pearl** How children learn to read; an experimental study. Ped. Sem., Dec., 1905. Vol. 12, pp. 496-502.

Boncour, G. P. See **Phillipe, Jean and Boncour, G. P.**

26. **Book, William F.** The high school teacher from the pupil's point of view. Ped. Sem., Sept., 1905. Vol. 12, pp. 239-288.

27. **Boone, Grace Rossman** The use of myths with children. Education, Jan., 1905. Vol. 25, pp. 303-310.

28. **Boyd, William** Ideational memory. Paidologist, Feb., 1905. Vol. 7, pp. 28-33.
Story told to see what points were remembered.

29. **Boyer, J.** De l'audition chez les anormaux. Bull. de la Soc. Libre, June, 1905. Vol. 5, pp. 667-676.

30. **Boyer, Louis.** L'Apprentissage comparé de la lecture et de l'écriture chez les enfants mentalement anormaux. Bull. de la Soc. Libre, Jan., 1905. Vol. 5, pp. 560-562.

31. **Boyle, A. Helen** Some points in the early treatment of mental and nervous cases; with special reference to the poor. Jour. of Mental Sci., 1905. Vol. 51, pp. 676-681.

32. **Bryant, Sara Cone** How to tell stories to children. Houghton, Mifflin & Co., Boston, 1905, pp. 260.

33. **Burn, John Henry** Children's answers; shrewd, witty, non-sensical and pathetic. A. Treherne & Co., London, 1905, pp. 267.

34. **Burnham, William H.** Education from the genetic point of view. Proc. N. E. A., 1905, pp. 727-732.

35. —— —— The hygiene of home study. Ped. Sem., June, 1905. Vol. 12, pp. 213-230.

36. **Butler, Amos W.** Importance of knowing complete history of feeble-minded individuals. Nat. Conf. Char. and Corr., 1905, pp. 525-526.

37. **Campbell, Charles Moss** Skin diseases of childhood, including advice on the care of the hair; ed. by Mrs. A. S. Ballin. Office of "Baby," the Mother's Magazine, London, 18—, pp. 60.

38. **Chamberlain, Alexander F.** Primitive hearing and hearing words. Am. Jour. of Psy., Jan., 1905. Vol. 16, pp. 119-130.

39. **Chamberlain, Alexander F. and Isabel C.** Studies of a child. III. Ped. Sem., Dec., 1905. Vol. 12, pp. 427-453.

40. **Chase, John H.** Street games of New York City. Ped. Sem., Dec., 1905. Vol. 12, pp. 503-504.

41. **Chubb, Percival** The value and place of fairy stories in the education of children. Proc. N. E. A., 1905, pp. 871-879.
The value of the fairy story to the child in asserting his spiritual lordship, developing passion for perfection, giving poetic truths and in cultivating emotional and imaginative powers.

42. **Ciaudo, Louis** Recherches sur les diamètres céphaliques de l'enfant dans les six premiers mois de la vie. H. Jouve, Paris, 1904, pp. 120.

43. **Claparède, Ed.** Psychologie de l'enfant et pédagogie expérimentale. H. Kundig. Genève, 1905, pp. 76.

44. **Clapp, Henry Lincoln** Unrecognized causes of corporal punishment. Education, Apr., 1905. Vol. 25, pp. 490-500.

44a. **Coelho, F. A.** Exercicios corporals e desenvolvimento moral.
As doutrinas. Boletim da Direc. Ger. da Instruc. Publ., Lisboa,
Anno 4, 1905, pp. 369-440.
The first section (on history of physical education) of a valuable and com-
prehensive monograph on "Bodily exercises and moral development."

45. **Cohn, M.** Schulschluss und Morbidität an Masern, Scharlach
und Diptherie, Zeits. f. Schulgesundheitspflege, 1905. Vol.
18, pp. 63-73.

46. **Combes, L.** Sur le langage des enfants. Bull. de la Soc.
Libre, Jan., 1905. Vol. 5, pp. 571-577.

47. **Cooper, Edward Herbert** The twentieth century child. J.
Lane, London, 1905, pp. 311.

48. **Danger, O.** Ein musikalischer Gehörkranker. Kinderfehler,
1905. Vol. 10, pp. 137-142.

49. **Davies, Edgar T.** Necessity for further preventive and pro-
tective child labor legislation. Nat. Conf. Char. and Corr., 1905,
pp. 143-148.

50. **Dawson, George E.** Levels of development in relation to
education. Jour. of Ped., Sept., 1905. Vol. 18, pp. 9-24.
A discussion of the biological view of the mind and the four levels of development.

51. **Dawson, Wm. J. G.** Care of feeble-minded as a preventive
of crime. Nat. Conf. Char. and Corr., 1905, pp. 529-530.

52. **DuBois, Patterson** Fireside child-study. Dodd, Mead &
Co., N. Y., 1903, pp. 159.
A plea for the universal study of children to get their point of view.
Written to stimulate intelligent observation on the part of parents.

53. **Erickson, Halford** Child labor legislation and methods of
enforcement in northern central states. Ann. Am. Acad. Pol.
& Soc. Sci., 1905. Vol. 25, pp. 467-479.

54. **Farabee, W. C.** Inheritance of digital malformations in
man. Papers Peab. Mus. Amer. Arch. and Ethn., Cambr.,
Mass., 1905. Vol. 3, pp. 69-77.
Treats of digital malformations observed in Pennsylvania.

55. **Field, W. Stanwood** The uses of recess time. Jour. of Ed.,
May 25, 1905. Vol. 61, pp. 567-568; June 8, 1905, pp. 623-624.

56. **Findlay, M. E.** Education of girls. Paidologist, July, 1905.
Vol. 7, pp. 83-93.
Contains practical suggestions based on experience.

57. **Fitz, Rachel Kent and Fitz, G. W.** Problems of babyhood ; building a constitution, forming a character. H. Holt
& Co., N. Y., 1906, pp. 127.

58. **Fleury, Maurice de** Nos enfants au collège ; le corps et l'âme de l'enfant. A. Colin, Paris, 1905, pp. 315.
A study of the child at school including hygiene and psychology.

59. **Foerster, Fr. W.** Jugendlehre ; ein Buch für Eltern, Lehrer und Geistliche. G. Reimer, Berlin, 1905, pp. 724.
A book of moral instruction on various topics including instruction in sex problems.

60. **Fox, Hugh F.** The operation of the new child labor law in New Jersey. Ann. Am. Acad. Pol. & Soc. Sci., 1905. Vol. 25, pp. 522-541.

61. **Frenzel, Franz** Die Hilfsschulen für schwachbegabte Kinder in ihrer Entwicklung, Bedeutung, und Organisation. L. Voss, Hamburg, 1903, pp. 88.

62. **Fumagalli, G.** Il senso della vita nell' educazione dell' infanzia. Rivista di Psicologia, July-Aug., 1905. Vol. 1, pp. 279-284.
The sense of life in the education of young children.

63. **Galton, Francis** Entwürfe zu einer Fortpflanzungs-Hygiene. Archiv f. Rassen-u. Gesellsch.-Biol., 1905. Vol. 2, pp. 812-829.
This is a translation of parts of No. 64.

64. —— —— Eugenics. Sociological Papers (Sociological Society, London, Eng.). Vol. 2, pp. 1-53. I. Restrictions in marriage. II. Studies in National Eugenics. III. Eugenics as a Factor in Religion.

65. **Geddes, Patrick** Adolescence. Paidologist. Feb., 1905. Vol. 7, pp. 33-41.
Review of President Hall's book.

66. **Gerhard, E. Schultz** The child's moral nature and its development. Am. Ed., Dec., 1905. Vol. 9, pp. 209-211.

67. **Gheorgov, I. A.** Die ersten Anfänge des sprachlichen Ausdrucks für das Selbstbewusstsein bei Kindern. Arch. f. d. Ges. Psy., 1905. Vol. 5, pp. 329-404.

68. **Giddings, Franklin H.** The social and legal aspect of compulsory education and child labor. Jour. of Ed., July 13, 1905. Vol. 62, pp. 107-108.

69. **Gounod, H. A.** The native language and native education. Jour. of the African Soc., Oct., 1905, pp. 1-14.

70. **Granger, Mrs. A. O.** The work of the general federation of women's clubs against child labor. Ann. Am. Acad. Pol. & Soc. Sci., 1905. Vol. 25, pp. 516-521.

71. **Griggs, Edward Howard** Principles of government in home and school. School Jour., Nov. 11, 1905. Vol. 71, pp. 491-492.

72. —— —— Work and play in education. Kindergarten Rev., Oct., 1905. Vol. 16, pp. 78-84.

73. **Grober, J.** Die Bedeutung der Ahnentafel für die biologische Erblichkeitsforschung. Archiv. f. Rassen-u. Gesellsch.-Biol., 1904. Vol. 1, pp. 664-681.

74. **Grudzinska, Anna** Child study in Poland. Ped. Sem., March, 1905. Vol. 12, pp. 97-98.

75. **Grünewald, Hermann** Die Grausamkeit der Kinder. Kinderfehler, 1905. Vol. 10, pp. 199-209.
Cruelty toward animals, and cultivation of kindness.

76. **Guillet, Cephas** The study of locality. Pop. Sci. Mo., Dec., 1905. Vol. 67, pp. 728-735.
What the author did with a class in the study of topography, physiography, and geology. Based on out-of-door work in their home vicinity in Ottawa, Canada.

77. **Gunckel, John E.** Boyville; a history of fifteen years' work among newsboys. Toledo Newsboys' Assoc., Toledo, 1905, pp. 219.

78. **Gutzmann, Hermann A. K.** Die Gesundheitspflege der Sprache, mit Einschluss der Behandlung von Sprachstörungen in den Schulen. F. Hirt, Breslau, 1895, pp. 152.

79. **Hadley, Arthur T.** Mental types in our schools. School Journal, July 1, 1905. Vol. 71, pp. 10-11.
Tells how the teacher must adapt her teachings to the different ambitions of children.

80. **Haines, Alice Calhoun** Japanese child life. Illus. by Alice Mar. F. A. Stokes Co., N. Y., 1905, v. p.

81. **Hales, F. N.** Materials for the psychogenetic theory of comparison. British Jour. of Psy., 1905. Vol. 1, pp. 205-239.
Treats of the comparison in the gesture-language of deaf-mutes and primitive peoples.

82. **Hall, G. Stanley** Adolescence; the need of a new field of medical practice. Mo. Cyclop. of Med. Practice, June, 1905. Vol. 8, pp. 241-243.

83. —— —— Child study in the university and college. Jour. of Ed. (Boston), July 20, 1905. Vol. 12, pp. 136-137.

84. —— —— New ideals of motherhood suggested by child study. Address at National Congress of Mothers, Washington, D. C., March 10, 1905. Report of Nat. Cong. of Mothers, Wash., D. C., 1905, pp. 14-27.

85. —— —— What children do read and what they ought to read. Proc. N. E. A., 1905, pp. 868-871. Also in Jour. of Ped., Sept., 1905. Vol. 18, pp. 46-51, and Public Libraries, Oct., 1905. Vol. 12, pp. 391-393.

86. **Halleck, Reuben Post** Why so many first year pupils leave the high school? How can they be induced to remain? Proc. N. E. A., 1905, pp. 436-443.
This article urges the need of altruism in the teacher of first year pupils of high schools.

87. **Hancock, John A.** Work and play. Education, Jan., 1905. Vol. 25, pp. 257-268.
The subject of growth is also discussed. Play is basis of work.

88. **Haney, James Parton** Manual training in the elementary schools. Education, May, 1905. Vol. 25, pp. 515-524. Also in Proc. N. E. A., 1905, pp. 253-259.
Its value in motor development and self expression.

89. **Hart, Hastings H.** The juvenile reformatory of the twentieth century. Nat. Conf. Char. and Corr., 1905, pp. 101-120.
From view point of creating and establishing right character in delinquents. Discusses educational methods, religious, intellectual and industrial training, equipment of institutions, agents and after care.

90. **Harvey, Lorenzo D.** Manual training in grades. Proc. N. E. A., 1905, pp. 121-134. Also in Jour. of Ed., July 13, 1905. Vol. 62, p. 107.
Concerning motor activities in relation to intellectual development.

91. **Heger, Alfred** Die Verkümmerung der Brustdrüse und die Stillungsnot. Archiv. f. Rassen.-u. Gesellsch.-Biol. 1905. Vol. 2. pp. 830-844.

92. **Heller, Harriet H.** Social life of the adolescent. Education, June, 1905. Vol. 25, pp. 579-589.

93. **Heller, Theodore** Ueberbürdungspsychosen bei minderwertigen Kindern. Zeits. f. Schulgesundheitspflege, 1905. Vol. 18, pp. 649-657.

94. **Henprich, K.** Zur modernen Kinderforschung. Part 2. Jahr. des Vereins für wissens. Päd., 1905. Vol. 27, pp. 56-82. (Continued from Vol. 26.)

95. **Hermann, ——** Zur Psychologie des kranken Kindes. Kinderfebler, 1905. Vol. 10, pp. 145-156.
Symptoms and treatment of child. Value in child study.

96. **Hierta-Retzius, Anna** Hirnentwicklung und Erziehung, zur Frage der Arbeitshygiene in der Schule. Stockholm, 1904, pp. 12.

97. **Hirsch, Emil G.** Child labor from the employer's point of view. Ann. Am. Acad. Pol. and Soc. Sci., 1905. Vol. 25, pp. 551-557.

98. **Hirt, Eduard** Typen nervös veranlagter Kinder und Aufgaben, Aussichten und Mittel ihrer Erziehung. Archiv. f. Rassen-u. Gesellsch.-Biol. 1904. Vol. 1. pp. 529-549.

99. **Holman, Henry** Some ways in which child study can give help and guidance to teachers. Paidologist, July, 1905. Vol. 7, pp. 73-83.

100. **Holmes, E. E.** Responsibility; an address to girls. Longmans, Green & Co., London, 1905, pp. 32.

101. **Houghton, Mrs. Louise Seymour** Telling Bible stories. C. Scribner's Sons, N. Y., 1905, pp. 286.

102.   **Hughes, Ada Marean** How does the routine of the kindergarten develop the child physically? Proc. N. E. A., 1905, pp. 347-350.
How the kindergarten develops definite action, control and co-ordination of muscles in songs, games, marching and table occupations.

103.   **Hutchinson, Woods** Dependence of brain on healthy body. Nat. Conf. Char. and Corr., 1905, pp. 427-428.

104.   **Ives, Ella Gilbert** The peculiar child.   Jour. of Ed., October 26, 1905. Vol. 62, pp. 463-464.

105.   **Jacobs, Bertha W.** Border line defectives; need of special treatment. Nat. Conf. Char. and Corr., 1905, pp. 532-533.

106.   **Janet, Pierre** Mental pathology.   Psy. Rev., March, May, 1905. Vol. 12, pp. 98-117.
Discusses fatigue, sleep, emotions, hysteria, obsessions, melancholia, because they are typical of all mental diseases.

107.   **Jastrow, Joseph** The natural history of adolescence. Pop. Sci. Mo., March, 1905. Vol. 66, pp. 457-465.
A discussion of G. Stanley Hall's 'Adolescence,' his authority for his statements, and the real, practical value of his conclusions.

108.   **Jean, L.** Etude sur les corrélations qu'on observe dans le caractère des enfants. Bull. de la Soc. Libre, June, 1905. Vol. 5, pp. 676-681.
A study of correlations observed in the character of children with special reference to the moral sentiments.

109.   **Jerusalem, W.** Marie Heurtin; Erziehungen einer blind und taub Geborenen. Österreichische Rundschau, 1905. Vol. 3, pp. 292-302.

110.   **Jewell, James Ralph** The psychology of dreams. Am. Jour. of Psy., Jan., 1905. Vol. 16, pp. 1-34.
Valuable study of dreams from extensive material.

111.   **Johnson, Alexander** Feeble-minded trained to become self-supporting. Nat. Conf. Char. and Corr., 1905, p. 537.

112.   **Jörger, J.** Die Familie Zero. Archiv. f. Rassen-u. Gesellsch.-Biol., 1905. Vol. 2, pp. 494-559.

113.   **Juba, Adolf** Die sog. "Eisenbahn"-Schuler.   Zeits. f. Schulgesundheitspflege, 1905. Vol. 18, pp. 803-814.
A study of the effects of daily railroad travel on school children.

114.   **Kappa.** Let youth but know; a plea for reason in education. Methuen & Co., London, 1905, pp. 256.

115.   **Karplus, J. P.** Ueber Familienähnlichkeiten an den Grosshirnfürchen des Menschen. Arb. a. d. Neurol. Inst. d. Wiener Univ., 1905. Vol. 12, pp. 1-58.
Gives results of author's investigations of 86 hemispheres as to family resemblances in the sulci of the cerebrum.

116.   **Kelley, Florence** Child labor legislation and enforcement in New England and the middle states. Ann. Am. Acad. Pol. & Soc. Sci., 1905. Vol. 25, pp. 480-490.

117. **Kelley, Florence** Examination for sense defects. Nat. Conf. Char. and Corr., 1905, p. 536.

118. —— —— Industrial causes of juvenile delinquency. Nat. Conf. Char. and Corr., 1905, pp. 148-149.
Exposure by employers of inexperienced children to temptation to steal and to contact with evil companions, and night work.

119. **Kemsies, Ferdinand** Beiträge zur Psychologie und Pädagogik de Kinderlügen und Kinderaussagen. Zeits. für päd Psy., Path. und Hygiene, 1905. Vol. 7, pp. 177-192.

120. **Kirkland, James H.** The school as a force against child labor. Ann. Am. Acad. Pol. & Soc. Sci., 1905. Vol. 25, pp. 558-562.

121. **Kirkpatrick, E. A.** Some simple methods of recognizing physical fitness and unfitness of school children. Proc. N. E. A., 1905, pp. 760-766.

122. **Kneeland, George J.** The largest summer school in the world. School Jour., Oct., 7, 1905. Vol. 72, pp. 339-341.
Tells the work that is being done in vacation schools for the children of Greater New York.

123. **Koch, Alexander** Ein Beitrag zur Wachstumsphysiologie des Menschen. Nach statistischen Erhebungen an der Stoyschen Erziehnungsanstalt in Jena. Zeits. f. Schulgesundheitspflege, 1905. Vol. 18, pp. 293-319; 400-416; 454-492.

124. **Koch-Grünberg, Theodor** Anfänge der Kunst im Urwald; Indianer-Handzeichnungen auf seinen Reisen in Brasilien gesammelt. E. Wasmuth, Berlin, 1905, pp. 145.
Valuable for comparing primitive art with children's drawings.

125. **Kölling, Elizabeth** Characterbilder schwachsinniger Kinder. Zeits. für Päd. Psy. Path. und Hygiene, 1905. Vol. 7, pp. 82-99.
Different types of feeble-minded children.

126. **Koppe, O.** Wie bestimmen wir die Konstitution der Schüler? Zeits. f. Schulgesundheitspflege, 1905. (Der Schularzt,) Vol. 3, pp. 47-52.

127. **Kotelmann, Ludwig** Schulgesundheitspflege. 2d rev. ed. C. H. Beck, München, 1904, pp. 216.

128. **Krause, F.** Hören und Sprechen; sechs Vorträge. P. S. Erben, Cöthen, 1905, pp. 198.

129. **Kretz, Richard** Ueber Infektionskrankheiten im schulpflichtigen Kindesalter. Zeits. f. Krankenpflege, 1905. No. 4, pp. 121-126.

130. **Lamini, V.** I giuochi delle bambine deficienti. Rivista di Psicologia. Mch.-Apr., 1905. Vol. 1, pp. 99-103.
Play of mentally deficient children.

131. **Law, M. W.** Our Ishmael. Am. Jour. of Sociol., 1902-3. Vol. 8, pp. 838-851.
A study of the psychology of the street-arab, and of the place and importance of the boys' club in efforts for elevating him.

132. **Lawrence, Isabel** A problem for women's clubs. Proc. N. E. A., 1905, pp. 724-727.
Referring to the co-operation of parents and teachers and the influence of the teacher upon the child.

133. **Leclére, Albert.** La genèse de l'émotion esthétique. Arch. de Psy., 1905. Vol. 4, pp. 155-205.

134. **Leighton, Robert L.** The boy and his school; what it can and what it cannot give him. J. Murray, London, 1905, pp. 97.

135. **Lemaitre, Auguste** Observations sur le langage intérieur des enfants. Arch. de Psy., 1905. Vol. 4, pp. 1-43.
A study of types of mental imagery.

136. **Leroy, Raoul** Pyromanie et puberté; examen médico-légal d'une jeune incendiaire. Arch. de Neurol., 1904. Vol. 18, pp. 449-454.

137. **Levinstein, Siegfried** Kinderzeichnungen bis zum 14. Lebensjahr. R. Voigtländer, Leipzig, 1905, pp. 133.
A remarkable collection of children's drawings.

138. **Lincoln, David Francis** The education of the feeble-minded in the United States. (U. S. Bureau of Educ. Rept. of the Comm., 1902. Vol. 2, pp. 2157-2197.)

139. **Lindley, Walter** The evils of institutional childhood. Nat. Conf. Char. and Corr., 1905, pp. 125-130.
A comparison of methods of caring for dependent children, with preference for family homes.

140. **Lindner, Gustav** Neuere Forschungen und Anschauungen über die Sprache des Kindes. Zeits. für päd. Psy., Path. u. Hygiene, 1905. Vol. 7, pp. 337-392.

141. **Lindsey, Ben B.** Child labor legislation and methods of enforcement in the western states. Ann. Am. Acad. Pol. and Soc. Sci., 1905. Vol. 25, pp. 508-515.

142. —— Juvenile courts. Nat. Conf. Char. and Corr., 1905, pp. 479-487.
Shows work being done in interest of delinquents by juvenile courts.

143. —— —— Recent progress of the juvenile court movement. Nat. Conf. Char. and Corr., 1905, pp. 150-167.

144. **Lindsey, Samuel McCune** The child labor campaign, national in scope. Charities, 1905. Vol. 13, pp. 525-531.

145. —— —— Proceedings of the annual meeting of the national child labor committee held in N. Y. City, Feb. 14-16, 1905. Ann. Am. Acad. Pol. and Soc. Sci., 1905. Vol. 25, pp. 563-585.

146. **Lobedank, Dr.** Die Gesundheitspflege des Schulkindes im Elternhause. L. Voss, Hamburg, 1904, pp. 219.

147. **Lobsien, Marx** Kinderzeichnung und Kunstkanon. Zeits. für päd. Psy., Path., u. Hygiene, 1905. Vol. 7, pp. 393-404.

148. **Lombroso, Paolo** Diplomacy of children. Grand Mag., Sept., 1905. Vol. 2, pp. 329-334.

149. **Loreta, U.** Contributo allo studio del senso estetico nel fanciullo. Rivista di Psicologia, July-Aug., 1905. Vol. 1, pp. 297-298.
   Contribution to the study of the æsthetic sense in children; a review of Vernon Lee's criticism of Baldwin.

150. **Lovejoy, Owen R.** Test of effective child-labor legislation. Ann. Am. Acad. Pol. and Soc. Sci., 1905. Vol. 25, pp. 459-466.

151. **Lowinsky, Victor** Hypothesen, Methoden und Anwendungen in der Hallschen Kinder-Psychologie. Zeits. für Päd. Psy., Path., & Hygiene, 1905. Vol. 7, pp. 100-125.
   A review of G. S. Hall and his work and that of his students in child study.

152. **Lyman, Ernest W.** The folly of over-indulging children. Kindergarten Rev., Feb., 1905. Vol. 15, pp. 368-369.

153. **McCleary, G. F.** Infantile mortality and infant's milk depots. P. S. King, London, 1905, pp. 135.

154. **MacClintock, Mrs. Porter Lander** The social life of children. Elem. School Teacher, 1904-1905. Vol. 5, pp. 232-240.

155. **McConkey, Bertha M.** Literature in elementary schools. Jour. of Ped., March, 1905. Vol. 17, pp. 225.230.
   A discussion of the kind of books children like to read.

156. **McDade, James E.** Child versus environment. School Jour., Sept. 16, 1905. Vol. 72, p. 266.

157. **MacDonald, D. B.** The moral education of the young among Muslims. Internat. Jour. of Ethics, 1905. Vol. 15, pp. 286-304.
   Gives Moslem view from the Koran and the Ihyā of al-Ghazzāli.

158. **MacDougall, R.** The significance of the human hand in the evolution of mind. Am. Jour. of Psy., 1905. Vol. 16, pp. 232-242.
   MacDougall holds that there is an intimate connection between the features of the hand and the soul of man.

Macy, Mrs. John See **Sullivan, Anne Mansfield.**

159. **Mack, Julian W.** Juvenile courts. Nat. Conf. Char. and Corr., 1905, pp. 480-481.
   Approval of the probation system.

160. **McKelway, A. J.** Child labor in southern industry. Ann. Am. Acad. Pol. and Soc. Sci., 1905. Vol. 25, pp. 430-436.

161. **Maclagan, R. C.** Additions to "The games of Argyleshire." Folk-Lore, 1905. Vol. 16, pp. 77-97; 192-221.

162. **McMillan, Margaret** Education through the imagination. S. Sonnenschein, London, 1904, pp. 196.

163. **Macnamara, Thomas James** Schoolroom humour. Simpkin, Marshall & Co., London, 1905, pp. 130.
     A collection of the unconscious witticisms of children, collected from teachers.

164. **Macomber, Mable E.** Crowds in the playground : their management. Jour. of Ed., July 6, 1905. Vol. 62, pp. 72-73.

165. **Madden, John** Education through motor stimulation. Nat. Conf. Char. and Corr., 1905, p. 533.

166. **Maestrini, Lina** Sguardo alla pedologia negli Stati Uniti ed in Europa. Zamorani e Albertazzi, Bolonga, 1905, pp. 67.
     An account of the rise and progress of child study in the United States and Europe.

167. **Mann, R.** Facial expression. Internat. Quar., 1905. Vol. 11, pp. 148-162.
     Education and inheritance constantly increase the differences between adults.

168. **Marcinowski** Zur Frage der "Lüge bei Kindern unter vier Jahren." Zeits. für Päd. Psy. Path. und Hygiene, 1905. Vol. 7, pp. 201-205.

169. **Marsh, Harriet A.** Child study in special clubs. Proc. N. E. A., 1905, pp. 721-724.
     Dealing particularly with the concern of any people *i. e.* the prolongation of life and improvement of health.

170. **Martin, George H.** Child labor and compulsory education. Jour. of Ed., July 20, 1905. Vol. 62, pp. 128-132.
     Asserts the child's right and men's duty; also his claim upon the world and on instruction.

171. —— —— Phases of manual training. Jour. of Ed., Feb. 2, 1905. Vol. 61, p. 115.

172. **Masselon, Rene** La démence précoce. A. Joanin, Paris, 1904, pp. 202.

173. **Medicus, Franz** Zür Frage des Ziehkinderwesens. Zeits. für Päd. Psy. Path. und Hygiene, 1905. Vol. 7, pp. 41-45.

174. **Meisner, Hugo** Isocephalie und Degeneration. Archiv f. Rassen-u Gesellsch.-Biol., 1905. Vol. 2, pp. 76-85.

175. **Mell, Alexander** Encyklopädisches Handbuch des Blindenwesens. A. Pichler's Witwe & Sohn, Wien, 1900, pp. 890.

176. **Meusy.**—Observations sur les enfants arriérés de la Salpêtrière. Bull. de la Soc. Libre, Jan., 1905. Vol. 5, pp. 559-560.

177. **Meyer-Rinteln, Wilhelm** Die Schöpfung der Sprache. F. W. Grunow, Leipzig, 1905, pp. 256.

178. **Miles, Eustace** Boy's control and self-expression. E. Miles, Cambridge, 1904, pp. 572.

179. **Miller, Louise Klein** Children's gardens for school and home; à manual of co-operative gardening. D. Appleton & Co., N. Y., 1904, pp. 235.

180. **Miller, Persis K.** School gardens in their relations to the three R's. Education, May, 1905. Vol. 25, pp. 531-542.

181. **Monroe, Will S.** Mental elements of dreams. Jour. of Philos. Psy. and Sci. Methods, Nov. 23, 1905. Vol. 2, pp. 650-652.

182. **Montgomery, Alice B.** The child of the juvenile court. Nat. Conf. Char. and Corr., 1905, pp. 167-172.
    Some influencing circumstances which the court must consider.

183. **Morgan, Conway Lloyd** Comparative and genetic psychology. Psy. Rev., March, May, 1905. Vol. 12, pp. 78-97.
    General principles and fundamental conceptions which underlie related problems of allied sciences.

184. **Morpurgo, E.** Il suicidio nei minorenni. Rivista di Psicologia, Sept.,Oct., 1905. Vol. 1, pp. 335-344.
    Suicide among minors.

185. **Mucke, Joh. Richard** Das Problem der Völkerverwandtschaft. J. Abel, Greifswald, 1905, pp. 368.
    Treats of the relationship of different ethnic stocks.

186. **Muirhead, John Henry** The scope and object of child study. Paidologist, July, 1905. Vol. 7, pp. 66-73.

187. **Munroe, James P.** The moral training of high school boys. Jour. of Ed., Feb. 23, 1905. Vol. 61, pp. 199-201.

188. **Murray, T. C.** The soul of a schoolboy. Am. Ed., Sept., 1905. Vol. 9, pp. 39-41.

189. **Muthesius, Karl** Kindheit und Volkstum. Thienemann, Gotha, 1899, pp. 54. (Bei. z. Lehrerbildung u. Lehrerfortbildung, pt. 13.)

190. **Myers, Charles S.** The taste names of primitive peoples. British Jour. of Psy., June, 1904. Vol. 1, pp. 117-126.

191. **Niceforo, Alfredo** Les classes pauvres. Giard et Brière, Paris, 1905, pp. 344.
    A study of physical differences in 3,147 children of Lausanne. Author concludes that the poorer classes are inferior to those in more comfortable circumstances, both physically and mentally.

192. **Oppenheim, Nathan** Die Entwicklung des Kindes Vererbung und Umwelt. E. Wunderlich, Leipzig, 1905, pp. 199.

193. —— —— The recognition of the physical development of the child in the training of kindergarteners. Proc. N. E. A., 1905, pp. 344-346.

194. **Oppermann, A.** Erste Untersuchung der Sehkraft der Augen bei den neueingeschulten Kindern. Zeits. f. Schulgesundheitspflege, 1905. Vol. 18, pp. 814-816.

195. **Perrin, John William** The truancy problem in Massachusetts, 1845-1890. Jour. of Ped., March, 1905. Vol. 17, pp. 214-224.

196. **Phillippe, Jean and Boncour, G. P.** Les anomalies mentales chez les écoliers; étude médico-pédagogique. F. Alcan, Paris, 1905, pp. 158.

197. **Piggott, Horace Edwin** Die Grundzüge der sittlichen Entwicklung und Erziehung des Kindes. H. Beyer, Langensalza, 1903, pp. 77. (Beitr. zur Kinderforschung, pt. 7.)

198. **Piper, Hermann** Schriftproben von schwachsinnigen resp. idiotischen Kindern. Fischer's Med. Buchhandlung, Berlin, 1893, pp. 17-64.

199. **Plate, L.** Prof. Dahl und die Abstammungslehre in der Schule. Einige Bemerkungen zu dem vorstehenden Aufsatze. Archiv. f. Rassen-u. Gesellsch.-Biol., 1904. Vol. 1, pp. 430-434.

200. **Platt, William** Child music: a study of the tunes made by quite young children. London, 1905, pp. 37.
    A valuable preliminary study of the beginning of the musical sense of the child.

201. **Pray, Florence** Children's dramatic games, ancient and modern. Education, Feb., 1905. Vol. 25, pp. 356-365.

202. **Pudor, Heinrich** Rousseau als Kinderarzt. Kinderfehler, 1905. Vol. 10, pp. 129-135.
    Summarizes Rousseau's study of hygiene for children.

203. **Puffer, J. Adams** Boys' gangs. Ped. Sem., June, 1905. Vol. 12, pp. 175-212.
    Study made at the Lyman School, Westborough, Mass.

204. **Queyrat, Frederic** Les jeux des enfants; étude sur l'imagination créatrice chez l'enfant. F. Alcan, Paris, 1905, pp. 161.
    The author advances no new theory of play, practically accepting that of Groos but as making specific application of the biological and educative value of play. The book has a special value for parents and teachers to whom it is addressed.

205. **Quirsfeld, Eduard** Zur physischen und geistigen Entwicklung des Kindes während der ersten Schuljahre. Zeits. f. Schulgesundheitspflege, 1905. Vol. 18, pp. 127-185.
    Based on measurements of 1,014 children.

206. **Ranke, Otto** Anthropometrische Untersuchungen an gesunden und Kranken Kindern mit besonderer Berücksichtigung des schulpflichtigen Alters. Zeits. f. Schulgesundheitspflege 1905. Vol. 18, pp. 719-745; 816-837.

207. **Reese, Lelia** The value of music in child training. Kindergarten Rev., May, 1905. Vol. 15, pp. 533-535.

208. **Reid, G. Archdall** Principles of heredity. Chapman, London, 1905, pp. 359.

209. **Retzius, Mrs. Anna Hierta-** Manual training of children between 7-14 years. Stockholm, 1900, pp. 15.

210. **Rich, Herbert M.** Infant mortality in Michigan and Detroit, with an inquiry concerning a normal infant mortality. Reprint 10 p. from 2. Arch. of Pediatrics, Oct., 1905. Vol. 22.

211. **Richman, Julia** The immigrant child. Jour. of Ed., July 13, 1905. Vol. 62, pp. 106-107. Also in Am. Ed., Sept., 1905. Vol. 9, pp. 17-18.
Effects of Americanization on the foreign born child and his parents.

212. **Riemann, G.** Psychologische Studien an Taubstumm-Blinden. T. Fröhlich, Berlin, 1905, pp. 35.

213. **Rogers Lina L.** How children are protected from disease in the public schools. Kindergarten Rev., March, 1905. Vol. 15, pp. 407-410.

214. **Rosen F.** Über Kindersparbüchsen in Deutschland und Italien. Globus, Brns., 1905. Vol. 87, pp. 277-281.
Describes German and Italian children's clay-banks in the shape of mammæ.

215. **Rösse, C.** Beiträge zur europäischen Rassenkunde und die Beziehungen zwischen Rasse und Zahnverderbnis. Archiv. f. Rassen-u. Gesellsch.-Biol. 1905. Vol. 2. pp. 689-798.

216. **Rouillon, Louis** The economics of manual training. Derry-Collard Co., N. Y., 1905, pp. 174.

217. **Rowe, Stuart H.** The child's physical development. School Jour., July 29, 1905. Vol. 71, p. 125. Also in Am. Ed. Sept. 1905. Vol. 9, p. 30.

218. —— —— The school and the child's physical development. Proc. N. E. A., 1905, pp. 742-749. Also in Jour. of Ed., July 13, 1905. Vol. 62, pp. 116-117.

219. **Sabin, Henry** The abnormally dull pupils in our schools. Jour. of Ed., May 4, 1905. Vol. 61, pp. 482-483.

220. **Saint-Hilaire, Etienne** La surdi-mutité; étude médicale. Maloine, Paris, 1900, pp. 300+55.

221. **Schaefer, Karl L.** Kommen Lügen bei Kindern vor dem vierten Jahre vor? Zeits. für päd. Psy., Path. und Hygiene, 1905. Vol. 7, pp. 195-201.

222. **Schallenberger, Margaret E.** Facts concerning the child mind and their application. Jour. of Ed., Nov. 16, 1905. Vol. 62, pp. 547-549.

223. **Schallmayer, W.** Zum Einbruch der Naturwissenschaft in das Gebiet der Geisteswissenschaften. Archiv. f. Rassen-u. Gesellsch.-Biol. 1904. Vol 1. pp. 586-597.

224. **Schoff, Mrs. Frederick** National outlook for childhood. Kindergarten Rev., Oct., 1905. Vol. 16, pp. 65-72.
Deals with mental, moral and physical life of children.

225. **Schoof, Hannah Kent** Experiences in the juvenile courts of Pennsylvania. Jour. of Ed., Jan. 12, 1905. Vol. 61, p. 36; Jan. 19, 1905, pp. 62-63; Feb. 2, 1905, p. 116.

226. **Schubert, Conrad** Einige Aufgaben der Kinderforschung auf Gebiete der künstlerischen Erziehung. Kinderfehler, 1905. Vol. 10, pp. 48-63; 97-109.
Influences of nature and surroundings on art; the duty of teachers.

227. **Schuyten, M. C.** De oorspronkelijke "Ventjes" der Antwerpsche schoolkinderen. Paedologisch Jaarboek, 1904. Vol. 5, pp. 1-87.
Résumé in French appended.

228. —— —— Over die toename der Spierkracht bij kinderen gedurende het Schooljaar. Paedologisch Jaarboek, 1904. Vol. 5, pp. 118-155.
Résumé in French appended.

229. —— —— Over Rechts-en Linkshandigheid bij kinderen. Paedologisch Jaarboek, 1904. Vol. 5, pp. 156-162.
Résumé in French appended.

230. **Seeley, Levi** Play as an educational factor. Jour. of Ped., Dec., 1905. Vol. 18, pp. 100-112.
Plays in the kindergarten. The difference between play and work and the value of playthings.

231. **Semon, Richard** Die Mneme als erhaltendes Prinzip im Wechsel des organischen Geschehens. W. Engelmann, Leipzig, 1904, pp. 353.

232. **Senet, Rodolfo** Quelques considérations sur la nyctophobie chez les enfants. Arch. de Psy., 1905. Vol. 4, pp. 350-357.
A study of night fears in children. 519 cases observed.

233. **Shearer, W. J.** Moral instruction in school. Jour. of Ed., Apr. 27, 1905. Vol. 61, pp. 451-452.

234. **Shipley, Mrs. S. Murray** Juvenile reformatory of the 20th century. Nat. Conf. Char. and Corr., 1905, pp. 541-542.
Need of play-houses in large cities to keep children out of mischief.

Simon, Th. See **Binet, Alfred and Simon, Th.**

235. **Smiles, Samuel** Physical education of the young; or, The nurture and management of children, founded on the study of their nature and constitution; ed. by Sir Hugh Beevor. W. Scott Pub. Co., London, 1905, pp. 221.

236. **Smith.** —— Defectives; examination for sense defects at entrance to school. Nat. Conf. Char. and Corr., 1905, pp. 524-525.

237. **Smith, Frank Webster** Child study in normal schools. Proc. N. E. A., 1905, pp. 714-719.
Dealing with the values of child study both from a physiological and psychical standpoint.

238. **Smith, Theodate L.** Child study at Clark University. Ped. Sem., March, 1905. Vol. 12, pp. 93-96.

239. —— —— Obstinacy and obedience. Ped. Sem., March, 1905. Vol. 12, pp. 27-54.
A study in the psychology and pedagogy of the will.

240. **Sorabji, Cornelia** Sun-babies; studies in the child-life of India. J. Murray, London, 1905, pp. 148.

241. **Souffret, Francois** De la disparité physique et mentale des races humaines et de ses principes. Godenne, Malines, 1892, pp. 322.
    Treats of the mental and physical ethnic differences and their relation to moral development.

242. **Spitzka, A.** The development of man's brain; American mind destined to dominate human powers of the earth. Connecticut Mag., 1905, pp. 319-355.
    Discusses cerebral localization, brains of intellectual persons, etc.

243. **Stadelmann, Heinrich** Schwachbeanlagte Kinder; ihre Förderung und Behandlung. O. Gmelin, München, 1904, pp. 40.

244. **Stelzle, Charles** Boys of the street; how to win them. Fleming H. Revell Co., N. Y., 1904, pp. 96.
    Considers all aspects of the problem practically, with reference especially to boys' clubs. Gives hints as to organization, gov't, etc.

245. **Stephens, Thomas** ed. The child and religion. G. P. Putnam's Sons, N. Y., 1905, pp. 371.

246. **Stern, William** Kinderaussagen und Aussagepädagogik. Zeits. für päd. Psy., Path. und Hygiene, 1905. Vol. 7, pp. 192-195.

247. **Storrs, O. S.** Importance of examination of troublesome children. Nat. Conf. Char. and Corr., 1905, pp. 535-536.

248. **Stratz, C. H.** Das Kind als Erzieher. Vierteljhrs. für körperliche Erziehung, 1905. Vol. I, pp. 17-22.
    We should not only educate children but we ought also to let them educate us.

249. **Strohmayer, W.** and **Stukenberg, W.** Bericht über die VI. Versammlung des Vereins für Kinderforschung am 14.-16. Oktober in Leipzig. Kinderfehler, 1905. Vol. 10, pp. 63-70; 111-120; 166-178; 212-220.

    Stukenberg, W. See No. 249.

250. **Sullivan, Anne Mansfield** The religious education of Helen Keller, the blind, deaf and dumb girl. A. C. Fifield, London, 1905, pp. 31.

251. **Szentesy, Bela** Die geistige Ueberanstrengung des Kindes (von einer noch nicht besprochenen Seite dargestellt.) Antien-Gesellschaft, Budapest, 1898, pp. 123.

252. **Tanner, Amy E.** Relation of the child's development to control of him. Proc. N. E. A., 1905, pp. 734-740.
    Dealing with the motor side of development.

253. **Terman, Lewis M.** A study in precocity and prematuration. Am. Jour. of Psy., April, 1905. Vol. 16, pp. 145-183.
    Valuable material on criminal, religious, and sexual precocity.

254. **Thayer, Alice** A study of children's interest in flowers. Ped. Sem., June, 1905. Vol. 12, pp. 107-140.

255. **Thurston, Henry D.** Probation in relation to schools. Nat. Conf. Char. and Corr., 1905, pp. 180-181.
Importance of giving children something interesting to do to keep them out of mischief and crime.

256. **Tögel, H.** 16 Monate Kindersprache. Kinderfehler, 1905. Vol. 10, pp. 156-165 ; 194-199.
Word formation. Words, sentences, and groups of sentences.

257. **Tomlinson, H. A.** Defectives. Nat. Conf. Char. and Corr., 1905, pp. 334-338 ; 523-539.
Treats of importance of institutions for feeble-minded, and necessity of examining children on entrance to school, that attention may be directed to their needs.

258. **Tovo, C.** Le forme del cranio nello sviluppo fetale. A. d. Soc. Rom. di Antropol., 1905. Vol. 11, pp. 27-44.
Gives results of examination by Sergi's method of 86 Piedmontese fetal skulls.

259. **Triplett, Norman** Pedagogical arrests and peculiarities. Ped. Sem., June, 1905. Vol. 12, pp. 141-157.
Deals with defects in teaching as cause of abnormalities, etc., in children.

260. **Troitzsch, Reinhold** Der Reinfeldersche Vielhörer und sein Gebrauch in der Klasse für schwerhörige Kinder. Kinderfehler, 1905. Vol. 10, pp. 178-182.
Description of apparatus, use, and value for children with defective hearing.

261. **Vaney, V.** Nouvelles méthodes de mesure applicables au degré d'instruction des elèves. L'Année Psychol., 1905. Vol. 11, pp. 146-162.
Tendency to advance backward children with bright ones. Mode of classification suggested. Tables of written work.

262. **Van Killpatrick, Evril** Ethical culture school as a source of educative experiment. School Jour., Sept. 2, 1905. Vol. 72, pp. 207-211.

263. **Variot, G.** L'atrophie infantile comme facteur de l'abaissement de la taille dans les faubourgs de Paris. Bull. de la Soc. d'Anthropol. de Paris, 1904. Ser. 5, Vol. 5, pp. 633-637.
From the observation of 3,000 children in 1892-1904 Dr. V. comes to the conclusion that digestive troubles and the inanition therefrom are a prime factor in lowering the stature of the Parisian man of the faubourgs.

264. **Vaux, George, Jr.** A plea for esthetic surroundings. Nat. Conf. Char. and Corr., 1905, pp. 120-125.

265. **Vincent, George E.** Group morality in children. Jour. of Ed., March 16, 1905. Vol. 61, pp. 289-290. Also an abstract in Proc. N. E. A., 1905, p. 214.

266. **Vincent, Ralph** The nutrition of the infant. 2d ed. Baillière, Tindall & Cox, London, 1904, pp. 321.

267. **Vossler, Karl** Sprache als Schöpfung und Entwicklung; eine theoretische Untersuchung mit praktischen Beispielen. C. Winter, Heidelberg, 1905, pp. 154.

268. **Weber, Ernst** Ursachen und Folgen der Rechtshandigkeit. C. Marhold, Halle, 1905, pp. 115.

269. **Wendtlandt, Otto** Das Kinderzimmer. Zeits. für Päd. Psy. Path. und Hygiene, 1905. Vol. 7, pp. 31-40.
Treats of hygienic requirements and furnishings.

270. **Wentworth, E. P.** Ethical culture in children's institutions. Nat. Conf. Char. and Corr., 1905, pp. 138-143.
Advocates giving children opportunities of choice, and assisting to right choice only when necessary.

271. **Wichmann, Ralf** Über besonders ermüdende und unangenehme Schulfächer gesunder und kranker Lehrerinnen. Zeits. f. Schulgesundheitsflege, 1905. Vol. 18, pp. 73-79.

272. —— —— Über die Nebenbeschäftigung gesunder und kranker Lehrerinnen. Zeits. f. Schulgesundheitspflege, 1905. Vol. 18, pp. 554-566.

273. **Wilk, E.** Das Werden der Zahlen und des Rechnens im Menschen und in der Menschheit auf Grund von Psychologie und Geschichte. Part 2. Jahr des Vereins für wissens. Päd., 1905. Vol. 37, pp. 207-251. (Continued from Vol. 35.)

274. **Williams, Alida S.** The investigation of fatigue from the teacher's point of view. Jour. of Ped., March, 1905. Vol. 17, pp. 199-213.
A discussion of mental and physical fatigue and the connection between atmospheric conditions and fatigue.

275. **Willson, Robert N.** The American boy and the social evil. J. C. Winston Co., Phila., 1905, pp. 159.

276. **Wilson, Erasmus** How to suppress the bad boy. Jour. of Ed., October 19, 1905. Vol. 62, pp. 435-436.

277. **Wilson, Mrs. L. P.** Right and wrong punishment. Kindergarten Rev., Mar., 1905. Vol. 15, pp. 411-415.

278. **Wilson, Louis N.** Bibliography of child study for the year 1904. Ped. Sem., Sept., 1905. Vol. 12, pp. 304-333.
List of 429 articles and books on child study published during the year.

279. —— —— Notes on a few books in child study. Proc. N. E. A., 1905, pp. 751-753.
Special mention of the best books for use in the subject of child study.

Wissler, Clark See **Boas, Franz and Wissler, Clark.**

280. **Witry, Dr.** Aus meiner Kinderpraxis. Kinderfehler, 1905. Vol. 10, pp. 135-136.
Study of two cases of emotional precocity.

281. **Wray, Angelina W.** Glimpses of child nature for teachers and parents. Public School Pub. Co., Bloomington, Ill., 1904, pp. 152.

282. **Ziehen, Dr.** Ueber Krampfkrankheiten im schulpflichtigen Alter. Zeits f. Schulgesundheitspflege, 1905. Vol. 18, pp. 252-254.

283. **Zindel-Kreissig, A.** Die Knabengesellschaft von Sargans. Schwz. A. f. Volksk., 1905. Vol. 8, pp. 52-55.
Gives the 25 articles of organization of the Knabengesellschaft or Youth's society, of Sargans in 1833.

284. Child study for parents. Paidologist, July, 1905. Vol. 7, pp. 96-99.

285. The cry of the children. Jour. of Ed. (Lond.), 1905. N. S., Vol. 27, pp. 749-750.

286. Dundee Social Union. Report on housing and industrial conditions and medical inspection of school children. J. Leng, Dundee, 1905, pp. 150.

287. Eye strain, and how it can be relieved. School Jour., Aug. 26, 1905. Vol. 72, p. 187.

288. Home for the training in speech of deaf children. Seventh report. Phila., 1904, pp. 28.

289. The hygiene of child life. Lancet, 1905. Vol. 2, p. 1926.

290. Infants in elementary schools. Lancet, 1905. Vol. 2, pp. 1116-1117.

291. London. Board of education. Regulations for secondary schools, from 1st August, 1904, to 31st July, 1905. Eyre & Spottiswoode, London, 1904, pp. 31.

292. London. Board of education. Regulations for the training of teachers and for the examination of students in training colleges. Wyman & Sons, London, 1904, pp. 57.

293. London. Board of education. Reports on children under five years of age in public elementary schools by women inspectors. Wyman & Sons, London, 1905, pp. 155.

294. London. Board of education. Suggestions for the consideration of teachers and others concerned in the work of public elementary schools. Wyman & Sons, London, 1905, pp. 155.

295. London County Council. Report of the education committee of the London county council submitting the report of the medical officer (education) for the year ended 31st March, 1905. Alexander & Shepheard, London, 1905, pp. 60.

296. Massachusetts. Commission on industrial and technical education. Report. Wright, Boston, 1906, pp. 196.
The report is one of the most thorough inquiries into the relations of children to our industries which has yet been made.

297. National Educational Association. Report of the committee on industrial education in schools for rural communities. N. E. A, 1905, pp. 97.

298. Out of the mouths of babes and sucklings. Jour. of Ed. (Lond.), 1905. N. S., Vol. 27, pp. 402-403.

299. Report of the National congress of mothers, held in Washington, D. C. March 10-17, 1905. Washington, 1905, pp. 272.

300. Some aspects of hygiene in schools. Jour. of Ed. (Lond.), 1905. N. S., Vol. 27, pp. 370-371.

---

301. Premier Congrès International d'Education et de Protection de l'Enfance dans la Famille. Liège, Sept., 1905.
   Vol. 1. Etude de l'enfance. p. 114.
   Vol. 2. Education familiale. Questions générales. pp. 343.
   Vol. 3. Education familiale avant l'âge d'école. pp. 93.
   Vol. 4. Education familiale pendant l'âge d'école. pp. 271.
   Vol. 5. Education familiale après l'école. pp. 176.
   Vol. 6. Les enfants anormaux. pp. 282.
   Vol. 7. Les œuvres d'éducation et de protection de l'enfance. pp. 248.
   Vol. 8. Compte rendu des assemblées et des expositions. pp. 369.
   Contains a large number of interesting papers on the various phases of child study.

---

302. Archiv fur Rassen.-und Gesellschafts Biologie. Archiv-Gesellschaft. Berlin. Vol. 2, 1905.

303. Beiträge zur Psychologie der Aussage. Barth. Leipzig, Vol. 2. 1905.

304. Eos. Witwe, Wien. Vol. 1, 1905.

305. Die Experimentelle Pädagogik. Nemnich. Leipzig. Vols. 1-2, 1905.
   These four journals (Nos. 302-303-304-305), none of which are much more than two years old, together with Die Kinderfehler (Langensalza, 1896), now in its eleventh volume, Zeitschrift fur pädagogische Psychologie, Pathologie und Hygiene (Berlin, 1899), and Zeitschrift fur Schulgesundheitspflege (Hamburg, 1888), mark a very distinct new educational movement in Germany which is of the utmost importance and of which few Americans have realized the full significance. They are the dawn of a new day for education in the land to which so many look for the best and most progressive educational ideals. Each represents a movement directed by a group of active workers who are far more scientific, modern and progressive than the rank and file of teachers in that or any other land.
   Reviewed in Ped. Sem., June, 1906. Vol. 13, pp. 255-256.

SUBJECT INDEX.

Abnormal, 18, 29, 30.
Abnormalities, 20, 21, 219, 280.
Adding, 8.
Adolescence, 65, 82, 92, 107, 114.
Æsthesiometer, 17.
Æsthetic Training, 264.
Æsthetics, 133, 147, 149.
Answers, 33.
Anthropometery, 24, 42, 123, 205, 206.
Antwerp, 227.
Arithmetic, 8, 273.
Art, Primitive, 124.
Art Instruction, 226.
Auditory Tests, 7.
Auxiliary Schools, 61.

Babies, 57.
Backward Children, 19, 259, 261.
Bad Boys, 255, 276.
Bible Stories, 101.
Bibliographical, 137, 140, 166.
Bibliography, 15, 94, 278, 279.
Biological, 50.
Blind, 175, 250.
Boys, 77, 134, 178, 187, 188, 227, 244, 255, 275, 276.
Boys' Clubs, 244.
Brain, 103, 115, 242.
Brain Development, 96.

Character, 14, 57, 108, 125.
Child and the Race, 189.
Child Labor, 1, 2, 3, 5, 6, 49, 53, 60, 68, 70, 97, 116, 120, 141, 144, 145, 150, 160, 170, 296.
Child-life, 80.
Child Mind, 222.
Child Study, 43, 47, 52, 74, 83, 94, 99, 132, 151, 166, 169, 186, 237, 238, 240, 249, 278, 279, 281, 284.
Childhood, 22, 224.
Children's Room, 269.
Clark University, 238.
Clay Banks, 214.
Comparative Psychology, 183.
Compulsory Education, 68, 170.
Congress at Liège, 301.
Control, 178.
Corporal Punishment, 44.
Counting, 8, 273.

Crime, 51, 118, 225.
Crowd, 164.
Cruelty, 75.

Deaf, 288.
Deaf Blind, 109.
Deaf Mutes, 81, 212, 220.
Defectives, 29, 30, 31, 93, 105, 130, 176, 198, 236, 257, 259.
Degeneration, 112, 174.
Delinquency, 118.
Delinquents, 131, 225, 234.
Dementia Praecox, 172.
Diplomacy, 148.
Discipline, 71, 252.
Diseases, 37, 95, 213.
Diseases, Infectious, 45, 129.
Dramatic Interests, 201.
Drawing, 124, 137, 147.
Dreams, 110, 181.
Dull, 219.
Dundee, 286.

Education, 114, 248.
Emotions, 133.
Environment, 156, 192.
Ethical Culture, 262, 270.
Ethnic Relations, 185.
Eugenics, 63, 64.
Evidence, 119, 246.
Evolution, 199.
Examination, 117.
Experimental Pedagogy, 43.
Eyesight, 287.

Face, 167.
Fairy Stories, 41.
Fatigue, 17, 106, 113, 274.
Fear, 232.
Feeble-minded, 36, 51, 111, 125, 138, 243.
Fingers, 11.
Fire, 136.
Flowers, 254.
Folk Lore, 161, 189.
Food, 263, 266.

Gangs, 203.
Gardens, 179.
Genealogy, 73.
General, 285, 298.

Genetic Psychology, 34, 183.
Girls, 56.
Grades, 90.
Groups, 265.
Growth, 24, 123, 263.

Hair, 37.
Hall, G. S., 65, 107, 151.
Hand, 158.
Head Measurements, 42.
Health, 57.
Hearing, 7, 29, 38, 48, 109, 128, 260.
Heredity, 11, 73, 112, 192, 208.
High School, 26, 86, 187.
Home, 71, 146.
Home Study, 35.
Humor, 163.
Hygiene, 35, 58, 63, 96, 103, 146, 202, 213, 269, 271, 272, 289, 300.
Hygiene, School, 15, 126, 127.

Imagination, 162, 204.
Immigrant Children, 211.
India, 240.
Indians, 124.
Individual Child Study, 12.
Indulgence 152.
Industrial Education, 296, 297.
Infantile Mortality, 153, 210.
Infants, 290, 293.
Inheritance, 54.
Institutional Life, 139.
Intellectual, 17, 20, 21.
Intelligence, 16, 18.
Interest, 254.
Internal Speech, 135.
Isocephaly, 174.

Japan, 80.
Jena, 123.
Journals, 302, 303, 304, 305.
Juvenile Courts, 142, 143, 159, 182.

Keller, Helen, 250.
Kindergarten, 102.

Language, 39, 46, 67, 69, 135, 267.
Leaving School, 86.
Lefthandedness, 229.
Legal Punishment, 10.
Legislation, 141.
Lies, 119, 168, 221.
Literature, 155.
Location, 76.

Manual Training, 4, 88, 90, 171, 209, 216.
Massachusetts, 195.

Measurements, 206.
Medical Inspection, 286, 295.
Memory, 28, 231.
Mental and Physical, 58, 102, 103.
Mental Defects, 196.
Mental Development, 39, 50.
Mental Pathology, 106.
Mental Strain, 251.
Mental Types, 79.
Milk, 153.
Moral Development, 195, 197.
Moral Education, 44a, 157.
Moral Instruction, 187, 233.
Moral Training, 66, 188, 197.
Morality, 265.
Morals, 59, 108, 275.
Motherhood, 84.
Mother-tongue, 69.
Mothers, 299.
Motor Training, 165.
Muscular Strength, 228.
Music, 48, 200, 207.
Myths, 27, 41.

Natural Science, 223.
Neglected Children, 10, 131.
Nervous System, 50.
Nervousness, 31, 98.
Newsboys, 77.
Night Fears, 232.
Normal Schools, 237.
Nutrition, 266.

Obedience, 239.
Obstinacy, 239.
Occupations, 1.
Overwork, 93.

Peculiar Children, 104, 247.
Physical Development, 102, 121, 193, 205, 217, 218.
Physical Education, 44a, 235.
Physical Training, 9.
Play, 40, 72, 87, 130, 291, 204, 230.
Playgrounds, 9, 164.
Poland, 74.
Poor, 31, 191.
Precocity, 253.
Prematuration, 253.
Pre-natal, 258.
Probation, 255.
Psychology of Expression, 246.
Puberty, 136.
Punishments, 277.
Pupil, 26.
Pyromania, 136.

Race, 185, 215.

Race Differences, 241.
Railroad Travel, 113.
Reading, 25, 30, 85.
Reason, 114.
Recess, 55.
Reform Schools, 89, 234.
Religious Ideas, 245.
Reports, 249.
Righthandedness, 229, 268.
Rousseau, J. J., 202.

School, 58, 71, 134, 163, 218.
School Diseases, 129, 213, 282.
School Gardens, 179, 180.
School Yard, 9.
School Work, 96.
Schools, 291, 292, 293, 294.
Self-consciousness, 67.
Self-expression, 178.
Sense Defects, 117, 236.
Sense of Life, 62.
Senses, 190.
Sex, 56, 59, 63, 100, 187, 275.
Sight, 109, 175, 194.
Skin-diseases, 37.
Sleep, 106.
Social, 154.
Social Sense, 92, 203, 265.
Societies, 283.
Sociological, 191.
Space Perception, 76.
Special Clubs, 169.
Special Schools, 19.

Speech, 13, 78, 128, 140, 177, 256.
Speech-defects, 78.
Story-telling, 32, 101.
Street-arab, 131.
Street Boys, 244.
Street Games, 40.
Study of Individual Child, 39.
Suckling, 91.
Suicide, 184.
Supernumerary Fingers, 11.

Taste, 190.
Teachers, 26, 271, 272, 292.
Teeth, 215.
Tone Deafness, 48.
Truancy, 195.
Underwork, 23.

Vacation Schools, 122.
Vision, 194.
Vital Sense, 62.

Weak-minded Children, 61.
Will, 14.
Woman's Clubs, 132.
Worcester, Mass., 24.
Work, 72, 87.
Writing, 30, 198.

Youth, 59.

Zero Family, 112.

PUBLICATIONS

OF THE

CLARK UNIVERSITY LIBRARY

WORCESTER, MASS.

EDITED BY LOUIS N. WILSON, LITT. D., LIBRARIAN

| VOL. 2. | August, 1907 | No. 5 |

Bibliography of Child Study for the Year 1906

Clark University Press

WORCESTER, MASS.

BIBLIOGRAPHY OF CHILD STUDY.

For the Year 1906.

By LOUIS N. WILSON, Librarian, Clark University.

1. **Adams, Myron E.** The causes of juvenile crime. Outlook, 1906. Vol. 83, pp. 796-801.
2. **Adkins, Frank J.** The school as a social centre. Jour. of Ed., Lond., 1906. N. S., Vol. 28, pp. 387-389.
3. **Adler, Felix** The punishment of children. Jour. of Ed., 1906. Vol. 63, pp. 402, 454, 481, 540, 596.
4. **Allen, Anne Elizabeth** Kindergarten and primary games. Elem. School Teacher, 1906. Vol. 7, pp. 13-15.
5. **Allen, Edward Ellis** Physical education of the blind. Amer. Phys. Ed. Rev., June, 1906. Vol. 11, pp. 65-74.
6. **Allinson, A. C. E.** The curriculum for girls. Nation, 1906. Vol. 83, pp. 198-199.
7. **Altenberg, Oskar** Etwas von moralischer Schwachsinnigkeit unter Schülern öffentlicher Schulen. Die Gesundh. der Schule, 1905. Vol. 3, pp. 58-72.
8. **Altschul, Theodor** Die Mitwirkung der Lehrer bei Gewinnung einer brauchbaren Morbiditätsstatistik in Schulen. Die Gesundh. der Schule, 1905. Vol. 3, pp. 134-138.
9. **Ament, Wilhelm** Fortschritte der Kinderseelenkunde, 1895-1903. 2d rev. ed. W. Engelmann, Leipzig, 1906. pp. 76.
10. —— —— Die Seele des Kindes. Kosmos, Stuttgart, 1906. pp. 96.
11. **American, Sadie** Vacation schools. Education, 1906. Vol. 26, pp. 509-518; 614-623.
12. **Arnold, Felix** The psychology of interest. Psy. Rev., 1906. Vol. 13, pp. 221-238; 291-315.
13. **Atkinson, J. H.** The preparatory school and the boy. Education, 1906. Vol. 27, pp. 227-230.
14. **Badley, J. H.** Co-education after fifteen; its value and its difficulties. Child Life, 1906. Vol. 7, pp. 12-19.
15. **Baginsky, Adolph** Ueber Waldsschulen und Walderholungsstätten. Zeits. für päd. Psy. Path. u. Hygiene, 1906. Vol. 8, pp. 161-177.

16. **Bair, Joseph Hershey** The development of thinking power in school children. Univ. of Colo. Invest. Depts. of Psy. and Ed., Apr., 1906. Vol. 3, pp. 45-51.

17. —— —— Human infancy, its causes, significance, and the limits of its prolongation. Univ. of Colo. Studies, Nov., 1905. Vol. 3, pp. 25-29.

18. —— —— Motor activity and mental selection. Univ. of Colo. Invest. Depts. of Psy. and Ed., 1905. Vol. 3, No. 1, pp. 28-32.

19. **Björkman, Frances M.** Children's court in American city life. Rev. of Revs., 1906. Vol. 33, pp. 305-311.

20. **Baldrian, Karl** Zur Pflege der Gesundheit taubstummer Kinder. Die Gesundh. der Schule, 1906. Vol. 4, pp. 129-134; 153-159.
    On the necessity of special physical care of deaf mute children, and need of special institutions for their care and training.

21. **Baldwin, W. A.** The school garden. Education, 1906. Vol. 26, pp. 447-461.

22. **Barrett, H.** Management of children. E. P. Dutton Co., N. Y., 1906.

23. **Bathurst, K.** The physique of girls. 19th Cent., 1906. Vol. 59, pp. 825-833.

24. **Baur, Alfred** Die Ernährung des Säuglings. Die Gesundh. der Schule, 1905. Vol. 3, pp. 73-75.

25. —— —— Grosse Muneli, kleine Rekruten. Die Gesundh. der Schule, 1905. Vol. 3, pp. 191-195.
    During the last few years Switzerland has become noted for its prize cattle, which have steadily increased in size and weight. This has been chiefly accomplished by feeding them milk, a steer which is being fattened for competition consuming as much as fifteen quarts daily. But while the cattle have increased in size and weight, the children have deteriorated until in the last year only 30% of the young men were available for military recruits. The chief cause of rejection was undersize and weight. This the anthor thinks is directly correlated with the feeding of milk to the cattle, and thus withdrawing it from the children, who are fed with Alpine rose tea as a substitute.

26. —— —— Die Hygiene des Ethosim Schulalter. Die Gesundh. der Schule, 1906. Vol. 4, pp. 30-42.
    A contribution to the hygiene of ethics. Discusses inherited ethical weakness, importance of nourishment from the beginning of life, questions of sex, etc.

27. —— —— Die Sophienhöhe bei Jena. Die Gesundh. der Schule, 1905. Vol. 3, pp. 171-177.
    Description of institute for feeble minded children at Jena, and brief outline of its methods.

28. **Beale, Dorothea** Presidential address delivered at the British Child-Study Association Conference, May, 1906. Paidologist, 1906. Vol. 8, pp. 66-70.

29. **Beale, Dorothea and others** Work and play in girls' schools. Longmans, Green & Co., London, 1901. pp. 433.

30. **Beebe, Katherine** Baby play. Kindergarten Rev., 1906. Vol. 17, pp. 67-72.
Shows importance of play in child's life.

31. **Beede, F. H.** The problem of the incorrigible boy. Jour. of Ed., 1906. Vol. 63, p. 335.

32. **Berger, Heinrich** Kreisarzt und Schulhygiene. L. Voss, Hamburg, 1902. pp. 88.

33. —— —— Die Schularztfrage für höhere Lehranstalten. L. Voss, Hamburg, 1904. pp. 162.

34. **Berninger, Johannes** Pädagogik und Hygiene; Schul-und Volksgesundheitspflege in der praktischen Berufstätigkeit des Lehrers. L. Voss, Hamburg, 1904. pp. 79.

35. —— —— Schul-und Volkshygiene; eine notwendige Forderung unserer Zeit. L. Voss, Hamburg, 1903. pp. 71.

36. **Biesalski,** —— Was können die Schulärzte zur Behandlung der skoliotischen Volksschulkinder tun? Zeits. fur Schulgesundheitspflege, 1906. Vol. 19, pp. 545-550; 610-627.

37. **Binet, Alfred and Simon, Th.** La misère physiologique et la misère sociale. L'Année Psy., 1906. Vol. 12, pp. 1-24.
A study of growth in height and weight of school children. Correlated with mental development, nutrition and social condition.

38. **Binet, Alfred and others** Recherches de pédagogie scientifique. L'Année Psy., 1906. Vol. 12, pp. 232-274.
Discusses the laboratory school of pedagogy of la rue Grange, aux Bells, and the measure of visual acuity in school children, pedagogic and medical methods, measure of auditory acuity, correct position for writing, better methods of estimating intelligence, the æsthetic sense, etc.

39. **Binswanger, O.** Ueber den moralischen Schwachsinn, mit besonderer Berücksichtigung der kindlichen Altersstufe. Samml. v. Abh. a. d. Geb. d. päd. Psy. u. Physiol., 1906. Vol. 8, No. 5, pp. 36.

40. **Blanchard, E. F.** Child-study. Education, 1906. Vol. 27. pp. 209-215.

41. **Boodin, John E.** Mind as instinct. Psy. Rev., 1906. Vol. 13, pp. 121-139.

42. **Borgquist, Alvin** Crying. Am. Jour. of Psy., Apr., 1906. Vol. 17, pp. 149-205.
A classification of crying states, analysis and effects and theories, but not wholly devoted to child study.

43. **Boulanger,** —— **and Hermant, Paul** Association des idées chez les idiots et les imbéciles. A. Vanderhaegen, Ghent, 1906. pp. 137.

44. **Bourneville,** —— **and Royer,** —— Imbécillité prononcée congénitale. Arch. de Neurol., 1906. Vol. 22, pp. 425-456.

45. **Bowne, J. T.** Classified bibliography of boy life, and organized work with boys. Internat. Comm. of Y. M. C. A., N. Y. 1906. pp. 36.

46. **Boyd, William** Changes in handwriting during adolescence. Paidologist, 1906. Vol. 8, pp. 106-109.

47. **Bradley, Rose M.** The children of Florence. 19th Cent., 1906. Vol. 60, pp. 618-631.

48. —— —— Soft Siena and her children. 19th Cent., 1906. Vol. 60, pp. 57-69.
An interesting article on child life in Siena.

49. **Burbank, Luther** Cultivate children like flowers. Elem. School Teacher, 1906. Vol. 6, pp. 457-460.

50. **Burgerstein, Leo** Schulhygiene, B. G. Teubner, Leipzig, 1906. pp. 138.

51. **Burnham, William H.** The hygiene and psychology of spelling. Ped. Sem., Dec., 1906. Vol. 13, pp. 474-501.

52. —— —— The hygiene of the teeth. Ped. Sem., Sept., 1906. Vol. 13, pp. 293-306.

53. —— —— Report of the committee on school hygiene of the Worcester public education association. Ped. Sem., June, 1906. Vol. 13, pp. 230-244.

54. **Burnite, Caroline** Beginnings of literature for children. Lib. Jour., 1906. Vol. 31, pp. 107-112.

55. —— —— Good and bad books for children. Pub. Lib., 1906. Vol. 11, pp. 360-362.

56. **Burr, Hanford M.** Studies in adolescent boyhood. Assoc. Seminar, 1906. Vol. 15, pp. 5-16; 45-61; 85-97.

57. **Büttner, Georg** Beobachtungen über körperliche Rückständigkeit bei geistiger Schwäche. Die Gesundh. der Schule, 1905. Vol. 3, pp. 243-247.
A comparative study of mental weakness and imperfect physical development.

58. —— —— Kurs der medizinischen Psychologie in Giessen mit besonderer Berücksichtigung der angebornenen Schwachsinnigen. Die Gesundh. der Schule, 1906. Vol. 4, pp. 139-145.
An account of the course at Giessen in medical psychology, which gives special attention to treatment and education of children who are weak minded from birth.

59. —— —— Ueber das Hilfsschulwesen. Die Gesundh. der Schule, 1906. Vol. 4, pp. 249-256; 276-289.
Contribution to pedagogical pathology, emphasizing the need of special classes for defective children.

60. —— —— Verschiedene Ursachen psychopathischer Erscheinungen bei Kindern. Die Gesundh. der Schule, 1905. Vol. 3, pp. 12-18.

61. **Byett, A. S.** Reform in infant schools. Paidologist, 1906. Vol. 8, pp. 77-90.

62. **Cannons, Harvey G. C.** *comp.* Descriptive handbook to juvenile literature. T. Bean & Son, London, 1906. pp. 312.

63. **Cantile, James** Physical efficiency; a review of the deleterious effects of town life upon the population of Great Britain, with suggestions for their arrest. G. P. Putnam's Sons, N. Y., 1906. pp. 216.

64. **Carus, Paul** Childhood and education in China. Open Court, 1906. Vol. 20, pp. 668-684.

65. —— —— First steps. Open Court, 1906. Vol. 20, pp. 495-499.

66. —— —— Our children; hints from practical experience for parents and teachers. Open Court Pub. Co., Chic., 1906.

67. **Chamberlain, Alexander Francis** Acquisition of written language of primitive peoples. Am. Jour. of Psy., Jan., 1906. Vol. 17, pp. 69-80.

Points out the ease with which North American Indian children learn to read and write their native tongues by means of syllabaries, special alphabets, etc.

68. —— —— Preterite forms, etc., in the language of English-speaking children. Mod. Lang. Notes, 1906. Vol. 21, pp. 42-44.

69. —— —— Some recent child-study and educational literature in Portuguese, Spanish and Italian. Psy. Bull., 1906. Vol. 3, pp. 371-383.

70. —— —— Variation in early human culture. Jour. Am. Folk-Lore, 1906. Vol. 19, pp. 177-190.

Treats among other things, of variation (due to environment) in nursery-rhymes, ideas of father and mother, etc.

71. **Chamberlain, Alexander Francis and Isabel C.** Hypnagogic images and bi-vision in early childhood. Am. Jour. of Psy., Apr., 1906. Vol. 17, pp. 272-273.

72. **Chambers, Will Grant** Memory types of Colorado pupils. Jour. of Philos. Psy. and Sci. Methods, 1906. Vol. 3, pp. 231-234.

73. —— —— The significance of motor activity in primary education. Jour. of Ped., 1906. Vol. 18, pp. 166-184.

74. **Claparède, Ed.** Psychologie du juge. L'Année Psy., 1906. Vol. 12, pp. 277-302.

A contribution to legal psychology considered under the two heads of judicial and criminal psychology.

75. **Colvin, Stephen S.** The child's world of imagination. Elem. School Teacher, 1906. Vol. 6, pp. 327-342.

76. **Colvin, Stephen S. and Meyer, I. F.** Imaginative element in the written work of children. Ped. Sem., March, 1906. Vol. 13, pp. 84-93.

77. **Compayre, Gabriel** La psychologie de l'adolescence. Rev. Philos., 1906. Vol. 61, pp. 345-377; 569-598.

78. **Cooke, Ebenezer** The method of nature is the archetype of all method. Paidologist, 1906. Vol. 8, pp. 28-35.

How to adapt drawing to the child's nature.
Continued from Vol. 7.

79. **Cramer, Ehrenfried** Ergebnisse der durch die ganze Schulzeit fortgesetzen augenärztlichen Beobachtung eines Klassenjahrganges des Gymnasiums in Cottbus. Zeits. für Schulgesundheitspflege, 1906. Vol. 19, pp. 305-317.

80. **Cromwell, A. D.** Practical child study. W. M. Welch Co., Chic., 1906.

81. **Croswell, T. R.** Self-government among children. Jour. of Ed., 1906. Vol. 63, pp. 451-452; 479-480.

82. **Dearborn, Walter Fenno** The psychology of reading. Science Press, N. Y., 1906. pp. 134. Also in Columbia Univ. Contrib. to Philos. and Psy. Vol. 14, No. 1.

83. **Decroly, O.** Les tests de Binet et Simon pour la mesure de l'intelligence. Arch. de Psy., 1906. Vol. 6, pp. 27-130.

84. **Delaporte, P. V.** Les petits enfants de cinq ans et au-dessous. A. Dewit., Bruxelles, 1906. pp. 326.

85. **Denyer, C. H.** Feeding of school children at public expense; summary of official reports. Econ. Jour., 1906. Vol. 16, pp. 617-622.

86. **Dexter, Edwin Grant** The effects of weather upon the child. Paidologist, 1906. Vol. 8, pp. 11-17.

87. **Dorsey, G. A.** Caddo customs of childhood. Jour. of Am. Folk-Lore, 1905. Vol. 18, pp. 226-228.
    Treats of customs to protect new-born children and the infant up to two years.

88. **Drawbridge, C. L.** Religious education, how to improve it. Longmans, Green & Co., N. Y., 1906. pp. 222.

89. **Drouot, E.** Les troubles de la parole à l'école primaire. Rev. Ped., 1906. N. S., Vol. 49, pp. 374-386.

90. **Dumont, Albert** Essai sur l'éphébie attique. Firmin-Didot & Cie, Leipzig, 1875-1876. 2 v.

91. **Edson, Andrew W.** The problem of the backward pupil. School Jour., 1906. Vol. 73, pp. 60-62.
    States reasons for backwardness.

92. **Elliott, C. A.** The cantines scolaires of Paris. 19th Cent., 1906. Vol. 59, pp. 834-841.

93. **Ellis, Havelock** The psychology of yellow. Pop. Sci. Mo., 1906. Vol. 68, pp. 456-463.
    See pages 456-458. Explanation and reason of child's interest in yellow.

94. **Enderlin, Max** Das Spielzeug in seiner Bedeutung für die Entwicklung des Kindes. Kinderfehler, 1906. Vol. 12, pp. 8-16; 65-71.

95. **Ernst, Lucy Hoesch and Meumann, Ernst** Das Schulkind in seiner körperlichen und geistigen Entwicklung. O. Nemnich, Leipzig, 1906. Pt. 1, pp. 165.

96. **Faggiani, I.** Il senso del tempo nei bambini. Atti del 5 Cong. Internat. di Psicologia, tenuto in Roma. Roma, 1905. p. 664.

This is a mere note, based upon considerable observational data, which states the theory that time sense in children is based upon the intervals between eating, that physiological stimulus which is referable to the digestive apparatus, which conduces to the development of this notion in both normal and defective children and even in animals. In normal children the habitual experience of these purely physiological sensations with the progress of mental development becomes transformed into a fact of the intelligence.

97. —— —— La memoria nei bambi ninormali e nei deficienti. Atti del 5 Cong. Internat. di Psicologia, tenuto in Roma. Roma, 1905. p. 609.

A brief account of memory tests made on 230 normal and deficient children of both sexes. The children were divided into three groups according to age, namely, 4-5 yrs., 5-6 yrs., and 7-13 yrs., and both quantitative and qualitative results were noted.

98. **Feltgen, Ernst** Schulhygienische Mitteilungen vom internationalen Tuberkulosekongress, Paris, 1905. Gesunde Jugend, 1905-6. Vol. 5, pp. 149-169.

99. **Fiebig, M.** Über Vorsorge und Fürsorge für die intellektuellschwache und sittlich gefährdete Jugend. Kinderfehler, 1906. Vol. 11, pp. 321-341 ; 353-376.

Fitz, George Wells See **Fitz, Rachel Kent and Fitz, G. W.**

100. **Fitz, Rachel Kent and Fitz, G. W.** Problems of babyhood. H. Holt & Co., N. Y., 1906. pp. 127.

101. **Förster, Wilhelm** Heilung und Vorbeugung jugendlicher Kriminalität. Zeits. für Schulgesundheitspflege, 1906. Vol. 19, pp. 246-251.

102. **Fraenkel, Arthur** Tuberkulose und Schule. Zeits. für Schulgesundheitspflege, 1906. Vol. 19, pp. 389-409.

A valuable statistical study.

103. **Frankenberg, H. von** Der Alkoholgenuss der Schulkinder. Zeits. für Schulgesundheitspflege, 1906. Vol. 19, pp. 695-707.

104. **French, William** Child-labor, compulsory education, and race suicide. Arena, 1906. Vol. 36, pp. 35-37.

105. **Fries, Theophil** Eine Lücke im Arbeitsfelde der empirischen Kinderpsychologie. Kinderfehler, 1906. Vol. 11, pp. 109-116.

106. **Gesell, Arnold** Jealousy. Am. Jour of Psy., Oct., 1906. Vol. 17, pp. 437-495.

A summary of jealousy during infancy, adolescence and adulthood, also its development and scope.

107. **Gheorgov, I. A.** Einiges über die grammatische Entwicklung der Kindersprache. Atti del 5 Cong. Intern. di Psicologia tenuto in Roma. Roma, 1905. pp. 203-210.

A study of the development of the different parts of speech in the language of children up to the age of three years.

108. **Goddard, Henry H.** Ideals of a group of German children. Ped. Sem., June, 1906. Vol. 13, pp. 208-220.

109. **Godley, Eveline C.** A century of books for children. Living Age, 1906. Vol. 249, pp. 689-698.

110. **Godtfring, O.** Die psychische Beeinflussung stotternder Schulkinder. Zeits. für Schulgesundheitspflege, 1906. Vol. 19, pp. 317-323.
Important suggestions for the treatment of stuttering children.

111. **Gorst, John E.** The children of the nation, how their health should be promoted by the state. Methuen & Co., London, 1906. pp. 297.

112. **Gray, Mary Richards** A visit to a Chinese kindergarten. Elem. School Teacher, 1906. Vol. 7, pp. 214-219.

113. **Greene, Cordelia A.** The art of keeping well; or, Common sense hygiene for adults and children. Dodd, Mead & Co., N. Y., 1906. pp. 418.

114. **Groszmann, Waldermar Heinrich** The position of the atypical child. Jour. of Nerv. and Ment. Disease, 1906. Vol. 33, pp. 425-446.

115. **Gulick, Luther H.** Why play must be taught. School Jour., 1906. Vol. 73, pp. 289-290.

116. **Gündel, A.** Zur Organisierung der Geistesschwachen-Fürsorge. C. Marhold, Halle, 1906. pp. 190.

117. **Gymer, Rose C.** Personal library work with children. Pub. Lib., 1906. Vol. 11, pp. 191-193.

118. **Hailmann, W. N.** Relation of Froebel's principles to hand work in the elementary school. Kindergarten Rev., 1906. Vol. 16, pp. 579-592.

119. **Hall, Granville Stanley** Boy life in a Massachusetts country town forty years ago. Ped. Sem., June, 1906. Vol. 13, pp. 185-191.

120. —— —— Youth: its education, regimen and hygiene. D. Appleton, N. Y., 1906. pp. 379.

121. **Halleck, Reuben Post** What kind of education is best suited to boys? School Rev., 1906. Vol. 14, pp. 512-521.

122. **Hamm,** —— Schwerhörige Schulkinder. Die Deutsche Schule, 1906. Vol. 10, pp. 287-291.

123. **Haney, James Parton** Education of the dullard in the public school. Jour. of Ed., 1906. Vol. 63, pp. 619-621.

124. **Harris, Ada Van Stone** The persistence of play activities throughout school life. Kindergarten Rev., 1906. Vol. 17, pp. 14-19.

125. **Henderson, C. Hanford** Naughty boys. Kindergarten Rev., 1906. Vol. 17, pp. 1-6.

126. **Hensgen, ——** Wie kann die Schule mitwirken zum Schutze gegen die Verbreitung der Tuberkulose. Die Gesundh. der Schule, 1905. Vol. 3, pp. 258-264.

Methods by which the schools may work against the spread of tuberculosis, and of diminishing dust. Open air summer schools emphasized.

Hermant, Paul See **Boulanger and Hermant, Paul.**

127. **Hill, Caroline Southwood** Notes on education for mothers and teachers. Seeley & Co., London, 1906. pp. 122.

128. **Hill, David S.** An experiment with pugilism. Ped. Sem., March, 1906. Vol. 13, pp. 125-131.

129. **Hill, Patty S.** The relation of play and work in modern education. Kindergarten Rev., 1906. Vol. 17, pp. 6-14.

130. **Hine, Lewis W.** The school in the park. Outlook, 1906. Vol. 83, pp. 712-719.

131. **Hodgson, Geraldine** Over-pressure. Jour. of Ed., Lond., 1906. N. S., Vol. 28, pp. 529-531.

132. **Hopf, Fr. E.** Uber die hygienische Bedeutung des Händewaschens, besonders in den Schulen. Zeits. fur Schulgesundheitspflege, 1906. Vol. 19, pp. 154-161.

133. **Horne, Herman Harrell** Practical and impractical ways of educating the will. Education, 1906. Vol. 27, pp. 85-91.

134. **Howe, Elizabeth** Can the collecting instinct be utilized in teaching? Elem. School Teacher, 1906. Vol. 6, pp. 466-471.

This article was written with a view to raising the question as to how the collecting instinct can be utilized in teaching.

135. **Hunt, Clara W.** Library for children a moral force. Lib. Jour., 1906. Vol. 31, pp. 97-103.

136. **Hunter, Robert** The social significance of underfed children. Internat. Quar., Jan., 1906. Vol. 12, pp. 330-349.

137. **Hylan, John P.** The apperceptive basis of manual training. Education, 1906. Vol. 26, pp. 324-341.

138. **Jackson, Arabelle H.** Library work with children. Lib. Jour., 1906. Vol. 31, pp. 89-97.

139. **Jessen, ——** Referate aus den einzelnen Gebieten der Schulgesundheitspflege. Die Gesundh. der Schule, 1906. Vol. 4, pp. 162-167.

Statistics in regard to the teeth of school children and their connection with disease.

140. **—— ——** Die Zahnverderbnis der Schuljugend und ihre Bekämpfung. Die Gesundh. der Schule, 1906. Vol. 4, pp. 77-93.

A detailed report of the results of the dental clinics established in connection with the schools and its beneficial effect on the general health of the children.

141. **Jewell, James Ralph** Place of nature study, school gardens, and agriculture in our schools. Ped. Sem., Sept., 1906. Vol. 13, pp. 273-292.

142. **Johnson, George E.** The country boy. Mass. Civic League Leaflets, 1906. No. 8. pp. 19.

143. **Jordan, Walter R.** The medical inspection of school children. Paidologist, 1906. Vol. 8, pp. 70-77.

144. **Kahn, Amy** Suggestive games for the first year. N. Y. Teachers' Monographs. Mch., 1906. Vol. 8, pp. 19-25.

145. **Kalischer, S.** Ueber Sorgenkinder für Schule und Haus. Die Gesundh. der Schule, 1905. Vol. 3, pp. 286-294.

   Two classes of children are here discussed, those who, though not to be classed as actually weak minded, make little progress in school, and morally weak children. Through an early recognition of such defects, much may be done for such children, while attempts to force them through secondary schools usually results in disaster.

146. —— —— Ueber tik-artige Bewegungen bei Kindern. Die Gesundh. der Schule, 1905. Vol. 3, pp. 267-270.

   Calls attention to certain automatisms in children as symptoms of nervous disorder and suggests proper modes of treatment.

147. **Kalle,** —— Zur Bekämpfung der Säuglingssterblichkeit durch die Schule. Die Gesundh. der Schule, 1905. Vol. 3, pp. 282-286.

   On the feeding of children under a year old; gives preparation and proportion of food and proper intervals of feeding.

148. **Karaman, L.** Hygienische Trinkbecherkasten für Schulen. Zeits. für Schulgesundheitspflege, 1906. Vol. 19, pp. 145-148.

149. **Katz, David** Ein Beitrag zur Kenntnis der Kinderzeichnungen. Zeits. f. Psy. u. Physiol. d. Sinnesorgane, 1906. Vol. 41, pp. 241-256.

150. **Kauffman, Warren S.** Kindergarten principles in later education. School Jour., 1906. Vol. 73, pp. 422-424.

151. **Kemsies, Ferdinand** Die sexuelle Aufklärung der Jugend. Zeits. für Päd. Psy. Path. u. Hygiene, 1906. Vol. 8, pp. 125-132.

   Sex information for children from the standpoint of the teacher.

152. **Kiefer, O.** Kindermisshandlung und Sexualität. Mutterschutz, 1906. Vol. 2, pp. 156-159.

153. **King, William** Special classes in the public schools of New York. Education, 1906. Vol. 27, pp. 95-100.

   How defective children are treated.

154. **Kirk, Florence** The training of children under five in elementary schools. Paidologist, 1906. Vol. 8, pp. 17-28.

   Methods employed in kindergarten work.

155. **Kluge, O.** Über das Wesen und die Behandlung der geistig abnormen Fürsorgezöglinge. Samm. v. Abh. a. d. Geb. d. päd. Psy. u. Physiol., 1906. Vol. 8, No. 4, pp. 18.

156. **Koester, Hermann L.** Geschichte der deutschen Jugendliteratur in Monographien. A. Janssen, Hamburg, 1906. Pt. 1, pp. 196.

157. **Kölling, Elizabeth** Persönlichkeitsbilder zweier schwachsinniger Kinder. Zeits. für Päd. Psy. Path. u. Hygiene, 1906. Vol. 8, pp. 241-267.

158. **Kraus, Siegfried** Die Berufsvormundschaft als Schutzorgan für die unehelichen Kinder. Mutterschutz, 1906. Vol. 2, pp. 237-242.

Kreiss, —— See **Munzel, Ed.** and **Kreiss, ——**

159. **Krumholz, August** Die Infektion durch Tuberkulose in den Lehrsälen der Normalschulen. Die Gesundh. der Schule, 1905. Vol. 3, pp. 216-221.
    Plea for the protection of school children against tuberculosis, propagated through unhygienic building construction and bad systems of ventilation.

160. **Kundius, Emil** "Wilhelm Tell" und das Kinderpublikum. Die Deutsche Schule, 1906. Vol. 10, pp. 434-439.

161. **Lalesque, Dr.** Congrès international des colonies scolaires de vacances, Bordeaux 17-20 avril, 1906. Rev. Ped., 1906. N. S., Vol. 48, pp. 535-547.

162. **Lamont, Hammond** Reading of children. Nation, 1906. Vol. 83, pp. 551-552.

163. **Larguier, J.** La psychologie judiciaire. L'Année Psy., 1906. Vol. 12, pp. 159-232.
    A psychological study of the value of children as witnesses. Takes up the work of Binet and Stern in this line.

164. **Laser, Hugo** Das Nägelbeissen der Schulkinder. Zeits. fur Schulgesundheitspflege, 1906. Vol. 19, pp. 219-225.

165. **Latter, Lucy R.** School gardening for little children. Swan Sonnenschein & Co., London, 1906. pp. 166.

166. **Lawrence, Isabel** How lead children to love good books. Pub. Lib., 1906. Vol. 11, pp. 179-183.

167. **Legg, F. and Legg, C.** School gardening for little children. Child Life, 1906. Vol. 8, pp. 172-175.

168. **Legorju, A.** La crise de l'enseignement secondaire; l'éducation et le droit social. Rey & Cie, Lyon, 1906. pp. 424.

169. **Lemaitre, A.** Troubles de la personnalité chez un garçon de 15 ans. Atti del 5 Cong. Internat. di Psicologia, tenuto in Roma. Roma, 1905. p. 482.
    A brief sketch of a case of multiple personality, characterized by nightmares, autoscopic hallucination and soliloquies.

170. **Libby, M. F.** Hall on growth; précis and comments. Univ. of Colo. Invest. Depts. of Psy. and Ed., 1905. Vol. 3, No. 1, pp. 3-23.

171. **Lipmann, Otto** Einige interessante Kinderlügen. Zeits. für päd. Psy. Path. u. Hygiene, 1906. Vol. 8, pp. 85-88.

172. **—— ——** Die Wirkung der Suggestivfragen. Zeits. für päd. Psy. Path. u. Hygiene, 1906. Vol. 8, pp. 89-96.

173. **Lobsien, M.** Ueber Differenzierungen des Gedächtnisses. Zeits. fur päd. Psy. Path. u. Hygiene, 1906. Vol. 8, pp. 330-343.

174. **Loch, C. H.** The feeding of school children. Yale Rev., 1906. Vol. 15, pp. 230-250.

175. **Loening, Edgar** Juvenile criminality in Germany. Rep. of Comm. of Ed. for 1904. Vol. 1, pp. 703-713.

176. **Lorentz, Friedrich** Erscheinungen der Literatur auf dem Gebiet der Schulhygiene im Jahre 1905. Zeits. für päd. Psy. Path. u. Hygiene, 1906. Vol. 8, pp. 389-407.

177. —— —— Sozialhygiene und Schule. L. Voss, Leipzig, 1906. pp. 162.

178. **Lovejoy, Owen R.** Child-labor and family disintegration. Independent, 1906. Vol. 61, pp. 748-750.

179. **Mackenzie, W. Leslie** The health of the school child. Methuen & Co., London, 1906. pp. 120.

180. **McMillan, Margaret** Citizens of to-morrow; medical inspection in schools. Independent Rev., 1906. Vol. 10, pp. 173-187.

181. **Major, David R.** First steps in mental growth; a series of studies in the psychology of infancy. Macmillan Co., N. Y., 1906. pp. 360.

182. **Maltby, A. B.** Library work with children. Outlook, 1906. Vol. 82, pp. 360-364.

183. **Martin, E. S.** The mind of a child. Harper's Mag., 1906. Vol. 114, pp. 70-75.

184. **Mathews, R. H.** Some initiation ceremonies of the aborigines of Australia. Zeits. f. Ethnol., 1905. Vol. 37, pp. 872-879.

185. **Mathewson, Albert M.** Boy's good government club, New Haven. Independent, 1906. Vol. 60, pp. 665-666.

186. **Maule, F.** Getting at the boys. Outlook, 1906. Vol. 81, pp. 822-826.

187. **Maximilian** —— Die Nasenerkrankungen in ihren Beziehungen zur Schule. Die Gesundh. der Schule, 1906. Vol. 4, pp. 9-19.
    An investigation of diseases of the nasal passage among school children, pointing out their results on the mental development and emphasizing need of medical supervision in the schools.

188. **Mead, Edwin D.** Peace teaching in schools. Jour. of Ed., 1906. Vol. 63, pp. 89-90.

189. **Mendel, Lafayette B.** Childhood and growth. F. A. Stokes Co., N. Y., 1906. pp. 54.

Meumann, Ernst See **Ernst, Lucy Hoesch** and **Meumann, Ernst.**

Meyer, I. F. See **Colvin, Stephen S.** and **Meyer, I. F.**

190. **Meyers, George Edmund** Moral training in the schools; a comparative study. Ped. Sem., Dec., 1906. Vol. 13, pp. 409-460.

191. **Miall, E.** Play. Child Life, 1906. Vol. 7, pp. 58-61.

192. **Miller, Elsa** Garden work. Elem. School Teacher, 1906. Vol. 6, pp. 246-252.
    Work done by the Francis W. Parker School, Chicago, in school gardens.

193. **Mills, Harriette Melissa** The child, his nature and needs. Kindergarten Mag., 1906. Vol. 19, pp. 85-05.

194. —— —— Veiled truths. Kindergarten Mag., 1906. Vol. 19, pp. 231-239.
    Significance of Christmas and its influence on child life.

195. **Milner, Mrs. Florence** When mercy seasons justice. Education, 1906. Vol. 27, pp. 216-221.

196. —— —— Youth and the sunshine. Education, 1906. Vol. 26, pp. 260-264.

197. **Mitchell, A. M.** Humane education; a plea for a humane and ethical system of elementary education. A. C. Fifield, London, 1906. pp. 32.

198. **Mobius, Paul Julius** *ed.* Gedanken über die Schule. G. Hirzel, Leipzig, 1906. pp. 64.

199. **Monroe, Will S.** American songs and school music. Jour. of Ed., 1906. Vol. 63, pp. 68-69.

200. —— —— German and American schools. School Rev., 1906. Vol. 14, pp. 217-222.
    A comparison of the nature and quantity of work done in the elementary schools of the two countries.

201. —— —— Kinderstudium in den Vereinigten Staaten. Die Kinderfehler, 1906. Vol. 11, pp. 203-207.

202. —— —— Use of pictures in teaching. Jour. of Ed., 1906. Vol. 63, p. 37.

203. **Morrissey, Elizabeth L.** Essentials of good books for children. Pub. Lib., 1906. Vol. 11, pp. 548-549,

204. **Moses, Julius** Zur Frage Jugendbelehrung. Kinderfehler, 1906. Vol. 11, pp. 166-177.

205. **Müller, E.** Über die Kleidung der Schulmädchen. Die Gesundh. der Schule, 1905. Vol. 3, pp. 88-91.

206. —— —— Was kann die Schule zur Verhütung der seitlichen Verkrümmung der Wirbelsäule (der Skoliose) tun? Die Gesundh. der Schule, 1906. Vol. 4, pp. 101-118.
    Suggestions for various means of guarding against spinal curvature in school children.

207. **Müller, E.** Was können Lehrer und Lehrerinnen tun, um die Entwicklung und das Fortschreiten der Kurzsichtigkeit bei ihren Schülern zu verhüten und die Augen derselben zu schärfen?· Die Gesundh. der Schule, 1905. Vol. 3, pp. 158-165; 186-191.

A discussion of what teachers can do to guard against near sightedness. Suggests various improvements in school material and practice and calls attention to dust in schoolrooms as prolific source of catarrh and eye troubles.

208. **Munroe, James P.** The joint educational responsibility of the school and the community. Ed. Rev., 1906. Vol. 31, pp. 439-450.

209. **Munzel, Ed.** and **Kreiss,** —— Bericht der Weimarer Schulärzte umfassend den Zeitraum des Schuljahres 1905-06. Die Gesundh. der Schule, 1906. Vol. 4, pp. 256-262.

Statistical report of the work of the school physicians at Weimar for the year 1905-06.

210. **Murdock, F. F.** Children in geography; how children can live in geography from the standpoint of the child's nature and needs. Jour. of Ed., 1906. Vol. 63, pp. 65, 177, 318, 431.

211. **Muthesius, Karl** Altes und Neues aus Herders Kinderstube. H. Beyer, Langensalza, 1905. pp. 35. Padagogisches Mag. Pt. 247.

212. **Nabours, Robert K.** Nature work in the schoolroom. Elem. School Teacher, 1906. Vol. 6, pp. 412-416.

213. **Nausester, W.** Die grammatische Form der Kindersprache. Zeits. fur Päd. Psy. Path. u. Hygiene, 1906. Vol. 8, pp. 214-233.

214. **Newman, George** Infant mortality; a social problem. Methuen & Co., London, 1906. pp. 356.

215. **Norris, George** Parental schools. School Jour., 1906. Vol. 72, pp. 241-242.

216. **Norsworthy, Naomi** Psychology of mentally deficient children. Science Press, N. Y., 1906. pp. 111. Arch. of Psy., Nov., 1906. No. 1.

217. **Noyes, William** The idle boy. Independent, 1906. Vol. 61, pp. 330-332.

218. **Ogden, Robert Morris** The foundations of character. Southern Ed. Rev., Nov., 1906. Vol. 3, pp. 126-131.

219. **Oliphant, James** Moral instruction. Internat. Jour. of Ethics, 1906. Vol. 16, pp. 401-418.

220. **Orr, William** Physical training in high schools. Ed. Rev., 1906. Vol. 32, pp. 42-55.

221. **O'Shea, M. V.** Development of ethical sentiment in the child. Internat. Jour. of Ethics, 1905. Vol. 16, pp. 68-76.

222. —— —— Tendencies in child and educational psychology. Psy. Bull., 1906. Vol. 3, pp. 357-363.

223. **Pabst,** —— Fürsorge der Städte fur kränkliche bezw. mit fehlerhaften Anlagen behaftete Schulkinder. Die Gesundh. der Schule, 1905. Vol. 3, pp. 165-171.

Account of municipal efforts for the betterment of the health of school children, especially those having bodily defects or weaknesses.

224. —— —— Die psychologische und pädagogische Bedeutung des praktischen Unterrichts. Die Gesundh. der Schule, 1906. Vol. 4, pp. 290-292.

Discusses the relation of motor training to mental development from the standpoint of modern psychology, showing the function of the former as a part of education.

225. **Palmer, Luella A.** Results of observations in the Speyer school experimental playroom. Kindergarten Rev., 1906. Vol. 17, pp. 140-147.

226. **Parker, J. M.** Child-training by bookkeeping. Outlook, 1906. Vol. 83, pp. 843-844.

227. **Patch, Kate Whiting** A child's thought of God. Kindergarten Rev., 1906. Vol. 16, pp. 257-265.

228. **Paulsen, Friederich** The village and the village school. Ed. Rev., 1906. Vol. 32, pp. 445-452.

229. **Paulsen, W.** Für die weltliche Schule. Die Deutsche Schule, 1906. Vol. 10, pp. 555-562.

230. **Payne, Bruce R.** How may manual training be made educative? School Rev., 1906. Vol. 14, pp. 425-428.

231. —— —— Is manual training as now taught educative? School Rev., 1906. Vol. 14, pp. 350-351.

232. **Perie, R.** L'instituteur et l'éducation morale. Rev. Ped., 1906. N. S., Vol. 48, pp. 205-226.

233. **Perrin, John W.** Indirect compulsory education; the factory laws of Massachusetts and Connecticut. Ed. Rev., 1906. Vol. 31, pp. 383-394.

234. **Piper, H.** Die pathologische Lüge. Zeits. für päd. Psy. Path. u. Hygiene, 1906. Vol. 8, pp. 1-15.

235. **Poole, Ernest** Child labor: the street. N. Y., 19—. p. 28.

236. **Poppelreuter, Walther** Zur Psychologie der Warheitsbewusstseins. Zeits. für päd. Psy. Path. u. Hygiene, 1906. Vol. 8, pp. 104-117.

237. **Porter, Charles** School hygiene and the laws of health. Longmans, Green & Co., N. Y., 1906. p. 313.

238. **Powell, Harold G.** Physical education of the blind. Amer. Phys. Ed. Rev., Mch., 1906. Vol. 11, pp. 7-11.

239. **Probst, M.** Les dessins des enfants Kabyles. Arch. de Psy., 1906. Vol. 6, pp. 131-140.

240. **Pudor, Heinrich** Hygiene als Unterrichtsgegenstand in den Schulen. Die Gesundh. der Schule, 1905. Vol. 3, pp. 93-98.

241. **Putnam, Mrs. Alice H.** The persistence of play activities in the school age, and their relation to work. Kindergarten Mag., 1906. Vol. 18, pp. 581-585.

242. **Ransehberg, P.** Vergleichende Untersuchungen an normalen und schwachbefähigten Schulkindern. Atti del 5 Cong. Internat. di Psicologia, tenuto in Roma. Roma, 1905, pp. 611-615.

    This is a comparative study on normal and weak minded children. The following points were tested, vocabulary and mental content; capability of comprehension and expression; memory; elementary arithmetical capability; ability to comprehend printed words of one and two syllables.

Ravenhill, Alice See **Scharlieb, Mary** and **Ravenhill, Alice.**

243. **Ray, John T.** Pupil self-government and training for good citizenship. School Jour., 1906. Vol. 73, pp. 339-340.

243 a. **Resta De Robertis** La psicologia dell' enfanzia nell' uso dei verbi. Atti del 5 Congresso Internationale di Psicologia tenuto in Roma dal 26 al 30 Aprile, 1905. Roma, 1905. pp. 678-691.

    A psychological study of the development of verbs in the vocabulary of children, and is a valuable contribution to the study of language.

244. **Richman, Julia** The incorrigible child. Ed. Rev., 1906. Vol. 31, pp. 484-506; also in Jour. of Ed., 1906. Vol. 63, pp. 286-290.

245. **Rietz,** —— Körperentwicklung und geistige Begabung. Zeits. fur Schulgesundheitspflege, 1906. Vol. 19, pp. 65-98.

    Results of the physical investigation of 20,400 school children corroborate Porter's conclusion that children of a higher school grade than that of others of the same age on the average show also better physical development.

246. **Riis, Jacob A.** Boy's fun in the old town. Outlook, 1906. Vol. 83, pp. 278-281.

247. —— —— Crippled children; the children's plea. Outlook, 1906. Vol. 82, pp. 753-755.

248. **Rischawy, G.** Die Bewegung zur Pflege der kunstlerischen Bildung und ihre Begründung. Die Deutsche Schule, 1906. Vol. 10, pp. 690-701.

249. **Rogers, Lina L.** How children are protected from disease in the public schools. Jour. of Ed., 1906. Vol. 63, p. 258.

250. **Roller, Karl** Des Lehrers hygienisches Wirken in der Aufnahmeklasse. Gesunde Jugend, 1905-06. Vol. 5, pp. 3-6.

351. **Roller, Karl** Erhebungen über das Mass der häuslichen Arbeitszeit, veranstaltet in einer Oberrealschulklasse. Zeits. für Schulgesundheitspflege, 1906. Vol. 19, pp. 1-28.

252. **Rosenfeld, Jessie** Special classes in the public schools of New York. Education, 1906. Vol. 27, pp. 92-100.

253. **Rosenfeld, Siegfried** Altersdispens und Unterrichtserfolg. Zeits. fur Schulgesundheitspflege, 1906. Vol. 19, pp. 141-145.

254. —— —— Schulbesuchsdauer und Morbidität. Zeits. fur Schulgesundheitspflege, 1906. Vol. 19, pp. 472-484.

A study of morbidity among Vienna school children, showing that the percentage of disease among school children, with the exception of contagious diseases, increases with the grades, although not necessarily from the fault of the school.

255. **Rosenthal, O.** Die sexuelle Aufklärung der Jugend. Zeits. für päd. Psy. Path. u. Hygiene, 1906. Vol. 8, pp. 16-28.

The question of sex instruction for children from the standpoint of the physician.

256. **Rouma, Georges** L'état de l'enseignement spécial pour enfants arriérés aux Pays-Bas. La Meuse, Liège, 1906. pp. 38.

257. **Rowe, Stuart Henry** Physical nature of the child, and how to study it. Macmillan Co., N. Y., 1906. pp. 211.

Royer See **Bourneville, and Royer.**

258. **Russell, Alys** The Ghent school for mothers. 19th Cent., 1906. Vol. 60, pp. 970-975.

259. **Rust, Horatio N.** A puberty ceremony of the Mission Indians. Amer. Anthropol., 1906. Vol. 8, pp. 28-32.

260. **Sadler, Michael E.** Report on secondary and higher education in Newcastle-upon-Tyne. Newcastle-upon-Tyne, 1905. pp. 89.

261. **von Sanden, Alfred** Zur Geschichte der Lissaer Schule. Ebbecke, Lissa, 1905. pp. 104.

262. **Schaffer, Mary Frances** Conservatism versus radicalism in the kindergarten. Education, 1906. Vol. 27, pp. 37-44.

263. **Schaeffer, N. C.** Moral training at school. Southern Ed. Rev., 1906. Vol. 3, pp. 95-100.

264. **Schäfer, J.** Die Bedeutung des Turnens für die sittliche Erziehung der Jugend. Zeits. für Schulgesundheitspflege, 1906. Vol. 19, pp. 210-218; 323-330.

265. **Schallmayer, W.** Die sociologische Bedeutung des Nachwuchses der Begabteren und die psychische Vererbung. Arch. f. Rassen-u. Ges. Biol., 1905. Vol. 2, pp. 36-75.

Discusses recent theories and investigations concerning the size of families of the more talented classes of the population.

266. **Scharlieb, Mary** and **Ravenhill, Alice** Physical training in Stockholm and Copenhagen. 19th Cent., 1906. Vol. 60, pp. 986-997.

267. **Schepp, F.** Typen von Schülern die bei einer gewissen pathologischen Beschaffenheit doch im allgemeinen Klassenunterricht mitgeführt werden können. Zeits. für päd. Psy. Path-u. Hygiene, 1906. Vol. 8, pp, 178-213.

268. **Schlesinger, Eugen** Die Folgen der Körperlichen Züchtigung der Schulkinder. Zeits. für Schulgesundheitspflege, 1906.
Vol. 19, pp. 775-780.

269. **Schmid, August** Über den Begriff der Natur in der Erziehung. Die Deutsche Schule, 1906. Vol. 10, pp. 370-373.

270. **Schmidt, F.** Gesundheitsgemässer Unterricht. Die Gesundh.
der Schule, 1906. Vol. 4, pp. 134-139.
   The author condemns certain methods of instruction and especially of
   examination as injurious to the health of pupils and an unnecessary nervous strain.

271. **Schnitzer, Hubert** Moderne Behandlung der Geister-
kranken. Zeits. für Pad. Psy. Path. u. Hygiene, 1906. Vol. 8,
pp. 35-57.

272. **Shreiber, H.** Beitrag zür fruchtbringenden Gestaltung des
Rechenungsunterricht in unseren Schulen für normale und
abnorme Kinder. Kinderfehler, 1906. Vol. 11, pp. 97-109.

273. **Schreuder, A. J.** Warum und wozu betriebt man Kinderstudium? Kinderfehler, 1906. Vol. 11, pp. 129-137; 161-166.

274. **Schulz, H.** Ausstellung für Schulgesundheitspflege in Hannover vom 3. bis 8. Oktober, 1905. Zeits. für Schulgesundheitspflege, 1906. Vol. 19, pp. 149-154.

275. **Schulze, Eduard** Inhaltsverzeichnis der ersten zehn Jahrgänge
der Zeitschrift für Kinderforschung (Die Kinderfehler). Langensalza, 1906. pp. 56.
   A bibliography of the articles on children, published in *Die Kinderfehler*
   during the ten years past.

276. **Schuyten, M. C.** Comment droit on mesurer la fatigue des
écoliers? Arch. de Psy., 1905. Vol. 4, pp. 113-128.
   Rapport au 1er Cong. internat. d'Hygiène scolaire à Nuremberg, 1904.

277. **Schwarz, Karl** Waldschulen. Die Gesundh. der Schule,
1905. Vol. 3, pp. 200-202.
   An appeal for open air schools during the summer.

278. **Scott, Colin Alexander** Children's self-organized work and
the education of leadership in the schools. Jour. of Ed., 1906.
Vol. 63, p. 33.

279. —— —— Secondhand science and children's reasoning. Ed.
Rev., 1906. Vol. 31, pp. 167-179.

280. **Seifart, H.** Kinderstudium in der Hilfsschule. Kinderfehler,
1906. Vol. 11, pp. 296-303.

281. **Sharp, Cecil** Music and folk songs in the elementary school.
Child Life, 1906. Vol. 8, pp. 79-83.

282. **Shaw, Adèle M.** Reading of children. Critic, 1906. Vol.
48, pp. 177-180.

283. **Sheldon, Winthrop D.** Some practical suggestions toward
a programme of ethical teaching in our schools. Education,
1906. Vol. 27, pp. 193-199.

284. **Shinn, Milicent Washburn** Körperliche und geistige Entwicklung eines Kindes in biographischer Darstellung; hrsg. von W. Glabbach and G. Weber. Langensalza, Gressley, 1905. pp. 645

285. **Shrubsall, F. C.** Comparison of the physical characters of hospital patients with those of healthy individuals from the same areas. Rept. Brit. Assoc. Adv. Sci., 1904 (1905). Vol. 74, pp. 702-704.
Children are much fairer than adults, and than healthy children. Blondes feel more acutely change of environment.

286. **Shute, Katherine H.** Literature in the elementary schools. School Rev., 1906. Vol. 14, pp. 484-491.

287. **Silber, Martha** Die Sprache meiner Kinder. Kinderfehler, 1906. Vol. 11, pp. 242-250; 268-275.

Simon, Th. See **Binet, Alfred** and **Simon, Th.**

288. **Sipe, Susan B.** School gardening at the national capital. Elem. School Teacher, 1906. Vol. 6, pp. 417-419.
Account of school gardening in the District of Columbia.

289. **Solbrig,** —— Die Regelung der Schulbankfrage im Regierungsbezirk Arnsberg. Zeits. fur Schulgesundheitspflege, 1906. Vol. 19, pp. 225-240.

290. **Spargo, John** The bitter cry of the children. Macmillan Co., N. Y., 1906. pp. 337.

291. **Starr, L.** Hygiene of the nursery. 7th ed. P. Blakiston, Phila., 1906.

292. **Stearns, Lutie E.** Problem of the girl in the library. Lib. Jour., 1906. Vol. 31, pp. 103-106.

293. **Steiner, Joseph A.** A study in modern philanthropies. Assoc. Seminar, 1906. Vol. 14, pp. 22-30; 49-52; 85-93; 129-137; 182-187; 205-214; 285-296; 349-358; 364-380.
A thesis which treats of children's aid societies, boys' clubs, juvenile courts, etc.

294. **Stetter, Konrad** Die Schulbank. Gesunde Jugend, 1905-6. Vol. 5, pp. 55-62; 104-111.

295. **Stevens, Kate** Child study in Great Britain. Ped. Sem., June, 1906. Vol. 13, pp. 245-249.

296. **Story, Elinor H.** Child-labor. Arena, 1906. Vol. 36, pp. 584-591.

297. **Stoudt, J. B.** Pennsylvania German riddles and nursery-rhymes. Jour. Am. Folk-Lore, 1906. Vol. 19, pp. 113-121.
Pages 119-121 contain counting-out rhymes, cradle-songs, etc.

298. **Stubbs, George W.** The mission of the juvenile court. Jour. of Ed., 1906. Vol. 63, pp. 171-173.

299. **Suck, Hans** Die schwellenlose Kombinationsschulbank. Zeits. fur Schulgesundheitspflege, 1906. Vol. 19, pp. 240-246.

300. **Swett, John** Practical nature study. Jour. of Ed., 1906. Vol. 63, pp. 199-200.
  Concerning some common-sense ways of interesting public school children in nature study.

301. **Szyc, Angelica** Flowers. Ped. Sem., Dec., 1906. Vol. 13, pp. 502-508.

302. **Tanner, Amy Eliza** Contributions from the child study department of Wilson college. Ped. Sem., Dec., 1906. Vol. 13, pp. 509-513.

303. **Tattersall, C. H.** Annual report of the medical officer of Salford for 1904. W. F. Jackson, Salford, 1905. pp. 59.
  This report treats of the inspection of schools. Eyesight in school children, anthropometric measurements, and defective children.

304. **Taylor, John Madison** Difficult boys. Pop. Sci. Mo., 1906. Vol. 69, pp, 338-351.
  Explanation of correct motor training of boys.

305. **Terman, Lewis M.** Genius and stupidity. Ped. Sem., Sept., 1906. Vol. 13, pp. 307-373.

306. **Thierack, H.** Sprachgebrechen. Die Gesundh. der Schule, 1905. Vol. 3, pp. 234-240.
  An appeal for the establishment of special institutions for the treatment of children with speech defects.

307. **Thompson, W. O.** The effect of moral education in the public schools upon the civic life of the community. Southern Ed. Rev., 1906. Vol. 3, pp. 87-94.

308. **Thurston, Henry W.** The social significance of the juvenile court. School Rev., 1906. Vol. 14, pp. 415-424.

309. **Toulouse, Eduard** and **Vaschide, N.** Mesure de l'odorat chez les enfants. Comptes rendus heb. des séances de la soc. de biol. 1899. Ser. 11, V. 1, pp. 487-489.

310. **Trüper, J.** Zur Frage der Behandlung unserer jugendlichen Missetäter. Kinderfehler, 1906. Vol. 11, pp. 138-144; 177-189; 201-203.

311. **Tyler, John M.** The boy and the girl in the high school. Education, 1906. Vol. 26, pp. 462-469.

312. —— —— The girl in the grammar grades. Education, 1906. Vol. 26, pp. 404-412.

313. **Ufer, Chr.** Kinderforschung und Pädagogik. Kinderfehler, 1906. Vol. 12, pp. 1-8; 33-40.

314. **Van, Lila** What children read. Pub. Lib., 1906. Vol. 11, pp. 183-185.

Vaschide, N. See **Toulouse, Eduard** and **Vaschide, N.**

315. **Viemann, Wilhelm** Beispiele von Kinderlügen bei grossen Männern. Zeits. für Pad. Psy. Path. u. Hygiene, 1906. Vol. 8, pp. 81-84.

316. **Walker, J. R.** Sioux games. Jour. Am. Folk-Lore, 1906. Vol. 19, pp. 29-36.
Pages 33-36 describe games of Indian boys and girls.

317. **Ward, Edward** Child study. Education, 1906. Vol. 27, pp. 209-215.

318. **Warnecke, A.** Vom pädagogischen Takt. Monatshefte f. d. Sprache u. Pädagogik, 1906. Vol. 7, pp. 33-38.

319. **Warwick, Frances E. M. G. countess of** A nation's youth; physical deterioration: its causes and some remedies. Cassell & Co., London, 1906. pp. 32.

320. **Watters, Caroline A.** Personal element. Effects upon the pupils produced by the teacher's sympathy and interest as well as friendship with them. Jour. of Ed., 1906. Vol. 63, pp. 60-61.

Waxweiler, Emile See **McLean, F. H.** and **Waxweiler, Emile.**

321. **Wehrmann, Martin** Die Begründung des evangelischen Schulwesens in Pommern bis 1563. A. Hoffmann, Berlin, 1905. pp. 72.

322. **Weis-Ulmenried, Anton** Gehorsam und Disziplin. Monatshefte f. d. Sprache u. Pädagogik, 1906. Vol. 7, pp. 109-113.

323. **Werner, Friedrich** Psychologische Begründung der deutschen Methode des Taubstummen-Unterrichts. Samml. v. Abh. a. d. Geb. d. päd. Psy. u. Physiol., 1906. Vol. 8, No. 6, pp. 50.

324. **Wetekamp, W.** J. P. Müllers System. Die Gesundh. der Schule, 1905. Vol. 3, pp. 34-40.

325. —— —— Neueste Erfahrung über das System Müller. Die Gesundh. der Schule, 1906. Vol. 4, pp. 45-48.
Another plea for more light in the schoolroom and better care of the eyes of school children.

326. **Weygandt, W.** Über Idiotie. Samml. Zwang. Abh. a. d. Geb. d. Nerv. u. Geistesk. 1906. Pt. 6-7, pp. 86.

327. **Wightman, H. J.** The child in the kindergarten and primary school. School Jour., 1906. Vol. 72, pp. 597-598.

328. **Wilberforce, R. G.** Education for country children. 19th Cent., 1906. Vol. 59, pp. 678-682.

329. **Wilson, Louis N.** Bibliography of child study for the year 1905. Ped. Sem., Sept., 1906. Vol. 13, pp. 374-397.
Bibliographic references to 305 articles and books on child study published during 1905.

330. **Winch, W. H.** Psychology and philosophy of play. Mind, 1906. N. S., Vol. 15, pp. 32-52; 177-190.

331. **Witte, Wilhelm**   Die sexuelle Aufklärung der Jugend. Zeits. für Pad. Psy. Path. u. Hygiene, 1906. Vol. 8, pp. 29-34.
The question of information concerning sex for children from the moral standpoint.

332. **Wolodekewitsch, Nicolai** Eine Untersuchung der höheren Geistesfähigkeiten bei Schulkindern. Zeits. für Päd. Psy. Path. u. Hygiene, 1906. Vol. 8, pp. 344-361.

333. **Wood, Casey A.** The sanitary regulation of the schoolroom with reference to vision. Elem. School Teacher, 1906. Vol. 7, pp. 62-71.

334. **Woodhull, Alfred A.**   Personal hygiene. J. Wiley & Sons, N. Y., 1906. pp. 221.

335. **Wright, William R.**   Some effects of incentives on work and fatigue. Psy. Rev., 1906. Vol. 13, pp. 23-34.

336. **Yerkes, Robert M.** Animal psychology and criteria of the psychic. Jour. of Philos. Psy. and Sci. Methods, 1906. Vol. 3, pp. 141-150.

337. **Zak, N. V.** Physical development of children in the secondary educational institutions of Moscow. Gerbek, Moscow, 1892, pp. 272.
Text in Russian with English translation.

338. **Zander, R.** Die Schädigung der Schuler durch die Sitztätigkeit und ihre Beseitigung. Die Gesundh. der Schule, 1905. Vol. 3, pp. 2-12.

339. **Ziehen, Th.** Die Geisteskrankheiten des Kindesalter. Reuther & Reichard, Berlin, 1906. pp. 130.
The work deals directly with mental diseases which develop during the school age.

----

340. American Academy of Political and Social Science. Annals. Philadelphia, 1906. Vol. 27.
Contains many valuable papers on child labor.

341. Bericht über den von mir gehaltenen Sprachheilkursus der sprachbeweglichen Kinder der I Bürgerschule im Schuljahre 1905-06. Die Gesundh. der Schule, 1905. Vol. 4, pp. 213-217.
Report of the results of the remedial courses for children with speech defects carried on in connection with the citizen schools.

342. Boston public library. List of books for teachers and students of the kindergarten. Boston Public Library. Mo. Bull., Dec., 1906. Vol. 11, pp. 406-412.

343. Child labor federation. To free the child-slaves. Cosmopolitan, 1906. Vol. 41, pp. 679-680 ; Vol. 42, pp. 109-112.

344. Children of the poor as cared for in Germany. Craftsman, 1906. Vol. 11, pp. 222-231.

345. The children's purgatory. Living Age, 1906. Vol. 249, pp. 719-728.

346. Cleverness of the young. Living Age, 1906. Vol. 248, pp. 751-755.

347. Craftsmanship for crippled children. Craftsman, 1906. Vol. 9, pp. 151-154.

348. Cry of the children. Quar. Rev., 1906. Vol. 205, pp. 29-53.

349. Edinburgh charity organization society. Report on the physical condition of fourteen hundred school children in the city, together with some account of their homes and surroundings. P. S. King, London, 1906. pp. 44 and 92 pl.

350. International congress for the welfare and protection of children. Legislation in regard to children. P. S. King, Westminster, 1906. pp. 88.

351. Jahrbuch für Volks-und Jugendspiele. Vol. 15. B. G. Teubner, Leipzig, 1906. pp. 327.

352. Kongress des Deutschen Vereins für Schulgesundheitspflege in Stuttgart. 6th. Die Gesundh. der Schule, 1905. Vol. 3, pp. 195-200.
  The chief subjects of discussion were the excessive time given to Greek and Latin to the detriment of biology and physiology—and overwork in the schools.

353. Kongress für Kinderforschung und Jugendfürsorge. Die Gesundh. der Schule, 1906. Vol. 4, pp. 67-70.
  Preliminary announcement of the Child Study Congress at Berlin, Oct. 1-4, 1906.

354. Library work with children in a few leading libraries. Pub. Lib., 1906. Vol. 11, pp. 193-202.

355. Massachusetts. Commission on industrial and technical education. Report. Wright, Boston, 1906. pp. 196.

356. Moral education board. Moral instruction in schools and colleges, 1906. p. 13

357. National conference of charities and corrections. Proceedings at the 33d annual session. F. J. Herr, Boston, 1906. pp. 687.
  Contains papers by various authors on defectives, industrial training playgrounds, juvenile court, etc.

358. New York State education department. Arbor day, Friday, May 4, 1906. N. Y. State educ. dept., Albany, 1906. pp. 32.

359. Proceedings of the second annual meeting of the National child labor committee. Ann. Am. Acad. Pol. and Soc. Sci., 1906. Vol. 27, pp. 371-399.

360. Public school girlhood. Saturday Rev., 1906. Vol. 102, pp. 539-540.

361. Report of an investigation of the teaching power in elementary schools, by a joint committee of the childhood and child study societies, assisted by Mr. Marshall Jackman. Paidologist, 1906. Vol. 8, pp. 36-44.

362. Die Schwächung des Gedächtnisses durch die Schule. Die Gesundh. der Schule, 1906. Vol. 4, pp. 118-120.
  Treats of the danger of permanently weakening the memory through the entrance into school and overstrain.

SUBJECT INDEX.

Abnormal, 60, 152.
Abnormalities, 155.
Adolescence, 46, 56, 77, 120, 170.
Æsthetics, 38.
Agriculture, 141.
Alcoholism, 103.
Amer. Indians, 67, 259, 316.
Animal psychology, 336.
Apperception, 137.
Arbor day, 358.
Arithmetic, 272.
Art, 248.
Association of ideas, 43.
Atypical child, 114.
Australia, 184.
Autobiographical, 119.
Automatisms, 146.
Auxiliary schools, 59, 280.

Backward children, 91, 123, 153, 256, 272.
Bad boys, 125, 304.
Bibliography, 9, 45, 69, 156, 176, 275, 329, 342.
Biographical, 181.
Blind, 5, 238.
Book-keeping, 226.
Books for children. *See* Literature.
Boy life, 119.
Boys, 13, 45, 56, 121, 142, 186, 217, 246.
Boys' clubs, 185.
Burbank, 49.

Caddo Indians, 87.
Canteens, 92.
Character, 218.
Child labor, 104, 178, 233, 235, 290, 296, 340, 343, 345, 348, 359.
Child life, 45, 48.
Child study, 9, 10, 24, 40, 80, 105, 193, 201, 222, 273, 275, 280, 284, 295, 302, 313, 317, 329, 351, 353.
Childhood, 64, 65, 66, 87.
China, 64, 112.
Christmas, 194.
City life, 19, 63.
Cleverness, 346.
Clothing, 205.

Co-education, 14.
Collecting instinct, 134.
Color, 93.
Colorado, 72.
Complexion, 285.
Connecticut, 233.
Copenhagen, 266.
Corporal punishment, 268.
Country children, 328.
Country life, 119, 142.
Crime, 1, 101, 175.
Criminology, 74.
Cripples, 247, 347.
Crying, 42.
Curriculum, 6, 253, 352.

Deaf, 122.
Deaf mutes, 20, 323.
Defectives, 59, 145, 153, 223, 357.
Degeneration, 319.
Discipline, 22, 195, 322.
Diseases, 8, 223, 249, 254.
Drawing, 78, 149, 239.
Drinking Cups, 148.
Dull, 123.

Education, 49, 64.
Elementary schools, 154, 200, 286, 327, 361.
Ethics, 197, 219, 221, 283.
Evidence, 163.
Eyesight, 79, 207.

Factory laws, 233.
Family, 178.
Father and mother, 70.
Fatigue, 276, 332, 335.
Feeble-minded, 7, 27, 39, 43, 57, 58, 96, 99, 116, 155, 157, 240, 242, 267.
Florence, 47.
Flowers, 301.
Folk-lore, 87.
Folk-songs, 281.
Food, 37, 85.
Friendship, 320.
Froebel, 118.
Fun, 246.

Games, 4, 94, 144, 174, 316.
Gardens, 192, 288.

Genius, 265, 305.
Geography, 210.
Germany, 108, 175, 200.
Ghent, 258.
Giessen, 58.
Girls, 6, 23, 29, 205, 312, 360.
God, 227.
Government, 185.
Grammar, 213.
Grammar schools, 312.
Great Britain, 63, 295.
Greece, 90.
Growth, 170, 189.

Hand work, 118.
Hannover, 274.
Hearing, 38, 112.
Herder, 211.
High school, 220, 311.
Home-work, 251.
Humanity, 197.
Hygiene, 20, 26, 32, 33, 34, 35, 36,
    38, 49, 51, 52, 79, 98, 103, 111,
    113, 126, 139, 143, 148, 177, 179,
    180, 206, 207, 209, 223, 237, 240,
    249, 250, 270, 274, 285, 291,
    303, 324, 325, 333, 334.
—— School, 53, 132, 140, 159, 176,
    187, 289, 349, 352.
Hypnagogic images, 71.

Ideals, 108.
Idiocy, 326.
Idleness, 217.
Illegitimate children, 158.
Imagination, 75, 76.
Imbecility, 44.
Incorrigibles, 31, 244.
Industrial education, 355.
Industrial training, 357.
Infant mortality, 147.
Infants, 17, 24, 84, 100.
Initiation ceremonies, 184.
Instinct, 41, 134.
Instruction, 224, 270.
Interest, 12, 93.
Italy, 47, 48.

Jealousy, 106.
Juvenile courts, 19, 298, 308, 357.
Juvenile delinquents, 215, 310.

Kabyle, 239.
Kindergarten, 4, 61, 112, 150, 154,
    262, 327, 342.

Language, 67, 68, 89, 107, 213, 242,
    243a, 287, 306.

Leadership, 278.
Legal psychology, 74.
Legislation, 350.
Libraries, 117, 135, 138, 182, 292,
    354.
Lies, 171, 234, 315.
Lissa school, 261.
Literature, 54, 55, 62, 109, 156,

    166, 203, 286, 314.
Manual training, 137, 230, 231,
    347.
Massachusetts, 119, 233.
Mathematics, 242.
Medical inspection of schools, 32,
    33, 36, 143, 180, 209.
Memory, 97, 173, 242, 362.
Memory types, 72
Mental and physical, 245.
Mental defectives, 216.
Mental development, 10, 16, 38,
    41, 60, 181, 183, 265.
Mental diseases, 271, 339.
Mental selection, 18.
Moral education, 356.
Moral imbecility, 99.
Moral training, 190.
Morals, 7, 26, 39, 219, 232, 263,
    307.
Moscow, 337.
Mother-school, 258.
Mothers, 127.
Motor ability, 73.
Motor activity, 18.
Müller, J. P., 324, 325.
Multiple personality, 169.
Music, 199, 281.

Nail-biting, 164.
Nature, 15, 269.
Nature study, 49, 141, 212, 300,
    301.
Nervousness, 146.
Newcastle, 260.
Normal and abnormal, 242.
Nose, 187.
Nursery, 291.
Nursery rhymes, 70, 297.
Nutrition, 24, 25, 37, 136, 147,
    174.

Obedience, 322.
Open air schools, 277.
Outings, 161.
Overwork, 131.

Parental school, 215.
Parks, 130.

Peace, 188.
Pedagogy, 313, 318, 361.
Pennsylvania, 297.
Personality, 243a.
Philanthropy, 293.
Physical development, 57, 63, 83, 95, 257, 285, 319, 337, 349.
Physical education, 5, 238, 264.
Physical training, 220, 266.
Physique, 23.
Pictures, 202.
Play, 29, 30, 94, 115, 124, 129, 191, 225, 241, 330.
Play grounds, 357.
Poor, 344.
Posture, 38, 330.
Preparatory schools, 13.
Psychology, 74, 82, 93, 110, 163.
Puberty, 90, 259.
Public schools, 360.
Pugilism, 128.
Punishment, 3.

Race suicide, 104.
Reading, 67, 82, 162, 282, 314.
Reasoning, 279.
Reform, 61.
Religion, 227, 321.
Religious education, 88.
Riddles, 297.

Rural schools, 228.
Salford, 303.
School, 198, 229.
School and community, 208.
School attendance, 254.
School colonies, 161.
School desks, 289, 294, 299.
School gardens, 21, 141, 165, 167, 288.
School system, 260.
Science, 279.
Scoliosis, 206.
Self-government, 81, 243.
Self-organization, 278.
Sex, 6, 13, 23, 29, 30, 56, 121, 152, 205, 311, 312.
Sex instruction, 151, 255, 331.
Siena, 48.

Smell, 309.
Sociological, 2, 81, 158, 168, 177, 208, 265, 308.
Songs, 199.
Sophienhöhe, 27.
Special classes, 252.
Speech, 213, 287.
Speech defects, 89, 306, 341.
Spelling, 51.
Speyer school, 225.
Stammering, 110.
Statistics, 8, 102.
Stimulus, 335.
Stockholm, 266.
Stupidity, 305.
Suggestion, 172.
Switzerland, 25.
Syllabaries, 67.
Sympathy, 320.

Teachers, 8, 34, 127, 250.
Teeth, 52, 139, 140.
Tics, 146.
Time-sense, 76.
Toys, 94.
Truth, 236.
Tuberculosis, 98, 102, 126, 159.

Underfeeding, 136.
United States, 201.

Vacation Schools, 11.
Variation, 70.
Vision, 71, 333.
Vital statistics, 214.

Washing, 132.
Weather, 86.
Weimar, 209.
Wilhelm Tell, 160.
Will, 133.
Wilson College, 302.
Witnesses, 163.
Worcester, Mass., 53.
Work, 29, 129.
Writing, 46, 67.
Written work, 76.

Youth, 120, 196, 319.

PUBLICATIONS

OF THE

CLARK UNIVERSITY LIBRARY

WORCESTER, MASS.

EDITED BY LOUIS N. WILSON, LITT. D., LIBRARIAN

| Vol. 2 | September, 1908 | No. 6 |

Bibliography of Child Study for the Year 1907

Clark University Press

WORCESTER, MASS.

BIBLIOGRAPHY OF CHILD STUDY

For the Year 1907

By LOUIS N. WILSON, Librarian, Clark University

1. **Abadie, Jean** Recensement des enfants anormaux des écoles publiques de garçons de la ville de Bordeaux. L'Educateur Moderne, 1907. Vol. 2, pp. 209-226.
2. **Addams, Jane** National protection for children. Ann. Am. Acad. Pol. & Soc. Sci., 1907. Vol. 29, pp. 57-60.
3. **Adler, Felix** Attitude of society towards the child as an index of civilization. Ann. Am. Acad. Pol. & Soc. Sci., 1907. Vol. 29, pp. 135-141.
4. **Agahd, Konrad** Jugendwohl und Jugendrecht. H. Schroe, del, Halle, 1907. pp. 231.
5. **Alexejeff, W. G.** Die arithmologischen und wahrscheinlich-keitstheoretischen Kausalitäten als Grundlagen der Strümpell-schen Klassifikation der Kinderfehler. Zeits. f. Phil. u. Päd., 1906. Vol. 14, pp. 145-159.
6. **Allemagne, Henry René d'** Historie des jouets. Hachette & Cie, Paris, 18——. pp. 316.
7. **Allen, Annie Winsor** Home, school and vacation ; a book of suggestions. Houghton, Mifflin & Co., Boston, 1907. pp. 220.
8. **Ament, W.** Eine erste Blütezeit der Kinderseelenkunde um die Wende des 18. zum 19. Jahrhundert. Zeits. f. päd. Psychol., 1907. Vol. 9, pp. 225-226.
9. **Andrew, M. F.** Unfortunates and their treatment. Education, 1907. Vol. 27, pp. 361-367.
10. **Andrews, Agnes** Moral training and the schools. Jour. of Ed. Boston, 1907. Vol. 65, pp. 200-201.
    Anfroy, Ernest See No. 11.
11. **Anfroy, Lucien et Anfroy, Ernest.** Enquête relative au vocabulaire connu des enfants. Bull. de la Soc. Libre, 1907. Vol. 7, pp. 25-41.
12. **Arrowsmith, John** Brain development through play. Paidologist, 1907. Vol. 9, pp. 52-64.
    Babonneix, L. See **Hutinel, V.** and **Babonniex, L.**

Previous installments of the BIBLIOGRAPHY OF CHILD STUDY have appeared in the *Pedagogical Seminary*, as follows : April, 1898, Vol. 5, pp. 541-589 ; Sept., 1899, Vol. 6, pp. 386-410 ; Dec., 1900, Vol. 7, pp. 526-556 ; Dec., 1901, Vol. 8, pp. 515-537 ; Dec., 1902, Vol. 9, pp. 521-542 ; Dec., 1904, Vol. 10, pp, 514-536 ; Sept., 1903, Vol. 11, pp. 292-327 ; Sept., 1905, Vol. 12, pp. 304-333 ; Sept., 1906, Vol. 13, pp. 374-397 ; Sept., 1907, Vol. 14, pp. 329-354.

13. **Baginsky, A.** Die Impressionabilität der Kinder unter dem Einfluss des Milieus. (Beitr. zur Kinderforsch. u. Heilerziehung, H. 27.) Langensalza, Beyer, 1907. pp. 21.

14. **Baldrian, Karl** Über Unterschiede in der Sprachaneignung auf natürlichem und künstlichem Wege. Eos, 1907. Vol. 3, pp. 101-127.
     A study of the differences in the acquirement of language between deaf and normal children.

15. **Barbier, Karl** Ertäubung und Verlust der Sprache. Zeits. f. Kinderforschung, 1907. Vol. 12, pp. 208-215.

16. **Barnard, Grace Everett** The American ideal in the kindergarten. Proc. of N. E. A., 1907. pp. 456-462.

17. **Barnes, Clifford W.** Moral training through the agency of the public school. Proc. N. E. A., 1907. pp. 373-378.

18. **Baur, Alfred** Grosse Muneli, kleine Rekruten. Gesundheitswarte der Schule, 1905. Vol. 3, pp. 191-195.
     Calls attention to the fact that in certain parts of Switzerland children deteriorate because milk is denied them in order to fatten prize cattle.

19. —— —— Fürsorge für die körperlich kranken Kinder in der Schule. Die Gesundh. der Schule, 1907. Vol. 5, pp. 148-161.
     —— —— See also No. 300.
     Beckwith, Marie E. See **Salisbury, Grace Emily** and **Beckwith, M. E.**

20. **Belot, A.** Les études relatives à la psychologie de l' enfant. Bull. de. la. Soc. Libre, 1907. Vol. 7, pp. 121-144.

21. **Berkhan, Oswald** Ein schwachsinniges Kind mit einer Ohrspitze im Sinne Darwin's. Zeits. f. d. Erforschung u. Behandlung d. jugendl. Schwachsinns, 1907. Vol. 1, pp. 504-507.
     An interesting description of the ear of a feeble minded child which showed a well marked development of Darwin's ear points.

22. **Betts, G.** Mind and its education. D. Appleton, N. Y., 1907. pp. 265.
     An elementary text-book in psychology. Has chapters on attention, habit, memory, imagination, etc. "Exercises" and "Suggested Readings" at the end of each of the 16 chapters.

23. **Beveridge, Albert J.** Child labor and the constitution. Nat. Conf. of Char. and Corr., 1907. pp. 188-196.

24. **Beyrand, Alfred** Les terreurs nocturnes de l'enfant. Vigot Vigot Frères, Paris, 1900. pp. 67.

25. **Biedenkapp, Georg** Schultaugenichtse und Musterschüler. H. Costenoble, Jena, 1907. pp. 232.
     Biographical data of 20 famous men who did not shine in school.

26. **Bienstock, Dr.** Die Waldschule in Mülhausen i. Els. Zeits. f. Schulgesundheitspflege, 1907. Vol. 20, pp. 219-235.

27. **Binet, Alfred** Das Problem der abnormen Kinder. Eos, 1905. Vol. 1, pp. 114-130.

28. —— —— La valeur médicale de l' examen de la vision par les instituteurs. Bull. de la Soc. Libre, 1907. Vol. 7, pp. 145-159.

29. —— —— Les nouvelles classes de perfectionnement. Bull. de la Soc. Libre, 1907. Vol. 7, pp. 170-183.

30. **Binet, Alfred** and **Simon, Théodore** Enfants anormaux. A. Colin, Paris, 1907. pp. 211.

31. **Blaisdell, Thomas C.** Dramatizing. Proc. N. E. A., 1907. pp. 485-491.

32. **Blanchard, Grace** The child and the public library. Pub. Lib., 1907. Vol. 12, p. 91.

33. **Block, Siegfried** Mental defectives; an attempt to treat some cases with medicines. Medical Record, 1907. Vol. 72, pp. 728-730.

34. **Boas, F.** Heredity in anthropometric traits. Amer. Anthrop., 1907. N. S., Vol. 9, pp. 453-469.
    Treats of length and width of head, breadth of face, etc., in 191 families, almost all Russian Jews in New York.

35. **Bolton, Frederick E.** Some ethical aspects of mental economy. Pop. Sci. Mo., 1907. Vol. 71, pp. 246-257.

36. **Bolton, Thaddeus L.** Some social laws of personal growth. Jour. of Ped., 1907. Vol. 20, pp. 29-56.

37. **Bourneville, Dr.** Die ärztlich-pädagogische Behandlung der idiotischen Kinder. Eos, 1907. Vol. 3, pp. 143-152.
    A discussion of the Seguin method of instruction, based on physical development, and European methods which place more emphasis on sense drill in training the feeble minded.

38. **Boutell, Carrie M.** True independence in childhood. Kindergarten Mag., 1907. Vol. 20, pp. 115-119.

39. **Bradley, Rose M.** Some London children at play. 19th Cent., 1907. Vol. 61, pp. 571-586.

40. **Braunschvig, Marcel** L' éducation esthétique de l' enfant par les jeux et les jouets. Revue Péd., 1907. Vol. 50, pp. 201-215.

41. **Brennemann, J.** The sacral or so-called "Mongolian" pigment spots of earliest infancy and childhood, with especial reference to their occurrence in the American negro. Amer. Anthrop., 1907. N. S. Vol. 9, pp. 12-30.

42. **Bresgen, Maximilian** Die Nasenerkrankungen in ihren Beziehungen zur Schule. Die Gesundh. der Schule, 1906. Vol. 4, pp. 9-19.
    Note. This was erroneously entered in the 1906 Bibliography under the name Maximilian ——.

43. —— —— Die Beziehung des Hörorgans zur schwachen Begabung. Die Gesundh. der Schule, 1907. Vol. 5, pp. 1-6.

44. **Brittain, Horace L.** A study in imagination. Ped. Sem., June, 1907. Vol. 14, pp. 137-207.
    Tests interest by favorite authors, favorite poems, memory tests, mental imagery, etc. Bibliography of 68 titles.

45. **Brown, J. Stanley** Meaning and function of manual training. Proc. N. E. A., 1907. pp. 701-705.

46. **Browne, Anna C.** Free play. Kindergarten Rev., 1907. Vol. 17, pp. 559-562.

47. **Brunner, M.** Der Geist des taubstummen Kindes.   Eos, 1905
and 1907.   Vol. 1, pp. 9-46; and vol. 3, pp. 1-17.
A psychological study of the deaf mute child.

48. **Buckbee, Anna**   The work of the primary school in the
development of character.   Jour. of Ped., 1907.   Vol. 19, pp.
214-230.
An excellent discussion of moral training in the elementary schools.

49. **Bunting, Evelyn M.** and others.   School for mothers.   H.
Marshall, Lond., 1907.   pp. 86.

50. **Burbank, Luther**   The training of the human plant.
Century Co., N. Y., 1907.   pp. 99.

51. **Burnham, Wm. H.** The hygiene of drawing.   Ped. Sem.,
Sept., 1907.   Vol. 14, pp. 289-304.
Discusses the principles of motor training, age of beginning drawing,
sequence of instruction, etc.   Bibliography of 59 titles.

52. **Burr, Hanford M.** Studies in adolescent boyhood, chapters
IV-VII.   Assoc. Seminar, 1907.   Vol. 15, pp.   124-135; 205-221;
241-259; 284-300.

53. **Butler, Amos W.** The burden of feeble-mindedness.   Nat.
Conf. of Char. and Cor., 1907.   pp. 1-11.

54. **Büttner, Georg**   Kongress für Kinderforschung und Jugendfürsorge zu Berlin.   Die Gesundh. der Schule, 1907.   Vol. 5, pp.
6-12 ; 25-32.

55. —— ——   Moralisch schwachsinnige Kinder.   Die Gesundh. der
Schule, 1907.   Vol. 5, pp. 52-57.

56. **Carpenter, Estelle** Vitalizing of the child through song.
Proc. N. E. A., 1907.   pp. 856-862.

57. **Carret, Edna P.** Directed play at recess.   Jour. of Ed.   Boston, 1907.   Vol. 65, pp. 68-69.

58. **Chabot, Charles** La cooperation de l'école et de la famille.
L'Année Psychologique, 1906.   Vol. 13, pp. 326-343.

59. **Chlopin, G. W.** Über Selbstmord und Selbstmordversuche
unter den Schülern der russischen mittleren Lehranstalten.
Zeits. f. Schulgesundheitspflege, 1907.   Vol. 20, pp. 574-578.

60. **Chrysostom, Brother**   The psychology of examinations.
Psy. Bull., 1907.   Vol. 4, pp. 219-220.

61. **Claretie, Leo** Les jouets; histoire, fabrication.   Lit. Impri-
meries Réunies, Paris, 18—.   pp. 325.

62. **Clark, David Wasgatt** American child and moloch of to-
day.   Eaton & Mains, N. Y., 1907.   pp. 81.
Treats of child labor.

63. **Clark, Mrs. Frances E.** Vitalizing of the child through song.
Proc. N. E. A., 1907.   pp. 862-865.

64. **Clemenz, B.** Die Beobachtung und Berücksichtigung der
Eigenart der Schüler.   Langensalza, Beyer, 1907.   pp. 40.

65. **Colvin, Stephen S.** The educational value of humor.   Ped.
Sem., Dec., 1907.   Vol. 14, pp. 517-524.
Suggests the development and utilization of humor in children.

66. **Conklin, Edmund S.** Psychology of young manhood; or, Observations on the psychology of later adolescence. Assoc. Seminar, 1907. Vol. 16, pp. 27-31; 55-66; 102-118.

67. **Corbin, Alice M.** Value in the Santa Claus myth. Kindergarten Mag., 1907. Vol. 20, pp. 129-130.

68. **Coriat, Isador H.** The mental condition of juvenile delinquents. Psy. Clinic, 1907. Vol. 1, pp. 125-137.

69. **Cotton, Alfred Cleveland** The care of children. Amer. School of Home Economics, Chic., 1907. pp. 208. (Lib. of home econ.)

70. **Cousinet, Roger** Le rôle de l'analogie dans les représentations du monde extérieur chez les enfants. Revue Philos., 1907. Vol. 64, pp. 159-173.

71. **Crampton, C. W.** The influence of physiological age upon scholarship. Psy. Clinic, 1907. Vol. 1, pp. 115-120.

72. **Curtis, Henry S.** The playground. Nat. Conf. of Char. and Corr., 1907. pp. 278-286.

73. —— —— The problem of city playgrounds. Kindergarten Mag., 1907. Vol. 20, pp. 23-30.

74. **Czerny, A.** Der Arzt als Erzieher des Kindes. Deuticke, Wien, 1907. pp. 105.

75. **Darroch, Alexander** The children; some educational problems. T. C. Jack, London, 1907. pp. 133. (Soc. problems ser. No. 1.)
   A shilling book of 14 chapters. Touches on medical examination of schools and children, also the feeding of school children.

76. **Davidson, John** The educational meaning and function of myth. Paidologist, 1907. Vol. 9, pp. 98-115.

77. **Delany, Selden P.** Morality and the public schools. Education, 1907. Vol. 28, pp, 97-112.

78. **Desfosses, P.** De la scoliose chez l'enfant. L'Educateur Moderne, 1907. Vol. 2, pp. 316-324.

79. **Deutsch, Julius** Die Kinderarbeit und ihre Bekämpfung. Rascher & Co., Zürich, 1907. pp. 247.

80. **Dewe, J. A.** The American boy; impressions of an Englishman. School Rev., 1907. Vol. 15, pp. 197-200.

81. **Dietrich, John** Sub-normal children. Jour. of Ed., Boston, 1907. Vol. 65, pp. 291-292.

82. **Dix, K. W.** Ueber hysterische Epidemien an deutschen Schulen. (Beitr. zur Kinderforsch. u. Heilerziehung, Heft 33.) Beyer, Langensalza, 1907. pp. 42.

83. **Döring, M.** Ein Versuch zur Erforschung elementarer ästhetischer Gefühle bei 7-9 jährigen Kindern. Exper. Päd., 1906. Vol. 3, pp. 65-74.

84. **Dörpfeld, F. W.** Beiträge zur pädagogischen Psychologie. 1 Tl. Denken und Gedächtnis. Eine psychologische Monographie. (10. Aufl.) Bertelsmann, Gütersloh, 1906. pp. 171.

85. **Doran, Edwin W.** A study of vocabularies. Ped. Sem., Dec., 1907. Vol. 14, pp. 401-438.
Brings out facts in regard to the vocabularies of grammar school and high school pupils and college students. Bibliography of 118 titles.

86. **Dresslar, Fletcher B.** Development of an adequate course of study in manual training for elementary grades. From the point of view of child study. Proc. N. E. A., 1907. pp. 766-771.

87. —— —— Superstition and education. University Press, Berkeley, Cal., 1907. pp. 239.
A careful and interesting study ; shows how prevalent superstition is in spite of our universal education. Bibliography of 26 titles.

88. **Droop, F.** Die sexuelle Aufklärung der Jugend. Heuser, Neuwied, 1907. pp. 17.

89. **Drummond, Margaret** Memory. Paidologist, 1907. Vol. 9, pp. 34-52.

90. **Drummond, W. B.** An introduction to child study. E. Arnold, London, 1907. pp. 348.

91. **Dürr-Borst, M.** Die Erziehung der Aussage und Anschauung des Schulkindes. (Diss. Zürich.) Exper. Päd., 1906. Vol. 3, pp. 1-30.

92. **Durand, Geo. Harrison** The study of the child from the standpoint of the home finding agency. Nat. Conf. of Char. and Corr., 1907. pp. 256-265.

93. **Eastman, Charles A.** The school days of an Indian. Outlook, 1907. Vol. 85, pp. 851-855; 894-899.

94. **Eberhardt, John C.** The examination of the eyes of school children. Elem. School Teacher, 1907. Vol. 7, pp. 263-268.

95. **Eder, M. D.** Disease in the schoolroom; a brief survey of the 2d International congress on school hygiene, held in Lond., Aug. 5-10, 1907. Pub. for the Committee for promoting the physical welfare of children by the M. D. C. of the Independent labour party. Lond., 1908. pp. 16.

96. **Edwards, Walter A.** History in the life of the child. Proc. N. E. A., 1907. pp. 513-518.

97. **Ehrig, C.** Die Fortbildungsschule der Hilfsschule für Schwachbefähigte in Leipzig. Zeits. f. Beh. Schwachs. u. Epilept., 1907. Vol. 23, pp. 99-110.

98. **Eiselmeier, J.** Unsere Jugendliteratur. Monats. f. d. Sprache u. Pädagogik, 1907. Vol. 8, pp. 173-176.

99. **Eliot, Charles W.** A better chance for the children of the slums. Outlook, 1907. Vol. 86, pp. 769-770.

100. **Ellis, Havelock** Religion and the child. 19th Cent., 1907. Vol. 61, pp. 764-775.

101. **Enderlin, Max** Das Spielzeug in seiner Bedeutung für die Entwicklung des Kindes. Zeits. f. Kinderforschung, 1907 Vol. 12, pp. 9-16; 98-124.

102. **Engelsperger,** —— and **Ziegler,** —— Beiträge zur Kenntnis der physischen und psychischen Natur der sechsjährigen in die Schule eintretenden Münchener Kinder. Zeits. f. päd. Psychol., 1907. Vol. 9, pp. 67-70.

103. **Ernst, O.** Des Kindes Freiheit und Freude. Haessel, Leipzig, 1907. pp. 50.

104. **Eulenburg, Albert** Schülerselbstmorde. Zeits. f. päd. Psy. Path. u. Hygiene, 1907. Vol. 9, pp. 1-31.

105. **Evans, Mrs. Glendower** What do you know of children after they leave your institution? Nat. Conf. of Char. and Corr., 1907. pp. 274-278.
Results of training the feeble minded.

106. **Evans, Lawton B.** Should the school attempt the circle of the child's training or address itself to the school segment? Southern Ed. Rev., 1907. Vol. 4, pp. 158-160; *also in* Proc. N. E. A., 1907. pp. 170-173.

107. **Fairbanks, Harold W.** Illustrative excursions for field sight. Proc. N. E. A., 1907. pp. 504-506.

108. **Feer, E.** Der Einfluss der Blutsverwandtschaft der Eltern auf die Kinder. S. Karger, Berlin, 1907. pp. 32.
Thinks the evil effects upon children of consanguinity of parents has been exaggerated.

109. **Féré, C.** Note sur l'érotisme de la puberté. Rev. de méd., 1907. Vol. 27, pp. 293.

110. **Ferrari, G. Cesare** Die Therapie der jugendlichen Kriminalität. Eos, 1907. Vol. 3, pp. 161-178.
A psychological analysis of criminal tendencies in the young with practical application.

111. **Findlay, J. J.** The growth of moral ideas in children. Educ. Times, 1907. Vol. 60, pp. 215-219.

112. —— —— Churches and the schools. Ed. Rev., 1907. Vol. 33, pp. 186-192.

113. —— —— The parent and the school. Int. Jour. of Ethics, 1907. Vol. 18, pp. 92-99.

114. **Findlay, M. E.** Design in the art training of young children. Child Life, 1907. Vol. 9, pp. 6-9; 97-100; 178-181.

115. **Fischer, R.** Erziehung und Naturgefühl. Ein Beitrag zur Kunsterziehung. Mod. Verlagsbureau, Leipzig, 1907. pp. 94.

116. **Fleming, Martha** The making of a play. Elem. School Teacher, 1907. Vol. 8, pp. 15-23.

117. **Fœrster, Fr. W.** Schule und Charakter. Schulthess & Co., Zürich, 1907. pp. 213.

118. —— —— Sexualethik und Sexualpädagogik. Eine Auseinandersetzung mit den Modernen. Kempton, Kösel, 1907. pp. 97.

119. **Forbush, William Byron** The broadening path. B. F. Bowen, Indianapolis, 1907. 2 v.

120. **Foresman, Robert** Essential characteristics of music as compared with other branches of school curriculum. Jour. of Ed., Boston, 1907. Vol. 65, pp. 97-102.

121. **Francioni, Carlo** Le sindromi motorie della prima infanzia, in rapporto con le condizioni di sviluppo del sistema nervo-muscolare. Riv. sper. di freniatria, 1907. Vol. 33, pp. 449-497; 780-819.
    A study of infantile diseases connected with motor disturbances and in relation to the development of the motor nervous system.

122. **Freiberg, Albert H.** Some ultimate physical effects of child labor. Ann. Am. Acad. Pol. and Soc. Sci., 1907. Vol. 29, pp. 19-25.

123. **Gache, M. F.** Le rôle des mères dans l'éducation. Revue Péd., 1907. Vol. 50, pp. 40-50.

124. **Gallo, G.** Educazione e cura dei bambini deficienti in Italia. Verdali, Napoli, 1907.

125. **Galton, F.** Probability, the foundation of eugenics. Pop. Sci. Mo., 1907. Vol. 71, pp. 165-178.

126. **Gansberg, F.** Streifzüge durch die Welt der Grossstadtkinder. B. G. Teubner, Leipzig, 1907. pp. 233.

127. **Gates, W. A.** Training of the incorrigible. Proc. N. E. A., 1907. pp. 995-999.

128. **Gibb, Spencer J.** The problem of boy-work. W. Gardner, London, 1906. pp. 96.

129. **Gibb, W. Travis** Criminal aspect of venereal diseases in children, based upon the personal examination of over 900 children, the alleged victims of rape, sodomy, indecent assault, etc. Medical record, 1907. Vol. 71, pp. 643-646.

130. **Godfrey, Elizabeth** *Pseud*. English children in the olden time. Methuen & Co., London, 1907. pp. 336.

131. **Godtfring, O.** Die Waldschule für schwachbefähigte Kinder. Zeits. f. Schulgesundheitspflege, 1907. Vol. 20, pp. 236-243.

132. **Gofflot, L. V.** Le théâtre au collège du moyen âge à nos jours. H. Champion, Paris, 1907. pp. 336.

133. **Gregoire, E.** Die Furchtsamkeit beim Blinden. Eos, 1905. Vol. 1, pp. 274-276.
    Timidity in the blind and its treatment.

134. **Groszmann, Maximilian P. E.** Some phases of eccentric mentality in children. Education, 1907. Vol. 28, pp. 90-96.

135. **Grudzinska, Anna** A study of dolls among Polish children. Ped. Sem., Sept., 1907. Vol. 14, pp. 384-390.
    Submitted 9 questions and received answers from 182 children in Warsaw Kiev, Posen, Kalisch and other parts of Poland.

136. **Guillet, Cephas** A study in interests. Ped. Sem., Sept., 1907. Vol. 14, pp. 322-328.
    168 boys and 151 girls—ages from 11 to 23—arranged 12 subjects in the order of their preference.

137. **Guillet, Cephas** Education in interests; a study in experimental pedagogy. Ped. Sem., Dec., 1907. Vol. 14, pp. 474-487.

138. **Gundobin, N.** Die Eigentümlichkeiten des Kindesalters. Jahrb. f. Kinderhk., 1907. Vol. 65, pp. 720-732.

139. **Gurlitt, Ludwig** Der Verkehr mit meinen Kindern. H. Ehbock, Berlin, 1907. pp. 195.

140. **Guthrie, Leonard G.** Contributions from history and literature to the study of precocity in children. Lancet, 1907. Vol. 173, pp. 1592-1596.

141. —————— Functional nervous disorders in childhood. H. Frowde, London, 1907. pp. 300.

142. **Guttler, Wilhelm** Die religiöse Kindererziehung im deutschen Reiche. W. Rothschild, Berlin, 1908. pp. 331.

143. **Guttmann, Max** Einige Beobachtungen über die Wirkung des Turnunterrichts auf abnormale Kinder. Eos, 1906. Vol. 2, pp. 295-302.
    Report on results of gymnasium work for feeble-minded children.

144. **Gutzmann, Hermann** Zur Untersuchung der Sprache schwachsinniger Kinder. Zeits. f. d. Erforschung u. Behandlung d. jugendl. Schwachsinns, 1907. Vol. 1, p. 1-14.
    A careful investigation of the relation of the speech of feeble-minded children to sight, hearing, touch, defects of speech organs, attention and intelligence.

145. **H., H. R.** The vacation school in London. Child Life, 1907. Vol. 9, pp. 201-204.

146. **Hall, Granville Stanley** and others. Aspects of child life and education. Ginn & Co., Boston, 1907. pp. 326.
    Contains papers on Contents of Children's Minds; Psychology of Day Dreams; Story of a Sand Pile; Study of Dolls; Collecting Instinct; Psychology of Ownership; Fetichism in Children; and Boy Life in a Mass. Country Town.

147. **Hamann, Chr.** Was unsere Kinder lesen. (Sammlung päd. Vorträge, 1891. Vol. 4. pp. 121-133.) A. Helmich, Bielefeld, 1891. pp. 13.

148. **Hancock, John A.** Mental depression in young women and children. Ped. Sem., Dec., 1907. Vol. 14, pp. 460-468.
    Summarizes returns from 225 young women, 8 young men, and 60 children in the grade schools of Minn.

149. **Haney, James Parton** Manual training as a preventive of truancy. Education, 1907. Vol. 27, pp. 634-641.

150. **Härtel, Fritz** Die funktionelle Behandlung der seitlichen Rückgratsverkrümmung (Skoliose). Gesunde Jugend, 1907. Vol. 6, pp. 145-157.

151. **Harris, James Arthur** Heredity. Bulletin of the Washington Univ. Assoc., St. Louis, 1908. Vol. 6, pp. 58-79.

152. **Harris, Mary Brocas** Some aspects of child life in 1807. Child Life, 1907. Vol. 9, pp. 205-209.

153. **Hartmann, Berthold** Die Analyse des kindlichen Gedankenkreises als die naturgemässe Grundlage des ersten Schulunterrichts. E. von Mayer, Lpz., 1906. pp. 232.
New edition of a classic.

154. **Hartmann, K. A. Martin** Die Hygiene und die höhere
Schule. Gesunde Jugend, 1907. Vol. 6, pp. 1-18.

155. **Hauri, N.** Das Märchen und die Kindesseele. E. Richter,
Zürich, 1907. pp. 36. (Praktische Haus-Bibliothek, No. 3.)
A number of the best known fairy tales from Grimm are epitomized and
commented upon in reference to their teaching for children.

156. **Heath, H. Llewellyn.** The infant, the parent and the state; a
social study and review. P. S. King, London, 1907. pp. 191.

157. **Heidenhain, A.** Sexuelle Belehrung der aus der Volksschule
entlassenen Mädchen. (Flugschriften d. d. Gesellschaft z.
Bekämpfung d. Geschlechtskrankheiten. Heft. 8.) J. A. Barth,
Lpz., 1907. pp. 15.

158. **Heller, T.** Psychasthenische Kinder. (Beitr. zur. Kinderforsch. u. Heilerziehung, H. 29.) Beyer, Langensalza, 1907.
pp. 14.

159. **Hellwig, B.** Die vier Temperamente bei Kindern. Ihre
Aeusserung und ihre Behandlung in Erziehung und Schule.
Als Anh.: Das Temperament der Eltern, Lehrer und Erzieher.
9. Aufl. Paderborn, Esser, 1907. pp. 74.

160. **Hémon, Félix** Les écoles d'art indigène et l'enseignement
primaire des filles en Algérie. Revue Péd., 1907. Vol. 50, pp.
305-319.

161. **Henderson, Chas. R.** Physical study of children. Nat. Conf.
of Char. and Corr., 1907. pp. 251-256.

162. **Henne am Rhyn, O.** Prostitution und Mädchenhandel.
Neue Enthüllungen aus dem Sklavenleben weisser Frauen und
Mädchen. 2 Aufl. Hedewig, Leipzig, 1907. pp. 96.

163. **Herts, A. M.** Children's educational theatre. Atlan. Mo.,
1907. Vol. 100, pp. 798-806.

164. **Hertz, Alice** Une école normale Anglaise; les élèves-maî-
tresses au jardin d'enfants. Child Life, 1907. Vol. 9, pp. 36-40.

165. **Hetherington, Clark W.** Organization and administration
of athletics. Proc. N. E. A., 1907. pp. 930-940.

166. **Heymans, G. u. Wiersma, E.** Beiträge zur speziellen Psychologie auf Grund einer Massenuntersuchung. Zeits. f. Psy.
u. Physiol. d. Sinnesorgane, 1906-07. Vol. 42, pp. 81-127; 258-
301. Vol. 43, pp. 321-373. Vol. 45, pp. 1-42.

167. **Hilles, Charles Dewey** Schools for juvenile delinquents.
Nat. Conf. of Char. and Corr., 1907. pp. 209-217.

168. **Hinz, P.** Wie können durch die unterrichtliche Behandlung der Kinder in der Volksschule Nerven und Geisteskrankheiten verhindert werden. Die Gesundh. der Schule, 1907.
Vol. 5, pp. 12-18.

169. **Hitcher, Theresa** Telling stories to children. Pub. Lib., 1907. Vol. 12, pp. 89-91.

170. **Hofer, Mari Ruef** Recreative games and plays for the schoolroom. Kindergarten Mag., 1907. Vol. 19, pp. 383-389.

171. **Home, Henrietta** The child mind. Mathews, Lond., 1906. pp. 48.
   Very brief and sketchy.
   Houston, H. E. See **Washburn, W. W. and Houston, H. E.**

172. **How, Frederick Douglas** The book and the child; an attempt to set down what is in the mind of children. Pitman, London, 1907. pp. 189.

173. **Hughes, J. L.** The vital revelation of Froebel. Child Life, 1907. Vol. 9, pp. 115-119; 172-177.

174. **Huntington, Edward A.** A juvenile delinquent. Psy. Clinic, 1907. Vol. 1, pp. 21-24.

175. **Hurley, Timothy D.** Juvenile probation. Nat. Conf. of Char. and Corr., 1907. pp. 225-232.

176. —— —— Origin of the Illinois juvenile court law. Visitation and Aid Soc., Chicago, 1907. pp. 189.

177. **Hutinel, V. and Babonneix, L.** Les fonctions nerveuses chez l'enfant. Leur développement. Gaz. d. hôp., 1907. Vol. 80, pp. 1093.

178. **Hyslop, Theo. B.** Brain fag in children. Jour. of Preventive Med., Oct., 1905. Vol. 13, pp. 603-612.

179. **Ingram, Mrs. Helene** The value of the fresh air movement. Nat. Conf. of Char. and Corr., 1907. pp. 286-294.

180. **Jaeger, J.** Prinzipien und Beweis der Willensfreiheit. Zeits. f. Kinderforschung, 1907. Vol. 12, pp. 129-139.

181. **Jessen, Ernst** Die praktische Lösung der Frage der Schulzahnkliniken. Gesunde Jugend, 1907. Vol. 6, pp. 188-192.

182. **Johnson, Fanny L.** The kindergarten games as a means of physical development. Kindergarten Rev., 1907. Vol. 17, pp. 327-330.

183. **Johnson, George Ellsworth.** Education by plays and games. Ginn & Co., Boston, 1907. 'pp. 234.

184. **Johnson, Harrold** Some essentials of moral education. Int. Jour. of Ethics, 1907. Vol. 17, pp. 475-483.

185. **Johnson, Martha J.** Relation of music to physical education. Proc. N. E. A., 1907. pp. 940-942.

186. **Jordy, Dr.** Bericht über die 8. Jahresversammlung des deutschen Vereins für Schulgesundheitspflege in Karlsruhe. Zeits. f. Schulgesundheitspflege, 1907. Vol. 20, pp. 485-493; 569-574.

187. **Kassel, Carl** Bemerkungen zur Schulgesundheitspflege. Zeits. f. Schulgesundheitspflege, 1907. Vol. 20, pp. 668-673.

188. **Kelley, Florence** Some ethical gains through legislation.
      Macmillan Co., N. Y., 1905. pp. 341.
      Discusses children's occupations and children's rights under the law.
189. **Kemsies, F.** Zur Frage der Kinderlügen. Zeits. f. päd.
      Psychol., 1907. Vol. 9, pp. 226-227.
190. **Kent, Ernst Beckwith** The constructive interests of chil-
      dren. Columbia Univ., N. Y., 1903. pp. 78.
191. **Key, E.** (Maro. F. Uebers.) Das Jahrhundert des Kindes
      Studien. Fischer, Berlin, 1907. pp. 230.
192. **Kiefer, O.** Körperliche Züchtigung bei der Kindererziehung
      in Geschichte und Beurteilung. A. Kohler, Berlin, 1904.
      pp. 196.
193. —— —— Zur Frage der körperlichen Züchtigung bei Kindern.
      Leipzig, 1907. pp. 54.
194. —— —— Zur Psychologie des Prügelns. Zeits. f. Kinderfor-
      schung, 1907. Vol. 12, pp. 169-172.
195. **Kiesgen, Lawrenz** Randglossen zur Jugendschriften-Frage.
      Kösel, Kempten, 1904. pp. 64.
196. **Kirk, Mrs.** The training of the colour sense in children.
      Child Life, 1907. Vol. 9, pp. 119-122.
197. **Kirk, John R.** Should the school furnish better training for
      non-average child? Proc. N. E. A., 1907. pp. 221-227.
198. **Kirkpatrick, E. A.** A vocabulary test. Pop. Sci. Mo., 1907.
      Vol. 70, pp. 157-164.
      Language of children.
199. **Kluge, O.** Über das Wesen und die Behandlung geistig abnor-
      mer Fürsorgezöglinge. Samml. von Abh. aus dem Gebiete
      der päd. Psy. und Physiol., 1905. Vol. 8, pt. 4, pp. 18.
200. **Knopf, S. A.** The duty of society to the child at school.
      Nat. Conf. of Char. and Corr., 1907. pp. 174-185.
      Note. Treatise on school hygiene.
201. **Kosog, O.** Wahrheit und Unwahrheit bei Schulkindern. Die
      Deutsche Schule, 1907. Vol. 11, pp. 65-78.
202. **Kotscher, L. M.** Das Erwachen des Geschlechtsbewusstseins
      und seine Anomalien. Eine psychologisch-psychiatrische
      Studie. (Grenzfr. d. Nerven. u. Seelenlebens, H. 52.) Berg-
      mann, Wiesbaden, 1907. pp. 82.
203. **Kraft, A.** Errichtung einer Schulzahnklinik in Zürich. Der
      Schularzt, 1907. Vol. 5, pp. 39-48.
204. —— —— Die VI Schweizerische Konferenz für das Idioten-
      wesen am. 28 und 29 Juni in Solothurn. Zeits. f. Schulgesund-
      heitspflege, 1907. Vol. 20, pp. 578-592.
205. **Krenberger, S.** Das Unterrichtsziel bei Schwachsinnigen und
      der Unterrichtsstoff in der Vorschule. Eos, 1906. Vol. 2, pp.
      188-198.
      On the psychology and pedagogy of weak-minded children.

206. **Kroh, Carl J.** Physical training a department of education. Elem. School Teacher, 1907. Vol. 7, pp. 241-246.

207. —— —— Physical training; a question of judicious support. Elem. School Teacher, 1907. Vol. 7, pp. 379-384.

208. **Lahy, J. M.** Das Wesen und die Entstehung des Bewusstseins. Eos, 1906. Vol. 2, pp. 1-21.

Discusses the relation of brain development to development of consciousness in infants and children.

209. **Lalliat,** —— Recherches d'anthropométrie sur des enfants d'école. Bull. de la Soc. Libre, 1907. Vol. 7, pp. 49-60.

210. **Lambkin, Nina B.** Play, its value and fifty games. Holbrook-Barker, Chic., 1907. pp. 91.

211. **Lang, L.** (Pilcz, A., Vorw.) Die kindliche Psyche und der Genuss geistiger Getränke. Safár, Wien, 1907. pp. 81.

212. **Lay, W. A.** Die plastiche Kunst des Kindes. Exper. Päd., 1906. Vol. 3, pp. 31-54.

213. **Leubuscher, G.** Schularzttätigkeit und Schulgesundheitspflege. B. G. Teubner, Leipzig, 1907. pp. 70.

214. **Levoz, Arthur** La protection de l'enfance en Belgique. Bruxelles, 1902. pp. 497.

215. —— —— L'éducation et la protection de l'enfance. Bruxelles, 1905. pp. 39.

216. **Lévy, Albert** L'air insalubre dans les écoles. Bull. de la Soc. Libre, 1907. Vol. 7, pp. 113-118.

217. **Ley, Aug.** L'arriération mentale; contribution à l'étude de la pathologie infantile. J. Lebègue & Cie, Bruxelles, 1905. pp. 259.

The book is a study of the pathology and psychology of defective children. Discusses ætiology, symptomology, diagnoses and treatment.

218. **Lindheim, Alfred von** Saluti juventutis; der Zusammenhang körperlicher und geistiger Entwicklung in den ersten zwanzig Lebensjahren des Menschen. F. Deuticke, Leipzig, 1907. pp. 564.

219. **Lippold,** —— Das Ehrgefühl und die Schule. Torgau, 1907. pp. 49.

220. **Lobsien, Marx** Ueber Zahlengedächtnis und Rechenfertigkeit. Zeits. f. päd. Psy., Path. u. Hygiene, 1907. Vol. 9, pp. 161-168.

221. **Loewenberg, J.** Geheime Miterzieher. Studien und Plaudereien für Eltern und Erzieher. 4. Aufl. Gutenberg-Verlag, Hamburg, 1907. pp. 201.

222. **Londonderry, Theresa.** School hygiene. 19th Cent., 1907. Vol. 62, pp. 388-394.

223. **Lorentz, Friedrich** Die Beziehungen der Sozialhygiene zu den Problemen sozialer Erziehung. Zeits. f.d. Erforschung u. Behandlung d. jugendl. Schwachsinns, 1907. Vol. 1, p. 244-256.

224. **Lovejoy, Owen R.** Child labor and education. Jour. of Ed., Boston, 1907. Vol. 66, pp. 90-91.

225. —— —— Child labor and philanthropy. Nat. Conf. of Char. and Corr., 1907. pp. 196-206.

226. **Low, Florence B.** The educational ladder and the girl. 19th Cent., 1907. Vol. 62, pp. 395-405.

227. **Lowd, Edna B.** Object drawing. Proc. N. E. A., 1907. pp. 843-848.

228. **Lugg, H. C.** Notes on some puberty and other customs of the natives of Natal and Zululand. Man, 1907. Vol. 7, pp. 115-119.

    Treats of puberty, pregnancy, death and burial customs in existence about 40 years ago and ¦which can be applied in a general sense to almost every tribe.

229. **Mabie, Hamilton W.** The contribution of the kindergarten to American education. Kindergarten Rev., 1907. Vol. 17, pp. 629-631.

230. **MacClintock, Porter Lander** Literature in the elementary school. University Press, Chicago, 1907. pp. 305.

    While a school book primarily has much of interest concerning children's reading, fairy tales, plays for children, etc.

231. **McCrady, L. L.** The child and the imaginative life. Atlantic Mo., 1907. Vol. 100, pp. 480-488.

232. **MacDonald, Arthur** Decay of family life and increase of child crime. Education, 1907. Vol. 28, pp. 30-36.

233. —— —— Reform of juvenile criminals. Ped. Sem., Dec., 1907. Vol. 14, pp. 496-505.

    There are three general classes of children especially needing protection and study—abandoned—vicious—criminal.

234. —— —— Studies of juvenile criminals. Medical Record, 1907. Vol. 72, pp. 101-103.

235. **McIver, M. N.** Aims of special education. Proc. N. E. A., 1907. pp. 984-986.

236. **McKeag, A. J.** The problem of defective children as discussed in the International Congress on school hygiene. Psy. Clinic, 1907. Vol. 1, pp. 210-216.

237. —— —— The second international congress on school hygiene. Ped. Sem., Dec., 1907. Vol. 14, pp. 512-516.

    The second triennial congress was held in London, Aug. 5-10, 1907.

238. **McKeever, William A.** The cigarette boy. Education, 1907. Vol. 28, pp. 154-160.

239. **McKelway, A. J.** The evil of child labor; why the South should favor a national law. Outlook, 1907. Vol. 85, pp. 360-364.

240. **MacMillan, D. P.** Types of children. Ed. Rev., 1907. Vol. 33, pp. 256-270.

241. **McMillan Margaret** Infant mortality. Ind. Labour Party, London, 1907. pp. 15.

242. **McNeill, I. C.** Expression by the hands. Proc. N. E. A., 1907. pp. 491-494.
Refers to oral reading.

243. **Mahony, John J.** The problem of the poor pupil. Education, 1907. Vol. 28, pp. 197-212.

244. **Major, D. R.** First steps in mental growth; a series of studies in the psychology of infancy. Macmillan, N. Y., 1906. pp. 14+360.

245. **Mangold, G. B.** Waste of child study. Pop. Sci. Mo., 1907. Vol. 70, pp. 549-556.

246. **Marsh, Harriet A.** An unstaked claim in psychology. Ped. Sem., Dec., 1907. Vol. 14, pp. 488-495.
Seeks some explanation of certain tendencies in school children. Why do some teachers, evidently well equipped, fail to inspire or control their classes?

247. **Martin, Eva M.** Children's competitions. 19th Cent., 1907. Vol. 61, pp. 587-592; 996-1003.

248. **Martindale, W. C.** Separation of insubordinate and incorrigible children from regular school. Jour. of Ed., Bost., 1907. Vol. 65, pp. 292-293.

249. **Masselon, René** L'affaiblissement intellectuel dans la démence précoce, la démence sénile et la paralysie générale. L'Année Psychologique, 1906. Vol. 13, pp. 260-274.

250. **Mecke, H.** Fröbelsche Pädagogik und Kinderforschung. (Beitr. zur Kinderforsch. u. Heilerziehung, Heft. 36.) Beyer, Langensalza, 1907. pp. 14.

251. **Meumann, E.** Æsthetische Versuche mit Schulkindern. Exper. Päd., 1906. Vol. 3, pp. 74-88.

252. **Miller, Wallace E.** Child study; the situation in Ohio and border states. Ann. Am. Acad. Pol. and Soc. Sci., 1907. Vol. 29, pp. 71-76.

253. **Mills, Harriette Melissa** Froebel's views concerning the nature and needs of the child. Kindergarten Mag., 1907. Vol. 19, pp. 373-382.

254. **Mitchell, Frank D.** Mathematical prodigies. Am. Jour. of Psy., Jan., 1907. Vol. 18, pp. 61-143.
Considers those who have shown unusual ability in mental arithmetic especially cases where the ability has developed at an early age.

255. **Mitchell, W.** Structure and growth of the mind. Macmillan Co., N. Y., 1907. pp. 512.

256. **Monroe, Will S.** Color sense of young children. Paidologist, 1907. Vol. 9, pp. 7-10.

257. —— —— Progress of education in Italy. Rept. of Comm. of Ed. for 1906. Wash., 1907. Vol. 1, pp. 73-90.
Gives an account of the institutions for defective, dependent, and delinquent children.

258. **Moses, Julius** Idiotenfürsorge und Fürsorgeerziehung. Zeits. f. Schulgesundheitspflege, 1907. Vol. 20, pp. 366-369. *Also in* Zeits. f. Kinderforschung, 1907. Vol. 12, pp. 267-270.

259. —— —— Der Kongress für Kinderforschung und Jugendfürsorge vom 1. bis 4. Oktober, 1906, in Berlin. Eos, 1907. Vol. 3, pp. 57-67.
Report of the 1st International Congress for Child Study at Berlin.

260. **Moses, Montrose J.** Children's books and reading. M. Kennerley, N. Y., 1906. pp. 272.

261. —— —— The children's library and the home. Outlook, 1907. Vol. 87, pp. 177-185.

262. **Mosley, Thomas S.** The problem of child idleness. No. Am. Rev., 1907. Vol. 185, pp. 515-517.

263. **Müller, Hugo** Die Gefahren der Einheitsschule für unsere nationale Erziehung. A. Töpelmann, Giessen, 1907. pp. 142.

264. **Neuert, G.** Ueber Begabung und Gehörsgrad der Zöglinge der badischen Taubstummenanstalten Gerlachsheim u. Meersburg. Eine statist. Studie, zugleich als Beitrag zur Trennungsfrage. (Päd. Monog. Bd. IV.) Nemnich, Leipzig, 1907. pp. 168.

265. **Neustaedter, M.** Some potent etiological factors in backward children. Medical record, 1907. Vol. 71, pp. 226-229.

266. **Newman, George** Infant mortality, a social problem. Methuen & Co., London, 1906. pp. 356+40.
Perhaps the most comprehensive and careful study of the subject in English.

267. **Newton, Richard Cole** The reawakening of the physical conscience. Pop. Sci. Mo., 1907. Vol. 71, pp. 156-164.
Note, physical training in schools.

268. **Nichols, J. B.** The numerical proportions of the sexes at birth. Mem. Amer. Anthrop. Assoc., 1907. pp. 247-300.

269. **Nix, Amalie** Home and school life in Germany. Proc. N. E. A., 1907. pp. 467-474.

270. **Norsworthy, Naomi** Psychology of mentally deficient children. Science Press, N. Y., 1906. pp. 111.

271. **Norton, Ruth W.** An experiment with children's gardens. Kindergarten Rev., 1907. Vol. 17, pp. 483-489.

272. **Oebbecke, ——** Besonderheiten der schulärztlichen Statistik und Technik. Der Schularzt, 1907. Vol. 5, pp. 153-165.

273. **Oliphant, James** Parental rights and public education. Int. Jour. of Ethics, 1907. Vol. 17, pp. 205-217.

274. **Oppler, Therese** Zur Frage der sexuellen Aufklärung der Jugend. Zeits. f. Schulgesundheitspflege, 1907. Vol. 20, pp. 22-27.

275. **O'Shea, Michael Vincent** Notes on ethical training. Ed. Rev., 1907. Vol. 33, pp. 368-373.

276. **O'Shea, Michael Vincent** The kindergarten spirit in Europe. Kindergarten Rev., 1907. Vol. 17, pp. 257-262.

277. —— —— Linguistic development and education. Macmillan Co., N. Y., 1907. pp. 347.

278. **Pabst, Alwin** Die Knabenhandarbeit in der heutigen Erziehung. B. G. Teubner, Leipzig, 1907. pp. 118.

279. **Palmer, Kate** Infancy and schools; should children under five attend school? Paidologist, 1907. Vol. 9, pp. 11-18.

280. **Patch, Kate Whiting** The sensitive child. Kindergarten Rev., 1907. Vol. 17, pp. 416-420.

281. **Patterson, John** The child and child education among the ancient Greeks. Education, 1907. Vol. 28, pp. 37-47.

282. **Payne, Bertha** Causes and cure of truancy in schools. Elem. School Teacher, 1907. Vol. 7, pp. 554-559.

283. **Peacock, H. M.** Village games. Child Life, 1907. Vol. 9, pp. 126-129.

284. **Pearse, Carrol G.** Separation of physically and mentally defective children from regular schools. Jour. of Ed., Boston, 1907. Vol. 65, pp. 287-289.

285. **Pearson, K.** On the relationship of intelligence to size and shape of head, and to other physical and mental characters. Biometrika, 1906. Vol. 5, pp. 105-146.

286. —— —— The scope and the importance to the state of the science of national eugenics. Pop. Sci. Mo., 1907. Vol. 71, pp. 385-412.

287. **Philippe, J.** Á propos d'une nouvelle classification des enfants anormaux. L'Educateur Moderne, 1907. Vol. 2, pp. 396-403.

288. **Plecher, Hans** Zur Psychologie der Schulprüfungen. Zeits. f. päd. Psy. Path. u. Hygiene, 1907. Vol. 9, pp. 302-311.

289. **Poelchau, G.** Fürsorgestellen für die Schuljugend, eine wünschenswerte Ergänzung der Schularzt-Einrichtung. Der Schularzt, 1907. Vol. 5, pp. 57-64; 75-87.

290. **Pohlmann, A.** The heredity of the upright position and some of its disadvantages. Monist, 1907. Vol. 17, pp. 570-582.

291. **Pokrowski, E.** Matériaux pour servir à l'étude de l'éducation physique chez les différents peuples de l'empire russe. Revue d'ethnographie, 1889. Vol. 7, pp. 520-567.
      Treats of the collection of 500 objects (clothing, cradles, toys, seats, walking-apparatus, etc.) used for children among the various peoples of the Russian empire.

292. **Poole, Ernest** Chicago's public playgrounds. Outlook, 1907. Vol. 87, pp. 775-781.

293. **Pottag, A.** Zur Mimik der Kinder beim künstlerischen Geniessen. (Päd. Magazin, Heft 302.) Beyer, Langensalza, 1907. pp. 17.

294. **Proal, L.** L'éducation et le suicide des enfants. Gaz. méd. de Nantes, 1907. Vol. 25, pp. 31-

295. **Purcell, Helen E.** Children's dramatic interest and how this may be utilized in education. Elem. School Teacher, 1907. Vol. 7, pp. 510-518.

296. **Queyrat, F.** (Krause, P. Uebers.) Das Denken beim Kinde und seine Pflege. Nach. d. 2. Aufl. Wunderlich, Leipzig, 1907. pp. 84.

297. **Racine, G.** Les jeux à l'école. L'Educateur Moderne, 1907. Vol. 2, pp. 247-251.

298. **Ranschburg, Paul** Leicht schwachsinnige als Zeugen. Eos, 1907. Vol. 3, pp. 81-101.
    A study of the capability of the slightly weak-minded for making correct statements.

299. **Rasmus, P.** Ein Fall von Seelenstörung im frühen Kindesalter. Jahrb. f. Kinderhk., 1907. Vol. 66, pp. 326-327.

300. **Baur, Alfred** Die Blinddarmentzündung in ihrer Beziehung zur Schule. Die Gesundh. der Schule, 1907. Vol. 5, pp. 124-137.

301. **Reeder, R. R.** Study of the child from the institutional standpoint. Nat. Conf. of Char. and Corr., 1907. pp. 265-274.

302. **Regener, Fr.** Auch ein Wort zur Aufsatzreform. Die Deutsche Schule, 1907. Vol. 11, pp. 676-698.

303. **Ribbing, S.** (Reyher, O., Uebers.) Die sexuelle Hygiene und ihre ethischen Konsequenzen. Gesundes Geschlechtsleben und seine Folgen fur die Sittlichkeit. Neuer Abdruck. Hobbing, Stuttgart, 1907. pp. 198.

304. **Ricci, C.** (Roncali, E., Übers., Lamprecht, K., Vorw.) Kinderkunst. Voigtländer, Leipzig, 1906. pp. 61.

305. **Richards, Charles R.** The problems of industrial education. Manual Training Mag., 1907. Vol. 8, pp. 125-132.

306. **Richman, Julia** Special classes and special schools for delinquent and backward children. Nat. Conf. of Char. and Corr., 1907. pp. 232-243.

307. **Rodenacker, Dr.** Schularzt und Moralunterricht. Gesunde Jugend, 1907. Vol. 6, pp. 24-26.

308. **Rogers, A. C.** The relation of the institutions for defectives to the public school system. Nat. Conf. of Char. and Corr., 1907. pp. 469-477.

309. **Rogers, James E.** City of Telhi, a Junior republic. Education, 1907. Vol. 27, pp. 271-280.

310. **Rotges, ——** Examen pédagogique de l'état de la vision à distance dans les écoles publiques de la ville de Bordeaux. Bull. de la Soc. Libre, 1907. Vol. 7, pp. 91-96.

311. **Rouma, Georges** Die Fürsorge für schwachsinnige und mit Sprachgebrechen behaftete Kinder in den Niederlanden. Eos, 1906. Vol. 2, pp. 266-295.
    Report on methods of instruction and curriculum for weak-minded children in the Netherlands.

312. **Rouma, Georges** L'organization de cours de traitement pour enfants troublés de la parole. Engelman, Leipzig, 1906. pp. 170.
A catalogue résumé of methods of treatment of speech defects with a survey of the schools and methods in other lands.

313. —— —— Eine Klasse abnormer Kinder. Eos, 1907. Vol. 3, pp. 264-298.
Report of observations on a class of 26 children in Brussels, giving methods of instruction and results. Heredity and environment of each child carefully examined.

314. —— —— Les troubles de la parole chez les enfants anormaux. L'Educateur Moderne, 1907. Vol. 2, pp. 199-203.

315. **Rousselle, G.** Étude silencieuse et étude bourdonnante. Bull. de la Soc. Libre, 1907. Vol. 7, pp. 163-168.

316. **Rowe, Stuart H.** Action and reaction in primary schools. Education, 1907. Vol. 27, pp. 420-429.

317. **Rowland, Eleanor Harris** A proposed method for teaching æsthetics. Psy. Bull., 1907. Vol. 4, p. 214.

318. **Ruediger, William C.** Adolescence: period of mental reconstruction. Jour. of Psy., 1907. Vol. 18, pp. 353-370.

319. —— —— Glimpses into the schools of Hamburg, Germany. Education, 1907. Vol. 28, pp. 224-232.

320. **Sachs, Julius** Co-education in the United States. Ed. Rev., 1907. Vol. 33, pp. 298-305.

321. **Sadler, S. H.** The higher education of the young; its social, domestic and religious aspects. G. Routledge, London, 1907. pp. 276.

322. **Saiz, Giovanni** Sul significato delle anomalie fisiche, in rapporto all'etiologia e patogenesi della demenza precoce. Riv. sper. di freniatria, 1907. Vol. 33, pp. 364-415.
A discussion of the significance of physical anomalies in relation to the etiology and pathology of dementia præcox.

323. **Salisbury, Grace Emily** and **Beckwith, M. E.** Index to short stories; an aid to the teacher of children. Rowe, Peterson & Co., Chic., 1907. pp. 118.

324. **Sanctis, Sante de** Typen und Grade mangelhafter geistiger Entwicklung. Eos, 1906. Vol. 2, pp. 97-115.
Tests for various types and grades of defective intellect.

325. **Sarason, D.** Zum Problem der Sexualbelehrung. Zeits. f. Schulgesundheitspflege, 1907. Vol. 20, pp. 733-746.

326. **Sarbó, Arthur von** Was für Prinzipien sind bei der Bekämpfung des Stotterns zu befolgen? Eos, 1905. Vol. 1, pp. 257-261.
Gives psychological principles on which treatment of stuttering should be based.

327. —— —— Über die Ursachen der Sprachstörungen bei Kindern. Eos, 1906. Vol. 2, pp. 255-266.
Discusses the causes of stuttering, stammering, etc.

328. **Schallenberger, Margaret E.** The American ideal of the kindergarten. Elem. School Teacher, 1907. Vol. 8, pp. 122-129.

329. —— —— Motive for kindergarten work. Proc. N. E. A., 1907. pp. 462-467.

330. **Schenk, Alwin** Die neunklassige Hilfsschule. Zeits. f. Kinderforschung, 1907. Vol. 12, pp. 197-202.

331. **Scherz, Anna T.** German songs and rhymes for children. Elem. School Teacher, 1907. Vol. 7, pp. 420-429.

332. **Schmidkunz, H.** Die oberen Stufen des Jugendalters. Zeits. f. päd. Psychol., 1907. Vol. 9, pp. 72-74.

333. **Schmidt, Heuert C. K.** Für die Rute in der Erziehung. Leipziger Verlag, 190-. pp. 56.

334. **Schreiber, Adele.** *ed.* Das Buch vom Kinde; ein Sammelwerk für die wichtigsten Fragen der Kindheit unter Mitarbeit zahlreichen Fachleute. B. G. Teubner, Lpz., 1907. 2 v. in 1.
    Das Buch vom Kinde is a collective work embracing the entire life of the child as an individual and in relation to the race. Noted physicians, psychologists, educators, jurists, and artists, have contributed the separate articles but the book is nevertheless unitary in character. The two sections of Vol. I deal respectively with problems relating to the physical welfare of the child and to pedagogy. Vol. II deals with public educational and protective institutions; the child in his social and legal relations, and lastly vocations and training for these. The book as a whole is one of the most important and valuable contributions which has been made to child study.

335. **Schreiber, H.** Die alten Kinderreime und ihre Anregung zu Selbstproduktionen der Kleinen. Zeits. f. Kinderforschung, 1907. Vol. 12, pp. 161-169.

336. **Schulze, Edward** Erziehung und Arbeit. Zeits. f. päd. Psy. Path. u. Hygiene, 1907. Vol. 9, pp. 169-190.

337. **Schulze, Rudolf** Die Mimik der Kinder beim künstlerischen Geniessen. Zeits. f. Kinderforschung, 1906. Vol. 12, pp. 139-151.

338. **Schwarz, Hermann** The study of experimental pedagogy in Germany. School Rev., 1907. Vol. 15, pp. 535-543.
    Schuyler, William See **Swift, Edgar James** and **Schuyler, William**

339. **Scupin, Ernst** and **Scupin, Mrs. Gertrud** Bubi's erste Kindheit. Th. Grieben, Leipzig, 1907. pp. 264.
    Scupin, Mrs. Gertrud See **Scupin, Ernst** and **Scupin, Mrs. Gertrud**

340. **Sheldon, Winthrop D.** Some practical suggestions toward a programme of ethical teaching in our schools. Education, 1907. Vol. 27, pp. 262-270; 353-360.
    Extensive bibliography.

341. **Shepardson, Everett** A preliminary critique of the doctrine of fundamental and accessory movements. Ped. Sem., March, 1907. Vol. 14, pp. 101-116.
Importance of the motor phases of schoolroom activities re-emphasized. Bibliography of 51 titles.

342. **Sherard, Robert Harborough** The child-slaves of Britain. Hurst & Blackett, Lond., 1905. pp. 267.

343. **Shields, Thomas Edward** Education of our girls. Benziger Bros., N. Y., 1907. pp. 299.
The Roman Catholic point of view.

344. **Sibenaler, —** L'âge du discernement; considérations juridiques et médico-légales sur la responsabilité de l'enfance coupable. (Thèse méd.) Bordeaux, 1906. pp. 108.

345. **Siebengartner, M.** Die erste Entwicklung des Kindes. Auf Grund der neueren Kinderforschung dargestellt. (Päd. Zeitfr., Heft, 13.) Höfling, München, 1907. pp. 52.

346. **Siebert, F.** Ein Buch für Eltern. Seitz & Schauer, München, 1903-04. 3 v. in 2. *Contents.* 1. Den Müttern heranreifender Töchter. 2. Den Vätern heranreifender Söhne. 3. Wie sag' ich's meinem Kinde?

347. **Siegrist, A.** Ueber die Notwendigkeit, die Augen der schulpflichtigen Kinder vor dem Schuleintritte untersuchen zu lassen. Klin. Monatsbl. f. Augenhk., 1907. Vol. 2, Suppl., pp. 1-25.

348. **Simon, Helene** Schule und Brot. Voss, Leipzig, 1907. pp. 90.
Bread comes before school and there should be public regulation of school feeding. Sketches a desirable law covering all present forms of the evil of underfeeding.

Simon Théodore See **Binet, Alfred** and **Simon, Théo-dore**.

349. **Slaughter, J. W.** Psychology and kindergarten method. Child Life, 1907. Vol. 9, pp. 59-61.

350. **Smith, Faith E.** Library work for children. Pub. Lib., 1907. Vol. 12, pp. 79-83.

351. **Smith, Franklin O.** Pupils' voluntary reading. Ped. Sem., June, 1907. Vol. 14, pp. 208-222.
Gives answers from 915 boys and 1,284 girls as to what and how much they read.

352. **Smith, Theodate L.** The Berlin Congress for Child Study. An account of the first international congress for child study held at the University of Berlin, Oct. 1-4, 1906. Ped. Sem., March, 1907. Vol. 14, pp. 130-134.

353. —— —— Bibliography of articles relating to the study of childhood and adolescence, which have been published in the Pedagogical Seminary and American Journal of Psychology. Ped. Sem., Sept., 1907. Vol. 14, pp. 355-365.
Lists 203 articles and adds 10 books, with a subject index.

354. **Smith, Theodate L.** Children's lies and training in truth. Kindergarten Rev., 1907. Vol. 18, pp. 129-134.
———— See also No. 146.

355. **Snedden, David Samuel** Administration and educational work of American juvenile reform schools. Teachers College, Columbia University, N. Y., 1907. pp. 206.

356. ———— History study as an instrument in the social education of children. Jour. of Ped., 1907. Vol. 19, pp. 259-268.

357. ———— The public school and juvenile delinquency. Ed. Rev., 1907. Vol. 33, pp. 374-385.

358. **Sollier, Paul** Les maladies nerveuses a l'école. Bull. de la Soc. Libre, 1907. Vol. 7, pp. 105-112.

359. **Spann, Othmar** Die Lage und das Schicksal der unehelichen Kinder. Mutterschutz, Sept., 1907. Vol. 3, pp. 345-358.
    Treats of birth rate of illegitimate children in Germany. Birth rate, relation of this to marriage laws, viability, environment, means of support ; physical, moral and social handicap.

360. **Spindler, F. N.** Memory types in spelling. Education, 1907. Vol. 28, pp. 175-181.

361. **Spraggon, Belle** Ambidextrous sewing. Kindergarten Rev., 1907. Vol. 17, pp. 269-273.

362. **Stadelmann, H.** Die kindliche Nervosität, ihre Beziehungen zur Schule und ihre Bekämpfung. Med. Klinik, 1907. Vol. 3, pp. 35-37.

363. ———— Der Stand des Unterrichts an den Schulen für Schwachbefähigte in Deutschland. Zeits. f. päd. Psy. Path. u. Hygiene, 1907. Vol. 9, pp. 275-290.

364. **Steinhaus, F.** Die hygienische Bedeutung des fünfstündigen Vormittagsunterrichts. Zeits. f. Schulgesundheitspflege, 1907. Vol. 20, pp. 533-569.

365. ———— Der Trinkspringbrunnen. Zeits. f. Schulgesundheitspflege, 1907. Vol. 20, pp. 746-757.

366. **Stephani, ——** Über Körpermessungen und einen neuen Körpermessapparat. Gesunde Jugend, 1907. Vol. 6, pp. 231-238.

367. **Stephens, George Asbury** The juvenile court system of Kansas. Mail & Breeze Pub. Co., Topeka, 1906. pp. 122.

368. **Stern, Mrs. Clara** and **Stern, William** Die Kindersprache. J. A. Barth, Leipzig, 1907. pp. 394.

369. **Stern, Otto** Der Zitterlaut R. Zeits. f. Kinderforschung, 1907. Vol. 12, pp. 289-299 ; 353-372.

Stern, William See **Stern, Mrs. Clara** and **Stern, William.**

370. **Stier, Dr.** Die Bedeutung der Hilfsschulen für den Militärdienst der geistig Minderwertigen. Zeits. f. Kinderforschung, 1907. Vol. 12, pp. 225-235; 257-267.

371. **Stilwell, Katharine M.** Educational problems of adolescence. Elem. School Teacher, 1907. Vol. 8, pp. 161-173.

372. **Summers, Maud** Kindergarten extension. Kindergarten. Rev., 1907. Vol. 17, pp. 385-388.
373. **Suzzalo, Henry** The story and the poem. Proc. N. E. A., 1907. pp. 478-482.
374. —— —— Training of the child's emotional life. Proc. N. E. A., 1907. pp. 905-910.
375. **Swift, Edgar James** and **Schuyler, William** The learning process. Psy. Bull., 1907. Vol. 4, pp. 307-311.
376. **Tanner, Amy E.** How best to develop character in children. Education, 1907. Vol. 27, pp. 546-549.
377. **Tate, J. H.** The education and employment of the deaf. Nat. Conf. of Char. and Corr., 1907. pp. 512-515.
378. **Tews, J.** Moderne Erziehung in Haus und Schule. B. G. Teubner, Leipzig, 1907. pp. 132.
379. **Thalhofer F.** Die sexuelle Pädagogik bei den Philanthropen. (Diss. Jena.) Kösel, Kempten, 1907. pp. 127.
380. **Thévenelle, Georges** L'assistance médicale par l'école. Revue Péd., 1907. Vol. 50, pp. 158-163.
381. **Thiele, Adolf** Reinlichkeit und Schule. Der Schularzt, 1907. Vol. 5, pp. 1-10; 19-29.
382. **Thomas, F.** Le Mensonge. Rev. Péd., 1907. Vol. 50, pp. 501.
383. **Thompson, H.** From the cotton field to the cotton mill. Macmillan Co., N. Y., 1906. pp. 284.
384. **Thomsen, Dr.** Dementia præcox und manisch-depressives Irresein. Allg. Zeits. f. Psychiat., 1907. Vol. 64, pp. 631-654.
385. **Thumser, Viktor** Strittige Schulfragen; ein Wort der Verständigung an die Eltern. F. Deuticke, Wien, 1907. pp. 34.
386. **Tillier, Jean** La gymnastique des enfants au Japon. L'Educateur Moderne, 1907. Vol. 2, pp. 441-443.
387. **Town, Clara Harrison** An infantile stammer (baby talk) in a boy of twelve years. Psy. Clinic, 1907. Vol. 1, pp. 10-20.
388. —— —— Public day schools for backward children. Psy. Clinic, 1907. Vol. 1, pp. 81-88.
389. **Trannoy,** —— La mythomanie. (Thèse méd.) Paris, 1906. pp. 81.
390. **Trüper, J.** Zum Hilfsschultag in Charlottenburg. Zeits. f Kinderforschung, 1907. Vol. 12, pp. 193-197.
391. **Tucker, Blanche** Notes on the care of babies and young children. Longmans, Green & Co., London, 1907. pp. 68.
392. **Tuczek, F.** Bericht über den Kongress für Kinderforschung und Jugendfürsorge zu Berlin, vom. 1. bis. 4 Oktober, 1906. Zeits. f. d. Erforschung u. Behandlung d. jugendl. Schwachsinns, 1907. Vol. 1, pp. 170-184.
393. **Tyler, John Mason** Growth and education. Houghton, Mifflin & Co., N. Y., 1907. pp. 294.

394. **Ufer,** —— Kinderforschung und Pädagogik. Zeits. f. päd. Psychol., 1907. Vol. 9, pp. 59-61.

395. **Uffenheimer, Albert** Erster Kongress für Kinderforschung, und Jugendfürsorge zu Berlin vom 1. —4. Oktober, 1906; ergänzendes Referat. Zeits. f. d. Erforschung u. Behandlung d. jugendl. Schwachsinns, 1907. Vol. 1, pp. 185-190.

396. **Urwick, W. E.** The child's mind, its growth and training. E. Arnold, London, 1907. pp. 269.

397. **Vogt, H.** Der Mongolismus. Zeits. f. d. Erforschung u. Behandlung d. jugendl. Schwachsinns, 1907. Vol. 1, pp. 445-488.

398. **Wachenheim, F. L.** Climatic treatment of children. Rebman Co., N. Y., 1907. pp. 400.

399. **Wade, W.** Beobachtungen an Taubblinden. Eos, 1905. Vol. 1, pp. 153-157.

400. **Wahrheit, A.** Die Bedeutung der Phantasie im Lichte der Jugendschutzbestrebungen. Ein Beitrag zur Frage der Sexualpädagogik. (Päd. Zeitfr. Heft, 12.) Höfling, München, 1906. pp. 43.

401. **Wake, C. Staniland** A widespread boy-hero story. Jour. of Am. Folk-Lore, 1907. Vol. 20, pp. 216-219.

402. **Walter, F.** Die sexuelle Aufklärung der Jugend. Notwendigkeit, Schranken und Auswüchse. Mit besonderer Berücksichtigung der sozialen Verhältnisse. Donauwörth, Auer, 1907. pp. 162.

403. **Washburn, W. W.** and **Houston, H. E.** On the naming of colors. Am. Jour. of Psy., Oct., 1907. Vol. 18, pp. 519-523.

404. **Washburne, Mrs. Marion Foster** Study of child life. Amer. School of Home Economics, Chicago, 1907. pp. 183. (Lib. of home econ.)

405. **Weigl, Franz** Aufklärungsarbeit über die Bewahrung der Jugend vor den Genussgiften. Zeits. f. päd. Psy. Path. u. Hygiene, 1907. Vol. 9, pp. 291-301; *also in* Die Gesundh. der Schule, 1907. Vol. 5, pp. 192-201.

406. —— Die Schulbank. Gesunde Jugend, 1907. Vol. 6, pp. 19-23.

407. —— —— Die Mittel zur Abhilfe in der Not geistiger Minderwertigkeit. Gesunde Jugend, 1907. Vol. 6, pp. 75-78.

408. **Weigle,** —— Der Einfluss der Jugendvereine auf die sittliche und religiöse Entwickelung der männlichen Jugend. 2. Aufl. Barmen, Westdeutsch. Jünglingsbund, 1907. pp. 37.

409. **Weiss, Anton** Schulhygienisches aus der theresianisch-josefinischen Zeit. Zeits. f. Kinderforschung, 1907. Vol. 12, pp. 202-208.

410. **Weygandt, W.** Idiotie und Dementia præcox. Zeits. f. d. Erforschung u. Behandlung d. jugendl. Schwachsinns, 1907. Vol. 1, pp. 311-332.
   Gives typical and classification of symptoms in idiocy and dementia præcox.

411. —— —— Psychisch-abnorme Kinder in der ambulanten Praxis. Med. Klinik, 1907. Vol. 3, pp. 1061-1064.
   Wiersma, E. See **Heymans, G.** and **Wiersma, E.**

412. **Wiesner, Anton** Die Nervosität der Kinder. Eos, 1906. Vol. 2, pp. 161-188.
   A discussion of the symptoms, causes and treatment of nervousness in children.

413. **Wigram, Eirene** Firm foundations; a guide for parents and others to religion and religious education. J. Murray, London, 1907. pp. 323.

414. **Wild, Pfarrer A.** Die körperliche Misshandlung von Kindern durch Personen welchen die Fürsorgepflicht für dieselben obliegt. Rascher & Co., Zürich (no date). pp. 162.
   A most painful anthology of the mistreatments of children in all ages.

415. **Williams, Linsly R.** Statistical information concerning the physical welfare of school children. Nat. Conf. of Char. and Corr., 1907. pp. 155-165.

416. **Wilson, George S.** Relation of industrial trades to the state schools for the blind. Nat. Conf. of Char. and Corr., 1907. pp. 500-507.

417. **Wilson, Louis N.** Bibliography of child study for the year 1906. Ped. Sem., Sept., 1907. Vol. 14, pp. 329-354.
   Gives 362 titles for the year 1906. Arranged alphabetically with a subject index. First issue appeared in 1898.

418. **Winteler, Jakob** Ergebnisse der experimentellen Pädagogik. Eos, 1907. Vol. 3, pp. 241-263.
   Some results of tests of sensation, sense discrimination, learning processes and memory. Gives a summary of work done by various experimenters.

419. **Witmer, Lightner** Clinical psychology. Psy. Clinic, 1907. Vol. 1, pp. 1-9.
   Article on the clinical method of studying defective children.

420. —— —— A case of chronic bad spelling—amnesia visualis verbalis due to arrest of post-natal development. Psy. Clinic, 1907. Vol. 1, pp. 53-64.

421. —— —— The fifteen months training of a feeble-minded child. Psy. Clinic, 1907. Vol. 1, pp. 69-80.

422. —— —— Retardation through neglect in children of the rich. Psy. Clinic, 1907. Vol. 1, pp. 157-174.

423. **Wohrizek, Theodor** Sonderschulen für Skolistische. Zeits. f. Schulgesundheitspflege, 1907. Vol. 20, pp. 175-179.

424. **Wolfsohn, Ryssia** Die Heredität bei Dementia præcox. Allg. Zeits. f. Psychiat., 1907. Vol. 64, pp. 347-362.

425. **Wolodkewitsch, Nicolai** Eine Untersuchung der höheren Geistesfähigkeiten bei Schulkindern. H. Walther, Berlin, 1907. pp. 61. *Also in* Zeits. f. päd. Psy. Path. und Hygiene, 1907. Vol. 8. pp. 344-361; 409-423. Vol. 9, pp. 32-58.

426. **Wycke, Richard T.** Story telling. Education, 1907. Vol. 28, pp. 76-79.

427. **Wygant, Elsie Amy** Reading for little children. Elem. School Teacher, 1907. Vol. 7, pp. 275-287. Vol. 8, pp. 104-110; 146-151; 197-202.

428. **Wyss, C. von** A study of children and seedlings. Child Life, 1907. Vol. 9, pp. 67-69.

429. **Yoshida, K.** Ueber japanische Erziehung und den Moralunterricht in den Schulen Japans. C. Marowsky, Minden, 1906. pp. 23.

Ziegler, —— See **Engelsperger, —— and Ziegler, ——**

430. **Ziehen, Prof.** Die Erkennung des angeborenen Schwachsinns. Zeits. f. Schulgesundheitspflege, 1907. Vol. 20, pp. 32-36.

---

431. Child labor. For various articles on child labor *see* Annals of the American Academy of Pol. and Social Science, 1907. Vol. 29. *Also* Charities and the Commons, Vol. 19.

432. Child labor in the United States. Govt. Print. Off., Wash., 1907. pp. 200. (U. S. Bur. of the Census. Bull. 69.)

433. Children 2,000 years ago; British Museum collection of toys, etc. Spectator, 1907. Vol. 98, pp. 970-971.

434. Classes d'anormaux psychiques. Revue Péd., 1907. Vol. 50, pp. 44-50.

435. Educational research club of Hartford county. Report on questionnaire No. 1, Likes and dislikes of teachers and pupils. Hartford press, Hartford, 1905. pp. 15.

436. Das Elend unserer Jugendliteratur; ein Beitrag zur kunstlerischen Erziehung der Jugend. B. G. Teubner, Leipzig, 1905. pp. 225.

437. The federal child labor bill. Nation, 1907. Vol. 84, p. 98.

438. General need for education in matters of sex. Society of Social Hygiene, Chicago, 1907.
    A very valuable and suggestive pamphlet of ten essays. Useful for all teachers.

439. II. Internationaler Kongress für Schulhygiene. Zeits. f. Schulgesundheitspflege, 1907. Vol. 20, pp. 443-454.

440. Kindertheater. Jugendschriften-Warte, 1896. Vol. 4, pp. 31-32.

441. Kongress für Kinderforschung und Jugendfürsorge. Bericht, 1906. Vol. 1. H. Beyer, Langensalza, 1907. pp. 432.

442. Moral training in the public schools; California prize essays by C. E. Rugh and others. Ginn & Co., Boston, 1907. pp. 203.
    Five practical papers by teachers who realize the importance of moral training as distinct from "religious instruction."

443. Mutter und Kind; wie man heikle Gegenstände mit Kindern behandeln kann. A. Töpelmann, Giessen, 1904. pp. 44.
444. National child labor committee. Proceedings of the annual meetings, 1905-1907. 1st-3d. N. Y., 1905-1907.
Vol. 1. Child labor. Vol. 2. Child labor, a menace. Vol. 3. Child labor and the republic.
445. The physician in the school. Nation, 1907. Vol. 85, p. 180.
446. Schoolboy English. Outlook, 1907. Vol. 86, pp. 314-316.
447. Das Seelenleben eines Erblindeten. Eos, 1905. Vol. 1, pp. 46-66.
Psychology of the blind, an article founded on the autobiography of Luigi Ansaldi, an Italian, who became blind in his seventh year.
448. Studies by Amer. Statistical Association. Physical welfare of children. Jour. of Ed., 1907. Vol. 66, pp. 510-511.

SUBJECT INDEX

Abnormal, 1, 30, 199, 287, 314, 411, 434.
Activity, 341.
Adolescence, 52, 66, 318, 371.
Æsthetics, 40, 251, 317.
Africa, 228.
Alcoholism, 211.
Algeria, 160.
Ambidexterity, 361.
American boy, 80.
Amer. Indians, 93.
Analogy, 70.
Ancient Greeks, 281.
Anthropometry, 34, 209, 285, 366.
Art, 114, 160, 212, 293, 304, 337.
Athletics, 165.
Auxiliary schools, 330, 370, 390.

Baby-talk, 388.
Backward children, 265, 284, 306, 388.
Belgium, 214.
Berlin congress, 54, 352, 392, 395, 441.
Bibliography, 20, 353, 417.
Blind, 133, 300, 416, 447.
Books for children. *See* Literature.
Bordeaux, 310.
Boy-hero, 401.
Boy-work, 128.
Boys, 52, 80.
Brain, 12.
Brain development, 208.
Brain-fag, 178.

Character, 48, 117, 376.
Charlottenburg, 390.
Child labor, 23, 62, 79, 122, 188, 224, 225, 239, 342, 383, 431, 432, 437, 444.

Child life, 152, 404.
Child study, 8, 86, 90, 139, 146, 161, 252, 259, 334, 339, 394, 428, 441.
Child types, 240.
Childhood, 38, 191.
Church, 112.
Cigarettes, 238.
City children, 126.
Civilization, 3.
Cleanliness, 381.
Climate, 398.
Clinical psychology, 419.
Co-education, 320.
Collections, 291.
Color sense, 196, 256, 403.
Competition, 247.
Consanguinity, 108.
Conscience, 267.
Consciousness, 208.
Contents of children's minds, 153.
Corporal punishment, 192, 193, 194, 333.
Crime, 68, 129, 232, 233, 234, 344.
Deaf blind, 399.
Deaf children, 14, 15, 47, 377.
Deaf mutes, 264.
Defectives, 5, 19, 29, 124, 236, 257, 284, 308.
Delinquents, 257, 306.
Dementia præcox, 249, 322, 384, 410, 424.
Dental clinics, 181, 203.
Dependents, 257.
Design, 114.
Development, 345.
Diseases, 95, 121.
Dolls, 135.
Drama, 31, 116, 132, 163, 295, 440.
Drawing, 51, 227.

Drinking fountains, 365.
Dunces, 25.

Ear, 21, 43.
Eccentric mentality, 134.
Education, 50, 378, 385.
Emotions, 280, 374.
England, 130, 164.
Environment, 13.
Epidemics, 82.
Erotism, 109.
Essays, 302.
Ethics, 35, 118, 275, 340.
Etiological, 265.
Eugenics, 50, 125, 286.
Europe, 276.
Evidence, 91.
Examinations, 60, 288.
Exercise, 179.
Experimental pedagogy, 338, 418.
Expression, 242.
External world, 70.
Eyesight, 28, 94, 310, 347.

Family, 232.
Fatigue, 178.
Fear, 24, 133.
Feeble minded, 21, 27, 37, 53, 97,
    105, 131, 143, 144, 205, 298, 301,
    311, 313, 324, 363, 421, 422,
    430.
Feelings, 83.
Folk-lore, 87, 401.
Folk-tales, 155.
Food, 348.
Form of head, 34, 285.
Freedom, 103.
Freedom of will, 180.
Fresh air, 179.
Froebel, 173, 250, 253.
Fundamental and accessory, 341.

Games, 170, 182, 183, 210, 283.
General works, 334.
Germany, 269, 331, 338, 363.
Girls, 160, 226, 343.
Grammar, 31.
Growth, 332, 393.
Gymnastics, 386.

Hamburg, 319.
Hand, 242.
Heredity, 34, 108, 151, 290, 424.
History, 96, 356.
Home, 7, 92, 261, 321, 378.
Home life, 269.
Honor, 219.
Humor, 65.

Hygiene, 49, 51, 69, 154, 186, 187,
    200, 222, 223, 237, 272, 303,
    364, 381, 391, 405, 409, 439.
——— School, 213.
Hysteria, 82.

Idiocy, 204, 258, 397, 410.
Idleness, 262.
Illegitimate children, 359.
Illinois juvenile courts, 176.
Imagination, 44, 231, 400.
Impressionability, 13.
Impure air, 216.
Incorrigibles, 127, 248.
Independence, 38.
Industrial education, 416.
Infant mortality, 241, 266.
Infants, 214, 215, 279, 339.
Institutions, 301.
Insubordinates, 248.
Intelligence, 285.
Interest, 136, 137, 190.
Italy, 124, 257.

Japan, 386, 429.
Junior republic, 309.
Juvenile courts, 176, 367.
Juvenile criminals, 110, 233, 234,
    344.
Juvenile delinquents, 68, 167, 174,
    175, 357.
Juvenile reform, 355.

Kansas, 367.
Kindergarten, 16, 164, 182, 229,
    253, 276, 328, 329, 349, 372.

Language, 11, 14, 15, 85, 198, 277,
    312, 368, 388, 446.
Learning process, 375.
Legends, 155.
Liberty, 38.
Libraries, 261, 350.
Lies, 189, 354, 382.
Likes and dislikes, 435.
Literature, 98, 119, 147, 195, 230,
    260, 351, 436.
London, 39, 145.

Maltreatment, 414.
Manual labor, 278.
Manual training, 45, 86, 149, 305.
Märchen, 155.
Mathematical prodigies, 254.
Medical inspection of schools, 28,
    75.
Medicine, 33.
Memory, 84, 89, 220, 360.
Mental and physical, 43.

Mental defectives, 33, 270, 299, 370, 407, 411, 434.
Mental depression, 148.
Mental development, 22, 171, 172, 218, 244, 296, 425.
Mental diseases, 168.
Mental economy, 35.
Mental evolution, 50, 255, 396.
Mental retardation, 422.
Mental training, 106, 197.
Milk, 18.
Mongolian spots, 41.
Moral education, 119.
Moral training, 10, 17, 48, 429.
Morals, 55, 77, 111, 184, 307, 408, 442.
Mothers, 49, 123.
Movements, 316, 341.
Mulhausen Waldschule, 26.
Music, 56, 63, 120, 185.
Mythomania, 389.
Myths, 67, 76, 401.

Native Schools, 160.
Nature, 115.
Negro, 41.
Nervous diseases, 358.
Nervousness, 141, 168, 177, 362, 412.
Night-fears, 24.
Non-average child, 197.
Nose, 42.
Number, 220.
Nutrition, 18, 75, 348.

Observation, 91.
Ohio, 252.

Parents, 113, 139, 156, 159, 221, 273.
Pathology, 217.
Peculiar children, 64, 138.
Pedagogy, 394.
Personal, 36.
Phonetics, 369.
Physical, 41, 267.
Physical development, 218, 415, 448.
Physical training, 185, 206, 207.
Physician, 74.
Physiological age, 71.
Play, 12, 39, 40, 46, 57, 170, 183, 210, 297.
Playgrounds, 72, 73, 292.
Playthings, 6, 40, 61, 101.
Pleasure, 103.
Poetry, 373.
Poland, 135.
Poor pupil, 243.

Precocity, 140.
Probation, 175.
Prostitution, 162.
Protection, 2.
Psychoasthenic, 158.
Psychology, 20, 166, 246, 316.
Puberty, 109.
Puberty customs, 228.
Public library, 32.

Reading, 260, 351, 427.
Religion, 100, 321, 408, 413.
Religious education, 142.
Rhymes, 335.
Russia, 59, 291.

Santa Claus, 67.
Scholarship, 71.
School, 7.
School and family, 58.
School desks, 406.
School excursions, 107.
School gardens, 271.
School hours, 364.
School physician, 272, 307, 380, 445.
School system, 263.
Scoliosis, 78, 150, 423.
Sense of honor, 219.
Sensitive, 280.
Sewing, 361.
Sex, 52, 88, 109, 118, 129, 162, 202, 226, 268, 274, 303, 325, 379, 402, 408, 438.
Sex instruction, 157, 346, 443.
Silence, 315.
Six-year-old child, 102.
Slums, 99.
Social education, 356.
Social sense, 36.
Societies, 408.
Sociological, 2, 3, 156, 200, 266.
Songs, 56, 63, 331.
Special schools, 423.
Special training, 235.
Speech, 144, 368.
Speech defects, 312, 314, 326, 327.
Spelling, 360, 420.
Stammering, 387.
State, 156.
Statistics, 5, 264, 415.
Stories, 323, 373.
Story-telling, 169, 426.
Strümpell, 5.
Study, 315.
Stuttering, 326, 327.
Subnormal, 81.
Suicide, 59, 104, 294.
Superstition, 87.

Teachers, 159.
Teeth, 181.
Telhi, 309.
Temperament, 159.
Theatre, 132, 163, 440.
Thought, 296.
Toys, 6, 61, 433.
Truancy, 149, 282.
Truth, 201, 354.

Unfortunates, 9.
Upright posture, 290.

Vacation schools, 145.
Vacations, 7.
Venereal diseases, 129.
Vision, 28, 196, 256.
Vocabulary, 11, 85, 198.

Waste, 245.
Work, 336.

Youth, 4, 88, 98, 195, 218, 274,
    289, 332, 400, 402, 405, 408,
    436.
Zürich, 203.

SUPPLEMENT TO BIBLIOGRAPHY OF ARTICLES
RELATING TO THE STUDY OF CHILDHOOD
AND ADOLESCENCE WHICH HAVE BEEN
PUBLISHED IN THE PEDAGOGICAL
SEMINARY AND THE AMERICAN
JOURNAL OF PSYCHOLOGY
1907-1912

SUPPLEMENT TO BIBLIOGRAPHY OF ARTICLES RELATING TO THE STUDY OF CHILDHOOD AND ADOLESCENCE WHICH HAVE BEEN PUBLISHED IN THE PEDAGOGICAL SEMINARY AND THE AMERICAN JOURNAL OF PSYCHOLOGY

1907-1912

In 1907 a bibliography of the University Publications relating to childhood and adolescence was printed in the September number of the Pedagogical Seminary. As, since that date, nearly one hundred additional studies have appeared, the present appendix is issued to bring the bibliography to date.

THEODATE L. SMITH

BIBLIOGRAPHY

Names of contributors who have not been connected with the University are marked with an asterisk.

1. ACHER, R. A. Spontaneous constructions and primitive activities of children analogous to those of primitive man. *Am. Jour. of Psy.*, Jan., 1910, vol. 21, pp. 114-150.
2. APPLETON, L. ESTELLE. [The] twentieth century crusades, and what they taught one member of the five hundred. *Ped. Sem.*, March, 1909, vol. 16, pp. 23-48.
3. *BUTTENWIESER, ELLEN CLUNE. [The] obstinate child. *Ped. Sem.*, Sept., 1911, vol. 18, pp. 315-328.
4. BOBBITT, FRANKLIN. [The] growth of Philippine children. *Ped. Sem.*, June, 1909, vol. 16, pp. 137-168.
5. BOLAND, GENEVIEVE. Taking a dare. *Ped. Sem.*, Sept., 1910, vol. 17, pp. 510-524.
6. BRITTAIN, HORACE L. [A] study in imagination. *Ped. Sem.*, June, 1907, vol. 14, pp. 137-207.
7. *BROWN, DAISY D. Young people's ideas of the value of Bible study. *Ped. Sem.*, Sept. 1910, vol. 17, pp. 370-386.
8. *BURGERSTEIN, LEO. Co-education and hygiene with special reference to European experience and views. *Ped. Sem.*, March, 1910, vol. 17, pp. 1-15.
9. *—— ——. [The] main problems of schoolroom sanitation and school work. *Ped. Sem.*, March, 1910, vol. 17, pp. 16-28.
10. *—— ——. Some remarks on the relations of body and mind. *Ped. Sem.*, March, 1910, vol. 17, pp. 29-39.
11. BURNHAM, WILLIAM H. Arithmetic and school hygiene. *Ped. Sem.*, March, 1911, vol. 18, pp. 54-73.
12. —— ——. European investigations in school hygiene. *Ped. Sem.*, Sept., 1910, vol. 17, pp. 525-544.
13. —— ——. [The] hygiene of drawing. *Ped. Sem.*, Sept., 1907, vol. 14, pp. 289-304.

14. ── ──. [The] hygiene of the nose. *Ped. Sem.,* June, 1908, vol. 15, pp. 155-169.
15. ── ──. School hygiene in the Children's Institute. *Ped. Sem.,* June, 1910, vol. 17, pp. 183-188.
16. ── ──. [The] scientific study of hygiene (abstract). *Ped. Sem.,* Dec., 1909, vol. 16, pp. 437-441.
17. CARRIGAN, THOMAS CHARLES. [The] law and the American child. *Ped. Sem.,* June, 1911, vol. 18, pp. 121-183.
18. CHAMBERLAIN, ALEXANDER F. Activities of children among primitive peoples. I. *Ped. Sem.,* June, 1909, vol. 16, pp. 252-255.
19. CHAMBERLAIN, ALEXANDER F. and ISABEL C. Studies of a child. IV. "Meanings" and "Definitions" in the forty-seventh and forty-eighth months. *Ped. Sem.,* March, 1909, vol. 16, pp. 64-104.
20. *CHANDLER, EDWARD H. How much children attend the theatre, the quality of the entertainment they choose and its effect upon them. *Ped. Sem.,* June, 1909, vol. 16, pp. 365-371.
21. CHASE, HARRY W. Work with the backward and subnormal in the Children's Institute. *Ped. Sem.,* June, 1910, vol. 17, pp. 189-203.
22. COLVIN, S. S. [The] ideational types of school children. *Ped. Sem.,* June, 1909, vol. 16, pp. 314-324.
23. *CRAIG, ANNE THROOP. [The] development of a dramatic element in education. *Ped. Sem.,* March, 1908, vol. 15, pp. 75-81.
24. *CRAMPTON, C. WARD. Anatomical or physiological age versus chronological age. *Ped. Sem.,* June, 1908, vol. 15, pp. 230-237.
25. CURTIS, ELNORA WHITMAN. [The] dramatic instinct in education. *Ped. Sem.,* June, 1908, vol. 15, pp. 229-246.
26. ── ──. Out-door schools. *Ped. Sem.,* June, 1909, vol. 16, pp. 169-194.
27. DAWSON, GEORGE E. [A] characterization of the prevailing defects in backward children and a method of studying and helping them. *Ped. Sem.,* Dec., 1909, vol. 16, pp. 429-436.
28. *DORAN, EDWIN W. [A] study of vocabularies. *Ped. Sem.,* Dec., 1907, vol. 14, pp. 401-438.
29. ELLISON, LOUISE. Children's capacity for abstract thought as shown by their use of language in the definition of abstract terms. *Ped. Sem.,* April, 1908, vol. 29, pp. 253-260.
30. *EMERY, GEORGE E. Medical inspection in two Worcester schools. *Ped. Sem.,* March, 1910, vol. 17, pp. 111-115.
31. FLEMING, PIERCE J. Moving pictures as a factor in education. *Ped. Sem.,* Sept., 1911, vol. 18, pp. 336-352.
32. GAULT, ROBERT H. [A] history of the questionnaire method of research in psychology. *Ped. Sem.,* Sept., 1907, vol. 14, pp. 366-383.
33. GODDARD, HENRY H. Four hundred feeble-minded children classified by the Binet method. *Ped. Sem.,* Sept., 1910, vol. 17, pp. 387-397.
34. ── ──. Research in school hygiene, in the light of experiences in an institution for the feeble minded. *Ped. Sem.,* March, 1910, vol. 17, pp. 50-53.
35. ── ── Two thousand normal children measured by the Binet measuring scale of intelligence. *Ped. Sem.,* June, 1911, vol. 18, pp. 232-259.
36. *GRUDZINSKA, ANNA. Report on the Polish child study association. *Ped. Sem.,* March, 1910, vol. 17, pp. 119-120.

37. *——— ———. [A] study of dolls among Polish children. *Ped. Sem.*, Sept., 1907, vol. 14, pp. 384-390.

38. GUILLET, CEPHAS. Education in interests. A study in experimental pedagogy. *Ped. Sem.*, Dec., 1907, vol. 14, pp. 474-487.

39. ——— ———. Retentiveness in child and adult. *Ped. Sem.*, July, 1909, vol. 20, pp. 318-352.

40. ——— ———. [A] study in interests. *Ped. Sem.*, Sept., 1907, vol. 14, pp. 322-328.

41. HALL, G. STANLEY. [The] culture-value of modern as contrasted with that of ancient languages. *Ped. Sem.*, Sept. 1908, vol. 15, pp. 370-379.

42. ——— ———. " Elements of strength and weakness in physical education as taught in colleges." *Ped. Sem.*, Sept., 1908, vol. 15, pp. 347-352.

43. ——— ———. [The] function of music in the college curriculum. *Ped. Sem.*, March, 1908, vol. 15, pp. 117-126.

44. ——— ———. General outline of the new child study work at Clark University. *Ped. Sem.*, June, 1910, vol. 17, pp. 160-165.

45. ——— ———. [The] medical profession and children. *Ped. Sem.*, June, 1908, vol. 15, pp. 207-216.

46. ——— ———. [The] national child welfare conference: its work and its relations to child study. *Ped. Sem.*, Sept., 1910, vol. 17, pp. 497-504.

47. ——— ———. [The] needs and methods of educating young people in the hygiene of sex. *Ped. Sem.*, March, 1908, vol. 15, pp. 82-91.

48. ——— ———. Psychology of childhood as related to reading and the public library. *Ped. Sem.*, March, 1908, vol. 15, pp. 105-116.

49. ——— ———. [The] psychology of music and the light it throws upon musical education. *Ped. Sem.*, June, 1908, vol. 15, pp. 358-364.

50. ——— ———. Recent advances in child study. *Ped. Sem.*, June, 1908, vol. 15, pp. 353-357.

51. HARTSON, LOUIS D. [The] psychology of the club; a study in social psychology. *Ped. Sem.*, Sept., 1911, vol. 18, pp. 353-414.

52. *HERTS, ALICE MINNIE. Dramatic instinct—its use and misuse. *Ped. Sem.*, Dec., 1908, vol. 15, pp. 550-562.

53. HILL, DAVID SPENCE. Comparative study of children's ideals. *Ped. Sem.*, June, 1911, vol. 18, pp. 219-231.

54. *HOLMES, ARTHUR. [The] psychological clinic. *Ped. Sem.*, Dec., 1909, vol. 16, pp. 488-491.

55. HOLMES, W. H. Plans of classification in the public schools. *Ped. Sem.*, Dec., 1911, vol. 18, pp. 475-522.

56. KAYLOR, M. A. Feelings, thought, and conduct of children toward animal pets. *Ped. Sem.*, June, 1909, vol. 16, pp. 205-239.

57. LIBBY, WALTER. [The] imagination of adolescents. *Ped. Sem.*, April, 1908, vol. 29, pp. 249-252.

58. LIBBY, WALTER AND OTHERS. [The] Contents of children's minds. *Ped. Sem.*, June, 1910, vol. 17, pp. 242-280.

59. MACDONALD, ARTHUR. Reform of juvenile criminals. *Ped. Sem.*, Dec., 1907, vol. 14, pp. 496-505.

60. McKEAG, ANNA J. [The] second international congress on school hygiene. *Ped. Sem.*, Dec., 1907, vol. 14, pp. 512-516.

61. MAGNI, JOHN A. Department of child linguistics. *Ped. Sem.*, June, 1910, vol. 17, pp. 213-218.

62. *MATEER, FLORENCE. [The] vocabulary of a four year old boy. *Ped. Sem.*, March, 1908, vol. 15, pp. 63-74.

63. MEYER, ADOLF. [The] dynamic interpretation of dementia prae-cox. *Am. Jour. of Psy.*, July, 1910, vol. 21, pp. 385-403.

64. *MITCHELL, FRANK D. Mathematical prodigies. *Ped. Sem.*, Jan., 1907, vol. 18, pp. 61-143.

65. NICE, LEONARD BLAINE. [The] disinfection of books. *Ped. Sem.*, June, 1911, vol. 18, pp. 197-204.

66. ORDAHL, GEORGE. Rivalry: its genetic development and pedagogy. *Ped. Sem.*, Dec., 1908, vol. 15, pp. 492-549.

67. *PELSMA, JOHN R. [A] child's vocabulary and its development. *Ped. Sem.*, Sept., 1910, vol. 17, pp. 328-369.

68. *SCHMITT, CLARA. [The] teaching of the facts of sex in the pub-lic school. *Ped. Sem.*, June, 1910, vol. 17, pp. 229-241.

69. SHAFER, GEORGE H. Health inspection of schools in the United States. *Ped. Sem.*, Sept., 1911, vol. 18, pp. 273-314.

70. *SIMONS, SARAH E. Imitative writing in the high school. *Ped. Sem.*, Sept., 1910, vol. 17, pp. 451-479.

71. *SMITH, FRANKLIN O. Pupils' voluntary reading. *Ped. Sem.*, June, 1907, vol. 14, pp. 208-222.

72. SMITH, P. A. Some phases of the play of Japanese boys and men. *Ped. Sem.*, June, 1909, vol. 16, pp. 256-267.

73. SMITH, THEODATE L. [The] Berlin Congress for child study. *Ped. Sem.*, March, 1907, vol. 14, pp. 130-136.

74. —— ——. Bibliography of articles relating to the study of child-hood and adolescence which have been published in the Peda-gogical Seminary and the American Journal of Psychology. *Ped. Sem.*, Sept., 1907, vol. 14, pp. 355-365.

75. —— ——. Correspondence department of the Children's Insti-tute. *Ped. Sem.*, June, 1910, vol. 17, pp. 176-182.

76. —— ——. Dr. Maria Montessori and her houses of childhood. *Ped. Sem.*, Dec., 1911, vol. 18, pp. 533-542.

77. Special child surveys in Worcester by Clark students. *Ped. Sem.*, June, 1910, vol. 17, pp. 219-228.

78. *STERN, WILLIAM. Abstracts of lectures on the psychology of tes-timony and on the study of individuality. *Amer. Jour. of Psy.*, April, 1910, vol. 21, pp. 270-282.

79. STRONG, ANNA LOUISE. [A] civic institute on child life. *Ped. Sem.*, Dec., 1910, vol. 17, pp. 545-546.

80. *SWETT, HARRY PREBLE. Her little girl. *Ped. Sem.*, March, 1910, vol. 17, pp. 104-110.

81. TANNER, AMY E. Experimental didactics in the Children's Insti-tute. *Ped. Sem.*, June, 1910, vol. 17, pp. 204-212.

82. WALLIN, J. E. WALLACE. [A] boy's exposition. *Ped. Sem.*, Sept., 1910, vol. 17, pp. 505-509.

83. —— ——. Human efficiency. A plan for the observational, clin-ical and experimental study of the personal, social, industrial, school and intellectual efficiencies of normal and abnormal in-dividuals. *Ped. Sem.*, March, 1911, vol. 18, pp. 74-84.

84. —— ——. [The] moving picture in relation to education, health, delinquency and crime. *Ped. Sem.*, June, 1910, vol. 17, pp. 129-142.

85. WHIPPLE, GUY MONTROSE, and WHIPPLE, Mrs. GUY M. [The] vo-cabulary of a three-year-old boy with some interpretative com-ments. *Ped. Sem.*, March, 1909, vol. 16, pp. 1-22.

86. WIGGAM, AUGUSTA. [A] contribution to the data of dream psy-chology. *Ped. Sem.*, June, 1909, vol. 16, pp. 240-251.

87. *WILLIAMS, TOM A. How inebriety might be prevented by early education. *Ped. Sem.*, June, 1909, vol. 16, pp. 195-204.

88. *—— ——. Intellectual precocity. Comparison between John
        Stuart Mill and the son of Dr. Boris Sidis. *Ped. Sem.*, March,
        1911, vol. 18, pp. 85-103.
89. WILSON, LOUIS N. Bibliography of child study. *Ped. Sem.*, Sept.,
        1907, vol. 14, pp. 329-354.
90. —— ——. Bibliography of child study. *Ped. Sem.*, June, 1908,
        vol. 15, pp. 400-429.
91. —— ——. Library facilities for the work of the Children's Insti-
        tute and the new buildings for this work. *Ped. Sem.*, June,
        1910, vol. 17, pp. 166-175.
92. WINCH, W. H. Color-names of English school-children. *Am.
        Jour. of Psy.*, July, 1910, vol. 21, pp. 453-482.

BOOKS RELATING TO CHILDHOOD AND ADOLESCENCE. PUBLISHED BY
    THOSE CONNECTED WITH CLARK UNIVERSITY, 1907-1912.

ANDERSON, LEWIS FLINT. History of Common School Education:
    an Outline Sketch. H. Holt & Co., New York, 1909, 308 p.
HALL, G. STANLEY. Educational Problems. D. Appleton & Co.,
    New York, 1911, 2 vols., 710 and 714 p.
MISAWA, TADASU. Modern Educators and Their Ideals. D. Ap-
    pleton & Co., New York, 1909, 304 p.
Proceedings of the Child Conference for Research and Welfare.
    Held at Clark University, July 6th-10th, 1909, and June 28th-
    July 2nd. G. E. Stechert & Co., New York, vol. 1, 1909, 257 p.;
    vol. 2, 1910, 286 p.

SUBJECT INDEX

Abstract Thought 29
Anthropological Measurements 4
Activities of Primitive Children 18
Adolescence 57
Anatomical Age 24
Ancient and Modern Languages 41
Anthropometry 4
Arithmetic 11

Backward Children 21, 27
Bible Study 7
Binet Tests 33, 35
Boasting 5
Body and Mind 10
Boys' Clubs 51
—Exposition 82

Child Study 36, 44, 46, 50
——Bibliography 74, 89, 90
——Congress 73
—Welfare Conference 46
Children's Ideals 53
—Institute 15, 21, 44, 61, 75, 81, 91
—Reactions to Animals 56
Civic Institute on Child Life 79
Classification 55
Child Surveys 77
Color Names 92
Contents of Children's Minds 58
Co-education 8

Definitions 19, 29
Dementia Praecox 63
Dolls 37
Drama 25
Dramatic Instinct 23, 25, 52
Drawing 13
Dreams 86

Efficiency 83
Emotions 66
English Schools 2
Experimental Pedagogy 38, 81

Feeble Mindedness 21, 33, 34

Gifted Children 83, 88
Growth of Philippine Children 4

Health Inspection 69
High Schools, in 38, 40, 57, 71
Hygiene, 8, 9, 11, 12, 13, 14, 16. 34, 60, 65

Ideational Types 22
Imagination 6, 57, Also in 23, 80
Imaginary Companion 80
Imitation, in 1, 72
Imitative Composition 70
Interest 38, 40; Also in 1, 6

Juvenile Delinquency 59, 84

Language 19, 29, 61, 62, 67, 85
Law and the Am. Child 17
Libraries 48, 91
Linguistics 61

Mathematical Prodigies 64
Medical Inspection 30
Medical Profession and Children 45
Memory Tests 6, 39
Mental Tests 33, 35
—Imagery 6, 22
Modern Languages 41
Montessori Method 76
Moral Degeneracy, in 59
Moving Pictures 31, 84
Music 43, 49

Obstinacy 3
Open Air Schools 26; Also in 2

Peoples' Institute, in 25
Physical Education 42
Physical Degeneration, in 2, 59
Play 72
Polish Child Study Assoc. 36
Precocity, 64, 88; Also in 83
Preferences in Reading 6
Prevention of Inebriety 87
Primitive Activities of Children 1
Psychological Clinic 54
Psychology of Testimony 78
Public Library 48

Questionnaire Method 32

Reading   48, 71
Retentiveness   39
Rivalry, 66; Also in   72

School Room Sanitation   9
Sex, In   72
Sex Differences, in   6. 28, 40
Sex Education   47, 68
Spontaneous Constructions   1

Studies of Individual Chil-
  dren   19, 39
Taking a Dare   5
Teasing, in   72
Temperance   87
Tests of Intelligence   33, 35
Theatre, 20; Also in   25

Vocabularies   28, 62, 67, 85

In addition to the articles listed many of the addresses given at the Child Conference for Research and Welfare were printed in the Ped. Sem., but as they are all included in the volumes of the conference reports, they have not been listed separately.

BOOK NOTES

Motion Study, a method for increasing the efficiency of the workman, by FRANK B. GILBRETH. New York, 1911, D. Van Nostrand Co. XXIII, 116 p., with introduction by Robert Thurston Kent, Editor of "Industrial Engineering."

Probably no more unique and profitable book of pedagogy has appeared in recent years than Gilbreth's "Motion Study." Its chief purpose is to point out how motions can be economized in the industries and more especially in the brick-laying trade. The text is well illustrated with half-tone cuts which recently appeared with much the same discussion in "Industrial Engineering." While most of the concrete illustrations are drawn from the brick-masons' trade, the work is much broader in scope and is pregnant with suggestions in every other field of human endeavor. The work indicates that Gilbreth is one of the chief authorities on conservation and the earning power of workmen.

The discussion appears under three main heads: First, the *worker,* including his anatomy, creed, contentment, experience, fatigue, habits, health, nutrition, size, etc., as variables affecting the amount of work done; second, *surroundings, tools,* etc., including clothes, letterings and colors, entertainment, heating, size and weight of unit moved, union rules, etc., as a second group of variables; third, *motion,* including acceleration, sequence, direction cost, work accomplished, length, inertia and many others as a third group of variables affecting the earning capacity of the workmen.

The problem is discussed from the humanity standpoint and not with a view to devising means for extorting the last ounce of energy from the laborer. Mr. Gilbreth reports that he has actually succeeded in doubling the efficiency of the workmen and at the same time sending them home in the evening less fatigued than when they worked under the less scientific but more "convenient" regulations. The motions per brick have been reduced from eighteen under the old method to one and three-fourths under the new system.

A single incident related in the introduction will serve to illustrate the wider application of the principles. Gilbreth was attracted in the Japanese-British Exposition to a girl putting papers on blacking boxes at a wonderful speed. He at once timed her, and it required forty seconds to do twenty-four boxes. However, he noticed that her speed was due to quick motions rather than to economy of motions. He interposed and showed the girl how to eliminate half of her motions, and on the first trial she did twenty-four boxes in twenty-six seconds. On the second trial she succeeded in twenty seconds, exactly doubling her output of a few minutes before. She was not working any harder, only making fewer motions.

The only purpose of the review in this connection is the hope that some thoroughly practical educator will become interested and work out the details by which the same conservation principles could be applied to the work of the school-room showing how the highest efficiency could be secured in the movements of teacher, pupils, classes, progress of recitation, convenience of materials, as the conditions would be found in any well ordered school or system of schools. The field is very promising and Mr. Gilbreth himself calls upon universities and university trained men to give their attention to the question in its more scientific aspects.

Much has already been done on two of the variables, but the third suggests a field of unexplored possibilities. The "worker" is being studied by the experts in the hygiene of the school child. The "surroundings, equipments and tools" is fairly well investigated by the students of the hygiene of the school equipment. These are the fields of most marked progress in recent years. No less interesting and valuable would be the subject of the hygiene of school motions for the conservation of the teacher's time and energy, the elimination of loss motion in school routine and the consequent increased efficiency of the school machine. Dinsmore, McMurry, Bagley and others have sensed the problem, but none have attempted its scientific treatment as Gilbert has done in the economic sphere.

The only obvious criticism of the book is in its form. The reader would gladly sacrifice some of the minuteness of detail in the illustrations, to be relieved of the irritating glare of the highly glazed pages. This feature is the more inexcusable in that it violates the author's own scientific findings and recommendations. It is to be hoped that publishers will not afflict the reading public with many such gross violations of the hygiene of reading. One is surprised to read, "there shall not be any polished surfaces in its [light] vicinity that will reflect an unnecessary bright spot anywhere that can be seen by the eyes of the worker," on a page that is impossible to adjust in proper light so that it will not give off bright spots.   L. W. Sackett

Le Croquis à L'Ecole Primaire, par J. J. Sauvage, M. et Mme. L. V. Vandenhouten. 1910. 284 p.

This is a very attractive presentation of the possibilities in the use of the barest outline sketches in all primary work. As the teacher talks she now and then represents the crucial points by a few lines, which serve as points of attachment for the children's vivid fancy. Some of the sketches to illustrate moral lessons, are most unconsciously and wittily brief, like the one to show the danger of drinking when one is hot—a running boy indicated by three lines, a glass and then—tragic end—a bed with an enormous bottle even bigger than the bed standing by. So the sad fate of the belligerent goats who met on the narrow bridge is shown by a criss-crossing of upheaving lines very suggestive indeed of the turmoil going on below.

The authors also use sketching to aid observation, representing all the common occurrences of daily life and its tools, utensils, etc. Letter boxes, carnival, streetsweeping, storms, drought, balloons, steamboats, flowers and fruits, animals in whole and part, the human body in the teaching of physiology—in short everything and anything. Nothing is too complex to be shown in a few lines, it would seem.

So where one began with admiration one ends with reservation. The sketches are used in very many instances where any teacher could bring the real object into the school or have the children go to it, and seem to be used instead of the object, not by way merely of recalling it. Again they are used in many cases where a good picture would be far preferable, as in showing the differences and similarities between related animals. In other instances they seem to be used as rather absurd mnemonic devices, for learning poetry, and while the authors say that sketches can not take the place of reasoning in arithmetic, still they seem to think that when Johnny has to find out how much his clothes cost altogether if his shoes cost 10 f., his cap 3 and his suit 16, it somehow helps him to have drawings of shoes, cap and suit with plus signs between. Similarly, 84l. —9l. is indicated by a hogshead and a pail with a minus sign between them.

No one would question for an instant the great value of ability on the part of a teacher to use sketches in the course of a lesson on any subject and at any grade from kindergarten through University. Indeed we seem to have made far more use in this country of drawing as a language than has been done abroad. But to use it so indiscriminately as is done here is, it seems to me, to encourage the teacher to use the easier instead of the better method. If the different forms of leaves or claws are to be taught, she will be satisfied with a rough outline drawing instead of a trip to the woods after the leaves or a searching through zoologies after the claws. And so through the list.

AMY E. TANNER

Woman's Part in Government, whether she votes or not, by WILLIAM H. ALLEN. New York, Dodd, Mead & Co., 1911. vii, 377 p.

In the preface the author states his belief that women will soon be both permitted and expected to vote, but the aim of the book is to show the ineffectiveness of the ballot and the large share women may take and do take to-day in government. Outside interests are now inside the home to stay and the most domestic of women must know enough not to be a problem creator—which can not be done by mere devotion to home or by contemplation of the paradise that lies at the feet of the mother. After discussion of the details of registration and voting, how to avoid fraud in both, protecting and interpreting the vote, qualifications for voters, form of the ballot, and value of initiative, referendum and recall, the author makes the point that the ballot does not make officials do their duty, but that public knowledge of their acts does. Misgovernment is due to public ignorance, and is stopped by getting evidence based upon definite units of inquiry, and using papers and magazines to publish this evidence.

Now, all this in all its details women and women's clubs can do. The ballot does not study proposed laws, nor watch legislation, nor systematize knowledge, nor make budgets, nor attend hearings, nor write reports. If women and women's clubs did these things for their own community they would go far to give it an efficient government, library, charities, and churches.

Ballots do not stop contagion, nor discover disease-bearing water, nor get clean milk, nor keep babies alive, nor detect impure foods and drugs, nor expose patent medicines, nor note factory conditions nor stop child labor nor locate housing evils nor clean streets nor dispose of refuse—but women can do all these things.

The schools, both public and private, need woman's help in just the same way, and so do the courts and police departments and various agencies for the suppression of vice. The author remarks grimly that a high death rate of infants is more indecent than open gambling but that any community that permits open gambling is very unlikely to fight infant mortality.

Altogether, the most ardent advocate of woman's suffrage who reads this book can not but have an uneasy feeling that after all a ballot is rather an ineffective tool as compared with the ability to throw a searchlight upon all forms of official activity. The book is impressive in that every generality is pointed by a series of detailed questions or suggestions, and references to organizations which have done the work under discussion and to the pamphlets describing such work. It tells how things can be done, where they have been done, and the results obtained by the doing. It should be in the library of every woman and woman's club—and it would do men no harm to get a few ideas from it.

AMY E. TANNER

The way of an eagle, by E. M. DELL. New York, G. P. Putnam's Sons, 1912. 406 p.

The theme of this tale is summed up in the quotation from Proverbs: "There be three things which are too wonderful for me, yea, four which I know not: The way of an eagle in the air; the way of a serpent upon a rock; the way of a ship in the midst of the sea; and the way of a man with a maid." The hero combines all these characteristics, showing the boldness of the eagle, the wiliness of the serpent, the staunchness of the good ship, and the love of the man. Other characters are perhaps intended to figure the weaknesses of each, while the heroine is the helpless prey, the fascinated bird, the storm tossed bark and the blushing maid. The plot is very well worked out and holds the reader to the very end.

Manual of style. A compilation of typographical rules governing the publications of the University of Chicago, with specimens of types used at the University Press. 3d ed. Chicago, University of Chicago Press, 1911. 118 p.

This is a codification of the typographical rules employed by the University of Chicago in connection with its official printing of publications issued through the university press. It originated nearly twenty years ago in single sheets of fundamentals jotted down by the first proof-readers, and has grown from year to year. It is a unique book and full of all sorts of information concerning not only kinds of type and style, but also illustrations, with plenty of information on all the topics.

World geography, by RALPH S. TARR and FRANK M. McMURRY. New York, The Macmillan Co., 1912. 536 p. (One-volume edition.)

The first 185 pages give the foundation for understanding such common things as food, shelter, soils, hills, valleys, industries, climate, government which are part of every child's environment. Secondly comes mountains, rivers, lakes and oceans. Part Three treats of North America and Part Four of general geography, wind, rain, oceans, races of mankind. Then follows South America, Europe, Africa, Australia and then comes a large collection of colored maps, relief study, maps illustrating climate, products, population and other maps. These are interspersed in the text and carefully chosen, and altogether the volume contains nearly 700 cuts with a voluminous bibliography and an appendix of statistics.

Black and white in South East Africa, by MAURICE S. EVANS. New York, Longmans, Green & Co., 1911. 341 p.

The underlying idea of this work is that there are social, mental and spiritual as there are obvious physical differences between the Abantu and the Europeans and that it will be most just to both races if the natives are consciously developed on lines indicated by the study of their characteristics than on the assumption that their intelligence and natures are those of white men. These ideas will probably gain the general consent as an abstract proposition, but when it comes to actually enforcing them, there are very great difficulties. After describing the country and the people, tribalism, missions and education, the author discusses the needs of black men and the demands of the white in labor and land, tells how the black man thinks and the effects of his mode of thought upon the white man, discusses past policies and present theories and attempts to peer into the future. It is an interesting and inspiring book.

The negro and his needs, by RAYMOND PATTERSON, with a foreword by William Howard Taft. New York, F. H. Revell Co., 1911. 212 p.

The southern man is too close to the negro, and the northern man too far away. This author seeks the middle ground and from his long experience as a journalist, which is commended by President Taft, his classmate. He discusses the problems of increase, temperament, the mulatto, morally, the environment, economic problems, his relations to the white planter, political issues, suffrage, and what the negro has done for himself, the southerner's point of view, theories, need of education. The latter he conceives as the great need at present.

India under Curzon and after, by LOVAT FRASER. London, William Heinemann, 1911. 496 p.

This volume is a well informed and very sympathetic account of Lord Curzon's rule in India, although Curzon did not suggest it, has not seen a line of it, and he has neither authorized nor inspired a single statement. The writer first describes the condition of things in India before Lord Curzon's day, the latter's preparation, and then his work. This he characterizes by departments, first the North-West Frontier, the tribal country, Chitral and Afghanistan; then Persia, Seistan and Tibet. He then takes up the land question, education, the princes and native states, the reconstruction of the government machinery, the problem of the plague, famine and irrigation, commerce, industry, the physical problems, army reforms and Lord Kitchener, unrest and kindred questions.

Java, Sumatra, and the other Islands of the Dutch East Indies, by A. CABATON. London, T. Fisher Unwin, 1911. 376 p. (Tr., with a preface by Bernard Miall.)

The writer, after generalities and a historical sketch, treats of the physical geography, divisions, natives, the Javanese mind, the oriental foreign element, Europeans, administration, products, forests and mines, other possessions, political and economic conditions of Sumatra, Borneo, Celebes, the Moluccas and Timor. The book has a number of illustrations and a map.

Psychology and pedagogy of writing, by MARY E. THOMPSON. Baltimore, Warwick & York, Inc., 1911. 133 p. (Educational Psychology Monographs.)

The author treats here of the historical development of the alphabet, gives a resumé of the experiments bearing on the psychology of reading and in a final chapter describes its pedagogy. The work was done under the direction of Dean Thomas N. Balliet of the University of New York. It is somewhat elementary, but seems to accomplish very well what it seeks and is a useful tract or pamphlet for teachers.

The utility of all kinds of higher schooling. An investigation by R. T. CRANE. Chicago, 1909. 331 p.

This severest critic which higher education has ever had in this country has brought his material now together in a rather stately book in which he starts with Spencer's definition and Eliot's five-foot shelf of books. Then comes a chapter of opinions of college men and others of those of college graduates, of business men, and criticism of their letters, on misrepresentations, professional men, college training and character, the making of statesmen and orators. He then takes up technical, medical, and scientific training, agriculture and manual training, tells how the University of Wisconsin " defrauds the state," and finally gives us a conclusion of the whole matter.

A primer of teaching practice, by J. A. GREEN and C. BIRCHENOUGH. New York, Longmans, Green & Co., 1911. 262 p., illustrated.

This book is the outcome of many attempts to organize the professional work of training college students. It does not offer a new theory of education but merely surveys the variety of activities that enter into the complex work of class teaching. The different chapters are efforts to treat these activities in isolation, feeling that it is best to attack them one by one. It is not intended to supplant the study of special preparation or courses of psychology, but rather to be a preparation for both. Among these chapters are work and play, narration, description, explanation, observation, expression, imitation, inference, investigation, questioning, corrections, illustrations, discipline.

Outlines of school administration, by ARTHUR C. PERRY, Jr. New York, The Macmillan Company, 1912. 452 p.

This is designed as a text-book upon the subject. Under Part 1, Organization, the author discusses the organic structure of the school system of the United States, Germany, France, Great Britain and other countries and the curriculum, in infant, elementary, secondary, higher and vocational education and also the normal public education in this country and elsewhere. Part Second treats of school direction in the United States and other countries; Part Three of supervision; Part Four of management; and Part Five of the training and status of teachers.

A joysome history of education, for use in schools and small families, to which is appended a somewhat hilarious appendix, by WELLAND HENDRICK. Nyack, N. Y., The Point of View, 1911. 67 p.

In this little book an author has indulged to the full a very quiet and rather effective sense of humor, of which it is difficult to give any adequate conception in a note. The natal morn of education was when the first mother " briskly laid the flat of her hand upon the most inviting rotundity of (their) children's bodies." A page or two are devoted to Jews, Greeks, Middle Ages, Rousseau, Komensky, Froebel, Herbart, and the rest is on modern teaching. A special skit is on " Pedaguese " at the expense of English by a Professor " O'Shaw " or something like it, where one claim gives the original and the other the meaning. A comic vocabulary is appended which is rather racy.

Some fundamental verities in education, by MAXIMILIAN P. E. GROSZMANN. Boston, Richard G. Badger, 1911. 118 p.

The writer here sets forth his pedagogical views with the endorsement of several prominent educators. Part one is devoted to manual culture and sense training; part two to culture and art expression. The work contains some thirty illustrations.

Studies in the history of classical teaching. Irish and continental, 1500-1700. By REV. T. CORCORAN, S. J. New York, Benziger Bros., n. d. 306 p.

This is historical, going back to William Bathe of Dublin, 1564-1614. Then comes the practice of classical education in the post-Renaissance period, and then there are various appendices. It is an interesting and thorough historical sketch.

The educational system of China, as recently reconstructed, by HARRY EDWIN KING. Washington, Govt. Printing Office, 1911. 105 p. (U. S. Bureau of Education Bull., 1911. No. 15, Whole No. 462.)

The first chapter treats of the growth of modern education in China up to 1898, then discusses the next two years which were those of reforms and then the development of modern education from 1900-1906, controlling agencies, primary, middle, collegiate, normal, technical and miscellaneous schools, Chinese students studying abroad. It is a timely paper.

Great educators of three centuries, by FRANK PIERREPONT GRAVES. New York, The Macmillan Co., 1912. 289 p.

This is an account of fourteen of the great educators from Milton to Spencer. It includes Francis Bacon, Ratich, Comenius, Locke, Francke, Rousseau, Basedow, Froebel, Lancaster, Bell and Horace Mann. It was well worth while to do these autobiographically and to bring them into a more accessible form and the work seems to be well done.

The social factors affecting special supervision in the public schools of the United States, by WALTER HENRY JESSUP. Columbia University, Contributions to Education, No. 43. N. Y., Teachers College, 1911. 123 p.

The author takes up music, drawing, manual training, domestic science, physical education, penmanship, distribution of specialists, salaries, sex selection, division of responsibility, with summaries and conclusions. He seeks to find sanctions back of the demand for the introduction of these subjects, and to find whether this demand comes from the school or outside, to point out typical ways of introducing new topics, and to determine their effects and certain quantitative aspects of the subject.

Provision for exceptional children in public schools, by JAMES H. VAN SICKLE, LIGHTNER WITMER and LEONARD P. AYRES. Washington, Govt. Printing Office, 1911. 92 p. (U. S. Bureau of Education, Bull., 1911. No. 14, Whole No. 462.)

The authors treat of the discovery of the exceptional children and their probable relations to normal children, classification methods of determining extent and degree, provision in school systems, grading and promotion, description of work done for exceptional children in about thirty cities.

The causes of the elimination of students in public secondary schools of New York city, by JOSEPH KING VAN DENBURG. New York, Teachers College, Columbia University, 1911. 206 p.

Part One is devoted to the study of entering population. Then follow the elimination, advancement in the school course, early promise, first term's mark, the human side.

Children at play and other sketches, by ROSE M. BRADLEY. London, Smith, Elder & Co., 1911. 316 p.

The chapters are: London children at play, Matty of Spitalfields, the children of Florence, Sienna and her children, days in a Paris convent, fête day at Avignon, day in Provence, the month of Mary, Frère Jacques, on the road in Corsica.

The use of the bible in the education of the young, by T. RAYMONT.
New York, Longmans, Green & Co., 1911. 254 p.

No educational writer hitherto has dealt with the subject of Bible
teaching from his own special point of view. Here, however, we have
in Part I the Old Testament, its literary aspects and a teacher's survey.
The New is treated in the same way and in the last part, the writer
gives a course of instruction and preparation for the teacher, a mode
of presentation, with bibliography, chronological tables and a comparative view of schemes treated in an appendix.

Child nature and child nurture, by EDWARD PORTER ST. JOHN. Boston,
Pilgrim Press, 1911. 106 p.

After distinguishing nature and nurture the writer discusses the
instincts that are associated with physical life, the appetite, nervousness, sex; then how to deal with the child's fears, then with its anger,
then with the love impulse, then how to train in kindness and unselfishness and respecting property rights. The plan is unique, direct,
and we should think would be most effective. It certainly marks a
new departure in work of this kind and ought to be read by everyone
interested in the moral and religious training of children.

The problem of race-regeneration, by HAVELOCK ELLIS. 71 p. And
The methods of race-regeneration, by C. W. SALEEBY. 63 p. (New
Tracts for the Times). London, Cassell & Co., Limited, 1911.

These two books are New Tracts for the Times and sold at six-
pence in England. Ten other pamphlets are in preparation on the relations of race-regeneration to national ideals, spiritual life, woman-
hood, education, social development, moral progress, religion, sex,
industrialism, birthrate. In the first tract Ellis treats the improvement of the environment, problems of to-day, next step in social reform, eugenics; and in the second Saleeby treats of natural and secondary methods of race-regeneration, first essentials, the positive or
Galtonian methods, and negative methods, and preventive methods and
racial poisons.

The declining birthrate; its national and international significance.
By A. NEWSHOLME. New York, Cassell & Co., Ltd., 1911. 64 p.
(New Tracts of the Times.)

The writer first reviews the rates of national increase of population and measures the effects of declining contributions of birth rates
in different countries and towns, causes of reduction, indirect factors,
possible effects of altered distribution of fertility, national and international forecasts and finally discusses some possibility of action.

We and our children, by WOODS HUTCHINSON. New York, Doubleday,
Page & Co., 1911. 371 p.

The sequence of themes is: before the little one comes, babies as
bulbs, the nursery age, the sweet tooth, kindergarten age, feeding the
human caterpillar, our ivory keepers at the gate, the child's self-
respect, brick walls and the growing child, eyes and ears, the worship
of the race stream, reluctant mothers, the American mother, the delicate child, fiction as a diet, overworked children in farm and school.

A digest of the laws and regulations of the various states relating to the reporting of cases of sickness, by JOHN W. TRASK. Washington, Govt. Printing Office, 1911. 191 p. (Public Health Bulletin, No. 45.)

This is an abstract of the state and territorial laws relating to the reporting of sickness to the health authorities to and through whom cases are reported, following the states in alphabetical order.

Tom and Tom Tit and other stories about schools, by C. W. BARDEEN. Syracuse, N. Y., C. W. Bardeen, Publisher, 1911. 286 p.

Editor Bardeen has here produced a number of very interesting school stories. He is preeminently the story writer of all American teachers.

Adolescence; being selections from the occasional poems and meditations of the author to his twenty-fifth year. By WERNER MATTHEWS. Cambridge, England, printed by Fabb & Tyler, 1911. 148 p.

This volume, consisting mostly of poems, is a contribution to the psychology of adolescence. It is interesting and typical. It abounds in aphorisms and enthusiasms and experiments with all sorts of rhyme and poetry.

The hygiene of the soul, by GUSTAV POLLAK. New York, Dodd, Mead & Co., 1910. 209 p.

This book is really an account of the life, character and writings of Feuchtersleben, the author of " The Dietetics of the Soul " which is here translated and epitomized. The work excited a merited attention in its day.

Poems of action. A collection of verses for youth, chosen and edited by DAVID R. PORTER. New York, Association Press, 124 E. 28th St., 1911. 259 p.

This author attempts to bring together all the poets using the English language which mature boys enjoy reading. It is a book for older boys but it is a little difficult to know precisely how he determined his choice of poems. On the whole his selections seem to be excellent.

Productive farming, by KARY CADMUS DAVIS. Philadelphia, J. B. Lippincott & Co., 1911. 357 p.

This book is intended to suit the needs of rural schools of all kinds and graded village and city schools chiefly below high school rank. Its parts are plant production, animal production, animal products, farm management, with an appendix and reference tables. The book is copiously illustrated and is in every way attractive.

Some old Egyptian libraries, by ERNEST CUSHING RICHARDSON. New York, Charles Scribner's Sons, 1911. 93 p.

This is an interesting research in an interesting subject which the author has treated in a very scholarly way.

Increasing human efficiency in business. A contribution to the psychology of business. By WALTER DILL SCOTT. New York, Macmillan, 1911. 339 p.

The writer discusses in successive chapters the possibility of increasing human efficiency and then imitation, competition, loyalty, concentration, wages, and pleasure, as means of increasing human efficiency. Then the relations between the latter and love of the game, relaxation, rate of movement, practice versus theory, making experience an asset, capitalizing it, and finally judgment and habit formation.

Commentary on the science of organization and business development, by ROBERT J. FRANK. Revised edition. Chicago, Chicago Commercial Publishing Co., 1910. 277 p.

This work treats first of organization, then in successive chapters of coöperate financing, management, re-organization and consolidation, and promotion of enterprises, with an appendix. It is a valuable addition to the now rapidly growing literature upon this subject.

Self-investment, by ORISON SWETT MARDEN. New York, Thomas Y. Crowell Co., 1911. 315 p.

This is a series of vocation talks to young people apparently on how to utilize their powers, what to do with their time, how to read, etc.

Whence and whither, or the evolution of life, by THOMAS F. NEIL. Altoona, Pa., Mirror Printing Co., n. d. 62 p.

This booklet presents the author's struggle for a comprehension of life. Beliefs must come from individual experience and from this point of view he gives his notions of the origin and progress of man, the progress of the soul, of religion, and the progress of civilization.

Circumstances or character, by CLEMENT F. ROGERS. London, Methuen & Co., 1911. 218 p.

The writer first states some fundamental principles, then discusses charity in the church, religion and belief and finally, order and disorder.

Heroes of everyday life, by FANNY E. COE. Boston, Ginn & Company, 1911. 169 p.

The diver, telegraph operator, civil engineer, day laborer, life saver, fireman, engineer at sea and the miner are discussed by different writers in a way to show the heroism that is often necessary and rarely wanting where heroism is needed in the active pursuit of their occupations.

Home life in all lands, by CHARLES MORRIS. Philadelphia, J. B. Lippincott Co., 1911. 344 p. (Book III, Animal Friends and Helpers.)

In the earlier volumes of the series, man as a maker of and dweller in the home was dealt with, but animals too have their home and home life and it is of this that this book treats. The chapters are household pets and comrades, our single hoofed helpers, cloven hoofed draught animals, animals which yield food, birds of the poultry yard, tuneful home pets, our cousin the monkey, other animals as pets, wild animals in man's service.

Wit and wisdom of G. K. Chesterton. New York, Dodd, Mead & Company, 1911. 233 p.

Farm mechanics and drawing. Syllabus for secondary schools, 1911. Education Department bulletin. Published fortnightly by the University of the State of New York. Number 500, Albany, N. Y., August 1, 1911. 32 p.

Six thousand common English words; their comparative frequency and what can be done with them. By R. C. ELDRIDGE. Niagara Falls, N. Y. 64 p.

The aims, values and methods of teaching psychology in a normal school, by J. MACE ANDRESS. Rep. from December, 1911, Journal of Educational Psychology, pp. 541-554.

United States history for schools, by EDMUND S. MEANY.. Ill. New York, Macmillan Co., 1912. 587 p.

L'education commune a' Buenos Aires, par PABLO A. PIZZURNO. Buenos Ayres, Attliers due Bureau Météorlogique Argentin, 1910. 87 p. (Extrait du Recensement Général L'Education Levé le 23 Mai 1909.)

Ophthalmia neonatorum, by J. W. KERR. Washington, Govt. Printing Office, 1911. 20 p. (Public Health Bulletin, No. 49, October, 1911.)

Proceedings of the Massachusetts Historical Society, October, 1910-June, 1911. Vol. XLIV. Boston, published by the Society, 1911. 787 p.

The report of the Philadelphia milk show; its organization, management and a description of the exhibits, edited by ARTHUR EDWIN POST. Ill. Published by the Executive Committee, 1911. 123 p.

The eight pillars of prosperity, by JAMES ALLEN. New York, Thomas Y. Crowell Co., 1911. 233 p.

Address by President Stewardson, of Hobart College, in memory of Henry Langdon Parker, with the proceedings of the Worcester County Bar and Superior Court. Worcester, Mass., 1911. 27 p.

NOTES

The activity in the field of experimental pedagogy in Russia is well illustrated by the Proceedings of the First Pan-Russian Convention of Experimental Pedagogy (held at St. Petersburg, December 26-31, 1910) 1911, which has just come to hand.

The contents of the volume are as follows:

The First Meeting. December 26th, 1910

G. E. Rossolimo. "Types of Profiles of Psychically Deficient Pupils.

A. M. Shubert. "An attempt at Application of the System of Binet to the Investigation of the Abilities of Defective Children."

N. P. Postovsky. "On Modifications in the Method of Sante De Sanctis for the Determination of the Anomalous Degrees of Intellect and Its Normal Level in Children of School Age."

The Second Meeting. December 27th, 1910

A. A. Shcheglov. "Heightened Liability to Fatigue of Pupils as a Symptom of Social Degeneration."

A. B. Vladimizsky. "The Problems of Neuro-Psychical Hygiene in Contemporary Pedagogical Life."

F. E. Ribakoff. "Capacity for Mental Work of Men Students and Women Students, members of the Higher Courses for Women." The women students of these courses are called, in distinction from men students in universities proper—*coursistes*.

A. F. Iazuzsky. "On the Natural Experiment."

A. P. Netschaev and G. M. Mininkhin. "Observation upon the Reading of Children, as one of the Forms of the Natural Experiment."

The Third Meeting. December 28th, 1910

P. Tsonev. "On Experimental Investigations of the Teaching of Free-Hand Drawing in Connection with Modelling."

A. H. Krogius. "Experimental Investigation of the Processes of Thinking."

P. E. Leikfeld. "The Law of Weber and the Law of Merkel."

G. E. Troshin. "On the Child's Induction."

I. I. Vabalass-Gaudeitiss. "A New Apparatus for the Investigation of Attention."

The Fourth Meeting. December 29th, 1910

I. V. Evergetov. "Experiment and Its Significance in the Solution of Questions of Moral Education."

N. S. Maltsev. "On the Activity of the Belgian Pedotechnical Society."

A. L. Shcheglov. "On the Investigation of Muscular Power and Muscular Fatigue in Schools."

T. K. Markaziantz. "The Capacity for Work of Adults and Children in Different Hours of the Day."

The Fifth Meeting. December 30th, 1910

L. G. Orshansky. "On the Pedagogical Significance of the Development of the Left Hand."

L. G. ORSHANSKY. "On Collection and Study of Children's Toys as Material for the Study of Child Psychics."
A. P. NETSCHAEV. "On an Experimental School at the Pedagogical Academy."
G. E. ROSSOLIMO. "An Attempt at Experimental Investigation of Candidates from Peasants' Boys for Scholarships in the Society of the Name of Lomonossoff in Moscow."
V. P. KASTCHENKO. "Should the Gifted Children be Singled out from the General Mass of Scholars?"

THE SIXTH MEETING. DECEMBER 31ST, 1910

M. L. MOROSOV. "Concerning the Problem of an Inquiry among Backward and Abnormal Children in Elementary Schools."
K. I. SHIDLOVSKY. "History of Organization of Auxiliary Schools in Moscow."
A. N. BAGENOV. "Organization of Auxiliary Classes for the Mentally Retarded."
F. A. GALINOVSKY. "Selection of Children for Auxiliary Classes."
V. P. KASTCHENKO. "Determination of the Degree of Mental Deficiency by the Method of De Sanctis."
V. P. BRAJASS. "Experimental Psychological Investigations of Color Sensations in Children."
A. I. ZATCHINIAEV. "On the Psychological Foundations of Teaching the Written Expression of Thought.
A. V. VLADIMIZSKY. "Concerning the System of Experimental Investigation of Personality." The Program of Lectures by Dr. R. Sommer.

The Board of Directors of the recently organized Kindergarten Association, 1 Madison Avenue, New York City, offer three prizes for essays on the benefits of the Kindergarten and suggest the following subjects: 1. Why should all our schools have Kindergartens? 2. What the Kindergarten does for the child. 3. The influence of the Kindergarten on the home. 4. The Kindergarten as an uplifting influence in the community. The prizes are: first, $100; second, $50; and third, $25; and the contest is open to all Kindergartners and Primary Teachers. Essays should not contain more than fifteen hundred words, written on one side of the paper only, and should be received by the Association not later than April 15th, 1912.

A new school of the science of education has recently been established at Geneva under the name of Institut J. J. Rousseau. Dr. Pierre Bovet has been called from the professorship of philosophy and pedagogy at the University of Neuchatel to assume the directorship. Professor Ed. Claperéde, professor of experimental psychology at the University of Geneva, is one of the teaching corps. The Institut will be both a school and a center for research. The principal subjects taught will be psychology, including general and child psychology, together with practice in the psychological laboratory and anthropometry as applied to schools; school hygiene with practical instruction on the diseases of children; a clinical and pedagogical course on backward and abnormal children; moral and social education; history and philosophy of the great educators; school administration and organization.

Classics In
Child Development

An Arno Press Collection

Baldwin, James Mark. **Thought and Things.** Four vols. in two. 1906-1915

Blatz, W[illiam] E[met], et al. **Collected Studies on the Dionne Quintuplets.** 1937

Bühler, Charlotte. **The First Year of Life.** 1930

Bühler, Karl. **The Mental Development of the Child.** 1930

Claparède, Ed[ouard]. **Experimental Pedagogy and the Psychology of the Child.** 1911

Factors Determining Intellectual Attainment. 1975

First Notes by Observant Parents. 1975

Freud, Anna. **Introduction to the Technic of Child Analysis.** 1928

Gesell, Arnold, et al. **Biographies of Child Development.** 1939

Goodenough, Florence L. **Measurement of Intelligence By Drawings.** 1926

Griffiths, Ruth. **A Study of Imagination in Early Childhood and Its Function in Mental Development.** 1918

Hall, G. Stanley and Some of His Pupils. **Aspects of Child Life and Education.** 1907

Hartshorne, Hugh and Mark May. **Studies in the Nature of Character. Vol. I: Studies in Deceit; Book One, General Methods and Results.** 1928

Hogan, Louise E. **A Study of a Child.** 1898

Hollingworth, Leta S. **Children Above 180 IQ, Stanford Binet:** Origins and Development. 1942

Kluver, Heinrich. **An Experimental Study of the Eidetic Type.** 1926

Lamson, Mary Swift. **Life and Education of Laura Dewey Bridgman, the Deaf, Dumb and Blind Girl.** 1881

Lewis, M[orris] M[ichael]. **Infant Speech:** A Study of the Beginnings of Language. 1936

McGraw, Myrtle B. **Growth: A Study of Johnny and Jimmy.** 1935

Monographs on Infancy. 1975

O'Shea, M. V., editor. **The Child: His Nature and His Needs.** 1925

Perez, Bernard. **The First Three Years of Childhood.** 1888

Romanes, George John. **Mental Evolution in Man:** Origin of Human Faculty. 1889

Shinn, Milicent Washburn. **The Biography of a Baby.** 1900

Stern, William. **Psychology of Early Childhood Up to the Sixth Year of Age.** 1924

Studies of Play. 1975

Terman, Lewis M. **Genius and Stupidity:** A Study of Some of the Intellectual Processes of Seven "Bright" and Seven "Stupid" Boys. 1906

Terman, Lewis M. **The Measurement of Intelligence.** 1916

Thorndike, Edward Lee. **Notes on Child Study.** 1901

Wilson, Louis N., compiler. **Bibliography of Child Study.** 1898-1912

[Witte, Karl Heinrich Gottfried]. **The Education of Karl Witte,** Or the Training of the Child. 1914